As we approach the thir[...] [...]tinue to take their toll on untold numbers [...] ar has become a topic of serious discussio[n] [...] n will fall within the jurisdiction of the In [...] rising that the global community conti[...] [...]sort to war, aggression, and the comr........ ꞏꞏ ꞏꞏassive war crimes. *Seeking Accountability for the Unlawful Use of Force*, edited by Professor Leila Sadat, could not be more timely or important. It contains thoughtful and accessible essays by some of the leading experts in the field of international criminal law. They trace its modern history and consider the future of mechanisms of accountability for war crimes. This excellent collection is essential reading for all interested in the relationship between law and war.

Justice Richard Goldstone,
Former Chief Prosecutor of the International Criminal
Tribunals for the former Yugoslavia and Rwanda

Leila Sadat is a towering figure in the field of international law, and it is no surprise that she has assembled in this thought-provoking enterprise many prominent legal experts and contributors. In international criminal law, there is continued debate over what constitutes reasonable use of force and what measures may be appropriate to deter and punish acts of aggression. This book offers rare insight into the legal debates, and provides compelling arguments for a rational use of force within the existing framework of international law.

Dr. Mark S. Ellis,
Executive Director, International Bar Association

The significance of this book cannot be underestimated. With the activation of the International Criminal Court's jurisdiction over the crime of aggression, the time is ripe to reflect on the way accountability for the unlawful use of force has been dealt with both by the ICC's predecessors as well as through other mechanisms. Moreover, it is important to take stock and reflect on the many challenges faced so far in order to better prepare for future accountability efforts. The collection brings together leading academics in the field who provide a holistic examination of the issue at hand, filling an important gap in the scholarship. I cannot recommend it highly enough.

Professor Olympia Bekou,
School of Law, University of Nottingham, U.K.

This collection of essays, written by eminent scholars in the field, could not be more timely, as we approach the activation of the ICC's jurisdiction over the crime of aggression on 17 July 2018, the very day of its twentieth anniversary. *Seeking Accountability for the Unlawful Use of Force* is an essential reading companion for those, scholars and practitioners alike, who seek a better understanding of the legacy of the Nuremberg and Tokyo trials against the backdrop of the shifting boundaries between *jus ad bellum* and *jus in bello* in the post-9/11 age.

Professor Christine Van den Wyngaert,
Judge at the International Criminal Court

SEEKING ACCOUNTABILITY FOR THE UNLAWFUL USE OF FORCE

Despite the conclusion of the International Military Tribunal at Nuremberg that aggression is the "supreme international crime," armed conflict remains a frequent and ubiquitous feature of international life, leaving millions of victims in its wake. This collection of original chapters by leading and emerging scholars from all around the world evaluates historic and current examples of the use of force and the context of crimes of aggression. As we approach the seventy-fifth anniversary of the Nuremberg War Crimes Tribunal, *Seeking Accountability for the Unlawful Use of Force* examines the many systems and accountability frameworks that have developed since the Second World War. By suggesting new avenues for enhancing accountability structures already in place as well as proposing new frameworks needed, this volume will begin a movement to establish the mechanisms needed to charge those responsible for the unlawful use of force.

Leila Nadya Sadat is the James Carr Professor of International Criminal Law at Washington University Law and Director of the Harris World Law Institute. Since 2012 she has served as Special Adviser on Crimes Against Humanity to the International Criminal Court (ICC) Prosecutor, and in 2008 launched the Crimes Against Humanity Initiative to address the scourge of global atrocity crimes and draft a treaty on their punishment and prevention. Sadat is an award-winning scholar who recently received an Honorary Doctorate from Northwestern University and the Arthur Holly Compton Faculty Achievement Award. She is incoming President of the International Law Association (American Branch) and a member of the U.S. Council on Foreign Relations.

Seeking Accountability for the Unlawful Use of Force

Edited by

LEILA NADYA SADAT

Washington University in St. Louis

CAMBRIDGE
UNIVERSITY PRESS

University Printing House, Cambridge CB2 8BS, United Kingdom

One Liberty Plaza, 20th Floor, New York, NY 10006, USA

477 Williamstown Road, Port Melbourne, VIC 3207, Australia

314–321, 3rd Floor, Plot 3, Splendor Forum, Jasola District Centre, New Delhi – 110025, India

79 Anson Road, #06–04/06, Singapore 079906

Cambridge University Press is part of the University of Cambridge.

It furthers the University's mission by disseminating knowledge in the pursuit of
education, learning, and research at the highest international levels of excellence.

www.cambridge.org
Information on this title: www.cambridge.org/9781107187535
DOI: 10.1017/9781316941423

First published 2018

Printed in the United States of America by Sheridan Books, Inc.

A catalogue record for this publication is available from the British Library.

Library of Congress Cataloging-in-Publication Data
NAMES: Sadat, Leila Nadya, author.
TITLE: Seeking accountability for the unlawful use of force / Leila Nadya Sadat,
    School of Law, Washington University in St. Louis.
DESCRIPTION: Cambridge [UK] ; New York, NY : Cambridge University Press, 2018. |
    Includes bibliographical references and index.
IDENTIFIERS: LCCN 2017055338 | ISBN 9781107187535 (hardback) |
    ISBN 9781316638118 (paperback)
SUBJECTS: LCSH: Aggression (International law) | War (International law) |
    Crimes against peace–Law and legislation. | International criminal law. |
    International Military Tribunal. | War crimes. | Nuremberg Trial of
    Major German War Criminals, Nuremberg, Germany, 1945-1946.
CLASSIFICATION: LCC KZ7140 .S23 2018 | DDC 341.6/3–dc23
    LC record available at https://lccn.loc.gov/2017055338

ISBN 978-1-107-18753-5 Hardback
ISBN 978-1-316-63811-8 Paperback

This book is dedicated to two pioneers of international criminal justice

Benjamin B. Ferencz and M. Cherif Bassiouni

and to the victims of war, everywhere,

and to Sam, Kyra, and Emily, that they may see peace in their time.

Contents

Notes on Contributors

M. Cherif Bassiouni (1937–2017) was Emeritus Professor of Law at DePaul University College of Law, Honorary President of the Siracusa International Institute for Criminal Justice and Human Rights, and Honorary President of the International Association of Penal Law. He served in twenty-two United Nations positions and as a consultant to the U.S. Departments of State and Justice on many projects. Professor Bassiouni received numerous distinctions and awards, including a 1999 nomination for the Nobel Peace Prize for his work in the field of international criminal justice and for his contribution to the creation of the International Criminal Court.

David M. Crane was appointed a Professor of Practice at Syracuse University College of Law in 2006. He is currently a Principal at Justice Consultancy International, LLC. From 2002 to 2005 he was the founding Chief Prosecutor of the Special Court for Sierra Leone. In 2006 he founded Impunity Watch and in 2011 created the "I Am Syria" campaign. He assisted in the creation of the new U.N. Syrian International Independent Mechanism and he currently chairs an international effort to build a case against all sides committing international crimes in the Syrian civil war called the Syrian Accountability Project.

Robert Cryer is Professor of International and Criminal Law at Birmingham Law School. He has written, among other things, on war crimes trials in Asia, most notably as the coauthor (with Neil Boister) of *The Tokyo International Military Tribunal: A Reappraisal* (2008). He is also coeditor of the *Journal of Conflict and Security Law* and a member of the editorial board of the *Journal of International Criminal Justice*. He is currently working on various projects, including a book on the application of international humanitarian law by international criminal tribunals.

Federica D'Alessandra is an international law and policy scholar currently on a visiting appointment at the Harvard Law School where she focuses on international justice, the law of armed conflict, and related aspects of public international law. At Harvard, D'Alessandra also serves as an Adviser to Dean Hempton's One-Harvard Initiative for Sustainable Peace, and she spent six years at the John F. Kennedy School of Government as the Benjamin B. Ferencz Fellow, and as Carr Center for Human Rights Policy Fellow focusing on international security, multilateral diplomacy, atrocity prevention, and transitional justice.

Yoram Dinstein is Emeritus Professor at Tel Aviv University. He is a member of the Institut de Droit International and the President of the Israel United Nations Association. He is the editor of the *Israel Yearbook on Human Rights* and the author of several books on the laws of war. He has served twice as Stockton Professor of International Law at the U.S. Naval War College; Humboldt Fellow at the Max Planck Institute for International Law; Meltzer Visiting Professor of Law at New York University; and Visiting Professor of Law at the University of Toronto.

Terje Einarsen is Professor of Law at the University of Bergen, Norway, where he teaches international criminal law. He is Senior Research Associate at the University of London. He is also a lawyer, with permission to appear before the Supreme Court, and member of the Norwegian Bar Association. Einarsen has been a judge at the Court of Appeals and Head of the Human Rights Committee of the Norwegian Judges' Association. He is founder of the Universal Crimes Project, and author of *The Concept of Universal Crimes in International Law* (2012).

Benjamin B. Ferencz is a Hungarian-born Harvard lawyer and a staunch advocate of the international rule of law and the International Criminal Court. He served in World War II under General Patton and became Prosecutor of the *Einsatzgruppen* case, one of the twelve trials conducted by the United States in Nuremberg, Germany. In "an appeal of humanity to law" he convicted twenty-two defendants of murdering over a million people. Now in his ninety-eighth year, he continues to dedicate his life to using international law to deter war and to help create a more humane and just world order. He has published more than 100 books and articles, including *An International Criminal Court: A Step toward World Peace* (1980), *Enforcing International Law: A Way to World Peace* (1983), and *New Legal Foundations for Global Survival* (1994).

Donald M. Ferencz is the Executive Director of the Planethood Foundation and Convener of the Global Institute for the Prevention of Aggression. He is a

Visiting Professor at Middlesex University School of Law in London and a Research Associate at the Oxford University Faculty of Law's Centre for Criminology. He served as an NGO adviser to the Special Working Group on the Crime of Aggression, charged with developing amendments to the Rome Statute of the International Criminal Court (ICC). His work in the field of international justice focuses primarily on strengthening the rule of law through universalization of core crimes of the ICC.

Robin Geiß is Professor of International Law and Security at the University of Glasgow School of Law. Previously, he worked as Legal Adviser to the International Committee of the Red Cross in Geneva. Professor Geiß is a member of the scientific advisory board of the German Institute for International and Security Affairs, editor of the *Yearbook on International Humanitarian Law*, and a member of the German national International Humanitarian Law (IHL) Committee. He was a Visiting Professor at Sciences Po, a member of the group of experts that drafted the Tallinn Manual on cyberwarfare and Rapporteur of the ILA Study Group on the conduct of hostilities in the twenty-first century.

John Hagan is MacArthur Professor of Sociology and Law at Northwestern University and the American Bar Foundation. He has received the Stockholm Prize in Criminology, the Edwin Sutherland and Harry J. Kalven awards, and is an elected fellow of the American Academy of Arts and Sciences and National Academy of Sciences. He lead-authored a trilogy of monographs on *Justice in the Balkans, Darfur and the Crime of Genocide*, and *Iraq and the Crimes of Aggressive War*. He is former President of the American Society of Criminology and has received the Guggenheim, German Marshall Fund, and C. Wright Mills awards.

Anna Hanson is a post-doctoral fellow at the Graduate Institute in Geneva. She is currently working in two areas of international/legal sociology. Her dissertation research examines the post–9/11 transnational regulatory regime of anti–money laundering/counter–terrorism financing, which she argues sits at the intersection of crime, finance, and risk. The second project she is working on is a collaborative project (with Professor John Hagan and Joshua Kaiser) that deals with issues surrounding human rights, atrocity crimes, and legal cynicism caused by the 2003 invasion and occupation of Iraq.

Catherine Harwood is a PhD candidate and staff member at the Grotius Centre for International Legal Studies at Leiden University. She graduated *cum laude* from Leiden University with an LLM in Advanced Studies in Public International Law in 2012. In 2009, she graduated from Victoria

University of Wellington, with a Bachelor of Laws (First Class Honors) and a Bachelor of Arts in Sociology. She has worked as a judge's clerk at the New Zealand Court of Appeal and has interned at the International Criminal Court (ICC) and the International Bar Association's Programme on the ICC.

Robert Heinsch is an Associate Professor at Leiden University, and the Director of its LLM Programme in Public International Law. He is also the Director of the Kalshoven-Gieskes Forum on International Humanitarian Law (IHL) and its IHL Clinic, and a member of the German National IHL Committee. Previously, he was Rapporteur of the ILA Study Group on the Conduct of Hostilities Under IHL, has held the position of Federal Dissemination Officer at the German Red Cross, has worked as a legal adviser at the Red Cross in Berlin, and as a legal officer in the Trial Chamber of the International Criminal Court (ICC) in The Hague.

Larissa van den Herik is the Vice Dean of Leiden Law School and Professor of Public International Law at the Grotius Centre for International Legal Studies, Leiden University. She is general editor of Cambridge Studies in International and Comparative Law. Professor Van den Herik is Chair of the ILA Study Group on U.N. Sanctions and International Law. She also holds the position of Vice-Chair of the Advisory Committee on Public International Law Issues to the Dutch Government and has advised the government in that capacity, inter alia, on drones, cyberwarfare, humanitarian assistance, and autonomous weapons systems. Her most recent publications include the *Research Handbook on UN Sanctions and International Law* (2017).

Larry May is W. Alton Jones Professor of Philosophy Emeritus and Professor of Law at Vanderbilt University. He is also Professor of Philosophy Emeritus at Washington University. He has published more than thirty books, winning awards in law, philosophy, and political science fields. He is an authority on Just War Theory and International Law. Professor May's work has been addressed at three conferences in Europe: at Leiden University (2009); the Grotius Institute, Peace Palace at The Hague (2012); and the School of International Relations at the University of St. Andrews (2013). He is currently working on a multivolume work on ancient legal thought.

Carrie McDougall is the Legal Adviser at Australia's Mission to the United Nations in New York. Previously, she served as Assistant Director of the International Law Section at the Australian Department of Foreign Affairs and Trade (DFAT), where she provided advice on a range of security law issues. Before joining DFAT, she was a lecturer at Melbourne Law School, and was a commercial litigator. Her book *The Crime of Aggression under the*

Rome Statute of the International Criminal Court was published by Cambridge University Press in 2013. Dr. McDougall holds a PhD, LLB (hons), and a BA (hons).

Mary Ellen O'Connell, the Robert and Marion Short Professor of Law at the University of Notre Dame, focuses her research on international law and the use of force, international dispute resolution, and international legal theory. She is the author or editor of numerous books and articles, including *The Power and Purpose of International Law* and *What Is War?* She is at work on a new book, *The Art of Law in the International Community*. Professor O'Connell was a vice president of the American Society of International Law and chair of the International Law Association's Committee on the Use of Force.

Douglas J. Pivnichny is an Associate Legal Officer at the International Atomic Energy Agency (IAEA). He previously served as a University Trainee at the International Court of Justice. He earned his BA with honors at the University of Oxford, his JD from Washington University in St. Louis, and a Master's in International Law from the Graduate Institute, Geneva. In summer 2014, he served as the Whitney R. Harris World Law Institute Fellow. He contributes to this volume in his personal capacity and not on behalf of any institution to which he is or has been affiliated.

Geoffrey Robertson is a human rights barrister, academic, author, and broadcaster. He is the founder and joint head of Doughty Street Chambers. He has been counsel in many landmark cases. He served part-time as an appeals judge at the Special Court for Sierra Leone. In 2008 the U.N. Secretary General appointed him as one of the three distinguished jurist members of the U.N.'s Internal Justice Council. Robertson authored *Crimes against Humanity: The Struggle for Global Justice* (4th ed. 2012). In 2011 he was awarded the New York Bar Association's prize for achievement in international policy and law.

Leila Nadya Sadat is the James Carr Professor of International Criminal Law at Washington University Law and Director of the Harris World Law Institute. Since 2012 she has served as Special Adviser on Crimes Against Humanity to the International Criminal Court (ICC) Prosecutor, and in 2008 launched the Crimes Against Humanity Initiative to address the scourge of global atrocity crimes and draft a treaty on their punishment and prevention. Sadat is an award-winning scholar who recently received an Honorary Doctorate from Northwestern University. She is incoming President of the International Law Association (American Branch) and a member of the U.S. Council on Foreign Relations.

Sergey Sayapin is an Assistant Professor in International and Criminal Law at KIMEP University's School of Law in Almaty, Kazakhstan. From 2000 to 2014, he held various posts at the ICRC Regional Delegation in Central Asia. Dr. Sayapin is the author of *The Crime of Aggression in International Criminal Law: Historical Development, Comparative Analysis and Present State* (2014), and a coeditor of *The Use of Force against Ukraine: Jus ad bellum, jus in bello, jus post bellum* (forthcoming). He is the founding Editor-in-Chief of the *Central Asian Yearbook of International and Comparative Law.*

William A. Schabas is Professor of International Law at Middlesex University School of Law in London, Professor of International Criminal Law and Human Rights at Leiden University, and Emeritus Professor of Human Rights Law at the National University of Ireland–Galway. Professor Schabas serves as a Steering Committee member for Washington University's Crimes Against Humanity Initiative. He has authored *The Universal Declaration of Human Rights: Travaux préparatoires* (Cambridge University Press, 2013); *Unimaginable Atrocities, Justice, Politics, and Rights at the War Crimes Tribunals* (2012); and *The International Criminal Court: A Commentary on the Rome Statute* (2010).

Ambassador David J. Scheffer is the Mayer Brown/Robert A. Helman Professor of Law and Director of the Center for International Human Rights at Northwestern University Pritzker School of Law. He previously served as the U.S. Ambassador at Large for War Crimes Issues (1997–2001) and led the U.S. delegation at U.N. talks establishing the International Criminal Court. He was the U.N. Secretary-General's Special Expert on United Nations Assistance to the Khmer Rouge Trials from 2012 to 2017, was selected by *Foreign Policy* magazine as one of the "Top Global Thinkers of 2011," and received the Berlin Prize in 2013.

Kirsten E. Sellars is Visiting Fellow, Coral Bell School of Asia Pacific Affairs, Australian National University. Her research focuses on public international law – specifically, the law governing uses of force, the law of the sea, and international criminal law – with particular emphasis on Asian perspectives. Her latest books, the monograph *"Crimes against Peace" and International Law* (2015) and edited volume *Trials for International Crimes in Asia* (2015), are published by Cambridge University Press.

Jennifer Trahan is Associate Clinical Professor, The Center for Global Affairs, NYU. She has served as counsel to the International Justice Program of Human Rights Watch, served as Iraq Prosecutions Consultant to the International Center for Transitional Justice, and worked on cases before the

Special Court for Sierra Leone and Rwanda Tribunal. She has written books on the case law of the Yugoslav and Rwanda Tribunals, several book chapters, and scores of law review articles. She has also taught at Columbia University, Fordham Law School, and Brooklyn Law School, and she lectures at Salzburg Law School's Summer Institute on International Criminal Law.

Manuel J. Ventura is a director of The Peace and Justice Initiative – an NGO assisting States in ICL–related matters – and an Associate Legal Officer in Chambers at the Special Tribunal for Lebanon. He is also an adjunct fellow at Western Sydney University's School of Law, a casual law lecturer at The Hague University, and a member of the Council of Advisers of the Global Institute for the Prevention of Aggression. Previously, he served in the ICTY's Office of the Prosecutor, in Defense at the International Criminal Court (ICC), and for Chief Justice Mogoeng Mogoeng at the Constitutional Court of South Africa and STL President Antonio Cassese.

Angela Walker is an attorney at Latham & Watkins in Washington, D.C., where she handles complex litigation and internal investigations, as well as war crimes matters. While earning her JD and LLM in International Human Rights at Northwestern University, she served as the editor-in-chief of the *Journal of International Human Rights*. Walker clerked at the International Criminal Court (ICC), the District Court for the Northern District of Illinois, and the Inter-American Court of Human Rights. She has led trainings on international law for government agencies, non-governmental organizations, and law professors. Walker's publications focus on international humanitarian law and international criminal procedure.

Foreword

GEOFFREY ROBERTSON

This is a good time for serious discussion about the international law crime of aggression, and this is a good book to begin it. After a deceptively false start at Nuremberg, and a tentative definition in 1974 endorsed by a General Assembly Resolution, it appeared elliptically in Article 5 of the Rome Statue a quarter-century later as a crime within the jurisdiction of the International Criminal Court, but a jurisdiction which would be suspended until an up-to-date definition could be agreed. Agreement was not reached until the Kampala Review conference in 2010, and thus potential liability for the commission of aggression went unmentioned in the debates over the Bush/Blair invasion of Iraq without Security Council approval in 2003. The Kampala Amendments required a minimum of thirty ratifications, and the new State of Palestine lodged the thirtieth in 2016, Crimea having been "annexed" in the meantime. That left a further year before activation of the jurisdiction by a two-thirds majority of State Parties, which happened on December 14th, 2017, after a bitter fight over its scope in the Assembly of States Parties.

In the result, the crime will be punishable if committed after 17th July 2018, but not by nationals of a non-ratifying State or on such a State's territory (although these cases should still be referable to the ICC by the Security Council). In the meantime, there has been the attack on a Syrian airbase ordered by President Trump, avowedly to punish President Assad for his likely (although not forensically proven) use of chemical weapons against civilians. This set the academic dovecotes fluttering: was it a blatant breach of the U.N. Charter, or justified as some form of humanitarian intervention, or by a derivative of Responsible to Protect (R2P), or a contorted version of self-defense? As mutterings are still coming from the White House about a possible attack on North Korea, it is time to contemplate the consequences – in this case through illuminating essays of experts who were assembled at an important conference at Washington University in St. Louis School of Law in 2015.

It is difficult to disagree with the sentiments of the Nuremberg judgment, that *"to initiate a war of aggression … is not only an international crime, it is the supreme international crime differing only from other war crimes in that it contains within itself the accumulated evil of the whole."*[1] Unfortunately, as several of these papers (and notably that by the indefatigable Bill Schabas) point out, the Court's derivation of individual liability for the crime from the Kellogg–Briand Pact was distinctly shaky. That Pact, in 1928, was a disingenuous promise by States (including the United States) to renounce war as an instrument of national policy, and to rely instead on "pacific means" to settle their disputes. The counts in the Nuremberg indictment of *"conspiracy to wage aggressive war"* (prosecuted by the Americans with the help of a movie-tone news account of Hitler's foreign conquests) and *"crimes against peace"* (prosecuted by the British) were overblown and hypocritical. As the U.K.'s Foreign Office historical adviser, E. L.Woodward, noted on the eve of the trial, *"up to September 1st 1939, His Majesty's Government was prepared to condone everything that Germany had done to secure her position in Europe."*[2]

If anyone had been guilty as an accessory to the crime of aggression it was Stalin, who approved the Molotov–Ribbentrop Pact of August 1939 with its secret protocol carving a slice of Eastern Europe for the Soviet Union as reward for acquiescence in captured Nazi *Lebensraum*. So damning was this secret protocol that Robert Jackson – in a rare example of prosecutorial misconduct – did not disclose it to the defense, but at Soviet insistence kept it locked up.[3] It was easy for Justice Pal, a bitter Indian nationalist, to discredit the Tokyo trial as "victors' justice" by pointing out in his dissent the illogic of inferring a crime of aggression from the Kellogg–Briand Pact – it gave some force to his otherwise disgraceful attempt to whitewash Japanese war crimes (his dissent was published as a book, under the title *On Japan Being Not Guilty*).[4] Understandably, there was a certain shame-facedness about the retroactivity of these Nuremberg crimes, and aggression did not much feature in condemnations of the USSR for invading Hungary or Czechoslovakia or in

[1] 1 Trial of Major War Criminals Before the International Military Tribunal, Nuremberg, 14 November–1 October 1946, Judgment, at 186 (1947), *available at* www.loc .gov/rr/frd/Military_Law/pdf/NT_Vol-I.pdf.

[2] *Quoted by* Michael Biddiss, *Victors' Justice? The Nuremberg Tribunal*, Hist. Today, May 1995, at 54.

[3] Richard Overy, Interrogations: The Nazi Elite in Allied Hands, 1945 54 (2001).

[4] *See* Yves Beigbeder, Judging War Criminals: The Politics of International Justice 72 (1999).

commentaries on military interventions by the United States, from Santa Domingo to Vietnam.

Nonetheless, the crime is now here to stay, confirmed by the General Assembly after Nuremberg, given a definition agreed by States in 1974,[5] included provisionally in the Rome Statute in 1998 and crystallized at Kampala in 2010. Today, it means

> the use of armed forced *by a state against the sovereignty, territorial integrity or political independence of another state, or in any other manner inconsistent with the Charter of the UN.*

This simply picks up Article 2(4) of the Charter, and turns its injunction to Member States to "refrain" from aggression into individual liability for leaders of States that fail to refrain, if that failure takes the form of

> *planning, preparation, initiation or execution, by a person in a position effectively to exercise control over or to direct the political or military action of a State, of an act of aggression which, by its character, gravity and scale, constitutes a manifest violation of the Charter of the United Nations.*

Various essays in this book helpfully decode the elements of the crime. It will apply to Presidents or Prime Ministers, and to their senior ministers and to generals and to acting military commanders (i.e., to those brought into the net by Article 28 of the Rome Statute on "Responsibility of Commanders and other Superiors"). It will not, however (perhaps because it derives from the draft of 1974 – halcyon days before Islamic terrorism) apply to leaders of Al-Qaeda or ISIS or commanders of any "caliphate" – it still requires a Westphalian connection to the command structure of a sovereign State. Bin Laden would not be guilty of the crime of aggression for ordering 9/11 – which strikes some as absurd, although the limitation to State commanders has the advantage of withdrawing a degree of dignity, or least of all recognition, from terrorist leaders. The definition does not cover cyberattacks – another sign of its age, although the exclusion may be justified because they do not take human life, or at least not yet.

There remains some question over those who direct armed attacks by proxy – by support to terrorists, cross-border raiders, factions in a civil war and so forth (Kirsten Sellers recounts the heated debates in 1974 over whether aggression was committed by States supporting "freedom fighters"). Among the examples given in Article 8*bis* (2)(g) is a State's *"substantial involvement"*

---

[5] G.A. Res. 3314 (XXIX), annex, Definition of Aggression, U.N. Doc. A/RES/3314(XXIX) (Dec. 14, 1974).

in sending *"armed bands, groups, irregulars or mercenaries, which carry out armed force against another state,"* but these marauders must be despatched by a State commander who can control and direct them: it would not incriminate funding or supplying them with arms, so Charles Taylor would escape liability as an aggressor for supporting the Revolutionary United Front in Sierra Leone, and President Reagan could not retrospectively be deemed guilty of aggression for supporting the *contras* in Nicaragua, although as Sergey Sayapin persuasively argues, it might well apply to Russia's *"substantial involvement"* in aggression committed against Ukraine. Creation of instability, and encouragement of coups by financing, propagandizing, bribery, and the various undercover means used by U.S. and Russian spies and diplomats during the Cold War and thereafter fall outside the scope of the new crime (although such evidence could be relevant to the "planning, preparation . . . ," etc., of an actual attack). So too would cyberattacks and promotion of "fake news" by hostile States in order to influence democratic elections – an accusation made against Russia in respect of interference in the 2016 U.S. Presidential election.

The value of this volume is in part that it illuminates issues that will become acute when the crime does fall within the jurisdiction of the Court. David Scheffer and Angela Walker, for example, identify the danger that States will hesitate to ratify the amendment (or will opt out of its application) for fear that it may incriminate any well-intentioned use of military power for humanitarian purposes. "Humanitarian Intervention" unsanctioned by the Security Council will generally amount to a "manifest breach" of Article 2(4) of the Charter, whenever the interveners put "boots on the ground" or missiles in the airspace of an inhumane or failed State. Jennifer Trahan answers this concern by pointing out that the crime will only be committed by a "manifest" violation of the Charter, determined by its *"character, gravity* and [the conjuncture is important] *scale."* She concludes that "bona fide *humanitarian intervention would not be prosecutable as not having the right 'character' to constitute a 'manifest' Charter violation."* Unfortunately, any breach of Article 2(4) of the Charter is "prosecutable" in theory, and an invasion for humanitarian reasons (e.g. to stop the State killing its own citizens) would be "manifest" – i.e., demonstrable – because of its gravity and scale. "Character" would, like the other two characteristics (*gravity* and *scale*), seem referable to its military nature rather than its political or humanitarian purpose. It is ironic that those States most likely to ratify the crime, because of their commitment to peace and international law, are the countries most likely to support a genuine humanitarian intervention, such as bombing to stop Serbia continuing its ethnic cleansing in Kosovo.

Rather than have such States opt out or decline to ratify the amendment, and in place of oxymoronic claims that humanitarian intervention is "unlawful but legitimate," the way forward is surely to define carefully what constitutes an exception to the Charter prohibition on the use of force against sovereign States. The U.K. government in 2013 at least made a start, claiming that military action against Syria would be lawful if the Security Council was poleaxed and such action was necessary to avoid the disaster of civilians being gassed by chemical weapons, so long as

(1) *There is convincing evidence, generally accepted by the international community as a whole, of extreme humanitarian distress on a large scale, requiring immediate and urgent relief;*
(2) *It must be objectively clear that there is no practicable alternative to the use of force if lives are to be saved; and*
(3) *The proposed use of force must be necessary and proportionate to the aim of relief of humanitarian need and must be strictly limited in time and scope to this aim.*[6]

This was the U.K. government's legal position in support of a mission to punish Assad for breaching President Obama's "red line" over use of chemical weapons, but Parliament saw no urgent necessity for it and Obama was faced down by Congress, although in 2017 President Trump did not bother to ask. The U.K. definition is inadequate: it should focus on stopping crimes against humanity; the intervener should have regional backing (or at least a "coalition of the willing") and the support of a majority on the Security Council notwithstanding a veto by a superpower; the intervener must disavow any prospect of profit (e.g. by requiring territory and resources) and promise to pick up the pieces by undertaking whatever reconstruction is necessary for a return to normality.[7] If all these preconditions are satisfied, the intervention would not be *"inconsistent with the Purposes of the United Nations,"* as Article 2(4) of the Charter describes the character of the aggressive action it prohibits, but rather in conformity with Charter purposes of protecting international peace and human rights.

A further danger is that the cause of aggression can be sidestepped by a reinterpretation of the "inherent right to self-defense against armed attack"

---

[6] Prime Minister's Office, Policy Paper on Chemical Weapon Use by Syrian Regime: UK Government Legal Position (Aug. 29, 2013), www.gov.uk/government/publications/chemical-weapon-use-by-syrian-regime-uk-government-legal-position/chemical-weapon-use-by-syrian-regime-uk-government-legal-position-html-version.

[7] See Geoffrey Robertson, Crimes Against Humanity: The Struggle for Global Justice 755–59 (2012).

provided as an all-purpose exemption by Article 51 of the Charter. In customary law, stemming from the *Caroline* example, an armed attack must be
"imminent" before the right arises. The Bush Doctrine of "pre-emptive"
self-defense stretched the imminence test beyond breaking point, and today
the Trump White House, like the Obama administration before it, justifies
drone strikes, cyberattacks, and other military assaults on sovereign States if
they are "unable or unwilling" to combat terrorists within their territories. As
Leila Sadat points out, this amounts to a rewriting of the rules of international
law by the United States to provide a veneer for the use of force to achieve
military objectives. The bellicosity of President Trump at the U.N. Summit in
September 2017 against Venezuela, Cuba, and Iran seemed to reflect a U.S.
foreign policy that will not only seek to undermine States that displease it (*plus
ça change*) but may actually attack them or arm their internal opponents. As
for North Korea, Trump's rhetoric, like that of former President Ahmadinejad
against Israel – wiping it *"off the face of the map"* – presages or at least implies
a threat to use nuclear weapons – a threat that is itself *"generally unlawful"*
according to the International Court of Justice in the *Nuclear Weapons* case.
North Korea could feel justified in using its nukes first if a U.S. strike were
thought by Trump's bellicose language to be imminent, and thus could be
met with a pre-emptive first strike. The elasticity of Article 51, at least as
currently promoted by the United States, casts confusion over whether the
crime of aggression would apply to reprisals, or even to first strikes where preemption is a proclaimed, if subjective, purpose.

*

In reality, there are likely to be few prosecutions for the new crime. States with
leaders so malign that they would seriously consider invading other countries
will not become members of the Court (it still lacks 70 State parties, including
the United States, Russia, and China) or else will refuse to accept the
aggression amendments or alternatively accept them but opt out of the Court's
jurisdictions, which may or may not amount to the same thing, although it
hardly matters – the fact is that aggressor States will have multiple ways of
avoiding the Court's jurisdiction. Unless, of course, the Security Council
refers their acts of aggression to the Court (as it currently may do with war
crimes, genocide, and crimes against humanity). In other words, any
non–Member States referred by the Security Council will be those without
an alliance with one of the "Big 5" – think perhaps Galtieri and his junta for
invading the Falklands, or Saddam Hussein for invading Kuwait. In similar
cases, the existence of the new crime may have a real deterrent impact.

But never will it threaten the leader of a superpower or one of its allies – not even President Assad, who has for six years survived demands that Syria should be referred to the ICC, notwithstanding 400,000 deaths, 5 million refugees (with 6 million internally displaced), and chemical weapons strikes against civilians. He is protected against any Security Council action by Russia, which needs him to maintain a Mediterranean base for the Russian fleet. But he is not protected against the vagaries of Donald Trump, who ordered the attack on a Syrian airbase while lunching with the President of China. It was a limited attack that did little structural damage (war planes were flying the next day) although six Syrian soldiers were killed. Would such an action amount to the crime of aggression, once Article 8 becomes operational? It was a clear enough breach of the Charter, where the only explicit defense is the Article 51 right of self-defense, but not even the United States (which stretched the concept to breaking point in an effort to excuse the 2003 invasion of Iraq) could claim that Assad's air force was likely to bomb Manhattan.

President Trump did not commit a war crime – he did not target schools and hospitals (a speciality of the Syrian air force) – and he was innocent of any crime against humanity, as his one-off attack was not "widespread and system-atic" (although if he carries out further attacks, these elements may coalesce). He could not invoke (as some of his defenders have suggested) the doctrine of R2P, which hinges on Security Council approval. So there is no prospect of him being arrested next time he plays golf in Scotland.

Nonetheless, the attack was "manifest" (in the sense of being legally clear-cut) as a breach of the U.N. Charter. But was it "manifest" in the sense of being blindingly obvious because of its *"character, gravity and scale?"* There would be wiggle room for an accused Trump here: the airfield was not severely damaged, no civilians were killed, and "only" six soldiers lost their lives. It is an uneasy example of a clear breach of the U.N. Charter that would, because of its comparatively limited scale and consequences, entail no crim-inal liability for the leader who ordered it.

The raid was condemned by most international law scholars but accepted – even applauded – by most States – an example, perhaps, of how "State practice" is developing in favor of humanitarian intervention if it is swift and sure and directed against States in the hope of stopping further crimes against humanity. The Trump assault, an instant reaction to punish, borne of his daughter's pity at seeing pictures on Instagram of gassed children, ignored the preconditions necessary to validate an attack for the humanitarian purpose of deterring further crimes against humanity. For a start, Syria's guilt was not proved – the Chemical Weapons Convention, which Trump proclaimed his action was intended to support, has an urgent "anytime anywhere"

investigative procedure for identifying culprits, which the United States did
not bother to activate.

There are cases when it is absurd to quarrel with breaches of the U.N.
Charter or to demean them as *"unlawful but legitimate,"* and they range from
the Israeli attack on Entebbe to release hostages in the dog days of Idi Amin to
the Indian army invasion to stop the Pakistani army committing genocide in
Bangladesh. Humane intervention has an honorable history, the first articulated modern example going back to the 1650s, when the Duke of Piedmont,
an independent State in Southern France, began executing Protestants who
refused to convert to Catholicism. The poet Milton, who worked as Cromwell's Kissinger, told how they were *"slain by the bloody Piedmontese that
rolled / mother with infant down the rocks."* Cromwell was moved to tears, and
he prepared an English invasion in order to stop the *"violation of the honest
maxims of humane policy."* The Duke quickly agreed to end the persecution,
before the British navy reached Nice.

A number of the essays in this book comment on the dire consequences of
the superpower veto, which has stultified Security Council action over Syria
and Yemen and caused its failure to realize the potential of R2P. This is not an
argument against adoption of the crime of aggression, of course, but only a
warning that Security Council references to the ICC will be confined to
attacks commanded by leaders of States without superpower support. In such
cases, the very existence of the crime may act as a deterrent to the use of force,
and if it is used, an appropriate basis for trial and punishment of rulers who
make war on their neighbors.

The real importance of the Kampala Amendments, now that the jurisdiction has been activated as from July 2018, is to influence the calculations and
deliberations of those politicians and generals in powerful nations who,
although legally or practically beyond its reach, will nonetheless be subject
to national and especially international obloquy if they ignore it. Whatever
aggression presidents may contemplate without much fear of ending in the
dock of The Hague, they must nevertheless take into account the diplomatic
and political consequences of committing what everyone can recognize as an
international crime. This factor alone will carry some deterrent effect: I really
doubt whether the United Kingdom would have joined the U.S. invasion of
Iraq – a "manifest" breach of the U.N. Charter – had the aggression jurisdiction then been in existence. British generals, and even Tony Blair himself,
would have hesitated before taking a step that would clearly have entailed
their criminal liability. As for other superpower leaders of countries unconstrained by membership of the ICC, the fact that its State Parties have put the
crime of aggression amendment on its statute book will be a "mind how you

go" before President Trump bombs North Korea or President Putin annexes Estonia. Commission of the crime will upset their alliances and besmirch their legacies, and may affect their future holiday plans as well as limit the countries to which they may travel for hospital operations. It is easy to appreciate why Lithuania, Latvia, and Estonia were among the first to ratify the crime: it will not stop a Russian invasion, but its very existence as an international law offense would give rootin' tootin' shootin' Putin some reason to hold fire.

The twenty-first century has seen a hunger for international justice, a phenomenon that often raises more expectations than it can deliver (think of those peaceful protesters in Damascus back in 2011 with their banners "El Assad to The Hague"). But with adoption of the Kampala Amendments the intellectual arsenal of international criminal law will be complete, irrespective of whether its weapons can in practice be used. The very fact that they might be used, should leaders commit the crime, will become a subject of international diplomacy and discussion, for reflections in popular media as well as learned journals, and a focus for public protest everywhere in the world.

It is for academic experts, as custodians of international law, not only to discourse about its development among themselves but to explain them to the multitude. This book achieves both purposes (although the second might be better served without references to *jus ad bellum, jus in bello, proprio motu,* and other phrases understood – if at all – only by international lawyers). It will become an essential primer on the history, interpretation, and potential consequences of the crime of aggression. The advent of that crime should enable a better response to future breaches of the U.N. Charter than to describe them as "unlawful but legitimate." The rule of law requires a more straightforward answer: they are either criminal, or they fall within the strict limits of the right to self-defense or humanitarian intervention.

Geoffrey Robertson AO, QC
Doughty Street Chambers
February 2018

Preface

LEILA NADYA SADAT

This book is the result of three years of hard work. But it builds upon centuries of inspired thinking and practical efforts to constrain war. As the chapters in this volume outline, the efforts to constrain violence and impose accountability on aggressors include Hammurabi's Code, the 1899 and 1907 Hague Treaties with their Martens Clauses, the Kellogg–Briand Pact, the Nuremberg and Tokyo trials and judgments, the establishment of the United Nations, the decisions of international courts, arbitral tribunals and fact-finding commissions, the development of just war doctrines and the Responsibility to Protect, and, most recently, the establishment of the International Criminal Court and the activation of the Kampala Amendments on the crime of aggression. These efforts show that even during the darkest days of war, men and women have never given up the dream of a world at peace in which violence is the exception, rather than the rule, and in which lawful violence is defined and cabined by robust legal frameworks.

This volume would never have been possible but for the generosity – and leadership – of both Ben and Don Ferencz, who helped with its conceptual framing, funding, and implementation both in their individual capacities and through the generosity of the Planethood Foundation. Ben's faith in the rule of law and its capacity to serve the interest of peace has been an inspiration for more than seven decades. Don, equally, has become a passionate advocate for the rule of law in the service of peace. I, personally, and the world entire, are indebted to them for their perseverance, clear-sightedness, wisdom, and faith in humankind's ability to do better than it has done in the past.

I am also grateful to Harris Institute Fellows Fizza Batool, Madaline George, Kristin Smith, and Tamara Slater, who worked on the volume from conception to realization, and to Bethel Mandefro, the Institute's Program Coordinator and Office Manager, who helped with the logistics of our

St. Louis Conference in 2015 and with shepherding the volume through publication. It would be remiss to omit the many students who worked on the volume as well, including Kaitlyn Byrne, Kelly Mullen, Jesus A. Osete, Brittany Sanders, and Caroline Tunca. I would also like to thank John Berger, my editor at Cambridge University Press, who has helped me with this as well as other publications.

Finally, just as this volume was going to press, one of its authors, the inimitable Professor M. Cherif Bassiouni passed from this world to the next. Perhaps foreseeing this, he wrote in his chapter of the baton being passed to the next generation in the long struggle for peace and international justice. We will miss his voice and his leadership, his brilliant mind, his creativity, and his vision. This book is dedicated to him, along with Ben Ferencz, with the deepest respect, admiration, and gratitude for their decades of leadership and service to humankind.

As the drums of war beat louder with each passing day, and world leaders seem insufficiently committed to the maintenance of peace, this volume – with its critical analyses, historic lessons, and proposed new frameworks – is more important than ever. I hope that the reader will find in it something of value, and that the work herein will contribute to the continuing establishment of rules designed to impose accountability on those who use violence to achieve political ends. For, as Albert Camus wrote during the dark days of the Second World War, "peace is the only battle worth waging."

Leila Nadya Sadat
St. Louis, Missouri
October 17, 2017

Table of Cases

Introduction

DONALD M. FERENCZ

That the life of an eccentric sixteenth-century Danish astronomer should be prominently featured among the sources of inspiration for a modern-day treatise on international law may be surprising to some, but will perhaps seem less so to those familiar with his story.

Tycho Brahe was born in 1546 in Denmark, to a well-connected family of noble lineage. It may fairly be said that he was a man possessed. While at university in Rostock, Germany, he survived a duel with a fellow student in which the greater part of his nose was cut clean off. He wore a prosthetic replacement made of an amalgam of metals for the rest of his life – but it had little to do with his later claims to fame.

Although Tycho lived and died prior to the invention of the telescope, by the date of his untimely death in 1601 he had meticulously charted the position of more than a thousand stars, using only the naked eye and instruments that were built to his own specifications. The English author Alfred Noyes (perhaps best known for his poem "The Highwayman") celebrated the astronomer's life of dogged determination in a poetic volume entitled *The Torch-Bearers: Watchers of the Sky*, published in 1922. I first heard of it as a young man from my father, who had read portions of it that had been poignantly quoted in the eloquent writings of the distinguished twentieth-century jurist Justice Benjamin Cardozo. Like Cardozo, he was inspired by Brahe's story, and felt it well worth sharing.

To say that Tycho's career began, quite literally, with a bang is no exaggeration. On the night of November 11, 1572, in the skies over the Herrevad Abbey in northern Denmark, the then-twenty-five-year-old observed something quite unexpected. A light that had never been seen before was shining brightly within the constellation Cassiopeia. According to present-day reporting by the National Aeronautics and Space Administration, what Tycho saw that night was the after-effect of "a thermonuclear explosion as bright as a billion stars."

Fortunately for Tycho – as well as for the rest of planet Earth – the blast had occurred over 6,500 light years away (a single light year being equal to 6 trillion miles). Though others had also seen it, its sighting is most notably associated with Brahe due to the publication in 1573 of his *De Nova et Nullius Aevi Memoria Prius Visa Stella* ("On the New and Never Previously Seen Star"). Never mind that it wasn't a new star at all, but rather the explosive burst of a supernova emanating from the death throes of an extinguished sun; its sighting was a game-changer. Since the time of Aristotle, classical Western thought had held that the heavens were immutable and unchanging. The appearance of Tycho's supernova dispelled such assumptions and flung open the doors to new ways of thinking about the ordering of the cosmos.

With his credentials already well established, Tycho managed to have most of his future star-charting efforts underwritten with royal patronage from Frederick II, King of Denmark and Norway. An elaborate research complex and observatory was built for him on the Island of Hven (now part of Sweden). He named it Uraniborg in tribute to Urania, the ancient Greek muse of the heavens. It was there that for most of the next twenty years he searched the skies by night and conducted experiments in alchemy by day. With the passage of time, however, there arose a new king whose ministers had little interest in projects with such ill-defined utility. As Noyes tells the story, when the new king's emissaries challenged Tycho as to the practical value of his work, he offered nothing more than the firm belief that his accurate recording of the positions of the stars would help bring future generations that much closer to a truer understanding of the nature of the universe:

> "We are sent," they said, "to see and to report
> What use you make of these estates of yours.
> Your alchemy has turned more gold to lead
> Than Denmark can approve. The uses now!
> Show us the uses of this work of yours."
> Then Tycho showed his tables of the stars,
> Seven hundred stars, each noted in its place
> With exquisite precision, the result
> Of watching heaven for five-and-twenty years.
> "And is this all?" they said ...
> "Not all, I hope,"
> Said Tycho, "for I think, before I die,
> I shall have marked a thousand."
> "To what end?
> When shall we reap the fruits of all this toil?
> Show us its uses."

"In the time to come,"
Said Tycho Brahe, "perhaps a hundred years,
Perhaps a thousand, when our own poor names
Are quite forgotten, and our kingdoms dust,
On one sure certain day, the torch-bearers
Will, at some point of contact, see a light
Moving upon this chaos. Though our eyes
Be shut for ever in an iron sleep,
Their eyes shall see the kingdom of the law ... "

Though my father was an ardent admirer, he had never actually read *The Torch-Bearers* until I managed to find a copy, which I presented to him in 1970. At about that same time, he began the process of winding down his private law practice, so as to be able to fully devote himself to work on criminalizing the illegal use of force. In doing so, he left behind the New York offices that he had shared for many years with Telford Taylor, who, in a prior life, had appointed him Chief Prosecutor of the *Einsatzgruppen Case* at the American-led subsequent proceedings at Nuremberg. In need of a new office, he had one constructed as an adjunct to our family home in New Rochelle. He spent so many hours of seclusion in research and writing there that one morning a handwritten notice mysteriously appeared, taped to his office door. It had been written and surreptitiously affixed there by my eldest sister, Keri, and it remains there to this day. It said simply: "Here lies Tycho Brahe *ad infinitum*" – and, as my father's Epilogue to this volume (written in his ninety-seventh year) bears witness, the *ad infinitum* characterization wasn't too far off the mark.

To help advance the effective rule of law, my family established the Plancthood Foundation in 1996. Together with the Whitney R. Harris World Law Institute, the foundation co-hosted a 2015 symposium at Washington University School of Law in St. Louis entitled "The Illegal Use of Force: Reconceptualizing the Laws of War." This treatise is a by-product of that symposium, and is intended to help move forward the discussion of how developments within the law may advance prospects for a more humane and peaceful world. In bringing it to press, the efforts of Professor Leila Sadat have been paramount, and we would like to express our sincere gratitude, not only to her, but also to each of the contributing scholars whose submissions are included herein.

As for Tycho, when support from the Danish Court dried up, he took what instruments he could to Prague, where, from 1599 until his sudden death two years later, he worked under the auspices of Rudolf II, the Holy Roman Emperor. As a consequence, his cherished star charts came to be known as the Rudolphine tables. They were published in 1624 by Johannes Kepler, who had assisted Brahe in Prague and who relied on their data in developing his groundbreaking laws of planetary motion – a milestone that is still considered among the most brilliant advances in all of science. The torch had been passed, and, by its continued passing, achievements that once seemed inconceivable now regularly unfold within the realm of the possible.

Tycho's observatory at Uraniborg has long since crumbled to decay, yet the flame of his example can still be seen in the constellation of those whose torches of insight and learning light a path forward to the kingdom of the law.

Donald M. Ferencz

January 11, 2017

PART I

Historic and Contemporary Perspectives on the Unlawful Use of Force

The Status of Aggression in International Law from Versailles to Kampala – and What the Future Might Hold

M. CHERIF BASSIOUNI

I. *JUS AD BELLUM* AND *JUS IN BELLO*: THEIR ORIGINS AND THEIR DIFFERENCES

What we refer to today as international humanitarian law, regulating the use of force by one group against another, began its evolution in several civilizations some 5,000 years ago, thus evidencing the existence of evolving commonly shared human and social values.[1] The principles that emerged from this evolution reveal a certain common humanitarian thread among diverse civilizations of the world, reflecting values such as the preservation of human life and the minimization of harm and hardship to noncombatants, particularly women, children, and the elderly. The observance of *jus in bello* has been marked by the protagonists' shared interests.

The history of *jus ad bellum*, the legal or moral justification for going to war, is distinct from that of *jus in bello*. Warring groups rarely share interests or reasons for fighting: more often than not, the protagonists who resort to using force do so to achieve their own particular goals of power and wealth. Because compliance with *jus ad bellum* has lacked the motivating factor of common interests between protagonists in armed conflict, notwithstanding the apparent

---

[1] *See* A Manual on International Humanitarian Law and Arms Control Agreements 5–15 (M. Cherif Bassiouni ed. 2000) [hereinafter Bassiouni, Manual]; *see also* Charles Freeman, Egypt, Greece and Rome: Civilizations of the Ancient Mediterranean (2d ed. 2004); Patrick Glenn, Legal Traditions of the World: Sustainable Diversity in Law (5th ed. 2014). *See generally* Andrew Clapham & Paola Gaeta, The Oxford Handbook of International Law in Armed Conflict (2014). *See generally* 1–12 Arnold Toynbee, Study of History (1934–61); 1–11 Will Durant & Ariel Durant, The Story of Civilization (1993). *See also* 1–2 Harry Austryn Wolfson, Philo: Foundations of Religious Philosophy in Judaism, Christianity, and Islam (1947, 1962); Aristotle, Nicomachean Ethics (Terence Irwin trans., 2d ed. 2000).

connection between *jus ad bellum* and *jus in bello*, their legal norms have evolved differently.[2]

The constraints that have emerged over time under *jus ad bellum* also reveal the influence of shared value-oriented goals that include the preservation of world order, the maintenance of peace, and the minimization of human harm and material damage.[3] While these constraints reflect some of the same human and social values contained in *jus in bello*, they are based on different policy considerations and are conditioned by state interests, which in part explains why *jus in bello* has been more consistent in its norms. Both, however, have had their enforcement challenges.

By the time the idea of the "just war" was reflected in St. Thomas Aquinas's *Summa Theologica*, published in 1485 CE,[4] various norms and standards of *jus in bello*, developed in different civilizations, were already some 4,000 years old.[5] But in the end, both *jus ad bellum* and *jus in bello* became identified with Western civilization, even though they originated elsewhere and were transmitted to the West through ancient Greek, Persian, Indian, and Arabic writings translated by Arab Muslim scholars.[6] That legacy shaped what

---

[2] For a policy-analysis approach focusing on the *jus ad bellum* see MYRES S. McDOUGAL & FLORENTINO P. FELICIANO, LAW AND MINIMUM WORLD PUBLIC ORDER: THE LEGAL REGULATION OF INTERNATIONAL COERCION (1961); Myres S. McDougal, Harold D. Laswell & W. Michael Reisman, *The World Constitutive Process of Authoritative Decision, in* 1 THE FUTURE OF THE INTERNATIONAL LEGAL ORDER: TRENDS AND PATTERNS 73 (Richard A. Falk & Cyril E. Black eds., 1969). For a different critical perspective based on contemporary political realism, *see* Mohamed S. Helal, *Justifying War and the Limits of Humanitarianism*, 37 FORDHAM INT'L L.J. 551 (2014) [hereinafter Helal, *Justifying War*].

[3] Political realists will challenge this premise expressed above, claiming instead that the outcome, mentioned above, is part of state interest and no commonality of shared moral or social values should be given more than marginal consideration. *See* Ian Ward, *The End of Sovereignty and the New Humanism*, 55 STAN. L. REV. 2091, 2106 (2003); Paul W. Kahn, *Speaking Law to Power: Popular Sovereignty, Human Rights, and the New International Order*, 1 CHI. J. INT'L L. 1, 9 (2000); Hans J. Morgenthau, *The Machiavellian Utopia*, 55 ETHICS 145, 146 (1945).

[4] ST. THOMAS AQUINAS, SUMMA THEOLOGICA (1485) [hereinafter AQUINAS]. *See also* discussion *infra* note 6 on Aquinas and others.

[5] *See* SUN TZU, THE ART OF WAR 76 (Samuel B. Griffith trans., 1963); THE LAWS OF MANU 230, tit. VII, ¶ 90 (Georg Bühler trans., 1886); MARCUS TULLIUS CICERO, DE OFFICIIS (Walter Miller trans., 1975); GEORG F. MARTENS, SUMMARY OF THE LAW OF NATIONS, FOUNDED ON THE TREATIES AND CUSTOMS OF THE MODERN NATIONS OF EUROPE (William Cobbett trans., 1795). *See also* JOHN KEEGAN, A HISTORY OF WARFARE 173 (1993); Bassiouni, MANUAL, *supra* note 1, at 5–21 and accompanying notes.

[6] These writings and principles went on to influence the writings of Western Christian scholars (transmitted mostly through Arab Muslim scholars) such as Vitoria (1486–1546), Ayala (1548–1584), Gentili (1552–1608), Suarez (1548–1617), and later to Hugo Grotius in his writings the *De Jure Belli ac Pacis* from 1625. These works were followed by Puffendorf, Burlemaqui, and de Vattel. FRANCISCUS DE VICTORIA, DE INDIS ET DE IVRE BELLI RELECTIONES (Classics

became Western European Christian conceptions of, and limitations on, *jus ad bellum* and *jus in bello*[7] that one can attribute to the migration of ideas or to

of International Law Ser. No. 7, vol. I, 1917); Balthazar Ayala, Three Books on the Law of War and on the Duties Connected with War and on Military Discipline (Classics of International Law Ser. No. 2, vol. II, 1912); Alberico Gentili, De Jure Belli Libri Tres (Classics of International Law Ser. No. 16, vol. I, 1933); Francisco Suarez, Selections from Three Works (Classics of International Law Ser. 20, vol. I, 1944); Hugo Grotius, De Jure Belli ac Pacis (1625); Samuel Pufendorf, De Jure Naturae Et Gentium Libri Octo bk. III (1672); Jean Jacques Burlamaqui, Principes Du Droit Naturel et Politique (1747); Emmerich De Vattel, Le Droit Des Gens (1758). For a discussion on Beccaria, Grotius, and de Vattel *see* Roscoe Pound, An Introduction to the Philosophy of Law (1922). Despite the idea of human values and their role in times of conflict existing in many different societies throughout early recorded history, it was only in about the thirteenth century CE that the concept of *jus ad bellum* developed as a consequence of the writings of St. Thomas Aquinas on the "just war." Aquinas was inspired by Augustine of Hippo, an Arab Tunisian Catholic bishop who lived from 354 to 430 CE and wrote about the war in North Africa between the invading barbarians of the European north, as they were referred to, and the Roman Byzantine troops that occupied parts of North Africa. At the time, the Roman governor was much less concerned with the conduct of war than he was with the pursuit of earthly pleasures, which led Bishop Augustine, who was later canonized, to argue for some theories, which we would in modern times call humane theories, in the use of war and limitations on the right to resort to war. Between 1265 and 1273, St. Thomas Aquinas, inspired by the writings of Augustine, drafted his *Summa Theologica* (though it was not published until 1485), which became the basis of the theory of the "just war" and the concept of *jus ad bellum*.

7   This is particularly evidenced in Islam's early prohibition of aggression. As stated by Professor Mohammad Hashim Kamali:

> During the first 13 years of his campaign in Makka, the Prophet Muhammad was not permitted to use force even in self defence. Islam was propagated only through peaceful engagement with the people, inviting them to give up idolatry and embrace the monotheistic call of Islam. The idolaters of Makka persecuted and forced a number of the Prophet's Companions to migrate, initially to Abyssinia, and later to Madina. Nevertheless, the Prophet kept reminding his Companions to be patient and to pursue their campaign peacefully. Some of them urged the Prophet if he would allow reciprocal treatment, which he declined due to repeated Quranic instructions:
>
>> So wait patiently (O Muhammad) for thy Lord's decree, surely thou art in Our sight (52:48);
>>
>> Then bear with them and say: peace. They will (eventually) come to know (43:89);
>>
>> So forgive, with a gracious forgiveness (15:85);
>>
>> Repel (evil) with what is better. Then will he between whom and thee was hatred become as it were thy friend and intimate! (41:34).
>
> As the persecution of Muslims reached its peak when the pagans of Makka conspired against the life of the Prophet, he migrated to Madina. Even then the Quranic permission to fight was not granted until a year later when the Makkans set out to attack the Muslim community some 270 k[ilometers] away in Madina. The first Quranic verse that permits fighting was then revealed:
>
>> Permission is granted to those who fight because they have been wronged, and God is indeed able to give them victory; those who were driven from their homes unjustly because they said: our Lord is God (78:39).

natural sharing of moral values or both, a convergence that contributed to the growth and development of human and social values that the world community has come to embrace.

It was not until 1648, when the Treaty of Westphalia recognized the putative sovereign equality of States, that the principle of States' respect for each other's existence and integrity formally emerged.[8] But that treaty was between European States[9] that were extricating themselves from the Thirty Years War, which was fought over the reformation of Christianity,[10] and the same States later showed that when it came to invading non-European States and territories, they did not feel bound by this limitation. These States freely engaged in what we generically have come to call aggression, carried out in the most brutal ways, particularly against non-Western and non-Christian communities, whether or not those communities were regarded as States in the European understanding of that

---

Mohammad Hashim Kamali, *Jihad and the Interpretation of the Quran: Contextualising Islamic Tradition*, in JIHAD AND ITS CHALLENGES TO INTERNATIONAL AND DOMESTIC LAW 39, 42–43 (M. Cherif Bassiouni & Amna Guellali eds., 2010). As stated by this writer in the same book:

> When the Prophet and his followers were forced to leave Makka (622 CE), they were attacked by non-Muslims, and a verse of the *Quran* was revealed about the right to self-defense against aggression: "Sanction is given unto those who fight because they have been wronged." Later, the *Quran* was more explicit:
>> *Surat al-Baqarah*: Fight in the way of God against those who fight against you, *but do not begin hostilities for God does not love aggression.* And slay them wherever you find them [the aggressors], and drive them out of their places whence they drove you out, for persecution is worse than slaughter. And fight not with them in the Inviolable Place of Worship until they attack you, then slay them. Such is the reward of disbelievers.

M. Cherif Bassiouni, *Evolving Approaches to Jihad: From Self-Defense to Revolutionary and Regime-Change Political Violence*, in JIHAD AND ITS CHALLENGES TO INTERNATIONAL AND DOMESTIC LAW, supra, at 11, 23.

[8] Treaty of Westphalia, Oct. 24, 1648, 1 Parry 271; 1 Parry 119. *See* Leo Gross, *The Peace of Westphalia, 1648–1948*, 42 AM. J. INT'L L. 20 (1948); DEREK CROXTON & ANUSCHKA TISCHER, THE PEACE OF WESTPHALIA: A HISTORICAL DICTIONARY (2002); WILLIAM P. GUTHRIE, THE LATER THIRTY YEARS WAR: FROM THE BATTLE OF WITTSTOCK TO THE TREATY OF WESTPHALIA (2003). *See also* BEYOND WESTPHALIA?: STATE SOVEREIGNTY AND INTERNATIONAL INTERVENTION (Gene M. Lyons & Michael Mastanduno eds., 1995).

[9] Or various analogs to monarchies, since "States" (as the term is now understood) did not then exist.

[10] *See generally* PETER H. WILSON, THE THIRTY YEARS WAR: EUROPE'S TRAGEDY (2011); RICHARD BONNEY, THE THIRTY YEARS' WAR 1618–1648 (2002); C. V. WEDGEWOOD, THE THIRTY YEARS WAR (2016).

form of political organization.[11] This is evident in the colonization by European States of territories in Africa, Asia, and North and South America.[12]

So even if *jus ad bellum* was a limitation on the power of States to resort to the use of force against other States, in practice it was limited to interactions between Christian Western European States and certainly not without exceptions. But except for moralists, it was not a universal principle of what was right or wrong or what was universally applicable to all cultures and peoples of the world. This meant that there were multiple standards and that some members of this amorphous international society benefited from exceptionalism, just as happens today when it suits the interests of major powers.[13]

With so many exceptions throughout history and so little enforcement over so long, sustaining the desideratum to refrain from the use of force except for a just reason (which was essentially self-defense but which, like many expandable legal concepts, was in practice frequently stretched to the limits of credibility) became increasingly difficult. Yet that concept survived in *jus ad bellum* and managed, by the time of the new millennium, to evolve to the point that major confrontations between States capable of inflicting terrible harm on the world have not only been contained but significantly reduced.

---

[11] JEAN-PAUL SARTRE, COLONIALISM AND NEOCOLONIALISM (Azzedine Haddour, Steve Brewer & Terry McWilliams trans., 2001); NORRIE MacQUEEN, COLONIALISM (2007); FREDERICK COOPER, COLONIALISM IN QUESTION: THEORY, KNOWLEDGE, HISTORY (2005).

[12] The exception was also extended by papal authority to four Crusades. Pope Urban II called for the First Crusade in 1095, which officially began the following year. The Second Crusade was announced by Pope Eugene III in 1147. The Third Crusade was undertaken at the behest of Pope Clement III in 1189, and the Forth Crusade began in 1202 during the term of Pope Innocent III. *Cf.* JONATHAN RILEY-SMITH, THE CRUSADES: A HISTORY (3d ed. 2014) [hereinafter RILEY-SMITH, THE CRUSADES: A HISTORY]; JONATHAN RILEY-SMITH, THE OXFORD HISTORY OF THE CRUSADES (2002) [hereinafter RILEY-SMITH, THE OXFORD HISTORY OF THE CRUSADES]. *See generally* AMIN MAALOUF, THE CRUSADES THROUGH ARAB EYES (1989). This practice prevailed in the Christian Western European history of colonialism over centuries, ending only in the last few decades with the era of decolonization. *See* sources cited *supra* note 11 (on colonialism). For information on decolonization *see* RAYMOND BETTS, DECOLONIZATION: THE MAKING OF THE CONTEMPORARY WORLD (2d ed. 2004); DIETMAR ROTHERMUND, THE ROUTLEDGE COMPANION TO DECOLONIZATION (2000).

[13] This situation is captured well in the classic 1970s novel *Animal Farm* (first published in 1945), in which George Orwell wrote, "some animals are more equal than others." GEORGE ORWELL, ANIMAL FARM 133 (1972). *See generally* Harold Koh, *Foreword: On American Exceptionalism*, 55 STAN. L. REV. 1479 (2003); MICHAEL IGNATIEFF, AMERICAN EXCEPTIONALISM AND HUMAN RIGHTS (2005); Anu Bradford & Eric A. Posner, *Universal Exceptionalism in International Law*, 52 HARV. INT'L L.J. 1 (2011).

But although the practice of States using force against other States and other peoples has decreased, the concepts and values reflected in the *jus ad bellum* – and its moral and legal validity – have been politically compromised. Despite the post-millennium decline in interstate armed conflicts,[14] States have still found ways to carry out their power and interest objectives, which attests to the success of *realpolitik*, or political realism in international affairs, over commonly shared human and social values.[15]

With the advent of the new millennium, *jus ad bellum* was tested by new means and methods of warfare, including the use by States of automated weapon systems (AWS), and new categories of protagonists, including non-state actors, who often provide support and assistance to combatants.[16] This

---

[14]   See *infra* Section VI and accompanying notes (on the changing nature of aggression).

[15]   *See generally* BERNARD WILLIAMS, IN THE BEGINNING WAS THE DEED: REALISM AND MORALISM IN POLITICAL ARGUMENT (Geoffrey Hawthorn ed., 2005); JOHN BEW, REALPOLITIK: A HISTORY (2015); KENNETH N. WALTZ, REALISM AND INTERNATIONAL POLITICS (2008); THE REALISM READER (Colin Elman & Michael A. Jensen eds., 2014); NORRIN M. RIPSMAN, JEFFREY W. TALIAFERRO, & STEVEN E. LOBELL, NEOCLASSICAL REALIST THEORY OF INTERNATIONAL POLITICS (2016); JACK DONNELLY, REALISM AND INTERNATIONAL RELATIONS (2000); Richard H. Steinberg & Jonathan M. Zasloff, *Power and International Law*, 100 AM. J. INT'L L. 64 (2006); Richard N. Haass, *Paradigm Lost*, FOREIGN AFF., Jan.–Feb. 1995, at 43.

[16]   *See* Azar Gat, *The Changing Character of War*, in THE CHANGING CHARACTER OF WAR 27 (Hew Strachan & Sibylle Scheipers eds., 2011); Mats Berdal, *The "New Wars" Thesis Revisited*, in THE CHANGING CHARACTER OF WAR 109 (Hew Strachan & Sibylle Scheipers eds., 2011); M. Cherif Bassiouni, *The New Wars and the Crisis of Compliance with the Law of Armed Conflict by Non-State Actors*, 98 J. CRIM. L. & CRIMINOLOGY 711 (2008) [hereinafter Bassiouni, *New Wars & Non-State Actors*]; Jaume Saura, *On the Implications of the Use of Drones in International Law*, 12 J. INT'L L. & INT'L R. 120 (2016); Stathis N. Kalyvas, *The Changing Character of Civil Wars, 1800–2009*, in THE CHANGING CHARACTER OF WAR, *supra*, at 202; EVGENI MOYAKINE, THE PRIVATIZED ART OF WAR: PRIVATE MILITARY AND SECURITY COMPANIES AND STATE RESPONSIBILITY FOR THEIR UNLAWFUL CONDUCT IN CONFLICT AREAS (School of Human Rights Research Ser. No. 67, 2015). *See generally* Louis Maresca & Eleanor Mitchell, *The Human Costs and Legal Consequences of Nuclear Weapons Under International Humanitarian Law*, 97 INT'L REV. RED CROSS 621 (2015); ARMED CONFLICTS AND THE LAW (Jan Wouters, Philip De Man & Nele Verlinden eds., 2016); YORAM DINSTEIN, THE CONDUCT OF HOSTILITIES UNDER THE LAW OF INTERNATIONAL ARMED CONFLICT (3d ed. 2016); LEILA NADYA SADAT, *America's Drone Wars*, 45 CASE W. RES. J. INT'L L. 215 (2012); Frédéric Mégret, *The Humanitarian Problem with Drones*, 2013 UTAH L. REV. 1283 (2013); MILENA STERIO, *The Covert Use of Drones: How Secrecy Undermines Oversight and Accountability*, 8 ALB. GOV'T L. REV. 129 (2015); Kristina Benson, *"Kill 'em and Sort It Out Later": Signature Drone Strikes and International Humanitarian Law*, 27 PAC. MCGEORGE GLOB. BUS. & DEV. L.J. 17 (2014); Alan Backstrom & Ian Henderson, *New Capabilities in Warfare: An Overview of Contemporary Technological Developments and the Associated Legal and Engineering Issues in Article 36 Weapons Reviews*, 94 INT'L REV. RED CROSS 483 (2012); Jackson Maogoto & Steven Freeland, *The Final Frontier: The Laws of Armed Conflict and Space Warfare*, 23 CONN. J. INT'L L. 165 (2007); Jameson W. Crockett, *Space Warfare in the Here and Now: The Rules of Engagement for U.S. Weaponized Satellites in the Current Legal Space Regime*, 77 J. AIR L. &

changing reality requires us to consider a new legal strategy to address aggression: one that helps deter States' decision makers from resorting to aggression; reduces their resorting to other methods and means of warfare, including the use of AWS; and reaches the ever-expanding groups of non-state actors and organizations (many of whom meet the definition of legitimate businesses and, in the case of certain multinational corporations, are beyond the reach of the law) engaging in such conduct. This new approach requires several paradigm shifts about international law enforcement modalities, particularly as to individual international criminal responsibility and its expansion to non-state actors.[17]

Although the brand name "aggression" no longer means what it did throughout the five centuries of evolution of *jus ad bellum*, we must not jettison the historical legacy of *jus ad bellum*. It is still the international law foundation of the prohibition of the use of force by one State against another State and against other people and, ideally, the use of force by non-state actors as well.[18] It must be noted, however, that the customary international law violation of *jus ad bellum* does not contain principles and norms for the criminalization of individuals' conduct leading to aggression. This is provided in another legal regime of international law, namely international criminal

COM. 671 (2012); CYBERWAR: LAW AND ETHICS FOR VIRTUAL CONFLICTS (Jens David Ohlin, Kevin Govern & Claire Finkelstein eds., 2015); MICHAEL E. O'HANLON, THE FUTURE OF LAND WARFARE (2015); MITCHELL D. SILBER, DANIEL B. GARRIE & RHEA D. SIERS, CYBERWARFARE: UNDERSTANDING THE LAW, POLICY AND TECHNOLOGY (2015); HEATHER HARRISON DINNISS, CYBER WARFARE AND THE LAWS OF WAR (2012). For more information on the United States' use of new technology in combat *see* MATTHEW ROSENBERG & JOHN MARKOFF, *At Heart of U.S. Strategy, Weapons That Can Think*, N.Y. TIMES, Oct. 26, 2016, at A1 ("Just as the Industrial Revolution spurred the creation of powerful and destructive machines like airplanes and tanks that diminished the role of individual soldiers, artificial intelligence technology is enabling the Pentagon to reorder the places of man and machine on the battlefield the same way it is transforming ordinary life with computers that can see, hear and speak and cars that can drive themselves. The new weapons would offer speed and precision unmatched by any human while reducing the number—and cost—of soldiers and pilots exposed to potential death and dismemberment in battle. The challenge for the Pentagon is to ensure that the weapons are reliable partners for humans and not potential threats to them. . . . Can a machine be trusted with lethal force? Who is at fault if a robot attacks a hospital or a school? Is being killed by a machine a greater violation of human dignity than if the fatal blow is delivered by a human?").

[17] *See* M. CHERIF BASSIOUNI, INTRODUCTION TO INTERNATIONAL CRIMINAL LAW 59–109 (2d rev. ed. 2012) [hereinafter BASSIOUNI, INTRO TO ICL].

[18] *Id.*

law (ICL).[19] But the two are complimentary. International law norms, like domestic ones, range in their legislative techniques and stages and include the enunciative, declarative, prescriptive, and proscriptive (which includes individual criminalization).[20] They are all on the same continuum.[21]

II. THE CONTROL AND PROHIBITION OF AGGRESSION IN CONTEMPORARY INTERNATIONAL LAW

In what would appear to be the pursuit of a shared goal, the prevention of aggression, States have taken three paths: defining "aggression," placing it under the jurisdiction of the United Nations Security Council, and criminalizing it under international criminal law. At the United Nations, the definition of aggression has gone through various stages and committees established by the General Assembly to draft a definition, culminating in a United Nations General Assembly resolution in 1974 after twenty-two years of work. More telling is the fact that the Security Council has never relied on that definition in any of its resolutions pertaining to the use of force by one State against another.

The United Nations Charter includes the prohibition of aggression in Article 39 and confers exclusive jurisdiction in matters affecting peace and security to the Security Council pursuant to Chapter VII. But in all the conflicts it has considered pursuant to its exclusive jurisdiction on matters affecting peace and security under Chapter VII of the Charter, the Security Council has never made a finding of aggression against any State. Throughout its history, the Security Council has dealt with such issues as political rather than legal matters, thus not relying on the 1974 Definition of Aggression. And because of the legal implications that could arise from a Security Council finding that one State committed aggression against another, it never made such a finding. The two major implications would be state responsibility and

---

[19] *See generally* BASSIOUNI, INTRO TO ICL, *supra* note 17; THE CAMBRIDGE COMPANION TO INTERNATIONAL CRIMINAL LAW (WILLIAM A. SCHABAS ed., 2016) [hereinafter CAMBRIDGE COMPANION]; ROGER O'KEEFE, THE OXFORD INTERNATIONAL LAW LIBRARY: INTERNATIONAL CRIMINAL LAW (2015); ANTONIO A. CASSESE et al., INTERNATIONAL CRIMINAL LAW: CASES AND COMMENTARY (2011). *See also* 1–4 HISTORICAL ORIGINS OF INTERNATIONAL CRIMINAL LAW (MORTEN BERGSMO et al. eds., 2014–15) [hereinafter HISTORICAL ORIGINS OF ICL].

[20] For a theory of normative evolution *see* M. Cherif Bassiouni, *The Proscribing Function of International Criminal Law in the Processes of International Protection of Human Rights*, 9 YALE J. WORLD PUB. ORD. 193 (1982).

[21] *Id.* at 195.

the international criminal responsibility of individual decision makers and senior executors of aggression under international criminal law.[22]

The criminalization of aggression under international criminal law also has gone through a variety of stages, from post–World War II up to the International Criminal Court (ICC) Kampala Amendments of 2010.[23] Thus what should have been a coordinated, complementary approach between *jus ad bellum* as it evolved in customary international law (the definition of aggression by the United Nations, the international criminal law definition of aggression by individual decision makers and senior executors) and the application of the principles of state responsibility from the harmful consequences caused by one State to another never materialized. The fragmented and unrelated series of developments ultimately weakened the *jus ad bellum* and its enforcement under international law. But then the world did not witness a Third World War, and the United Nations engaged in a number of peacekeeping operations, all of which indicated a relatively positive outcome, even though outside the historical legal framework that was also apparently being championed.[24] This may well illustrate the wide gap between the perception of academics, or their wishful thinking, and reality.

If one sets the birth of *jus ad bellum* at 1485 CE, the date of the publication of the *Summa Theologica*,[25] the principle has survived more than 500 years, and one can argue that the reasons for *jus ad bellum* in the time of St. Thomas Aquinas still exist today. But in the postmillennial era of globalization,[26] a time in which the post–World War II push for collective peace and security, human rights, and international criminal accountability is facing new domestic sociopolitical challenges and greater nationalistic unilateralism under the questionable claims of national security and national interest, this five-century evolution may well have outlived its political usefulness.

The concept of *jus ad bellum* establishes the justification for the prohibition of aggression on the basis of the unarticulated premise that the concept of the "just war" presupposes the existence of a contrasting principle of the "unjust

---

[22] *See infra* note 40 (on the Nuremberg Charter [also known as the London Charter], Tokyo Charter, and Control Council Law No. 10).

[23] Rome Statute of the International Criminal Court art. 8*bis*, 15*bis*, 15*ter*, *adopted on* July 17, 1998, 2187 U.N.T.S. 91 (entered into force July 1, 2002) [hereinafter Rome Statute or Kampala Amendments].

[24] *See infra* notes 79–96 and accompanying text (on peacekeeping operations, humanitarian intervention, and the responsibility to protect).

[25] *See* discussion on Aquinas, *supra* note 4 and accompanying text.

[26] *See generally* GLOBALIZATION AND ITS IMPACT ON THE FUTURE OF HUMAN RIGHTS AND INTERNATIONAL CRIMINAL JUSTICE (M. Cherif Bassiouni ed., 2015) [hereinafter Bassiouni, GLOBALIZATION, HRs AND ICJ].

war." But between what is deemed a just and unjust war lies a schism filled by contrasting philosophical, theological, political, and legal views – and more important, the absence of any system capable of applying a fair and impartial standard to all States and enforcing it. The struggle that centers on the specificity of a proscriptive norm occurs at the political level, while the criminalization of aggression follows another tortuous course that started only after the end of World War I, when the then-unspecified concept of aggression was retroactively and ambiguously included in Article 227 of the Treaty of Versailles, which identified Kaiser Wilhelm II of Germany as the perpetrator of what was then an unknown international crime.[27] This initiative separated the previously prescriptive stage of aggression, which could be thought to have started with the publication of the *Summa Theologica* in 1485,[28] and the first effort at proscribing aggression in 1919, more than 430 years later. The initiative was presumably a tangible expression of the values of humankind and an attempt to regulate the conduct of States by holding a given head of state individually criminally accountable for the international crime of aggression. But that initiative was one of the most successful legal deceptions ever undertaken in the history of international criminal law.[29]

It started in the aftermath of the defeat of Germany, Austria-Hungary, and the Ottoman Empire in 1918, when the victorious Allies, namely Great Britain, France, Italy, Japan, and the United States[30] demanded a heavy toll of punitive reparations from Germany.[31] These reparations were

---

[27] *See* Treaty of Versailles, *infra* note 30, art. 227; 1–4 FRED L. ISRAEL, MAJOR PEACE TREATIES OF MODERN HISTORY 1698–1967 (1967–80).

[28] AQUINAS, *supra* note 4 and accompanying text.

[29] M. Cherif Bassiouni, *World War I: "The War to End all Wars" and the Birth of a Handicapped International Criminal Justice System*, 30 DENV. J. INT'L. L. & POL'Y 244 (2002) [hereinafter Bassiouni, WWI]; *see* CLAUD MULLINS, THE LEIPZIG TRIALS: AN ACCOUNT OF THE WAR CRIMINALS' TRIALS AND A STUDY OF GERMAN MENTALITY 35 (1921); JAMES F. WILLIS, PROLOGUE TO NUREMBERG: THE POLITICS AND DIPLOMACY OF PUNISHING WAR CRIMINALS OF THE FIRST WORLD WAR 9–10 (1982); James Brown Scott, *The Trial of the Kaiser, in* WHAT REALLY HAPPENED AT PARIS: THE STORY OF THE PEACE CONFERENCE, 1918–1919, at 231, 240 (EDWARD MANDELL HOUSE & CHARLES SEYMOUR eds., 1921).

[30] The following States were also described by the Treaty of Versailles as the Principal Allied and Associated Powers: Belgium, Bolivia, Brazil, China, Cuba, Ecuador, Greece, Guatemala, Haiti, the Hedjaz, Honduras, Liberia, Nicaragua, Panama, Peru, Poland, Portugal, Romania, the Serb-Croat-Slovene State, Siam, Czechoslovakia, and Uruguay. Treaty of Peace Between the Allied and Associated Powers and Germany (Treaty of Versailles), June 28, 1919, 2 Bevans 235 (entered into force Jan. 10, 1920) [hereinafter Treaty of Versailles].

[31] *See* FREDERICK TAYLOR, THE DOWNFALL OF MONEY: GERMANY'S HYPERINFLATION AND THE DESTRUCTION OF THE MIDDLE CLASS (2015). *See also* MARGARET MACMILLAN, PARIS 1919: SIX MONTHS THAT CHANGED THE WORLD (2003); PATRICK J. BUCHANAN, CHURCHILL, HITLER,

reminiscent of discredited practices mostly known in the Roman era, and continuing up to the end of the Middle Ages. Germany's economy was devastated and its peoples severely penalized, making life so difficult in the ensuing two decades that they helped bring about national-socialism and World War II.[32]

Europeans were not, however, satisfied with reparations. They wanted to humiliate the Germans by prosecuting their Emperor, which resulted in Article 227 in the Treaty of Versailles.[33] But that was not the end of the story, as Kaiser Wilhelm II was artfully charged to be prosecuted for "a supreme offence against international morality and the sanctity of treaties."[34] No such crime existed at the time, and the artful crafting of Article 227 in 1919, when the Treaty of Versailles was signed,[35] was intended to assuage those who had been aggrieved by the German aggression that began on July 28, 1914, with the onset of the First World War. At the same time, the ambiguity of the provision ensured that the German Emperor could never be prosecuted for something that, as defined, did not constitute a crime under international law – or for that matter, a crime under the laws of any State.[36] But it did satisfy Western public opinion. The Kaiser sought refuge in The Netherlands, which found that no such crime existed under its laws or international law and said that even if the Allies requested, it would not extradite him to be submitted to an international tribunal that would prosecute him.[37] The rest of the world blamed The Netherlands, but the grandchildren of Great Britain's Queen Victoria,

AND "THE UNNECESSARY WAR": HOW BRITAIN LOST ITS EMPIRE AND THE WEST LOST THE WORLD (2009).

[32] See BARRY A. JACKISCH, THE PAN-GERMAN LEAGUE AND RADICAL NATIONALIST POLITICS IN INTERWAR GERMANY, 1918–39 (2012). See also JOHN M. STEINER, POWER POLITICS AND SOCIAL CHANGE IN NATIONAL SOCIALIST GERMANY: A PROCESS OF ESCALATION INTO MASS DESTRUCTION (1975).

[33] This was true even though Kaiser Wilhelm II was Queen Victoria's grandson. CATRINE CLAY, KING, KAISER, TSAR: THREE ROYAL COUSINS WHO LED THE WORLD TO WAR (2006); CORRESPONDANCE ENTRE GUILLAUME II ET NICOLAS II, 1894–1914 (Marc Semenoff trans., 1924).

[34] Treaty of Versailles, *supra* note 30, art. 227.

[35] The Article was crafted by someone representing Great Britain at Versailles, where the treaty was drafted. See Bassiouni, WWI, *supra* note 29, at 268–72; *see also* M. Cherif Bassiouni, *Combating Impunity for International Crimes*, 71 U. COLO. L. REV. 409, 411 (2000).

[36] See sources cited *supra* note 29 (on WWI prosecutions).

[37] See Bassiouni, WWI, *supra* note 29, at 248–49. See also Scott, *supra* note 29, at 243–44; WILLIS, *supra* note 29, at 107–08; M. Cherif Bassiouni, *From Versailles to Rwanda in Seventy-Five Years: The Need to Establish a Permanent International Criminal Court*, 10 HARV. HUM. RTS. J. 11, 18–20 (1997) [hereinafter Bassiouni, *Need for Permanent ICC*].

including the Kaiser,[38] and the rest of the European monarchy could breathe a sigh of relief that no head of state was held internationally accountable.[39]

Although Article 227 of the Treaty of Versailles did not establish a criminal offense for which the Kaiser could be prosecuted, its inclusion in the treaty was the first time in history that a head of state was targeted to be tried before an international judicial body for what became known as "crimes against peace" after World War II[40] and "aggression" in the Kampala Amendments of 2010."[41]

A few years later, a number of European States, spurred in part by the United States, entered into the Kellogg–Briand Peace Pact in 1924, which implicitly prohibited State Parties from using force against each other. Although the text contained no absolute prohibition against the use of armed

---

[38] *See* sources cited *supra* note 33 and accompanying text (on Queen Victoria's heirs). *See also* WILLIS, *supra* note 29.

[39] *See infra* note 62 and accompanying text (on the 1474 trial of Peter von Hagenbach). To date, the immunity of sitting heads of state is part of customary international law as affirmed by the International Court of Justice decision in *Arrest Warrant of 11 April 2000 (Dem. Rep. Congo v. Belg.)*, notwithstanding the Rome Statute's Article 27, which removes it. *See* discussion *infra* note 43 (on *Democratic Republic of the Congo v. Belgium*). *See also* M. CHERIF BASSIOUNI, THE LEGISLATIVE HISTORY OF THE INTERNATIONAL CRIMINAL COURT: INTRODUCTION, ANALYSIS, AND INTEGRATED TEXT (2005) [hereinafter BASSIOUNI, LEGISLATIVE HISTORY OF THE ICC]; 1 THE LEGISLATIVE HISTORY OF THE INTERNATIONAL CRIMINAL COURT 18 (M. Cherif Bassiouni & William Schabas eds., 2d rev. ed. 2016) [hereinafter Bassiouni & Schabas]; MARK LEWIS, THE BIRTH OF THE NEW JUSTICE: THE INTERNATIONALIZATION OF CRIME & PUNISHMENT, 1919–1950, at 36–39 (2014).

[40] *See* Charter of the International Military Tribunal – Annex to the Agreement for the Prosecution and Punishment of the Major War Criminals of the European Axis art. 6(a), Aug. 8, 1945, 82 U.N.T.S. 279 [hereinafter London Charter]; *see also* Charter of the International Military Tribunal for the Far East art. 5(a), Jan. 19, 1946, *amended* Apr. 26, 1946, T.I.A.S. No. 1589 [hereinafter Tokyo Charter]; Allied Control Council Law No. 10, Punishment of Persons Guilty of War Crimes, Crimes Against Peace and Against Humanity art. II(1)(a), Dec. 20, 1945, *reprinted in* 3 Official Gazette of the Control Council for Germany at 50–55 (1946) [hereinafter Control Council Law No. 10].

[41] *See* Kampala Amendments, *supra* note 23. *See also* the 1974 Definition of Aggression: G.A. Res. 3314 (XXIX), arts. 2–4, Definition of Aggression, U.N. Doc. A/RES/3314(XXIX) (Dec. 14, 1974) [hereinafter G.A. 1974 Res. Defining Aggression].
For an historical and detailed information/perspective on defining aggression *see* 1–2 BENJAMIN B. FERENCZ, DEFINING INTERNATIONAL AGGRESSION, THE SEARCH FOR WORLD PEACE: A DOCUMENTARY HISTORY AND ANALYSIS (1975); M. Cherif Bassiouni & Benjamin B. Ferencz, *The Crime Against Peace and Aggression: From Its Origins to the ICC, in* 1 INTERNATIONAL CRIMINAL LAW: SOURCES, SUBJECTS, AND CONTENTS 207 (M. Cherif Bassiouni ed., 3d ed. 2008) [hereinafter Bassiouni, ICL Vol. 1]. *See also* Bassiouni & Schabas, *supra* note 39, at 60–130; Michael P. Scharf, *Universal Jurisdiction and the Crime of Aggression*, 53 HARV. INT'L L.J. 357 (2012). *See generally* M. CHERIF BASSIOUNI, CRIMES AGAINST HUMANITY: HISTORICAL EVOLUTION AND CONTEMPORARY APPLICATION (2011) [hereinafter Bassiouni, CAH].

force by one State against another, the pact was another small step forward, another confirmation of the *jus ad bellum* prohibition of aggression.[42]

The historical record shows that aggression was not prohibited outright and certainly was not criminalized, but it also shows the slow growth of customary international law between 1919 and 1924. After World War II it became the legal building block for the proscription of aggression as "crimes against peace" and for holding accountable those responsible for it, including heads of state.[43]

What the Kellogg–Briand Pact did in 1924 was reinforce the customary international law prohibition of aggression, which was firmly in the historical track of *jus ad bellum*, even though it was not in the international criminal law track of individual criminalization of the violation of *jus ad bellum*. Yet by necessity after World War II, this became the makeshift bridge between the *jus ad bellum* and the individual criminalization of its violation in the post–World War II prosecutions, when the victorious Allies felt compelled to deal with Nazi Germany's and Japan's acts of aggression. At that time, they had little customary international law to rely on except the Kellogg–Briand Pact of 1924, which by necessity became the foundational basis for "crimes against peace," as enunciated in 1945 in the International Military Tribunal (IMT) Charter's Article 6(a), the International Military Tribunal for the Far East (IMTFE)

---

[42] Article 1 provides that

> ARTICLE I. The High Contracting Parties solemnly declare in the names of their respective peoples that they condemn recourse to war for the solution of international controversies, and renounce it, as an instrument of national policy in their relations with one another.

General Treaty for Renunciation of War as an Instrument of National Policy (Kellogg–Briand Pact), Aug. 27, 1928, 94 L.N.T.S. 57 [hereinafter Kellogg–Briand Pact].

[43] *See* sources cited *supra* note 40 and accompanying text (on the Nuremberg and Tokyo Charters and Control Council Law No. 10). *See also* sources cited *infra* note 44 (on "crimes against peace"). Later in 1998, the Rome Statute provides the following:

> 1. This Statute shall apply equally to all persons without any distinction based on official capacity. In particular, official capacity as a Head of State or Government, a member of a Government or parliament, an elected representative or a government official shall in no case exempt a person from criminal responsibility under this Statute, nor shall it, in and of itself, constitute a ground for reduction of sentence.
> 2. Immunities or special procedural rules which may attach to the official capacity of a person, whether under national or international law, shall not bar the Court from exercising its jurisdiction over such a person.

Rome Statute, *supra* note 23, art. 27. But the International Court of Justice in its opinion in *Democratic Republic of the Congo v. Belgium* held that customary international law still prevailed, in that heads of state in office still benefit from temporal immunity and not substantive immunity for international crimes. Arrest Warrant of 11 April 2000 (Dem. Rep. Congo v. Belg.), Judgment, 2002 I.C.J. Rep. 3 (Feb. 14).

Statute's Article 5(a), and the four major Western Allies' Control Council Law No. 10.[44] Almost at the same time, the United Nations Charter was adopted, but it shied away from using the then-current term of "crimes against peace," preferring the more flexible term "aggression."[45] The United Nations Charter's prohibition of aggression did not, however, include individual criminal responsibility for those who decided and/or carried out such acts, even though the U.N. language was adopted about the same time as the IMT Charter and the IMTFE Statute and the prosecution of individuals before the two international tribunals for "crimes against peace."[46] This was a politically artful

---

[44] For all practical purposes, between 1624 and the international community's reaction to the atrocities of World War II in 1945, history reveals how hard it was to achieve any progress to advance international criminal justice against political obstacles. *See* M. Cherif Bassiouni, *Challenges to International Criminal Justice and International Criminal Law, in* Cambridge Companion, *supra* note 19, at 353 [hereinafter Bassiouni, Challenges to ICJ & ICL]. And it was not until post–World War II that the international community adopted the London Charter on August 8, 1945, for the European theater, the Tokyo Charter on January 19, 1946, and Control Council Law No. 10 on December 20, 1945, that international criminal justice caught up with the commonly shared values of most people of the world, and its promotion was supported by the political will of States. *See* London Charter, *supra* note 40; Tokyo Charter, *supra* note 40; Bassiouni, Legislative History of the ICC, *supra* note 39, at 49–53; Bassiouni & Schabas, *supra* note 39, at 20–33. Yet even then, the London Charter, the Tokyo Charter, and Control Council Law No. 10 defined aggression respectively as follows:

> London Charter art. 6(a): Crimes Against Peace: namely, planning, preparation, initiation or waging of a [declared] war of aggression, or a war in violation of international treaties, agreements or assurances, or participation in a common plan or conspiracy for the accomplishment of any of the foregoing;
>
> Tokyo Charter art. 5(a): Crimes against Peace: Namely, the planning, preparation, initiation or waging of a declared or undeclared war of aggression, or a war in violation of international law, treaties, agreements or assurances, or participation in a common plan or conspiracy for the accomplishment of any of the foregoing;
>
> Control Council Law No. 10 art. II(1)(a): Crimes against Peace. Initiation of invasions of other countries and wars of aggression in violation of international laws and treaties, including but not limited to planning, preparation, initiation or waging a war of aggression, or a war of violation of international treaties, agreements or assurances, or participation in a common plan or conspiracy for the accomplishment of any of the foregoing.

London Charter, *supra* note 40, art. 6(a); Tokyo Charter, *supra* note 40, art. 5(a); Control Council Law No. 10, *supra* note 40, art. II(1)(a).

[45] As described *supra* in note 44. *See also* U.N. Charter arts. 1(1), 39, allowing the use of force only for self-defense under Articles 51 and 52 and whenever it is authorized by the Security Council under Charter VII of the Charter. In time, the attempt to expand it to humanitarian intervention and to the "obligation to protect" were brought to a standstill. *See* Helal, *Justifying War, supra* note 2, at 577–642.

[46] To the best of this author's knowledge, there was only one case in which "crimes against peace" was successfully prosecuted under Control Council Law No. 10. *See "The Ministries Case,"* in 14 Trials of War Criminals Before the Nuernberg Military Tribunals Under Control Council Law No. 10, Judgment, 308 (1949), *available at* www.loc.gov/rr/frd/Military_Law/pdf/NT_war-criminals_Vol-XIV.pdf.

severance of the postulates of the new international legal order reflected in the U.N. Charter: The Charter not only failed to address the criminalization of "aggression"; it did not even define it. It left this task to the Security Council, subject to the veto power of its Permanent Members.[47]

The political work evidenced in the Charter amounted to a functional decoupling of "aggression" as a political concept from the prohibition of aggression under customary international law and the international crime of "crimes against peace" under international criminal law, for which individual criminal responsibility attaches,[48] up to and including heads of state.[49] And so it remains to date except for the forward progress of the Kampala Amendments, subject to all their limitations.[50]

III. THE SITUATION AFTER WORLD WAR II

The historic evolution described above occurred mostly after World War II and in particular during and after the Cold War. During the Cold War years, from 1948 to 1989, States used the same political games and maneuvers they had used in the past, namely the manipulation of international institutions and the exploitation of the gaps and contradictions that existed in international

---

[47] In 1993–1994, the Security Council relied on the Charter to establish two *ad hoc* tribunals, the International Criminal Tribunal for the former Yugoslavia (ICTY) and International Criminal Tribunal for Rwanda (ICTR), to prosecute individuals for genocide, crimes against humanity, and war crimes but not aggression. *See* U.N. Security Council, Statute of the International Criminal Tribunal for the former Yugoslavia (as amended on July 7, 2009), S.C. Res. 827, U.N. Doc. S/RES/827 (May 25, 1993) (establishing the ICTY); U.N. Security Council, Statute of the International Criminal Tribunal for Rwanda (as amended on Dec. 16, 2009), S.C. Res. 955, U.N. Doc. S/RES/955 (Nov. 8, 1994) (establishing the ICTR). Aggression thus continued to be generically prohibited under customary international law, but not legally defined, and no individual criminal accountability measures were established for its transgression.

[48] As in the London Charter and Tokyo Charter, *supra* note 40, and the Rome Statute's Kampala Amendments, *supra* note 23.

[49] *See* London Charter, *supra* note 40, art. 7 ("The official position of defendants, whether as Heads of State or responsible officials in Government Departments, shall not be considered as freeing them from responsibility or mitigating punishment."); Tokyo Charter, *supra* note 40, art. 6 ("Neither the official position, at any time, of an accused, nor the fact that an accused acted pursuant to order of his government or of a superior shall, of itself, be sufficient to free such accused from responsibility for any crime with which he is charged, but such circumstances may be considered in mitigation of punishment if the Tribunal determines that justice so requires."); Control Council Law No.10, *supra* note 40, art. II(4)(a) ("The official position of any person, whether as Head of State or as a responsible official in a Government Department, does not free him from responsibility for a crime or entitle him to mitigation of punishment.").

[50] *See* sources cited *infra* notes 114–134 and accompanying text (discussion of the Kampala Amendments).

law. The powerful States' manipulation of the United Nations' organs and its bureaucracy shows how different stages can be set for different political plays and players in order to convey something to the international community that may not necessarily be the actual outcome. This is what occurred with aggression as described in this Section during the post–World War II era. What follows briefly describes multiple processes in connection with defining and criminalizing aggression and establishing an international criminal jurisdiction and then the International Criminal Court, which has jurisdiction over the perpetrators of that international crime.[51]

The events of 1939 and 1940 outdistanced customary international law on the topics of aggression, war crimes, and what became known as "crimes against humanity."[52] Nazi Germany blatantly invaded Czechoslovakia and Poland and rolled across Belgium before it invaded France and prepared to invade the United Kingdom. By the time Germany invaded the Soviet Union in June 1941, World War II was well underway. About six months later, on December 7, 1941, Germany's ally the Empire of Greater Japan, which had already invaded China's Manchuria in 1937 and committed brutal, mass atrocities against the civilians of Nanking,[53] surreptitiously attacked the United States at Pearl Harbor.[54]

The conduct of Germany and Japan met any conceivable definition of aggression and certainly fell within the original scope of the limitations on the

---

[51] For crimes within the ICC's jurisdiction see the Rome Statute, *supra* note 23, art. 5. For ICC jurisdiction over heads of state, see *id.* art. 27(1)-(2). For the definition and provisions relating to the crime of aggression in the Kampala Amendments *see* the Kampala Amendments, *supra* note 23.

[52] *See* M. Cherif Bassiouni, *International Law and the Holocaust*, 9 CAL. W. INT'L L.J. 201, 209–14 (1979) [hereinafter Bassiouni, Holocaust]; Bassiouni, CAH, *supra* note 41, at 1–50. *See also* THE ROUTLEDGE HISTORY OF THE HOLOCAUST (Jonathan C. Friedman ed., 2010); DOMINICK LaCAPRA, REPRESENTING THE HOLOCAUST: HISTORY, THEORY, TRAUMA (1994); TIMOTHY SNYDER, BLACK EARTH: THE HOLOCAUST AS HISTORY AND WARNING (2015); JEREMY BLACK, THE HOLOCAUST: HISTORY AND MEMORY (2016).

[53] In December 1937, more than 300,000 Chinese civilians and soldiers were raped, tortured, and murdered by Japanese forces. But that was of no interest or concern of the victorious Western Allies. *See* IRIS CHANG, THE RAPE OF NANKING: THE FORGOTTEN HOLOCAUST OF WORLD WAR II (2012). The Japanese military, with the assistance of the Japanese government, also sexually and physically exploited more than 100,000 women throughout Asia by forcing them into enforced prostitution. These women, referred to as "comfort women" were forced into "comfort stations" established throughout Asia by Japan to be repeatedly raped and assaulted by Japanese soldiers. Shellie K. Park, *Broken Silence: Redressing the Mass Rape and Sexual Enslavement of Asian Women by the Japanese Government in an Appropriate Forum*, 3 ASIAN-PAC. L. & POL'Y J. 23 (2002). *See also* GEORGE HICKS, THE COMFORT WOMEN: JAPAN'S BRUTAL REGIME OF ENFORCED PROSTITUTION IN THE SECOND WORLD WAR (1997); YOSHIMI YOSHIAKI, COMFORT WOMEN: SEXUAL SLAVERY IN THE JAPANESE MILITARY DURING WORLD WAR II (Suzanne O'Brien trans., 2000).

[54] *See* JOHN KEEGAN, THE SECOND WORLD WAR (2005).

jus ad bellum that St. Thomas Aquinas first formulated and that became part of what is now known as natural law.[55] But beyond the anemic language of the Kellogg–Briand Peace Pact,[56] no positive international law norm was applicable at the time to the blatant acts of aggression carried out in World War I and in World War II, however defined.[57] In fact, one could even say that the international community's inability to agree beyond such an anemic definition in 1919 emboldened Germany and Japan, only twenty years after the

---

[55] *See generally* THE NATURAL LAW READER (Brendan F. Brown ed., 1960); *see also* LLYOD L. WEINREB, NATURAL LAW AND JUSTICE 56–63 (1987); Carl J. Friedrich, *Philosophical Reflections of Leibniz on Law, Politics, and the State*, 11 NAT. L.F. 89 (1966); Luis Legaz y Lacambra, *Political Obligation and Natural Law*, 2 NAT. L.F. 119 (1957). For a naturalist perspective, *see* JACQUES MARITAIN, LES DROITS DE L'HOMME ET LA LOI NATURELLE (1942). *But see* H.L.A. HART, THE CONCEPT OF LAW (1961); H.L.A. Hart, *Positivism and the Separation of Law and Morals*, 71 HARV. L. REV. 593 (1958), *but cf.* PATRICK DEVLIN, THE ENFORCEMENT OF MORALS (1965). *Compare with* Morris Cohen, *Moral Aspects of the Criminal Law*, 49 YALE L.J. 987 (1940); JEREMY BENTHAM, A FRAGMENT ON GOVERNMENT AND AN INTRODUCTION TO THE PRINCIPLES OF MORALS AND LEGISLATION (Wilfrid Harrison ed., 1948). LLYOD L. WEINREB, NATURAL LAW AND JUSTICE 280 n.7, 47 (1987) (Cicero referred to the *jus gentium* as law derived from nature or reason. "For Cicero, 'the universality of a principle is a proof of its naturalness and hence of its validity, for the law of Nature is no mere ideal, it is a binding law and no enactment of the people or senatus-consult can prevail against it. The argument, though not put in these words, is obvious: if all races of mankind acknowledge a practice it must be because it has been taught them by their universal mother, Nature. Cicero thus identifies the law of Nature with the *ius gentium* in the sense of law common to all peoples.'") (citations omitted) ("The incorporation of natural law into Christian thought is often traced to St. Paul's statement in the Epistle to the Romans: '[W]hen the Gentiles, who have not the law, do by nature those things that are of the law, these having not the law, are a law to themselves; who shew the work of the law written in their hearts, their conscience bearing witness to them.' Paul is responding to the argument that pagans, not having the benefit of Revelation in the Old Testament, should not be blamed for failing to follow the law. Although his words are at least suggestive of a moral law accessible to reason, biblical scholars do not all agree that in fact he had a conception of natural law in mind. Whether he did or not, his words were so construed by early Christian writers, who referred to them as a textual basis for the doctrine of natural law. There is nothing philosophically new in the use of the doctrine. But it is now identified with the law of God, taught to men by Christ; it is a specifically theological concept and much more concrete than the natural law of the Stoics.").

[56] *See* Kellogg–Briand Pact, *supra* note 42.

[57] *Id.* Thus to criminalize aggression as "crimes against peace" in the London Charter and Tokyo Charter in 1945–1946 violated the well-established "principle of legality" in almost every legal system in the world. For information on the legal principle *nullum crimen sine lege* or "no crime without law," *see* Marc Ancel, *La Regle Nulla Poena Sine Lege, dans les Legislations Modernes, in* 2 ANNALES DE L'INSTITUT DE DROIT COMPARÉ DE L'UNIVERSITÉ DE PARIS 245 (1936); GIULIANO VASSALLI, NULLUM CRIMEN SINE LEGE (1939). For information on "general principles of international law," *see* M. Cherif Bassiouni, *A Functional Approach to "General Principles of International Law"*, 11 MICH. J. INT'L L. 768, 770–73 (1990) [hereinafter Bassiouni, *General Principles*].

devastations of the First World War, to engage in acts of aggression against other States and usher in World War II.

After the surrender of Germany and Japan in May and August of 1945,[58] the international community struggled with how to respond. By then, efforts had already been undertaken to take a big step forward in history, namely to hold accountable those who had committed acts that were considered crimes against international law in keeping with the early historic concept of *hostes humani generis*, which was first developed in Roman law for those who committed crimes against the Empire and were thus deemed the enemies of humankind.[59]

The historical concept of *hostes humani generis*, as it evolved from Roman law into the post-1300s writings of publicists, culminating with the writings of the Dutch jurist Hugo Grotius in 1624 and many others after him,[60] became the foundational concept of international criminal law and certainly in connection with the drafting of the Charter of the International Military Tribunal, the International Military Tribunal for the Far East Statute, and Law No. 10 of the Allied Control Council (the governing body of the Allied occupation zones in Germany after the end of World War II in Europe). These were the first three international normative instruments that posited "crimes against peace" and "crimes against humanity" as international crimes subject to prosecution;[61] "war crimes" had already been established under international

---

[58] Germany formally announced its surrender on May 7, 1945, and Japan followed in suit on August 14, 1945. *See* KEEGAN, SECOND WORLD WAR, *supra* note 54.

[59] *See* BASSIOUNI, INTRO TO ICL, *supra* note 17, at 137–38; *see also* CICERO, DE OFFICIIS (L.H.G. Greenwood trans., 1953). Except that in the Roman conception it was limited to the Roman Empire and did not extend beyond it. Nevertheless, in subsequent times it was found to be a valid legal concept that became internationalized, in part through the writings of Hugo Grotius in 1624, who embodied the notion of *aut dedere aut punire* in his work *De Jure Belli ac Pacis Libri Tres*, later reflected in Cesare Beccaria's *Dei Delitti e Delle Pene*. *See* GROTIUS, *supra* note 6; M. CHERIF BASSIOUNI & EDWARD M. WISE, AUT DEDERE AUT JUDICARE: THE DUTY TO EXTRADITE OR PROSECUTE IN INTERNATIONAL LAW (1995). *See also* M. CHERIF BASSIOUNI, INTERNATIONAL EXTRADITION: UNITED STATES LAW AND PRACTICE 420–25 (6th ed. 2014); BASSIOUNI, ICL Vol. 1, *supra* note 41, at 129–31; CESARE BECCARIA, DEI DELITTI E DELLE PENE (1764).

[60] *See* BASSIOUNI, INTRO TO ICL, *supra* note 17, at 137–38. *See also* CICERO, *supra* note 59; sources cited *supra* note 6 (on early writers on international criminal law).

[61] *See* FERENCZ, *supra* note 41, at 205–25, 415–91; BASSIOUNI & FERENCZ, *supra* note 41, at 210–14; BASSIOUNI & SCHABAS, *supra* note 39, at 27–33. *See generally* BASSIOUNI, CAH, *supra* note 41, at 111–66; SCHARF, *supra* note 41, at 369–74. *See also* EUGENE DAVIDSON, THE TRIAL OF THE GERMANS: AN ACCOUNT OF THE TWENTY-TWO DEFENDANTS BEFORE THE INTERNATIONAL MILITARY TRIBUNAL AT NUREMBERG (1997).

At the IMT, these two crimes were charged for the first time in Counts One and Two, specifically:

humanitarian law but had never been prosecuted by an internationally established tribunal.[62]

The primary challenge in prosecuting "crimes against peace" was that until then, it did not exist as an international crime under normative international law.[63] The criminalization of "crimes against peace" and the prosecution of its perpetrators under the Nuremberg and Tokyo Charters was founded on the existing prohibition in the Kellogg–Briand Pact, even though the language of that treaty offers little support for the recognition that aggression or "crimes against peace" as defined in the Nuremberg and Tokyo Charters constituted a crime under international law.[64] This and other shortcomings led some to

> When finally completed by the several staffs, the indictments contained four counts. Count One charged the defendants, during a period of years preceding May 8, 1945, with participating in a common plan or conspiracy to commit crimes against peace, war crimes, and crimes against humanity, as defined in the Charter. Particulars of the nature and development of the alleged common plan were specified and the Nazi Party was described as the central core of the plan.
>
> Count Two charged the defendants, during a period of years preceding May 8, 1945, with participating in the planning, preparation, initiating, and waging wars of aggression. The actions against Austria and Czechoslovakia were not specified as aggressive wars; but it was charged that wars of aggression were waged against Poland, the United Kingdom and France, Demark and Norway, Belgium, the Netherlands and Luxembourg, Yugoslavia and Greece, the U.S.S.R., and the United States of America.

WHITNEY R. HARRIS, TYRANNY ON TRIAL: THE TRIAL OF THE MAJOR GERMAN WAR CRIMINALS AT THE END OF WORLD WAR II AT NUREMBERG, GERMANY, 1945–1946, at 30 (rev. ed. 1999) [hereinafter HARRIS, TYRANNY ON TRIAL]. The above-cited author, Mr. Whitney R. Harris, worked under Justice Robert Jackson as a prosecutor at the IMT trials at Nuremberg and was a Lieutenant Commander in the United States Navy.

[62] The exception is the 1474 trial of Peter von Hagenbach, who was hired by the French Duke of Burgundy to occupy the city of Breisach and compel taxes from its residents. The townspeople rebelled and von Hagenbach followed the Duke's orders to sack, pillage, and burn the city. Von Hagenbach was subsequently prosecuted by leaders from member States of the Holy Roman Empire, which for all practical purposes established the first international criminal tribunal. At trial, von Hagenbach attempted to exhibit the written orders of the Duke, but the judges refused his request and by refusing to accept von Hagenbach's defense, they shielded the Duke from responsibility. BASSIOUNI, INTRO TO ICL, supra note 17, at 1048–50. The post–World War I Leipzig trials prosecuted by the German Reichsgericht (Supreme Court) are detailed in BASSIOUNI, INTRO TO ICL, supra note 17, at 419–21. See also WILLIS, supra note 29, at 118.

[63] See FERENCZ, supra note 41, at 205–25, 415–91; Bassiouni & Ferencz, supra note 41, at 210–14; Bassiouni & Schabas, supra note 39, at 27–33. See generally BASSIOUNI, CAH, supra note 41, at 111–66; SCHARF, supra note 41, at 369–74.

[64] And that the tenuous language of the Kellogg–Briand Pact did not violate the "general principles of international law," which include the "principles of legality" recognized in almost every national criminal justice system in the world. See BASSIOUNI, GENERAL PRINCIPLES, supra note 57. See also the definitions of "crimes against the peace," applied through the London Charter, Tokyo Charter, and Control Council Law No. 10, supra note 40.

refer to these two sets of proceedings as "victors' justice,"[65] even though those who were prosecuted had committed acts that by any stretch of the imagination would still be within the meaning of "crimes against peace" in existing customary international law.

In addition to the prosecutions under the Nuremberg Charter, the Tokyo Charter, and Control Council Law No. 10 (which was applicable only to the European theater),[66] other prosecutions were undertaken by States within their domestic legal systems and by nationally established military commissions and other *ad hoc* courts. Such bodies were established by Australia and China,[67] and in the Far East by France, The Netherlands, the United

---

[65] AUGUST VON KNIERIEM, THE NUREMBERG TRIALS 101–05 (1959). *See also* Otto Pannenbecker, *The Nuremberg War-Crimes Trial*, 14 DePAUL L. REV. 348 (1965); Otto Kranzbuhler, *Nuremberg Eighteen Years Afterwards*, 14 DePAUL L. REV. 333 (1965); Herbert Kraus, *The Nuremberg Trial of the Major War Criminals: Reflections After Seventeen Years*, 13 DePAUL L. REV. 233 (1964); Carl Haensel, *The Nuremburg Trial Revisited*, 13 DePAUL L. REV. 248 (1964); HARRIS, TYRANNY ON TRIAL, *supra* note 61, at 567–70. *See generally* WHITNEY R. HARRIS, THE TRAGEDY OF WAR (2004). The prosecutions under the IMTFE in Tokyo were far less rigorous than those under the IMT at Nuremburg, and such legal niceties as whether "crimes against peace" existed in international law were given short shrift in Tokyo. Subsequently, German national prosecutions and de-Nazification law did not include "crimes against peace" or "aggression." *See* Tokyo Judgment, *reprinted in* 1 THE TOKYO JUDGMENT: INTERNATIONAL MILITARY TRIBUNAL FOR THE FAR EAST 1 (Bernard V.A. Röling & Fritz Reuter, eds., 1977); see also the dissent of Justices Röling and Pal in these proceedings, 2 THE TOKYO JUDGMENT, *supra*, at 1041 and 517 respectively. *See also* BASSIOUNI, INTRO TO ICL, *supra* note 17, at 558–66; BASSIOUNI, CHALLENGES TO ICJ AND ICL, *supra* note 44, at 356–59. For Far East prosecutions, see generally ARNOLD C. BRACKMAN, THE OTHER NUREMBERG: THE UNTOLD STORY OF THE TOKYO WAR CRIMES TRIALS (1987); SABURO SHIROYAMA, WAR CRIMINAL: THE LIFE AND DEATH OF HIROTA KOKI (1977); DOCUMENTS ON THE TOKYO INTERNATIONAL MILITARY TRIBUNAL: CHARTER, INDICTMENT AND JUDGMENTS (Neil Boister & Robert Cryer eds., 2008); RICHARD H. MINEAR, VICTORS' JUSTICE: THE TOKYO WAR CRIMES TRIAL 160–80 (1971); THE TOKYO WAR CRIMES TRIAL: AN INTERNATIONAL SYMPOSIUM (Chihiro Hosoya et al. eds., 1986); PHILIP R. PICCIGALLO, THE JAPANESE ON TRIAL: ALLIED WAR CRIMES OPERATIONS IN THE EAST 1945–1951 (1979); BASSIOUNI, LEGISLATIVE HISTORY OF THE ICC, *supra* note 39, at 49; R. John Pritchard, *British Postwar War Crimes Courts: The Gift of Clemency Following the British War Crimes Trials in the Far East, 1946–1948*, 7 CRIM. L.F. 15 (1996). *See also* Bassiouni & Schabas, *supra* note 39, at 27–33.

[66] In addition to the prosecutions by the IMT and the IMTFE, the four major Allies also prosecuted the same crimes in Germany pursuant to Allied Control Council Law No. 10. *See* TELFORD TAYLOR, FINAL REPORT TO THE SECRETARY OF THE ARMY ON THE NUERNBERG WAR CRIMES TRIALS UNDER CONTROL COUNCIL LAW No. 10 (1949); TELFORD TAYLOR, THE ANATOMY OF THE NUREMBERG TRIALS: A PERSONAL MEMOIR (1992). To this writer's best knowledge, only in *"The Ministries Case"* was "crimes against peace" successfully prosecuted. *See The Ministries Case, supra* note 46. Since then, to this writer's knowledge, there have been no national prosecutions for "crimes against peace" or "aggression."

[67] From 1942 onward, the Australian government undertook numerous war crime investigations that resulted in 300 trials involving 812 mostly Japanese alleged war criminals. Narrelle Morris, *Obscuring the Historical Origins of International Criminal Law in Australia: The Australian*

Kingdom, and the United States.[68] The United States also established military commissions in Europe to prosecute war crimes committed throughout the

War Crimes Investigations and Prosecutions of Japanese, 1942–1951, in 2 HISTORICAL ORIGINS OF ICL, *supra* note 19, at 355. These trials took place in Morotai, Wewak, Labuan, Rabaul, Darwin, Singapore, Hong Kong, and Manus Island from 1945 to 1951. The charges were brought under the War Crimes Act of 1945 and the Regulations for the Trial of War Criminals. *Id.* at 379. *See* GEORGINA FITZPATRICK, TIM MCCORMACK & NARRELLE MORRIS, AUSTRALIA'S WAR CRIMES TRIALS 1945–51 (2016).

Even while World War II was ongoing, as early as 1942 the Republic of China had indicated that Japan would be held responsible for the crimes committed in China. Zhang Tianshu, *The Forgotten Legacy: China's Post-Second World War Trials of Japanese War Criminals, 1946–1956, in* 2 HISTORICAL ORIGINS OF ICL, *supra* note 19, at 267, 272. Potential war crimes were investigated by the Investigation Commission on Crimes of the Enemy and the Investigation Commission on Damage and Loss of War. *Id.* After the war ended, an additional commission was established regarding the crimes committed in Nanjing (Nanking). *Id.* The Republic of China acted on its intent to prosecute, and Chinese military courts were established at ten different locations by the end of April 1949. These courts were located in Nanjing, Shanghai, Peking, Hankou, Guangzhou, Shenyang, Xuzhou, Jinan, Taiyuan, and Taipei and sentenced 145 people to death and more than 300 people to prison. Ling Yan, *The 1956 Japanese War Crimes Trials in China, in* 2 HISTORICAL ORIGINS OF ICL, *supra* note 19, at 215, 215.

An additional forty-five Japanese nationals were prosecuted for war crimes before a Special Military Tribunal (SMT) in Taiyuan and Shenyang in 1956. *Id.* at 216. At the time of the SMT trials, there was a new Chinese government that had abolished all laws enacted before 1949 by the former government. Therefore, a Decision on the Handling of Japanese War Criminals under Detention Who Committed Crimes during the Japanese Invasion War was adopted in April 1956 and provided for the prosecution of Japanese war criminals by the Special Military Tribunal as well as the court's jurisdiction. *Id.* at 222–23. The SMT's temporal jurisdiction ranged from September 1931 when the Imperial Japanese Army first invaded Manchuria until Japan's World War II surrender in September 1945. The majority of crimes prosecuted by the SMT fell under the international crimes of war crimes and crimes against humanity, as well as the crime of aggression. *Id.* at 225. Further, only individuals were held accountable for crimes; none of the accused was part of the group that formulated a state policy of aggression or made the decision to wage war. *Id.* at 226.

[68] The British conducted war crimes trials of Japanese in Singapore for crimes committed on the Japanese-occupied islands of Andaman and Car Nicobar. Cheah Wui Ling, *Post-Second World War British Trials in Singapore: Lost in Translation at the Car Nicobar Spy Case, in* 2 HISTORICAL ORIGINS OF ICL, *supra* note 19, at 301. Japanese military personnel were alleged to have subjected residents of the two islands to torture, summary trials, executions, and mass killings during World War II, and survivors traveled to Singapore to give testimony at the trials. *Id.* at 302. Sixteen Japanese defendants were prosecuted for crimes committed against civilians. *Id.* at 305–06. *See also* David J. Cohen, *The Singapore War Crimes Trials and Their Relevance Today,* 31 SING. L. REV. 3 (2013). The British established the British War Crimes Courts in Hong Kong, which had jurisdiction over war crimes committed against any British or Commonwealth citizens or suspects captured within Hong Kong. *See* HONG KONG'S WAR CRIMES TRIALS (Suzannah Linton ed., 2013).

In 1945, the French Permanent Military Tribunal in Saigon (FPMTS, or Saigon trials) was established and tried 230 Japanese war criminals in Indochina. Ann-Sophie Schoepfel-Aboukrat, *The War Court as a Form of State Building: The French Prosecution of Japanese War*

continent that did not include "crimes against peace."[69] National prosecutions were also brought in the domestic legal systems of Czechoslovakia, France, Germany, Poland, the Soviet Union, and Yugoslavia,[70] but they,

Crimes at the Saigon and Tokyo Trials, in 2 HISTORICAL ORIGINS OF ICL, *supra* note 19, at 119, 120.

    Additional World War II criminal trials were established by The Netherlands in the then–Dutch East Indies (now Indonesia) before the Temporary Courts Martial in Batavia for "minor" Japanese war criminals. Nina H. B. Jørgensen & Danny Friedmann, *Enforced Prostitution in International Law Through the Prism of the Dutch Temporary Courts Martial at Batavia, in* 2 HISTORICAL ORIGINS OF ICL, *supra* note 19, at 335. These courts primarily prosecuted the crime of enforced prostitution, and all the victims were either Indo-European or Dutch nationals, most of whom had been taken from internment camps to brothels, where they were sexually assaulted, raped, and beaten by men in "an organized system directed by the military with civilian collaboration." *Id.* at 339. To prosecute these crimes, the Lieutenant Governor-General of the Dutch East Indies passed four ordinances to allow the Temporary Courts Martial to try war crimes, including enforced prostitution, in accordance with international law. *Id.* at 338. *See* Matthew Lippman, *Prosecution of Nazi War Criminals Before Post-World War II Domestic Tribunals,* 8 U. MIAMI INT'L & COMP. L. REV. 1, 5–7 (2015).

    The United States also conducted war crimes trials. The most well known, *In re Yamashita,* took place in Manila in the Philippines and later went to the United States Supreme Court. *See, e.g., In re Yamashita,* 327 U.S. 1, 26–81 (1946), which reviewed the U.S.-established military courts in the Philippines' ability to prosecute Japanese military personnel occupying the Philippines. These proceedings were found flawed by Justices Murphy and Rutledge in a dissenting opinion because of General Douglas MacArthur's command influence. *See* ALLAN A. RYAN, YAMASHITA'S GHOST: WAR CRIMES, MACARTHUR'S JUSTICE, AND COMMAND ACCOUNTABILITY (2012). These military commissions conducted trials for the Category B and C offenders (as defined by the Tokyo Charter) at the Yokohama trials. These Class B and C Japanese war crimes trials were tried by different courts established by the Allies in various places, including Manila, Singapore, Saigon, Rabaul, Hong Kong, Kwajalein Atoll, and Batavia. *See* Robert W. Miller, *War Crimes Trials at Yokohama,* 15 BROOK. L. REV. 191 (1949); Ling Yan, *The 1956 Japanese War Crimes Trials in China, in* 2 HISTORICAL ORIGINS OF ICL, *supra* note 19, at 215.

[69] The United States established military commissions in Rome, Dachau, and Wiesbaden. David Glazier, *Precedents Lost: The Neglected History of the Military Commission,* 46 VA. J. INT'L L. 5 (2005).

[70] Trials were held in Czechoslovakia for crimes against the State, crimes against people, and informing. Czechoslovakia also established a special court, the National Court, to prosecute pro-Nazi collaborators. Veronika Bílková, *Post-Second World War Trials in Central and Eastern Europe, in* 2 HISTORICAL ORIGINS OF ICL, *supra* note 19, at 697, 701.

    The French also tried 2,345 Germans for war crimes in France in the Permanent Military Tribunals in France. SCHOEPFEL-ABOUKRAT, *supra* note 68, at 121. From 1946 until 1948, Poland established special criminal courts to try individuals for crimes committed in Polish territory, and after 1948 alleged war criminals were tried by courts of general jurisdiction. Malgorzata Tryuk, *Interpretation at the Trials of Nazi Criminals in Poland After World War II, in* TRANSLATION UND "DRITTES REICH" 79, 79–80 (Dörte Andres, Julia Richter & Larisa Schippel eds., 2016). In Germany, domestic prosecutions were aimed at Nazi collaborators and crimes committed by the German military, police, and government apparatus during occupation of other countries during the war. 3 INTERNATIONAL CRIMINAL LAW: INTERNATIONAL ENFORCEMENT 304 (M. Cherif Bassiouni ed., 3d ed. 2008) [hereinafter

too, did not involve "crimes against peace" as defined in the Tribunal Charters and Control Council Law No. 10.[71]

The post-World War II international criminalization of aggression under the *rubrique* "crimes against peace" was short lived and ended with the IMT and IMTFE. Other than *The Ministries Case*, no convictions for that crime are known by this writer to have taken place under Control Council Law No. 10 in the European theater by any of the four major Allies.[72]

Separately and independently, two other political and legal tracks developed within the emerging United Nations system. But the criminalization of aggression remained a contested subject from 1947 until 1998, when that crime was included in the Statute of the International Criminal Court, though it remained undefined until the Kampala Amendments.[73]

IV. AGGRESSION IN THE UNITED NATIONS CHARTER

The prohibition of aggression first arose under the United Nations Charter, despite the Charter's lack of a definition thereof and failure to provide for international criminal accountability for its transgression. The process of parceling aggression into different legal regimes continued, which did not strengthen the overall legal effect of the prohibition of aggression or the international criminal accountability of its perpetrators.

As stated in Article 1 of the Charter, the United Nations was established

> To maintain international peace and security, and to that end: to take effective collective measures for the prevention and removal of threats to the peace, and *for the suppression of acts of aggression* or other breaches of the peace, and to bring about by peaceful means, and in conformity with the principles of justice and international law, adjustment or settlement

Bassiouni, ICL ENFORCEMENT]. The Soviet Union prosecuted more than 80,000 individuals for crimes taking place during World War II under its 1943 Punishment Decree, which established military field courts. BÍLKOVÁ, *supra*, at 716–17. Between 1944 and 1946, Yugoslavia also prosecuted individuals for war crimes under a newly passed Act on Criminal Offences Against People and the State. *Id.* at 709.

[71] *See supra* note 44 (on definitions of "crimes against peace").

[72] *See* Henry T. King Jr., *Nuremberg and Crimes against Peace*, 41 CASE W. RES. J. INT'L L. 273, 277–78 (2009).

[73] Kampala Amendments, *supra* note 23.

of international disputes or situations which might lead to a breach of the peace.[74]

Paragraph 4 of Article 2 requires that all Members "refrain in their international relations from the threat or use of force against the territorial integrity or political independence of any state, or in any other manner inconsistent with the Purposes of the United Nations."[75] The Charter then charges the Security Council, an organ of the United Nations, in Article 39 with responsibility to "determine the existence of any threat to the peace, breach of the peace, or *act of aggression* and ... make recommendations, or decide what measures shall be taken in accordance with Articles 41 and 42, to maintain or restore international peace and security."[76]

The Charter mandated the Security Council to determine the existence of acts of aggression even though the term remained undefined until 1974.[77] The tortuous path to the definition of aggression that followed evidenced the political manipulations of States seeking to delay, if not undermine, an enforceable definition of aggression as referred to in Article 39 of the Charter.

While the Security Council was intended to determine the existence of acts of aggression, it was not intended to be a collective security system. Instead, it was a reflection of the experiences of World War II and the realization that nuclear weapons existed and could be used by major powers and other States to the world's detriment. France, the Soviet Union, the United Kingdom, and the United States saw themselves as the guardians of peace who by their collective action could ensure such outcomes even if occasionally small

---

[74] U.N. Charter art. 1(1) (emphasis added).

[75] *Id.* art. 2(4).

[76] *Id.* art. 39 (emphasis added). *See also* WOLFGANG FRIEDMANN, THE CHANGING STRUCTURE OF INTERNATIONAL LAW 60 (1964). Despite the mandate of the Security Council being limited to maintaining international peace and security, a State-centric view of international law, in the 1990s increased focus on human rights gave rise to the idea that human beings, not States, should be the primary beneficiaries of international legal protections. This was known as the humanization of international law, and it impacted the perceived role of the Security Council in regard to international security. *See generally* Paul W. Kahn, *Speaking Law to Power: Popular Sovereignty, Human Rights, and the New International Order*, 1 CHI. J. INT'L L. 1, 5 (2000); THEODOR MERON, THE HUMANIZATION OF INTERNATIONAL LAW (2006); Menno T. Kamminga, *Humanisation of International Law*, in CHANGING PERCEPTIONS OF SOVEREIGNTY AND HUMAN RIGHTS: ESSAYS IN HONOUR OF CEES FLINTERMAN 29 (Ineke Boerefiijn & Jenny Goldschmidt eds., 2008).

[77] Aggression was finally defined after a long journey that began in part in 1947 (but mostly in 1952) and ended in 1974. G.A. 1974 Res. Defining Aggression, *supra* note 41.

conflicts erupted, as long as those conflicts did not threaten what the major powers saw as international peace and security.[78]

[78] This was described by one author as follows:

> First and foremost, however, the foundation of peace was believed to be the prevention of conflict between the great powers. With their superior militaries and political influence, it was assumed that only these states could seriously undermine international security. Therefore, the architects of the UN system established a great power concert, in the form of the Security Council, to oversee international security relations. The negotiations over the prerogatives of the Security Council and the powers of its permanent members demonstrated that the Council was indeed designed as a great power concert and not, as many assume, a collective security system. Under collective security, an attack against one is an attack against all. Nowhere in the Charter, however, does the UN make such a pledge to its members. Nowhere is the security, territorial integrity, and political independence of states guaranteed. Never was it promised that the Security Council would vigilantly subdue all aggressors and indiscriminately protect all victims. Once this reality of UN "collective security" is understood, it becomes apparent that the Security Council's record of selectivity, politicization, and double standards are neither defects nor failures, but inherent features of the system.

Mohamed S. Helal, *Am I My Brother's Keeper? The Reality, Tragedy, and Future of Collective Security*, 6 HARV. NAT'L SEC. J. 383, 470 (2015) [hereinafter Helal, *Am I My Brother's Keeper?*]. *See also, id.* at 470 n.389 (citing Peter Opitz, *Collective Security, in* A CONCISE ENCYCLOPEDIA OF THE UNITED NATIONS 38 [Helmut Volger ed., 2d ed. 2009] [the "tendency of the permanent members toward selective action" is a deficit of U.N. collective security]); *id.* at 398 ("A solution that is repeatedly proposed to overcome these challenges is to institute a system of collective security. To many scholars, the United Nations Charter represents the latest attempt to establish such a system. This, I contend, misunderstands the UN's purposes and structure. The UN security regime, with the Security Council at its epicenter, is not a collective security organization. Rather, it resembles a great power concert designed to contribute to preventing conflict between the leading states in the international political system.") (citations omitted); *id.* at 400–01 ("The second characteristic of collective security is that its members are granted legal assurances that the collectivity will unfailingly come to their aid in the event of aggression. This certainty of a collective response 'permits no *ifs* or *buts*.' In other words, collective security functions in a nondiscriminatory manner; all aggressors will be equally opposed and all victims will be equally defended. Therefore, participation in a collective effort to confront aggression must be forthcoming regardless of the identity of either the aggressor or the victim and independently of whether the threat or act of aggression jeopardizes vital interests of the participating state.") (citations omitted).

See also GARY WILSON, THE UNITED NATIONS AND COLLECTIVE SECURITY 5 (2014); Oscar Schachter, *Authorized Uses of Force by the United Nations and Regional Organizations, in* LAW AND FORCE IN THE NEW INTERNATIONAL ORDER 65 (Lori Damrosch & David Scheffer eds., 1991); José E. Alvarez, *Judging the Security Council*, 90 AM. J. INT'L L. 1, 2 (1996); Ved P. Nanda, *Preemptive and Preventive Use of Force, Collective Security, and Human Security*, 33 DENV. J. INT'L L. & POL'Y 7 (2004) [hereinafter Nanda, *Preemptive and Preventive Use of Force*]; Thomas M. Franck, *Collective Security and UN Reform: Between the Necessary and the Possible*, 6 CHI. J. INT'L L. 597, 605 (2006); Christine Gray, *The Charter Limitations on the Use of Force: Theory and Practice, in* THE UNITED NATIONS SECURITY COUNCIL AND WAR: THE EVOLUTION OF THOUGHT AND PRACTICE SINCE 1945, at 86, 86–87 (Vaughan Lowe et al. eds., 2008); RUTH B. RUSSELL, A HISTORY OF THE UNITED NATIONS CHARTER: THE ROLE OF THE

While the Security Council was never intended to serve as a collective security body, the experiences of World War II and the existence of nuclear weapons led to the acceptance that the United Nations, at times, needed to serve as a peacekeeper among nations, both through bureaucratic and political processes as well as through peacekeeping operations. Only three years after the United Nations was established, the Security Council passed a resolution establishing the United Nations Truce Supervision Organization (UNTSO) to "assist the United Nations Mediator and the Truce Commission in supervising the observance of the truce in Palestine" in 1948.[79] One year later, again by resolution, the Security Council assigned the UNTSO to monitor four armistice agreements between Israel and the neighboring countries of Egypt, Jordan, Lebanon, and the Syrian Arab Republic.[80] These two resolutions sparked the lengthy history of United Nations peacekeeping operations, which includes seventy-one missions undertaken since 1948.[81] Currently there are sixteen ongoing U.N. peacekeeping operations, across four continents.[82] According to Article 17 of the U.N. Charter, every Member State is legally obligated to pay its respective share toward United Nations peacekeeping operations, and in addition to their financial contributions, 128 States have voluntarily contributed uniformed personnel to such operations.[83] The budget for these peacekeeping operations has grown from about $4 million in 1948[84] to approximately $7.87 billion for 2016–2017.[85] Some studies about the effectiveness of U.N. peacekeeping operations have been conducted, but none has been comprehensive enough to prove that these operations have contained or controlled aggression or the extent to which they have limited the human harm that conflicts have inflicted. One has to assume that they have had some positive effect, even though the cost–benefit analysis of these bureaucratically driven operations is generally negative. But if we add the positive outcomes of these operations to the Security Council's involvement in situations affecting peace and security (even when referring to them as aggression), can we assume that these disparate efforts reduced occurrences of

---

UNITED STATES, 1940–1945, at 960 (1958); ROBERT C. HILDERBRAND, DUMBARTON OAKS: THE ORIGINS OF THE UNITED NATIONS AND THE SEARCH FOR POSTWAR SECURITY 2 (1990).

[79] S.C. Res. 50, U.N. Doc. S/RES/50 (May 29, 1948).

[80] S.C. Res. 73, U.N. Doc. S/RES/73 (Aug. 11, 1949).

[81] *United Nations Peacekeeping Operations Fact Sheet: 31 May 2017*, UNITED NATIONS, www.un.org/en/peacekeeping/documents/bnotelatest.pdf.

[82] *Id.*

[83] *Id.*

[84] Michael Renner & Global Policy Forum, *Peacekeeping Operations Expenditures: 1947–2005*, GLOB. POL'Y, www.globalpolicy.org/images/pdfs/Z/pk_tables/expend.pdf.

[85] *United Nations Peacekeeping Operations Fact Sheet*, *supra* note 81.

aggression? The answer, in light of the past millennium's reduction of conflicts involving States (as described in Section VI) tends to be positive, though no scientific causal connection can be established between the decline in the number of aggressions by one State against another and the policies and practices of the United Nations. Nevertheless, inferences can be drawn with due consideration to other factors affecting such an outcome.

Despite the United Nations' historical failure to prevent conflicts or to intervene in conflicts to minimize their harmful effects, the major powers have resisted the call for unilateral humanitarian intervention. The first of these occurred in 1971, just about twenty-five years after the establishment of the United Nations,[86] when Indian forces entered what is now Bangladesh (then East Pakistan) in response to massive human rights abuses amounting to war crimes and crimes against humanity against the people of East Pakistan by the West Pakistani military.[87] The situation forced an estimated eight million refugees to flood into India,[88] and between 300,000 and three million Bangladeshis lost their lives.[89]

Following the invasion, India justified its use of force through unilateral intervention to the United Nations, stating that the duty to refrain from using military force did not apply because Bangladesh had become "a victim of colonial rule and was not a self-governing territory" and such force was necessary to prevent loss of life and promote self-determination.[90] The invasion and stated rationale brought to the forefront the debate over the role of

---

[86] *See generally* Thomas M. Franck & Nigel S. Rodley, *After Bangladesh: The Law of Humanitarian Intervention by Military Force*, 67 AM. J. INT'L L. 275 (1973) (for pre-1900 acts of humanitarian intervention).

[87] A representative of the International Commission of Jurists described the conduct/treatment to the U.N. Sub-Commission on the Prevention of Discrimination and Protection of Minorities as "killing and torture; mistreatment of women and children; mistreatment of civilians in armed conflict; religious discrimination; arbitrary arrest and detention; arbitrary deprivation of property; suppression of the freedom of speech, the press and assembly; suppression of political rights; and suppression of the right of migration." And "[o]ther reports have indicated that a 'coldblooded, planned' attempt at systematic and selective killing of the leaders of the Awami League, Bengali military and police officials, and intellectuals (especially university teachers, writers and students), was undertaken purportedly to deprive East Pakistan of any future leadership." Ved P. Nanda, *Self-Determination in International Law: The Tragic Tale of Two Cities—Islamabad (West Pakistan) and Dacca (East Pakistan)*, 66 AM. J. INT'L L. 321, 332 (1972) [hereinafter Nanda, *Self-Determination in International Law*].

[88] *See* Nanda, *Self-Determination in International Law, supra* note 87, at 323 n.9.

[89] Independent researchers put the number at 300,000 to 500,000 victims, while the Bangladesh government estimates as many as three million victims. Mark Dummett, *Bangladesh War: The Article that Changed History*, BBC NEWS (Dec. 16, 2011), www.bbc.com/news/world-asia-16207201.

[90] Franck & Rodley, *supra* note 86, at 276.

the United Nations, and more particularly the Security Council, with respect to the concept of collective force and with it the concept of humanitarian intervention as we understand it today.

The concept of unilateral humanitarian intervention has generally been rejected by the international community. But the rejection of unilateral humanitarian intervention did not stop the United States, acting through NATO from March until June, 1999, from using force against Serbia after events in Kosovo led to the expulsion of an estimated 800,000 ethnic Albanians living in Kosovo.[91] Over eleven weeks, NATO bombarded Serbia in the largest allied military operation in Europe since World War II, causing significant civilian casualties and destroying Serbian weapons, helicopters, and infrastructure.[92] For all intents and purposes, no further developments have been made with respect to the doctrine of humanitarian intervention.[93] But the debate continues: despite U.N. Secretary-General Kofi Annan's concern over NATO's use of force in Serbia, one year later, in 2000, he posed the question to all Member States: "If humanitarian intervention is, indeed, an unacceptable assault on sovereignty, how *should* we respond to a Rwanda, to a

---

[91] *See* SONJA BISERKO, YUGOSLAVIA'S IMPLOSION: THE FATAL ATTRACTION OF SERBIAN NATIONALISM 283 (2012).

[92] Ved P. Nanda, *NATO's Armed Intervention in Kosovo and International Law*, 10 U.S. A.F. ACAD. J. LEGAL STUD. 1 (1999–2000). The airstrikes raised concerns of the then–Secretary General of the United Nations Kofi Annan, as they were undertaken without Security Council authorization. *Id.* at 8.

[93] *See* Sean D. Murphy, *Criminalizing Humanitarian Intervention*, 41 CASE W. RES. J. INT'L L. 341 (2009); Louis Henkin, *Humanitarian Intervention*, 26 STUD. TRANSNAT'L LEGAL POL'Y 383 (1994); Harold Koh, *The War Powers and Humanitarian Intervention*, 54 HOUS. L. REV. 971 (2016) [hereinafter Koh, *The War Powers and Humanitarian Intervention*]; A.P.V. Rogers, *Humanitarian Intervention and International Law*, 27 HARV. J.L. & PUB. POL'Y 725 (2004). *See also* Carsten Stahn, *Responsibility To Protect: Political Rhetoric or Emerging Legal Norm?*, 101 AM. J. INT'L L. 99 (2007); Alex J. Bellamy, *Whither the Responsibility to Protect? Humanitarian Intervention and the 2005 World Summit*, 20 ETHICS & INT'L AFF. 143 (2006) [hereinafter Bellamy, *Whither the Responsibility to Protect?*]; David Scheffer, *Atrocity Crimes Framing the Responsibility to Protect*, 40 CASE W. RES. J. INT'L L. 111 (2007) [hereinafter Scheffer, *Atrocity Crimes*]; Ben Saul, *The Dangers of the United Nations' "New Security Agenda": "Human Security" in the Asia-Pacific Region*, 1 ASIAN J. COMP. L. 1 (2006); William W. Burke-White, *Adoption of the Responsibility to Protect, in* THE RESPONSIBILITY TO PROTECT: THE PROMISE OF STOPPING MASS ATROCITIES IN OUR TIME 17, 18 (Jared Genser & Irwin Cotler eds., 2012); GARETH EVANS, THE RESPONSIBILITY TO PROTECT: ENDING MASS ATROCITY CRIMES ONCE AND FOR ALL 38–50 (2008); Christopher C. Joyner, *"The Responsibility to Protect": Humanitarian Concern and the Lawfulness of Armed Intervention*, 47 VA. J. INT'L L. 693, 720 (2007); ALEX J. BELLAMY, RESPONSIBILITY TO PROTECT: THE GLOBAL EFFORT TO END MASS ATROCITIES 84 (2009) [hereinafter BELLAMY, THE GLOBAL EFFORT].

Srebrenica—to gross and systematic violations of human rights that offend every precept of our common humanity?"[94]

What these and other cases reveal is the existence of a political and legal gap between what international law posits and prohibits and what the United Nations is capable of doing to prevent aggression and its harmful consequences for civilian populations. The effort to fill this gap by the doctrine of humanitarian intervention had a short life span, no matter what the human consequences were. A few years later, a promising new international initiative was developed, but it was stillborn.

In 2000, the concept of the "Responsibility to Protect" was first actively developed by the International Commission on Intervention and State Sovereignty,[95] and at the 2005 World Summit all United Nations Member States formally agreed to help protect the world from genocide, war crimes, and crimes against humanity.[96] It was a grand declaration, subscribed by many heads of state in a formal ceremony, but again the world was duped. The declaration was never acted upon, and soon thereafter it became another of those historical legal appendages intended to make the peoples of the world feel better about a system that was not likely to become better.

Dividing aggression into a political concept, subject to the political considerations of the Security Council, including the veto power of its five Permanent Members; a legal definition; and the individual criminalization of those who engage in it (namely, its leaders and senior executors) has worked brilliantly to the benefit of States' interests and to the detriment of the world's peoples. This history – and what follows in Section V – are an extraordinary, perhaps unique, example of how States have played the games of *realpolitik* by using U.N. bodies and mechanisms to mandate different committees with different tasks to pursue different ends, creating the appearance of action while actually fostering the *status quo*.

---

[94] U.N. SECRETARY-GENERAL, *We the Peoples: The Role of the United Nations in the 21st Century*, at 48, U.N. DOC. A/54/2000 (Mar. 27, 2000).

[95] The Commission described the concept as "the idea that sovereign states have a responsibility to protect their own citizens from avoidable catastrophe – from mass murder and rape, from starvation – but that when they are unwilling or unable to do so, that responsibility must be borne by the broader community of states." INT'L COMM'N ON INTERVENTION AND STATE SOVEREIGNTY, THE RESPONSIBILITY TO PROTECT VIII (2001), http://responsibilitytoprotect.org/ICISS%20Report.pdf.

[96] G.A. Res. 60/1, 2005 World Summit Outcome, U.N. Doc. A/RES/60/1, ¶¶ 138–39 (Sept. 16, 2005).

V. THE POST–WORLD WAR II EFFORTS TO DEFINE AGGRESSION AND THE ESTABLISHMENT OF INDIVIDUAL INTERNATIONAL CRIMINAL RESPONSIBILITY

A. *Collective Responsibility*

Historically, defeated tribes or nations have paid a heavy price to the victors, a collective responsibility that stopped only when the victors had exacted from the vanquished land material goods or other forms of payment. The victors usually argued that these payments were either a penalty for the defeated group's decision to wage war or reparations for damages it had inflicted in fighting – two forms of collective punishment that reached their end with the Treaty of Versailles in 1919, when the victorious Allies exacted costly reparations from Germany.[97] France obtained the territories of Alsace-Lorraine and, beginning in 1921, occupied the Ruhr industrial district of Germany, which produced eighty percent of the country's coal,[98] and all former German overseas colonies became League of Nations mandates.[99] The result of this type of collective punishment, under the guise of reparations, was later identified as one of the causes for the rise of national-socialism in Germany and for World War II.[100]

By the 1940s, however, many in the international community had decided that this kind of collective punishment was unfair because it violated the rights of those who opposed the war, those who did not engage in it, and future generations who should not be responsible for what their ancestors had done. But that shift still allowed for some new concepts of collective criminal responsibility to arise, though that took some time in the different legal systems throughout the world. In common-law countries, those who participated in a crime or aided and abetted its commission were held as criminally responsible as those who actually carried out the crime. In other legal systems, participation in organized criminal groups, such as the Mafia in Italy and other groups known in the French criminal code as *"association de malfaiteurs,"* became criminalized no matter how much the individual participated in or initiated

---

[97] See generally LEONARD GOMES, GERMAN REPARATIONS, 1919–1932: A HISTORICAL SURVEY (2010); DONNA HARSCH, GERMAN SOCIAL DEMOCRACY AND THE RISE OF NAZISM (1993).

[98] NICHOLAS ROOSEVELT, *The Ruhr Occupations*, 4 FOREIGN AFF. 113 (1925).

[99] *Holocaust Encyclopedia: Treaty of Versailles, 1919*, U.S. HOLOCAUST MEM'L MUSEUM, www.ushmm.org/wlc/en/article.php?ModuleId=10005425.

[100] As the German people struggled to survive under the enormous burden of the reparations, the loss of their major coal industry and an important economically productive territory had harsh consequences. *See generally* ROOSEVELT, *supra* note 98.

the goals of the criminal organization. The IMT also recognized this form of criminality in establishing the responsibility of the members of the SS (an abbreviation of *Schutzstaffel*, the black-uniformed elite corps and self-described "political soldiers" of the Nazi Party who had immense police and military powers), and the SA (the brown-shirted Storm Troopers, another paramilitary organization).[101] This meant that mere membership in an organization deemed criminal carried with it individual criminal responsibility, irrespective of what the individual did.[102] The individuals' actual conduct was left for the judge to consider when making decisions for purposes of punishment.

International criminal law (ICL), since its early beginnings with the prohibition of certain crimes under *jus in bello*, then piracy and the slave trade, remained focused on the individual actors involved in the actual commission of the crime or any of its elements. It did not bring organizations into its scope. It is only recently, in the millennial era, that ICL has defined certain international crimes such as terrorism as including elements of collective criminal responsibility. The jurisprudence of the International Criminal Tribunal for the former Yugoslavia (ICTY) did establish the doctrine of "joint criminal enterprise" (JCE), which is a form of group criminality but not of collective criminal responsibility.[103] This is an important distinction to keep in mind

---

[101] *SS Police State*, U.S. HOLOCAUST MEM'L MUSEUM, www.ushmm.org/outreach/en/article.php?ModuleId=10007675.

[102] London Charter, *supra* note 40, art. 10 ("In cases where a group or organisation is declared criminal by the Tribunal, the competent national authority of any Signatory shall have the right to bring individuals to trial for membership therein before national, military or occupation courts. In any such case the criminal nature of the group or organisation is considered proved and shall not be questioned."); *see also* BASSIOUNI, INTRO TO ICL, *supra* note 17, at 96–104.

[103] Joint criminal enterprise had its roots in Nuremberg conspiracy law but was largely created by the jurisprudence of the ICTY. Under the joint criminal enterprise theory, "an individual may be held responsible for all crimes committed pursuant to the existence of a common plan or design that involves the commission of a crime provided for in the Statute if the defendant participates with others in the common design." BASSIOUNI, INTRO TO ICL, *supra* note 17, at 373–74. The ICTY and ICTR judges found joint criminal enterprise implicitly, though not explicitly, included in Article 7(1) and Article 6(1) of the respective Statutes on the issue of commission. *See* S.C. Res. 827, *supra* note 47, art. 7(1) ("1. A person who planned, instigated, ordered, committed or otherwise aided and abetted in the planning, preparation or execution of a crime referred to in articles 2 to 5 of the present Statute, shall be individually responsible for the crime."); S.C. Res. 955, *supra* note 47, art. 6(1) ("1. A person who planned, instigated, ordered, committed or otherwise aided and abetted in the planning, preparation or execution of a crime referred to in articles 2 to 4 of the present Statute, shall be individually responsible for the crime."). *See also* Prosecutor v. Krajišnik, Case No. IT-00-39, Judgment, ¶¶ 871–93 (Sept. 27, 2006); Prosecutor v. Plavšić, Case No. IT-00-39 & 40/1, Judgment Summary, § 2

when considering who should be included in the international criminaliza-tion of aggression.[104]

Aggression is more complex and more complicated, as are different types of massive criminality evident in the crimes committed during the Nazi regime and in the communist regime that started in Russia in 1917 and for all practical purposes lasted until 1989. While the number of victims in Nazi Germany – including Jews, Slavs, Gypsies, the mentally ill, and others – is estimated at twenty million people, the number of victims in the Soviet Union is also estimated at twenty million, though no one can verify either of those figures.[105] But surely the scope of the victimization is so broad that it does not really matter how precise the numbers are. Germany paid reparations to Israel and to individual victims pursuant to the Luxembourg Agreements,[106] but

(Feb. 27, 2003); *Case Information Sheet: "Kosovo, Croatia, and Bosnia" (IT-02–54) Slobodan Milošević*, INT'L CRIM. TRIBUNAL FOR THE FORMER YUGOSLAVIA, www.icty.org/x/cases/slobodan_milosevic/cis/en/cis_milosevic_slobodan_en.pdf; Kai Ambos, *Joint Criminal Enterprise and Command Responsibility*, 5 J. INT'L CRIM. JUST. 159 (2007); Allison Marston Danner & Jenny S. Martinez, *Guilty Associations: Joint Criminal Enterprise, Command Responsibility, and the Development of International Criminal Law*, 93 CAL. L. REV. 75 (2005); Antonio Cassese, *The Proper Limits of Individual Responsibility under the Doctrine of Joint Criminal Enterprise*, 5 J. INT'L CRIM. JUST. 109 (2007).

[104] While it may be easy to identify a dictatorial head of state for ordering planes, missiles, ships, and/or troops to cross a national border and attack another State, it may be more difficult to identify those in a cabinet or national security council or armed forces council who shared in the collective decision-making process. The common law–based legal systems have no such problems because their systems include the crime of conspiracy. But that crime exists in some fifty States of the world out of 198. Nevertheless, other States have developed similar concepts or enhanced their traditional concepts of group criminality.

[105] The number of people killed as a result of Nazi policies is estimated to be about twenty million, though no single document created by the Nazis totals the precise number of victims. *Documenting Numbers of Victims of the Holocaust and Nazi Persecution*, U.S. HOLOCAUST MEM'L MUSEUM, www.ushmm.org/wlc/en/article.php?ModuleId=10008193. As for victims of the Soviet Union, in 1989 a major Russian newspaper reported that twenty million had died during Stalin's regime. *See* Bill Keller, *Major Soviet Paper Says 20 Million Died as Victims of Stalin*, N.Y. TIMES (Feb. 4, 1989), www.nytimes.com/1989/02/04/world/major-soviet-paper-says-20-million-died-as-victims-of-stalin.html.

[106] Further, when West Germany and East Germany unified in 1990, the agreement expressly stated that the united country would continue its obligations to pay reparations. *See* David Binder, *Germany to Pay Jewish Victims of Nazis*, N.Y. TIMES (Nov. 7, 1992), www.nytimes.com/1992/11/07/world/germany-to-pay-jewish-victims-of-nazis.html. For the text of the Luxembourg Agreements, see Agreement Between the State of Israel and the Federal Republic of Germany, Isr.-Germ., Sept. 10, 1952, 162 U.N.T.S. 205; Protocol No. 1 Drawn up by Representatives of the Federal Republic of Germany and of the Conference on Jewish Material Claims Against Germany, Sept. 10, 1952, 162 U.N.T.S. 270; Protocol No. 2 Drawn up by Representatives of the Federal Republic of Germany and the Conference on Jewish Material Claims Against Germany, Sept. 10, 1952, 162 U.N.T.S. 298. *See also* Kurt Schwerin, *German Compensation for Victims of Nazi Persecution*, 67 Nw. U.L. REV. 479 (1972).

Russia never did.[107] As history shows, rarely has any Western European country[108] ever been made to pay reparations to the indigenous population it has colonized, including those they exterminated.[109]

While all these considerations are valid, we should remember that international endeavors to define aggression or criminalize the responsibility of those who engage in it have carefully avoided the issue of whom to include in what is necessarily a larger circle than in other forms of criminality. This necessarily has to include group criminal responsibility for the principal decision makers and principal executors of the aggression plan. More importantly, the consequences that flow from aggression – such as genocide, war crimes, and crimes against humanity – should also include individual and group criminality.

The exclusion of collective criminal responsibility for aggression is a valid consideration under international human rights law, and this impacts how to deal with victim compensation for those who have suffered the consequences of aggression as provided for in the U.N. Declaration of Basic Principles of Justice for Victims of Crime and Abuse of Power.[110] But this does not eliminate the responsibility of States for wrongful conduct.[111]

---

[107] Even further, Russian lawmakers are in talks over the possibility of Russia requesting reparations from Germany for Russians killed during WWII. P. Spinella, *Russian Lawmakers Want Germany to Pay Reparations for World War II*, Moscow Times (Feb. 3, 2015), https://themoscowtimes.com/news/russian-lawmakers-want-germany-to-pay-reparations-for-world-war-ii-43525.

[108] An exception to this was the payment of reparations by Austria to Austrian victims of the Holocaust and their heirs. Agreement Between the United States of America and Austria, U.S.-Austria, Jan. 23, 2001, T.I.A.S. No. 13,143, www.state.gov/documents/organization/129563.pdf.

[109] This includes the United States in connection with the extermination of the Native Americans as well as major colonial powers such as the United Kingdom, France, Portugal, Belgium, and The Netherlands.

[110] G.A. Res. 40/34, Declaration of Basic Principles of Justice for Victims of Crime and Abuse of Power, U.N. Doc. A/RES/40/34 (Nov. 29, 1985). *See also* M. Cherif Bassiouni, *Victims' Rights and Participation in ICC Proceedings and in Emerging Customary International Law*, in Contemporary Issues Facing the International Criminal Court 233, 233 (Richard H. Steinberg ed., 2016); M. Cherif Bassiouni, *International Recognition of Victims' Rights*, 6 Hum. Rts. L. Rev. 203 (2006). At times, truth commissions are also established in order to try to better meet the needs of victims. *See* Int'l Ctr. for Transitional Justice & Kofi Annan Found., Challenging the Conventional: Can Truth Commissions Strengthen Peace Processes? (2014).

[111] G.A. Res. 56/83, Responsibility of States for Internationally Wrongful Acts, U.N. Doc. A/RES/56/83 (Jan. 28, 2002). *See also* James Crawford, *The ILC's Articles on Responsibility of States for Internationally Wrongful Acts: A Retrospect*, 96 Am. J. Int'l L. 874 (2002); Robert Rosenstock, *The ILC and State Responsibility*, 96 Am. J. Int'l L. 792 (2002); Alan Nissel, *The Duality of State Responsibility*, 44 Colum. Hum. Rts. L. Rev. 793 (2013); Edith Brown Weiss, *Invoking State Responsibility in the Twenty-First Century*, 96 Am. J. Int'l L. 798 (2002).

After all is said and done, the option of collective responsibility has been abandoned and rejected, and the responsibility of States for wrongful conduct is far from effective.[112] Victim compensation has worked for Holocaust victims because of political pressure, but not for others. And the major powers' opposition to the Declaration of Basic Principles of Justice for Victims of Crime and Abuse of Power continues unabated, making sure United Nations resolutions do not even refer to it.[113] What is left are the Kampala Amendments.

B. *Defining Aggression and Establishing Individual Criminal Responsibility*

After the extraordinary developments in international criminal justice after World War II, notwithstanding their weaknesses and faults, the international community was buoyed by the hope that it could establish a permanent international criminal court. That meant developing a codification of international crimes and a statute for an international court that would directly enforce the proscription of criminal conduct in what later became the Draft Code of Offences Against the Peace and Security of Mankind, in addition to the existing indirect or state enforcement regime.[114] In 1946, the U.N. General Assembly adopted a resolution embodying what were then called the

---

[112] This may be a reason why for so long many States opposed the Declaration of Basic Principles of Justice for Victims of Crime and Abuse of Power, which includes reparations. *See* Declaration of Basic Principles of Justice for Victims of Crime and Abuse of Power, *supra* note 110. *See also* Military and Paramilitary Activities in and Against Nicaragua (Nicar. v. U.S.), Merits Judgment, 1986 I.C.J. Rep. 14 (June 27).

[113] As the United Nations Independent Expert who drafted those Guidelines, I can attest to that opposition. M. Cherif Bassiouni (Independent Expert), *Rep. of the Independent Expert on the Right to Restitution, Compensation and Rehabilitation for Victims of Grave Violations of Human Rights and Fundamental Freedoms, Mr. M. Cherif Bassiouni, Submitted Pursuant to Commission on Human Rights Resolution 1998/43*, U.N. Doc. E/CN.4/1999/65 (Feb. 8, 1999); M. Cherif Bassiouni (Independent Expert), *Final Rep. on the Right to Restitution, Compensation, and Rehabilitation for Victims of Gross Violations of Human Rights and Fundamental Freedoms, Submitted in Accordance with Commission Resolution 1999/33*, U.N. Doc. E/CN.4/2000/62 (Jan. 18, 2000); M. Cherif Bassiouni (Independent Expert), *The Basic Principles and Guidelines on the Rights to a Remedy and Reparation for Victims of Gross Violations of International Human Rights Law and Serious Violations of International Humanitarian Law*, U.N. Doc. E/CN.4/2005/L.48 (Apr. 13, 2005). *See also, e.g.*, G.A. Res. 60/147, U.N. Doc. A/RES/60/147 (Dec. 16, 2005).

[114] *See* BASSIOUNI, ICL ENFORCEMENT, *supra* note 70. At the time, this was the code that was being developed for the codification of international crimes, but ultimately it was not used in the establishment of the International Criminal Court.

Nuremberg Principles,[115] and in 1947 the General Assembly mandated a committee to prepare the draft code of offences, which began its work two years later.[116] In 1950, the General Assembly established a separate committee to draft a statute for a permanent international criminal court.[117] By that time, however, the Cold War was underway and enthusiasm for the codification of international crimes and enforcement through a permanent international court had waned. Aggression, one of the crimes that was to be included in the draft code of offenses, was the most contentious, especially for the United States and the Western Alliance, along with the Soviet Union, and the Eastern Bloc, as the prospects of war or lesser military engagements were very real.

Although the idea of having a definition of aggression that proscribed certain conduct and established individual criminal responsibility was not met with much enthusiasm from the two opposing blocs, the process was already in motion. A committee had been established to prepare a draft code, including aggression, and a separate committee was working on a statute for a permanent international criminal court. Stopping the process *tout court* would have been very difficult – and probably would have encountered considerable opposition, particularly in the West, so another approach was needed. In an artful bureaucratic manner, one that suited both the Soviet Union and the Eastern Bloc, the preparatory "dirty work" was left to the States of the West, which controlled the U.N. bureaucratic and institutional mechanisms, and that launched a splintered process that lasted for several decades. (This long and twisted process has been described in detail in several works.[118]) In brief, this was the splintering process: first, the concept of aggression was removed from the mandate of the committee working on the draft code, and a special committee was established in 1952 to define the crime.[119] What once had been a coherent, cohesive process was fragmented: three different committees worked in three different locations at three different times – each with

---

[115] G.A. Res. 95 (I), Affirmation of the Principles of International Law Recognized by the Charter of the Nürnberg Tribunal, U.N. Doc. A/RES/95(I) (Dec. 11, 1946).

[116] G.A. Res. 177 (II), Formulation of the Principles Recognized in the Charter of the Nürnberg Tribunal and in the Judgment of the Tribunal, U.N. Doc. A/RES/177(II) (Nov. 21, 1947); *Summary Records and Documents of the First Session Including the Report of the Commission to the General Assembly*, [1949] 1 Y.B. Int'l L. Comm'n VI, U.N. Doc. A/CN.4/13 and Corr. 1–3.

[117] Rep. of the Comm. on Int'l Criminal Jurisdiction, U.N. GAOR, 7th Sess., Supp. No. 11, U.N. Doc. A/2136 (1952).

[118] *See generally* BASSIOUNI, LEGISLATIVE HISTORY OF THE ICC, *supra* note 39, at 54–90; 1–2 Bassiouni & Schabas, *supra* note 39. *See also* BASSIOUNI, CAH, *supra* note 41, at 176–83; Bassiouni, *Challenges to ICJ and ICL*, *supra* note 44, at 385–87.

[119] G.A. Res. 688 (VII), Question of Defining Aggression, U.N. Doc. A/RES/688(VII) (Dec. 20, 1952).

its own members, resources, and staff support. Lack of coordination basically ensured that the committees would create distinct products, released at different times, that would not necessarily be compatible. And so it went: in 1953, the committee working on the draft statute for the court produced its final report, which was tabled by the U.N. General Assembly because the committee on the code of offenses had not completed its work.[120] That committee did so in 1954, but the General Assembly promptly tabled that draft code because the committee on aggression had not completed its work.[121] The Special Committee on Aggression, which consisted of government representatives (not experts, like the other two committees) took its time and produced its report in 1974, a full twenty-two years after it had been established.[122]

By then the draft code had been tabled for twenty years and was in need of significant updates, if not completely obsolete. The draft statute on an international criminal court, tabled for twenty-one years, also required updating. But to do this, the General Assembly had to provide a new mandate for a new committee to look into the three drafts. That alone took four more years, and by 1978 the General Assembly re-mandated the draft code to the International Law Commission (ILC), but without reference to the draft statute for the court, which remained in limbo.[123]

It was not clear whether the new mandate to the ILC included the definition of aggression that the General Assembly had adopted in 1974.[124] The ILC appointed a new rapporteur[125] who had difficulties finding his way through the maze and produced a report in 1991,[126] and the process went straight downhill from then on. The final report, which boiled down the elaborate draft code of twelve crimes to only five, was submitted to the General Assembly in 1996 but

---

[120] G.A. Res. 898 (IX), International Criminal Jurisdiction, U.N. Doc. A/RES/898(IX) (Dec. 14, 1954).

[121] Int'l Law Comm'n, Rep. Covering the Work of Its Sixth Session, U.N. Doc. A/2693, at 149–52 (1954); *see* BASSIOUNI, LEGISLATIVE HISTORY OF THE ICC, *supra* note 39, at 58–60; Bassiouni & Schabas, *supra* note 39, at 60–67.

[122] G.A. 1974 Res. Defining Aggression, *supra* note 41.

[123] G.A. Res. 33/97, Draft Code of Offenses Against the Peace and Security of Mankind, U.N. Doc. A/RES/33/97 (Dec. 16, 1978).

[124] G.A. 1974 Res. Defining Aggression, *supra* note 41.

[125] Int'l Law Comm'n, Rep. on the Work of Its Thirty-Fifth Session, U.N. Doc. A/38/10, at 13 (1983).

[126] Int'l Law Comm'n, Rep. on the Work of Its Forty-Third Session, U.N. Doc. A/46/10, at 94–98 (1991) [hereinafter 1991 Draft Code of Crimes Against the Peace and Security of Mankind]. *See also Commentaries on the International Law Commission's 1991 Draft Code of Crimes Against the Peace and Security of Mankind*, 11 NOUVELLES ETUDES PÉNALES 1 (1993).

was never voted on.[127] On the topic of aggression, there was no progress. The establishment of an international criminal court moved forward some time later, in part, as a result of the Security Council's establishment of the International Criminal Tribunal for the former Yugoslavia (ICTY)[128] and the International Criminal Tribunal for Rwanda (ICTR).[129]

Finally, in 1998, a statute for an international criminal court was adopted in Rome. Article 5 included "aggression" as one of the crimes within the court's jurisdiction, but at the time the statute was adopted it did not contain a definition for the crime.[130] It was not until twelve years later that the Kampala Amendments were adopted at the Review Conference, defining aggression in Article 8*bis* and amending the International Criminal Court's jurisdiction over the crime of aggression in Article 15*bis*. The full articles include many details, but the Kampala Amendments generally define "aggression" as "the use of armed force by a State against the sovereignty, territorial integrity or political independence of another State, or in any other manner inconsistent with the Charter of the United Nations."[131] Article 8*bis*(1) defines a "crime of aggression" as the

> planning, preparation, initiation or execution, by a person in a position effectively to exercise control over or to direct the political or military action of a State, of an act of aggression which, by its character, gravity and scale, constitutes a manifest violation of the Charter of the United Nations.[132]

[127] Int'l Law Comm'n, Rep. on the Work of Its Forty-Eighth Session, U.N. Doc. A/51/10, at 17 (1996) [hereinafter 1996 Draft Code of Crimes Against the Peace and Security of Mankind]. *See also* BASSIOUNI, ICL ENFORCEMENT, *supra* note 70, at 121.

[128] S.C. Res. 827, *supra* note 47.

[129] S.C. Res. 955, *supra* note 47.

[130] Rome Statute, *supra* note 23, art. 5(2).

[131] Kampala Amendments, *supra* note 23, art. 8*bis*(2). As of June 2017, thirty-four States have ratified the Kampala Amendments, subject to any legal issues pertaining to Palestine being considered a State for the purposes of the International Criminal Court. Those thirty-four States are Andorra, Argentina, Austria, Belgium, Botswana, Chile, Costa Rica, Croatia, Cyprus, Czech Republic, El Salvador, Estonia, Finland, Georgia, Germany, Latvia, Liechtenstein, Lithuania, Luxembourg, Malta, Mauritius, The Netherlands, Norway, Poland, Portugal, Samoa, San Marino, Slovakia, Slovenia, Spain, Switzerland, Macedonia, Trinidad and Tobago, and Uruguay. *Status of Ratification and Implementation of the Kampala Amendments on the Crime of Aggression, Update No. 27*, CRIME OF AGGRESSION (May 1, 2017), http://crimeofaggression.info/the-role-of-states/status-of-ratification-and-implementation/.

[132] *Id.* art. 8*bis*(1). As evidenced by the text of the Kampala Amendments, the definition adopted in 2010 refers to the 1974 General Assembly Resolution adopting the Definition of Aggression, and the enumerated acts constituting aggression follow the 1974 definition verbatim.
    Compare G.A. 1974 Res. Defining Aggression, *supra* note 41, art. 3(a)-(g) *with* Kampala Amendments, *supra* note 23, art. 8*bis*(2)(a)-(g). Both definitions also explicitly refer to acts of aggression as violations of the United Nations Charter, and both definitions apply regardless of

Those opposed to defining "aggression" had hoped that such a day would never come, but a few committed States and nongovernmental organizations were not about to give up.[133]

Even with a definition, however, the ICC does not have jurisdiction over the "crime of aggression" with regard to other States that have not specifically opted into the Kampala Amendments, even if those Amendments are ratified by the requisite thirty States Parties.[134] The Kampala Amendments are, however, what I consider the life-support system for the individual criminalization of the crime of aggression.

VI. THE CHANGING NATURE OF AGGRESSION IN THE NEW MILLENNIUM

Two basic considerations or assumptions should be assessed here. The first: have human and social values been able to limit States' pursuit of power and wealth through acts that violate those values and the international law that embodies them? The second: was an international legal system ever meant to protect the collective security of all States and all peoples?

any declaration of war. *See* 1974 G.A. Res. Defining Aggression, *supra* note 41, art. 2; Kampala Amendments, *supra* note 23, art. 8*bis*(1). There are, however, two important differences between the definitions, namely individual criminal responsibility and the role of the United Nations Security Council. The Kampala Amendments explicitly provide for individual criminal responsibility, stating that conduct "by a person in a position effectively to exercise control over or to direct the political or military action of a State," may constitute an act of aggression. Kampala Amendments, *supra* note 23, art 8*bis*(1). There is no comparable provision in the 1974 Definition of Aggression. Also differentiating the two definitions is the role of the Security Council in determining acts that constitute aggression. Under the 1974 definition, the enumerated acts are not exhaustive and the Security Council may determine other acts constituting aggression. 1974 G.A. Res. Defining Aggression, *supra* note 41, art. 2. The Kampala definition does not contain a similar understanding. Another, albeit more minor, distinction is that the Kampala definition explicitly applies to acts committed against "the sovereignty, territorial integrity or political independence of a State" while the 1974 definition refers only to acts committed against a State. *Compare* 1974 G.A. Res. Defining Aggression, *supra* note 41, art. 2 *with* Kampala Amendments, *supra* note 23, art. 8*bis*(2).

[133] It must be said that Kampala would not have taken place had it not been for the concerted efforts of a number of persons, chief among them Ambassador Zeid Ra'ad Al Hussein of Jordan, who served as President of the Assembly of States Parties (ASP), and Ambassador Christian Wenaweser of Liechtenstein, who was also a former President of the ASP. A number of NGOS and other individuals representing civil society organizations and academia were also very active and effective, including Benjamin B. Ferencz. The Coalition for the International Criminal Court also deserves recognition.

[134] The Amendments will not enter into force, giving the Court jurisdiction over the crime of aggression, until sometime after January 1, 2017, when a decision is made by States Parties to activate jurisdiction, and they will apply only to the States Parties that have opted in.

These questions include a number of related questions, such as whether the United Nations system was ever intended to be a collective security system or whether it was meant to be a much more modest and basic process reflecting past experiences and seeking to avoid repeating them. If the latter is true, then the United Nations' system, and particularly its veto mechanism in the Security Council for five Permanent Members, is nothing more than a reflection of the reality of political power. If so, no further discussion is needed. This answer, that the United Nations was established to help avoid the repetition of past, harmful experiences, explains the Security Council's failure to act as a collective security mechanism in so many world conflicts,[135] the failure of the practice of humanitarian intervention,[136] and the failure of the Responsibility to Protect.[137]

All the changes witnessed in the practices of various U.N. organs are essentially variations on this theme, reminiscent of what Giuseppe di Lampedusa stated in his novel *The Leopard*: "[i]f we want things to stay as they are, things will have to change."[138] This explains States' tergiversations, and not only within the United Nations, but since the early days of the evolution of *jus ad bellum*.[139] It also reveals how States have used various legal, political, and bureaucratic techniques to create the impression – over long periods of time – that humanitarian values were embodied in international legal norms and standards concerning the prescription and proscription of aggression. What is more telling than the practice and pronouncements of the Security Council in light of its mandate and Articles 1, 39, and 53 on "aggression,"[140] is that not once since 1945 has the Security Council deemed any conflict anywhere in the world to constitute "aggression." And not once has the Security Council referred to the 1974 General Assembly Resolution defining "aggression."[141]

This is relevant to the future insofar as the political interests of the major powers remain somehow balanced. In the end, for the world's major powers and for most developed States, the major concerns are the prevention of wars,

---

[135] *See* 1–2 THE PURSUIT OF INTERNATIONAL CRIMINAL JUSTICE: A WORLD STUDY ON CONFLICTS, VICTIMIZATION, AND POST-CONFLICT JUSTICE (M. Cherif Bassiouni ed., 2010) [hereinafter Bassiouni, STUDY ON CONFLICTS].

[136] *See* sources cited *supra* notes 86–94 and accompanying text; *see also* sources cited *infra* note 164 and accompanying text (on humanitarian intervention).

[137] For the definition of the Responsibility to Protect *see supra* notes 94–96. *See also* sources cited *infra* note 165 and accompanying text (on the Responsibility to Protect).

[138] GIUSEPPE TOMASI DI LAMPEDUSA, THE LEOPARD 40 (Archibald Colquhoun trans., Everyman's Library 1991) (1958).

[139] *See* AQUINAS, *supra* note 4.

[140] U.N. Charter arts. 1, 39, 53.

[141] 1974 G.A. Res. Defining Aggression, *supra* note 41.

the protection of their security and economic interests, and when conflict occurs, minimizing it.[142] The techniques employed to achieve these outcomes have varied as required by the changing means, methods, and weapons of war.[143]

Since the United Nations was established in 1945, the world has witnessed more than 300 conflicts,[144] some of which were defined under international humanitarian law (IHL) as "conflicts of an international character," others as "conflicts of a non-international character" and "purely internal conflicts" (to which IHL does not apply). These classifications, which were adopted by the States that formulated the four Geneva Conventions of August 12, 1949,[145] reflected the interests of States in a narrow way that limited the applicability of international humanitarian law to only the first two categories, even though the same protected human values were at stake in "purely internal conflicts."[146] This was done to give States greater leeway with what could otherwise be deemed violations of international humanitarian law when these acts were committed against their own populations.[147] Even so, under "conflicts of

---

[142] This is evident in the present conflict in Syria. *See* discussion and sources cited *infra* note 150.

[143] *See* sources cited *supra* note 16 (on new wars).

[144] *See* Christopher Mullins, *Conflict Victimization and Post-Conflict Justice, 1945–2008, in* BASSIOUNI, STUDY ON CONFLICTS, *supra* note 135, at 122.

[145] *See* Geneva Convention (I) for the Amelioration of the Condition of the Wounded and Sick in Armed Forces in the Field art. 3, Aug. 12, 1949, 75 U.N.T.S. 31; Geneva Convention (II) for the Amelioration of the Condition of Wounded, Sick, and Shipwrecked Members of the Armed Forces at Sea art. 3, Aug. 12, 1949, 75 U.N.T.S. 85; Geneva Convention (III) Relative to the Treatment of Prisoners of War, Aug. 12, 1949, 75 U.N.T.S. 135; Geneva Convention (IV) Relative to the Protection of Civilian Persons in Time of War art. 3, Aug. 12, 1949, 75 U.N.T.S. 287.

[146] It is worth mentioning that the State Parties in 1949 purposely wanted to distinguish between the two types of conflicts, irrespective of the identity of the human and social interests protected in these instruments. Thus violations of the four Conventions in the context of "conflicts of an international character" were deemed "grave breaches," requiring prosecution and eventually punishment, while with respect to "conflicts of a non-international character," violations of the same practices were contained in a single article, namely Common Article 3, which were not called "grave breaches" but "violations." *See* Theodor Meron, *The Humanization of Humanitarian Law*, 94 AM. J. INT'L L. 239 (2000); Theodor Meron, *Classification of Armed Conflict in the Former Yugoslavia: Nicaragua's Fallout*, 92 AM. J. INT'L L. 236 (1998); Theodor Meron, *The Geneva Conventions as Customary Law*, 81 AM. J. INT'L L. 348 (1987).

[147] Theodor Meron, *International Criminalization of Internal Atrocities*, 89 AM. J. INT'L L. 554 (1995); Theodor Meron, *On a Hierarchy of International Human Rights*, 80 AM. J. INT'L L. 1 (1986); Theodor Meron, *On the Inadequate Reach of Humanitarian and Human Rights Law and the Need for a New Instrument*, 77 AM. J. INT'L L. 589 (1983); Theodor Meron & Allan Rosas, *A Declaration of Minimum Humanitarian Standards*, 85 AM. J. INT'L L. 375 (1991); Asbjørn Eide, Allan Rosas & Theodor Meron, *Combating Lawlessness in Gray Zone Conflicts Through Minimum Humanitarian Standards*, 89 AM. J. INT'L L. 215 (1995).

a non-international character," the main compliance incentive of granting insurgents "prisoner of war" (POW) status has been renounced, and only under "belligerency"[148] can similar rights and obligations in "conflicts of an international character" be applied. That this discrepancy in the two legal regimes still exists, even though the same humanitarian values are at stake, is a contradiction in the application of these values and a disincentive to comply with the laws of armed conflicts.[149] As to "purely internal conflicts," none of these humanitarian norms applies, even though the same human and social interests are involved. As always, state interests prevail.[150]

The number of conflicts of an "international character" as well as those of a "non-international character" began to decline around the end of the first decade of the new millennium, and by 2016 only eight conflicts involving opposing forces from different States continued to exist. They were the following: Iraq (with United States and Iranian forces acting in support of the government); Syria (with Russian and Iranian forces acting in support of the Assad regime in power, and with the United States and others engaging in limited military activities against the group known as the Islamic State of Iraq

---

[148] See Yair M. Lootsteen, *The Concept of Belligerency in International Law*, 166 MIL. L. REV. 109, 109–10 (2000).

[149] See Marco Sassòli, *Taking Armed Groups Seriously: Ways to Improve Their Compliance with International Humanitarian Law*, 1 J. INT'L HUMANITARIAN LEGAL STUD. 5 (2010); Jean-Marie Henckaerts, *The Development of International Humanitarian Law and the Continued Relevance of Custom*, 3 ASIA-PACIFIC Y.B. INT'L HUMANITARIAN L. 1 (2007); Michel Veuthey, *Implementation and Enforcement of Humanitarian Law and Human Rights Law in Non-International Armed Conflicts: The Role of the International Committee of the Red Cross*, 33 AM. U.L. REV. 83 (1983); Yves Sandoz, *International Humanitarian Law in the Twenty-First Century*, 6 YB. INT'L HUMANITARIAN L. 3 (2003); MARIE-LOUISE TOUGAS, DROIT INTERNATIONAL SOCIÉTÉS MILITAIRES PRIVÉES ET CONFLIT ARMÉ (2012).

[150] In the first category, the conflict has to be between two States and in the second, the conflict, which exists in one State, has to involve an internal insurgent group and a foreign State. As defined, and more so as interpreted, States have much leeway to interpret the terminology and standards of international humanitarian law as a way of avoiding the characterization of the conflict, and thus avoiding responsibility under international humanitarian law – as is evident in the current conflict in Syria, in which Russia and Iran, as well as the United States and Turkey, are militarily involved, but so far the conflict has not been legally characterized. This allows Russia and Iran, as well as the Syrian regime, to claim that it is a purely internal conflict and that international humanitarian law – let alone "aggression" – does not apply. *Russia Launches Third Day of Syria Strikes from Iran*, REUTERS (Aug. 18, 2016), www.reuters.com/article/us-mideast-crisis-russia-iran-idUSKCN10T15I; Anne Barnard & Somini Sengupta, *Syria and Russia Appear Ready to Scorch Aleppo*, N.Y. TIMES (Sept. 25, 2016), www.nytimes.com/2016/09/26/world/middleeast/syria-un-security-council.html; Rick Gladstone & Somini Sengupta, *Unrelenting Assault on Aleppo Is Called Worst Yet in Syria's Civil War*, N.Y. TIMES (Sept. 26, 2016), www.nytimes.com/2016/09/27/world/middleeast/aleppo-syria.html; Ben Hubbard, *"Doomsday Today in Aleppo": Assad and Russian Forces Bombard City*, N.Y. TIMES (Sept. 23, 2016), www.nytimes.com/2016/09/24/world/middleeast/aleppo-syria-airstrikes.html.

and Syria [ISIS] but not operations connected with the civil war between opposition forces and the Assad regime); Afghanistan (with U.S., U.K., and some NATO forces[151] in support of the Afghan government against Taliban nationalist fighters from within Afghanistan and across its borders with Pakistan); Pakistan (with U.S. drones engaging in bombings against selected individuals believed to be involved in Taliban operations in Afghanistan); Yemen (with Saudi Arabia and Egypt engaging in aerial bombings against Yemenis who have seized power in an internal conflict in the country with the support of the United States); Libya (where troops from the United States, the United Kingdom, France, and Italy are on the ground in Benghazi to support the U.N.-sponsored government [which has yet to be recognized by the separate parliament in Tripoli] engaging in military operations against Libyan militias in the Misrata area presumed to be affiliated with ISIS);[152] Somalia (with the United States engaging in special operations on the ground and air support against al-Shabaab, a dominant dissident Islamist group opposing the makeshift government); and Ukraine (with Russian forces supporting rebel Ukrainian forces in Eastern Ukraine and the occupation by Russian forces of Crimea). The United States, France, the United Kingdom, and maybe other States also engage in covert military "special operations" in certain States, with French forces being reported present in Mali, Niger, and Chad.[153]

Compared to the number of conflicts in the last decades of the previous millennium, the number of involvements by governments using their military forces in the territories of other States and the amount of resulting human harm as reported by various United Nations, intergovernmental organizations (IGO), and NGO sources is significantly lower.[154] Thus, in a technical legal sense, today we have many fewer "conflicts of an international character" than a decade ago and even fewer when compared to the number over the last fifty years, though a number of "conflicts of a non-international character" and "purely internal conflicts" involving the interests of other States still exist.

[151] *Resolute Support Mission (RSM): Key Facts and Figures*, N. Atl. Treaty Org. (July 2016), https://www.nato.int/nato_static_fl2014/assets/pdf/pdf_2016_07/20160707_2016-07-RSM-Placemat.pdf.

[152] M. Cherif Bassiouni, Libya: From Repression to Revolution, a Record of Armed Conflict and International Law Violations, 2011–2013 (2013).

[153] Elisha Bala-Gbogbo, *France, Nigeria to Intensify Military Efforts Against Boko Haram*, Bloomberg (May 14, 2016), www.bloomberg.com/news/articles/2016-05-14/france-nigeria-to-intensify-military-efforts-against-boko-haram.

[154] Admittedly these sources are not necessarily reliable, and they are also selective insofar as they ignore conflict zones in Asia in particular, where they have little or no presence or access.

Those numbers, however, also have declined since 2008, as has the amount of human harm.[155]

All this seems to have contributed to the decrease in interest in aggression by the international community. Facts have caught up with political reality: aggression, as it had been known since 1945 until recently, no longer constitutes the type of threat to world peace and security that existed during the Cold War, and it therefore no longer demands political and legal efforts to prohibit and criminalize it. The changing reality since 1989, the official end of the Cold War, has gradually marginalized the threat of aggression – and as a result, its legal consequences.

States still pursue power and wealth through various means, including coercive ones, but these no longer fall within the historic meaning of aggression. This raises the question of whether aggression, as conceived of in the post–World War II era, is the type of international activity that still needs to be criminalized *per se*, as opposed to reinforcing the criminalization of its consequences.

The protagonists engaged in today's armed conflicts are very different from those of previous decades, and the means and methods of warfare have also changed. New technology has added new challenges, namely automated weapons systems, which include drones and other tools with which attacks can be committed without the forces of one State actually entering the territory of another.[156] These new tools – and the definition of those who use them – no longer fit into the traditional categories of aggression, and international humanitarian law will have to be altered to apply to such new methods and means, including the responsibility of its actors, however defined.[157] That is also likely to mean that the painstaking progress made

---

[155] *See* BASSIOUNI, STUDY ON CONFLICTS, *supra* note 135. "The decline in international or interstate war started in the 1970s, but at the same time civil wars surged, thus diverting attention from the decline in international war. With the end of the Cold War, however, international war declined further and civil wars began to decline as well. After 2001, there was another increase in civil wars, but it does not even begin to suggest a return to the high civil war levels of the pre-1900 period." Kathryn Sikkink, Federica D'Alessandra & Aroop Mukharji, *Memo: Has International Law Diminished the Illegal Use of Armed Force?* 4 (Feb. 3, 2016) (Carr Center for Human Rights Policy White Paper, unpublished, on file with author).
[156] *See* sources cited *supra* note 16 (on AWS, drones, cyber warfare, and new wars).
[157] Will this be limited to the AWS operators or extend to their commanders? And how will that technological chain of command be established? Will it include the scientific and technological developers of such weapons systems? The next generation of AWS may also employ the use of artificial intelligence and robotics, pushing further out any traditional concepts and standards of responsibility.

against the prevalence of *realpolitik* over human and social values will have to start all over again – or certainly take many steps backward.

Academics, including this writer, who have relied on *jus cogens* for the non-derogable prohibition of certain international crimes such as aggression, genocide, crimes against humanity, war crimes, torture, and slavery, may well have to revisit the sustainability of that doctrinal source of law in light of new realities.[158] Admittedly, it is hard to justify this source of higher law in light of the absence of state practice. The academic bestowment of the *jus cogens* label to a given type of activity is not in itself evidence of its existence, particularly in the absence of state practice to sustain it.[159] Just as we need to

---

[158] Anthony D'Amato, *It's a Bird, It's a Plane, It's* Jus Cogens!, 6 CONN. J. INT'L L. 1 (1990). *See* M. Cherif Bassiouni, *International Crimes:* Jus Cogens *and* Obligatio Erga Omnes, LAW & CONTEMP. PROBS., Autumn 1996, at 63 (discussing *jus cogens* crimes); BASSIOUNI, INTRO TO ICL, *supra* note 17, at 236–46. *See also* Gordon A. Christenson, Jus Cogens: *Guarding Interests Fundamental to International Society*, 28 VA. J. INT'L L. 585, 587 (1988); N. G. Onuf & Richard K. Birney, *Peremptory Norms of International Law: Their Source, Function and Future*, 4 DENV. J. INT'L L. & POL'Y 187 (1974); Mark W. Janis, *The Nature of* Jus Cogens, 3 CONN. J. INT'L L. 359, 360 (1988); CRISTOS L. ROZAKIS, THE CONCEPT OF JUS COGENS IN THE LAW OF TREATIES (1976); Alfred Verdross, Jus Dispositivum *and* Jus Cogens *in International Law*, 60 AM. J. INT'L L. 55, 57 (1966); Egon Schwelb, *Some Aspects of International* Jus Cogens *as Formulated by the International Law Commission*, 61 AM. J. INT'L L. 946, 949 (1967); Bassiouni, *General Principles, supra* note 57, at 801 ("The very words '*jus cogens*' mean 'the compelling law' and, as such, a *jus cogens* principle holds the highest position in the hierarchy of all other norms, rules, and principles. It is because of that standing that *jus cogens* principles have come to be known as 'preemptory norms.' However, scholars are in disagreement as to what constitutes a preemptory norm and how a given rule, norm, or principle rises to that level. The basic reason for this is that the underlying philosophical premises of the scholarly protagonist view are different. These philosophical differences are also aggravated by methodological disagreements."); Karen Parker & Lyn Beth Neylon, Jus Cogens: *Compelling the Law of Human Rights*, 12 HASTINGS INT'L & COMP. L. REV. 411 (1989). The Vienna Convention on the Law of Treaties uses the term "peremptory norm." Vienna Convention on the Law of Treaties, May 23, 1969, 1155 U.N.T.S. 331. The Law of Treaties indeed embodies customary rules that have emerged from international and national legal experience, as well as national legal principles of the law of contracts. RESTATEMENT OF THE FOREIGN RELATIONS LAW OF THE UNITED STATES (REVISED) § 102 (Tent. Draft No. 6, 1985).

[159] D'Amato, *supra* note 158 (on *jus cogens*). Article 38(d) of the Statute of the International Court of Justice (ICJ) recognizes as one of the sources of international law, "the teachings of the most highly qualified publicists of the various nations," but what may be sufficient as an eventual source of law for the ICJ in light of its narrow jurisdictional scope may not be so with respect to international criminal law insofar as there exists the "principles of legality" in any criminalization of individual conduct, whether it emanates from an international or national source. Statute of the International Court of Justice art. 38(d), June 26, 1945, 59 Stat. 1055, 3 Bevans 1179. While this problem has not arisen before the ICTY and ICTR in their respective articles on war crimes or the laws and customs of war, the legal issue nevertheless remains that international as well as national criminalization requires certainty in the definition of the crime as well as notice to its potential perpetrators. It is hard to think of how non-state actor combatants in various arenas in Africa and Asia, who may not even know how to read and write

reassess the sustainability of *jus cogens* as a source of higher law, we should assess the past to better confront the issues of the future.

VII. ASSESSING THE PAST TOWARD DEVELOPING A NEW STRATEGIC APPROACH FOR THE FUTURE

The First World War witnessed a rise in popular demand by the aggressed peoples of the world for the accountability of those who committed aggression against them. The word "aggression" was used in popular literature in Europe and in the everyday discourse of the people of Belgium, France, and England. It was the first time in history that a popular movement of the sort succeeded in achieving a legal reality (in Article 227 of the Treaty of Versailles).[160] But political considerations prevailed, and no one, including the German Emperor, was ever prosecuted for aggression.[161]

Those who were invaded and many others needed no legal expertise to recognize that Germany's invasion of France and Belgium during World War I was an act of aggression, as was Japan's World War II invasion of China and attack on Pearl Harbor, ordered and executed by the principal decision makers in these countries.[162] The value-oriented limitations on the power of States in their use of force were popularly understood throughout the world, no matter how complex they were for theologians, philosophers, and jurists. For most of the world's people, the prohibition of aggression, no matter how defined, was common sense.

But this was not so for those who practiced *realpolitik* (or whatever other term was advanced by politicians and academics who defended the pursuit of power and wealth objectives by state actors claiming justification for the self-identified interests of the State or States in question).[163] This became evident in the 1970s with the emergence of the controversial doctrine of "humanitarian intervention,"[164] and later in the early 2000s with the concept of the

and who certainly have no access to copies of the Geneva Conventions (let alone an understanding of what the "laws and customs of war" may mean in other societies) can be held accountable for something that they do not know. Bassiouni, *New Wars & Non-State Actors, supra* note 16.

[160] Treaty of Versailles, *supra* note 30.

[161] *See* Bassiouni, WWI, *supra* note 29, at 281–86; Bassiouni, *Need for Permanent ICC, supra* note 37, at 19–22.

[162] *See* Bassiouni, WWI, *supra* note 29, at 256–58. *See also* M. Cherif Bassiouni, *Perspectives on International Criminal Justice*, 50 VA. J. INT'L L. 269, 312–13 (2010).

[163] Helal, *Justifying War, supra* note 2, at 558.

[164] *See* Nanda, *Self-Determination in International Law, supra* note 87; Murphy, *supra* note 93; Henkin, *supra* note 93; Koh, *The War Powers and Humanitarian Intervention, supra* note 93;

"Responsibility to Protect."[165] None of these counterpart doctrines to *realpolitik*'s manipulations of justifications to engage in aggression succeeded.[166] And so it was for *jus ad bellum*, which has been around since the time of St. Thomas Aquinas in the 1200s CE[167] in Western Christian Europe – nothing much has changed, notwithstanding the trials and tribulations of those who are dismissed by their opponents in the political realism field as unrealistic idealists. Yet ever since certain moral and social values emerged in different civilizations, sustaining the validity of *jus ad bellum* and *jus in bello*, including the implication that the conduct in question should be proscribed and its violators held accountable, the political defenders of the unbridled pursuit of power and wealth used their bag of tricks to arrest, deviate, or alter this value-oriented expectation. And this caused the political demise of aggression and its legal status.

There was a time when the *realpoliticians* opposed outright political and legal efforts to have aggression declared an international crime and to have that crime enforced. But then they found other covert ways to undermine it. After the First World War, it was the artful definition of Article 227 of the Treaty of Versailles on the responsibility of the Kaiser that prevented the prosecution of the Emperor (or anyone else) for aggression.[168] Then, in the brief period between 1919 and 1939 with Italy's blatant aggression in Ethiopia (Abyssinia), world powers again saw the need to stymie any efforts to proscribe

---

Rogers, *supra* note 93. *See also* Stahn, *supra* note 93; Bellamy, *Whither the Responsibility to Protect?*, *supra* note 93.

[165] G.A. Res. 60/1, *supra* note 96, ¶¶ 138–39; David Scheffer, *The Fate of R2P in the Age of Retrenchment, in* BASSIOUNI, GLOBALIZATION, HRs AND ICJ, *supra* note 26, at 617; Ved P. Nanda, *The Future Under International Law of the Responsibility to Protect After Libya and Syria*, 21 MICH. ST. INT'L L. REV. 1 (2013); David Scheffer, *Atrocity Crimes, supra* note 93; Saul, *supra* note 93. *See also* Burke-White, *supra* note 93, at 17, 18; EVANS, *supra* note 93, at 38–50; Joyner, *supra* note 93, at 720; BELLAMY, THE GLOBAL EFFORT, *supra* note 93, at 84; Helal, *Am I My Brother's Keeper?, supra* note 78, at 453–54 ("In 2005, the UN hosted the World Summit, which was celebrated as 'the largest gathering of world leaders in history.' At its conclusion, the World Summit Outcome Document (WSOD) was unanimously adopted by the General Assembly. Although the WSOD included matters spanning the entire breadth of the UN's work, it was the adoption of RtoP that attracted the most attention, was hailed as a 'millennial change' in international relations, and celebrated by some scholars as marking a constitutional moment in which the principle of 'civilian inviolability' became a foundational norm in international law" [citations omitted]).

[166] So blatant is the resistance of *realpolitik* and other self-proclaimed political realists from Harvard and the University of Chicago law faculty that there is now a frontal attack on all human rights. *See* ERIC A. POSNER, THE TWILIGHT OF HUMAN RIGHTS LAW (2014).

[167] *See supra* note 4 and accompanying text (discussion of St. Thomas Aquinas).

[168] *See* Bassiouni, WWI, *supra* note 29, at 257–60.

acts of aggression.[169] But by then the League of Nations had been formed,[170] and its political processes were thwarted. Then the major Western European powers needed justifications to preserve and protect their colonial regimes, which were inflicted on other peoples by means of aggression. This, too, was not new.[171]

Then came World War II, whose unprecedented, horrible consequences could not be ignored. Once again, people all over the world had no difficulty identifying Nazi-German aggression in Europe and imperial Japanese aggression in Asia and against the United States. This time, the crimes committed were too egregious to be overlooked and their consequences were so devastating that they could not be covered up politically. Thus the successful Allies pursued the criminalization of some of the major perpetrators before the IMT, the IMTFE, and under Control Council Law No. 10.[172] Still, politics played a role, and the term "aggression" was carefully avoided, as was the prosecution of the Emperor of Japan.[173]

---

[169] *See generally* George W. Baer, *Sanctions and Security: The League of Nations and the Italian-Ethiopian War 1935–1936*, 27 INT'L ORG. 165 (1973).

[170] Anne Deighton, *The European Union, Multilateralism and the Use of Force, in* THE CHANGING CHARACTER OF WAR, *supra* note 16, at 315, 316–18; *History: from the League of Nations to the United Nations*, UNITED NATIONS OFFICE AT GENEVA, www.unog.ch/ 80256EDD006AC19C/(httpPages)/242056AEA671DEF780256EF30037A2A8? OpenDocument#.

[171] As of the twelfth century, *jus ad bellum* was transcended by the papal justifications for four Crusades and the established right for these Western Christian States to discover other people's lands and occupy them by subjugating those non-Western Christians to slavery and colonial occupation and what we have to call "inhumane and degrading treatment and punishment." *See generally* RILEY-SMITH, THE CRUSADES: A HISTORY, *supra* note 12; RILEY-SMITH, THE OXFORD HISTORY OF THE CRUSADES, *supra* note 12; *see* Convention Against Torture and Other Cruel, Inhuman or Degrading Treatment or Punishment, Dec. 10, 1984, 1465 U.N.T.S. 85 (entered into force June 26, 1987); J. HERMAN BURGERS & HANS DANELIUS, UNITED NATIONS CONVENTION AGAINST TORTURE: A HANDBOOK ON THE CONVENTION AGAINST TORTURE AND OTHER CRUEL, INHUMAN, OR DEGRADING TREATMENT OR PUNISHMENT (1988); JOSÉ LUIS DE LA CUESTA ARZAMENDI, EL DELITO DE TORTURA (1990); NIGEL RODLEY & MATT POLLARD, THE TREATMENT OF PRISONERS UNDER INTERNATIONAL LAW (3d ed. 2011); M. Cherif Bassiouni & Daniel Derby, *An Appraisal of Torture in International Law and Practice*, 48 REV. INT'LE DE DROIT PÉNAL 23 (1977); M. Cherif Bassiouni, *An Appraisal of the Growth and Developing Trends of International Criminal Law*, 45 REV. INT'LE DE DROIT PÉNAL 405 (1974), translated and reprinted as *Il Diritto Penale Internazionale: Contenuto e Scopo Nel Suo Sviluppo Storico*, LA GIUSTIZIA PENALE, Feb. 1979, at 55. Exceptionalism was born then and continues to live on. *See* sources cited *supra* note 13 (on exceptionalism).

[172] *See* London Charter, *supra* note 40; Tokyo Charter, *supra* note 40; Control Council Law No. 10, *supra* note 40.

[173] The Emperor of Japan, by decision of General Douglas MacArthur, was spared prosecution before the IMTFE or any other body because of the Japanese people's reverence of his person. DOUGLAS MACARTHUR, REMINISCENCES (1964).

After the post–World War II criminalization of "crimes against peace" came the attempt, starting in 1947, to codify and criminalize "offenses against the peace and security of mankind,"[174] although that attempt still did not refer to aggression. One year later, in 1948, the Cold War menaced the world's peace and security, but by then the two main protagonists had weapons of mass destruction, including nuclear, chemical, and biological weapons. With these weapons, particularly nuclear ones, the world's very existence was at stake.[175] The conduct of war changed, and surrogates were successfully used to avoid confrontation between the United States and the Soviet Union. This was not the time to talk about proscribing aggression.

As is evident in the practice of the United Nations Security Council, between 1945 and 2016 the term aggression was not used once and the Security Council did not find one case of aggression. The Security Council also never referred to the General Assembly 1974[176] Definition of Aggression, as mentioned before,[177] even though articulating that definition took twenty-two years. The *realpoliticians* also buried the half-century effort to draft a code of international crimes, as the United Nations referred to it first as the Draft Code of Offenses Against the Peace and Security of Mankind[178] from 1947 to 1988, and thereafter as the Draft Code of Crimes Against the Peace and Security of Mankind.[179] Neither one was ever adopted by the United Nations. Both were politically and bureaucratically buried and with them aggression, notwithstanding the 1974 Definition of Aggression adopted by the General Assembly. Then in June 2010, when the International Criminal Court's Kampala Amendments defined the crime of aggression, the moribund legal proscription of aggression as an international crime received some life support. Kampala saved it *in extremis.*[180]

---

[174] G.A. Res. 177 (II), *supra* note 116.

[175] *See* sources cited *supra* note 16 (on new wars, drones and non-state actors).

[176] *See* G.A. 1974 Res. Defining Aggression, *supra* note 41.

[177] *See* discussion *supra* Sections I and II (on defining "aggression").

[178] Int'l Law Comm'n, Rep. on the Work of Its Thirty-Ninth Session, U.N. Doc. A/42/10, at 12–13 (1987).

[179] *Id.*

[180] Review Conference of the Rome Statute of the International Criminal Court, *The Crime of Aggression*, Res. RC/Res.6, arts. 15*bis*(2)-(3), 15*ter*(2)-(3) (June 11, 2010), *available at* https://asp .icc-cpi.int/iccdocs/asp_docs/Resolutions/RC-Res.6-ENG.pdf; Rome Statute, *supra* note 23. *See generally* BASSIOUNI, LEGISLATIVE HISTORY OF THE ICC, *supra* note 39; Bassiouni & Schabas, *supra* note 39; David Scheffer, *States Parties Approve New Crimes for International Criminal Court*, ASIL INSIGHTS (June 22, 2010), www.asil.org/insights/volume/14/issue/16/ states-parties-approve-new-crimes-international-criminal-court; Niels Blokker & Claus Kreß, *A Consensus Agreement on the Crime of Aggression: Impressions from Kampala*, 23 LEIDEN

How long this life-support system will last – and how effective it will be – remains to be seen, but its moral legacy is not to be underestimated, for, if nothing else, the Kampala Amendments reinforced the human and social values that condemn aggression and exposed to the international community those States that failed to ratify or accede to the definition of aggression.[181] I fear, however, that this will have insignificant impact on world political opinion.

As I have discussed, since World War II, the changed nature of armed conflict has resulted in fewer international conflicts between or involving States – but more conflicts involving non-state actors.[182] This changing reality has added to the *realpoliticians'* arguments that aggression is no longer a necessary legal concept requiring proscription and individual criminal accountability. The argument, deceiving as its purposes are, is nonetheless plausible. But it does not take into account the many other means by which aggression and its intended outcomes can be achieved in this era of globalization, particularly with the use of automated weapons systems. Political, economic, and financial means, as well as other subversive means, can be effectively used to achieve the same results that the post–World War I and post–World War II formulations of aggression could, with much lower costs and fewer harmful consequences.[183] This means that international law and all its specialized disciplines such as international humanitarian, human rights, and criminal law must converge on this new reality and develop the necessary and appropriate legal means and methods likely to deter these new forms of aggression and to hold accountable those who will be less visible in the commission of human harm.

That will take forms other than the *caduc* concept (the French term best expresses the political status of aggression) that has legally fallen into *désuétude* with respect to its practice.[184] The fact that aggression remains unacceptable conduct in the human and social values of most peoples of the world does not alter its record of nonenforcement.

Ideally, the next stage of enforcing aggression will be to secure a more genuinely universal acceptance of commonly shared values and goals of condemning and preventing aggression, including but not limited to, means

---

J. INT'L L. 889 (2010); Stefan Barriga & Leena Grover, A *Historic Breakthrough on the Crime of Aggression*, 105 AM. J. INT'L L. 517 (2011).

[181] For a list of States Parties that have ratified the Kampala Amendments see *supra* note 131 and accompanying text.

[182] *See* sources cited *supra* note 16 (on new wars, drones, and non-state actors).

[183] *Id.*

[184] A "consistent state practice" is an element of customary international law.

of collective security[185] and the application of principles and methods of international and national criminal accountability for those at the highest levels of government and in the military and security apparatuses of States as well as those in the technological and scientific fields of developing auto-mated weapons systems and robotics. But in light of history, that outcome is doubtful. Ideals may exist at the national and international levels, but their enforcement, let alone their effective and impartial enforcement, are not a certain consequence.

Aggression, as reflected in the hollow promises of the United Nations Charter, has fallen into *désuétude,* and its consequence among the peoples of the world has been to discredit international law as a tool of the powerful.[186] Nevertheless, though it cannot be empirically demonstrated, the human and social values sustaining the prohibition of aggression and the goal of holding its perpetrators criminally accountable may have had the beneficial effect of limiting wars between major powers and the escalation of conflicts of an "international character." In a pragmatic sense, this reality of States refraining from resorting to aggression in the traditional sense has some benefit. This should be the new point of departure for a new approach to the proscription of aggression – by holding its protagonists internationally criminally responsible for its consequences.

The response to this historical transformation requires an imaginative approach to international criminal responsibility to ensure accountability of heads of state, senior military commanders, senior decision makers in the intelligence communities, and others for using aggression through new means and methods of warfare and coercive techniques.

If the end goal is to deter people from engaging in aggression as a means of minimizing the resulting harm, the pursuit of alternative legal ways is the course of the future. The objective should not be the survival of the brand name "aggression" but of the transformation of the technique of prevention by enhancing the deterrent through international and national criminal account-ability for the consequences of what would be implicitly recognized as aggression. How the *realpoliticians* will react will probably echo their histor-ical reactions against any limitations on the powers of States to pursue, through non-state actors, power and wealth no matter what human and material harm is inflicted on others.

[185] Wilson, *supra* note 78, at 5; Schachter, *supra* note 78, at 65; Alvarez, *supra* note 78, at 2; Nanda, *Preemptive and Preventive Use of Force, supra* note 78; Franck, *supra* note 78, at 605.
[186] *See* sources cited *supra* note 13 (on exceptionalism).

How successful such a new strategy may be depends on the capability of some States and international civil society's ability to join forces to resist the efforts of *realpolitik* now so well linked to intergovernmental organizations' bureaucracies. And so the struggle goes on, passed as a baton in the relay of generations by those trying to make this world a better place for everyone.

Maybe the best policy solution is to leave aggression in the category of a legal concept in limbo, neither dead nor alive but somehow capable of being brought back to life if and when needed. Perhaps new efforts should be directed toward other international crimes, which are the outcome or consequence of aggression as it is customarily understood, to fill the gap of criminal accountability for the perpetrators. Thus, what may *de facto*, but not *de jure*, start as aggression may end up as crimes against humanity or war crimes.[187] Even though the *jus ad bellum* reveals that what is generically called aggression is politically dead, legally moribund, and on life support, it is stoically alive in the commonly shared values of most peoples of the world.

---

[187] International humanitarian law in this respect is not particularly useful. In fact, it is a hindrance to the achievement of international criminal accountability for the consequences of aggression because of the division of international humanitarian law into the three sublegal regimes. That division, as mentioned, was designed to shield States and state actors from international criminal accountability, other than in the situations of conflicts of an "international character" and the more narrowly circumscribed conflicts of a "non-international character" which are reflected in Common Article 3 of the Geneva Conventions and Protocol II. *See* Geneva Conventions, *supra* note 145. In large part due to the political influence of the United States, Protocol II, which now has 168 State Parties, has not been recognized as being part of the customary law of armed conflicts. Protocol Additional to the Geneva Conventions of 12 August 1949, and Relating to the Protection of Victims of Non-International Armed Conflicts, June 8, 1977, 1125 U.N.T.S. 609 (entered into force Dec. 7, 1978) [Protocol II]. The same is true of Additional Protocol I of 1977, which applies to conflicts of an "international character" and which for the same reasons as in the case of Protocol II is still not recognized as being part of customary international law despite having 174 State Parties. Protocol Additional to the Geneva Conventions of 12 August 1949, and Relating to the Protection of Victims of International Armed Conflicts, June 8, 1977, 1125 U.N.T.S. 3 (entered into force Dec. 7, 1978) [Protocol I]. The solution mentioned above is at best a short-term palliative, though not one to be underestimated. The example of the Syria conflict is once again relevant, as it is politically impossible and legally difficult to charge, but surely "crimes against humanity" and "war crimes" can be charged against Syrian, Russian, and Iranian military operatives in the field, and more importantly, against their commanders under command responsibility. But that of course requires political will, which is presently lacking— though maybe not permanently. For sure, new norms are needed to address the new technologies of AWS, though that, too, requires political will. The use of drones is a reality, as are certain forms of cyberattacks that presage the potential expansion of this new form of aggression.

2

Nuremberg and Aggressive War

WILLIAM A. SCHABAS

I. INTRODUCTION

Responding to a motion filed by the defendants challenging the charge of crimes against peace as a violation of the principle of legality, the International Military Tribunal held that the maxim *nullum crimen sine lege* "has no application to the present facts." According to the four judges,

> Occupying the positions they did in the Government of Germany, the defendants, or at least some of them must have known of the treaties signed by Germany, outlawing recourse to war for the settlement of international disputes; they must have known that they were acting in defiance of all international law when in complete deliberation they carried out the designs of invasion and aggression.

They said their view was "strongly reinforced by a consideration of the state of international law in 1939, so far as aggressive war is concerned."[1]

The Tribunal cited many sources, notably the 1928 Kellogg–Briand Pact, confirming the prohibition of aggressive war, but it did not provide any authority supporting its criminalization. That individuals might be punished following criminal trial for their involvement in acts of aggressive war had of course been debated since 1919 when France, apparently at Clemenceau's personal instigation,[2] submitted a discussion paper to the Commission on Responsibility stating:

---

[1] 1 Trial of Major War Criminals Before the International Military Tribunal, Nuremberg, 14 November – 1 October 1946, Judgment, at 219 (1947), *available at* www.loc.gov/rr/frd/Military_Law/pdf/NT_Vol-I.pdf [hereinafter IMT Judgment].

[2] Kirsten Sellars, *Trying the Kaiser: The Origins of International Criminal Law, in* 1 Historical Origins of International Criminal Law 195, 199–202 (Morten Bergsmo, Cheah Wui Ling & Yi Ping eds., 2014).

[T]hat there is between nations as between individuals a true *regime of right, namely, the principle of the responsibility, not only political but legal,* of the people who go to war in order to steal from a neighbouring State some provinces against the will of their populations and because they either wish to secure the wealth these provinces contain or to ruin their industries and their commerce. [3]

However, Sub-Commission II recommended that German leaders, including the Emperor, should not be charged for "the acts which provoked the war and its initiation."[4] The finding was confirmed in the final report of the Commission:

The premeditation of a war of aggression, dissimulated under a peaceful pretence, then suddenly declared under false pretexts, is conduct which the public conscience reproves and which history will condemn, but by reason of the purely optional character of the institutions at The Hague for the maintenance of peace (International Commission of Inquiry, Mediation and Arbitration) a war of aggression may not be considered as an act directly contrary to positive law, or one which can be successfully brought before a tribunal such as the Commission is authorized to consider under its terms of reference.[5]

When the paragraph was being debated in the Commission, the French delegate asked if the wording might be "softened," but Robert Lansing of the United States insisted that "[a] new doctrine advocated by a very few men should not be permitted to change the standing rule of the world."[6] Lansing said "he was fully of opinion that a war of aggression ought to be declared to be a crime against international law, but this had never been done and the paragraph should therefore stand as drafted."[7]

The work of the Commission was not followed by the Supreme Council when it finalized the penalty clauses of the Treaty of Versailles. Article 227 of the Treaty arraigned the Kaiser "for a supreme offence against international

---

[3] F. Larnaude & A. de Lapradelle, *Inquiry into the Penal Liabilities of the Emperor William II, in* COMMISSION ON THE RESPONSIBILITY OF THE AUTHORS OF THE WAR AND ON THE ENFORCEMENT OF PENALTIES, MINUTES OF MEETINGS OF THE COMMISSION 4, 10 (1919) [hereinafter COMMISSION ON RESPONSIBILITY MINUTES] (emphasis in original).

[4] *Report of Sub-Commission II on the Responsibility of the Authors of the War, in* COMMISSION ON RESPONSIBILITY MINUTES, *supra* note 3, at 45–46.

[5] *Commission on the Responsibility of the Authors of the War and on Enforcement of Penalties: Report Presented to the Preliminary Peace Conference,* 14 AM. J. INT'L L. 95, 118 (1920).

[6] *Minutes of the Ninth Meeting, March 25, 1919, at 10.30 a.m., in* COMMISSION ON RESPONSIBILITY MINUTES, *supra* note 3, at 97, 99.

[7] *Id.* at 100.

morality and the sanctity of treaties." This is often cited as a precursor of the criminalization of aggression. But condemning Germany's violation of a treaty enshrining Belgian neutrality was not the same thing as a criminal prohibition of resort to war to settle international disputes. After the Dutch objected to the extradition request, Clemenceau replied that,

> *il ne s'agit pas dans la circonstance d'une accusation publique ayant le caractère juridique quant au fond, mais d'un acte de haute politique international imposée par la conscience universelle dans lequel les formes du droit ont été prévues uniquement pour assurer à l'accusé un ensemble de garanties tel que le droit publique n'en a jamais connu.*[8]

During the interwar years there was marked progress in the law governing the use of force as well as in the development of an international criminal court. But there is little evidence during this period of further reflection on whether acts of aggression might be described as an international crime. The debate only resumed during the early study of criminal prosecutions that took place during the Second World War.

II. THE CAMBRIDGE COMMISSION

In July 1942, Professor Hersch Lauterpacht presented a paper to the International Commission for Penal Reconstruction and Development, which was based in Cambridge, considering "the responsibility for the premeditated violation of the General Treaty for the Renunciation of War as lying within the sphere of criminal law."[9] He seems to have been uncertain about this, however, as in the subsequent version of his paper published in the *British Yearbook of International Law* Lauterpacht expressed concern that a prosecution on this basis might be deemed a political offense and therefore provide an exception to extradition.[10] The *Tentative List of War Crimes* prepared by Lauterpacht for the Cambridge Commission in 1942 did not include the crime of aggression.[11] Lauterpacht's hesitation in this area may have been influenced by Sir Arnold McNair, who had been his doctoral supervisor, and

---

[8] Paul Mevis & Jan Reijntjes, *Hang Kaiser Wilhelm! But For What? A Criminal Law Perspective*, in 1 HISTORICAL ORIGINS OF INTERNATIONAL CRIMINAL LAW, *supra* note 2, at 213, 216.

[9] KIRSTEN SELLARS, 'CRIMES AGAINST PEACE' AND INTERNATIONAL LAW 50 (2013).

[10] Hersch Lauterpacht, *The Law of Nations and the Punishment of War Crimes*, in 5 INTERNATIONAL LAW: BEING THE COLLECTED PAPERS OF HERSH LAUTERPACHT: DISPUTES, WAR AND NEUTRALITY, PARTS IX–XIV 491, 532 (Elihu Lauterpacht ed., 2004).

[11] Hersch Lauterpacht, *Tentative List of War Crimes*, in 5 INTERNATIONAL LAW: BEING THE COLLECTED PAPERS OF HERSH LAUTERPACHT, *supra* note 10, at 538, 538–41.

who opposed the criminalization of aggression when the matter was considered in Committee III of the United Nations War Crimes Commission, in mid-1944.[12] The Cambridge Commission did not make definite recommendations or produce a comprehensive report. There is no reference to any discussion of the crime of aggression in the account of its work provided in the *History of the United Nations War Crimes Commission*.[13]

Kirsten Sellars also traces the idea of criminal prosecution of aggression to the writings of Soviet jurist Aron Naumovich Trainin, noting that this began to attract attention outside the country when Soviet media began disseminating his writings, in August 1943.[14] Trainin's book *Hitlerite Responsibility Under Criminal Law*, published in Russian in July 1944 and in an English translation the following year, set out a case for prosecuting "crimes against peace." "The direct and most dangerous form of offence against peace is the attack of one State on another – aggression – which directly breaks the peace, and forces war on the peoples," wrote Trainin. "Aggression is, therefore, the most dangerous international crime."[15]

III. THE LONDON INTERNATIONAL ASSEMBLY

The first serious debates and elaborate studies concerning the prosecution of aggression or crimes against peace would appear to have been undertaken under the aegis of the London International Assembly. It was an unofficial body, established in September 1941 on the initiative of Viscount Cecil. The London International Assembly was composed of public intellectuals, activists, and representatives of the governments-in-exile then based in London. Membership included nationals of Australia, Belgium, China, Czechoslovakia, Ethiopia, France, Greece, India, The Netherlands, New Zealand,

---

[12] U.N. War Crimes Comm'n, *Note by Sir Arnold McNair on the questions submitted, namely, whether (i) the preparation for and launching of the present war by individuals, and (ii) preparatory acts by individuals which are themselves criminal acts, can or ought to be treated by the Commission as "war crimes,"* Doc. C.43 (Aug. 18, 1944), *available at* www.legal-tools.org/uploads/tx_ltpdb/File_3224-3232.pdf [hereinafter *Note by Sir Arnold McNair*]; ARIEH J. KOCHAVI, PRELUDE TO NUREMBERG: ALLIED WAR CRIMES POLICY AND THE QUESTION OF PUNISHMENT 98 (1998); SELLARS, *supra* note 9, at 59–60.

[13] U.N. WAR CRIMES COMM'N, HISTORY OF THE UNITED NATIONS WAR CRIMES COMMISSION AND THE DEVELOPMENT OF THE LAWS OF WAR 94–99 (1948), *available at* www.cisd.soas.ac.uk/documents/un-war-crimes-project-history-of-the-unwcc,52439517 [hereinafter HISTORY OF THE UNITED NATIONS WAR CRIMES COMMISSION].

[14] SELLARS, *supra* note 9, at 49.

[15] A. N. TRAININ, HITLERITE RESPONSIBILITY UNDER CRIMINAL LAW 37–39 (1945).

Norway, the Soviet Union, Poland, the United Kingdom, the United States, and Yugoslavia. Its purpose was to

> serve the common cause of all those nations that are resisting aggression by providing greater opportunities for the People of Great Britain and each of the Allied and Associated Nations to understand more fully each other's history ... and to consider the principles of post-war policy and the applica-tion of these principles to the problems of national and international affairs.[16]

The Assembly addressed a broad range of issues.

At its second meeting on October 20, 1941, Lord Cecil proposed that the members of the Assembly should "concentrate their attention upon the following points ... (2) The measures that might be desirable to ensure the trial of war criminals."[17] Arthur Lehman Goodhart, a member of the Ameri-can group and a professor of jurisprudence at the University of Oxford, presented a report stating:

> [T]he occupied countries wish to be assured that justice will be done to the war criminals. This was promised in the Versailles Treaty, but it failed completely. It will not be difficult to constitute after the war a proper Court for such trials, but it will be far more difficult to define what acts are to be considered criminal and who is to be held responsible for them. These questions ought to be considered now. Moreover, it might be possible to suggest some method by which evidence could be collected at the present time so that it could be established for the future.[18]

The Assembly agreed to set up a commission to study "Proposals for the trial of war criminals at the end of the war."[19] Commission I of the London Inter-national Assembly[20] eventually produced a lengthy report, published in December 1943 just as the United Nations War Crimes Commission was being set up. Several of the major participants in the War Crimes Commission had been actively engaged in the work of Commission II of the London International Assembly.

Marcel de Baer, the Belgian judge who chaired Commission II of the London International Assembly, wrote to its members in July 1942 explaining that although he favored establishing an international criminal court with jurisdiction over all war crimes, he understood that others thought this should

---

[16] London Int'l Assembly, Reports on Punishment of War Crimes (1943).
[17] London Int'l Assembly, *Proceedings of the Second Meeting, 20 October 1941*, at 3 (1941).
[18] *Id.* at 8.
[19] *Id.* at 14.
[20] It was initially Commission II of the Assembly.

be limited. Asking for members of the Commission to provide him with their views, he listed cases in an annex that he felt ought to be within the jurisdiction of the proposed international court: "The following are cases: 1. as to which it is assumed that some of the Courts of the Allied Nations have *no* jurisdiction or; 2. which are not adequately covered by the penal law of some of the Allied Countries: I. Crimes Against the State: (a) the crime of war (breach of the Kellogg Pact). . . ."[21] This was a controversial proposal, however, and Dr. Victor Lehman of the United Kingdom opposed consideration of violation of the Kellogg–Briand Pact by the Commission because it did not contain "specific penalties for specific crimes," adding that "any *ad hoc* legislation would have to be retrospective. This would be against the principle *nulla poena sine lege*, which in my view, should be observed under all circumstances."[22]

De Baer presented Commission II's interim conclusions to the twelfth meeting of the London International Assembly on September 28, 1942. He began:

> This war calls for retribution. The Germans and Japanese and other Axis partners must be punished for what they have done to us. At the end of the last war the effect of victory was lost because the aggression remained unpunished: Germany was not made to suffer, and the individual criminals were not punished. This must not be allowed to happen again. It must be brought to the knowledge of future generations that, with each war, the aggressor will be made to suffer more severely, and that *it does not pay* to attack other nations.[23]

De Baer spoke of the penal provisions of the Treaty of Versailles, Articles 227–230, noting that the scheme was not "sufficiently thought out," that it was "unsound" and a "fiasco." He said "the Germans were quick in seeing their weak points, and the first wedge was driven in the Peace Treaty by attacking its penal provisions."[24]

René Cassin, one of three Vice Presidents of the Assembly, intervened in the debate in order to stress the importance of the issue of aggressive war:

> The declaration of war in violation of the Briand–Kellogg Pact was in itself a war crime. It was a violation of a Treaty accepted by all the nations, including Germany, Italy and Japan. In its Resolution the London International

---

[21] *Annex to the Letter of 22nd July 1942 by M. de Baer, to members of Commission II on the Trial of War Criminals, in* LONDON INT'L ASSEMBLY, *supra* note 16, at 90, 91.

[22] *Commission II on the Trial of War Criminals, 4 July 1942, in* LONDON INT'L ASSEMBLY, *supra* note 16, at 33, 33.

[23] *Proceedings of the Twelfth Meeting held at the Goldsmiths' Hall, Forster Lane, Cheapside, EC2, at 3 pm on Monday, September 28th, 1942, in* LONDON INT'L ASSEMBLY, *supra* note 16, at 122, 124.

[24] *Id.* at 124–25.

Assembly should also draw attention to the fact that in 1927 the Assembly of
the League of Nations had voted in favour of a proposal – put forward by the
Polish delegation – whereby any aggression was an international crime.
Germany, Italy and Japan were then members of the League and had voted
in favour of this proposal. It was important that mention should be made in
the Resolution, not only of the fact that war was illegal but also that it was an
international crime and was recognised as such by Treaty.[25]

Cassin proposed that a paragraph be added to the resolution under consideration: "Whereas the war of aggression waged by the Axis Powers is an
international crime, as per the terms of the resolution of the ordinary Assembly
of the League of Nations of 1927, for which these powers voted. . . ."[26] Cassin's
amendment was seconded by W. R. Bisschop, who said "he would like to go a
bit further." Bisschop said that if it was a crime to violate the Kellogg–Briand
Pact, "then every act committed during the war of aggression was a crime in
itself and all the persons taking part in that international crime were war
criminals."[27] To this suggestion, an objection was raised by Viscount Cecil,
the President of the Assembly, who cautioned that "it would render our work
fruitless if we said that everything done in an aggressive war was a crime in
itself."[28] Statements of support for Cassin's amendment were made by de Baer
of Belgium and Liang of China.[29] On Viscount Cecil's motion, adoption of
the resolution was postponed to the next meeting of the Assembly. On
October 12, 1942, the Assembly adopted a resolution that began as follows:

> Whereas the Assembly of the League of Nations declared by resolution in
> November 1927 that aggression was an international crime, and
>
> Whereas the Pact of Paris condemned recourse to war for the settlement of
> international controversies, and
>
> Whereas the Axis Powers have violated both the resolution and the Pact of
> Paris to which they were parties, and
>
> Whereas in the course of and in connection with the war of aggression waged
> by the Axis Powers, heinous crimes have been and are being committed by
> nationals of the Axis Powers . . . [30]

[25] *Id.* at 135.
[26] *Id.*
[27] *Id.* at 136.
[28] *Id.*
[29] *Id.*
[30] *Proceedings of a Special Meeting held at Gas Industry House, Hyde Park Corner, London, SW 1,
at 2.00 pm on Monday, October 12th, 1942, in* LONDON INT'L ASSEMBLY, *supra* note 16, at
115, 121.

The materials produced by Commission I make it clear that the "concept of war crimes" had evolved from one limited to violations of the laws and customs of war so as to include other categories. "[A]s the discussions of other questions progressed and as political statements such as the Declaration of December 17, 1942 and others were made, it appeared more and more necessary to include in our research" crimes committed against Germans and stateless persons, practical measures to deal with quislings and collaborators, "and also to consider the punishability of the waging of an aggressive war."[31] In particular, the Commission noted this was prompted by the November 6, 1943, broadcast by Stalin stating "punishment of those responsible for the waging of the war as being one of the purposes which the United Nations have in view."[32]

The studies and other materials generated by Commission II were published in a 419-page mimeographed volume in 1943, a rare copy of which can be found in the British Library. It includes two relevant papers, both of them dated November 1943. The first is an eight-page article by Bohuslav Ečer entitled *The Crime of Aggressive War*. A representative of the Czech government-in-exile, Ečer had served as deputy mayor of Brno from 1935–1939.[33] The second is a six-page article by Marcel de Baer of Belgium entitled *The Crime of Aggression: Considerations of Present Interest on the Pact of Paris*. The two were not in agreement on the criminal nature of aggressive war.

"There is no doubt that before the League of Nations was set up international law permitted all kinds of war, even a war of aggression, as a legal means of settling international disputes," Ečer began.[34] He briefly reviewed the debates in the Commission on Responsibilities of the Paris Peace Conference and the early efforts of the League of Nations to prohibit aggressive war, noting that the covenant "stopped short half way. It lessened the possibility of war, but it did not forbid war, even aggressive war, nor declare it to be an international crime."[35] Ečer cited the preamble of the 1924 Geneva Protocol: "Recognising the solidarity of its members, asserting that a war of aggression

---

[31] *The Concept of War Crimes, Introductory Note*, in LONDON INT'L ASSEMBLY, *supra* note 16, at 154, 155.

[32] *Id.*

[33] Eduard Stehlik, *Bohuslav Ečer and the Prosecution of War Crimes*, in PROCEEDINGS OF THE INTERNATIONAL CONFERENCE: EUROPEAN CONSCIENCE AND COMMUNISM 53–63 (June 2–3, 2008), *available at* www.ustrcr.cz/data/pdf/konference/sbornik-svedomi-en.pdf; Kerstin von Lingen, *Setting the Path for the UNWCC: The Representation of European Exile Governments on the London International Assembly and the Commission for Penal Reconstruction and Development, 1941–1944*, 25 CRIM. L.F. 45 (2014).

[34] Bohuslav Ečer, *The Crime of Aggressive War*, in LONDON INT'L ASSEMBLY, *supra* note 16, at 172a, 172a.

[35] *Id.* at 172b.

constitutes a violation of this solidarity and an international crime. . . ." He also cited one of the rapporteurs, Nicolaos Politis, who had said in a speech to the Assembly of the League of Nations that aggressive war *"se trouve non seulement condamnée, non seulement considérée comme un crime inter-national, mais encore entourée des sanctions, accompagnée du châtiment nécessaire pour la prévenir et au besoin pour le réprimer."* Ečer said that this was "the language of criminal law: crime, penalty, prevention, repression," and it was an interpretation that was approved by the Assembly of the League.[36]

Ečer then turned to the Kellogg–Briand Pact, noting that it was not framed in the language of criminal law, which is why, in his view "it completely failed as an instrument of prevention." Ečer acknowledged that some academic interpreters of the Pact considered that it recognized aggressive war as an international crime or *délit*; however, he noted that the Nazis were responsible for so many atrocities and war crimes that it was not necessary, in order to ensure they be properly punished, to charge them with criminal responsibility for waging aggressive war. However, he insisted that they should also be "expressly condemned for this greatest and most fundamental crime of theirs: the preparation and launching of the Second World War. This is also in the interest of the new world order of peace."[37]

According to Ečer, the Kellogg–Briand Pact provided a sufficient basis for criminal prosecution. He said that the Axis Powers were aware when they started the war that they were "committing an act which had been declared by an international instrument, binding upon them, to be illegal, an unlawful act. This is sufficient for guilt."[38] Ečer described the waging of aggressive war as a "chain" of ordinary crimes, including murder, arson, and robbery, for which severe penalties were provided in all legal systems. In this way, he managed to dismiss the *nulla poena* argument. "Whose legal conscience will be troubled when the international court sends the authors of this war as accomplices in mass murder, arson, robbery etc. to the only place where the national court sends those guilty of murder, namely to the scaffold?" he wrote.[39]

But Ečer also contended that even if the principle of legality was not fully satisfied, "the man guilty of a monstrous crime never imagined before must be

---

[36] *Id.* at 172a, 172c.
[37] *Id.* at 172e.
[38] *Id.*
[39] *Id.* at 172f.

punished, even though no law has so far pronounced his act to be a crime."[40]
He concluded:

> a. Aggressive war is a crime, and by its character an international crime, because it aims against peace and international order. The total aggressive war started by Germany and her allies in 1939 is additionally an international crime in its territorial extent and the number of victims of the aggression.

> b. Not only the aggressor States as such but also their rulers and military leaders are personally responsible in the eyes of the law for the gigantic chain of crimes which compose this war and which are punishable under the criminal law of the countries affected.

> c. The penalty according to all these laws is death.[41]

Ečer criticized the approach proposed by Marcel de Baer, who proposed that upon defeat or surrender the Axis leaders should recognize the criminality of their acts as a way of overcoming objections based upon the principle of legality. "Whether the Germans agree or not, is, of course, of minor importance here," said Ečer. "If the courts only tried and condemned those murderers who agreed to it by recognising the criminality of their act, justice would be in a poor way."[42]

De Baer insisted that *"there is no such thing as a crime of international law, since no punishment has been provided for any such crimes."*[43] According to de Baer, just as there was no way of punishing a State for breaching a treaty, it was also impossible to punish an individual unless the act has been made a punishable crime under national law.[44] De Baer thought that he had a solution to what he called "the old '*ex post facto*' horse." Domestic legislation would first be adopted criminalizing the waging of aggressive war. Then, Hitler and his associates would be prosecuted for acts perpetrated after the enactment of the law. "Even if we abide by Beccaria's rule 'nullum crimen sine lege' and cannot hold Hitler criminally responsible *for the waging* of the war, at least he can be punished, legally, for *continuing an occupation*," wrote de Baer.[45] He said it might be "more difficult for an Anglo-Saxon jurist than for a Continental to accept this theory of continuous offences, but it is well

[40] *Id.*
[41] *Id.* at 172h.
[42] *Id.* at 172g.
[43] Marcel de Baer, *The Crime of Aggression: Considerations of Present Interest on the Pact of Paris,* *in* LONDON INT'L ASSEMBLY, *supra* note 16, at 172i, 172i–172n (emphasis in the original).
[44] *Id.* at 172j.
[45] *Id.* at 172m.

established in all other European countries, including Germany."[46] De Baer did not speak to what would seem to be a fatal flaw in his approach: if the country in question was occupied, how was it to enact criminal legislation that might apply?

IV. THE UNITED NATIONS WAR CRIMES COMMISSION

Unlike the London International Assembly, the United Nations War Crimes Commission was a truly intergovernmental organization. In addition to delegates from the United States and the United Kingdom, participants came from several of the other Allied Powers as well as the governments-in-exile. Several of its members had been active in the work of the London International Assembly. The name of the body suggested that its authority was confined to violations of the laws and customs of war. But in 1944, as its activities got underway, the Commission debated whether to take an expansive approach whereby it would also consider those categories of international crime that were later labelled "crimes against humanity" and "crimes against peace."

In April 1944, Bohuslav Ečer, representing the Czech government-in-exile, returned to the arguments he had advanced in the London International Assembly. He proposed that Committee III of the Commission include within its ambit the crime of the waging of aggressive war. He had devised a new argument, insisting that the Second World War was not only "a simple aggressive war" but rather "a total, thus a criminal war both in purpose and in methods." He continued: "The launching of such criminal war is a crime. The very fundamental crime without which there would not be 'war crimes.' The fact is in comparison with 1914–18 a new one."[47] Ečer appeared to downplay the significance of the Kellogg–Briand Pact. Two weeks later, Ečer submitted a supplementary paper in which he developed his arguments, drawing more or less verbatim on the text he had published in the report of the London International Assembly in November 1943.[48] Committee III proposed a set of "Conclusions" by which the scope of its work was interpreted

---

[46] *Id.* at 172n.
[47] Rapporteur Dr. B. Ečer, *Scope of the Retributive Action of the United Nations According to Their Official Declarations (The Problem of "War Crimes" in connection with the Second World War)*, at 9, Doc. III/4 (Apr. 27, 1944), *available at* www.legal-tools.org/uploads/tx_ltpdb/File_7019-7038.pdf.
[48] Rapporteur Dr. B. Ečer, *Scope of the Retributive Action of the United Nations According to Their Official Declarations (The Problem of "War Crimes" in connection with the Second World War), Explanatory and Additional Note by Dr. Ečer to his Report (Doc. III/4)*, Doc. III/4(a) (May 12, 1944), *available at* www.legal-tools.org/uploads/tx_ltpdb/File_7039-7045.pdf.

to include "crimes committed for the purpose of preparing or launching the war, irrespective of the territory where these crimes have been committed."[49]

The proposal was presented by Stefan Glaser of Poland, the Chairman of Committee III, to the plenary Commission at its meeting on May 23, 1944. Glaser considered that "what was controversial in the proposal was not the objects sought but the question whether they involved an enlargement of the Commission's functions which it was not competent to effect." Doubts were expressed about whether governments would agree, and about the expediency of enlarging the scope of the Commission's work.[50] The Commission returned to this issue on June 6, 1944. It decided to refer the matter back to Committee III for further consideration.[51] On June 13, 1944, the Committee reported to the Commission that it had set up a subcommittee, to be composed of Ečer, J. M. de Moor of The Netherlands, and Lieutenant Colonel Hodgson of the United States, to examine "the question whether preparation for and launching of a war of aggression and individual acts of preparation for such a war were crimes."[52] Sir Arnold McNair, the distinguished British legal scholar who was Vice-Chancellor of the University of Liverpool at the time, appears to have been added subsequently as a member of the subcommittee.[53]

McNair prepared a paper arguing strenuously for the view that there could be no criminality attached to the waging of aggressive war. It received the approval of a majority of the subcommittee, with Ečer dissenting. McNair started with the proposition that a "human agent" of a State could only be guilty for a criminal act if the State itself could commit a crime. "What judicial or literary authority is there for saying that a State can be the subject of criminal liability?" he asked.

> I do not think that anyone can produce any judicial or arbitral decision to that effect. The breach by a State of a rule of customary international law or

[49] *Scope of the Retributive Action of the United Nations. Conclusions Proposed by the Drafting Committee*, Doc. III/5 (May 12, 1944), *available at* www.legal-tools.org/uploads/tx_ltpdb/File_7046.pdf; *Scope of the Retributive Action of the United Nations: Resolution Proposed by Committee III*, Doc. C. 20 (May 16, 1944).

[50] U.N. War Crimes Comm'n, *Minutes of Nineteenth Meeting held on May 23rd 1944*, at 3, Doc. M.19, *available at* www.legal-tools.org/uploads/tx_ltpdb/File_596-601_01.pdf.

[51] U.N. War Crimes Comm'n, *Minutes of Twenty-First Meeting held on June 6th 1944*, at 4, Doc. M.21 (June 7, 1944), *available at* www.legal-tools.org/uploads/tx_ltpdb/File_606-612_01.pdf.

[52] U.N. War Crimes Comm'n, *Minutes of Twenty-Second Meeting held on 13 June, 1944*, at 2, Doc. M.22, *available at* www.legal-tools.org/uploads/tx_ltpdb/File_613-622_01.pdf.

[53] U.N. War Crimes Comm'n, *Rep. of the Sub-Comm. Appointed to Consider Whether the Preparation and Launching of the Present War Should be Considered "War Crimes"*, Doc. C.55 (Sep. 27, 1944), *available at* www.legal-tools.org/uploads/tx_ltpdb/File_3286.pdf.

of a treaty has hitherto been regarded as analogous to a breach of contract or to a delict[,] but not to a crime, as is evidenced by the general rule that only compensatory damages, and not penal or vindictive damages, can be awarded against a State[.][54]

McNair considered in some detail the argument that the Kellogg–Briand Pact might have altered the situation. He said that "however desirable it may be *de lege ferende* to take steps which will enable Governments in future to punish the procuring of aggressive war as a criminal act – I do not consider that *de lege lata* a judge would hold that the effect of the Peace Pact was to make it a criminal act." McNair referred to the "grave inconvenience of discussing whether those responsible for the Russian invasion of Poland or of Finland in 1939 committed crimes."[55] McNair said he would expect a United Nations tribunal to honor the principle *nullum crimen sine lege*, concluding: "A conviction which was secured from a legal tribunal in violation of the principles of law would in the long run damage the countries which were responsible for it and would discredit rather than strengthen the rule of law upon which alone international society must rest."[56]

Committee III adopted the view that acts perpetrated "merely for the purpose of preparing for and launching aggressive war" were not, *lege lata*, war crimes. It said such acts,

> and especially the acts and outrages against the principles of the laws of nations and against international good faith perpetrated by the responsible leaders of the axis powers and their satellites in preparing and launching this war are of such gravity that they should be made the subject of a formal condemnation in the peace treaties.

Furthermore the Committee said it was "desirable that for the future penal sanctions should be provided for such grave outrages against the elementary principles of international law."[57]

The original draft of Committee III's report said that "[t]he other members, including Sir Arnold McNair, have met and considered a note which the latter has been good enough to prepare (Doc. C.43). As the result of their discussions, the members Hodgson and de Moor recommend Committee III to

---

[54] *Note by Sir Arnold McNair, supra* note 12, at 1–2.
[55] *Id.* at 4.
[56] *Id.* at 9.
[57] *Rep. of the Sub-Comm. Appointed to Consider Whether the Preparation and Launching of the Present War Should be Considered "War Crimes"*, Doc. C.55, *supra* note 53.

adopt the following conclusion.... ."[58] The final version, as adopted by the Committee, said: "Lieut.-Col. Hodgson, Dr. de Moor and Sir Arnold McNair have met and considered a note which the latter has been good enough to prepare (Doc. C.43). As the result of their discussions, Lieut.-Col. Hodgson and Dr. de Moor recommend Committee III to adopt the following conclusions.... ."[59] Bohuslav Ečer seems to have been excluded, or perhaps he excluded himself, from the interaction with McNair. On September 26, Ečer informed the Commission that he was resigning from Committee III and that he was considering resigning from the Commission itself.[60] Ečer did not, in fact, leave the Commission, continuing to serve well into 1945 in various functions. Reacting to the McNair document and its effective endorsement by Committee III, Ečer prepared a minority or dissenting report.[61]

The majority and minority reports were presented to the Commission in early October.[62] Ečer spoke first, repeating the arguments that he had made in his earlier submissions. He referred to the failed efforts at prosecution following the First World War, explaining that the approach he was proposing would avoid similar difficulties:

> If we accept the fundamental point of view that the preparation and launching of the present total war are crimes because the whole policy which is the background of the present war is a criminal one, we will better understand such crimes as the extermination of foreign races, and we shall be able to put these crimes into the right light. That is, we shall be able to judge them according to their real substance, i.e. not as simple "violations of laws and customs of war" but as instruments of a general criminal policy and as part of a criminal war.[63]

He took issue with McNair's paper, noting that "we must take the consequences" if "we admit that the invasion of The Netherlands in 1940 was not a

[58] U.N. War Crimes Comm'n, *Rep. of the Sub-Comm. Appointed to Consider Whether the Preparation and Launching of the Present War Should be Considered "War Crimes"*, Doc. III/9 (Sep. 15, 1944), *available at* www.legal-tools.org/uploads/tx_ltpdb/File_7055.pdf.
[59] *Rep. of the Sub-Comm. Appointed to Consider Whether the Preparation and Launching of the Present War Should be Considered "War Crimes"*, Doc. C.55, *supra* note 53.
[60] U.N. War Crimes Comm'n, *Minutes of Thirty-Third Meeting held on 26th September, 26th, 1944*, at 1, Doc. M.33, *available at* www.legal-tools.org/uploads/tx_ltpdb/File_711-718_01.pdf.
[61] U.N. War Crimes Comm'n, *Supplement to the Minority rep. presented by Dr. B. Ecer on the question whether the preparation and launching of the present war should be considered as crimes being within the scope of the United Nations War Crimes Commission*, Doc. C.56a (Oct. 6, 1944), *available at* www.legal-tools.org/uploads/tx_ltpdb/File_3287-3302.pdf.
[62] SELLARS, *supra* note 9, at 63–64 (debates are reviewed in detail).
[63] U.N. War Crimes Comm'n, *Minutes of Thirty-Fifth Meeting held on 10th October 1944*, at 4, Doc. M.35, *available at* www.legal-tools.org/uploads/tx_ltpdb/File_738-751_01.pdf.

crime." This would mean, said Ečer, that "the general devastation prepared by the Germans in The Netherlands is in principle a legitimate measure permitted by international law."[64] Any violations that might be punishable would be attributable to military officials, reducing any trial "to the secondary – although important – question of the degree, extent, or intensity of the general devastation: but the devastation in itself would be assumed, according to international law, to have been legitimate."[65] He continued:

> Would that be just? I think not. We cannot allow the Germans to abuse international law. In my opinion we must refuse the Germans the plea of military necessity, because they were not forced to invade the Netherlands. They had no right to attack the country, and consequently they cannot plead a necessity which, in fact, was no necessity on their part, but a situation deliberately created by them. The invasion was a crime; and consequently the invader cannot, according to the general principles of law, acquire any right on the basis of his crime. A burglar trapped in a house cannot set it on fire, and then plead necessity. The supreme court of my country established in a judgment a rule that nobody can plead necessity who voluntarily or intentionally put himself in such a situation.[66]

Ečer concluded by referring to the draft resolution prepared by the London International Assembly in November 1943, noting that it had been approved by the Assembly on August 23, 1944.[67]

When Ečer concluded his presentation, Robert Wright of Australia voiced his agreement with the minority report. He said "the preparation for and launching of the present totalitarian war constituted a war crime and should be treated by the Commission as such."[68] Lord Wright referred to his own legal culture of the common law where importance was placed on "developing principles." In support he also noted the list of "instructed writers on international law" invoked in Ečer's minority opinion, adding that "this corresponds to what the moral sense of humanity demands."[69] Wuncz King of China, Zivkovic of Yugoslavia, Burdekin of New Zealand, and Cyprian of Poland also associated themselves with Ečer's views.[70]

---

[64] *Id.*

[65] *Id.* at 5.

[66] *Id.*

[67] *Id.* at 6.

[68] *Id.* at 7.

[69] *Id.* at 8.

[70] *Id.* at 10–11; U.N. War Crimes Comm'n, *Minutes of Thirty-Sixth Meeting held on 17th October, 1944*, at 3–8, Doc. M.36, *available at* www.legal-tools.org/uploads/tx_ltpdb/File_751-773_01.pdf.

Noting that he was the only member of the subcommittee who was present to argue for the majority report, de Moor insisted that "total war" was not in itself a crime but rather "an accumulation of recognised war crimes." As for aggressive war, although it was "terrible and illegal" he said that "unhappily not until now" has it been recognized as a punishable crime under international law. "It *ought* to be declared a crime," he said, and "it is the duty of the United Nations War Crimes Commission emphatically to draw the attention of the United Nations Governments to this gap."[71] Lieutenant Colonel Cowles of the United States, Gros of France, and Stavropoulos of Greece, supported the majority opinion that the waging of war was not an international crime.[72] It was impossible to reach agreement, despite further remarks by both de Moor and Ečer. The Commission decided to adjourn the matter for six weeks, enough time for them to share the detailed minutes of the debate with their governments and to receive instructions on how to proceed.[73]

Sir Cecil Hurst, who chaired the Commission, reported to the British Foreign Minister, Sir Anthony Eden, that this had become an issue in the Commission because of fears that those responsible for the war would go unpunished.[74] The Foreign Office replied to Hurst expressing its view that aggressive war *per se* was not a war crime. He then circulated a memo to the Commission recommending that no vote be taken on the issue, and his advice was followed. Hurst said he was concerned that the debate could be misinterpreted by public opinion and that opposition to the concept of prosecution for waging aggressive war might be construed as a general rejection of the criminality of the Nazi leaders, which it was not.[75]

The subject returned to the agenda in early December. Zivkovic formally presented the view of the government of Yugoslavia that the Kellogg–Briand Pact provided a sufficient basis to include aggressive war on the list of international crimes.[76] Ečer confirmed that the views in his minority report were those of the government of Czechoslovakia.[77] Burdekin reported that the government of New Zealand had endorsed his remarks in the debate but that

---

[71] *Id.* at 10 (emphasis in the original).

[72] *Id.* at 11–16.

[73] *Id.* at 20.

[74] Kochavi, *supra* note 12, at 99.

[75] U.N. War Crimes Comm'n, *Examination of the question whether the preparation and launching of the present war can be considered a "war crime"*, Doc. C.64 (Nov. 30, 1944); Kochavi, *supra* note 12, at 100; History of the United Nations War Crimes Commission, *supra* note 13, at 184.

[76] U.N. War Crimes Comm'n, *Minutes of Forty-First Meeting held on 6th December, 1944*, at 4–5, Doc. M.41, *available at* www.legal-tools.org/uploads/tx_ltpdb/File_821-826__M41__01.pdf.

[77] *Id.* at 5.

it also considered that it was open to the Commission to propose that punishment of the leaders of the Axis could result from "political rather than judicial action."[78] Before adjourning the debate, the Chairman suggested that the Commission "seemed likely" to reject the majority report.[79]

The Commission never did vote to either adopt or reject the report from Committee III on aggressive war. At the March 14, 1945, meeting of the Commission, Ečer observed that no agreement had been reached on the question.[80] The issue returned somewhat indirectly in May 1945 following the presentation of a report by Committee II destined for the San Francisco Conference. Indeed, this may have been an attempt by some members of the Commission to find some conclusion to the impasse. Committee II's draft report reviewed the debates of the previous year, noting that Committee III had been opposed to including the preparation of aggressive war within the scope of the Commission's work but that it had also recommended that penal sanctions be provided in the future for such acts. The draft report also referenced the minority report submitted by Bohuslav Ečer. Committee II proposed that the following clause be inserted in the Charter of the United Nations:

> Any person in the service of any State who has violated any rule of inter-national law forbidding the threat or use of force, or any rule concerning warfare, especially the obligation to respect the generally recognised prin-ciples of humanity, shall be held individually responsible for these acts, and may be brought to trial and punishment before the civil or military tribunals of any State which may secure custody of his person.[81]

The draft report attempted to summarize the debates within the Commis-sion with respect to the criminal nature of a war of aggression. It suggested that "the existence of opposite views ... may also indicate that the meaning of the Kellogg–Briand Pact, which was the primary ground for both sets of opinions, is not clear in this regard."[82] It continued:

> If the Kellogg–Briand Pact is ambiguous in the mentioned respect and it was intended, as maintained by some members of the Commission, that

---

[78] *Id.*

[79] *Id.* at 6.

[80] U.N. War Crimes Comm'n, *Minutes of the Fifty-Second Meeting held on 14th March, 1945*, at 5, Doc. M.52.

[81] U.N. War Crimes Comm'n, *Draft Recommendation to the Governments Concerning Penal Sanctions for the Threat or Use of Force, Submitted by Comm. II*, at 2, Doc. C.100 (May 2, 1945), *available at* www.legal-tools.org/uploads/tx_ltpdb/File_3494-3498.pdf.

[82] *Id.*

individual criminal responsibility should attach to those who launched an aggressive war, it would seem highly desirable that its meaning be clarified and that its original intent be clearly declared to that effect.[83]

The Commission debated the draft report at its May 2, 1945, meeting. André Gros read into the minutes the position of the government of France:

> I must now state that the French interpretation of the Briand–Kellogg Pact is the following: the fact of having prepared for, and launched the present war constitutes a violation of international law as it was laid down in the Paris Pact, but cannot be treated as a war crime in the state of international law in 1939.[84]

Lord Wright of Australia, who by now was Chairman of the Commission, said he supported the report and "saw no ambiguity in the Briand–Kellogg Pact."[85] Colonel Hodgson of the United States said his personal view was that the Kellogg–Briand Pact did not create any form of individual criminal liability. However, "many distinguished persons in the Commission" took a different view, he acknowledged. He said he was prepared to leave the answer to his government.[86] The report was adopted at the next meeting.[87]

V. THE LONDON CONFERENCE

In October 1944, the United Nations War Crimes Commission had proposed that an international criminal court be established for the purpose of post-war prosecutions.[88] This did not resonate very favorably when transmitted to the British government. Already, the major powers were contemplating the establishment of a "military tribunal" that might be set up quite quickly and in which the smaller countries that had been so active in the debates about criminal prosecution would not participate. In January 1945, a memorandum to President Roosevelt reported that the United Nations War Crimes Commission "has been widely and publicly criticised for the paucity of the results

---

[83] *Id.*

[84] U.N. War Crimes Comm'n, *Minutes of Fifty-Eighth Meeting held on May 2nd, 1945*, at 5, Doc. M.58, *available at* www.legal-tools.org/uploads/tx_ltpdb/File_901-906_01.pdf.

[85] *Id.*

[86] *Id.* at 6.

[87] U.N. War Crimes Comm'n, *Minutes of Fifty-Ninth Meeting held on May 3rd, 1945*, at 2–3, Doc. M.59, *available at* www.legal-tools.org/uploads/tx_ltpdb/File_907-910_01.pdf.

[88] *See* William A. Schabas, *The United Nations War Crimes Commission's Proposal for an International Criminal Court*, 25 CRIM. L.F.171, 174 (2014).

of its work. In recent months its activities have been marked by dissensions."[89] The memorandum proposed that a trial be held on a range of charges including "the waging of an illegal war of aggression with ruthless disregard for international law and the rules of war."[90]

Well into 1945, the British had still not abandoned the idea of some form of summary execution of the Nazi leaders. In an April 1945 note to the United States, the British highlighted some of the legal difficulties in holding a trial. Noting that any trial ought to include charges concerning "the unprovoked attacks which, since the original declaration of war, [Hitler] has made on various countries," the British said: "These are not war crimes in the ordinary sense, nor is it at all clear that they can properly be described as crimes under international law."[91]

Preliminary discussions took place at the Yalta Conference, but it was at the San Francisco Conference, in May 1945, that France, the United States, the Soviet Union, and the United Kingdom agreed on establishing an international military tribunal. In his June 6, 1945, report to President Truman, the head of the American delegation to the London Conference, Justice Robert Jackson, set out his vision of a war of aggression as an international crime.[92] Jackson's proposal to include aggressive war within the subject-matter jurisdiction of the Tribunal was submitted to the other three powers on June 14, 1945, and then formally presented on June 26 to the London Conference. It was the same day as the San Francisco Conference was outlawing the use of force in the Charter of the United Nations, as Benjamin Ferencz has pointed out.[93] The American proposal included "[l]aunching a war of aggression" among the crimes that would be punishable.[94] A United Kingdom submission issued a few days later concurred on this point.[95] Soviet enthusiasm for the

---

[89] Robert H. Jackson, *Memorandum to President Roosevelt from the Secretaries of State and War and the Attorney General, January 22, 1945, in* U.S. DEP'T OF STATE PUB. NO. 3080, REPORT OF ROBERT H. JACKSON, UNITED STATES REPRESENTATIVE TO THE INTERNATIONAL CONFERENCE ON MILITARY TRIALS 3, 4 (1949) *available at* www.loc.gov/rr/frd/Military_Law/pdf/jackson-rpt-military-trials.pdf [hereinafter REPORT OF ROBERT H. JACKSON].

[90] *Id.* at 6.

[91] *Aide-Mémoire from the United Kingdom, April 23, 1945, in* REPORT OF ROBERT H. JACKSON, *supra* note 89, at 18, 19.

[92] Robert H. Jackson, *Report to the President by Mr. Justice Jackson, June 6, 1945, in* REPORT OF ROBERT H. JACKSON, *supra* note 89, at 42, 42–54.

[93] Benjamin B. Ferencz, *Defining Aggression: Where It Stands and Where It's Going,* 66 AM. J. INT'L L. 491, 492 (1972).

[94] *Revision of American Draft of Proposed Agreement, June 14, 1945, in* REPORT OF ROBERT H. JACKSON, *supra* note 89, at 55, 55–60.

[95] *Amendments Proposed by the United Kingdom, June 28, 1945, in* REPORT OF ROBERT H. JACKSON, *supra* note 89, at 86, 87.

prosecution of aggression had never really been in doubt, the international law arguments in support having been developed by its leading specialist, Professor A. N. Trainin.

The issue was discussed at length on July 19. The French delegate, André Gros, questioned whether the four-power conference could legitimately make new law on the subject, and he expressed the view that France did not consider the waging of aggressive war to be a crime that incurred individual liability.[96] Gros had made similar statements in the United Nations War Crimes Commission.[97] The delegates considered whether or not aggression should be defined, but leaned towards referring only to applicable international agreements that might have been violated by Germany. Accordingly, the British delegation submitted a proposal that listed the following crime: "Domination over other nations or aggression against them in the manner condemned or foresworn in (*inter alia*) the following Pacts or Declarations. . . ."[98]

By July 31 the United States had reformulated the provision as "The Crime of War."[99] It included a specific reference to the Kellogg–Briand Pact. At the August 2 session,[100] Britain pointed out that the Soviet specialist, Professor Trainin, had treated aggression not as a "crime of war" but a "crime against peace," and agreement was quickly reached on this minor change in terminology. In the final version, adopted August 8, "crime" became "crimes," presumably for the sake of parallelism with "crimes against humanity," and the specific mention of the Kellogg–Briand Pact was removed in favor of a general reference to "international treaties, agreements or assurances."

VI. CONCLUSIONS

B. V. A. Röling, the Dutch judge at the Tokyo trial, stated in an interview with Professor Antonio Cassese that "in my view aggressive war was not a crime under international law at the beginning of the war."[101] In its final judgment, the Nuremberg Tribunal essentially conceded the fact that punishing crimes

---

[96] *Minutes of Conference Session, July 19, 1945, in* REPORT OF ROBERT H. JACKSON, *supra* note 89, at 295, 297.

[97] *Minutes of Fifty-Eighth Meeting held on May 2nd, 1945, supra* note 84, at 5.

[98] Robert H. Jackson, *Proposed Revision of Definition of "Crimes" (Article 6), Submitted by British Delegation, July 20, 1945, in* REPORT OF ROBERT H. JACKSON, *supra* note 89, at 312.

[99] Robert H. Jackson, *Revision of Definition of "Crimes," Submitted by American Delegation, July 31, 1945, in* REPORT OF ROBERT H. JACKSON, *supra* note 89, at 395.

[100] Robert H. Jackson, *Minutes of Conference Session, August 2, 1945, in* REPORT OF ROBERT H. JACKSON, *supra* note 89, at 399, 416–17.

[101] B.V.A. RÖLING & ANTONIO CASSESE, THE TOKYO TRIAL AND BEYOND 98 (1993).

against peace amounted to retroactive prosecution. It appeared to view prosecution for aggressive war as a legitimate exception to the general rule:

> To assert that it is unjust to punish those who in defiance of treaties and
> assurances have attacked neighboring states without warning is obviously
> untrue, for in such circumstances the attacker must know that he is doing
> wrong, and so far from it being unjust to punish him, it would be unjust if his
> wrong were allowed to go unpunished.[102]

At the time, *nullum crimen* does not seem to have had the sacred, non-
derogable status that it would later take on.[103]

But when the judges at Nuremberg and at Tokyo came to punish persons
who had been convicted of the "supreme crime," they hesitated.[104] Nobody
found guilty of crimes against peace and not of the other two categories,
war crimes and crimes against humanity, was sentenced to death. For example,
Rudolph Hess was convicted of crimes against peace and acquitted of war
crimes and crimes against humanity. He received a sentence of life imprisonment and eventually died in detention in 1987. On the other hand, Julius
Streicher was convicted of crimes against humanity and acquitted of crimes
against peace. He was sentenced to death and was executed within weeks of the
final judgment. In other words, when the judges came to impose the "supreme
penalty," aggressive war no longer appeared to be the "supreme crime."

The conclusion that the "supreme international crime" formulation of the
judges at Nuremberg may have been a bit of judicial hyperbole is not in any
way intended to trivialize the importance of punishment of aggression. But it
is certainly striking to observe that the uncertainty about the role of aggression
within the overall system of international criminal law is not only characteristic of the debate that immediately preceded Nuremberg, but it is also manifested in the approach to the issue in the decades that were to follow the
landmark trial. The difficulty faced by the United Nations War Crimes
Commission in taking a position on whether or not aggressive war should
be a crime[105] seems remarkably like the indecision at the Rome Conference,

---

[102] IMT JUDGMENT, *supra* note 1, at 219.

[103] *See, e.g.*, International Covenant on Civil and Political Rights, art. 4(2), Dec. 16, 1966, 999
U.N.T.S. 171 (entered into force Mar. 23, 1976).

[104] *See* RÖLING & CASSESE, *supra* note 101, at 67, 99.

[105] Eventually, the United Nations War Crimes Commission did take a position on the subject,
but only after the London Conference. A resolution adopted on January 30, 1946, declared that
"crimes against peace and against humanity, as referred to in the Four Power Agreement of
August 8th, 1945, (i.e., the Nuremberg Charter), were war crimes within the jurisdiction of the
Commission." HISTORY OF THE UNITED NATIONS WAR CRIMES COMMISSION, *supra* note 13,
at 187.

more than half a century later. After haunting the corridors of the FAO building for weeks, aggression was finally slipped into the final package submitted by the Bureau to the Committee of the Whole of the Diplomatic Conference on July 17, 1998, but only barely, in Article 5. A dozen years later, the Kampala Review Conference adopted detailed provisions for the Rome Statute that entered into force in 2013. These became fully operational when the ability to exercise jurisdiction over the crime of aggression was activated by the Assembly of States Parties on 14 December 2017,[106] pursuant to articles 15*bis* (3) and 15*ter* (3). The general rule of territorial jurisdiction does not apply. Moreover, according to the prevailing interpretation, the Court can only proceed with respect to aggression attributable to the nationals of States Parties that have also ratified the amendments on the crime of aggression. Thus, the work that began in Paris and that continued in London, then Nuremberg, and later in Rome and Kampala, remains unfinished and incomplete.

---

[106] Res. ICC-ASP/16/Res.5, Activation of the jurisdiction of the Court over the crime of aggression (Dec. 14, 2017).

3

The Tokyo International Military Tribunal and Crimes Against Peace (Aggression)

Is There Anything to Learn?

ROBERT CRYER

I. INTRODUCTION

The Nuremberg International Military Tribunal (also known as the Nuremberg IMT or Nuremberg Tribunal) judgment is known for many things. Naturally, the most famous, and foundational, pronouncement of that Tribunal being that "crimes against international law are committed by men, not abstract entities, and only by punishing individuals who commit such crimes can the provisions of international law be enforced ... individuals have international duties which transcend the national obligations of obedience imposed by the individual state."[1] A silver medal may, however, be given to its statement that, in relation to crimes against peace,

> War is essentially an evil thing. Its consequences are not confined to the belligerent States alone, but affect the whole world.

> To initiate a war of aggression, therefore, is not only an international crime; it is the supreme international crime differing only from other war crimes in that it contains within itself the accumulated evil of the whole.[2]

This finding of the Nuremberg IMT, as we will see, is something that is often misunderstood. The Tokyo Tribunal's views on point are often, in contrast to its European counterpart, largely ignored.[3] It is the intention of this

---

[1] 1 TRIAL OF MAJOR WAR CRIMINALS BEFORE THE INTERNATIONAL MILITARY TRIBUNAL, NUREMBERG, 14 NOVEMBER – 1 OCTOBER 1946, Judgment, at 223 (1947), *available at* www.loc.gov/rr/frd/Military_Law/pdf/NT_Vol-I.pdf [hereinafter IMT JUDGMENT].

[2] *Id.* at 186.

[3] For a notable counterexample *see* KIRSTEN SELLARS, CRIMES AGAINST PEACE AND INTERNATIONAL LAW (2013), which concentrates heavily on the Tokyo IMT in this regard. *See also* Kirsten Sellars, *The Legacy of the Tokyo Dissents on "Crimes Against Peace," in* 1 THE CRIME OF AGGRESSION: A COMMENTARY 113 (Claus Kreβ and Stefan Barriga eds., 2017) [hereinafter THE CRIME OF AGGRESSION: A COMMENTARY].

Chapter to attempt to remedy this lack of focus on the Tokyo Tribunal, much of which has contemporary relevance, ironically, perhaps more than its sibling at Nuremberg on this, as at Nuremberg, the issues were reasonably clear.[4]

This Chapter will proceed as follows: it will explain the background and legal nature of the Tribunal and its relationship to the Nuremberg IMT, then address the way in which the judgment(s) dealt with crimes against peace as well as some of the judges' extra-curial writings. It finishes with an evaluation of the legacy of the Tokyo Tribunal with respect to the crime of aggression, and the influence that it has had on the debate in the post-War era, and that which it ought to.[5]

II. THE BACKGROUND OF THE TOKYO IMT

The image of the Nuremberg IMT, in the modern era, is that it was designed to prosecute the authors and implementers of the Holocaust. This view is somewhat anachronistic. Many of those most responsible for the vast criminality that was involved in that genocide were prosecuted, rightly convicted,[6] and received heavy sentences, up to and including (under the norms of the time) the death penalty.[7] However, at the time, the Nuremberg Trial, and its judgment, was largely focused on the charges of aggression.[8]

The Tokyo Trial was even more focused on the crime of aggression, not least as it was, when compared to the Nuremberg IMT, which was a multi-national cooperative exercise, far more dominated by the United States, who

---

[4] Although, *see* William Schabas, *Nuremberg and Aggressive War*, in this volume.

[5] It would be vastly remiss of me not to make clear that my thinking here has been heavily influenced by my friend and co-author Neil Boister, *see, e.g.*, NEIL BOISTER & ROBERT CRYER, THE TOKYO INTERNATIONAL MILITARY TRIBUNAL: A REAPPRAISAL (2008); [hereinafter BOISTER & CRYER]. Professor Boister and I have also edited a collection of documents relating to the Trial. DOCUMENTS ON THE TOKYO INTERNATIONAL MILITARY TRIBUNAL (Neil Boister & Robert Cryer eds., 2008) [hereinafter Boister & Cryer, DOCUMENTS]. This reprints the relevant documents with original pagination as annotations, where the judgments are cited in this chapter, the original pagination is provided.

[6] Even the unapologetic Nazi *Krönjurist*, Carl Schmitt, accepted that the crimes against humanity charges, the rubric under which those responsible for the Holocaust were convicted, were lawful. *See, e.g.*, Claus Kreβ, *Versailles—Nuremberg—The Hague: Germany and International Criminal Law*, 40 INT'L LAW. 15, 22 (2006). For Schmitt's unpleasant and unconvincing attempt to explain his role under the Nazi regime, *see* CARL SCHMITT, EX CAPTIVITATE SALUS (Andreas Kalyvas & Federico Finchelstein eds., 2017).

[7] IMT JUDGMENT, *supra* note 1, at 365–67. On the deliberations on point see TELFORD TAYLOR, THE ANATOMY OF THE NUREMBERG TRIALS (1992).

[8] *See, e.g.*, DAVID LUBAN, LEGAL MODERNISM ch. 8 (1997).

initially conceived of the Trial as being one, in essence, for the prosecution of
those responsible for the attack on the United States at Pearl Harbor. [9] It was
only after the realization that the other Allies would not be amenable to a
Tribunal that was solely focused on that attack that the ambit of the proposed
(at the time) Tribunal was expanded. As the Dutch Judge (Justice Röling) at
the Tokyo IMT wrote some years later,

> One wish did exist in American military and political circles, and that was to
> revenge the attack on Pearl Harbor, the surprise attack which had crippled
> the American Pacific Fleet, taking 4000 American lives. For the United
> States, Pearl Harbor was the symbol of Japanese guile, if not of Japanese
> criminality. For this attack without declaration of war the responsible leaders
> should be punished exemplarily. That was the opinion of General Douglas
> MacArthur, as he told me personally.[10]

Such a limitation would have undermined the ideals of the inspirational
opening speech given by Justice Robert Jackson at the opening of the Nuremberg trial, a piece of rhetoric that could serve as an ideal of international
criminal justice more gernerally:

> We must never forget that the record on which we judge these defendants
> today is the record on which history will judge us tomorrow. To pass these
> defendants a poisoned chalice is to put it to our own lips as well. We must
> summon such detachment and intellectual integrity to our task that this Trial
> will commend itself to posterity as fulfilling humanity's aspirations to do
> justice.[11]

As a result, charges of aggression against other States (many of whom were
the colonial authorities of the relevant territories, such as the United Kingdom
in Burma and India, the Netherlands in what is now Indonesia, and the
United States in the Philippines) were also added, as well as charges of murder
(on which see later) and war crimes.[12] The political nature of the charges of
aggression is one that plagues debates on this crime to this day,[13] as does the

---

[9]   See generally BOISTER & CRYER, *supra* note 5, chs. 1–2.
[10] Bert V.A. Röling, *The Nuremberg and Tokyo Trials in Retrospect, in* 1 A TREATISE ON
      INTERNATIONAL CRIMINAL LAW 590, 597 (M. Cherif Bassiouni & Ved Nanda eds., 1973).
[11] 2 TRIAL OF THE MAJOR WAR CRIMINALS BEFORE THE INTERNATIONAL MILITARY TRIBUNAL:
      PROCEEDINGS, 14 NOVEMBER 1945 – 30 NOVEMBER 1945, Second Day, Wednesday,
      21 November 1945, at 100 (1947), *available at* www.loc.gov/rr/frd/Military_Law/pdf/NT_
      Vol-II.pdf.
[12] See generally Indictment, *reprinted in* Boister & Cryer, DOCUMENTS, *supra* note 5, at 16.
[13] Martti Koskenniemi, "A Trap for the Innocent ... ," *in* 2 THE CRIME OF AGGRESSION:
      A COMMENTARY, *supra* note 3, at 1359.

matter of the relationship between the crime itself and the modes of liability, a matter to which we will return.

A. *The Tokyo IMT Statute*

The Tokyo IMT was created in January 1946 by virtue of an executive order of General Douglas MacArthur, acting as the Supreme Commander of the Allied Powers and (while perhaps not personally, but by virtue of his role) the occupying authority in Japan. Pursuant to the Japanese instrument of Surrender, the Tokyo IMT was set up to implement Principle 10 of the Potsdam Declaration, which promised "stern justice" for "war criminals." The ambit of this term, and the legal nature of the Tribunal was a matter of some contention,[14] although it was probably lawfully established as an international Tribunal.[15]

Owing to the objectives of the Tokyo IMT, which, in spite of its expanded focus on crimes against peace committed against States other than the United States, and other crimes, was to be concentrated on aggression, the jurisdiction of the Court was limited to what were called "Class A" war criminals. They were to be prosecuted for crimes against peace, with the other charges being, to some extent, parasitic upon those charges. The centrality of crimes against peace, and indeed, the limitation of the jurisdiction of the Tokyo IMT to such defendants was inherent to the Tokyo IMT's Statute, Article 5 of which provided:

> *Jurisdiction Over Persons and Offenses.* The Tribunal shall have the power to try and punish Far Eastern war criminals who as individuals or as members of organizations are charged with offenses which include Crimes against Peace.[16]

Hence it was structured into the Tokyo IMT's mandate that it was only to prosecute those who were, in addition to any other offenses, indicted for crimes against peace. Others (known as Class "B" or "C" criminals) were prosecuted in various domestic tribunals, which, when compared to those in the European sphere, are relatively understudied, at least in the English-speaking world.[17]

---

[14] For further detail, *see* BOISTER & CRYER, *supra* note 5, ch. 2.

[15] *Id.*

[16] Charter of the International Military Tribunal for the Far East, Jan. 19, 1946, *amended* Apr. 26, 1946, T.I.A.S. No. 1589 [hereinafter Tokyo Charter]. The cultural backdrop of the terminology is hard to pass by, *see generally* EDWARD SAID, ORIENTALISM (1978).

[17] There has been considerable recent work on point though. *See, e.g.*, TRIALS FOR INTERNATIONAL CRIMES IN ASIA chs. 1–6 (Kirsten Sellars ed., 2016); HONG KONG'S WAR

Article 5(a) of the Tokyo IMT's Charter granted the Tribunal jurisdiction over aggression, in a provision clearly modelled on Article 6(a) of the Nuremberg IMT's Statute. It provided for the competence of the Tribunal over

> Crimes against Peace: Namely, the planning, preparation, initiation or waging of a declared or undeclared war of aggression, or a war in violation of international law, treaties, agreements or assurances, or participation in a common plan or conspiracy for the accomplishment of any of the foregoing;[18]

The final clause of Article 5(a) is important, as we will see, owing to the fact that the charges of aggression were closely linked to the prosecution's theory of there being an overarching, long-term "wheel" conspiracy to take over Asia, and perhaps the world.

A lesser discussed aspect is Article 5(c), which allowed the Tribunal, by the time of the indictment, to assume jurisdiction over

> Crimes against Humanity: Namely, murder, extermination, enslavement, deportation, and other inhumane acts committed *against any civilian population*, before or during the war, or persecutions on political or racial grounds in execution of or in connection with any crime within the jurisdiction of the Tribunal, whether or not in violation of the domestic law of the country where perpetrated. Leaders, organizers, instigators and accomplices participating in the formulation or execution of a common plan or conspiracy to commit any of the foregoing crimes are responsible for all acts performed by any person in execution of such plan.[19]

The story behind this provision is complex, and relates to a specific theory developed by the prosecution. This was, in short, that all killings (including of combatants) that occurred in an unlawful (i.e., aggressive) armed conflict were not covered by belligerent privilege, and were thus, simply, murder.[20] In the first iteration of the Tokyo IMT's Statute, the words in italics were included, but, at the request of the prosecution, three days prior to the submission of the indictment, they were removed, so that the prosecution could attempt to charge the defendants with the equivalent of the domestic offense of murder through this means.

CRIMES TRIALS (Suzannah Linton ed., 2013); AUSTRALIA'S WAR CRIMES TRIALS 1945–51 (Georgina Fitzpatrick, Tim McCormack & Narrelle Morris eds., 2016).

[18]   Tokyo Charter, *supra* note 16, art. 5(a).

[19]   *Id.*, art. 5(c) (emphasis added).

[20]   *See* JOSEPH B. KEENAN & BRENDAN F. BROWN, CRIMES AGAINST INTERNATIONAL LAW ch. VII (1950). For comment and critique, *see* BOISTER & CRYER, *supra* note 5, ch. 6.

B. *The Indictment*

Unlike the indictment that was submitted to the Nuremberg IMT, which was relatively brief and limited to four counts (i.e., the overall conspiracy, crimes against peace, crimes against humanity, and war crimes),[21] the indictment submitted to the Tokyo IMT was a huge and over-complicated document. It was controversial owing both to what it included, and who it did not.[22] The first thirty-six counts related to crimes against peace and various conspiracies to commit such offenses against various States and also to take over Asia.[23] Counts thirty-seven to fifty-two were the murder charges mentioned above. War crimes were only covered by the final three counts (fifty-three to fifty-five). The suggestion of an overall conspiracy that included all of the defendants, even though they in many instances did not know much of one another, was controversial, even among the prosecutors in Tokyo.[24]

At least as controversial was the choice of defendants,[25] especially the IMT's failure to indict the Shōwa Emperor (Hirohito) for his role in initiating the various conflicts. This omission was likely due to considerations of *realpolitik*, in particular the role that he was expected to (and did) play in the occupation and reconstruction of Japan.[26] As Yoriko Otomo phrases it, "[t]he dominant school of thought proposes that the Supreme Commander General Douglas MacArthur 'saved' Hirohito to preserve public order within newly occupied Japan."[27] There is good evidence for this. As will be seen, this raised comment both politically and judicially. The specific role that Hirohito played, or could have played, in preventing and/or ending the war(s) is one that remains controversial.[28] There is, however, little doubt that the decision to insulate him from prosecution (and keep discussion of his role out of the Trial itself

---

[21] 1 TRIAL OF THE MAJOR WAR CRIMINALS BEFORE THE INTERNATIONAL MILITARY TRIBUNAL, 1 OCTOBER 1945, Indictment, at 27 (1947), *available at* www.loc.gov/rr/frd/Military_Law/pdf/ NT_Vol-I.pdf.

[22] For a reprint, *see* Boister & Cryer, DOCUMENTS, *supra* note 5; for comment *see* BOISTER & CRYER, *supra* note 5, ch. 3.

[23] For a summary, *see* BOISTER & CRYER, *supra* note 5, at 70–73.

[24] *Id.* at 206–08.

[25] *See* Awaya Kentarō, *Selecting Defendants at the Tokyo Trial, in* BEYOND VICTOR'S JUSTICE? THE TOKYO WAR CRIMES TRIAL REVISITED 55, 57 (Yuki Tanaka, Tim McCormack & Gerry Simpson eds., 2011) [hereinafter BEYOND VICTOR'S JUSTICE].

[26] *See generally* BOISTER & CRYER, *supra* note 5, at 65–69. In greater, and more theoretical detail, *see* Yoriko Otomo, *The Decision Not to Indict the Emperor, in* BEYOND VICTOR'S JUSTICE, *supra* note 25, at 63.

[27] Otomo, *id.* at 63.

[28] *See, e.g.,* JOHN W. DOWER, EMBRACING DEFEAT: JAPAN IN THE WAKE OF WORLD WAR II (1999).

[with one slip, that both the prosecution and defense arranged to have, to all intents and purposes, retracted]) had little to do with legal considerations, much to the chagrin of some of the prosecuting States, and indeed some of the judges.[29]

III. THE TRIAL

As might be predicted, particularly by contemporary commentators who had taken note of the arguments raised at the Nuremberg IMT,[30] the prosecution and defense argued very different positions with respect to the crimes against peace charges; the prosecution arguing in part on naturalistic, and in part on positivistic grounds, that aggression was criminal under international law by the late 1920s.[31] Unsurprisingly, the defense, on strictly positivistic grounds, countered that this was simply not the case.[32] The details of their arguments have been set out elsewhere,[33] and need not be repeated here. Although they are of historical interest, they are not of such great importance going forward, not least as the Tokyo IMT's majority judgment declared its fidelity to the earlier Nuremberg IMT's opinion on both the preexisting criminal nature of crimes against peace, and the hortatory, rather than binding, nature of the *nullum crimen sine lege* principle.[34]

Naturally, this Chapter will deal with this aspect of the judgments, but, owing to space constraints, it will not trace the arguments of the parties in detail. They are also covered in exhaustive detail in the various opinions that were given, or expressed quietly between the judges in Tokyo that are canvassed below, and the question of whether or not aggression is now a crime under international law is one that is now basically settled,[35] although the precise customary definition is at least arguably not completely codified.[36]

---

[29] BOISTER & CRYER, *supra* note 5, at 67–68.

[30] Of which it seems clear some had. *See, e.g.,* Gordon Ireland, *Uncommon Law in Martial Tokyo,* 4 Y.B. WORLD AFF. 54 (1950).

[31] This is a style of argument I tend to call "presentational positivism." Robert Cryer, *International Criminal Tribunals and the Sources of International Law: Antonio Cassese's Contribution to the Canon,* 10 J. INT'L CRIM. JUST. 1045, 1048 (2012). Although the U.S. Chief Prosecutor was happy enough to be avowedly naturalistic. *See, e.g.,* KEENAN & BROWN, *supra* note 20, at v–vi.

[32] *See, e.g.,* BOISTER & CRYER, *supra* note 5, ch. 10.

[33] *Id.*

[34] Judgment, *reprinted in* Boister & Cryer, DOCUMENTS, *supra* note 5, at 48, §§ 437–39 [hereinafter IMTFE Judgment].

[35] R. v. Jones [2006] UKHL 16, [2007] [12]-[19] (Lord Bingham).

[36] On the controversies on point, *see, inter alia,* Claus Kreβ, *The State Conduct Element, in* THE CRIME OF AGGRESSION: A COMMENTARY, *supra* note 3, at 412.

The discussion in this Chapter will center more on what we can learn from the Tokyo IMT's judicial opinions on aggression, and how they may help us think of the crime today. This Chapter contends that many of the issues that were in question at Tokyo have not gone away.

IV. THE MAJORITY JUDGMENT

The Majority judgment needs to be understood, as perhaps more modern judgments of international criminal tribunals, against its background, in particular, the fact that the judgment postdated the Nuremberg IMT's decision. It also, and very importantly (albeit something only noted in the interstices of the Tokyo IMT's judicial deliberations), postdated the U.N. General Assembly's Resolution affirmation of the principles that were recognized in the Nuremberg IMT's Charter, as well as "similar" principles adopted in the Tokyo IMT's Statute.[37] Hence, by 1948, the time of the Tokyo Judgment, the consensus of U.N. members was that the Nuremberg Charter and Judgment were an accurate reflection of international law both then and before.[38]

Whether this was an accurate assessment of the status of the relevant international law in the late 1920s (in other words at the time of the Kellogg–Briand Pact) may be open to question.[39] The agreement between U.N. member States (who were not necessarily representative of the majority of people on the planet) was that the Nuremberg IMT's Statute, and the judgment that came from that body, was reflective of the relevant (intertemporal) international law (i.e., that the law was as stated by the drafters and judges at the time of the conduct of the defendants). There is evidence that, both practically and whether or not it was given in to politically, this was raised before the judges at Tokyo.[40]

The Majority at Tokyo took a diffident approach to the law that it had to apply, and essentially ratified the findings of the Nuremberg IMT, saying in a comment in their judgment that

> After this Tribunal had in May 1946 dismissed the defence motions and upheld the validity of its Charter and its Jurisdiction thereunder, stating that

---

[37] G.A. Res. 95 (I), Affirmation of the Principles of International Law Recognized by the Charter of the Nürnberg Tribunal, U.N. Doc. A/RES/95(I) (Dec. 11, 1946) (adopted by consensus).

[38] For a characteristically insightful note *see* Antonio Cassese, Introductory Note, *Affirmation of the Principles of International Law recognised by the Charter of the Nürnberg Tribunal*, UNITED NATIONS (2009), *available at* http://legal.un.org/avl/pdf/ha/ga_95-I/ga_95-I_e.pdf.

[39] Carrie McDougall, *The Crimes Against Peace Precedent*, *in* THE CRIME OF AGGRESSION: A COMMENTARY, *supra* note 3, at 49.

[40] SELLARS, *supra* note 3, at 181–82, 241.

the reasons for this decision would be given later, the International Military Tribunal sitting at Nuremberg delivered its verdicts on the first of October 1946. That Tribunal expressed inter alia the following opinions: "The Charter is not an arbitrary exercise of Power on the part of the victorious nations but is the expression of international law existing at the time of its creation." The question is what was the legal effect of this pact (Pact of Paris August 27, 1928)? The Nations who signed the pact or adhered to it unconditionally condemned recourse to war for the future as an instrument of policy and expressly renounced it. After the signing of the pact any nation resorting to war as an instrument of national policy breaks the pact. In the opinion of the Tribunal, the solemn renunciation of war as an instrument of national policy necessarily involves the proposition that such a war is illegal in international law; and that those who plan and wage such a war, with its inevitable and terrible consequences, are committing a crime in so doing. "The principle of international law which under certain circumstances protects the representative of a state cannot be applied to acts which are condemned as criminal by international law. The authors of these acts cannot shelter themselves behind their official position in order to be freed from punishment in appropriate proceedings." The maxim "nullum crimen sine lege" is not a limitation of sovereignty but is in general a principle of justice. To assert that it is unjust to punish those who in defiance of treaties and assurances have attacked neighboring states without warning is obviously untrue for in such circumstances the attacker must know that he is doing wrong, and so far from it being unjust to punish him, it would be unjust if his wrong were allowed to go unpunished.... With the foregoing opinions of the Nuremberg Tribunal and the reasoning by which they are reached this Tribunal is in complete accord.... In view of the fact that in all material respects the Charters of this Tribunal and the Nuremberg Tribunal are identical, this Tribunal prefers to express its unqualified adherence to the relevant opinions of the Nuremberg Tribunal rather than by reasoning the matters anew in somewhat different language to open the door to controversy by way of conflicting interpretations of the two statements of opinions.[41]

In short, the Majority essentially expressed, in relation to crimes against peace, its complete fidelity to the Nuremberg IMT's views on point (i.e., that developments in the inter-War period culminating in the Kellogg–Briand Pact, and the subsequent resolutions rendered aggression criminal, irrespective of the intentions of the drafters of the Pact of Paris).

Whether they were right to do so is a matter for some doubt, but given the Nuremberg "precedent" and General Assembly Resolution 95(I), the Majority

---

[41] IMTFE Judgment, *supra* note 34, at 377–78.

was probably at least on stronger legal ground than the Nuremberg IMT here. Equally, there is evidence that some of the Allied powers did all they could to ensure, by hook or by crook, that their judges did not do anything that might be seen to undermine the Nuremberg judgment.[42] It is difficult to avoid the feeling that the Majority was renouncing its obligation to establish its own authority and taking the easy way out on this.

When it turned to the facts, the Majority took the view that there was an overarching conspiracy among high-level Japanese officials since the late 1920s. There are serious questions about the extent to which the Majority drew many people and events together, when they may or may not have been directly or indirectly linked. They were often linked together by a theory of a broad conspiracy, which was probably not proved to a criminal standard. This is a point that emphasizes the links between the definitions of crimes and the principles of liability that tend to have a large role in international criminal law. This is particularly the case with regard to the crime of aggression, which has the requirement, in the ICC regime at least, that a person must be in a position to effectively control the policy of the State as to whether to engage in armed conflict.[43] The Majority's interpretation of the facts, though, showed more signs of a conspiracy theory than nuanced understanding of East Asian politics in the early to mid-twentieth century.[44] This is not to say that Japanese policy in that era was altruistic, but the idea that there was a large, long-term conspiracy was probably stretching the evidence a little too far.[45]

---

[42] SELLARS, *supra* note 3.

[43] This is the position adopted in the Kampala Amendments to the Rome Statute. *See* Rome Statute of the International Criminal Court *adopted on* July 17, 1998, 2187 U.N.T.S. 91 (entered into force July 1, 2002) [hereinafter Rome Statute]. Rome Statute as amended (for those who have ratified them) by Amendments on the Crime of Aggression arts. 8*bis* and 25*bis*, *adopted on* June 11, 2010, C.N.651.2010.TREATIES-8 (entered into force May 8, 2013). [hereinafter Rome Statute, as amended].

For critique, *see* Kevin Jon Heller, *Retreat from Nuremberg: The Leadership Requirement in the Crime of Aggression*, 18 EUR. J. INT'L L. 477 (2007), and Mark A. Drumbl, *The Push to Criminalize Aggression: Something Lost Amid the Gains?*, 41 CASE W. RES. J. INT'L L. 291 (2009).

[44] For a balanced view *see* MARIUS B. JANSEN, THE MAKING OF MODERN JAPAN 335–675 (2000).

[45] *Id.* For a more critical view of the approach of the Majority to the facts, *see* RICHARD MINEAR, VICTOR'S JUSTICE: THE TOKYO WAR CRIMES TRIAL Ch. V (1971); for the opposite view, *see* DAVID BERGAMINI, JAPAN'S IMPERIAL CONSPIRACY (1971).

V. THE SEPARATE AND DISSENTING OPINIONS ON CRIMES AGAINST PEACE IN THE TOKYO IMT

The Nuremberg IMT only had a brief and largely forgotten dissent by the Soviet Judge Iona Nikitchenko, who concentrated on the fact that he wanted Rudolf Hess to be sentenced to death for crimes against peace.[46] Indeed, the separate and dissenting opinions on crimes against peace in Tokyo have been a central part of the legal and political debate on the Tokyo Trial. This part of the Chapter explains the heterogeneous legal and factual bases upon which their concurrences, separate opinions, and dissents are premised.

A. *Judge Jaranilla*

Judge Delfin Jaranilla's concurring opinion is one that is difficult to appraise acontextually, owing to the fact that his hostility to the defendants is abundantly clear, not least as he was a victim of the Bataan Death March in the Philippines, charged before the Tokyo IMT. As such, he would have been required to recuse himself in most national courts (and as we now have seen in, for example, the International Criminal Tribunal for the former Yugoslavia [ICTY], in international criminal tribunals).[47] His opinion on the modes of liability rather than the existence of crimes against peace and the facts found, upon which he agreed with the majority, was even broader on the ambit of liability for the defendants.[48] It ought not to be forgotten that a good part of liability for international crimes relates to the modes of liability, as the drafters of the Kampala amendments clearly saw.[49] Jaranilla would have gone further on point.

---

[46] Dissenting Opinion of Judge I. T. Nikitchenko, *available at* http://digitalcommons.law.uga .edu/cgi/viewcontent.cgi?article=1006&context=imt. It is notable that the version of the judgment that is most frequently referenced, that in the *American Journal of International Law*, 41 Am. J. Int'l L. 172 (1947), does not include Nikitchenko's opinion. For a very useful analysis *see* Sellars, *supra* note 3, at 113ff.

[47] For further details *see* Robert Cryer, *Delfin Jaranilla, in* The Oxford Companion to International Criminal Justice 391 (Antonio Cassese et al. eds., 2010) [hereinafter Oxford Companion].

[48] Concurring Opinion by the Honorable Justice Deflin Jaranillla, Member from the Philippines, *reprinted in* Boister & Cryer, Documents, *supra* note 5, at 642, §§ 7–10, §§ 19–23.

[49] Roger Clark, *General Principles of International Criminal Law, in* The Crime of Aggression: A Commentary, *supra* note 3, at 590.

B. *Judge Bernard*

The next opinion for discussion is the dissenting opinion of Judge Henri Bernard, the French Judge. In contradistinction to the Majority, he did not accept that the judges had no independent right to challenge the Charter,[50] and so he engaged in a separate evaluation of the crimes against peace charges in the period covered in the indictment. Bernard was critical of the Majority's reason on the existence of crimes against peace in positive international law at the time dealt with by the Prosecution's submission, but, in part because of his background in natural law,[51] Bernard found that the drafters of the Kellogg–Briand Pact simply thought they were writing down what was obvious to all. As he opined,

> The signatories of the pact were able to outlaw the war as an instrument of national policy without troubling themselves to know to what extent society would be authorized to go towards repression of eventual violations of their agreement. But the fact that these signatories did not wish to, or simply did not consider deciding that war as an instrument of national policy or that aggressive war was a crime does not in the least imply that they believed it was not a crime.... There is no doubt in my mind that such a war is and always has been a crime in the eyes of reason and universal conscience – expressions of natural law upon which an international tribunal can and must base itself to judge the conduct of the accused tendered to it.... There is no doubt either that the individual cannot shelter behind the responsibility of the community the responsibility which he incurred by his own acts. Assuming that there exists a collective responsibility, obviously the latter can only be added to the individual responsibility and cannot eliminate the same. It is because they are inscribed in natural law and not in the constitutive acts of the Tribunal by the writers of the Charter, whose honor it is, however, to have recalled them, that those principles impose themselves upon the respect of the Tribunal.... In the light of these considerations will appear the justification of the rejection of the objections of the Defense based upon the principle "nullum crimen sine lege," upon the principle of the non-retroactivity of laws, or upon the nullity of the dispositions of article of the Charter setting forth the principle of individual responsibility.[52]

[50] Dissenting Judgment of Justice Henri Bernard, Member from France, *reprinted in* Boister & Cryer, DOCUMENTS, *supra* note 5, at 662, §§ 8–10 [hereinafter Bernard Dissent].

[51] *Id.* at 18. For a brief biography *see* Robert Cryer, *Henri Bernard, in* OXFORD COMPANION, *supra* note 47, at 255.

[52] Bernard Dissent, *supra* note 50, §§ 10–11.

Suffice it to say, the philosophical positions adopted by Bernard were more than controversial. Indeed, Thomas Baty, while not an impartial observer, described them as "Hitlerian."[53] While Baty's use of invective is unfortunate, and hyperbolic, Bernard's adoption of a purely objectivist approach to the intention of the drafters, in his words, "simply did not consider" that aggressive war "was a crime" but did not, at the same time, "imply that they believed it was not a crime" is hardly usual in international law, either then or now. That said, Bernard's dissent was stemmed in large part from his frustration with the procedure adopted by the Tribunal, which he thought so flawed with respect to the rights of the defense that it made fact-finding impossible. He explained (in a manner that is not always clear) as follows:

> A verdict reached by a Tribunal after a defective procedure cannot be a valid one. The Majority having expressed their verdict, I will however make known mine also subject to caution and revisable as it is. . . . In spite of the violation of rules the respect of which was essential to the defense of the Accused, and perhaps because of it, I reached the conclusion that the culpability of the Accused regarding the accusation of crimes against peace cannot be regarded as certain.[54]

As discussed below, the difficulty of obtaining evidence in relation to crimes against peace is a matter that will be seen to be a lesson of Tokyo.

C. *President Webb*

The President of the Tribunal, William Webb, was also a natural lawyer, who may have been compromised as well, owing to the fact that he had previously been involved in writing reports on alleged (albeit later proved) Japanese war crimes, particularly in Papua New Guinea. He rendered a separate opinion.[55] Webb's initial views were set out in a memorandum to the other members of the Tribunal, in a huge separate and dissenting opinion, which relied very heavily on natural law, raising the ire of many of his more positivist colleagues.

---

[53] *See* THOMAS BATY, INTERNATIONAL LAW IN TWILIGHT 188 (1954). BOISTER & CRYER, *supra* note 5, at 280–81. On Baty more generally *see* Shinya Murase, *Thomas Baty in Japan: Seeing Through the Twilight*, 73 BRIT. Y.B. INT'L L. 315 (2003).

[54] Bernard Dissent, *supra* note 50, § 21.

[55] On whom, *see generally* Robert Cryer, *W. F. Webb, in* OXFORD COMPANION, *supra* note 47, at 570.

It was based heavily on a memorandum submitted (at his request) from Father Peter Herzog of Sophia University in Tokyo.[56]

Webb's memorandum was heavily criticized. As a result, in a surprising development, he was not, as President, part of the drafting committee for the Majority judgment. Nonetheless, as he began his final opinion, Webb withdrew his opinion to the extent to which he would not disagree with the Majority.[57] Hence the published version of his opinion is a somewhat emaciated version of his earlier views,[58] which largely did not disagree with the Majority opinion, referring to the same resolutions that led up to the Kellogg–Briand Pact. Webb, however, made his natural law sympathies tolerably clear,[59] in a similar manner to Judge Bernard, that the "conclusion is irresistible that the illegality of aggressive war and its criminality were perceived and acknowledged." No evidence is provided, although it is notable that Webb voted against the death penalty for any of the defendants in Tokyo.[60]

D. *Judge Pal*

Probably the most controversial member of the Tokyo IMT was Judge Pal, who upon his arrival in Tokyo announced his intention to dissent from any convictions. [61] Judge Pal challenged both the legality of the charges of crimes against peace on the basis of the *nullum crimen sine lege* principle, and the facts that the Majority found. His dissent is important, and requires considerable time to discuss, both at the level of law and politics.

Pal began with a lengthy explanation of why he believed that the crimes against peace charge could only be justified if it was based on existing

---

[56] Draft Judgment of Sir William Flood Webb, The International Military Tribunal for the Far East, 1946–1948: Reasons for the Judgment of the President and Member from Australia, 14 January 1947, Papers of William Flood Webb, Series 1, Wallet 8, 3DRL/2481, Australian War Memorial.

[57] The Separate Opinion of President of the Tribunal, Sir William Flood Webb (Member From Australia), *reprinted in* Boister & Cryer, Documents, *supra* note 5, at 629, § 1.

[58] *Id.*

[59] *Id.* §§ 9, 11.

[60] *See* Boister & Cryer, *supra* note 5, at 254–55.

[61] Elizabeth Kopelman, *Ideology and International Law: The Dissent of the Indian Justice at the Tokyo War Crimes Trial*, 23 N.Y.U. J. Int'l L. & Pol. 373 (1991); Ashis Nandy, *The Other Within: The Strange Case of Radhabinod Pal's Judgment on Culpability*, 23 New Literary Hist. 45 (1992). *See also* Robert Cryer, *Radhabinod Pal*, in Oxford Companion, *supra* note 47, at 449–50. Given his prejudgment it could legitimately be questioned whether he ought to have been considered an appropriate member of the bench. It is a basic principle of judicial propriety that a judge decides a case on the basis of that which is presented at trial, rather than sit with a predetermnined outcome (whichever it is) in mind.

international law. In his view, the Charter itself could not create offenses, but only give jurisdiction over previously existing offenses. As he opined,

> [T]he criminality or otherwise of the acts alleged must be determined with reference to the rules of international law existing at the date of the commission of the alleged acts. In my opinion, the charter cannot and has not defined any such crime and has not, in any way, limited our authority and jurisdiction to apply the rules of international law as may be found by us to the facts alleged in this case.[62]

In addition, Pal determined that to hold otherwise would simply be an example of victors' justice, insofar as they imposed a new crime without the authority to do so.[63]

Furthermore, Pal looked, in detail, at the criminality of aggression at the relevant period. His decision, while lengthy, and at times abstruse on point, is convincing. Looking to the extant international law at the time, pursuant to the Kellogg–Briand Pact, Pal quite rightly found that while it may have outlawed non-defensive use of force, it did not criminalize it. He concluded:

> In my judgment no category of war became a crime in international life up to the date of commencement of the world war under our consideration. Any distinction between just and unjust war remained only in the theory of the international legal philosophers. The Pact of Paris did not affect the character of war and failed to introduce any criminal responsibility in respect of any category of war in international life. No war became an illegal thing in the eye of international law as a result of this Pact.[64]

This is a conclusion with which the large majority of academic opinion now, if not always then, would concur.[65]

Judge Pal also dealt with the fact that a number of the States that had ratified the Kellogg–Briand Pact had reserved the right to determine themselves what did, or did not, amount to self-defensive force, which meant that the Pact lacked any normative "bite."[66] As he put it,

---

[62] Judgment of the Member from India, The Honourable Mr. Justice Pal, *reprinted* in Boister & Cryer, DOCUMENTS, *supra* note 5, 809, § 26 [hereinafter Pal Dissent]; *see also id.* at 33ff.

[63] *Id.* §§ 41–68.

[64] *Id.* §§ 151–52.

[65] For an overview, *see, e.g.,* McDougall, *The Crimes Against Peace Precedent, supra* note 36, at 21–48; *Contra* Quincy Wright, *The Law of the Nuremberg Trial,* 41 AM. J. INT'L L. 38, 49–51 (1947) (although the case he made has not stood the test of history, nor was it considered canonical at the time, *see, e.g.,* Georg Schwarzenberger, *The Judgment of Nuremberg,* 21 TUL. L. REV. 329 (1947)).

[66] Pal Dissent, *supra* note 62, at 86ff.

My own view is that war in international life remained, as before, outside the province of law, its conduct alone having been brought within the domain of law. The Pact of Paris did not come within the category of law at all and consequently failed to introduce any change in the legal position of a belligerent state or in the jural incidents of belligerency.[67]

This was related to the fact that Pal also was heavily critical of the fact that the Charter of the Tokyo IMT failed to define aggression, hence rendering it open to "interested interpretation," and failing to appreciate that colonialism could also be considered as such.[68] Similar concerns about the definition of aggression have plagued discussions of the crime ever since, even after the adoption of the Kampala Amendments to the Rome Statute.[69]

Perhaps inconsistently, Judge Pal then engaged in a detailed evaluation of the facts of the case, largely agreeing with the defense that Japan had been engaged in a conflict that was both a response to the actions of China, the Netherlands, the United States, and the United Kingdom, and was intended to liberate Asia from European colonialism.[70] In doing so, Pal engaged in what Gerry Simpson has accurately described as a "dissident narrative," one that is rare from the member of a bench of an international criminal tribunal.[71] If the judgment of the Majority can be criticized for adopting a simple narrative drawn from the prosecution, then Pal can be said to be the flip side of this, adopting a similarly binary approach to the question of aggression, related to his own, entirely understandable, view of European colonization of Asia (and elsewhere). His view of the Japanese response to it, though, may be considered to be rather sanguine.

E. *Judge Röling*

One of the most sophisticated judges of the Tokyo IMT was the Dutch jurist B.V.A. Röling, who remained throughout his life a firm, and often lonely, defender of the Tokyo Trials, in particular the principles that it embodied. He asserted these views during the Vietnam War, even though in many places in the

---

[67] *Id.* § 116.

[68] *See, e.g., id.* §§ 136–37.

[69] On which *see* Leena Grover, *Interpreting the Crime of Aggression, in* THE CRIME OF AGGRESSION: A COMMENTARY, *supra* note 3, at 375; *Id.*, Kreβ, *The State Conduct Element, supra* note 36, at 412; and, at a more conceptual level, Koskenniemi, *supra* note 13.

[70] Pal Dissent, *supra* note 62, §§ 349–1014.

[71] Gerry Simpson, *Didactic and Dissident Histories in War Crimes Trials*, 60 ALB. L. REV. 801 (1997); *see generally* GERRY SIMPSON, LAW, WAR AND CRIME: WAR CRIMES TRIALS AND THE REINVENTION OF INTERNATIONAL LAW ch. 5 (2007).

West, such positions were unwelcome.[72] Röling was also uncomfortable with the approach of the Majority to the positive law basis of crimes against peace (although he came under pressure from his home Government to accept it).[73]

Röling did not bow to that pressure, and, like some of the other dissenters, rejected the argument (that was accepted by, for example, Judge Jaranilla and probably the Majority) that the Charter bound them whether they agreed with it or not.[74] Röling, therefore, disagreed with the Majority about the existence of crimes against peace, on the basis that as a matter of positive law, the criminality of crimes against peace was not clearly established at the time as a matter of positive law.[75] Nonetheless, Röling found an alternative basis for putting people in prison for conduct that amounted to crimes against peace, albeit on an idiosyncratic basis. This was that the victors in a *bellum justum* (i.e., just war) had the right, as occupiers, to incarcerate those who were a possible threat to the security of the occupier, and therefore what was being done there was an implementation of that right.[76] Röling supported this by reference to the sentencing practice of the judges of the Nuremberg IMT,[77] who other than Nikitchenko,[78] would not have sentenced anyone to death on crimes against peace charges alone. Perhaps the difficulty is that, in spite of his positivist framing, Röling was, in the end a naturalist, and could not explain why any incarceration other than for security reasons, in a manner accepted by law, would not simply be a violation of human rights and/or humanitarian law.[79]

On the other major issues, that of factual findings, Röling took a careful line. In his view, while the Majority opinion was unnuanced as to the facts, so were the positions of some of the other judges. As such, he rejected the idea that there had been an overarching conspiracy among the defendants going back at least to the Mukden incident in 1931 but agreed that such a conspiracy did exist later on, involving some, although not all, of the accused.[80] In part, he based this on his realization that some of the relevant documents relied upon by the Majority (and the prosecution) had probably been mistranslated.[81]

---

[72] *See* B.V.A. RÖLING & ANTONIO CASSESE, THE TOKYO TRIAL AND BEYOND (1992); Robert Cryer, *Röling in Tokyo: A Dignified Dissenter*, 8 J. INT'L CRIM. JUST. 1109 (2010).

[73] *Id.*

[74] Opinion of The Member from the Netherlands, Bernard Victor Röling, *reprinted in* Boister & Cryer, DOCUMENTS, *supra* note 5, at 679, §§ 1–8 [hereinafter Röling Dissent].

[75] *Id.* §§ 14–53.

[76] *Id.* §§ 46–53.

[77] *See supra* note 46.

[78] Röling does not mention this in his dissent.

[79] Although the positive international law of human rights was, at that time, shall we say, nascent.

[80] Röling Dissent, *supra* note 74, §§ 63–177.

[81] *Id.* §§ 79, 83.

VI. THE LESSONS OF THE TOKYO IMT

The question that now falls for discussion is what the Tokyo IMT teaches modern international criminal law (and lawyers) about the crime of aggression. It is the contention of this Chapter that it has a great deal of contemporary relevance, at the purely legal, practical, and conceptual levels, as well as the interrelationship of these aspects of the crime.[82]

The first, legal, aspect is that of the creation, or recognition, of crimes under international law. The position of the various judges on this point was telling. At Nuremberg, although some equivocation on this point; it can be deduced from the main opinion (and its reliance on its Charter as binding on the judges, but then the engagement, framed as for the avoidance of doubt, with the question of customary law), the judges largely cohered around the lawfulness of the charges.[83] This was the case, they opined, in part because the *nullum crimen sine lege* principle was more a guideline for justice than an absolute principle.[84]

This was not so in Tokyo, where there was vocal dissensus on point. In spite of the Majority's reliance on Nuremberg (and probably the reaction of the General Assembly's essential ratification of it in Resolution 95[I]), this did not convince all of the judges. So Judges Bernard, Webb, Röling, and most notably, Pal, evidenced their disagreement with the idea that the Charter was binding on them, and, independently evaluated the existence, on whichever basis they chose, of the legality of the crimes included in the Tokyo IMT's Charter. A question upon which they differed.

This, in and of itself is interesting, insofar as more recently there have been suggestions that judges at international criminal tribunals are bound to follow these statutes where jurisdiction is present, and need not consider the question of customary law. Upon occasion, there has been some judicial support for this view,[85] but there has been considerable academic critique

---

[82] On the relationship between many of these *see* DAVID KENNEDY, INTERNATIONAL LEGAL STRUCTURES (1987).

[83] *See supra* note 4.

[84] *Id.* In terms of the law, at the time, which predated modern human rights law, they may have been accurate. *See generally* KENNETH S. GALLANT, THE PRINCIPLE OF LEGALITY IN INTERNATIONAL AND COMPARATIVE CRIMINAL LAW (2009).

[85] Prosecutor v. Fofana, Case No. SCSL-2004-14-AR72, Decision on Challenge to Jurisdiction *Materiae*: Nature of the Armed Conflict, ¶¶ 2–25 (May 25, 2004). Prosecutor v. Tadić, Trial Chamber Decision, ¶¶ 49–51 as cited in Prosecutor v. Tadić, Case No. IT-94-1-AR72, Decision on Interlocutory Appeal on Jurisdiction, ¶ 79 (Oct. 2, 1995). *See generally* Robert Cryer, *The Relationship of International Humanitarian Law and War Crimes: International Criminal Tribunals and Their Statutes, in* CONTEMPORARY CHALLENGES TO THE LAWS OF

on point.[86] This is on the basis of, in relation to, in particular non-States Parties to the Rome Statute, the possibility that the Kampala Amendments on aggression may not reflect customary law, and therefore may fall afoul of the (now, if not in the '40s) firmer *nullum crimen* principle.

This reflects the controversy over the issue of the definition of aggression. If the cliché that one person's terrorist is another's freedom fighter, a similar consideration, in the absence of a clear definition of aggression, has plagued the question of the ambit of that crime. One person's aggressor may be another's defender of the State, national security, or humanity, as the sometimes bitter debates about the lawfulness of the conflicts in Kosovo and Iraq showed.[87] Indeed, some of the arguments brought by the defense in Tokyo, that matters of self-defense were non-justiciable as they were a matter of high policy, saw a notable echo in the U.S. position in the *Nicaragua* case.[88] Such arguments are likely to surface again if the ICC takes up a case relating to aggression.

WAR: ESSAYS IN HONOUR OF PROFESSOR PETER ROWE 117 (Caroline Harvey, James Summers & Nigel White eds., 2014).

[86] Marko Milanović, *Aggression and Legality: Custom in Kampala*, 10 J. INT'L CRIM. JUST. 165 (2012); Marko Milanović, *Is the Rome Statute Binding on Individuals? (And Why We Should Care)*, 9 J. INT'L CRIM. JUST. 25 (2011).

[87] For a smattering of the literature *see* IAN BROWNLIE, INTERNATIONAL LAW AND THE USE OF FORCE BY STATES, 185–94 (1963); YORAM DINSTEIN, WAR, AGGRESSION AND SELF-DEFENCE (5th ed. 2011). That there was disagreement on the law on the use of force was not, however, the stated view in 1950 when the Nuremberg principles were discussed in the Sixth Committee of the G.A. (UNGAOR 5th Session, 6th Committee, 231st meeting); *see* Christian Tomuschat, *Crimes against the Peace and Security of Mankind and the Recalcitrant Third State*, 24 ISR. Y.B. HUM. RTS. 41, 53 (1995); M. Cherif Bassiouni & Benjamin Ferencz, *The Crime against Peace, in* 1 INTERNATIONAL CRIMINAL LAW 313 (M. Cherif Bassiouni ed. 2d. 1999). On the controversy relating to Kosovo and Iraq, *see, e.g.,* Bruno Simma, *NATO, the UN and the Use of Force: Legal Aspects*, 10 EUR. J. INT'L. L. 1 (1999); Antonio Cassese, *Ex Iniuria Ius Oritur? Are We Moving Towards International Legitimation of Forcible Humanitarian Countermeasures in the Word Community?*, 10 EUR. J. INT'L. L. 23 (1999); William H. Taft & Todd F. Buchwald, *Preemption, Iraq, and International Law*, 97 AM. J. INT'L L. 557 (2003); Vaughan Lowe, *The Iraq Crisis: What Now?*, 52 INT'L & COMP. L. Q. 859 (2003).

[88] Case Concerning Military and Paramilitary Activities in and Against Nicaragua (Nicar. v U.S.), Counter-Memorial of the United States (Jurisdiction and Admissibility), 1984 I.C.J. Vol. II, ¶¶ 450–519 (17 Aug.). *See* Abram Chayes, *Nicaragua, the United States and the World Court*, 85 COL. L. REV. 1445 (1985). The Contention was unanimously rejected by the Court. Military and Paramilitary Activities in and Against Nicaragua (Nicar. v. U.S.), Judgment on Jurisdiction and Admissibility, 1984 I.C.J. Rep. 392, ¶¶ 96–98 (Nov. 26). *See, e.g.,* Abram Chayes, *Nicaragua, the United States and the World Court*, 85 COL. L. REV. 1445 (1985); Oscar Schachter, *Disputes Involving the Use of Force, in* THE INTERNATIONAL COURT OF JUSTICE AT A CROSSROADS 223 (Lori F. Damrosch ed., 1987); Domingo E. Acevedo, *Disputes Under Consideration by the Security Council of the United Nations in id.* at 242; *contra* Eugene V. Rostow, *Disputes Involving the Use of Force in id.* at 264.

The legal position on point, as a matter of customary law if care is taken by induction from the post-War trials and other practice,[89] was far from the sole basis of the discussions at Rome and after. At Rome, the arguments on whether or not aggression ought to be included turned, to some extent, on the absence of a codified definition.[90] To some extent, these were both principled, and pretextual, as they were at Tokyo.

It could be argued that the naturalist dissenters in Tokyo, Bernard, Webb, to some extent Röling, and, more controversially, Justice Pal, could explain this on the basis that there is/was a clear definition of aggression in the law of nature, but that argument simply begs the question of whether such a law of nature exists. This was not the majority position of States after the post-War trials were over.[91] Also, the suggestion that international crimes are, for the most part, *mala in se*, may not apply so readily to the crime of aggression (even though it might be the case that it ought to be). The law on the use of force is not always clear, and it is possible that an accused may claim that the law on the use of force is sufficiently unclear (and the law of aggression contains a *renvoi* to that law) that there ought not to be a conviction in his case. Such cases are likely to be both self-interested and at best only possibly plausible.[92]

This reflects back on the comments of the 1919 commission about the ability of lawyers to deal with the nature of aggression – it seems that aggression is difficult (albeit not impossible) to reduce to matters of law.[93] The creation of narratives in this area rely on various factors, as the Tokyo IMT showed. The first is the simple fact of evidence. When it comes to proving aggression, it will be immensely rare that such evidence will be readily available. The Nuremberg IMT was in an extraordinary position in that the vast majority of the evidence was available in documentary form. The same was not the case for the Tokyo IMT. As such, the prosecution had to rely on inference, and, in particular, that of a broad idea of conspiracy that relied on induction from activity (which is not necessarily the worst form of proof, but nor is it the best). As we have seen even in domestic inquiries, such as the Chilcot inquiry into

---

[89] For a useful compilation *see Historical Review of Developments Relating to Aggression*, UNITED NATIONS (2003), *available at* http://legal.un.org/cod/books/HistoricalReview-Aggression.pdf.

[90] Andreas Zimmermann, *Article 5(2)*, *in* COMMENTARY ON THE ROME STATUTE OF THE INTERNATIONAL CRIMINAL COURT: OBSERVERS' NOTES, ARTICLE BY ARTICLE 119–25 (Otto Triffterer & Kai Ambos eds., 3d. 2015).

[91] *See* BOISTER & CRYER, *supra* note 5, at 277–99.

[92] Aggression is probably not unique on this point when we are dealing with international crimes.

[93] For a comparable argument, *see* PAYAM AKHAVAN, REDUCING GENOCIDE TO LAW (2012). That said, this is not a counsel of despair, all things that exist are subject to the (perhaps reductionist) structures of law one way or another. Difficulty is not to be confused with impossibility.

the U.K.'s approach to the run-up to the use of force in Iraq, getting the relevant evidence, even in a national jurisdiction, is not simple.[94]

As the Tokyo Trial showed, in the absence of direct evidence, the temptation to revert to inference, rather than direct proof, is always there. In addition to the issue of how much evidence is available, the difference in the interpretation[95] of the evidence, and what may or may not have been destroyed or deliberately withheld, makes an assessment of the situation difficult. This is not to say that inferences cannot be drawn, but it is more to say that they are often made on the basis of open, or subjective, political views, as the opposable views of the Majority and Judge Pal show.

This also relates to the ability of even a fair process to render a full history of what has led to any armed conflict. Judge Bernard, in the Tokyo IMT, raised the point very directly, as mentioned previously.[96] Irrespective of whether he was correct (and he may have been), the link he drew between the fairness of the proceedings and its ability to render an accurate rendering of the facts upon which its judgment is based is one that cannot be ignored.

This is perhaps, but only perhaps, rendered more relevant when the crime of aggression is at issue, as the 1919 Commission identified, and has been dealt with in detail by Gerry Simpson.[97] To deal with international crimes, including aggression, involves constructing a narrative of right and wrong, which may not always be simple, as the distinctions between the opinions of the Majority, Judge Pal, and Judge Röling showed. As such, the Tokyo Trial shows that on the basis of the notionally same evidence, very different ways of approaching that evidence are maybe plausible, and will be read differently by different constituencies.[98] Both sides perhaps reflect Martti Koskenniemi's comment that

> [The classic, "liberal" view] fails to recognise the (tragic) necessity of some war, sometimes – or at least the need to integrate that necessity into the conceptual world where one moves. It is a view where the "good" politics are not a "politics" at all, while everything that one's adversary does is suspect and "political."[99]

---

[94] For the approach of the Committee *see* Sir John Chilcot, *Report of the Iraq Inquiry*, THE IRAQ INQUIRY ¶¶ 39–94 (2016), *available at* www.iraqinquiry.org.uk/the-report/.

[95] Including the translation of that interpretation, and the nuances which may or may not be caught in the translation process.

[96] *See supra* note 56.

[97] *See supra* note 74.

[98] BOISTER & CRYER, *supra* note 5, ch. 11.

[99] Koskenniemi, *supra* note 13, at 1380.

The debate over the various interpretations of history is also heavily influenced by the question of jurisdiction, both territorial and temporal. The context of conflicts is rarely simple, and the extent to which they are more broadly linked can be very difficult to deal with. To take one example, the Majority judgment in the Tokyo IMT determined that its jurisdiction reached back to the Lake Khassan and Nomonohan "incidents" between Japan and the Soviet Union, on the basis that they were related to an overall conspiracy, an issue that was cogently critiqued by Judge Röling on the basis that these were not really linked in any way to the conflict that the Tribunal was set up to adjudicate upon.[100] Those incidents, as correctly identified by Judge Röling, were really separate to the Pacific sphere of World War II. This is an issue that may arise with the International Criminal Court (ICC), in terms of whether a "situation" that arises and is suggested to be subject to the jurisdiction of the Court may be adjudicated upon. This may particularly be the issue when it comes to those who may be found liable under the broader parts of Article 25 (3) of the Rome Statute rather than as direct perpetrators.[101]

VII. CONCLUSION

Leaving aside the appropriately moribund idea of the "murder" charges that the prosecution sought to bring at the Tokyo IMT, the proceedings there are very telling when it comes not only to their time but also to international criminal law more generally – especially when it comes to the writing of contentious histories. The way in which people see such histories is often structured through how court decisions have been made, be they positive or negative.[102] This is perhaps most significant in relation to the crime of aggression, which was bitterly contested, as a matter of law, philosophy, fact finding, and narrative. As the ICC now has, in certain, limited, circumstances,[103] jurisdiction over the crime of aggression, it may be useful to look

---

[100] Röling Dissent, *supra* note 74, §§ 9–10.

[101] For very useful discussion on point, *see* Clark, *supra* note 49.

[102] *See* MADOKA FUTAMURA, WAR CRIMES TRIBUNALS AND TRANSITIONAL JUSTICE: THE TOKYO TRIAL AND THE NUREMBERG LEGACY (2008). For more general reflections on point *see* MARK OSIEL, MASS ATROCITY, COLLECTIVE MEMORY, AND THE LAW (1997); IAN BURUMA, THE WAGES OF GUILT: MEMORIES OF WAR IN GERMANY AND JAPAN (1994); JEFFREY HERF, DIVIDED MEMORY: THE NAZI PAST IN THE TWO GERMANYS (1999).

[103] Rome Statute, *supra* note 43, art. 5; Res. ICC-ASP/16/Res.5, Activation of the jurisdiction of the Court over the crime of aggression (Dec. 14, 2017). The Resolution was adopted by consensus on that date. On the ICC's jurisdiction over agression *see* the Rome Statute, as amended, *supra* note 43, art. 15*bis*, 15*ter* (for the parties to those changes). There are, as of December 2017, 35 parties to these amendments.

back to the Tokyo IMT on these issues, while also looking forward to what the ICC can do. Some of the problems may have gone away, but some sub-structural issues remain and cannot be ignored. The Tokyo IMT raises many of these, and to fail to look to the lessons of the past, both positive and negative, is likely to lead to the repetition of the same mistakes. It may be that this is a cliché of international criminal lawyers,[104] but that does not mean that it does not contain a kernel of truth. The Tokyo IMT has its lessons for us, in particular on aggression. Sometimes to look to the past is to give something of a guide for the future, and what happened in Tokyo can give us lessons, both positive and negative, for what we look to do now, in particular on the thorny issue of what is, and is not, aggressive.

---

[104] The usual citation used is that to an aphorism of GEORGE SANTAYANA, THE LIFE OF REASON: REASON IN COMMON SENSE 284 (1905), although this is unlikely to be the first expression of such a sentiment.

4

The Just War in Ancient Legal Thought

LARRY MAY

I. INTRODUCTION

In the four-thousand-year recorded history of legal thought, one of the most enduring questions has been, when is it just to engage in war? The discussion of whether a State could go to war for reasons other than self-defense is as old as recorded history. The answers to this question have been varied and fascinating and include opportunity, necessity, vengeance (and punishment). Over the centuries, the most commonly recognized just war is a war of national defense, although even in ancient times wars of humanitarian intervention were recognized as just.[1]

There is an especially interesting perspective on the justness of war that we can find in ancient legal texts, especially from Mesopotamia and the ancient Near East, although I will also refer to texts from ancient China and Egypt as well. And despite what many may think, the perspective on war that is found in these ancient legal texts can provide clear guidance today, despite the differences between the time of Hammurabi, around 1750 BCE, and now. In particular, we will find that the dominant perspective of humanitarianism of many ancient rulers manifested itself in a strong concern for achieving peace, and a peace that involved minimizing oppression. And the emphasis on eliminating or minimizing oppression can give us a model for understanding how wars for national defense or for rescuing those who are oppressed can be justified.

Because there were many wars occurring in these very ancient times, one of the puzzles then, as well as now, is how to reconcile humanitarian motivations with the waging of war. The just war of the ancient Near East, I will argue,

---

[1] This Chapter is taken from Chapter 12 of my book manuscript, *Ancient Legal Thought*, currently in draft. *See infra* note 40.

involved war that was aimed at pacification. But the peace that just war aimed at was one that diminished oppression in the target States. And so we have the idea that later emerged in humanitarian intervention wars, although these ancient just wars were inspired by a stronger sense of humanitarianism than is often seen today.[2]

In the first half of this Chapter I will look at some of the most interesting ancient responses to the question, when is war just? Then in the second half of the Chapter I will assess these various responses for normative guidance today. I will draw often on ancient sources in order to show how old the controversy is and how often the answers were different from but relevant to our situation today. My thesis is that from the earliest of times the only relatively sure grounding for a just war is defense of those who are oppressed, either oppressed by aggressors from without or oppressors from within.

II. OPPORTUNITY

The nearly constant wars in the early history of Mesopotamia and the rest of the ancient Near East are often discussed in terms of one or another city-state seeking to gain advantage over others whenever the opportunity presented itself.[3] But there is an alternative explanation for why there were so many wars in ancient times – various city-states tried to gain control over enough territory so that pacification could be accomplished, thereby putting an end to the previously constant threat of invasion.[4]

The pure desire for increased territory, or for the gain in wealth or resources, is condemned from a very early point in legal history. We can turn to Hammurabi whose writings take us back to roughly 1750 BCE. Here is how he describes himself in the Epilogue to his stela that propounds his "code" of law:

> I am Hammurabi, noble king. I have not been careless or negligent toward humankind, granted to my care by the god Enlil, and with whose shepherding the god Marduk charged me. I have sought for them peaceful places, I removed serious difficulties, I spread light over them. With the mighty weapons which the gods Zababa and Ishtar bestowed upon me, with

---

[2] I am not claiming that the model of humanitarianism that I will discuss in these ancient texts was accepted by ancient rulers, or even by most of them. I am instead interested in describing a conceptual framework that one can, perhaps surprisingly, find in ancient texts that speak to us today.

[3] *See* 1 ALEXANDER GILLESPIE, THE CAUSES OF WAR: 3000 BCE TO 1000 CE, pt. II (2013).

[4] *See* Benjamin R. Forester, *Water Under the Straw: Peace in Mesopotamia, in* WAR AND PEACE IN THE ANCIENT WORLD 66, 66–80 (Kurt A. Raaflaub ed., 2007).

the wisdom of the god Ea allotted to me, with the ability which the god Marduk gave me, I annihilated enemies everywhere, I put an end to wars, I enhanced the well being of the land, I made the people of all settlements lie in safe pastures, I did not tolerate anyone intimidating them. The great gods have chosen me, I am indeed the shepherd who brings peace, whose scepter is just.[5]

There is a scholarly debate about whether we should trust Hammurabi's words here,[6] but my point is just that in this very early legal text Hammurabi feels that he should explain that the reason for the many wars he initiated was to pacify a region, between the Tigris and Euphrates Rivers, which had had very little peace during hundreds of years of war up to his time.

There is a similar statement on a stone cylinder erected by Cyrus the Great of Persia, who conquered Babylon more than a thousand years after Hammurabi. In 500 BCE Cyrus says:

I am Cyrus king of the universe, king of the city of Anshan. . . . When I went as a harbinger of peace into Babylon I founded my sovereign residence within the palace amid celebration and rejoicing. Marduk, the great lord bestowed on me my destiny the great magnanimity of one who loves Babylon, and I every day sought him out in awe. My vast troops were marching peaceably in Babylon, and the whole of Sumer and Akkad had nothing to fear. I sought the safety of the city of Babylon and all its sanctuaries. As for the population of Babylon . . . who as if without divine intervention had endured a yoke not decreed for them. I soothed their weariness; I freed them from their bonds.[7]

Here Cyrus claims that his conquest of Babylonia and much of the rest of Asia Minor was aimed at liberating the peoples of this region from tyranny and oppression.

Indeed, the Greek historian Xenophon tells us of this (probably imaginary) speech of Cyrus:

Cyrus: "Now I am going to let you who have been captured go home and consult with the rest of the Chaldaeans whether you wish to have war with us or be our friends. And if you choose war, do not come this way again without weapons, if you are wise; but if you decide that you desire peace, come

---

[5] Hammurabi, *The Laws of Hammurabi* (c. 1750 BCE), *reprinted in* LAW COLLECTIONS FROM MESOPOTAMIA AND ASIA MINOR 71, 133 (Martha T. Ross ed. & trans., 2d ed. 1997).

[6] *See* MARC VAN DE MIEROOP, KING HAMMURABI OF BABYLON: A BIOGRAPHY (2005).

[7] Irving Finkel, *The Cyrus Cylinder: the Babylonian Perspective, in* THE CYRUS CYLINDER: THE KING OF PERSIA'S PROCLAMATION FROM ANCIENT BABYLON 4, 6 (Irving Finkel ed., 2013).

without arms. I shall see to it that you have no cause for complaint, if you become our friends."

And when the Chaldaeans heard this, they commended Cyrus highly, shook hands with him heartily, and departed for home.[8]

Again, there is scholarly support for thinking that Cyrus was not always so gentle and generous to his captives,[9] but what is of interest is how this early legal text, and the commentary by Xenophon writing a generation later, describes Cyrus's conquest: not in terms of opportunity for gain, but in terms of opportunity to defend a population from oppression and to pursue peace.

There are certainly early accounts of war that stress the precious metals and land that is brought into the hands of a conqueror.[10] But in the discussion of conquest, in some of the very earliest legal texts, there is also the expression of the view that the conquest should be conducted for the good of the people, especially for their defense against being the victims of constant war or against oppression by their despotic rulers. We can see in the pronouncements of Hammurabi and Cyrus the incipient and controversial idea of humanitarian intervention that has today nearly replaced national defense as the primary basis of a just war. The opportunity to do good is what is stressed even as it is acknowledged that borders were crossed and military might was used to suppress tyrants.

III. NECESSITY

Recourse to war has often been purportedly justified by various forms of necessity. The main claim of necessity over the centuries has had to do with providing defense against enemy soldiers that are crossing the border, and who have not been provoked to do so. We will talk about this just cause to engage in war again by reference to some legal texts from the ancient Near East. Here is a passage from a treaty between Niqmepa of Alalakh and Ir-Adad/Tesup of Tunip from the fifteenth century BCE:

If someone from my territory enters your territory to survive, you shall certainly keep them (alive) as though they were of your land. (But) you

[8]   Xenophon, Cyropaedia [The Education of Cyrus] bk. III, ch. 2, §§ 13–14 (Walter Miller trans., 1914), *available at* www.perseus.tufts.edu/hopper/text?doc=Perseus%3Atext% 3A1999.01.0204%3Abook%3D3%3Achapter%3D2%3Asection%3D13.
[9]   *See* Matt Waters, Ancient Persia: Concise History of the Achaemenid Empire, 550–330 BCE (2014).
[10]   *See* Gillespie, *supra* note 3.

shall surely not detain them within your territory, and must return them to my territory, you may not confine (even) one family within your land."[11]

There are several issues intertwined here. First, and most relevant for us at the moment, is that the mere crossing of borders is not thought to trigger a justified war. Indeed, those who transgress a State's borders are not to be killed. For other writers such as the Chinese theorist Mozi, this is at least in part because it is not necessary to kill them in order to protect the homeland.[12] There is also another necessity issue here as well, namely that in certain circumstances a State has the obligation to provide for the survival of people from another State.

War was not to be engaged in if it were not necessary for achieving a result that would be considered to be just. The terms for justice in the earliest legal writings encompass both strict legal justice and also the more wide-ranging idea of equity as a distinctly moral concept. It is important to note that achieving equity was often characterized in terms of what the gods expected or demanded of their people. This is a significant difference between ancient times and our own. But there is also often a secular reason as well that is intertwined with the theological.

In the prologue to his laws, Hammurabi speaks of how the god Marduk instructed him to create the stela that lists the laws. This seems to give the law a theological significance. But Hammurabi also speaks of how he has duties as the shepherd of his flock, especially to protect the most vulnerable members of the society. This secular reason is intertwined with the theological in that Hammurabi sees his role of shepherd also as commanded by the gods. But this aspect of Hammurabi's role is as often linked to considerations of humanity as to any specific god's command.

Again, Hammurabi intimates that he only goes to war when it is necessary to achieve a lasting peace after other measures have failed. We can see this when Hammurabi speaks of showing mercy to those who are not true threats even as they have given cause for his wrath to come down on them.[13] The idea seems to be that even though Hammurabi has had reason to strike against his enemies, he has resisted and shown mercy unless these enemies threaten the well-being of his own citizenry. There is no explicit discussion of necessity in these ancient texts, but the sentiment of restraint is so powerful that one can

---

[11] 1 Treaty, Law, and Covenant in the Ancient Near East 311 (Kenneth A. Kitchen & Paul J. N. Lawrence eds. & trans., 2012).

[12] *See* The Mozi: A Complete Translation (Ian Johnson trans., 2010).

[13] *See* Hammurabi, *supra* note 5, at 76–81.

easily infer that war was only considered just if it was necessary to wage it to counter threats to the well-being of the citizenry.

Hugo Grotius, a Dutch jurist writing in 1625 CE, takes a related although differently grounded position. Grotius offers a strong and clear statement of what he thinks necessity requires:

> therefore the Dread ... of our Neighbour's increasing Strength, is not a warrantable Ground for making War upon him. To justify taking up Arms in our own Defense, there ought to be a Necessity for doing so, which there is not, unless we are sure, with a moral Certainty, that he has not only Forces sufficient, but a full Intention to injure us.[14]

For Grotius, reasons such as vengeance may be justifying reasons but only if war is the only way that vengeance can be meted out.[15] Indeed, Grotius argues strongly that past injury is not a just cause to go to war; only the mitigation of truly threatening injury can satisfy the necessity condition.

The difference between Grotius and Hammurabi, who seems to hold similar views about necessity despite living 3,500 years earlier, concerns the rationale behind a fairly strict construal of necessity. Hammurabi is motivated, he tells us, by humanitarian ideals concerning the minimization of oppression. Grotius also says he is motivated by humanitarian concerns but these are linked to mutual restraint of powerful nations rather than a concern for the oppressed and downtrodden.

Contemporary accounts are not as clear concerning the importance of satisfying a necessity condition for a just war as was true in ancient times. There is not as much discussion now as one would have hoped concerning diplomacy and other non-lethal strategies rather than violently confronting enemy soldiers.[16] If we were to think about such matters from the standpoint of a two-person case, we would want to know if retreat or building up defenses could be engaged in instead. And today it is rare to find concern for such humanitarian issues.

IV. VENGEANCE AND PUNISHMENT

Rulers have sometimes claimed that retaliation, revenge, or the right to punish give them justification for recourse to war. Indeed, until quite recently some

---

[14] HUGO GROTIUS, DE JURE BELLI AC PACIS [On the Law of War and Peace] 1102 (Francis Kelsey trans., Oxford Clarendon Press 1925) (1625).

[15] *Id.* at 1097.

[16] *See* LARRY MAY, CONTINGENT PACIFISM: REVISITING JUST WAR THEORY (2015).

just war theorists have said that punishment is a just cause to go to war. The idea is that in international affairs, where there is no sovereign, rulers will think that they are free to engage in aggression unless other rulers express a willingness to punish the aggressors.

Some ancient texts have supported the idea of punishment as a just cause to initiate war. And in some cases it seemed plausible that this should be so. Think of the case of an envoy or emissary who is killed while serving in his official role in a foreign capital. We can find threats of war and actual occasions of war in very ancient times when such officials were killed or harmed. For example, in a letter from the Hittite king to another Anatolian king, dating from around the sixteenth century BCE, the Hittite king threatens to "subdu[e] by force of arms" the Anatolian king if the envoy named Walmu is not returned.[17] In such cases, there was both a threat of punishment if the wrong was not quickly corrected, and there was the threat used as something to fear if the wrongdoer harmed the nation by killing one of its agents.

The idea that those who are guilty can have wars waged against them is ancient in origin, although it is not always as straightforward as it has seemed to some commentators. The argument was often couched in terms of what is the righteous path. Mencius, second only to Confucius among ancient Chinese sages, says the following:

> 7B2 . . . there are no just wars. It does happen that some are better than others. "Punishment" involves superiors attacking inferiors. Opposing armies do not "punish" each other . . .

> 7B4 . . . If the ruler of a state loves humaneness, he will have no enemy in the world. . . . To punish is to correct. With everyone wishing to be corrected, what is the need of fighting?[18]

Later, Mencius argues that killing people is not truly a kind of punishment since they will not be alive to be corrected.

Mencius, who lived in China at roughly 350 BCE during the period where there were many wars occurring, also had this to say:

> 4A14. From this it can be seen that one who enriched a ruler who was not given to the practice of humane government was cast off by Confucius. How much more would this be true in the case of one bent on making war? Wars that arise from territorial contests kill so many people that the fields are

---

[17] See *Letter from a King of Hatti to an Anatolian Ruler,* in HITTITE DIPLOMATIC TEXTS no. 23A, at 145–46 (Gary Beckman & Harry A. Hoffner, Jr. eds., 2d ed. 1999).

[18] MENCIUS 156–57 (Philip J. Ivanhoe ed., Irene Bloom trans., 2009).

packed with corpses; wars that arise from contests over cities kill so many people that cities will be packed with corpses.[19]

Mencius, like some ancient Mesopotamian rulers, thought that considerations of humanity and humanness were crucial moral concepts in assessing war.

In the treaties of the most ancient times, we find threats of war understood in terms of punishment for violation of the treaty. Here we can look to some of the earliest treaties, those between Sumerian and Egyptian rulers. At the end of the treaties (as is also true of certain "codes" of law) there are listed "threats" that will befall those who break the treaty, as well as "benefits" that will occur to those who keep the treaty, as internal mechanisms of compliance that could prove useful to international humanitarian law.

Consider a representative treaty between Eannatum of Lagash and the Ruler of Umma (c. 2500 BCE):

If I do transgress, then may the great casting-net of Enlil, by which I swore an oath be cast down from heaven upon Umma ...

If for any reason, for any cause, a leader of Umma goes back on this agreement against Enlil my King; if he opposes or contests this agreement; if he sets aside this agreement; then may the great casting-net of Enlil be cast down from heaven upon Umma![20]

If for any reason, any cause, an Umma leader breaks this agreement [against Ninki] – if he opposes (or) contests the agreement; if he sets aside this agreement; (then) may Ninki, by whom I have sworn an oath, cause snakes out of the earth to bite Umma's feet![21]

And in the following treaty, punishment in terms of the gods exercising recourse to war is something that is clearly threatened for those who break the treaty:

Anyone who transgresses these words, Adad/Tesup, lord of divination and Shamash, the lord of judgment, the god Sin and the great gods shall destroy his name and his seed ... from the lands, let them bring down his throne and his [scepter].[22]

The parties invoke the gods who will both seek vengeance and administer a kind of divine punishment for the party who breaks the treaty. Of course, it is the parties that will administer the divine punishment. The underlying

[19] *Id.* at 81.
[20] Treaty, Law, and Covenant in the Ancient Near East, *supra* note 11, at 7.
[21] *Id.* at 15.
[22] *Treaty between Niqmepa of Alakh and Ir-Adad/Tesup of Tunip* (c. 15th century BCE), *reprinted in* Treaty, Law, and Covenant in the Ancient Near East, *supra* note 11, at 313.

assumption is then that the aggrieved party may wage war against the treaty-breaking party on behalf of the gods. Yet also in treaties from this period the rationale not to break a treaty comes from a concern for the benefits the treaty promotes, especially insofar as the people of the nations in question are kept safe.

V. NATIONAL DEFENSE AND ANCIENT RULES OF WAR

The history of writing is normally traced back to the first cuneiform clay tablets found in ancient Mesopotamia around 3000 BCE. Legal documents were among the very first of the written texts to be recovered from this period, including bills of sale and rudimentary contracts.[23] A millennium after the invention of writing, sovereign rulers were putting their agreements in writing.

In the middle of the fourteenth century BCE, we have a record of a treaty struck between a Hittite ruler Suppiluliuma I and Aziru of Amurru. This is largely a vassal treaty that Aziru was probably forced to sign. But what is interesting is that Aziru agrees to aid the Hittite ruler in both defensive and offensive wars. And what is important for us is that the treaty to aid each other in offensive wars is couched in defensive terms:

> If the King of Hatti [Hittite kingdom] goes against the land of Hurri, or Egypt, or Babylonia, or the land of Ashtata, or the land of Alshi – whatever foreign lands located near your borders are hostile to My Majesty, or whatever friendly lands – [that is, friendly to My Majesty] – located near your borders – the land of Mukish, the land of Kinza, the land of Nuhashshi – turn and become hostile to the King of Hatti – when the King of Hatti goes to attack this enemy, if you, Aziru, do not mobilize wholeheartedly with infantry and chariotry, and do not fight him wholeheartedly, you will have transgressed the oath.[24]

Here we have an exchange of oaths to come to one another's aid in seemingly offensive wars, but where even offensive war alliances were justified by references to hostile and threatening forces to be combated. This wording was repeated in several other treaties of the Hittites and their close neighbors.[25]

In 1285 BCE, after a major battle, the Pharaoh Ramses II of Egypt and the Hittite King, Hattusili III, completed an agreement that is often cited as one of the first truly "international" treaties for which a record exists. In this

[23] *See* DOMINIQUE CHARPIN, WRITING, LAW, AND KINGSHIP IN OLD BABYLONIAN MESOPOTAMIA (2010).

[24] HITTITE DIPLOMATIC TEXTS, *supra* note 17, treaty 5, at 37–38.

[25] *See id.* treaties 7 and 9.

important document, there is a non-aggression pact that is its centerpiece. Here the alliance is portrayed as purely defensive – aiding in the defense of one another against foreign attacks:

> And if someone else, an enemy, comes against Egypt, and Ramses, Beloved of Amon, King of Egypt, your brother, send to Hattusili, King of Hatti, his brother: "Come to my aid against him," then Hattusili, King of Hatti, shall send his infantry and his chariotry, and they will defeat his enemy.[26]

And in the next section, the treaty also calls for these States to aid each other from internal attacks as well.

Of special importance is the part of this agreement concerning fugitives, which was a common feature of the treaties at this time. And while fugitives, including fugitive slaves, were to be returned, "they shall not punish them for their offenses" or "destroy their households, together with their wives and sons."[27] There is here a clear statement that prisoners are not to be treated inhumanely, and also a separation between those who were warriors and those who were civilians, with a prohibition on destroying the civilians.

In the Middle Hittite Period, we see even a reference to what today would be called the rules concerning the end of war. The treaty among the Elders of Several Anatolian Communities requires that

> after the campaign you shall not violate the wife or daughter of a man, [nor] shall you injure them. After the campaign no one shall steal a man, woman, son, daughter, slave, slave girl, sheep, [horse], mule, ass, silver, gold, bronze, or copper implements.[28]

Here we have a strong statement of *jus post bellum*.

VI. HUMANITARIAN INTERVENTION

If the easy case of a just war is war waged for national defense, then one might think that humanitarian intervention in some cases is at least as easy. For in some cases of humanitarian intervention, war is waged to protect another State when that other State cannot protect itself from external aggression by one of its neighbors. However, the most common case of humanitarian intervention is not of this sort, but rather the case in which a State is oppressing its own people and intervention occurs to protect these people not from invasion but

---

[26] *Id.* treaty 15, at 98.
[27] *Id.* treaty 15, at 99.
[28] *Id.* at 165.

from their own despotic rulers, or from armed groups that attack other less-well-defended groups within the same State.

Ancient legal texts often express strong humanitarian sentiments. As I pointed out at the beginning of this Chapter, two of the best-known rulers of the ancient Near East, Hammurabi and Cyrus, cite protection of the oppressed as the reason for waging war. In addition, in some of the earliest law "codes" of Mesopotamia we see the beginnings of the ideas of human rights and dignity that are so crucial for humanitarianism today. Here is one example from the epilogue of Laws of Lipit-Ishtar (c. 1930 BCE), which is very interesting:

> In accordance with the true word of the god Utu, I made the lands of Sumer and Akkad hold fair judicial procedure. . . . I made right and truth shine forth, and I brought well-being to the lands of Sumer and Akkad. [. . .] all human-kind. When I established justice in the lands of Sumer and Akkad, I erected this stela.[29]

Lipit-Ishtar also says:

> At the time I liberated the sons and daughters of the city of Nippur, the sons and daughters of the city of Ur, the sons and daughters of the city of Isin, the sons and daughters of the lands of Sumer and Akkad, who were subjugated [by the yoke(?)], and I restored order.[30]

The reference here is clearly to waging wars to "liberate" oppressed people in these various city-states, and the justification is couched in terms of concern for humanity, and all of this from nearly 4,000 years ago.

A defense of humanitarian intervention seemingly could be mounted by considering some of what we have already discussed under the headings of opportunity and necessity. The wrongful waging of war for opportunity is for increasing territory or natural resources or access to the sea. These causes for war do not count as just because, among other things, the cost of war, especially its inevitable loss of innocent life, is not outweighed by such causes. But there are less problematic cases of waging war for opportunity, such as waging war to secure peace in a region that had been ravaged by a tyrannical ruler.

The idea of waging war to stop a war or to stop oppression, and thereby restore the peace, also does not seem obviously problematic. Indeed, if

---

[29] MARTHA T. ROTH WITH A CONTRIBUTION BY HARRY A. HOFFNER, JR., LAW COLLECTIONS FROM MESOPOTAMIA AND ASIA MINOR 33–34 (Piotr Michalowski ed., 2d ed. 1997) (bracketed text in the source).
[30] *Id.* at 25.

war can be justly waged at all, it seems that Augustine was right to say it would be most clearly so for the cause of protecting others who are innocent. In Augustine's view, war was generally suspect on grounds of the killing of the innocent. But in some situations, war was necessary in order to save innocent lives. Some wars can be considered just insofar as the war is waged for what today we would call humanitarian reasons.[31]

In addition to the idea of opportunity to save or protect the innocent, we can add the idea that some wars can be justly waged out of necessity, which meant primarily that there was an imminent threat that could not be thwarted by means other than war. In some cases of humanitarian intervention, necessity could be satisfied. The cases will be rare, though, since it is often very difficult to calculate what would be successful as well as when it is clear that there are no other non-lethal means available to achieve the humanitarian goal. In addition, there will be worries about the spending of lives and treasure to rescue people in a distant part of the world whose condition is not such as would allow the State to say that it was necessary to intervene.

The rationale for humanitarian intervention also runs up against the rationale for national defense. If a State's borders provide a normative reason to allow self-determination wide latitude, then such considerations will also at least partially weigh against crossing a State's borders to wage a humanitarian war. And the normal reasons to warrant such invasions – to stop an impending threat against one's own State, for instance – are not typically available in such cases.

It might seem that humanitarian intervention wars are still wars and hence do not appear to be very humane, belying the name for this kind of war. There is something odd about mounting the enormous lethal potential of armies in order to engage in humanitarian action. Defenders of humanitarian intervention will again have to contend with the death of the rescuing soldiers and of those meant to be saved that inevitably results from humanitarian intervention. Humanitarian wars have outcomes that are difficult to predict since these wars are often waged when there are no clear military targets. But the rescuing of those who are oppressed was seen as so important in ancient legal thought that only the positive aspects of such interventions were seen to be of overriding importance.

---

[31] *See* AUGUSTINE, CITY OF GOD bk. 19, § 6 (426), *reprinted in* LARRY MAY, ERIC ROVIE & STEVE VINER, THE MORALITY OF WAR: CLASSICAL AND CONTEMPORARY READINGS 16 (2006).

VII. RECONSIDERING NATIONAL DEFENSE AND HUMANITARIAN INTERVENTION

It is often said that in all cases defense of nation is a just cause to go to war. Today it is common for such a defense to be mounted in terms of self-determination of a people.[32] A conquering army deprives the people of the attacked State of their choice to remain unconquered. But of course the right of self-determination is not an absolute value – and things can be especially difficult when there is dispute within a State about what the people want. Various communitarians have tried to argue that what matters is what the majority of people in a State want,[33] but this has not been an easy argument to mount, as the case of a majority oppressing a minority within a State makes abundantly clear.

The ancient defense of nation in some Mesopotamian texts is often drawn in terms of protection against those from outside who would oppress the citizenry. The assumption is that people do not want to be oppressed, and it is an unalloyed good for oppression to be confronted.[34] A consideration of the value of confronting oppression gives to the idea of self-determination some extra weight as self-defensive war is justified.

Also, in some cases, diplomacy (suing for peace) might be a reasonable alternative to mounting armed violence when an enemy army is at the gates. Indeed, the enemy may be provoked into invading, as in the case of the Romans who had kidnapped the Sabine women causing the Sabines to invade Rome.[35] And this raises the question of whether the State first to cross another State's borders should always be seen as the aggressor.[36] For some ancient writers and texts, the idea seems to be that aggressors are those who would oppress, not merely those who would cross boundaries.

Another question often discussed was whether it was better to raise armies than to raise defensive structures. In ancient Egypt, huge defensive structures were built all along the Nile, and pharaohs bragged that such actions

---

[32] *See* MICHAEL WALZER, JUST AND UNJUST WARS: A MORAL ARGUMENT WITH HISTORICAL ILLUSTRATIONS (1st ed. 1977).

[33] *See* Avishai Margalit & Joseph Raz, *National Self-Determination*, 87 J. PHIL. 439 (1990).

[34] Oppression is the term used in the various translations of ancient texts, but it is not clear whether or not this corresponds exactly to what is meant by this term today, especially in the debates about racial discrimination.

[35] See Livy's account of this historical example in LIVY, HISTORY OF ROME bk. I, § IX, lines 1–12, at 33–37 (B. O. Foster trans., Harvard University Press 1919).

[36] *See* LARRY MAY, AGGRESSION AND CRIMES AGAINST PEACE (2008).

averted war.[37] Even in cases where war was in self-defense, certain texts challenged whether even this cause of going to war was just if non-lethal actions were not exhausted. Today, some theorists have raised similar challenges, wondering whether police actions and deterrent strategies might not be able to avert war in many cases.[38]

Defensive war remains the least controversial just war today, despite the apparent problems with this idea. One of the problems that we saw in some of the historical sources concerns the fact that States claim to be engaging in defensive war when they have mixed motives including gain. And here is where the historical discussion of necessity is so important. The attack of the aggressive State must be imminent before the defensive war that is waged is considered just. This raises various questions about preemptive, anticipatory, and preventive self-defense.[39] And, on the account I have outlined in this Chapter, the war is most likely to be just if the invading State seeks to oppress the population of the target State. Many ancient sources provide quite a different conceptual frame for understanding such matters than we find today.

Some legal sources from ancient Mesopotamia, as well as from other parts of the ancient world, provide us with a humanitarian conceptual framework for understanding law and politics. By this I mean that rulers and judges saw law as a way for the most powerful members of the society to be held accountable for exploiting the least powerful. The test of being considered a good ruler was that he or she was a good shepherd for the flock – where the shepherd always cared most about those who could not easily fend for themselves.

The humanitarian model contrasts to the way that ancient rulers and legal systems are often understood. This comes out most clearly in the imputation of a punitive model of *lex talionis* ("an eye for an eye") that was thought, correctly, to epitomize ancient Mesopotamian and other ancient societies' criminal law. One of the most difficult parts of the larger argument of establishing the humanitarianism of many ancient rulers is to show that *lex talionis* can have a humanitarian face. Part of the argument is to show that the kind of *lex talionis* doctrine espoused in ancient Mesopotamia is based in the idea of proportionality – where the punishment must fit the crime, and most importantly, must be no harsher than that. For ancient legal thought of

---

[37] *See* MARC VAN DE MIEROOP, A HISTORY OF ANCIENT EGYPT (2010).

[38] *See* Gabriella Blum, *The Dispensable Lives of Soldiers*, 2 J. LEGAL ANALYSIS 69 (2010); LARRY MAY, WAR CRIMES AND JUST WAR (2007).

[39] *See* YORAM DINSTEIN, WAR, AGGRESSION, AND SELF-DEFENCE (3d ed. 2001).

Mesopotamia and the Near East, *lex talionis* stands against the idea that those seeking revenge could justify utter disregard of the humanity of the wrongdoer.[40]

The Mesopotamian conceptual scheme that we can learn from is a philosophical orientation to law and rulership that is humanitarian in that those who are most vulnerable are of greatest concern. And the cornerstone of ancient humanitarianism is the idea of equity, or fundamental fairness, which is thought to stand in contrast to a narrower sense of justice that treats all equally according to the law, not taking account of specific conditions that make one person much more likely to be harmed by a given practice than another person. It is perhaps surprising but not lacking in evidence how thoroughly equity informed law and its interpretation in ancient Mesopotamia long before the idea is often thought to have arisen in ancient Roman legal philosophy.[41]

In the ancient legal thought of Mesopotamia and the Near East, equity called for rulers to protect those who were the most vulnerable members of their societies. The two domains in which rulers most boasted of their accomplishments were the fields of law and war. Ending corruption of ministers and making sure that people did not go hungry were often mentioned as key legal accomplishments. Winning battles where oppression was ended were also often mentioned as key military accomplishments.

As we have seen in this Chapter, the two clearest cases of just wars in some ancient legal texts were both waged to end or prevent oppression: wars of national defense – wars waged to prevent a State from violating self-determination or causing oppression of a population; and wars of humanitarian intervention – wars waged to stop a foreign ruler from oppressing his own people. For these rulers, the other classic bases for a just war – opportunity, necessity, and punishment – were all related to the humanitarian goal of stopping oppression.

The contemporary debates about how to understand a just war as well as the debates about aggression can be well served by the ancient debates. Most importantly, since a war of humanitarian intervention is still not generally acknowledged as a just war, our ancient sources can provide a needed conceptual framework for such wars. The key is to find a way to find a similar basis of support, as I have argued in humanitarianism, for humanitarian intervention wars and wars of national defense. The wars of national defense

---

[40] *See* Larry May, Ancient Legal Thought, ch. 9 (unpublished manuscript currently in draft).
[41] *See* 1 G. R. DRIVER & JOHN C. MILES, THE BABYLONIAN LAWS (1952).

are sometimes under attack as well. The ancient conceptual scheme helps to provide support for these wars as just wars, although not all of them. Aggression is to be condemned as unjust when it has the effect of oppressing or risking the oppression of a population – the mere transgression of borders is not sufficient.[42] Here what counts as an unjust war tracks acts that are clearly unjust in terms of violations of equity, as we next see.

VIII. WHY JUSTICE MATTERS IN INTERNATIONAL LAW

What is legal and what is just are not the same, as thousands of years worth of discussion in legal thought have shown. So, it is not initially clear what justice has to do with matters of international law. Let me take up this topic in this, the last, Section of this Chapter. As Aristotle argued, there are two kinds of justice – legal justice and a type of justice that is more important than legal justice, which Aristotle labeled equity.[43] Indeed, we find legal thinkers as far back as Hammurabi drawing a distinction between types of justice in similar ways. Hammurabi could proclaim his debt relief edicts as conforming to the broader justice category of equity, even as a strict approach to legal justice would have required him to respect all of the debt contracts of his day.[44] And ancient Greek and Roman rulers could declare amnesties at the end of wars as a way to pay homage to a god's mercy. Mercy is a normative category that is related to equity in ancient times and also in our own.[45]

Equity has its source not in statutes or treaties but in a fundamental sense of fairness, upon which a legal system can be grounded. Discussion of just wars is a discussion largely of equity considerations rather than strict justice. So, one could ask about a given war being just even if the state of international law were crystal clear. Although, of course, international law leaves room for equity, both as a matter of customary international law and in the Statute of the International Court of Justice's provision of allowing decisions on the basis of "*ex aequo et bono.*"[46]

In ancient times, the source of equity was often thought to be the laws of the gods, or as it later came to be understood by the time of the Greeks and Romans, the source was in natural law. Today, there are still some lawyers

---

[42] *See* MAY, AGGRESSION AND CRIMES AGAINST PEACE, *supra* note 36.

[43] ARISTOTLE, NICOMACHEN ETHICS bk. V, § 10 (350 BCE).

[44] *See* Larry May, Law, Equity, and Debt Forgiveness in Ancient Mesopotamia, Workshop Paper Presented at Washington University Political Theory Group (Dec. 2015).

[45] *See* Martha Nussbaum, *Equity and Mercy*, 22 PHIL. & PUB. AFF. 83 (1993).

[46] Statue of the International Court of Justice art. 38(2), June 26, 1945, 59 Stat. 1055, 3 Bevans 1179.

who recognize natural law as a source of law, especially international law. And other lawyers and law scholars recognize certain moral principles, enshrined in the old canons of equity, as sources of law – Ronald Dworkin was the most important theorist to take this position.[47]

The point is that a discussion of whether war is just does not fall wholly outside the framework of law. Indeed, I have argued for the last decade in a series of books that there is considerable overlap between the idea of just war especially in the work of early modern theorists like Vitoria, Suarez, Grotius, Pufendorf, and Vattel on the one hand, and contemporary discussions in international law on the other hand.[48] At the very least, it seems clear that early twentieth-century international legal theorists were heavily influenced by the sixteenth-, seventeenth-, and eighteenth-century theorists in the just war tradition. This seems particularly true for theorists like Hersch Lauterpacht and Justice Robert Jackson.[49] The Nuremberg Tribunal was by design grounded in natural law principles. So, for at least some leading international lawyers, the discussion of what wars are just is not merely a philosophical exercise. What I have argued in this Chapter is that we can go much further back historically than the sixteenth and seventeenth centuries CE, indeed to before the seventeenth century BCE.

There are pragmatic and moral reasons for thinking that it matters whether a given war is just. Globalization has so shrunk the world that no State can last for long if it is isolated from the community of States. The label "just war" is assigned to those wars that are not seen as violating the norms of the community of States. So, it behooves all States to be known for only fighting just wars if they have any hope of benefitting from the reciprocal good will of the rest of the States.

The more controversial question is what moral reasons there are for thinking that it matters if a given war is just. At least in part this is controversial because some international lawyers do not see morality as generally mattering

---

[47] See RONALD DWORKIN, LAW'S EMPIRE (1986); *see also* Dworkin's last essay, Ronald Dworkin, *A New Philosophy for International Law*, 44 PHIL. & PUB. AFF. 2 (2013).

[48] See LARRY MAY, CRIMES AGAINST HUMANITY: A NORMATIVE ACCOUNT (2004); MAY, WAR CRIMES AND JUST WAR, *supra* note 38; MAY, AGGRESSION AND CRIMES AGAINST PEACE, *supra* note 36; LARRY MAY, GENOCIDE: A NORMATIVE ACCOUNT (2010); LARRY MAY, AFTER WAR ENDS (2012).

[49] See Hersch Lauterpacht, *The Grotian Tradition in International Law*, 23 BRIT. Y.B. INT'L L. 1 (1946), *reprinted in* GROTIUS AND LAW 469–521 (Larry May & Emily McGill eds., 2014); *see also* Opening Statement for the United States of America by Robert H. Jackson, Chief of Counsel for the United States, Trial of the Major War Criminals before the International Military Tribunal (Nov. 21, 1945), *reprinted in* PHILOSOPHY OF LAW 435–40 (Larry May & Jeff Brown eds., 2010).

for international law.[50] Some state leaders and some international lawyers as
well see only political considerations as mattering. Yet nearly everyone would
agree that there are two domains relevant for international law, *lex lata*, what
the law *is*, and *lex ferenda*, what the law *should be*. And while issues about
what the law should be are not solely moral issues, morality gains a strong
foothold once it is indeed recognized that *lex ferenda* issues matter to international law.

Morality as understood over the millennia has a claim to objective, not
merely subjective, standing. This has to do with the close connection between
natural law and morality from the earliest of times. Today it is the idea of
human rights that continues to claim a kind of objective status for morality –
one has a right by virtue of being human, not merely if a ruler happens to
think the ruler's subjects are deserving of this status. Morality extends over all
of humanity and is grounded in the idea that there are norms that affect all
humans – this is the claim to objectivity. Of course, this is not to say that
human rights always trump all other considerations.

In the earliest records of legal thought the idea of humanity is of central
importance. In the epilogue to the laws of Lipit-Ishtar, which date from 1930
BCE, he tells us:

> In accordance with the true word of the god Utu, I made the lands of Sumer
> and Akkad hold fair judicial procedure. In accordance with the utterance of
> the god Enlil, I, Lipi-Ishtar, son of Enlil, eradicated enmity and violence ...
> I made right and truth shine forth, and I brought well-being to the lands of
> Sumer and Akkad ... [and to] all humankind.[51]

And as quoted earlier, in 1750 BCE Hammurabi says that "I have not been
careless or negligent toward humankind."[52]

Henry Sumner Maine has a very useful definition of equity that allows us to
see how in the history of legal thought equity could be a model for morally
assessing international law. Equity is "any body of rules existing by the side of
the original civil law, founded on distinct principles and claiming incidentally
to supersede the civil law in virtue of superior sanctity inherent in those
principles."[53] Maine then links this understanding of equity with what in
Roman law was called "Jus Naturale, or the Law of Nature"[54] upon which
the edicts of the Praetor were based. Maine also links the modern idea of

---

[50] *See* JACK L. GOLDSMITH & ERIC A. POSNER, THE LIMITS OF INTERNATIONAL LAW (2005).
[51] ROTH, *supra* note 29, at 33–35.
[52] *Id.* at 133.
[53] HENRY SUMNER MAINE, ANCIENT LAW 28 (1861).
[54] *Id.* at 46.

international law, "a law common to all nations," to these early ideas of natural law.[55] And in his lectures on international law, Maine adds this comment: "The number of ancient institutions which bear the marks of a design to stand in the way of war, and to provide an alternative to it, is exceedingly great."[56]

In this Chapter I have tried to give a sense of what some of the oldest legal texts tell us about what makes a war just. The idea that has remained is that the least problematic of just causes to go to war is defense of one's nation from invasion that was not provoked and where the invasion risked oppression of the citizenry. And the second least problematic cause is war waged also for humanitarian reasons, especially to stop oppression of tyrants of their people. For these ancient legal texts, all other causes for going to war were seen to be highly problematic.

---

[55] *Id.* at 49.
[56] Henry Sumner Maine, *Lecture One: Its Origins and Sources, in* INTERNATIONAL LAW: A SERIES OF LECTURES DELIVERED BEFORE THE UNIVERSITY OF CAMBRIDGE IN 1887, at 11, ¶ 12 (1888).

5

Definitions of Aggression as Harbingers of International Change

KIRSTEN E. SELLARS

I. INTRODUCTION

Debates about the definitions of aggression are responses to deadlock and harbingers of change. Each, in its own way and in its own time, has heralded a transition from an old to a new set of legal and institutional arrangements. The definitions in the early 1930s, which emerged in response to the failings of the League of Nations, signaled the shift away from the old dichotomy of belligerency and neutrality, and toward a new regime based on legitimate and illegitimate wars. The definitions of the early 1950s, responding to the Cold War Security Council deadlock, presaged the United Nations' transition from collective security organization to conflict mediator. The General Assembly's definition of 1974, negotiated during the era of détente, might, had the "new" Cold War not intervened, have heralded new alignments between powerful States. And the definition in the 2010 Kampala Amendments, anticipating shifts from a unipolar to a multipolar world, proposes dual sources of authority – the Security Council and International Criminal Court – on the handling of aggression.

Although debates about definitions herald change, they have also given rise to remarkably durable patterns of state behavior, patterns still being repeated to this day. The most consistent advocates of automatic yardsticks of aggression have been States vulnerable to attack or excluded from either the League Council or Security Council. These "excluded" States have not only looked to definitions for legal protection against the vicissitudes of international life, but have also tried to use them to break the powerful States' monopoly over the determination of aggression. This pattern was first discernible during the interwar years. In 1933, for example, the Soviet Union (a vulnerable State), backed by France (another vulnerable State), broached a definition at the Conference for the Reduction and Limitation of Armaments (Disarmament

Conference). During the Cold War decades, smaller States, beguiled by the prospect of undermining the Security Council's mandate under Article 39, kept the definitional flame alight. And today a legion of small, middling, and quite large "excluded" States posit International Criminal Court jurisdiction over the crime of aggression as an alternative (or, more diplomatically, a supplement) to Security Council determination.

By contrast, the most powerful States, as the "included" members of the League Council or Security Council, have been consistently *inconsistent* in their approach to definitions of aggression, and oscillate according to the force fields of other powerful States. They do not want to surrender their own control over decisions about aggression, but for limited and expedient ends – say, to exert pressure on another powerful State – they are sometimes prepared to initiate or support definitions. The past master of this was the Soviet Union, which was happy to pose as either an upholder of Security Council prerogatives or champion of the "excluded" majority, depending on whether it was voting for or vetoing Council resolutions. Alongside the Russians, the most consistently inconsistent of them all has been the United States, which proposed a definition in 1933, opposed a definition at the 1945 San Francisco Conference, proposed a definition at the 1945 London Conference, opposed a definition in the First Committee in 1950, proposed a definition in the U.N. Special Committee on the Question of Defining Aggression in 1969, and opposed a definition at the 1998 Rome Conference.

With these recurring motifs in mind, I will examine three pivotal moments in the evolution of definitions of aggression – 1933, 1950, and 1974 – and will, in their light, conclude with an assessment of the latest definition proposed at Kampala in 2010.[1]

II. LITVINOV'S BLUEPRINT

After the League of Nations' collective security machinery stalled over Manchuria in 1931–32, insecure States began to look to other legal mechanisms for protection against aggression. Prominent among them was the Soviet Union, whose leadership feared a war on both flanks against both Japan and Germany, and was particularly alarmed by Adolf Hitler's assumption of power on January 30, 1933.

Just seven days later, at the League-sponsored Disarmament Conference, the Soviet Foreign Minister Maxim Litvinov proposed attaching a "Definition

---

[1]   Some Sections of this Chapter have also appeared in: Kirsten Sellars, 'Crimes Against Peace' and International Law (Cambridge, 2013).

of 'Aggressor'" to the convention on security and disarmament under discussion. Rather than interpreting aggression as being a State's refusal to submit to international remedies (as had previous interwar treaties), it instead set out a list of illustrative examples of state aggression, starting with "declaration of war." This list was the blueprint for all of the subsequent enumerative definitions advanced from then to the present day.

After a preamble acknowledging the right to national independence, territorial inviolability, security, and self-defense, Litvinov's definition, with its emphasis on the chronology of events (note the use of "first"), stated:

> The aggressor in an international conflict shall be considered that State which is the *first* to take any of the following actions:
>
> a) Declaration of war against another State;
> b) The invasion by its armed forces of the territory of another State without declaration of war;
> c) Bombarding the territory of another State by its land, naval or air forces or knowingly attacking the naval or air forces of another State;
> d) The landing in, or introduction within the frontiers of, another State of land, naval or air forces without the permission of the Government of such a State, or the infringement of the conditions of such permission, particularly as regards the duration of sojourn or extension of area;
> e) The establishment of a naval blockade of the coast or ports of another State.[2]

This enumeration of aggressive acts was followed by the warning that "[n]o considerations whatsoever of a political, strategical or economic nature ... shall be accepted as justification of aggression."[3] These considerations prohibited various pretexts for the use of force based on the internal situation of a given State: "Political, economic or cultural backwardness of a given country"; "Alleged mal-administration"; "Possible danger to life or property of foreign residents"; "Revolutionary or counter-revolutionary movement, civil war, disorders or strikes"; and "The establishment or maintenance in any State of any political, economic or social order."[4]

This was followed by exclusions of the use of force on the grounds of national policies, such as the infringement of international agreements, the

---

[2]   League of Nations, Conference for the Reduction and Limitation of Armaments, *Definition of "Aggressor": Draft Definition*, Doc. Conf. D/C.G.38 (Feb. 6, 1933), *in* RECORDS OF THE CONFERENCE FOR THE REDUCTION AND LIMITATION OF ARMAMENTS (ser. B, vol. II), at 237–38 (1936) (emphasis added).

[3]   *Id.* at 238.

[4]   *Id.*

rupture of diplomatic or economic relations, the repudiation of debts, the non-admission or limitation of immigration, or religious or anti-religious measures. *The Economist* noted that the list included "every excuse … that any country has ever offered for attacking the Soviet Union."[5] But it was also designed to appeal to other States, including nations that had erected barriers to Japanese immigration, such as Australia and the United States; nations that had boycotted a foreign occupier's goods, such as China and India; and the European and Latin American nations that were indebted to the United States.

A. An Objective Standard

When Litvinov proposed his definition, he did not refer to any aggressor by name, but conveyed the Soviets' concerns about their security in the immediate future, which were linked to assaults to which they had been recently subjected, such as the Entente Powers' attacks on the new State in 1918–21. Could they expect international decisions by similarly motivated powers to be wholly impartial? Litvinov thought not. It was not so long ago, he said, that "the phenomenon of a Soviet socialist State was so distasteful to the whole capitalist world that, at the time, attempts were even made by way of intervention to restore capitalism in our country."[6] He added that some capitalist governments still made the "crusade against the Soviet Union almost the centre of their foreign policy."[7]

To rectify this state of affairs, Litvinov proposed his simple and objective marker of aggression: which nation attacked first? Because determination was automatic, there was no need for international bodies to *interpret* events. Litvinov's emphasis on the first strike was designed to compel them to act impartially, no matter which States happened to be involved in the dispute.

Although Litvinov had couched his proposal in terms of Soviet national self-interest, it attracted support from the majority of States, including France, Poland, Turkey, Chile, Persia, and the "Little Entente" States. The smaller nations in particular looked to international law, however flimsy the protections it offered, as upholding, on the principles of universality and equity, the

[5] *The Disarmament Conference*, ECONOMIST, Feb. 11, 1933, at 284, 285.
[6] League of Nations, Conference for the Reduction and Limitation of Armaments, *Plan for General Disarmament and the Organisation of Peace, Submitted by the French Government: General Discussion of the Memorandum by the French Delegation Dated November 14th, 1932 (continuation)* (Feb. 6, 1933), *in* RECORDS OF THE CONFERENCE FOR THE REDUCTION AND LIMITATION OF ARMAMENTS (ser. B, vol. II), *supra* note 2, at 230, 236.
[7] *Id.*

interests of the weak as well as the strong. Litvinov's definition, which set an unyielding standard for the identification of an aggressor, appealed to this sentiment.

In response, the delegations from the most powerful nations – the United States and Britain – couched their objections to the definition in emollient terms. While their private view was that it would restrict their actions, their public argument was that aggression was too complex and multifarious a matter to be adequately defined. The British delegate Anthony Eden quoted another British official to the effect that "it would seem impossible to decide, even in theory, what constitutes an act of aggression,"[8] while the American Hugh Gibson suggested that there "would always be ways of resorting to force which remained technically outside any definition that man in his finite wisdom could conceive."[9]

Before long, though, the Americans and British undermined their own arguments by advancing definitions of their own. On May 16, 1933, Franklin Roosevelt sent a message to the conference proposing that nations "individually agree that they will send no armed force of whatsoever nature across their frontiers."[10] (This definition, overlooked in subsequent commentaries, infuriated the British, who had not been consulted.) Six days later, the American delegation leader, Norman Davis, suggested that "the simplest and most accurate definition of an aggressor is one whose armed forces are found on alien soil in violation of treaties."[11] And a week after that, the Americans and British, still mindful of Litvinov, worked out a spoiler definition: "a state in violation of treaties, invades with its armed forces the territory of another state, whether by land, sea or air and whether with or without a declaration of war."[12] All these definitions made it clear that the opposition to Litvinov's version was not based on principle.

---

[8] League of Nations, Conference for the Reduction and Limitation of Armaments, *Definition of Aggression: Draft Declaration Proposed by the Delegation of the Union of Soviet Socialist Republics: General Discussion*, Minutes of the Eighth Meeting of the Political Commission, Doc. Conf. D/C.G./P.V.38 (Mar. 10, 1933), *in* Records of the Conference for the Reduction and Limitation of Armaments (ser. D, vol. V) at 47, 53 (1936).

[9] *Id.* at 55.

[10] League of Nations, Conference for the Reduction and Limitation of Armaments, *Message to the Conference from the President of the United States of America*, Minutes of the Fifty-Ninth Meeting of the General Commission, Doc. Conf. D/C.G./P.V.59 (May 19, 1933), *in* Records of the Conference for the Reduction and Limitation of Armaments (ser. B, vol. II), *supra* note 2, at 461, 462.

[11] Davis to Secretary of State (May 19, 1933), *in* 1 Foreign Relations of the United States Diplomatic Papers, 1933, at 154, 157 (1950).

[12] *Id.* at 176.

Britain's real motives for rejecting it emerged in a memorandum written by the Foreign Office Legal Advisor William Malkin (and summarized here by one of his diplomatic successors):

> Our main reasons for disliking this proposal (apart from an inherent prefer-ence for approaching each case on its merits) were: (a) that it was based upon a restrictive continental view of frontiers etc., which might well prove in an emergency militarily embarrassing to us (indeed it was suspected that the proposal was drafted with this aim in view); (b) that the list was in any case not exhaustive and could be got around with a little ingenuity by a deter-mined aggressor; and (c) that it was inherently bad and dangerous in basing itself . . . on "the purely chronological test that the aggressor is that party to the dispute *who is the first to commit* any of the specified acts."[13]

B. *Aggression Through Proxies*

The question of the definition was referred to the conference's Committee on Security Questions, presided over by Nicolas Politis – a longstanding partici-pant in debates about aggression.[14] His report, *An Act Relating to the Defin-ition of the Aggressor*, presented on May 24, 1933, was essentially a reworking of, rather than a departure from, the Litvinov proposal. The most significant change was the removal of the clause on the landing of military forces in another country without its permission, and its replacement with another clause relating to indirect aggression (aggression through proxies) carried out by armed bands.

This "armed bands" clause was inserted on the insistence of Turkey, which at the time was attempting to crush a Kurdish rebellion on its eastern border (in 1930, the Turks had deployed 60,000 troops against Kurdish incursions from Mount Ararat, located in neighboring Persia).[15] Bulgaria opposed the clause on the grounds that the Treaty of Neuilly prevented it from possessing a border force large enough to control the movement of armed bands, and it had no wish to be punished as an aggressor for this deficiency.[16] The clause stood, however, and appeared in the Politis–Litvinov draft as follows:

---

[13] Holmer, Recapitulating Malkin's Minute of 13 October 1933, FO 371/95721 (Mar. 2, 1951) (THE NATIONAL ARCHIVES [U.K.]) (emphasis in original).

[14] Politis was a frequent contributor to the French-language literature on aggression, along with Paul Bastid, Albert de Lapradelle, Louis Le Fur, Yves Leroy de la Brière, Robert Redslob, Georges Scelle, René Vignol, and others.

[15] *The Kurdish Rising*, TIMES (U.K.), July 25, 1930, at 11.

[16] Leeper minute, FO 371/17361 (May 31, 1933) (THE NATIONAL ARCHIVES [U.K.]).

Provision of support to armed bands formed in its territory which have
invaded the territory of another State, or refusal, notwithstanding the request
of the invaded State, to take in its own territory all the measures in its power
to deprive these bands of all assistance and protection.[17]

As it turned out, the Politis–Litvinov formula was shelved, but a few
months later the Soviets resurrected the resolution (retaining the clause
about armed bands) as the core of three Moscow-sponsored treaties, each
entitled Convention for the Definition of Aggression, signed on July 3, 4,
and 5, 1933, with Afghanistan, Czechoslovakia, Estonia, Latvia, Lithuania,
Persia, Poland, Romania, Turkey, and Yugoslavia.[18] But by the time these
treaties were ratified, the League's experiment in collective security was
virtually over. Japan withdrew from the League over Manchuria on
February 25, 1933, and Germany walked out of the Disarmament Conference, and thence the League, over arms limitations on October 14.
Thereafter, rearmament rather than disarmament dominated the international agenda.

III. COLD WAR SCHEMES

A. *Litvinov Redux*

After the Second World War, the League expired, and a new organization, the
United Nations, rose from its ashes. The first phase of the United Nations'
existence – the era of collective security – was characterized by the Security
Council's regulation of force and the prioritization of global security over
justice. But the second phase of its existence – the era of superpower conflict –
was defined by the breakdown of collective security and the emergence of
"just cause" as a justification for the use of force. The recasting of the United
Nations' role during this second phase meant that, once again, some of the
"excluded" States began to cast around for alternative mechanisms to safeguard themselves and their interests. This resulted in a campaign for a

[17] League of Nations, Conference for the Reduction and Limitation of Armaments, *Rep. of the Comm. on Security Questions: Act Relating to the Definition of the Aggressor*, Doc. Conf. D/C.G./108 (May 24, 1933), *in* 2 CONFERENCE FOR THE REDUCTION AND LIMITATION OF ARMAMENTS: CONFERENCE DOCUMENTS at 679, 683 (1935).
[18] *See, e.g.*, Convention for the Definition of Aggression, Afg.-Est.-Lat.-Persia-Pol.-Rom.-Turk.-U.S.S.R.-Fin., July 3, 1933, 147 L.N.T.S. 69.

definition of aggression for use in the event of the Security Council being deadlocked.

This process began in the General Assembly's First (Political and Security) Committee on November 4, 1950, when Andrei Vishinsky, the Soviet Foreign Minister, tabled a definition of aggression. This was a dramatic about-turn driven by political circumstances – in 1945, Soviet delegates had, along with other powers, successfully opposed the incorporation of a definition into both the U.N. Charter and the Nuremberg Charter. By late 1950s, though, all had changed with the collapse of the collective security system and growing fears of a third world war. The formation of NATO in 1949, and its breach of the Berlin "blockade" a month later, had forced the Soviets onto the defensive. In January 1950, they walked out of the Security Council after failing to unseat nationalist China in favor of communist China. But when the remaining Security Council members capitalized on the Soviets' absence and dispatched a U.N. army to intervene in the war in Korea, the Soviets abandoned their protest and returned to veto further action.

The ensuing Security Council deadlock prompted both the Soviet Union *and* the United States to attempt to rewrite the by then partly obsolescent U.N. Charter, each aiming to strengthen its own position in the new era of superpower rivalry. On November 3, 1950, the Americans tried to bypass the veto deadlock by introducing the Uniting for Peace Resolution, which would, in the event of Security Council paralysis, pass responsibility for the determination of "any threat to the peace, breach of the peace, or act of aggression" to the General Assembly.[19] The following day, Vishinky – who recognized that the Security Council no longer had a monopoly on the decision-making process, and hoped to preempt further American initiatives – proposed the aforementioned definition of aggression as a belated bid to set the terms of the debate in the General Assembly.

Vishinsky's definition[20] was closely modelled on the original definition submitted to the Disarmament Conference by his predecessor, Maxim Litvinov. Like Litvinov's, Vishinsky's covered declaration of war, invasion, bombardment, naval blockade, and keeping forces in another State without

---

[19] G.A. Res. 377 A (V), Uniting for Peace, U.N. Doc. A/RES/377(V) (Nov. 3, 1950), www.un.org/ga/search/view_doc.asp?symbol=A/RES/377(V).

[20] Union of Soviet Socialist Republics: Draft Resolution on the Definition of Aggression, U.N. Doc. A/C.1/608 (Nov. 4, 1950), *reprinted in* 1950 U.N.Y.B. 210, U.N. Sales No. 1951.I.24 [hereinafter Soviet Draft Resolution on the Definition of Aggression].

permission, and was advanced for much the same reason: to firm up the *status quo* and deflect attacks on the Soviet Union. Both definitions emphasized that the first strike was the automatic marker of aggression, and both were advanced in exceedingly dangerous international circumstances – indeed, the *perceived* perils of 1950 might have exceeded those of 1933: while Litvinov anticipated a traditional military assault by Germany or Japan, Vishinsky feared an American nuclear strike. (The Soviets were deeply concerned about the Americans' superior bomb technology and delivery systems, and had earlier proposed that the General Assembly declare that "the Government which will be the *first* to use the atomic weapon ... will commit a crime against mankind."[21])

When Vishinsky tabled his definition, other First Committee delegates, especially those from the NATO countries, responded with a predictable lack of enthusiasm. The American and Canadian representatives focused, among other things, on what the Soviet motion omitted: it did not, for example, apply to land "blockades" such as the Soviet's Berlin "blockade;" and it did not cover "indirect aggression," such as communist subversion and fomentation of civil strife.[22] The Canadian delegate further noted that the definition offered no help in deciding who had initiated a conflict such as the Korean War because "all that an aggressor would have to do to frustrate the purpose of the Soviet proposal would be to claim that the other party had attacked first, which was what North Korea had actually alleged."[23]After a tense debate, the Syrian and Bolivian delegates proposed that the definition be transferred from the First Committee to the International Law Commission. The Eastern Bloc representatives protested that the definition, being linked with the Security Council's work, was "primarily political and not legal."[24] But the motion was carried, and, as State Department Legal Advisor Herman Phleger recalled, the Soviet item was "shunted off" to the jurists in the International Law Commission.[25]

[21] Andrey Yanuaryevich Vyshinsky, *For Peace and Security of the Peoples Against the Threat of a New War* (Sept. 20, 1950), *in* THE SOVIET UNION AT THE FIFTH SESSION OF THE U.N.O., 1950, SEPTEMBER 20–OCTOBER 23 (Soviet News Booklet 1950) (emphasis added).
[22] Soviet Draft Resolution on the Definition of Aggression, *supra* note 20, at 211.
[23] *Id.*
[24] *Id.* at 212.
[25] Phleger to Lodge, U.S. Mission to the U.N. (Jan. 20, 1955) (Box 22, RG84, U.S. Mission to the U.N., Central Subject Files (1946–63), NATIONAL ARCHIVES AND RECORDS ADMINISTRATION [U.S.]). The Soviet proposal was referred to the International Law Commission by G.A. Res. 378 B (V), U.N. Doc. A/RES/378(V) (Nov. 17, 1950), www.un.org/en/ga/search/view_doc.asp?symbol=A/RES/378(V).

B. *Plans for an International Criminal Court*

What is notable about this discussion in 1950 is that no one, least of all Vishinsky himself, suggested that this definition should be used as a guide to criminal proceedings before an international criminal court. This is significant because at the time, precisely such a court, with jurisdiction over "crimes against peace" (the forebear of the crime of aggression), was being discussed within the United Nations. Significantly, this idea enjoyed the support of two Permanent Members of the Security Council. One of these was France, which in 1947 in the U.N. Committee on the Progressive Development of International Law, broached the idea of a court with jurisdiction over the same crimes as the Nuremberg Tribunal. (This was rejected by the Soviet Union, a consistent opponent of an international court, on the grounds that it was outside the Committee's terms of reference.[26]) The other Security Council member was the United States, which not only drew up plans for an international criminal court, but also envisaged one with explicit jurisdiction over "crimes against peace" – a fact that might give pause to those familiar with the Americans' more recent oppositional stance at the 1998 Rome Conference and the 2010 Kampala Conference.

A month after the debate about a definition in the First Committee, the General Assembly passed Resolution 489 (V) on "International Criminal Jurisdiction," deciding that seventeen States should meet in August 1951 to draft the founding documents and statute of the proposed court.[27] This time, the Soviets objected on the grounds that such a court would be contrary to the principle of state sovereignty.[28] But the Americans pressed ahead, to the extent of drafting their own resolution and statute as the starting point for discussion, based on the Nuremberg and Tokyo Charters and the Statute of the International Court of Justice.[29] On June 1, 1951, John Maktos, the U.S. State Department's Legal Advisor, circulated these documents around the

---

[26] Enclosure, Politzer to Taft, U.S. Mission to the U.N., at 1 (July 5, 1951) (referring to U.N. Doc. A/AC.10/52 [June 17, 1947]) (Box 90, RG 84, U.S. Mission to the U.N., Central Subject Files [1946–63], NATIONAL ARCHIVES AND RECORDS ADMINISTRATION [U.S.]).

[27] G.A. Res. 489 (V), International Criminal Jurisdiction, U.N. Doc. A/RES/489(V) (Dec. 12, 1950), www.un.org/en/ga/search/view_doc.asp?symbol=A/RES/489(V).

[28] Enclosure, Politzer to Taft, *supra* note 26, at 2.

[29] Maktos, First Draft of a U.N. General Assembly Resolution and First Draft of the Statute of the Proposed International Criminal Court, at 2 (June 1, 1951) (Box 22, RG 59, Bureau of U.N. Affairs [1941–51], NATIONAL ARCHIVES AND RECORDS ADMINISTRATION [U.S.]).

Department prior to their submission, explaining that the proposed court was "a temple of justice open to those willing to enter."[30]

The American draft resolution began and ended as follows:

> The General Assembly,
>
> *Conscious* of the responsibility of the United Nations to encourage the development of international law and to promote judicial inquiry into serious crimes of international scope, such as those recognized in the Charter of the Nuremberg Tribunal and in the judgment of the Tribunal ...
>
> *Resolves* to establish the International Criminal Court which shall be constituted and shall exercise its functions in accordance with the annexed Statute.[31]

The prominence given to the Nuremberg Charter and judgment in the opening stanza indicates that "crimes against peace" – the central charge brought at Nuremberg – was envisaged as being part of the proposed court's roster.

The American draft statute continued in a similar vein. Its authors explained:

> It was first thought that the article relating to jurisdiction over the subject matter might possibly read as follows:
> "The jurisdiction of the Court shall extend to the following:
>
> a. Crimes against peace;
> b. War Crimes, namely, violations of the laws or customs of war;
> c. Crimes against humanity;
> d. Genocide;
> e. Any other acts which are crimes under international law;
> f. Crimes over which jurisdiction shall have been given to the Court pursuant to a convention concluded under United Nations' auspices or, with the approval of the General Assembly, pursuant to any other convention."[32]

So "crimes against peace" was given pole position, just as it had been in the Nuremberg Charter. But the authors suspected that questions might be raised about why some crimes under international law had been enumerated while

---

[30] *Id.*
[31] Draft Resolution: Establishment of an International Criminal Court, at 1, 2 (May 28, 1951) (Box 22, RG 59, Bureau of U.N. Affairs [1941–51], NATIONAL ARCHIVES AND RECORDS ADMINISTRATION [U.S.]).
[32] *Id.* at 24–25.

others had not.[33] As a result, in the final draft, the section made reference only to generic "serious crimes of an international scope." It read:

1. The jurisdiction of the Court shall extend to serious crimes of an international scope over which jurisdiction shall have been conferred on it pursuant to a treaty or convention concluded under United Nations auspices or, with the approval of the General Assembly, pursuant to any other treaty or convention, provided such treaty or convention shall have been accepted by a state in the manner required by its laws before its nationals or persons found within its jurisdiction can be subjected to the jurisdiction of the Court.
2. By a resolution of the General Assembly adopted by a majority of the Members present and voting, any crime may be brought before the Court if the state having jurisdiction over the offense and the accused relinquishes jurisdiction to it.[34]

While the language of the American final draft appeared to be impeccably disinterested, it was nonetheless colored by Cold War thinking. The authors explained that the second paragraph might cover cases of expatriate Americans accused of international crimes: "Soviet law may, for instance, provide penalties for 'war propaganda' and an American may be accused under that law. It would certainly be preferable to have him tried by an international rather than by a Soviet court."[35] When discussing the number of sitting judges, the authors commented: "In view of the existing differences in political ideologies and the nature of the crimes that may come before the Court it would seem preferable to have a larger number than three judges in a chamber. Two of them may happen to be nationals of the Soviet bloc."[36] This draft was signed off by James Simsarian (of the State Department's Office of United Nations Economic and Social Affairs), and passed, with reservations, by Durward Sandifer (Deputy Assistant Secretary of State for United Nations Affairs).[37]

C. *Proposals to Define Aggression*

In the United Nations, the idea of convening an international criminal court with the jurisdiction to try individuals for crimes against peace and other crimes began to run out of steam in 1951. But at the same time, the alternative

---

[33] *Id.* at 25.
[34] *Id.* at 22.
[35] *Id.* at 24.
[36] *Id.* at 15.
[37] Sandifer to Maktos (July 18, 1951) (Box 8, RG 59, Files of Durward V. Sandifer [1944–54], NATIONAL ARCHIVES AND RECORDS ADMINISTRATION [U.S.]).

approach – a definition of aggression as a yardstick for *State* behavior – gathered pace. Many middling and small countries, suspicious of the powerful States, fearful of their nuclear arsenals, and resentful of their veto power, thought some good might come of it. Although the International Law Commission failed to reach agreement on whether or how aggression should be defined, the General Assembly in January 1952 nevertheless decided that it was still both "possible and desirable" to define aggression,[38] and convened the first of four Special Committees on the Question of Defining Aggression.[39] These debates were held intermittently between 1952 and 1974.

During this period, the Soviets usually led the demands for a definition of aggression. While they relished playing the anti–*status quo* card – condemning, for example, warmongering and imperialism as aggression – their radical stance masked an essentially conservative purpose. Their primary aim was to safeguard their own security, first, by suppressing any dissent bubbling up within the Soviet Bloc satellites (by presenting challenges to the regional *status quo* as aggressive acts), and second, by automatically designating the first strike as aggression, thereby precluding the West's nuclear States from engaging in anticipatory self-defense.

The Soviet Union was not alone in calling for a definition of aggression. At the same time, many Non-Aligned States were reworking older arguments for definition – that it would deter aggression, enhance international law, and guide States considering military action – to serve their own ends. Ideological and economic warfare were cast as aggression. So, too, was colonialism. In 1960, they voted through the *Declaration on the Granting of Independence to Colonial Countries and Peoples*, which, in its first article, stated that "alien subjugation, domination and exploitation" was "an impediment to the promotion of world peace and co-operation"[40] – in short, that colonialism was

---

[38] G.A. Res. 599 (VI), Question of Defining Aggression, U.N. Doc. A/RES/599(VI) (Jan. 31, 1952), www.un.org/en/ga/search/view_doc.asp?symbol=A/RES/599(VI).

[39] The first Committee, of 1952–1954, was established by G.A. Res. 688 (VII), Question of Defining Aggression, U.N. Doc. A/RES/688(VII) (Dec. 20, 1952). The second Committee, of 1954–1956, was established by G.A. Res. 895 (IX), Question of Defining Aggression, U.N. Doc. A/RES/895(IX) (Dec. 4, 1954). The third Committee, of 1957–1967, established by G.A. Res. 1181 (XII), Question of Defining Aggression, U.N. Doc. A/RES/1181(XII) (Nov. 29, 1957), was directed to decide "when it shall be appropriate for the General Assembly to consider again the question of defining aggression" – it was decided in 1959, 1962, 1965, and 1967 that it was not appropriate to consider again. The fourth and final Committee, of 1967–1974, was established by G.A. Res. 2330 (XXII), Need to Expedite the Drafting of a Definition of Aggression in the Light of the Present International Situation, U.N. Doc. A/RES/2330(XXII) (Dec. 18, 1967).

[40] G.A. Res. 1514 (XV), Declaration on the Granting of Independence to Colonial Countries and Peoples, U.N. Doc. 1514(XV) (Dec. 14, 1960), www.un.org/en/ga/search/view_doc.asp?symbol=A/RES/1514(XV).

aggression (and struggles against colonialism were not). The colonial powers, not wishing to incur opprobrium by voting against this motion, abstained, thus establishing a pattern of third-world assertiveness and first-world defensiveness that lasted the decade.

IV. DRAFTING THE 1974 DEFINITION

A. *Détente-Era Negotiations*

In this highly politicized environment, could the negotiations over a definition of aggression rise above the self-interested demands of its various protagonists? The debate over the "Definition of Aggression,"[41] which was raised in 1967, and passed by the General Assembly in 1974, suggests that it could not.

Unlike the proposals broached during the previous decades, the 1974 definition was conceived not during the Cold War, but during the period of détente. As a consequence, the negotiations were dominated less by disagreements between the West and the Soviet Bloc, which were able to tolerate and sometimes even collaborate with each other, and more by disputes between the West and the Non-Aligned States. (As a British official noted in 1973, "the difference between the East Europeans and the West had not been the real problem in recent years" – rather, the difficulties had arisen "mainly from the situation in the Middle East."[42])

Every party to the negotiations was compelled to make significant concessions. The Western powers were ambivalent at best, and hostile at worst, to the idea of defining aggression, but not long into the negotiations, the United States and its closest allies acknowledged that demand for a definition would not simply go away. Instead of dismissing the idea as unworkable, as they had done previously, they decided to try to set the terms of the debate by submitting a definition themselves.[43] Meanwhile, the Soviet Union, which was having problems with its satellites, eventually decided to soften its stance on an issue that had previously been central to its approach – the "first strike" (by now dubbed "the priority principle"). And the Non-Aligned States, having realized that U.N. resolutions voted through by impressive majorities had no legal traction if opposed by the powerful States, agreed to embark on

---

[41] G.A. Res. 3314 (XXIX), annex, Definition of Aggression, U.N. Doc. A/RES/3314(XXIX) (Dec. 14, 1974), www.un.org/en/ga/search/view_doc.asp?symbol=A/RES/3314(XXIX).

[42] Freeland (New York) to Martin, FCO 58/757 (Mar. 15, 1973) (THE NATIONAL ARCHIVES [U.K.]).

[43] The Americans mooted this idea in May 1968, and the first joint draft definition – co-sponsored by Australia, Canada, Italy, Japan, the United Kingdom, and the United States – was submitted in 1969.

negotiations concluded not by majority vote but by consensus.[44] Ultimately, though, these compromises could not hide the fact that the three groups had irreconcilable differences. Yet instead of abandoning the attempt to define aggression, they incorporated these contradictions into the definition itself, prompting one prominent critic, Julius Stone, to entitle his 1977 book on the negotiations *Conflict Through Consensus*.

B. *Objective and Subjective Criteria*

What, according to the 1974 definition, was aggression? Article 1, upholding the U.N. Charter, stated: "Aggression is the use of armed force by a State against the sovereignty, territorial integrity or political independence of another State, or in any other manner inconsistent with the Charter of the United Nations, as set out in this Definition."[45] And Article 2 set out the criteria on which a determination of aggression could be made. This brought proponents of the priority principle into conflict with advocates of the Security Council's power to decide the issue. The dispute went unresolved, and Article 2 set out both views:

> The first use of armed force by a State in contravention of the Charter shall constitute *prima facie* evidence of an act of aggression although the Security Council may, in conformity with the Charter, conclude that a determination that an act of aggression has been committed would not be justified in the light of other relevant circumstances, including the fact that the acts concerned or their consequences are not of sufficient gravity.[46]

The priority principle was embodied in the opening words, "first use," but Security Council paramountcy was restored by the phrases "*prima facie* evidence" and "other relevant circumstances," which suggested that aggression could be determined by non-chronological criteria. The concluding *de minimis* clause excused the Security Council from taking action over what it deemed to be insufficiently important incidents. The American delegation was pleased with this outcome, cabling Washington that

> (a) "Prima facie evidence"... would result from first use of force only if this use of force was in contravention of the Charter. Language thus leaves totally unaffected the typical case in which there is question as to whether there was

---

[44] W. Michael Reisman, *The Cult of Custom in the Late 20th Century*, 17 CAL. W. INT'L. L.J. 133, 137–38 (1987).

[45] G.A. Res. 3314 (XXIX), *supra* note 41, annex, art. 1.

[46] *Id.*, annex, art. 2.

Charter violation. (b) Even in the case of a first use of force in violation of the Charter the Security Council could refrain from making a determination of aggression, after considering the "other relevant circumstances" of the case.[47]

C. The Acts of Aggression

The heart of the definition was Article 3, which set out an illustrative but non-exhaustive list of acts that qualified as acts of aggression. In summary, these acts were: invasion or attack; bombardment; blockade; attacks on land, sea, or air forces; overstay on another State's territory; use of another State's territory for attack on a third State; and the "sending by or on behalf of a State of armed bands."[48]

The Western States, which had insisted on reinforcing the primacy of Security Council determination in Article 2, were keen to ensure that Article 3 followed suit. Disagreement arose not only over the acts themselves, but how those acts should be introduced. The 1973 consolidated text, which provided the basis for the final negotiations in 1974, opened with the words: "Any of the following acts, regardless of declaration of war, shall constitute an act of aggression."[49] But this formula, with the imperative phrase "shall constitute," smacked of automaticity. Should a State operating under a Security Council mandate automatically be deemed an aggressor because, say, it blockaded a port? The Western States thought not. Late in the negotiations, the American delegate, Robert Rosenstock, made his move, insisting that the words, "shall ... constitute" be replaced with the weaker "shall ... qualify as" an act of aggression.[50] In the final version, Article 3 began: "Any of the following acts, regardless of a declaration of war, shall, subject to and in accordance with the provisions of article 2, qualify as an act of aggression."[51] The words "subject to and in accordance with the provisions of article 2" shackled Article 3 to

---

[47] U.S. Mission to the U.N. (Geneva) to State Department, Definition of Aggression Committee: Priority and Intent, 1973GENEVA02274 (May 15, 1973) (NATIONAL ARCHIVES AND RECORDS ADMINISTRATION ACCESS TO ARCHIVES DATABASE [U.S.]). Note, the American cables are written in telegraphese.

[48] G.A. Res. 3314 (XXIX), *supra* note 41, annex, art. 3(g).

[49] Rep. of the Special Comm. on the Question of Defining Aggression, Apr. 25–May 30, 1973, 28 U.N. GAOR, Supp. No. 19, app. A, art. 3, U.N. Doc. A/9019 (1973) [hereinafter Rep. of the Special Comm. on the Question of Defining Aggression, U.N. Doc. A/9019].

[50] U.N. Special Committee on the Question of Defining Aggression [...] Report of the United Kingdom Delegation (Steel Draft), FCO 58/820, at 8 (Apr. 1974) (THE NATIONAL ARCHIVES [U.K.]) (bracketed ellipses indicate abbreviated document titles throughout this Chapter).

[51] G.A. Res. 3314 (XXIX), *supra* note 41, annex, art. 2.

Article 2, subjecting the listed acts to Security Council determination, while the words "shall ... qualify" made clear that the acts did not *constitute* aggression, but merely *qualified as* possible aggression prior to determination.

Two of the seven listed acts of aggression aroused particular controversy. The first of these, Article 3(d), dealt with assaults on forces and fleets. In its final form it read, "[a]n attack by the armed forces of a State on the land, sea or air forces, or marine and air fleets of another State."[52] The British introduced the phrase "marine and air fleets of another State" at the 1973 session, ostensibly to alleviate Japan's concerns about potential assaults on its merchant fleet, and particularly its oil tankers. The use of the word "fleets" signaled that the acts under consideration involved more than isolated incidents or single vessels. The British delegate, Rodney Batstone, reported to the Foreign Office: "This naturally aroused the suspicion and also the opposition of certain Delegations that the purpose of this addition was to justify as self-defence naval protection to fishery vessels harassed by another state."[53] (This tongue-in-cheek comment alluded to the ongoing "Second Cod War" between Britain and Iceland, in which British trawlers received the protection of Royal Navy frigates while fishing in zones policed by the Icelandic Coast Guard.) Even so, the Foreign Office acknowledged that the coastal States had a point:

> The non-aligned ... have in some ways a legitimate interest in excluding distant-water fishing fleets from this formula, especially in the light of the gathering momentum behind the concept of the 200-mile exclusive economic zone at the Law of the Sea Conference. The Delegation should therefore explore alternative formulations which would allay fears that every interference with a fishing vessel could be taken as an act of aggression.[54]

The point was reiterated somewhat more forcefully by the Ecuadoran delegation, which reserved its position on "marine and air fleets" at the end of the negotiations. As delegate Mario Alemán explained, "it was a legitimate exercise of national sovereignty for a country to detain and impose penalties upon any foreign vessel or aircraft engaged in unlawful activities within its territorial waters or airspace."[55] Taking a rather different view, the Japanese

---

[52] *Id.*, annex, art. 3(d).
[53] Special Committee on the Question of Defining Aggression [...] Report of the United Kingdom Delegation, FCO 58/757, at 8 (May 1973) (THE NATIONAL ARCHIVES [U.K.]).
[54] Brief for the U.K. Delegation [...], FCO 58/820, at 5 (May 12, 1974) (THE NATIONAL ARCHIVES [U.K.]).
[55] Rep. of the Special Comm. on the Question of Defining Aggression, March 11–April 12, 1974, 29 U.N. GAOR, Supp. No. 19, at 15, U.N. Doc. A/9619 (1974) [hereinafter Rep. of the Special Comm. on the Question of Defining Aggression, U.N. Doc. A/9619].

delegate, Iguchi Takeo, stated that Japan attached importance to Article 3(d) "since such an attack on his country's fleet would be equivalent to a blockade of Japan's coast."[56] He added that while the provision was not intended to apply to minor or isolated incidents, he could not accept "a remedial measure taken by a coastal State which contravened international law."[57]

After the Special Committee had agreed on the definition, it was passed to the Sixth (Legal) Committee, where Article 3(d) once more encountered opposition from the coastal States. The Canadian delegate raised a reservation; Peru, Brazil, and India threatened an amendment; and China reserved its position. The British delegate Henry Steel tried to calm their nerves. He argued that nothing in the clause would prejudice decisions made about coastal States' jurisdiction over adjacent waters at the concurrent Law of the Sea Conference, or impugn legitimate enforcement actions in those waters.[58] At the same time he issued a threat: "It is totally unrealistic to think that we can start picking away at the individual components of the definition without a grave risk of bringing the whole structure crashing down."[59] Steel later reported that this speech had gone down well not only with fellow maritime powers such as the Soviet Union and the United States, but with some of the coastal States as well. This, he observed, "shows that you can fool all of the people some of the time."[60]

D. *The Debate over Proxies*

The debate over Article 3(g) on "indirect aggression" by armed bands proved to be even more troublesome. The essence of this provision, as one delegate pointed out, was that "a State may not do covertly what it may not do overtly."[61] The final version, harking back to the Turkish amendment of 1933, identified as a potential act of aggression: "[t]he sending by or on behalf of a State of armed bands, groups, irregulars or mercenaries, which carry out acts of armed force against another State of such gravity as to amount to the acts listed above, or its substantial involvement therein."[62]

---

[56] *Id.* at 16.

[57] *Id.*

[58] H. Steel, Statement delivered at Sixth Committee, FCO 58/820, at 6–7 (Oct. 15, 1974) (THE NATIONAL ARCHIVES [U.K.]).

[59] *Id.* at 8.

[60] Steel to Martin, FCO 58/820, at 1 (Oct. 16, 1974) (THE NATIONAL ARCHIVES [U.K.]).

[61] Rodney K. Batstone, United Kingdom Representative, Speech delivered at Sixth Committee, FCO 58/757, at 2 (May 29, 1973) (THE NATIONAL ARCHIVES [U.K.]).

[62] G.A. Res. 3314 (XXIX), *supra* note 41, annex, art. 3(g).

The difficulty with this provision is that different States had different relationships with proxies, some positive and some negative. As a British Foreign Office memorandum indicated,

> The Arabs are thinking of Palestine guerrillas; the Latin Americans are thinking of Castro-type subversion from outside; the Africans are thinking of "freedom fighters" although some of them are also themselves vulnerable to subversion (e.g. Sudan, Ethiopia, Ghana, Nigeria); the Italians are thinking of Alto Adige; the communists are thinking of alleged subversion of the satellites; Canada may think of Quebec; Asians may think of Chinese subversion; we have to think of Rhodesia and Northern Ireland.[63]

The States produced various formulae with different thresholds of state responsibility. In 1969, for example, the Soviets produced a permissive draft with a high threshold that defined indirect aggression as:

> The use by a State of armed force by sending armed bands, mercenaries, terrorists or saboteurs to the territory of another State and engagement in other forms of subversive activity involving the use of armed force with the aim of promoting an internal upheaval in another State or a reversal of policy in favour of the aggressor shall be considered an act of indirect aggression.[64]

This was designed to condemn States that actively *sent* armed bands, but not those that passively tolerated them operating from their territory. As the British noted of this draft: "It is carefully tailored to exclude Arab guerrillas (not use of force by a State) and catch alleged Western activity in Eastern Europe, e.g. which they said preceded the Soviet invasion of Czechoslovakia."[65]

By contrast, the Americans, helped by the British (who backed the Americans on this in return for support against provisions on self-determination), pushed hard for a low threshold of indirect aggression, covering not just active support for armed bands but also simple connivance in their activities. They had good reason for prioritizing this issue. First, they thought it likely that the U.S. Department of Defense would at some time need to respond to indirect uses of force with direct uses of force. If indirect aggression was listed, they could claim to be acting in self-defense; without it, their actions might be

[63] Steering Committee on International Organisations [...], FCO 58/757, at 12 (July 10, 1970) (THE NATIONAL ARCHIVES [U.K.]).
[64] Draft Proposal submitted by the Union of Soviet Socialist Republics, U.N. Doc. A/AC.134/L.12 (Feb. 26, 1969), *in* Rep. of the Special Comm. on the Question of Defining Aggression, U.N. Doc. A/9019, *supra* note 49, annex 1, at 8.
[65] Steering Committee on International Organisations [...], *supra* note 63.

deemed *prima facie* evidence of aggression under Article 2.[66] Second, they wanted to watch the backs of the Israelis carrying out reprisals against insurgents operating out of the Arab States.[67]

The Americans and British therefore campaigned for much stronger language than had appeared in the 1973 consolidated text, which read:

> The sending by or on behalf of a State of armed bands, groups, irregulars or mercenaries, which carry out invasion or attack involving acts of armed force against another State of such gravity as to amount to the acts listed above, or its open and active participation therein.[68]

They were particularly moved to change the phrase "open and active participation," which implied that covert and passive participation was acceptable. Alongside "sending" they tried to insert "organising or assisting" (or, on the initiative of Indonesia, a State also concerned about insurgency, "support").[69] They also tried to tack an additional phrase to the end of the text, which read: "or knowing acquiescence in organized activities within its own territory directed toward and resulting in the commission of such acts."[70] Finally, they tried to remove the *de minimus* clause, "of such gravity."[71] Most of these attempts came to nothing: the best they could manage was the replacement of "open and active participation" with "substantial involvement."[72] The motives for this flurry of activity did not escape the other delegates. The Mexican delegate, Francisco Correa, said:

> Article 3(g) could under no circumstances be interpreted as adding to the number of situations in which the right of self-defence in accordance with the Charter could be invoked. It would be counterproductive if a State could use that provision to invoke the right of self-defence if it used armed force against another State when acts of subversion or terrorism took place in its

---

[66] Special Committee on the Question of Defining Aggression [...] Report of the United Kingdom Delegation, *supra* note 53, at 8–9.

[67] Brief for the UK delegation [...], *supra* note 54, at 5–6.

[68] Consolidated Text of the Reports of the Contact Groups and of the Drafting Group, app. A, art. 3(g), U.N. Doc. A/AC.134/L.42 (May 28, 1973), *in* Rep. of the Special Comm. on the Question of Defining Aggression, U.N. Doc. A/9019, *supra* note 49, annex II.

[69] Brief for the UK delegation [...], *supra* note 54, at 6.

[70] Proposals submitted to the Working Group, app. B, U.N. Doc. A/AC.134/L.42 (May 28, 1973), *in* Rep. of the Special Comm. on the Question of Defining Aggression, U.N. Doc. A/9019, *supra* note 49, annex II.

[71] U.N. Special Committee on the Question of Defining Aggression [...] Report of the United Kingdom Delegation (Steel Draft), *supra* note 50, at 9.

[72] *Id.*

territory. The definition of aggression, instead of discouraging the use of armed force, would then serve to legitimize it.[73]

It should be noted that some of the negotiating positions on Article 3(g) and other articles were driven by extraordinarily short-sighted objectives. Late in the negotiations, for example, the British Foreign Office instructed their delegates to try to remove the word "armed" from the phrase "armed force" in Article 3(g) and elsewhere in the definition. This was because British delegates participating at the Helsinki-based Conference on Security and Cooperation in Europe did not want to make any concessions to the Soviet Bloc argument that U.N. Charter Article 2(4) referred to non-military as well as military force.[74] Back at the aggression negotiations, Henry Steel initially thought they might succeed in doing this, but only because some Non-Aligned delegates thought the word "force" without the word "armed" could be interpreted as economic and ideological as well as armed aggression. Not for long, though. As Steel recounted,

> [T]he Russians then got into the act and argued strenuously for the retention of the existing text. . . . I am not clear whether they realised what lay behind the point in our minds: the argument was being conducted by Federov but Kolesnik was sitting behind him at that stage and I would therefore guess that they knew what it was all about. From our point of view, of course, it would have been absolutely fatal to have revealed the true motives of our making the suggestion.[75]

Caught between the Non-Aligned States and the Soviets, the British abandoned this position.

E. A Non-Exhaustive Definition

Just as Article 2 was tightly linked with Article 3, so Article 3 was also tightly linked with Article 4, a little-heralded but crucially important part of the definition. In the final version, this stated that: "The acts enumerated above [in Article 3] are not exhaustive and the Security Council may determine that other acts constitute aggression under the provisions of the Charter."[76]

---

[73] Rep. of the Special Comm. on the Question of Defining Aggression, U.N. Doc. A/9619, *supra* note 55, annex I, at 39.

[74] Special Committee on the Question of Defining Aggression [. . .] Report of the United Kingdom Delegation (Steel Draft), *supra* note 50, at 5.

[75] Steel to Martin, FCO 58/820, at 2 (Apr. 15, 1974) (The National Archives [U.K.]).

[76] G.A. Res.3314 (XXIX), *supra* note 41, annex, art. 4.

The Soviets originally broached this idea in 1969,[77] and the other four Permanent Members of the Security Council quietly but firmly endorsed it. This was because Article 4 gave the Security Council *overriding* discretion over the determination of acts of aggression, whether they were listed in Article 3 or not. By the same token, the acts listed could not *automatically* be considered to be aggression; they were merely illustrative examples requiring Security Council confirmation before being elevated to that status. This was, of course, a crucial concession to Security Council power – and the dagger to the heart of the definition. A few, such as the Colombian delegate, hoped that Article 4 might be used to add new acts of aggression to the list.[78] But most other delegates recognized it for what it was: the price they had to pay for securing Security Council support for a consensus definition. As mute testimony to this collective understanding, Article 4 was rarely discussed during the negotiations, and scarcely mentioned in the concluding speeches (the usually voluble British and French delegates both said that "no comment" was required on it[79]). It seems that no one, not even the beneficiaries, wished to draw attention to the high cost paid by all for Security Council endorsement.

F. *Delinking Aggression and Crime*

The guiding principles of the definition were set out in Article 5, an omnibus three-clause text covering the consequences of aggression. The legacy of Litvinov's definition could be found in the first clause, which stated: "No consideration of whatever nature, whether political, economic, military or otherwise, may serve as justification for aggression."[80] And shades of U.S. Secretary of State Henry Stimson's contemporaneous non-recognition doctrine could be found in the third clause, which stated: "No territorial acquisition or special advantage resulting from aggression is or shall be recognized as lawful."[81]

The second clause, Article 5(2), was a source of substantial disagreement between, on the one hand, the Soviet Union and the Non-Aligned States, and on the other, the Western States. The Soviets, guided by the Brezhnev

---

[77] Draft Proposal submitted by the Union of Soviet Socialist Republics, *supra* note 64.

[78] Rep. of the Special Comm. on the Question of Defining Aggression, U.N. Doc. A/9619, *supra* note 55, annex I, at 27.

[79] H. Steel, Statement delivered at Sixth Committee, FCO 58/820, at 3 (Apr. 12, 1974) (THE NATIONAL ARCHIVES [U.K.]); Rep. of the Special Comm. on the Question of Defining Aggression, U.N. Doc. A/9619, *supra* note 55, at 22.

[80] G.A. Res. 3314 (XXIX), *supra* note 41, annex, art. 5(1).

[81] *Id.* art. 5(3).

Doctrine prohibiting satellites from making "aggressive" moves toward autonomy within the Eastern Bloc, insisted that the definition make reference to
aggression being a crime. So too did the Non-Aligned States, which were
seeking to strengthen their hand when it came to the anticipated reopening of
negotiations over an international criminal court. Britain, backed by the
United States, led the Western States' opposition to these proposals.

The battle lines were drawn early, with the Soviet and Non-Aligned States'
drafts inclined toward designating aggression a crime. But the early drafts were
not necessarily an accurate guide to the participants' priorities during the
negotiations. States will defend a few hard-and-fast positions, which they
cannot give up at almost any cost, but they will also be prepared to concede
less important points, which they use as bargaining chips in exchange for
concessions. They will therefore often open proceedings by proposing or
supporting an ideal draft, with some positions either under- or overstated to
allow concessions to be made further down the line. In the case of Article 5(2),
the Soviets and Non-Aligned States eventually negotiated away the reference
to acts of aggression being crimes, while the British and Americans defended it
to the last.

The "consolidated text," which formed the basis for the 1974 negotiations,
stated the relevant part as follows: "Aggression constitutes [...] against international peace giving rise to responsibility under international law."[82] In the
ensuing debates, some proposed filling the brackets with the words "a grave
violation," or "a crime," or "criminal violation."[83] Others proposed replacing
the text with the virtually meaningless phrase, "[a]ggression gives rise to
responsibility under international law," or having no provision at all.[84]

The final version was slightly longer, but managed to drain all meaning
from the idea that an act of aggression was a crime. It read:

> A war of aggression is a crime against international peace. Aggression gives
> rise to international responsibility.[85]

In the first sentence, the negotiators succumbed to British insistence that the
words "war of" be inserted before the word "aggression," ostensibly to bring the
draft in line with the Nuremberg Charter, but in effect narrowing the scope of
what could be deemed "a crime against international peace." This change

---

[82] Consolidated Text of the Reports of the Contact Groups and of the Drafting Group, *supra* note
68, app. A, art. 6.

[83] Contact Group 4, FCO 58/757, at 1 (May 23, 1973) (THE NATIONAL ARCHIVES [U.K.]).

[84] *Id.*

[85] G.A. Res. 3314 (XXIX), *supra* note 41, annex, art. 5(2).

acquired its full import when read in conjunction with Article 3, which listed various *acts* of aggression – the crucial word being "act" – such as invasion, bombardment, or blockade. In other words, the acts listed in Article 3 were not *wars* of aggression, and consequently could not be described as "a crime against international peace." The British also insisted on breaking the original sentence into two, the full stop severing the link between "crime" and "international responsibility."

The second sentence of Article 5(2) introduced deliberate ambiguity into the concept of "responsibility." The Western delegates wished to avoid any hint of individual criminal responsibility because this would reopen the debate about an international criminal court, and the British thus pressed for the insertion of the word "state" before "responsibility."[86] They lost this battle to the Soviets, who argued that the word "state" tipped the balance too far away from individual responsibility and thus prejudiced the future growth of international law.[87] The delegates finally compromised on the anodyne phrase "international responsibility," which, while mildly hinting at either international criminal jurisdiction or Security Council determination, was vague enough to satisfy everyone.

G. *New Bedfellows*

The debates over Articles 2 and 5(2) suggest that the Western and Soviet delegates were perpetually at loggerheads. On this occasion, though, appearances were deceptive. Détente was in the air, and behind the scenes the Soviets were working with the British and the Americans to iron out problems as they emerged. On March 8, 1974, for example, during negotiations in New York, the Soviet delegate Dmitri Kolesnik went to lunch with the American, William "Tap" Bennett. Kolesnik explained to Bennett that the Soviets "felt strongly about obtaining language on aggression as 'a crime,'" and he cautioned the Americans against pushing the Non-Aligned States too hard on indirect aggression and self-determination, as it might "spoil what appeared to be a good chance for agreement."[88] Bennett replied that the Americans would

---

[86] U.S. Mission to the U.N. (New York) to State Department, Definition of Aggression, 1974USUNN01169 (Apr. 6, 1974) (National Archives and Records Administration Access to Archives Database [U.S.]).

[87] U.K. Mission (New York) to FCO, FCO 58/820, at 2 (Apr. 4, 1974) (The National Archives [U.K.]).

[88] U.S. Mission to the U.N. (New York) to State Department, Definition of Aggression, 1974USUNN00812 (Mar. 8, 1974) (National Archives and Records Administration Access to Archives Database [U.S.]).

try to make their points as unprovocatively as they could, "but that we needed some progress on both these issues."[89]

Three weeks later, on April 1, Kolesnik met John Scali and the British delegate Henry Steel at another lunch. Scali reported that "Kolesnik stated that before he left Moscow he had been called in by [Foreign Minister] Gromyko and told of importance Gromyko attached to producing a definition."[90] Kolesnik pointed out to Scali and Steel that he had helped and would help the Western delegates, by, for example, "giving Arabs and Africans virtually no support in their opposition to indirect means ... and say[ing] nothing to stimulate Africans regarding self-determination."[91]

Steel enquired of Kolesnik whether the Soviets absolutely required the controversial "aggression is a crime" formulation. As the British reported back to the Foreign Office:

> Steel told him that we had no room to move on this point and warned him that, if we were pressed too hard on it, it might lead to a collapse of the whole exercise though we should then take care, of course, to see that this was not the only issue left unagreed. He asked Kolesnik to do what he could to prevent that situation arising. Kolesnik was surprisingly relaxed and sympathetic. He said he had difficulties with his political masters "who did not understand the legal issues involved" but that he would consider how he could help.[92]

The British delegation was genuinely concerned that the negotiations would stall unless Kolesnik could "turn the heat off."[93] Kolesnik managed it by cabling Moscow and securing instructions permitting him to accept "wars of aggression."[94] Yet Article 5(2) in its final form continued to stir debate as the draft definition made its way from the Special Committee to the Sixth Committee, compelling Steel to respond that

> [I]t would be a mistake to treat the paragraph as though it were a sort of mythic text, pregnant with hidden meanings.... There are no angels

---

[89] *Id.*

[90] U.S. Mission to the U.N. (New York) to State Department, Definition of Aggression – Soviet Conduct, 1974USUNN01071 (Apr. 1, 1974) (NATIONAL ARCHIVES AND RECORDS ADMINISTRATION ACCESS TO ARCHIVES DATABASE [U.S.]).

[91] *Id.*

[92] U.K. Mission (New York) to FCO, FCO 58/820, at 2 (Mar. 28, 1974) (THE NATIONAL ARCHIVES [U.K.]).

[93] *Id.*

[94] Definition of Aggression – Soviet Conduct, *supra* note 90.

dancing on the point of this needle. The paragraph means exactly what it says: no more and no less. Fanciful and speculative theories, based on *a contrario* interpretations ... really do not help.[95]

H. *The Self-Determination Exception*

While the Russians, Americans, and British were discussing their respective positions, it was clear that one outcome of this was to jointly exert pressure on the Non-Aligned States to abandon cherished positions. As John Scali reported back to Washington:

> Deloff [Scali] and Steel both suggested to Kolesnik that while his failure actively stir up trouble on sensitive issues was positive step toward agreed definition he would also need privately press Africans and Arabs not seek too much. Kolesnik acknowledged this but said he had to be careful since Starcevic (Yugo) and others spreading rumor US and USSR had agreed on text and were now slowly jamming it down throats. Comment: we have heard same rumors and Starcevic, Teymour (Egypt), Ceauscu (Romania) main instigators. . . . It clear that Kolesnik came to do a deal and he is making good faith efforts to meet our reasonable needs.[96]

The debate over Article 7 would show that these rumors about the Americans and Soviets "slowly jamming" their own pre-agreed definition down the throats of the Non-Aligned nations were not without foundation. In the discussion about this article, the Non-Aligned States insisted that those fighting for their own or for others' self-determination be exempt from the designation of aggression. The Western nations opposed this interpretation. The final article read:

> Nothing in this Definition, and in particular article 3, could in any way prejudice the right to self-determination, freedom and independence, as derived from the Charter, of peoples forcibly deprived of that right and referred to in the Declaration on Principles of International Law concerning Friendly Relations and Co-operation among States in accordance with the Charter of the United Nations, particularly peoples under colonial and racist régimes or other forms of alien domination; nor the right of these peoples to struggle to that end and to seek and receive support, in accordance with the

---

[95] H. Steel, Statement delivered at Sixth Committee, *supra* note 58, at 8–9.
[96] Definition of Aggression – Soviet Conduct, *supra* note 90.

principles of the Charter and in conformity with the above-mentioned Declaration.[97]

This article illustrates the differences between those who believed that dominated peoples and their foreign supporters could legitimately use armed force to bring about self-determination, and those who either did not believe this or did not wish to see it universally acknowledged. Both factions looked to the U.N. Charter: the Non-Aligned States to Article 1 (which upheld the self-determination of peoples), and the Western States to Article 2(4) (which precluded the threat or use of force against the territorial integrity or political independence of any State).

On the face of it, the Non-Aligned States' views on self-determination appear to be well represented. The word "struggle" apparently validated the use of force for liberationist ends (and earlier Western efforts to insert "by all legitimate means" after "struggle" were successfully rebuffed).[98] Furthermore, the reference to Article 3 suggests that invasion, bombardment, blockade, and so on, were not proscribed in this struggle. More specifically, the phrase "seek and receive support" appears to override Article 3's injunction against state support for rebel activities against another State. Finally, the repeated use of the word "right" rebuffed those Western States that had argued that there was no "right" of self-determination, and that it was merely a "principle."[99] From a different perspective, however, it appears that the Western delegates secured their objectives. The word "struggle" was not preceded by the word "armed," although some Non-Aligned delegates had campaigned for this. Moreover, the Western delegates insisted in linking the article to previous prescriptions on the use of force, which is why the U.N. Charter is mentioned on no fewer than three occasions. In addition, the West had demanded the insertion of the word "forcibly" before the word "deprived," thus denying the right of self-determination to those dominated by non-forcible means.[100]

The negotiations over Article 7 were particularly hard fought. At first, the Western delegates attempted to exclude self-determination from the definition altogether, and when it became apparent that the Non-Aligned States were not going to give way, they battled over each phrase. In April 1974, Stephen

---

[97] G.A. Res. 3314 (XXIX), *supra* note 41, annex, art. 7.

[98] U.S. Mission to the U.N. (New York) to State Department, Definition of Aggression, 1974USUNN01025 (Mar. 28, 1974) (NATIONAL ARCHIVES AND RECORDS ADMINISTRATION ACCESS TO ARCHIVES DATABASE [U.S.]).

[99] Brazil, United Nations Special Committee on Principles of International Law, at 11 (Feb. 22, 1966) (Ser. no. A1838/1, 938/11, Pt. 8, Annex, THE NATIONAL ARCHIVES OF AUSTRALIA [Austl.]).

[100] U.S. Mission to the U.N. (New York) to State Department, Definition of Aggression, 1974USUNN01169 (Apr. 6, 1974), *supra* note 86.

Schwebel cabled the delegates in New York to express his disquiet: "Despite usefulness of provisions on 'forcibly deprived' and 'by all legitimate means,' we remain discontent[ed] with proposed article," he wrote, because:

> (a) its inclusion in a definition of aggression clearly imports that "wars of liberation" are an exception from proscriptions against aggression; (b) the proposed draft cuts back on like provisions of the friendly relations definition ... (c) acceptance of proposed text may place increased burden upon USG [U.S. Government] efforts to exclude a like escape clause from revised conventions on law of war.[101]

He added: "Critical point is that, if we agree that revolutionary forces may receive support, we are saying in effect that what would be an aggressive act – lending such armed support – is not aggression because, in subjective judgment of some, support is being lent to a struggle in pursuit of self-determination."[102]

But the clashes between the Western and the Non-Aligned delegates masked an important fact: while all parties, with different degrees of enthusiasm, upheld the right of self-determination, none was *wholly* committed to it – not even the Non-Aligned States. By 1974 the decolonization struggle was drawing to an end. Many nations were grappling with post-independence realities such as the agitation of minorities for self-determination within their own borders. As a result, the Non-Aligned States had shifted their attention to economic inequality, and narrowed their focus to the "colonial and racist" pariahs: Portugal, South Africa, and Israel. (The emphasis on "peoples under colonial and racist régimes or other forms of alien domination"[103] hinted at this more limited set of priorities.) The Soviet Union, meanwhile, offered ready rhetorical support to struggles in Southern Africa and the Middle East, but obviously not to those within their own bloc – where they maintained a State's right to take "police action" against dissident movements.[104] And, finally, while the Western powers were willing to support the struggle for self-determination if it accorded with their own objectives – they too had their favored causes, such as those of South Korea, South Vietnam, and Israel – they were not prepared to open the door to unruly challenges to the global

---

[101] State Department to U.S. Mission to the U.N. (New York), Definition of Aggression, 1974STATE065434 (Apr. 1, 1974) (NATIONAL ARCHIVES AND RECORDS ADMINISTRATION ACCESS TO ARCHIVES DATABASE [U.S.]).
[102] *Id.*
[103] G.A. Res. 3314 (XXIX), *supra* note 41, annex, art. 7.
[104] Julius Stone, *Hopes and Loopholes in the 1974 Definition of Aggression*, 71 AM. J. INT'L. L. 224 (1977).

status quo. Given this collective ambivalence toward the unfettered struggle for self-determination, it is not unreasonable to assume that the stalemate embodied within Article 7 suited almost everyone. Equilibrium – if not actual consensus – was achieved after all.

The General Assembly adopted Resolution 3314 (XXIX), with its annexed Definition of Aggression, on December 14, 1974. Though praised by the delegates, it could hardly be heralded as a breakthrough. It merely declared that certain acts might qualify as aggression, and preserved the very thing that many of the small and middling powers were most interested in usurping: the Security Council's determinative powers. Instead of being an alternative, the definition was reduced to offering "guidance" to the Security Council – and neglected guidance at that.[105] As the delegate from New Zealand noted at the time, the definition was, when all was said and done, "a very small mouse to emerge from beneath such a mountain of work."[106]

V. THE INTERNATIONAL CRIMINAL COURT AND THE CRIME OF AGGRESSION

While the end of the Cold War led to a relaxation of the hostilities between the superpowers, it also hastened the disintegration of some of the smaller States, such as Yugoslavia and Somalia, on the peripheries of the old power blocs. This combination of factors revived interest in judicial solutions to problems that were proving unresponsive to U.N. mediation and peacekeeping efforts, such as "rogue" States, terrorism, and the drug trade. The result was the 1998 Rome Statute establishing the International Criminal Court, which had operative jurisdiction over three crimes – genocide, crimes against humanity, and war crimes – and nominal jurisdiction over the fourth, the "crime of aggression."[107] In June 2010, States Parties at the Kampala Conference agreed upon amendments to the Rome Statute designed to activate jurisdiction over aggression.[108] The Court could, in theory, begin to hear

---

[105] G.A. Res. 3314 (XXIX), *supra* note 41, ¶ 4 (recommending that the Security Council "should, as appropriate, take account of that Definition as guidance in determining, in accordance with the Charter, the existence of an act of aggression").

[106] N.Z. Mission to the U.N. (New York) to External Affairs (Wellington), ABHS 950 W5422 (Oct. 9, 1974) (Box 169, 111/29/1, Pt. 1, THE NATIONAL ARCHIVES OF NEW ZEALAND [N.Z.]).

[107] Rome Statute of the International Criminal Court art. 5, adopted on July 17, 1998, 2187 U.N.T.S. 91 (entered into force July 1, 2002) [hereinafter Rome Statute].

[108] Review Conference of the Rome Statute of the International Criminal Court, *The Crime of Aggression*, Res. RC/Res.6 (June 11, 2010), https://asp.icc-cpi.int/iccdocs/asp_docs/Resolutions/RC-Res.6-ENG.pdf.

cases against individuals for aggression sometime after 2017. The whole issue was highly contentious, however. The "included" States wished to uphold their prerogative, as members of the Security Council, to determine when aggression has occurred and how to respond to it. And the "excluded" States, in the course of pushing for a less politicized body to determine aggression, continued their campaign stretching back to the interwar decades to break the powerful States' stranglehold over the decision-making process.

Since Kampala, many commentators have focused either on the "compromise" in Article 15*bis*, which allows States to exempt themselves from jurisdiction over aggression, or on the first paragraph of Article 8*bis*, which defines a crime of aggression. Far fewer commentators have discussed the transplantation of the 1974 definition into Article 8*bis*. This article opens as follows:

1. For the purpose of this Statute, "crime of aggression" means the planning, preparation, initiation or execution, by a person in a position effectively to exercise control over or to direct the political or military action of a State, of an act of aggression which, by its character, gravity and scale, constitutes a manifest violation of the Charter of the United Nations.

2. For the purpose of paragraph 1, "act of aggression" means the use of armed force by a State against the sovereignty, territorial integrity or political independence of another State, or in any other manner inconsistent with the Charter of the United Nations. Any of the following acts, regardless of a declaration of war, shall, in accordance with United Nations General Assembly resolution 3314 (XXIX) of 14 December 1974, qualify as an act of aggression. . . .[109]

Thereafter, Article 8*bis* reproduces the list of seven illustrative acts from the 1974 definition, starting with invasion, bombardment, and blockade, and finishing with the sending of armed bands.

What conclusions might be drawn from this? As with previous examples, the current demand for a definition is both a response to a set of current problems arising from a unipolar world, and an anticipation of a new set of institutional arrangements encompassing multipolar forms of authority. At the same time, it represents a recurrence of the enduring pattern: the "excluded" States' attempts to challenge the powerful States' decision-making powers on aggression.

But the Kampala definition also breaks new ground. For one thing, it wrenches an old definition out of its intended domain regulating *state*

[109] *Id.*, annex I, art. 8*bis*(1)-(2).

conduct, and inserts it into another one governing *individual behavior*. This is an unorthodox step.[110] It is also contrary to the intent of those who negotiated the 1974 definition. As we have seen, they deliberately adopted a State-centric view. They did not just overlook personal criminal liability; they actively repudiated it. Some States' early drafts nodded in the direction of criminalizing acts of aggression (to put it no more strongly than that), but they abandoned these positions under pressure from Britain and the United States. The final version of Article 5(2), which severed the connection between "crime" and "acts of aggression," was intended to signal the rejection of future international criminal jurisdiction over aggression.

Not only that, but during the negotiations, States were highly vigilant about the wording of each act of aggression, making sure that no potential avenues to prosecution were opened up. For example, when discussing Article 3(e) on armed forces remaining in another State after the termination of an agreement, the British delegate Rodney Batstone noted that

> If we have another dispute with [Dom] Mintoff [leader of the Maltese Labour Party] about the presence of British forces and we do not remove them quickly enough for his liking, we should not wish to concede that he could prosecute the local commanding officer for crimes against the peace.[111]

Furthermore, States expressly avoided anything like the "planning, preparation, initiation" formula that appears in the first paragraph of Kampala's Article 8*bis*. For example, when addressing Article 3(g) on armed bands, the French delegate, Jean-Michel Bessou, stated for the record that "[u]ntil they had been dispatched, no act of aggression had occurred; the mere fact of organizing or preparing armed bands did not of itself constitute an act of aggression."[112] Given these examples, it is safe to say that had the authors of the 1974 definition been aware that the list would later be transplanted into a criminal jurisdiction, they would either have drafted a different list, or refused to participate in the negotiations at all.

In Article 8*bis*, however, the 1974 definition has been selectively filleted to include the seven acts of aggression, but to exclude the contextualizing material. This, too, is an audacious act. The carefully crafted relationship

---

[110] The only other example was Robert Jackson's unsuccessful attempt to add a definition of aggression (borrowed from the Convention for the Definition of Aggression, signed by the Soviet Union and other States on July 3, 1933) to the "crimes against peace" provision in the 1945 Nuremberg Charter.

[111] Batstone to Martin, FCO 58/757, at 3 (May 26, 1973) (THE NATIONAL ARCHIVES [U.K.]).

[112] Rep. of the Special Comm. on the Question of Defining Aggression, U.N. Doc. A/9619, *supra* note 55, at 22.

between Articles 2, 3, and 4 in the earlier definition – encompassing the idea that the Security Council exercised discretion over a non-exhaustive list of acts of aggression – was not transmitted into the new definition. But the ghosts of this old relationship still haunt the Kampala proposal. Take, for example, the idea set out in Article 4 that the enumerated acts of aggression were not exhaustive, and could not be imposed automatically. The definition in Article 8*bis*, stripped of this provision, does not indicate whether the list of acts is conclusive or just illustrative. There are two potential approaches to this problem. On one hand, it might be concluded that the list *is not* exhaustive, and admits the possibility of considering analogous forms of aggression. This would allow the Court, operating at the behest of the Security Council, to consider acts that, though manifestly in violation of the U.N. Charter, were not listed (or perhaps not envisaged) four decades ago. On the other hand, it might be assumed that the Article 8*bis* list *is* exhaustive, foreclosing the consideration of analogous unlisted acts. The first option chimes with the aim of giving international bodies the latitude to make determinations on all the facts; the second option accords with the principle of non-retroactivity set out Article 22 of the Rome Statute.[113] One cannot have both.

VI. CONCLUSION

Will demands for definitions of aggression continue to arise from deadlock and act as catalysts for change? Possibly not. During the modern era, powerful States have attempted to manage interstate conflict in very distinct ways, and this is expressed in specific legal forms. During the "European century" concluding with the First World War, power was manifested through the doctrines of belligerent and neutral rights. Because there was no legal stigma attached to aggression, there were no demands for its definition. During the ensuing "American century," power was articulated through the concepts of lawful and unlawful uses of force. This distinction naturally gave rise to demands for definitions of aggression. But as an "Asian century" beckons, one might expect different legal regimes to emerge for dealing with conflict. This process is far from complete; and law, being conservative, will only confirm, not precede, a new reality. But given many Asian States' frustrations with the U.N. system and lack of interest in international criminal jurisdiction, it is possible to predict a move away from the current approaches to uses of force – and perhaps an abandonment of the concept of aggression altogether.

---

[113] Rome Statute, *supra* note 107, art. 22.

6

International Humanitarian Law in an Age of Extremes

Unlawful Uses of Force by Non-State Actors

DAVID M. CRANE

I. INTRODUCTION

A good practice carried to an extreme and worked in accordance with the letter of the law becomes a positive evil.[1]

A military historian once remarked that the history of man is the history of war and the history of war is the history of man.[2] History tells us that peace is not the norm despite mankind's efforts to achieve lasting peace. For much of history, conflict has been a barbaric clash of wills with the strong prevailing. In large measure, good rarely triumphed over evil. Though early attempts were made to extend some type of civility to the battlefield, use of law and regulation in protecting combatants is a modern phenomenon.[3] Only in the past fifty years have we seen a comprehensive legal regime evolve that attempts to regulate conduct in conflict.[4]

Despite the establishment of the laws of armed conflict in the past century, modern conflict involves actors who do not follow any international norms and who ignore basic humanitarian principles.[5] The dirty wars of the twenty-first century will mirror conflict not seen since the Dark Ages. Actors in these

---

[1] Swami Vivekananda, *Chapter X: The Method and the Means*, COMPLETE WORKS OF SWAMI VIVEKANANDA, http://ramakrishnavivekananda.info/vivekananda/volume_3/bhakti-yoga/the_method_and_the_means.htm.

[2] *See generally* JOHN KEEGAN, A HISTORY OF WARFARE (1993).

[3] *Development of IHL*, AM. RED CROSS (Apr. 2011), www.redcross.org/images/MEDIA_CustomProductCatalog/m3640105_IHL_Development.pdf.

[4] *Development of Modern International Humanitarian Law*, INT'L COMM. OF THE RED CROSS (May 13, 2010), www.icrc.org/eng/who-we-are/history/since-1945/history-ihl/overview-development-modern-international-humanitarian-law.htm.

[5] *See generally* Jed Odermatt, *Between Law and Reality: 'New Wars' and Internationalised Armed Conflict*, AMSTERDAM L.F., Summer Issue 2013, at 19, http://amsterdamlawforum.org/article/view/321/494.

conflicts choose to use fear, terror, and suffering as a weapon of war, preying upon the most vulnerable members of society – mainly women and children.

The international community is not prepared to predict, prevent, and fight in these types of conflicts. Even though the development of law in this area has flourished and the jurisprudence from the various international tribunals has developed the ability to hold combatants who do not follow the rule of law on the battlefield accountable, conflict itself has moved backward in many parts of the world where the standard is "no quarter."[6] Kill or be killed is the new norm in this evolving century.

Along with this devolution in conflict, we see the world in extremes as the final visages of the fifty-year-long Cold War slide away into history. It can be argued that the twentieth century was almost a century-long conflict that historians have broken up into three wars: World War I, World War II, and the Cold War.

With this change, further subtle yet significant events have taken place. Though the concept of the nation-state continues to be a center of power, States are no longer *the* center of power.[7] The Westphalian model of power arrangements centered on the nation-state has changed since the fall of the Berlin Wall. Multinational actors are now players on the international stage.[8] Corporations, worldwide criminal syndicates, and even nongovernmental organizations are centers of power. The most compelling change in power is the power given to the individual. With the World Wide Web and the availability of information at the fingertips of everyone who has access to the Internet, all the knowledge of mankind is available to everyone. We will not know or fully appreciate this impact for some time. Additionally, social media has linked citizens around the world, passing on information at lightning speed while the nation-state is increasingly unable to control it.

Despite these changes, international organizations are changing and losing influence. The United Nations paradigm remains valid but is not influential. As influence shifts and expands, the Security Council now reflects the tensions between and political aspirations of three powers, China, Russia, and the United States.[9] With their veto power, this circumstance has neutralized the

---

[6]   *Customary IHL: Rule 46. Orders or Threats That No Quarter Will Be Given*, INT'L COMM. OF THE RED CROSS, www.icrc.org/customary-ihl/eng/docs/v1_rul_rule46.

[7]   *See generally* Eric A. Engle, *The Transformation of the International Legal System: The Post-Westphalian Legal Order*, 23 QUINNIPIAC L. REV. 23 (2004).

[8]   *Id.*

[9]   *See generally* Sahar Okhovat, The United Nations Security Council: Its Veto Power and Its Reform (Ctr. for Peace and Conflict Studies, Working Paper No. 15/1, 2011), https://sydney.edu .au/arts/peace_conflict/docs/working_papers/UNSC_paper.pdf.

U.N.'s ability to be a force for good not seen since the stasis stemming from the Cold War.

Long relied upon regional security arrangements are no longer valid. As the threats to international peace and security change, the old security arrangements that stemmed from the Cold War are losing their relevancy. The North Atlantic Treaty Organization (NATO) is a shell of itself, only influential because of the presence of the United States. European armies have little to no ability to exert power in Europe or elsewhere and are considered a nonthreat to potential adversaries.[10]

Europe is no longer a significant geopolitical player. For centuries, the center of geopolitical power revolved around Europe, but this is no longer a reality. The European Union remains one of the great geopolitical developments in the modern era, but as a player on the world stage, it only is significant economically.[11] Simply put, Europe has become a tourist destination.

International law is no longer a stabilizing influence. In this age of extremes with the increasing threat of non-state actors, international law is ignored in conflict.[12] The basic premise of law by consent is increasingly being challenged around the world. With this phenomenon comes a consequential weakening of accountability through international criminal law. Actors, both State and non-state, are simply stepping over principles that govern the international community.

All of this augurs poorly for the rule of law generally and the laws of armed conflict in particular. This Chapter will seek to establish an understanding that despite the challenges ahead, the rule of law is more powerful than the rule of the gun – and can be maintained.

This Chapter will start out broadly with a look at the twentieth century and how power centers have shifted. We will then consider the general principles of the laws of armed conflict, followed by a discussion of what can be called the age of accountability. The Chapter concludes with how non-state actors in

---

[10] *See generally* Robert Cooper, *The Goals of Diplomacy, Hard Power, and Soft Power, in* AMERICAN POWER IN THE 21ST CENTURY 167–80 (David Held & Mathias Koenig-Archibugi eds., 2004).

[11] *See generally* Desmond Dinan, *Fifty Years of European Integration: A Remarkable Achievement,* 31 FORDHAM INT'L L.J. 1118 (2007), http://ir.lawnet.fordham.edu/cgi/viewcontent.cgi?article=2111&context=ilj.

[12] *See generally* Mattias Kumm, *The Legitimacy of International Law: A Constitutionalist Framework of Analysis,* 15 EUR. J. INT'L L. 907 (2004), http://ejil.org/pdfs/15/5/397.pdf.

upcoming dirty wars challenge the general principles of the laws of armed conflict, yet with the assertion that the laws that govern conflict do not have to be changed, only followed.

II. POWER SHIFTS IN THE BLOODY TWENTIETH CENTURY

Approximately 262 million human beings died as a result of government actions during the twentieth century.[13] Of those, around 115 million died at the hands of totalitarian governments.[14] Even more startling, most of those victims died during the Cold War, which was one of the most destructive conflicts in history. How so?

World War I was a clash of empires struggling for dominance in Europe.[15] An unintended conflict, the war sucked in the rest of the world, including the United States, because the world was truly Eurocentric. The result of this tragic human event was the loss of the German, Austro-Hungarian, Russian, and Ottoman Empires.[16] Their loss left a power vacuum with consequences felt throughout the rest of the twentieth century. Politicians on both sides of the conflict struggled to shape and mold a political outcome that would allow what was left of Europe to move forward.

The Treaty of Versailles was an attempt to create a victor's justice ensuring the survival of the last two remaining empires, the British and French, and their hold on vast territories around the world.[17] The empires and countries who lost gathered together what was left of their governments, economies, and social structures and sought out new political directions – and an explanation they could give their citizens as to why they lost. Some moved forward and restructured from monarchies to republican forms of government. Through revolution, the Russian Empire became what would be called a Soviet State,

[13] R. J. Rummel, *20th Century Democide*, Univ. of Haw., www.hawaii.edu/powerkills/ 20TH.HTM. Up to 101 million human beings died as a result of the 313 armed conflicts from 1945 to 2008. *See* Christopher Mullins, *Conflict Victimization and Post-Conflict Justice 1945–2008*, in 1 The Pursuit of International Criminal Justice: A World Study on Conflicts, Victimization, and Post-Conflict Justice 67, 67 (M. Cherif Bassiouni ed., 2010). Of those, the largest amount of conflict casualties occurred during purely internal conflicts and instances of state repression, 64–69 million including 22 million in the USSR alone during the Cold War. *Id.* at 103–07.
[14] R. J. Rummel, *The Democratic Peace: A New Idea*, Univ. of Haw., www.hawaii.edu/ powerkills/POLSYS.ART.HTM.
[15] *World War One: 10 Interpretations of Who Started WWI*, BBC News (Feb. 12, 2014), www.bbc .com/news/magazine-26048324.
[16] *Overview of World War I*, Dig. History, www.digitalhistory.uh.edu/era.cfm?eraid=12.
[17] Ruti G. Teitel, Globalizing Transitional Justice 83 (2014).

centered on an economic theory called communism. In the end, however, that use of the theory was only a power grab by an oligarchic group of individuals who perpetrated one of the great atrocities and frauds ever seen in history.[18]

Though seemingly a democratic government, the remnants of the old Ottoman Empire (Turkey) formed around a strongman and sought a scapegoat for the loss of their empire – the Christian Armenians.[19] The Armenian genocide lasted for several years and destroyed a large percentage of the Armenian people.[20] This was the first horrific result of the First World War. More atrocities would follow to be sure.

Over the next decade, mankind sought to create a world peace through the League of Nations and even outlaw war in the Kellogg–Briand Pact.[21] Neither was effective as various nations rearmed.[22] A humiliated Germany sulked and tried out democracy during the Weimar Republic.[23] Ironically, it was this very concept of democracy that would see a right-wing nationalist come to power on the political platform of restoring Germany to its rightful place in Europe and the world as well as correcting the wrongs stemming from the Versailles Treaty.[24]

Once in power Adolf Hitler began his dream of a thousand-year Reich that would result in a Second World War.[25] This conflict would see the destruction of an estimated 50–70 million human beings and the largest genocidal event in history – the attempted elimination of all the Jews of Europe.[26] During these dark five years the rule of law was pushed aside once again

[18] *See generally Lenin and the First Communist Revolutions, I*, MUSEUM OF COMMUNISM, http://econfaculty.gmu.edu/bcaplan/museum/hisfram1.htm.

[19] John Kifner, *Armenian Genocide of 1915: An Overview*, N.Y. TIMES, www.nytimes.com/ref/timestopics/topics_armeniangenocide.html.

[20] *Id.*

[21] *Kellogg–Briand Pact*, ENCYCLOPAEDIA BRITANNICA, www.britannica.com/event/Kellogg-Briand-Pact.

[22] *Id.*

[23] Paul Bookbinder, *Why Study Weimar Germany?*, FACING HIST. & OURSELVES, www.facinghistory.org/weimar-republic-fragility-democracy/readings/why-study-weimar-germany.

[24] It must be pointed out that on the other side of the world Japan began to develop a plan called the Greater Co-Prosperity Sphere that would eventually see almost all of Asia engulfed into the Japanese Empire.

[25] *See generally* Roger Moorhouse, *Germania: Hitler's Dream Capital*, HIST. TODAY, Mar. 2012, www.historytoday.com/roger-moorhouse/germania-hitlers-dream-capital.

[26] World War II: In Depth, U.S. HOLOCAUST MEM'L MUSEUM, www.ushmm.org/wlc/en/article.php?ModuleId=10007314; Bruce Robinson, *World War Two: Summary Outline of Key Events*, BBC (Mar. 30, 2011), www.bbc.co.uk/history/worldwars/wwtwo/ww2_summary_01.shtml; *By The Numbers: World-Wide Deaths*, NAT'L WWII MUSEUM, www.nationalww2museum.org/learn/education/for-students/ww2-history/ww2-by-the-numbers/world-wide-deaths.html.

while nations fed on each other in an attempt to achieve world domination or to counter such attempts. Fear and despair were the ruling human emotions.[27]

At the end of World War II the world order was forever changed. The last two empires were finished. Britain and France would never recover from the losses. Despite the failure of the League of Nations, the international community joined together one more time and created the United Nations paradigm – to settle disputes peaceably, resorting to the use of force only as a last resort.[28] Additionally, the four Allied Powers chose to use the rule of law in holding accountable at Nuremberg and Tokyo those who perpetrated the conflict's horrors – the first-ever attempt by mankind and the cornerstone for future modern international criminal tribunals and courts.[29] Additionally, the world entered the nuclear era after the creation of atomic and hydrogen weapons that did and would continue to threaten the destruction of whole peoples. Despite this, would the world now resort to the rule of law as a governing principle to maintain and restore international peace and security?

The answer was not really. Split in two by emerging power centers, the world slid slowly into the morass that was the Cold War, the third global conflict of the twentieth century.[30] Arguably the most destructive of the three conflicts, the Cold War gave the appearance of a "peaceful" standoff under the madness of the concept called "mutually assured destruction," yet in the darker corners of the world governments were destroying their own citizens by the tens of millions.[31] Protected by either the United States or the Soviet Union, dictators and thugs were allowed to do whatever they felt was necessary to govern and maintain power as long as they were aligned with one of the superpowers.

The important work completed by the international community during the first four years after World War II was thus negated or at least neutralized. The principles laid down by Nuremberg, the United Nations Charter, the Universal Declaration of Human Rights, the Genocide Convention, and the Geneva Conventions were pushed aside as both centers of political power struggled in a death grip for world influence.

These important principles would not be realized until after the Soviet Union dissolved and the Berlin Wall came down. Power shifted back to the

---

[27] *See generally* MAX HASTINGS, INFERNO: THE WORLD AT WAR, 1939–1945 (2011).
[28] *Maintain International Peace and Security*, UNITED NATIONS, www.un.org/en/sections/what-we-do/maintain-international-peace-and-security/.
[29] *Milestones: 1945–1952: The Nuremberg Trial and the Tokyo War Crimes Trials (1945–1948)*, U.S. DEP'T OF STATE, https://history.state.gov/milestones/1945-1952/nuremberg.
[30] *Cold War*, ENCYCLOPAEDIA BRITANNICA, www.britannica.com/event/Cold-War.
[31] R. J. Rummel, *How Many Did Communist Regimes Murder?* UNIV. OF HAW., www.hawaii.edu/powerkills/COM.ART.HTM.

United Nations paradigm and a "new world order." How little did the international community understand what that world order would become – not the democratic peace diplomats hoped for and academics lauded.

III. REGULATING CONFLICT AND ACCOUNTABILITY

As stated, in the middle of the bloody twentieth century, 1945–1949, the world paused after World War II to establish principles that have become the cornerstone of a new world order to restore international peace and security, using force only as a last resort.[32] These principles would eventually form the legal basis for modern international criminal law.

The International Military Tribunals in Nuremberg and Tokyo were groundbreaking efforts to hold accountable those leaders who perpetrated the recent conflict and brought about the subsequent deaths of 50–70 million human beings.[33] New international crimes were laid out based largely on customary international law. The leaders of Germany and Japan were charged with war crimes, crimes against humanity, and crimes against peace.[34] These laws and legal principles were adopted by the new United Nations General Assembly as the Nuremberg Principles.[35]

The United Nations was established with the hope that mankind and the nations of the world could settle their disputes peaceably.[36] Use of force became a last resort. This marker laid down in 1945 still stands today as the standard by which we deal with threats to international peace and security. For the first time mankind had formed a political, legal, and practical way to avoid war and conflict. Coupled with the Nuremberg Principles of accountability, the rule of law was established as the paradigm as to how the international community governed itself.

In 1948 the Universal Declaration of Human Rights declared simply that human beings have a legal right to exist.[37] This simple concept allowed the United Nations to establish future tribunals to prosecute as criminals those who violated that right to exist.[38] One of the most important and compelling

---

[32] UNITED NATIONS, *supra* note 28.

[33] U.S. DEP'T OF STATE, *supra* note 29.

[34] *Id.*

[35] G.A. Res. 95 (I), Affirmation of the Principles of International Law recognised by the Charter of the Nüremberg Tribunal, U.N. Doc. A/RES/1/95 (Dec. 11, 1946).

[36] UNITED NATIONS, *supra* note 28.

[37] G.A. Res. 217 (III) A, Universal Declaration of Human Rights, U.N. Doc. A/810 (Dec. 10, 1948).

[38] *Id.*

instruments of the twentieth century, this Declaration further established the rule of law for the modern era.

One year later the international community adopted the Genocide Convention as well as the Geneva Conventions. The Genocide Convention is the first treaty to outlaw the crime of crimes: the destruction of a people in whole or in part.[39] The Geneva Conventions took all of existing customary international law and related international instruments and codified those principles into rules by which we protect individuals found on the battlefield – the wounded and sick, prisoners of war, as well as civilians.[40] The Geneva Conventions, along with the Hague Rules and other treaties that limit or ban certain methods or weapons of war comprise the law of armed conflict (LOAC).[41]

These important rule-of-law principles of accountability, settling disputes peaceably, protecting the rights of human beings, outlawing genocide, and protecting individuals found on the battlefield were largely forgotten and certainly politically neutered as the world plunged into the Cold War, a forty-five year ideological struggle for world domination by the Soviet Union. The relative "peace" of the Cold War era was superficial as the West and capitalism faced down the Soviet Union and communism. The deadlock between the Soviet Union and the other three permanent members of the United Nations Security Council neutralized any effective ability to uphold the aforementioned principles, and leaders of brutal governments were assured immunity from prosecution. The Berlin Wall was the symbol of that cynical time.

When the Berlin Wall was pulled down, signaling the beginning of the end of the Soviet Union, the world hoped that this was the start of what President George H. W. Bush called the beginning of a new world order.[42] He was right, but his implied meaning of a world of democratic peace was a pipe dream. It was a new world order that would plunge the world into chaos.

---

[39] Convention on the Prevention and Punishment of the Crime of Genocide, Dec. 9, 1948, 78 U.N.T.S. 277.

[40] *The Geneva Conventions of 1949 and their Additional Protocols*, INT'L COMM. OF THE RED CROSS (Oct. 29, 2010), www.icrc.org/eng/war-and-law/treaties-customary-law/geneva-conventions/overview-geneva-conventions.htm.

[41] Transcripts and summaries of presentations at *The Law of Armed Conflict: Problems and Prospects*, CHATHAM HOUSE (April 18–19, 2005), www.chathamhouse.org/sites/files/chathamhouse/public/Research/International%20Law/ilparmedconflict.pdf.

[42] Stephen Knott, *George H. W. Bush: Foreign Affairs*, UNIV. OF VA., http://millercenter.org/president/biography/bush-foreign-affairs.

The first genocide since World War II was perpetrated in the Balkans, followed shortly by the horrific genocide in Rwanda, both within several years of the beginning of this new world order. Despite the political dust surrounding these events, the international community responded in an unusual way – it created mechanisms to hold those who were responsible for committing international crimes, war crimes, crimes against humanity, and genocide accountable. These *ad hoc* tribunals, called the International Criminal Tribunal for the former Yugoslavia and the International Criminal Tribunal for Rwanda, were created under Chapter VII of the United Nations Charter.[43] New statutes were drafted that began what is now modern international criminal law.

During this time frame, discussion began about establishing once again a permanent international criminal court. This dream of decades was realized in Rome in 1998, when the new International Criminal Court was established.[44] Additionally, the United Nations and Sierra Leone created a new international hybrid tribunal called the Special Court for Sierra Leone to hold accountable those who bore the greatest responsibility for war crimes and crimes against humanity during the civil war that devastated vast regions of West Africa from 1991–2002.[45]

Thus began what some called an "age of accountability." For the first time in history the international community created mechanisms to hold accountable those who targeted their own citizens and the citizens of other countries. This hopeful development was almost derailed when four planes were flown into three buildings in the United States in 2001, causing the only superpower to enter into its own "war on terror," slipping down a dark slope of torture, death, secret camps, and unlawful killing.

IV. UNLAWFUL USES OF FORCE: THE AGE OF EXTREMES AND KALEIDOSCOPIC CONFLICT

It is not clear whether our culture can ever develop sufficient knowledge, rigor, imagination, and humility to grasp the phenomenon of [ISIS]. But for now, we should admit that we are not only horrified but baffled.[46]

---

[43] *See generally Impact of the Yugoslav and Rwanda Tribunals: Lessons for the International Criminal Court*, Int'l Ctr. for Transitional Justice (Nov. 30, 2009), www.ictj.org/news/impact-yugoslav-and-rwanda-tribunals-lessons-international-criminal-court-0.

[44] *About the Court*, Int'l Criminal Court, www.icc-cpi.int/about?ln=en.

[45] Residual Special Court for Sierra Leone, www.rscsl.org/.

[46] Anonymous, *The Mystery of ISIS*, N.Y. Review Books (Aug. 13, 2015), www.nybooks.com/articles/2015/08/13/mystery-isis/.

As the Wall was coming down and the Soviet Union was dissolving, the United States fought with several dozen allies from around the world in what may possibly be the last industrial-age conflict – Operation Desert Storm. Using the latest information-age technology and new weapon systems, the U.S.-led coalition destroyed Saddam Hussein's Iraqi Army in a mere one hundred hours.[47] Shortly after this astonishing victory that very same information-age army found itself fighting a few hundred Somali insurgents/ rebels armed with crude weapons in Operation Restore Hope *and lost*.[48] This was the first dirty war of a new upcoming century, and the world's only superpower was completely unprepared to handle the nuances of tribal warfare waged by non-state actors.[49] This is the conflict of the future and to date we still have not developed any capability to handle such a fight.

Conflicts are evolving into uncivilized events. During Operation Desert Storm the allies took in around 70,000 prisoners of war.[50] All were processed and cared for according to the Geneva Conventions. All of the combatants were lawful combatants, carrying arms openly, with a fixed and distinct insignia, following a chain of command who followed the laws of armed conflict.[51] This conflict may be the last conflict that was civilized (as much as combat can be civilized). Persons found on the battlefield were largely protected, though there were incidents where the Iraqi forces abused their prisoners.

The twenty-first century thus far has shown that in large measure conflict has become uncivilized with little adherence to the rule of law. The attacks on September 11, 2001, were unprovoked terrorist events on unsuspecting civilians. From there the United States chose a darker approach to dealing with the perpetrators and those individuals, organizations, and countries that supported them in a misguided "war on terror." A country that historically did choose to follow the laws of armed conflict now characterized them as "quaint" and not relevant, declaring that "the rules have changed."[52] In places

---

[47] *Operation Desert Storm*, U.S. HISTORY, www.ushistory.org/us/60a.asp.

[48] *Operation Restore Hope*, GLOB. SEC., www.globalsecurity.org/military/ops/restore_hope.htm.

[49] *Id.*

[50] *See* John F. Bilbo, *Enemy Prisoners of War (EPW) Operations During Operation Desert Storm* ii (USAWC Military Studies Program Paper, 1992), www.dtic.mil/dtic/tr/fulltext/u2/ a251209.pdf; James F. Gebhardt, *The Road to Abu Ghraib: US Army Detainee Doctrine and Experience* 83 (Global War on Terrorism Occasional Paper No. 6, 2005), http://www.au.af.mil/ au/awc/awcgate/army/csi_gebhardt_road.pdf.

[51] *Id.*

[52] Memorandum from George J. Tenet, Dir. of Central Intelligence, Subj: We're at War (Sept. 16, 2001), http://nsarchive.gwu.edu/news/20051209/at_war.pdf ("All the rules have changed."); Memorandum from Alberto Gonzales, White House Counsel, Subj: Decision RE

like Guantanamo, Abu Ghraib, Bagram Air Base, in unknown or unnamed secret prisons throughout Europe and the Middle East, America changed the way civilians, prisoners of war, and others were treated in conflict. Torture was the rule, not the exception if at all. Until September 2001, the United States never tortured; after those attacks the United States went over to the dark side.

Today, in other places around the globe, internal armed conflicts rage with no regard for the rule of law: South Sudan, Burundi, Georgia, the Crimea, Colombia, Guatemala, Eastern Ukraine, Yemen, Sri Lanka, and of course the Levant region of the Middle East, Iraq, and Syria. In the so-called age of accountability, we see little accountability as tens of thousands of civilians are killed and many more become refugees. The number of refugees today fleeing conflict or other strife is as large as those in and around World War II.[53]

Combatants are increasingly criminal. In many of these internal armed conflicts the actors are criminals and unlawful combatants. Up to and including Operation Desert Storm, there were few unlawful combatants found on the battlefields of the twentieth century. Though there were exceptions in various jungles of Southeast Asia and Central America, most individuals found in combat were lawful.[54] That certainly has changed where the majority of combatants are now unlawful, hence criminal. There is no combatant immunity for these individuals and they can be prosecuted for their conduct either by the State they are operating in or by another State willing and able to prosecute them.[55] This is not happening.

Respect for the laws of armed conflict is diminishing or nonexistent as this criminal element of conflict increases. Because of this increased criminality found on the battlefield the laws of armed conflict are neither taught nor followed in the dirty wars of this new century. It is a free-for-all in which terror, torture, and sheer violence rule the day.

Conflicts are less political with uncertain origin and scope. These conflicts are never just nor justifiable under law. Though politically driven, at times conflict is being shaped by new, even unheard factors such as personal gain,

---

Application of the Geneva Convention on Prisoners of War to the Conflict with al Qaeda and the Taliban (Jan. 25, 2002) (draft), www.gwu.edu/~nsarchiv/NSAEBB/NSAEBB127/02.01.25.pdf ("In my judgment, this new paradigm renders obsolete Geneva's strict limitations on questioning of enemy prisoners and renders quaint some of its provisions . . .").

[53] Adrian Edwards, Leo R. Dobbs, ed., *World Refugee Day: Global forced displacement tops 50 million for first time in post-World War II era*, UNITED NATIONS HIGH COMMISSIONER FOR REFUGEES (June 20, 2014), www.unhcr.org/53a155bc6.html.

[54] DAVID GALULA, COUNTERINSURGENCY WARFARE: THEORY AND PRACTICE (2006).

[55] Knut Dörmann, *The Legal Situation of "Unlawful/Unprivileged Combatants,"* 85 INT'L R. RED CROSS 45 (2003), www.icrc.org/eng/assets/files/other/irrc_849_dorman.pdf.

greed, influence, intolerance, and terror. These factors creep out of nowhere, suddenly, or explode after simmering for decades. The results end up in an atrocity devolving into ungovernable combat.

The combatants are mere pawns in a deadly criminal enterprise. Many of the actors in these conflicts are part of non-state criminal activity with little understanding of why they are fighting. They run amok destroying all that is around them on orders of criminals fighting for, in large measure, their individual criminal gain.

Conflicts are less national and more regional. Though States are involved or are caught up in these various conflicts, the true actors owe little or no allegiance to any State and operate without borders, crossing back and forth at random attacking all who oppose their uncertain or unknown objectives. Whole regions become consumed as the conflict ebbs and flows across a region that is reluctant to be a part of the action. The so-called Islamic State of Iraq and Syria (ISIS) is the perfect example of this new combatant/actor found on the battlefield: criminal, brutal, unlawful, and using tactics that are tantamount to international crimes.

We are not prepared to handle such conflict. The international community has not seen the likes of this since the Middle Ages, and our rule-of-law-based societies have no answer to the threat. Our state-centric, Westphalian approach to world order has no influence on the non-state actors, criminals, terrorists, and misguided thugs who now perpetrate conflict. The idea of settling disputes peacefully and only using force as a last resort is abhorrent to their methods of interaction with others. International peace and security run counter to their aims.

The results are kaleidoscopic in nature.[56] *Where one thing changes in a crisis or conflict everything changes.* The premise is that in solving a problem regarding the past, there is a certainty in understanding that the more things change the more they remain the same. As to the present there is a predictability – things are changing and we react to these changes using the past as solution models. The future problems may be solvable in the old planning cycle, yet things are now kaleidoscopic ... one thing changes and all things change; there are no solution models.

The dilemma is that organizational theory and planning are based on lessons learned and past experience. We look back to learn lessons and plan forward based on the past. Our problem-solving process focuses on solutions and end-states. Set-piece warfare and current doctrine related to that type of

[56] David M. Crane, *Kaleidoscopic Warfare Theory* (forthcoming).

warfare are based on this planning process. Yet geopolitical events and twenty-first century conflict are evolving quickly beyond this deliberate planning cycle into unimaginable circumstances where none of the above matters. The result is uncertainty and unpredictability, rendering planning obsolete, causing doctrinal failures, confused reaction, and leading to unexpected outcomes and even failure ... and kaleidoscopic change.

Is there a solution – a fix? Even trying to solve the dilemma makes us fall into the kaleidoscopic trap. Currently there are no base models to solve. Current and even future planning and scenario-driven solutions need to be questioned. At this point an awareness that kaleidoscopic conflict may be the future is a start – a new lens through which to view these challenges. By this awareness, considerate discussion may point to a workable and perhaps sustainable result. *We may have to accept that there is no solution. At the end of the day we may only be able to manage international peace and security, not restore that peace and security.*

Are we really entering a new paradigm in which we can only manage international peace and security? With the current standoff between the three powers that have the real strength to impose their will on the international community, China, Russia, and the United States, the United Nations may not be able to build a consensus to act when one or two of the three permanent members of the Security Council refuses to cooperate. Sensing this new world "disorder," non-state actors around the world now have an opening to move forward with their agendas. We now see the likes of terrorist groups, international criminal cartels, gun runners, commodity dealers, as well as rogue States flourishing and clearly upsetting peace and security.

Boko Haram, al-Qaeda, ISIS, Hezbollah, and criminal or insurgent groups such as the Sinaloa cartel, Lord's Resistance Army, and Forces Démocratiques pour la Libération du Rwanda (FDLR) are wreaking havoc across the globe and there is little ability in the international community through the United Nations or regional security coalitions to deal with their threats. Terror, murder, mutilation, maiming, pillaging, and plunder are the new weapons of the dirty wars that the international community will have to deal with and account for.

Yet these methods of war fly in the face of international norms. The Westphalian model simply can't counter this new paradigm without resorting to extreme methods that could cause a diminution of the rule of law. The reaction by the United States to the attacks by al-Qaeda on that fateful September day in 2001 is a good example of throwing out the rules, making torture and inhumane treatment, as well as violations of civil liberties of all Americans, a new norm in fighting its so-called "war on terror." The more we react this way to violations or the ignoring of the rule of law by non-state actors the more we step away from the very international norms the international community has tried to adhere to these many decades. Given this reaction by the United States, a nation which once followed the rule of law, one can certainly understand why some are saying that Osama bin Laden succeeded in his attacks against the West by causing the United States to throw out the law and use the very methods terrorists use to gain an advantage in conflict.

V. CONCLUSION

Patient diplomacy backed by flexible and adaptable military capability centered on the rule of law can maintain, manage, and even restore international peace and security. The United States, Europe, and other nation-states that adhere to the rule of law must maintain that generalized course. The laws of armed conflict have the capacity to deal with the actions of non-state actors in the future. The key to success is avoiding, managing, and identifying future stresses that can lead to conflict and taking those stresses away. Much of those stresses are the result of domestic social and economic factors that can be addressed in a medium and long-term strategy. The use of force does not prevent these kaleidoscopic dirty wars.

Retired General Stanley McChrystal is correct when he states:

> In the time it took us to move a plan from creation to approval, the battlefield for which the plan had been devised would have changed. By the time it could be implemented, the plan – however ingenious in its initial design – was often irrelevant. . . .

> The key lies in shifting our focus from *predicting to reconfiguring*. By embracing humility – recognizing the inevitability of surprises and unknowns – and concentrating on systems that can survive and indeed benefit from such surprises, we can triumph over volatility.[57]

---

[57] STANLEY MCCHRYSTAL, TEAM OF TEAMS 69, 80 (2015).

PART II

Mechanisms for Restraining the Unlawful Use of Force and Enhancing Accountability

7

Commissions of Inquiry and the *Jus ad Bellum*

CATHERINE HARWOOD AND LARISSA VAN DEN HERIK

I. INTRODUCTION

Commissions of inquiry are not among the protagonists within the *jus ad bellum* architecture. Nonetheless, historically, several international commissions have been established in different institutional settings specifically to inquire into situations involving the use of force. These include the Dogger Bank Inquiry into Russian firing at a U.K. trawler,[1] the Lytton Inquiry regarding Japanese military action in Manchuria in 1931,[2] and the 1961 Red Crusader Inquiry into a naval incident involving the United Kingdom and Denmark.[3] A few contemporary commissions have also addressed *jus ad bellum* questions, even if not all were explicitly mandated to do so. These contemporary inquiries include international commissions established by the U.N. Security Council,[4] Secretary-General,[5] and

---

[1] Dogger Bank Inquiry, established by St. Petersburg Declaration on November 12, 1904. *Report of the Commissioners, drawn up in accordance with Article VI of the declaration of St. Petersburgh of the 12th (25th) November, 1904 (Great Britain v. Russia), reprinted in* 2 AM. J. INT'L L. 931 (1908).

[2] Commission of Enquiry, established by Council Resolution on December 10, 1931. *Report of the Commission of Enquiry*, League of Nations Doc. C.633.M.320 (1932).

[3] Red Crusader Inquiry, established by Exchange of Notes between the Government of the United Kingdom of Great Britain and Northern Ireland and the Government of the Kingdom of Denmark Establishing a Commission of Enquiry to Investigate Certain Incidents Affecting the British Trawler "Red Crusader," U.K.- Den., Nov. 15, 1961.

[4] Commission of Inquiry in connection with the Republic of the Seychelles, established by S.C. Res. 496, U.N. Doc. S/RES/496 (Dec. 15, 1981); Security Council Commission on Angola, established by S.C. Res. 571, U.N. Doc. S/RES/571 (Sept. 20, 1985).

[5] *See, e.g.*, Secretary-General's Panel of Inquiry on the 31 May 2010 Flotilla Incident, established pursuant to U.N. Secretary-General, Letter dated Aug. 2, 2010, from the Secretary-General addressed to the President of the Security Council, U.N. Doc. S/2010/414 (Aug. 3, 2010).

Human Rights Council (HRC);[6] regional commissions[7] and national commissions.[8] The Human Rights Council in particular has been very active lately in establishing commissions of inquiry. Despite the identity of their parent body, the HRC commissions have generally made reference to areas of law beyond human rights, particularly international humanitarian law and international criminal law.

Given their direct engagement with law, commissions of inquiry have loosely been characterized as a new form of adjudication[9] offering some accountability prospects. As these commissions tend to operate in peace and security contexts, this Chapter assesses the current and potential role of commissions of inquiry in the overall legal framework regarding the use of force. The Chapter aims to locate commissions of inquiry within the greater *jus ad bellum* architecture. It portrays the diversity of the inquiry landscape and zeroes in on the Kosovo and Iraq Inquiries as concrete examples of inquiry practice operating in situations that evoked fundamental *jus ad bellum* questions. The Chapter also offers thoughts on the accountability potential of commissions of inquiry and on how they relate to other *jus ad bellum* actors.

[6] *See, e.g.*, Commission of Inquiry on Lebanon, established by Human Rights Council Res. S-2/1, The Grave Situation of Human Rights in Lebanon Caused by Israeli Military Operations, U.N. Doc. A/HRC/RES/S-2/1 (Aug. 11, 2006) [hereinafter Lebanon Commission]; U.N. Fact-Finding Mission on the Gaza Conflict, established by Human Rights Council Res. S-9/1, The Grave Violations of Human Rights in the Occupied Palestinian Territory, Particularly Due to the Recent Israeli Military Attacks Against the Occupied Gaza Strip, U.N. Doc. A/HRC/RES/S-9/1 (Jan. 12, 2009) [hereinafter Goldstone Commission]; International Fact-Finding Mission to Investigate Violations of International Law Resulting from the Israeli Attacks on the Flotilla of Ships Carrying Humanitarian Assistance, established by Human Rights Council Res. 14/1, The Grave Attacks by Israeli Forces Against the Humanitarian Boat Convoy, U.N. Doc. A/HRC/RES/14/1 (June 2, 2010) [hereinafter Flotilla Commission].
[7] Independent Fact Finding Committee on Gaza, established by the League of Arab States on January 26, 2009, LEAGUE OF ARAB STATES, REP. OF THE INDEPENDENT FACT FINDING COMMITTEE ON GAZA: NO SAFE PLACE (2009), *reproduced in* Letter dated Oct. 1, 2009, from the Permanent Observer of the League of Arab States to the United Nations addressed to the President of the Security Council, U.N. Doc. S/2009/537 (Oct. 14, 2009) [hereinafter ARAB LEAGUE COMMISSION REPORT]; Independent International Fact-Finding Mission on the Conflict in Georgia, established by Council Decision 2008/901, 2008 O.J. (L 323) 66 (EU) [hereinafter Georgia Commission].
[8] *See, e.g.*, Commission of Inquiry on Iraq (The Netherlands), established pursuant to Parliamentary Documents II, 2008/09, 31847 No. 1 (Neth.) and Parliamentary Documents I, 2008/09, 31847 No. A (Neth.); Iraq Inquiry, PARL. DEB., H.C. (2009) 23 (U.K.), *available at* www.iraqinquiry.org.uk [hereinafter Chilcot Inquiry], established pursuant to Parliamentary Statement of Prime Minister Gordon Brown on June 15, 2009, *available at* www.publications.parliament.uk/pa/cm200809/cmhansrd/cm090615/debtext/90615-0004.htm.
[9] *See, e.g.*, Dapo Akande & Hannah Tonkin, *International Commissions of Inquiry: A New Form of Adjudication?*, EJIL: TALK! (Apr. 6, 2012), *available at* www.ejiltalk.org/international-commissions-of-inquiry-a-new-form-of-adjudication.

Section II first presents the most relevant contemporary international, regional, and domestic commissions of inquiry and interrogates how they have construed a *jus ad bellum* dimension into their mandates. Given the Human Rights Council's activity in establishing commissions of inquiry, it is specifically examined whether, given the recent activation of the International Criminal Court's (ICC's) jurisdiction over the crime of aggression,[10] future HRC commissions of inquiry may be expected to become more active in the *jus ad bellum* domain. Next, in Section III, the Chapter offers some more concrete insights into practice by zooming in on the Kosovo and Iraq inquiries, which both dealt with situations that raised fundamental *jus ad bellum* questions. Subsequently, in Section IV, the Chapter situates commissions of inquiry within the greater *jus ad bellum* architecture in both institutional and normative senses. Finally, Section V concludes with some last reflections on whether and how commissions of inquiry can offer some form of accountability for illegal uses of force.

II. A PRESENTATION OF RELEVANT COMMISSIONS OF INQUIRY AND *JUS AD BELLUM* DIMENSIONS OF THEIR MANDATES

In the arena of international peace and security, commissions of inquiry operate on different levels and within different institutional settings. Not all of these commissions have an express *jus ad bellum* mandate. At the international level, the U.N. Security Council is the primary organ responsible for maintaining international peace and security, and it has the authority to establish commissions of inquiry in the exercise of this responsibility.[11] The Security Council has full discretion regarding the contours of mandates of these commissions. It may delegate its power to establish commissions of inquiry to the Secretary-General, who may also establish commissions on his or her own motion.[12] For the purposes of this Chapter, the most relevant

---

[10] *Id.* at 9; Rome Statute of the International Criminal Court arts. 8*bis* and 15*bis*, *adopted on* July 17, 1998, 2187 U.N.T.S. 91 (entered into force July 1, 2002) [hereinafter Rome Statute]; Res. ICC-ASP/16/Res.5, Activation of the jurisdiction of the Court over the crime of aggression (Dec. 14, 2017).

[11] This power is conferred in U.N. Charter Article 34 and is also implied from the Security Council's functions. *See* Reparation for Injuries Suffered in the Service of the United Nations, Advisory Opinion, 1949 I.C.J. Rep. 174 (Apr. 11); HENRY G. SCHERMERS & NIELS BLOKKER, INTERNATIONAL INSTITUTIONAL LAW: UNITY WITHIN DIVERSITY ¶¶ 232–36 (5th ed. 2011); Edouard Fromageau, *Collaborating with the United Nations: Does Flexibility Imply Informality?*, 7 INT'L ORG. L. REV. 405 (2010).

[12] *See, e.g.*, Larissa J. van den Herik, *An Inquiry into the Role of Commissions of Inquiry in International Law: Navigating the Tensions Between Fact-Finding and Application of*

inquiry created by the Secretary-General concerned the 2010 Gaza flotilla incident, chaired by Geoffrey Palmer (the Palmer Commission). This commission had a rather broad mandate, namely to "examine and identify the facts, circumstances and context of the incident" and to "consider and recommend ways of avoiding similar incidents in the future."[13] Pursuant to this highly fact-oriented mandate, the commission repeatedly emphasized its non-legal methodology.[14] Nonetheless, the commission did present its conclusions "against the backdrop of the exposition of principles of public international law."[15] Yet, the overall legal analysis and the most pertinent and extensive *jus ad bellum* interpretations and analyses were not included in the principal report but rather in an Appendix prepared by the Chair and Vice-Chair.[16]

At the national level, Turkey and Israel also launched their own inquiries into the legality of the Gaza flotilla incident. An Israeli commission was asked to investigate whether the blockade and Israel's actions to enforce it complied with "rules of international law."[17] However, it limited its analysis to human rights and international humanitarian law.[18] A Turkish inquiry was asked to examine "legal implications and consequences of these acts."[19] It included considerations of the *jus ad bellum* and other fields of international law in its analysis. Previously, domestic commissions had also operated in parallel with international commissions. For instance, the Winograd Commission established by Israel to inquire into the 2006 Lebanon War had a HRC counterpart.[20] On other occasions, Israel's Ministry of Foreign Affairs has published legal

---

International Law, 13 CHINESE J. INT'L L. 1, 20 (2014). According to the *Declaration on Fact-finding by the United Nations in the Field of the Maintenance of International Peace and Security*, the Security Council and General Assembly should prefer to entrust the conduct of a fact-finding mission to the Secretary-General. G.A. Res. 46/59, U.N. Doc. A/RES/46/59, ¶ 15 (Dec. 9, 1991).

[13] U.N. Secretary-General, *Rep. of the Secretary-General's Panel of Inquiry on the 31 May 2010 Flotilla Incident*, ¶ 3 (Sept. 2, 2011), *available at* www.un.org/News/dh/infocus/middle_east/Gaza_Flotilla_Panel_Report.pdf [hereinafter Palmer Commission Report].

[14] *Id.* ¶¶ 14–15, 67.

[15] *Id.* ¶ 67.

[16] *Id.* app. 1, at 76–102.

[17] TURKEL COMM'N, THE PUBLIC COMMISSION TO EXAMINE THE MARITIME INCIDENT OF 31 MAY 2010, at 17 (2010), *available at* www.turkel-committee.gov.il/files/wordocs/8808report-eng.pdf.

[18] *See id.* pt. 1.

[19] TURKISH NAT'L COMM'N OF INQUIRY, REPORT ON THE ISRAELI ATTACK ON THE HUMANITARIAN AID CONVOY TO GAZA ON 31 MAY 2010, at 10 (2011), *available at* www.mfa.gov.tr/data/Turkish%20Report%20Final%20-%20UN%20Copy.pdf.

[20] *See* Lebanon Commission, *supra* note 6; Press Release, Winograd Commission Submits Interim Report, Isr. Ministry of Foreign Affairs (Apr. 30, 2007), *available at* http://www.mfa.gov.il/mfa/pressroom/2007/pages/winograd%20inquiry%20commission%20submits%20interim%20report%2030-apr-2007.aspx.

analyses of other Israeli military operations, but these have not been styled as independent commissions of inquiry.[21] Other relatively recent domestic inquiries with an express or potential *jus ad bellum* dimension have been launched in relation to the 2003 Iraq War as further analyzed in the next Section.

Moving back to the international plane, it can be noted that the Human Rights Council has also been very active in creating commissions of inquiry to investigate and report on situations of gross human rights violations, including when committed in times of conflict. The Council's activism has been replicated by regional organizations, which have created comparable commissions of inquiry at the regional level. Yet, in contrast to the Security Council and domestic authorities, the Human Rights Council, and to a lesser extent regional organizations, are more limited as regards the design of commissions. In line with its mandate, the international commissions that the Human Rights Council establishes are predominantly human-rights oriented. Since many commissions operate during times of armed conflict, and given the interplay between human rights and international humanitarian law, some HRC commissions of inquiry have also investigated and reported on violations of international humanitarian law.[22] In a similar vein, HRC commissions increasingly invoke international criminal law as the law of enforcement of human rights and international humanitarian law,[23] in line with the idea that

---

[21] *See, e.g.*, STATE OF ISR., THE 2014 GAZA CONFLICT: FACTUAL AND LEGAL ASPECTS (2015), *available at* http://mfa.gov.il/ProtectiveEdge/Documents/2014GazaConflictFullReport.pdf; STATE OF ISR., THE OPERATION IN GAZA: FACTUAL AND LEGAL ASPECTS (2009), *available at* http://mfa.gov.il/MFA_Graphics/MFA%20Gallery/Documents/GazaOperation%20w%20Links.pdf.

[22] Some HRC commissions were instructed in their mandates to investigate violations of international humanitarian law. *See, e.g.*, the Independent Commission of Inquiry on the Gaza Conflict established by Human Rights Council Res. S-21/1, Ensuring Respect for International Law in the Occupied Palestinian Territory, including East Jerusalem, U.N. Doc. A/HRC/RES/S-21/1 (July 23, 2014); Flotilla Commission, *supra* note 6; Goldstone Commission, *supra* note 6. Other HRC commissions made findings of international humanitarian law violations. *See, e.g.*, Rep. of the Ind. Int'l Comm'n of Inquiry on the Syrian Arab Republic, U.N. Doc. A/HRC/21/50 (Aug. 16, 2012); Rep. of the High-Level Fact-Finding Mission to Beit Hanoun Established Under Council Resolution S-3/1, U.N. Doc. A/HRC/9/26 (Sept. 1, 2008) [hereinafter Beit Hanoun Commission Report]. *See also* Philip Alston, Jason Morgan-Foster & William Abresch, *The Competence of the UN Human Rights Council and its Special Procedures in Relation to Armed Conflicts: Extrajudicial Executions in the 'War on Terror,'* 19 EUR. J. INT'L L. 183, 207 (2008); *contra* Daphné Richemond-Barak, *The Human Rights Council and the Convergence of Humanitarian Law and Human Rights Law, in* COUNTERINSURGENCY LAW: NEW DIRECTIONS IN ASYMMETRIC WARFARE 3 (William Banks ed., 2013).

[23] *See, e.g.*, Rep. of the United Nations Fact-Finding Mission on the Gaza Conflict, U.N. Doc. A/HRC/12/48, at 76, ¶ 286 (Sept. 25, 2009) [hereinafter Goldstone Commission Report]. *See also* Larissa van den Herik & Catherine Harwood, *Commissions of Inquiry and the Charm of International Criminal Law: Between Transactional and Authoritative Approaches, in* THE

human rights protections are "significantly advanced when individuals were held to account for their acts."[24] Certain commissions have recommended the International Criminal Court as a forum for prosecutions, in the event that concerned States fail to investigate and prosecute.[25] The recent codification of the crime of aggression in the Rome Statute of the International Criminal Court may therefore impact HRC commissions' engagement with the *jus ad bellum*.[26] Such engagement might also be linked to the human right to peace[27] and the rights of victims of serious violations of international humanitarian law and human rights law to the truth and to a remedy.[28]

Nonetheless, there are limits to the extent to which HRC commissions engage with areas of law other than human rights proper. For instance, the Syrian government's call for the HRC commission of inquiry on Syria to also consider international law on terrorism, and in particular relevant Security Council resolutions,[29] was only taken up by that commission to the extent that acts of terror violated international humanitarian law and human rights law.[30] Hence, the Syria Commission only expanded its mandate to include areas of international law that have a direct interplay with human rights and thus inform the application of human rights law, or which articulate the

TRANSFORMATION OF HUMAN RIGHTS FACT-FINDING 233 (Philip Alston & Sarah Knuckey eds., 2016); Catherine Harwood, *Human Rights in Fancy Dress? The Use of International Criminal Law by Human Rights Council Commissions of Inquiry in Pursuit of Accountability* 58 JAPANESE Y.B. INT'L L. 71 (2015), *available at* http://papers.ssrn.com/sol3/papers.cfm?abstract_id=2627058.

[24] Rep. of the Office of the High Comm'r for Human Rights, Outcome of the Expert Consultation on the Issue of Protecting the Human Rights of Civilians in Armed Conflict, ¶ 7, U.N. Doc. A/HRC/11/31 (June 4, 2009).

[25] *See, e.g.*, Goldstone Commission Report, *supra* note 23, ¶ 1969(c); Rep. of the Detailed Findings of the Commission of Inquiry on Human Rights in the Democratic People's Republic of Korea, U.N. Doc. A/HRC/25/CRP.1, ¶ 1225(a) (Feb. 7, 2014).

[26] For arguments in favor of insulating human rights from the *jus ad bellum*, *see* Marko Milanovic, *Extraterritorial Derogations from Human Rights Treaties in Armed Conflict, in* THE FRONTIERS OF HUMAN RIGHTS: EXTRATERRITORIALITY AND ITS CHALLENGES 55 (Nehal Bhuta ed., 2016).

[27] Human Rights Council Res. 32/28, Declaration on the Right to Peace, U.N. Doc. A/HRC/RES/32/28 (July 18, 2016).

[28] G.A. Res. 60/147, Basic Principles and Guidelines on the Right to a Remedy and Reparation for Victims of Gross Violations of International Human Rights Law and Serious Violations of International Humanitarian Law, U.N. Doc. A/RES/60/147 (Dec. 16, 2005).

[29] Note Verbale dated Dec. 21, 2011, from the Permanent Rep. of the Syrian Arab Republic addressed to the Commission (Dec. 21, 2011), *reproduced in* Rep. of the Ind. Int'l Comm'n of Inquiry on the Syrian Arab Republic, U.N. Doc. A/HRC/19/69, annex II, at 26 (Feb. 22, 2012).

[30] Rep. of the Ind. Int'l Comm'n of Inquiry on the Syrian Arab Republic, U.N. Doc. A/HRC/24/46, ¶ 11 (Aug. 16, 2013); *see also* ARAB LEAGUE COMMISSION REPORT, *supra* note 7, ¶¶ 412–22 (refusing to engage with "uncertain and undefined norms of international terrorism").

consequences of findings of violations of human rights law, and it avoided
further "jurisdictional overlap" with the Security Council as much as possible.
The institutional equilibrium with the Security Council was also indirectly
tested by attempts to establish a HRC inquiry on Yemen. While a draft
resolution to that effect was not adopted in 2015, in 2017 the HRC established
a group of experts to examine "all alleged violations and abuses of international human rights and other appropriate and applicable fields of international law committed by all parties to the conflict since September 2014."[31]
It is possible that this body may probe *jus ad bellum* dimensions of the
conflict.[32] However, the direction to examine "appropriate" legal fields might
imply a restrained approach. The HRC setting and diplomacy thus displayed a
certain reservation in respect of the Security Council's prerogatives in peace
and security matters.

Yet, in other instances, HRC commissions overlapped with the Security
Council's working space more directly. On several occasions, HRC commissions have indeed been created for situations that encompassed *jus ad bellum*
dimensions. These included the 2006 Lebanon Inquiry, the 2008 Beit
Hanoun Inquiry, and the 2009 Gaza Inquiry led by Justice Richard Goldstone
(the Goldstone Commission). These commissions had to grapple with the
question whether and to what extent they would draw on the *jus ad bellum* in
the fulfillment of their mandates. The mandate of the Lebanon Commission
articulated three concrete responsibilities,[33] but the Commission indicated
that it would interpret its mandate broadly in light of international law, and
more specifically, human rights and international humanitarian law.[34] The
broad reference to international law potentially opened the door for engagement with the *jus ad bellum*. Indeed, despite its overall focus on international
humanitarian law, the Commission did make some pertinent *jus ad bellum*
findings and even observed that Israel's military actions, which had already

---

[31] *See, e.g.*, Nick Cumming-Bruce, *Saudi Objections Halt U.N. Inquiry of Yemen War*, N.Y.
TIMES (Sept. 30, 2015), www.nytimes.com/2015/10/01/world/middleeast/western-nations-drop-
push-for-un-inquiry-into-yemen-conflict.html?_r=0; Human Rights Council Res. 36/31,
Human rights, technical assistance and capacity-building in Yemen, U.N. Doc. A/HRC/36/31 ¶
12(a) (Sept. 29, 2017).

[32] *See* S.C. Res. 2216, U.N. Doc. S/RES/2216 (Apr. 14, 2015). *See also* Tom Ruys & Luca Ferro,
*Weathering the Storm: Legality and Legal Implications of the Saudi-led Military Intervention in
Yemen*, 65 INT'L & COMP. L.Q. 61, 61–98 (2016).

[33] Lebanon Commission, *supra* note 6, ¶ 7.

[34] *See* Rep. of the Comm'n of Inquiry on Lebanon Pursuant to Human Rights Council
Resolution S-2/1, U.N. Doc. A/HRC/3/2, at 3, 24, ¶¶ 10, 63 (Nov. 23, 2006) [hereinafter
Lebanon Commission Report].

been labeled as offensive by the Security Council,[35] had "the characteristics of an armed aggression, as defined by General Assembly resolution 3314 (XXIX)."[36] The Beit Hanoun Commission included one paragraph on the *jus ad bellum* in its report, observing that, as it was unable to visit Israel, it was not able to reach firm findings.[37] *Jus ad bellum* issues came up in quite a different constellation in the context of the Goldstone Commission. In this case, allegations of bias were made against one of the commissioners, namely Professor Christine Chinkin.[38] Prior to her appointment, Professor Chinkin had signed a statement published in the *Sunday Times* rejecting Israel's claims of self-defense and labeling the Israeli actions instead as aggression, inter-twined with the commission of war crimes.[39] The disqualification petition was rejected by the members of the Goldstone Commission, indicating that the question of the legality of the Israeli military response was not an issue that fell within its mandate and the petition was thus misplaced.[40] Despite Israel's reliance on the doctrine of self-defense, engagement with the *jus ad bellum* by the Beit Hanoun and the Goldstone Commissions thus remained limited.

This rather reserved stance of the HRC commissions stands in contrast with regional approaches and, more specifically, the 2009 Fact-Finding Committee on Gaza established by the League of Arab States. Even though its mandate was phrased in quite similar terms as the HRC commissions', namely to investigate and report on violations of human rights and international humani-tarian law during an Israeli military operation, the Committee articulated express, albeit reserved, views on the *jus ad bellum*.[41] Coincidentally, another regional inquiry commission, which investigated a wholly different

---

[35] In Security Council Resolution 1701, the Security Council called for "a full cessation of hostilities based upon, in particular, the immediate cessation by Hizbollah of all attacks and the immediate cessation by Israel of all offensive military operations." S.C. Res. 1701, U.N. Doc. S/RES/1701, ¶ 1 (Aug. 11, 2006).

[36] Lebanon Commission Report, *supra* note 34, at 23, ¶ 61. G.A. Res. 3314 (XXIX), Definition of Aggression, U.N. Doc. A/RES/3314(XXIX) (Dec. 14, 1974).

[37] Lebanon Commission Report, *supra* note 34, at 14, ¶ 46.

[38] U.N. Watch, Request to Disqualify Prof. Christine Chinkin from UN Fact Finding Mission on the Gaza Conflict (Aug. 20, 2009), *available at* www.unwatch.org/wp-content/uploads/2016/01/2207UN_Watch_Request_to_Disqualify_Christine_Chinkin_from_UN_Goldstone_Mission_on_Gaza_20_August_2009.pdf.

[39] *Letter: Israel's Bombardment of Gaza is Not Self-Defence – It's a War Crime*, SUNDAY TIMES (Jan. 11, 2009), *available at* www.timesonline.co.uk/tol/comment/letters/article5488380.ece.

[40] *Statement by the UN Fact Finding Mission on the Gaza Conflict*, JEWISH CHRON. LONDON (Aug. 25, 2009), *reprinted in* U.N. *Goldstone Inquiry Rejects 'So-Called Petition of UN Watch'; Denies Mission is Quasi-Judicial*, U.N. WATCH (Aug. 30, 2009), *available at* https://www.unwatch.org/un-goldstone-inquiry-rejects-so-called-petition-of-un-watch-denies-mission-is-quasi-judicial/.

[41] ARAB LEAGUE COMMISSION REPORT, *supra* note 7, ¶¶ 405–11.

conflict, also deliberately and lengthily addressed the *jus ad bellum* in a more progressive, if not largely *de lege ferenda,* manner. This was the Independent International Fact-Finding Mission on the Conflict in Georgia established by the Council of the European Union in 2008. Although this mission was also mandated to investigate violations of international humanitarian and human rights law, its broader assignment was to investigate the origins and course of the conflict.[42] This set the stage for the extensive *jus ad bellum* coverage in its reports[43] resulting in far-reaching, perhaps excessive, legal interpretations.[44]

Hence, on the basis of the practice summarily analyzed in this Section, a provisional conclusion can be drawn that commissions of inquiry created by the Security Council and Secretary-General as well as domestic inquiries can be vested with mandates that include an explicit *jus ad bellum* dimension. In contrast, HRC commissions are generally focused on acts committed during an armed conflict rather than on the initiation of the conflict *per se* and in their practice they have been reserved in relation to *jus ad bellum* questions. Moreover, their parent body is not devoid of political considerations and pressures influencing its practice as regards the establishment of inquiry commissions in *jus ad bellum* contexts. Regional commissions can navigate between these extremes, but the record of the two commissions analyzed here, and particularly the Georgia Commission, demonstrates a greater keenness to broach *jus ad bellum* issues than the HRC commissions.

III. SPOTLIGHTING THE KOSOVO AND IRAQ INQUIRIES

As is apparent from the previous Section, the engagement of commissions of inquiry with the *jus ad bellum,* even if relatively sparse, can concern a variety of legal issues. Commissions have considered questions regarding the qualification of aggression, the applicability of self-defense specifically also against non-state actors, the interpretation of Security Council resolutions, and the existence of extra-Charter justifications. This Section offers some deeper

---

[42] Georgia Commission, *supra* note 7, art. 1.
[43] 1 Independent International Fact-Finding Mission on the Conflict in Georgia Report at 22, ¶ 19 (2009), *available at* http://echr.coe.int/Documents/HUDOC_38263_08_Annexes_ENG.pdf [hereinafter Georgia Commission Report Vol. I]; 2 Independent International Fact-Finding Mission on the Conflict in Georgia Report 244 (2009), *available at* www.caucasus-dialog.net/Caucasus-Dialog/Activities_&_Docs_files/IIFFMCG_Volume_II%20Kopie.pdf [hereinafter Georgia Commission Report Vol. II].
[44] For an appraisal, *see* Christian Henderson & James A. Green, *The Jus Ad Bellum and Entities Short of Statehood in the Report on the Conflict in Georgia,* 59 Int'l & Comp. L.Q. 129, 133 (2010).

insight into the *jus ad bellum* inquiry practice through a focus on inquiries into two distinct operations that each evoked fundamental *jus ad bellum* discussions, i.e., the 1999 NATO intervention in Kosovo and the 2003 invasion of Iraq.

A. *The Independent International Commission on Kosovo*

Inquiry practice is generally marked by *ad hoc*-ism and great diversity, as was illustrated in Section II. Within this landscape of variety, the Independent International Commission on Kosovo is, in an institutional sense, perhaps still even more unique than other commissions, as it was not integrated in any formal setting.[45] It was proposed by the Swedish Prime Minister, Hans Göran Persson, but the direct involvement of the Swedish government was restricted to initial funding and inviting the two chairpersons, Richard Goldstone and Carl Tham.[46] In addition, Sweden sought the backing of leading countries and it secured the U.N. Secretary-General's support, who ultimately also accepted to formally receive the report.[47] Despite these formal linkages, the commission members – selected by the two chairpersons – each participated in their personal capacity. Although the commission was thus not formally established as part of a concrete organizational setting, it did build on and refer to previous and coinciding formal inquiry initiatives in terms of spirit and approach, most notably those of the United Nations regarding the fall of Srebrenica[48] and the United Nations' failure to prevent the genocide in Rwanda[49] as well as the Brahimi Inquiry.[50] The Kosovo Commission formulated its mission statement very similarly to those inquiries by including, but not limiting itself to, a legal evaluation and adding a strong future-oriented focus with a lessons-learned exercise. Its mission statement read:

---

[45] INDEP. INT'L COMM'N ON KOSOVO, THE KOSOVO REPORT: CONFLICT, INTERNATIONAL RESPONSE, LESSONS LEARNED (2000) [hereinafter Kosovo Report].

[46] *Id.* ¶¶ 21–22.

[47] *Id. See also* Richard Goldstone, *The Independent International Commission on Kosovo, in* 7 INTERNATIONAL PEACEKEEPING: THE YEARBOOK OF INTERNATIONAL PEACE OPERATIONS 331, 331–332 (Michael Bothe & Boris Kondoch eds., 2001).

[48] U.N. Secretary-General, *Rep. of the Secretary-General Pursuant to General Assembly Res. 53/35, The Fall of Srebrenica*, U.N. Doc. A/54/549 (Nov. 15, 1999).

[49] Rep. of the Independent Inquiry into the Actions of the United Nations During the 1994 Genocide in Rwanda, U.N. Doc. S/1999/1257 (Dec. 16, 1999).

[50] Rep. of the Panel on United Nations Peace Operations (Brahimi Report), U.N. Doc. A/55/305-S/2000/809 (Aug. 21, 2000).

The Independent International Commission on Kosovo will examine key developments prior to, during and after the Kosovo war, including systematic human rights in the region. The Commission will present a detailed, object- ive analysis of the options that were available to the international community to cope with the crisis. It will focus on the origins of the Kosovo crisis, the diplomatic efforts to end the conflict, the role of the United Nations and NATO's decision to intervene militarily. It will examine the resulting refugee crisis including the responses of the international community to resolve the crisis. The effect of the conflict on regional and other states will also be examined. Furthermore, the Commission will examine the role of humani- tarian workers, NGOs and the media during the Kosovo war. Finally, the Commission will identify the norms of international law and diplomacy brought to the fore by the Kosovo war and the adequacy of present norms and institutions in preventing and responding to comparable crises in the future. In addition, the Commission will take up: the future status of Kosovo, Lessons learned for Kosovo and Lessons learned for the future.[51]

The report included a separate forty-page chapter on "International Law and Humanitarian Intervention" that addressed both questions of *jus ad bellum* as well as *jus in bello*.[52] As regards the legality of the NATO air campaign, the commission concluded that it was illegal, yet legitimate.[53] A significant chunk of the legality chapter was subsequently devoted to developing a framework for principled humanitarian intervention, articulating three threshold principles and eight contextual principles, as well as concrete suggestions for revisions of the U.N. Charter.[54] As is well known, after Kosovo the general discussion on humanitarian intervention was reframed and continued under the Responsi- bility to Protect concept.[55] Since the ICJ (International Court of Justice) litigation on the NATO actions was discontinued for lack of jurisdiction,[56] the report's judicial relevance and accountability potential was not further tested at that level, but it has informed parliamentary debates and may have

---

[51] Kosovo Report, *supra* note 45, at 24–25.

[52] *Id.* ch. 6, at 163–200.

[53] *Id.* at 186. Goldstone later indicated that the choice of the word "legitimate" was perhaps unfortunate. He clarified that what was meant was to indicate that the NATO actions were morally and politically justifiable. Goldstone, *supra* note 47, at 336.

[54] Kosovo Report, *supra* note 45, at 192–95.

[55] Int'l Comm'n on Intervention and State Sovereignty, The Responsibility to Protect (2001).

[56] Legality of the Use of Force (Serb. and Montenegro v. Belg.), Preliminary Objections Judgment, 2004 I.C.J. Rep. 279 (Dec. 15) and related judgments entered in the cases against Canada, France, Germany, Italy, The Netherlands, Portugal, Spain, the United Kingdom, and the United States of America.

independent value,[57] although of course its findings and conclusions have been subject to the same intense debates and criticisms that have also marked the discussion on humanitarian intervention more generally.[58]

B. *The Iraq Inquiries*

Inquiries into the Iraq War have also been established, but then formally as national inquiries in several jurisdictions. In 2004, a U.S. Presidential Inquiry was established to, *inter alia*, investigate errors in the Iraq intelligence.[59] Its report concluded that the Iraq intelligence was wrong in almost all respects, and that this constituted a major intelligence failure.[60] However, it did not offer conclusions as to whether the intelligence had purposefully been manipulated.[61] In contrast, Dutch and Danish commissions of inquiry had more legally oriented mandates. In 2012, Denmark established a commission to investigate the Danish decision to participate in the Iraq War, including "whether there was a basis for the assessment of the legality of the Danish participation according to Denmark's international obligations."[62] In 2015, a new Danish government aborted the commission prematurely. The Dutch Commission of inquiry had a more fruitful ending. It was established in 2009 and mandated to investigate preparations and decision-making with regard to The Netherlands' support for the invasion of Iraq, including "matters pertinent to international law."[63] Consequently, it discussed *jus ad bellum* matters at

---

[57] *Cf.* Goldstone, *supra* note 47, at 339.

[58] For a fierce rejection of the report's findings, *see* David Rieff, *The Hypocrisy of Humanitarian Intervention, in* 7 INTERNATIONAL PEACEKEEPING: THE YEARBOOK OF INTERNATIONAL PEACE OPERATIONS, *supra* note 47, at 351.

[59] Commission on the Intelligence Capabilities of the United States Regarding Weapons of Mass Destruction, established by Exec. Order No. 13,328, 69 Fed. Reg. 6901 (Feb. 11, 2004).

[60] CHARLES S. ROBB & LAURENCE H. SILBERMAN, COMM'N ON THE INTELLIGENCE CAPABILITIES OF THE U.S. REGARDING WEAPONS OF MASS DESTRUCTION, REPORT TO THE PRESIDENT OF THE UNITED STATES 46 (2005), *available at* http://govinfo.library.unt.edu/wmd/report/wmd_report.pdf.

[61] *Id.* at 8.

[62] Peter Otken, *Correspondents' Reports, Government Commission – Establishment of a Commission of Inquiry on the Danish Participation in the Armed Conflicts in Iraq and Afghanistan,* 16 Y.B. INT'L HUMANITARIAN L. 1 (2013), *available at* www.asser.nl/media/1395/denmark-yihl-16-2013.pdf.

[63] RAPPORT COMMISSIE VAN ONDERZOEK BESLUITVORMING IRAK 521, ¶ 1.4 (2010), *available at* www.rijksoverheid.nl/documenten-en-publicaties/rapporten/2010/01/12/rapport-commissie-davids.html [hereinafter DAVIDS COMMISSION REPORT]. A proposal aiming at a parliamentary inquiry was rejected. The President of the inquiry commission, a former Supreme Court President, composed the commission, which included one international lawyer. *Id.* ¶¶ 1.1 and 1.3.

length in a full chapter on issues of legality of the use of force and offered extensive legal treatment of how relevant Security Council resolutions had to be interpreted, concluding that these did not offer an adequate legal basis.[64]

The Dutch Commission, also called the Davids Commission after its chair, was the first formal commission of inquiry to consider whether the Iraq War amounted to an unlawful use of force. In its 2010 report, the Dutch Commission concluded that the war was illegal under international law, because the use of force was not justified on the basis of self-defense, nor had the Security Council authorized the use of force.[65] The Dutch government's view that the Security Council had indeed authorized the use of force had been based on the "corpus" theory (also known as the "revival" theory). According to this theory, authorization could be inferred from an interconnected reading of consecutive Security Council resolutions, notably Resolutions 678 (1990), 687 (1991), and 1441 (2002). Resolution 678 authorized the use of force to implement an earlier resolution that demanded Iraq's withdrawal from Kuwait. Resolution 687 required Iraq to disarm and to cooperate with U.N. inspectors and the IAEA (International Atomic Energy Agency), and Resolution 1441 decided that Iraq had been and remained in material breach and gave Iraq a final opportunity to meet its disarmament obligations as specified in Resolution 687. The Council also resolved that if Iraq failed to meet its obligations, it would convene to consider the situation and warned that Iraq would face "serious consequences" in case of continued violation.[66] The words "material breach" were used in analogy to Article 60 of the Vienna Convention on the Law of Treaties on the termination or suspension of treaties, thereby implying that Resolution 687 would be suspended and hence the authorization of Resolution 678 would revive. However, the Davids Commission rejected the revival theory, referencing statements made at the adoption of Resolution 1441 that it contained no "hidden triggers" and no "automaticity."[67] The Commission further observed that Resolution 1441 did not include the words "all necessary means,"[68] so that it did not, without further authorization, permit States to use military force to compel Iraq to comply.[69] The Commission also found that the consequences of a material breach involving the use of force and the right to take forcible measures rested solely with the Security Council, so that The Netherlands was

---

[64] *Report of the Dutch Committee of Inquiry on the War in Iraq,* 57 NETH. INT'L L. REV. 81, 134–35 (2010) [hereinafter *English Translation of the Davids Commission Report*].

[65] *Id.* at 134–35.

[66] S.C. Res. 1441, U.N. Doc. S/RES/1441, ¶ 13 (Nov. 8, 2002).

[67] *English Translation of the Davids Commission Report, supra* note 64, at 102.

[68] *Id.* at 132.

[69] DAVIDS COMMISSION REPORT, *supra* note 63, at 530, ¶ 18.

not entitled to use force by dint of its own determination that Iraq was in material breach of its obligations.[70] Interestingly, one member of the Commission added a gloss to the conclusion that there had not been an adequate legal basis. Although he agreed with that particular conclusion, he did add that, in his view, the rules of international law should not constitute the only guiding frame of a government, and that urgent demands of international politics such as the prevention of nuclear proliferation might and could also independently inform governmental decision making.[71] Although the Dutch Prime Minister Jan Peter Balkenende did not immediately embrace the Commission's reading and interpretations, the Dutch government ultimately did accept the report and its findings.

The series of inquiries into the British government's decision to go to war were, in contrast to the Dutch Commission, not mandated to directly assess the legality of that decision. An inquiry in 2003 tangentially considered the credibility of British intelligence of Iraqi weapons of mass destruction.[72] Its limited conclusions resulted in widespread public discontent. A second inquiry also examined the intelligence used to justify the Iraq War. It concluded that the intelligence was unreliable and unsubstantiated, and had been overstated by the government.[73] Public discontent continued to fuel demands for a wider inquiry, which was eventually established in 2009.[74] The Chilcot Commission had the mandate to "[consider] the UK's involvement in Iraq, including the way decisions were made and actions taken, to establish, as accurately as possible, what happened and to identify the lessons that can be learned."[75] The mandate did thus not include an *express* instruction to consider the legality of the use of force, but it was also not explicitly excluded.

---

[70] *English Translation of the Davids Commission Report*, at 136.

[71] DAVIDS COMMISSION REPORT, *supra* note 63, at 270 (Kanttekening Commissielid Van Walsum).

[72] LORD HUTTON, REPORT OF THE INQUIRY INTO THE CIRCUMSTANCES SURROUNDING THE DEATH OF DR DAVID KELLY C.M.G. (2004), *available at* https://fas.org/irp/world/uk/huttonreport.pdf.

[73] COMM. OF PRIVY COUNSELLORS, REVIEW OF INTELLIGENCE ON WEAPONS OF MASS DESTRUCTION (2004), *available at* http://news.bbc.co.uk/nol/shared/bsp/hi/pdfs/14_07_04_butler.pdf.

[74] Mark Phythian, *The Politics of Commissions of Inquiry into Security and Intelligence Controversies in Britain, in* COMMISSIONS OF INQUIRY AND NATIONAL SECURITY: COMPARATIVE APPROACHES 55, 67 (Anthony Stuart Farson & Mark Phythian eds., 2011). Phythian writes that the Chilcot Inquiry was "conceded from a position of weakness." *Id.* at 68.

[75] Sir John Chilcot, Chairman of the Iraq Inquiry, Statement at a News Conference (July 30, 2009), *available at* www.iraqinquiry.org.uk/the-inquiry/news-archive/2009/2009-07-30-opening/statement-by-sir-john-chilcot-chairman-of-the-iraq-inquiry-at-a-news-conference-on-thursday-30-july-2009 [hereinafter Statement by John Chilcot].

In June 2010, Sir John Chilcot specifically invited international lawyers to offer their analysis of the arguments relied on by the U.K. government regarding the legal basis for the use of force against Iraq. Although ample advice was offered by individuals of the highest caliber,[76] ultimately, the Chilcot Report did not articulate a direct view on legality. It did make findings with legal implications, such as the finding that "the UK chose to join the invasion of Iraq before the peaceful options for disarmament had been exhausted," and thus that "military action at the time was not a last resort."[77] It also found that the circumstances in which the government decided that there was a legal basis were "far from satisfactory," and that by acting in the absence of majority support, the United Kingdom had undermined the Security Council's authority.[78] Bypassing judgment on the revival theory, the Chilcot Report noted that pursuant to the legal view presented by the government, the invasion would only have been lawful if indeed there had been evidence of further material breaches by Iraq.[79] It thus framed the matter as a factual question, and sidestepped the core legal question. Notwithstanding this approach, the Chilcot Report is still relevant also from a legal perspective. It may of course be used and referenced by other actors including even the International Criminal Court. The specific question of the legality of the use of force in Iraq in 2003 does not fall within the Court's jurisdictional parameters, as Prosecutor Bensouda pointed out in response to an article by *The Telegraph* published just prior to the release of the Chilcot Report.[80] Yet, as she had earlier also indicated, "the findings of the relevant investigations conducted by the UK authorities" can be taken into account by the ICC Prosecutor to inform her decision making more generally as regards the situation of Iraq.[81]

From an accountability perspective, inquiries can thus have independent value by stating facts and elucidating processes and decision-making practices surrounding the given use of force. In addition, inquiries may lead to or

---

[76] *See generally* Dapo Akande, *Iraq Inquiry to Publish Submissions on International Law*, EJIL: TALK! (Oct. 22, 2010), *available at* www.ejiltalk.org/iraq-inquiry-to-publish-submissions-on-international-law; COMM. OF PRIVY COUNSELLORS, THE IRAQ INQUIRY (2016), *available at* http://www.iraqinquiry.org.uk/the-report. *See also* Philippe Sands, *A Grand and Disastrous Deceit*, 38 LONDON REV. BOOKS, July 28, 2016, at 9–11.

[77] Statement by Sir John Chilcot, *supra* note 75, at 1.

[78] *Id.* at 4.

[79] *Id.* at 5.

[80] Office of the Prosecutor, Statement of the Prosecutor Correcting Assertions Contained in Article Published by The Telegraph (July 4, 2016), *available at* www.icc-cpi.int/Pages/item .aspx?name=160704-otp-stat.

[81] OFFICE OF THE PROSECUTOR, REPORT ON PRELIMINARY EXAMINATION ACTIVITIES ¶ 44 (2015), *available at* www.icc-cpi.int/iccdocs/otp/OTP-PE-rep-2015-Eng.pdf.

inform other accountability processes at domestic or international levels, of political or juridical nature.

IV. LOCATING COMMISSIONS OF INQUIRY IN THE GREATER *JUS AD BELLUM* ARCHITECTURE

Notwithstanding the variety of commissions of inquiry, generally speaking, a commission's report is nonbinding and prepared for, and delivered to, its parent body. Nonetheless, as the previous Section also illustrated, inquiry reports may have wider normative ramifications and they can sensitize other institutions and international mechanisms. In particular, at the international level, inquiry findings can initiate or inform international judicial action before the International Court of Justice or prospectively at the International Criminal Court. Moreover, through its findings, a commission may contribute to creating a certain normative consensus or it may highlight an absence of such consensus.

A. *Institutional Implications*

Inquiry reports interact with judicial proceedings in two key ways: first, as a form of evidence; second, as a driver for judicial proceedings. First, established "inquiry facts" may be invoked in judicial proceedings by one of the parties and relied on by courts. Specifically, *jus ad bellum* inquiry findings can assist in proving that an attack has taken place[82] and whether a State reasonably and correctly relied on intelligence. Moreover, "inquiry facts" may also be useful for necessity and proportionality tests.[83] For instance, the Winograd Commission's finding that the Israeli government did not consider all options before launching a major operation in Lebanon in 2006 might imply that a military response was not strictly necessary in accordance with the rules of self-defense. In a different context, findings of domestic commissions with respect to the reasonableness of reliance on intelligence to justify the invasion of Iraq are also relevant in greater discussions on the legality of the Iraq War.

---

[82] *See, e.g.*, Oil Platforms (Iran v. U.S.), Merits Judgment, 2003 I.C.J. 161, 195–98, ¶¶ 71–76 (Nov. 6).

[83] Theodora Christodoulidou & Kalliopi Chainoglou, *The Principle of Proportionality From a* Jus ad Bellum *Perspective, in* THE OXFORD HANDBOOK OF THE USE OF FORCE IN INTERNATIONAL LAW 1187, 1198 (Marc Weller ed., 2015). *See, e.g.*, Gerry Simpson, *The War in Iraq and International Law*, 6 MELBOURNE J. INT'L L. 167, 182 n.94 (2005); J. M. Spectar, *Beyond the Rubicon: Presidential Leadership, International Law & the Use of Force in the Long Hard Slog*, 22 CONN. J. INT'L L. 47, 90 (2006).

In previous cases at the International Court of Justice, parties have submitted fact-finding reports in support of their claims, and the Court has accepted these documents as evidence. For instance, in the *Armed Activities* case, reports were submitted by a Special Rapporteur of the Commission on Human Rights, the Secretary-General on MONUC (Mission in the Democratic Republic of Congo), U.N. panels of experts, and non-governmental organizations.[84] The Court cited several fact-finding reports as credible and corroborative evidence of serious violations of international humanitarian law and human rights.[85]

International criminal courts and tribunals have also drawn on inquiry reports, albeit with more care and subject to principles of criminal law. The International Criminal Court has acknowledged fact-finding reports at different phases of the trial process as well as in ancillary proceedings.[86] Since the Kampala Amendments have entered into force, giving the International Criminal Court jurisdiction over the crime of aggression,[87] inquiry reports might thus also be used in this context.

In addition to a certain informative or evidentiary value, inquiry reports have catalyzed the initiation of international criminal proceedings. For instance, Security Council commissions of inquiry on the former Yugoslavia and Rwanda preceded the establishment of international criminal tribunals for those situations. In the ICC context, inquiry reports have contributed to the initiation of proceedings in different ways. In 2005, the Security Council referred Sudan to the International Criminal Court following its receipt of an inquiry report of serious violations in Darfur.[88] In 2013, the Union of the Comoros referred the situation upon vessels in a flotilla bound for Gaza, annexing as supporting material the HRC commission's report on that incident.[89] That report was also cited in the Prosecutor's analysis of whether

---

[84] Armed Activities on the Territory of the Congo (Dem. Rep. Congo v. Uganda), Judgment, 2005 I.C.J. 168, 201, ¶ 60 (Dec. 19).

[85] *Id.* ¶¶ 207, 211.

[86] *See, e.g.,* Carsten Stahn & Dov Jacobs, *The Interaction Between Human Rights Fact-Finding and International Criminal Proceedings: Towards a (New) Typology, in* THE TRANSFORMATION OF HUMAN RIGHTS FACT-FINDING, *supra* note 23, at 255.

[87] *See* Review Conference of the Rome Statute of the International Criminal Court, *The crime of aggression*, Res. RC/Res.6 (June 11, 2010).

[88] *See* S.C. Res. 1593, U.N. Doc. S/RES/1593 (Mar. 31, 2005) (citing Rep. of the Int'l Comm'n of Inquiry on Darfur, U.N. Doc. S/2005/60 [Feb. 1, 2005]).

[89] Gov't of the Union of Comoros, *Referral Under Articles 14 and 12(2)(a) of the Rome Statute Arising from the 31 May 2010, Gaza Freedom Flotilla Situation* (May 14, 2013), *appended to* Letter from Ramzan Aritürk & Cihat Gökdemir, Attorneys, Elmadağ Law Firm, to Fatou Bensouda, Prosecutor, Int'l Criminal Ct. (May 14, 2013), *available at* www.icc-cpi.int/iccdocs/otp/Referral-from-Comoros.pdf.

to proceed with an investigation.[90] The Prosecutor cited the Georgia Commission's report in the request to open an investigation of war crimes and crimes against humanity allegedly committed in and around South Ossetia.[91] In the future, inquiry reports might also lay the groundwork for prosecutions of the crime of aggression.

The utility of inquiry reports as sources of evidence and as catalysts of prosecutions render them an attractive resource for bodies concerned with ensuring accountability for violations, such as the Human Rights Council. Once the International Criminal Court gains jurisdiction over the crime of aggression, the Human Rights Council might be emboldened to establish inquiries with mandates encompassing *jus ad bellum* dimensions. Nonetheless, forays into the *jus ad bellum* might be perceived as overstepping the Human Rights Council's mandate as illustrated in the previous Section, and commentators have already questioned the Council's jurisdiction to consider matters beyond human rights, in respect of international humanitarian law.[92] However, if an alleged act of aggression is linked with serious human rights violations, the Human Rights Council might treat the violations as sufficiently connected to warrant investigation. Thus, a new *jus ad bellum* space might open up for the Human Rights Council. Alternatively, or in addition, the Security Council might also consider establishing inquiries as a preliminary step before referring aggressor States to the International Criminal Court.

While commissions may theoretically play a role in inducing compliance with the *jus ad bellum* and promoting the use of enforcement mechanisms in response to alleged violations, surrounding political dimensions should not be overlooked. At the international level, most commissions are established by political bodies, and in national jurisdictions, decisions to establish commissions rest with the executive or legislative branches of government. Thus, a critical mass of political will is necessary to establish an inquiry, and, accordingly, political factors can stymie efforts for their establishment.

---

[90] OFFICE OF THE PROSECUTOR, SITUATION ON REGISTERED VESSELS OF COMOROS, GREECE AND CAMBODIA: ARTICLE 53(1) REPORT (2014), *available at* https://www.icc-cpi.int/iccdocs/otp/OTP-COM-Article_53%281%29-Report-06Nov2014Eng.pdf.

[91] Office of the Prosecutor, Situation in Georgia: Request for Authorisation of an Investigation Pursuant to Article 15, No. ICC-01/15-4 (Oct. 13, 2015), *available at* www.legal-tools.org/uploads/tx_ltpdb/doc2087876.pdf.

[92] *See, e.g.*, Richemond-Barak, *supra* note 22.

B. *Normative Implications*

In addition to institutional linkages with judicial bodies, it may be considered whether commissions' *jus ad bellum* findings have normative authority beyond their institutional settings. Of course, inquiry reports are not binding, and commissions are not adjudicative bodies. Many commissions acknowledge this point expressly. For instance, the Palmer Commission wrote:

> We observe that the legal views of Israel and Turkey are no more authoritative or definitive than our own. A Commission of Inquiry is not a court any more than the Panel is. The findings of a Commission of Inquiry bind no one, unlike those of a court. So the legal issues at large in this matter have not been authoritatively determined by the two States involved and neither can they be by the Panel.[93]

Nonetheless, commissions' reports may still possess a certain normative authority. In this respect, Akande and Tonkin write that commissions' reports "may end up being just as authoritative, in the public eye and in relevant political and legal bodies, as proper judicial processes."[94] Although many scholars impliedly accept that commissions possess some kind of normative authority, this has not been theorized in depth. Some scholars treat commissions as "quasi-judicial" bodies. For instance, in Russell Buchan's chapter on inquiries into the Gaza flotilla incident, he explains that he used the term "quasi-judicial" because those commissions

> [S]atisfy the definition outlined by [José] Alvarez in his seminal work on this topic. For Alvarez, a quasi-judicial body is a body that can be "characterized by some serious attempt, primarily through rules for the type of expertise required of the dispute settlers, their method of selection, or their tenure in office (or all three), to recognize the 'independent' status of the third party decision-maker from the governments involved in their creation." ... The four bodies under consideration in this chapter can be regarded as quasi-judicial because their members were selected on the basis of their professional standing; namely, their expertise in international law and/or experience and knowledge of international relations. Consequently, there was a serious attempt by their creators to establish bodies that were capable of independently adjudicating the dispute.[95]

---

[93] Palmer Commission Report, *supra* note 13, at 10, ¶ 14.

[94] Akande & Tonkin, *supra* note 9.

[95] Russell Buchan, *The Mavi Marmara Incident and the Application of International Humanitarian Law by Quasi-Judicial Bodies*, in APPLYING INTERNATIONAL HUMANITARIAN LAW IN JUDICIAL AND QUASI-JUDICIAL BODIES: INTERNATIONAL AND DOMESTIC ASPECTS 479,

Other scholars characterize commissions as a type of scholarship. For instance, Koutroulis refers to fact-finding reports as "subsidiary sources of international law as manifestations of legal doctrine. At best, they can be regarded as informed doctrine, due to the expertise of the missions' members."[96]

Commissions' contributions to the clarification and incremental development of international law may also be explained on the basis of sociological accounts, where international law is conceived of as an argumentative practice.[97] These scholars theorize actors' contributions to law making using concepts such as "semantic authority,"[98] "legal legitimacy"[99] and "de facto authority."[100] For instance, citing Jan Paulsson,[101] Koutroulis argues that the value of a fact-finding mission's legal analysis depends on whether markers of legal legitimacy are evident in its establishment and work products. Such markers include "the quality of legal reasoning as well as on the authority, impartiality, and independence of the members of the mission."[102] Koutroulis observes that many fact-finding reports lack detailed legal reasoning in support of findings, and hypothesizes that this may result from the absence of express mandatory permission to apply the *jus ad bellum*, as well as a "conscious focus on behalf of the members on the dispute settlement function of the mission."[103] Other scholars have impliedly invoked markers of legal legitimacy when evaluating the persuasiveness of commissions' reports. For instance, Henderson and Green considered the Georgia Commission's "'brushstrokes'

---

481 n.14 (Derek Jinks, Jackson Maogoto & Solon Solomon eds., 2014) (quoting José E. Alvarez, International Organizations as Law-makers 459 [2005]).

[96] Vaios Koutroulis, *The Prohibition of the Use of Force in Arbitrations and Fact-Finding Reports*, in The Oxford Handbook of the Use of Force in International Law, *supra* note 83, at 605, 612.

[97] Sociological accounts have also been embraced to some extent by some legal formalists. *See, e.g.*, Jean d'Aspremont, *Non-State Actors and the Social Practice of International Law*, in Non-State Actors in International Law: Studies in International Law ¶¶ 2.1–2.6 (Math Noortmann, August Reinisch & Cedric Ryngaert eds., 2015).

[98] *See, e.g.*, Ingo Venzke, *Semantic Authority*, in Fundamental Concepts of International Law (Jean d'Aspremont & Sahib Singh eds., forthcoming 2017), *available at* http://papers.ssrn .com/sol3/papers.cfm?abstract_id=2723851.

[99] *See, e.g.*, Alvarez, *supra* note 95, at 570; Alan Boyle & Christine Chinkin, The Making of International Law 310 (2007).

[100] Karen J. Alter, Laurence R. Helfer & Mikael Rask Madsen, *How Context Shapes the Authority of International Courts*, 79 L. & Contemp. Probs. 1 (2016).

[101] Koutroulis, *supra* note 96, at 611 (citing Jan Paulsson, *The Role of Precedent in Investment Arbitration*, in Arbitration Under International Investment Agreements: A Guide to the Key Issues 699, 704 [Katia Yannaca-Small ed., 2010]).

[102] *Id.* at 612.

[103] *Id.* at 628.

approach to international law" undesirable, especially in light of the political importance of the report. "Whilst the Mission made it clear it was not a tribunal, it was still required as part of its mandate to address the facts under international law."[104] The authors considered that instead of systematically ascertaining and applying international law, the Commission "confused the desirable development of the law with its current content."[105] "Any arguments to make the law more 'coherent,' whilst welcome, need to be pronounced as *lex ferenda* and have no place in a Report of this nature."[106]

As regards normative authority, it can also be observed that commissions' most far-reaching legal assessments of the *jus ad bellum* have occurred in "non-official" portions of reports, particularly the Appendix to the Palmer Commission's report and Volume II of the Georgia Commission's report.[107] Although the reports are nonbinding in their entirety, relegation of legal analyses to subordinate portions of a report may result from the fact that not all commissioners agree with their content (as was the case for the Palmer Commission)[108] and thus reduce their normative weight even further.

Hence, from a positivist perspective, the main value of reports of commissions of inquiry is indirect in that they may stimulate the production of material sources of international law. States may rely on commissions' normative pronouncements for guidance in respect of disputed or unsettled issues and they may invoke inquiry reports in support of their positions.[109] As observed by Koutroulis, this process may promote normative stability, demonstrating the extent of state support or disagreement of commissions' articulations on the *jus ad bellum*.[110] Inquiry reports may therefore assist in the development of state practice and *opinio juris*. In addition, there is a growing body of scholarship critically appraising commissions' interpretations of legal rules, and judicial bodies have, on occasion, had overt regard to commissions'

---

[104] Henderson & Green, *supra* note 44, at 138.

[105] *Id.*

[106] *Id.*

[107] According to its preface, Volume II of the Georgia Commission's report contains a "selection of contributions by experts" that constituted the basis for Volume I, although "opinions expressed in these texts do not necessarily reflect the views of the Mission. In this regard, the views and findings as laid out in Volume I shall be considered as authoritative." GEORGIA COMMISSION REPORT, VOL. II, *supra* note 43, at 1.

[108] Mr. Süleyman Özdem Sanberk, the Representative from Turkey, formally registered his disagreement in the Appendix. Palmer Commission Report, *supra* note 13, at 105, app. II.

[109] *See e.g.*, Application of the International Convention on the Elimination of All Forms of Racial Discrimination (Geor. v. Russ.), Preliminary Objections of the Russian Federation, ¶ 1.1 (Dec. 1, 2009), *available at* http://www.icj-cij.org/files/case-related/140/16099.pdf.

[110] Koutroulis, *supra* note 96, at 625.

articulations of international law.[111] Thus, commissions not only generate legal discourse, but also contribute, at least indirectly, to the production of law through the traditional sources of international law.

V. CONCLUDING THOUGHTS

The survey of practice in this Chapter shows that several national, regional, and international commissions of inquiry have interpreted rules of the *jus ad bellum* and applied them to factual situations under investigation. Some inquiries discussed this legal field briefly, raising questions about the legality of the use of force before turning to assess alleged violations of international humanitarian and human rights law. However, others, including the Georgia Commission and the Palmer Commission, engaged in a more sustained analysis. In particular, domestic inquiries may have a direct accountability effect as shown by the Iraq examples,[112] even if such commissions refrain from expressly articulating views on legality.

Some interpretations by commissions of inquiry reflected settled law and orthodox perspectives, while others might be characterized as *lex ferenda*, or were even expressly meant to develop the law as in the case of the Kosovo Inquiry. Post–September 11, 2001, States have challenged some traditional parameters of the *jus ad bellum*, including the contours of self-defense and the interpretation of Security Council resolutions. Commissions have cautiously acknowledged developments in state practice while rejecting certain aspects as illegitimate, such as the "revival" theory of interpreting Security Council resolutions, or they have made findings that the law remains unsettled, such as in the scope of the right to self-defense to respond to armed attacks by non-state actors. Although their normative pronouncements are not binding according to traditional theories of the sources of international law, findings of inquiry commissions can have considerable *de facto* significance.

Commission reports are not intended to replace judicial decisions, but rather to create an authoritative narrative of events and possibly encourage appropriate follow-up action by stakeholders. When situations are unlikely to be formally litigated, commissions' findings may be valuable as a means of moral censure and may build political pressure for non-repetition. Reports

---

[111] *See, e.g.,* David Re, *Fact-Finding in the Former Yugoslavia: What the Courts Did, in* QUALITY CONTROL IN FACT-FINDING 279, 279 (Morten Bergsmo ed., 2013).

[112] *Cf. also* the quote included in Philippe Sands's essay of a grandfather of one of the British servicemen killed in Iraq, "we are vindicated." Philippe Sands, *A Grand and Disastrous Deceit, supra* note 76, at 9–11.

may, however, also catalyze the initiation of judicial proceedings and can be adduced as evidence. An open question in this regard is how the entry into force of the Kampala Amendments might affect the current scheme on aggression. As aggression can now be prosecuted as an individualized crime, the Human Rights Council might seek to establish inquiries into situations of aggression, especially where there is prolonged inaction or a stalemate in the Security Council. It is debatable what practical or normative force the findings of these commissions should have, and in particular whether findings and recommendations of commissions established by the Security Council should carry greater weight than those created by the Human Rights Council, as a result of the former's prerogatives in regard to the *jus ad bellum*. On the other hand, normative developments based on a human rights–oriented and an individualized understanding of the *jus ad bellum* and, particularly, aggression may well qualify these prerogatives and create space for a more pronounced role for other actors, including Human Rights Council commissions. The future role of commissions of inquiry in the field of the *jus ad bellum* thus seems to be undecided.

8

The International Court of Justice and the Use of Force

DOUGLAS J. PIVNICHNY

I. INTRODUCTION

The International Court of Justice (ICJ) began operation in 1946 as the primary judicial organ of the United Nations.[1] It is one of the six principal organs of the United Nations organization, the post-war manifestation of the alliance against fascism and our principal attempt to repair the failings of the earlier League of Nations. Consequently, one might expect the Court to have a role in matters of international peace and security, which are among the United Nations' chief concerns.[2] The Court has performed this role by hearing the cases brought before it and handing down judgments thereon. This Chapter reviews this history and the contribution of the Court in relation to the use of force.

This Chapter will first examine the jurisdictional barriers to the Court's consideration of cases involving the use of force. These are often considerable and have on multiple occasions frustrated States seeking redress for the unlawful use of force. Second, the Chapter will turn to the doctrinal contributions of the Court's jurisprudence on the use of force. Significant among these have been the Court's role in interpreting the U.N. Charter and determining the content of customary international law. Third, the Chapter will consider how the Court has used the principle of non-use of force as an interpretive principle to determine the scope of application of other international legal norms. Fourth, the Chapter will consider the Court's role in providing alternatives to force through the judicial resolution of disputes. Finally, this Chapter will consider what the future likely holds for the Court and its jurisprudence.

---

[1] *See* U.N. Charter art. 92.
[2] U.N. Charter pmbl.

In order to accomplish this, some questions will be excluded. For example, the Permanent Court of International Justice is outside the scope of this Chapter for two reasons. First, the Permanent Court heard no cases concerning the use of force.[3] Although international law did regulate the use of force in the first half of the twentieth century, through classical *jus ad bellum*[4] and modern conventions,[5] the Permanent Court was never seized of a case concerning the topic. Second, the law on the use of force has changed since the Permanent Court was replaced in 1946. Superseded by the U.N. Charter, older conventions and custom have lost their relevance. Indeed, as will be discussed, custom has since evolved to mirror the Charter.

Additionally, the scope of this Chapter is limited to questions of the principle of the non-use of force. As other contributions to this volume make clear, international law also regulates the conduct of armed conflict through, among others, international humanitarian law and international criminal law. While the Court has had opportunities to engage these fields,[6] this Chapter will focus on the Court's contributions to determining whether prosecuting a conflict as a whole was lawful and to preventing armed conflict in general.

II. JURISDICTIONAL BARRIERS

The contributions of the Court on the question of the use of force are limited by the Court's narrow jurisdiction. As established in its Statute, the function of the Court is to "decide in accordance with international law such disputes as are submitted to it."[7] In contentious cases, such submissions are limited by the Court's personal jurisdiction. Under Article 34(1) of the Court's Statute,

---

[3] *See generally* U.N. OFFICE OF LEGAL AFFAIRS, SUMMARIES OF JUDGMENTS, ADVISORY OPINIONS AND ORDERS OF THE PERMANENT COURT OF INTERNATIONAL JUSTICE, U.N. Doc. ST/LEG/SER.F/1/Add.4, U.N. Sales No. E.12.V.18 (2012).

[4] *See, e.g.*, 2 L. OPPENHEIM, INTERNATIONAL LAW: A TREATISE: WAR AND NEUTRALITY (2d ed. 1912) [hereinafter OPPENHEIM, WAR]. Oppenheim writes, for example, "war is not inconsistent with, but a condition regulated by, International Law." *Id.* § 53.

[5] E.g., General Treaty for Renunciation of War as an Instrument of National Policy, Aug. 27, 1928, 94 L.N.T.S. 57.

[6] *See, e.g.*, Application of the Convention on the Prevention and Punishment of the Crime of Genocide (Croat. v. Serb.), Merits Judgment, 2015 I.C.J. 3 (Feb. 3) [hereinafter Genocide (Croat. v. Serb.) Merits Judgment]; Armed Activities on the Territory of the Congo (Dem. Rep. Congo v. Uganda), Judgment, 2005 I.C.J. 168, ¶¶ 196–221 (Dec. 19) [hereinafter Armed Activities Judgment]; Military and Paramilitary Activities in and Against Nicaragua (Nicar. v. U.S.), Merits Judgment, 1986 I.C.J. 14, ¶¶ 254–56 (June 27) [hereinafter Nicaragua Merits Judgment].

[7] Statue of the International Court of Justice art. 38(1), June 26, 1945, 59 Stat. 1055, 3 Bevans 1179 [hereinafter ICJ Statute].

"[o]nly states may be parties in cases before the Court."[8] In a world where armed conflict is mostly non-international in character,[9] this jurisdictional limitation poses an important barrier to access to the Court. Two parties to a non-international armed conflict can never find themselves directly opposed before the Court, for example, as did Iran and the United States in the *Oil Platforms* case.[10]

Even in contentious cases in which each side is a State, the requirement of consent limits the Court's jurisdiction. As the Court stated in *East Timor*, "one of the fundamental principles of its Statute is that it cannot decide a dispute between States without the consent of those States to its jurisdiction."[11] This distinguishes it from internationalized mechanisms charged with finding individual criminal responsibility for unlawful uses of force where individual consent is never necessary and the consent of a territorial or national State often is not either. For example, the Security Council did not need the consent of the former Yugoslav States or Rwanda to create the U.N. international criminal tribunals,[12] nor did it need the consent of Sudan or Libya to refer their situations to the International Criminal Court (indeed, those States involved protested the Council's action).[13] Conversely, in the *Corfu Channel* case, the Security Council could only "[r]ecommend[ ] that the United Kingdom and

---

[8]   *Id.* art. 34(1).

[9]   For example, in 2012, of thirty-eight armed conflicts, one was an active international armed conflict, nine were belligerent occupations of part of one State by another and twenty-eight were non-international armed conflicts. THE WAR REPORT: 2012, at 3–4, 14–15 (Stuart Casey-Maslen ed., 2013). In 2013, of thirty-nine conflicts, two were active international conflicts, nine were belligerent occupations of one State by another and twenty-eight were non-international armed conflicts. THE WAR REPORT: ARMED CONFLICT IN 2013, at 9–10, 28–29 (Stuart Casey-Maslen ed., 2014). For 2014, those figures were forty-two, three, ten and twenty-nine respectively. THE WAR REPORT: ARMED CONFLICT IN 2014, at 7–8, 23–25 (Annyssa Bellal ed., 2015). In 2016, there were forty-nine armed conflicts, including three active international armed conflicts, ten belligerent occupations, and thirty-six non-international armed conflicts. ANNYSSA BELLAL, THE WAR REPORT: ARMED CONFLICTS IN 2016, at 15, 28–30 (2017).

[10]   Oil Platforms (Iran v. U.S.), Merits Judgment, 2003 I.C.J. 161 (Nov. 6) [hereinafter Oil Platforms Merits Judgment].

[11]   East Timor (Port. v. Austl.), Judgment, 1995 I.C.J. 101, ¶ 26 (June 30).

[12]   U.N. Security Council, Statute of the International Criminal Tribunal for Rwanda (as amended on Dec. 16, 2009), S.C. Res. 955, U.N. Doc. S/RES/955 (Nov. 8, 1994); U.N. Security Council, Statute of the International Criminal Tribunal for the former Yugoslavia (as amended on July 7, 2009), S.C. Res. 827, U.N. Doc. S/RES/827 (May 25, 1993). In Resolution 955, the Security Council notes Rwanda's request for a tribunal, but does not base its authority to establish one on that request. S.C. Res. 955, *supra*, ¶ 1; *see also* Letter dated Sept. 28, 1994, from the Permanent Rep. of Rwanda to the United Nations addressed to the President of the Security Council, 4, U.N. Doc. S/1994/1115 (Sept. 29, 1994).

[13]   S.C. Res. 1970, U.N. Doc. S/RES/1970 (Feb. 26, 2011); S.C. Res. 1593, U.N. Doc. S/RES/1593 (Mar. 31, 2005).

Albanian Governments ... refer the dispute to the International Court of Justice."[14] The United Kingdom filed a unilateral application seizing the Court, arguing that the Security Council resolution was sufficient to establish the Court's jurisdiction.[15] The Court disagreed, noting that nothing in the Charter authorized the Security Council to extend the Court's jurisdiction by recommendation.[16] Instead, it determined that it had jurisdiction on the basis of Albania's consent expressed, albeit vaguely, in a letter to the Court's Deputy-Registrar.[17] It remains open whether the Security Council can bind a State to the Court's jurisdiction by a decision under Chapter VII of the Charter.[18]

The Statute of the Court establishes two mechanisms by which a State can consent to the exercise of the Court's jurisdiction: by agreement[19] or through the so-called optional clause.[20] States can agree to submit a dispute to the Court either before it arises, through the insertion of a compromissory clause in a treaty, or afterward through a special agreement (*compromis*, in French). The former option has been exercised in more than three hundred treaties,[21] some applicable to broad categories of dispute, for example the European Convention for the Peaceful Settlement of Disputes,[22] and some much narrower, like the Genocide Convention.[23] The latter option of a special agreement is typically used by States jointly to submit boundary disputes to the Court.[24] Additionally, the principle of *forum prorogatum* allows States to agree to the Court's jurisdiction after an application is filed.[25]

---

[14] S.C. Res. 22, U.N. Doc. S/RES/22 (Apr. 9, 1947).

[15] Corfu Channel (U.K. v. Alb.), Preliminary Objections, 1948 I.C.J. 15, 23 (Mar. 25) [hereinafter Corfu Channel Preliminary Objections].

[16] *Id.* at 24.

[17] *Id.* at 18. *Corfu Channel* is thus considered a case where the Court exercised its jurisdiction on the basis of *forum prorogatum*. *See* Andreas Zimmermann, *Competence of the Court*, *in* THE STATUTE OF THE INTERNATIONAL COURT OF JUSTICE: A COMMENTARY 585, 615 (Andreas Zimmermann et al. eds., 2d ed. 2012); *see also infra* note 25 and accompanying text.

[18] *See* U.N. Charter art. 41.

[19] ICJ Statute, *supra* note 7, art. 36(1).

[20] *Id.* art. 36(2).

[21] Rep. of the Int'l Court of Justice, 1 August 2014–31 July 2015, ¶ 44, U.N. Doc. A/70/4 (Aug. 1, 2015).

[22] *E.g.*, European Convention for the Peaceful Settlement of Disputes, Apr. 30, 1958, 320 U.N.T.S. 244.

[23] *E.g.*, Convention on the Prevention and Punishment of the Crime of Genocide, Dec. 9, 1948, 78 U.N.T.S. 278.

[24] There are two exceptions: Gabčíkovo-Nagymaros Project (Hung./Slovk.), 1997 I.C.J. 7 (Sept. 25) and Asylum (Colom./Peru), 1950 I.C.J. 266 (Nov. 20).

[25] *See supra* note 17 and accompanying text; *see also, e.g.*, Certain Questions of Mutual Assistance in Criminal Matters (Djib. v. Fr.), 2008 I.C.J. 177 (June 4).

The optional clause allows States a more generalized mechanism to accept the Court's jurisdiction. Under Article 36(2) of the Statute, States may "declare that they recognize as compulsory *ipso facto* and without special agreement, in relation to any other state accepting the same obligation, the jurisdiction of the Court."[26] As of July 2017, seventy-two States maintained such declarations.[27] States may, however, and frequently do, tailor their acceptance of the Court's compulsory jurisdiction with reservations that often limit the Court's jurisdiction over cases involving the use of force. For example, both India and Djibouti have made the following reservation excluding from the Court's jurisdiction

> disputes relating to or connected with facts or situations of hostilities, armed conflicts, individual or collective actions taken in self-defence, resistance to aggression, fulfilment of obligations imposed by international bodies, and other similar or related acts, measures or situations in which India is, has been or may in future be involved.[28]

Even if a respondent State has not made a relevant reservation, it may still rely on any of its counterparty's reservations on the basis of reciprocity,[29] which can serve to further limit the Court's jurisdiction.

These limitations have impacted the Court's ability to hear cases concerning the use of force. For example, the contours of parties' instruments expressing consent have often excluded the U.N. Charter from the Court's subject-matter jurisdiction. In the *Military and Paramilitary Activities* case, direct consideration of the Charter was excluded by one of the U.S. reservations in its optional clause declaration relating to the application of multilateral treaties.[30] The *Oil Platforms* case was filed on the basis of the compromissory clause in the 1955 Treaty of Amity, Economic Relations, and Consular Rights between the United States and Iran,[31] so Iran's claims were limited to violations of that treaty.[32] In the *Genocide* cases, the Court's subject-matter jurisdiction was

---

[26] ICJ Statute, *supra* note 7, art. 36(2).

[27] Rep. of the Int'l Court of Justice, *supra* note 21, ¶ 43.

[28] Declaration by Djibouti recognizing as compulsory the jurisdiction of the International Court of Justice, in conformity with Article 36, paragraph 2, of the Statute of the International Court of Justice, ¶ 3, Sept. 2, 2005, 2332 U.N.T.S. 3; Declaration by India recognizing as compulsory the jurisdiction of the International Court of Justice, in conformity with Article 36, paragraph 2, of the Statute of the International Court of Justice, ¶ 4, Sept. 15, 1974, 950 U.N.T.S. 15.

[29] *See* Interhandel (Switz. v. U.S.), Preliminary Objections, 1959 I.C.J. 6, 23 (Mar. 21).

[30] Nicaragua Merits Judgment, *supra* note 6, ¶ 48.

[31] Treaty of Amity, Economic Relations, and Consular Rights, Iran-U.S., Aug. 15, 1955, 284 U.N.T.S. 93 [hereinafter Treaty of Amity, Economic Relations, and Consular Rights].

[32] Oil Platforms (Iran v. U.S.), Preliminary Objections, 1996 I.C.J. 803, ¶ 16 (Dec. 12) [hereinafter Oil Platforms Preliminary Objections].

limited to questions of the law of genocide, rather than use of force questions.[33] On other occasions, the contours of the parties' consent have excluded the cases altogether on the basis of successful jurisdictional challenges. For example, the *Legality of Use of Force* cases filed by the Federal Republic of Yugoslavia against NATO members challenging their intervention in Kosovo were all dismissed on jurisdictional grounds.[34] So was the *Armed Activities* case filed by the Democratic Republic of the Congo against Rwanda.[35] In the recent *Sovereign Rights and Maritime Spaces* case, Nicaragua's claims under Article 2(4) of the U.N. Charter against Colombia were excluded from the Court's jurisdiction because prior correspondence between the parties did not indicate the existence of a dispute on the question.[36] The *Application of the Convention on the Elimination of All Forms of Racial Discrimination* case combined the latter two categories.[37] Georgia brought a claim against Russia respecting the 2008 invasion of South Ossetia and the related conflict in Abkhazia.[38] Had the case gone forward, the Court's subject-matter jurisdiction would have been limited to violations of the International Convention on the Elimination of All Forms of Racial Discrimination by its compromissory clause.[39] But the case was dismissed at the preliminary objection stage on jurisdictional grounds relating to

[33] Genocide (Croat. v. Serb.) Merits Judgment, *supra* note 6; Application of the Convention on the Prevention and Punishment of the Crime of Genocide (Bosn. & Herz. v. Serb. & Montenegro), Merits Judgment, 2007 I.C.J. 43 (Feb. 26).

[34] Legality of the Use of Force (Serb. & Montenegro v. Belg.), Preliminary Objections, 2004 I.C.J. 279 (Dec. 15); Legality of the Use of Force (Serb. & Montenegro v. Can.), Preliminary Objections, 2004 I.C.J. 429 (Dec. 15); Legality of the Use of Force (Serb. & Montenegro v. Fr.), Preliminary Objections, 2004 I.C.J. 575 (Dec. 15); Legality of the Use of Force (Serb. & Montenegro v. Ger.), Preliminary Objections, 2004 I.C.J. 720 (Dec. 15); Legality of the Use of Force (Serb. & Montenegro v. It.), Preliminary Objections, 2004 I.C.J. 865 (Dec. 15); Legality of the Use of Force (Serb. & Montenegro v. Neth.), Preliminary Objections, 2004 I.C.J. 1011 (Dec. 15); Legality of the Use of Force (Serb. & Montenegro v. Port.), Preliminary Objections, 2004 I.C.J. 1160 (Dec. 15); Legality of the Use of Force (Yugoslavia v. Belg.), Provisional Measures (Removal from List), 1999 I.C.J. 761 (June 2); Legality of the Use of Force (Yugoslavia v. U.S.), Provisional Measures (Removal from List), 1999 I.C.J. 916 (June 2).

[35] Armed Activities on the Territory of the Congo (New Application: 2002) (Dem. Rep. Congo v. Rwanda), Preliminary Objections, 2006 I.C.J. 6 (Feb. 3).

[36] Alleged Violations of Sovereign Rights and Maritime Spaces in the Caribbean Sea (Nicar. v. Colom.), Preliminary Objections, ¶ 78 (Mar. 17, 2016), www.icj-cij.org/files/case-related/155/155-20160317-JUD-01-00-EN.pdf.

[37] Application of the International Convention on the Elimination of All Forms of Racial Discrimination (Geor. v. Russ.), Preliminary Objections, 2011 I.C.J. 70 (Apr. 1) [hereinafter ICERD Preliminary Objections].

[38] *Id.* ¶ 16.

[39] *See* International Convention on the Elimination of All Forms of Racial Discrimination art. 22, Mar. 7, 1966, 660 U.N.T.S. 195.

the procedural condition of prior negotiations.[40] In only one example, *Armed Activities on the Territory of the Congo (Democratic Republic of the Congo v. Uganda)*, did the Court go directly to the merits of a use of force dispute.[41]

In light of the limitations on the contentious jurisdiction of the Court, it is unsurprising that the political organs of the United Nations have used the ICJ's advisory opinion mechanism to submit questions related to armed conflict to the Court. However, this jurisdictional path is also limited. The most obvious such limitation is the advisory nature of the resulting opinion.[42] Other limitations include the Charter's restrictions on standing to request an advisory opinion. Under Article 96(1) of the Charter, the General Assembly and Security Council are generally competent to request advisory opinions on "any legal question."[43] This has resulted in force-related topics coming before the Court, for example, in *Legal Consequences of the Construction of a Wall in the Occupied Palestinian Territory*[44] and *Legality of the Threat or Use of Nuclear Weapons*.[45] Under Article 96(2) of the Charter, the General Assembly is also competent to invite other U.N. organs or specialized agencies to request advisory opinions only "on legal questions arising in the scope of their activities."[46] Most cases arising under this jurisdiction involve technical questions of the law establishing the requesting organization or its relations with either Member States or staff.[47] However, in 1993, the World Health Organization decided to request an advisory opinion on this question:

> In view of the health and environmental effects, would the use of nuclear weapons by a State in war or other armed conflict be a breach of its obligations under international law including the WHO Constitution?[48]

The Court determined that it did not have jurisdiction because the question fell outside the scope of WHO activities.[49] This suggests that the scope for

---

[40] ICERD Preliminary Objections, *supra* note 37, ¶ 186.

[41] Armed Activities Judgment, *supra* note 6.

[42] *Compare* U.N. Charter art. 94(1), *with* art. 96.

[43] *Id.* art. 96(1).

[44] Legal Consequences of the Construction of a Wall in the Occupied Palestinian Territory, Advisory Opinion, 2004 I.C.J. 136 (July 9) [hereinafter Wall Advisory Opinion].

[45] Legality of the Threat or Use of Nuclear Weapons, Advisory Opinion, 1996 I.C.J. 226 (July 8) [hereinafter Nuclear Weapons Advisory Opinion].

[46] U.N. Charter art. 96(2).

[47] *E.g.*, Judgment No. 2867 of the Administrative Tribunal of the International Labour Organization upon a Complaint Filed Against the International Fund for Agricultural Development, Advisory Opinion, 2010 I.C.J. 10 (Feb. 1).

[48] World Health Assembly Res. WHA46.40, *Health and Environmental Effects of Nuclear Weapons* (May 14, 1993).

[49] Legality of the Use by a State of Nuclear Weapons in Armed Conflict, Advisory Opinion, 1996 I.C.J. 66, ¶ 31 (July 6).

additional organs or agencies to request advisory opinions on questions relating to force is limited.

III. CONTRIBUTIONS ON PRIMARY OBLIGATIONS

In cases in which the Court's jurisdiction has been established, the Court has made significant doctrinal contributions through its jurisprudence. These have concerned primarily Article 2(4) of the U.N. Charter, its relationship with other sources of international law, and the right of self-defense.

A. *The Content of the Principle of Non-Use of Force*

The predominant source of the international law regulating the use of force is Article 2(4) of the U.N. Charter. Article 2(4) provides:

> All Members shall refrain in their international relations from the threat or use of force against the territorial integrity or political independence of any State, or in any other manner inconsistent with the Purposes of the United Nations.[50]

In the *Nuclear Weapons* case, the Court clarified the nature of this rule, making clear that it is concerned only with the fact of force, not the manner in which it is used.[51] As the Court stated, the provisions apply "to any use of force, regardless of the weapons employed. The Charter neither expressly prohibits, nor permits, the use of any specific weapon."[52] This, instead, is a concern for international humanitarian law.[53]

B. *Use of Force*

The lead case on the use of force remains *Military and Paramilitary Activities in and Against Nicaragua*, brought by Nicaragua against the United States regarding the latter's support for the Contra rebels.[54] *Military and Paramilitary Activities* is distinct within the Court's jurisprudence for its discussion of what the principle of the non-use of force actually proscribes.[55] In its discussion, the

---

[50] U.N. Charter art. 2(4).
[51] *Nuclear Weapons Advisory Opinion, supra* note 45, ¶ 39.
[52] *Id.*
[53] *See id.* ¶¶ 52–54; *see also, e.g.*, Convention on Cluster Munitions, May 30, 2008, 2688 U.N.T.S. 39; Convention on the Prohibition of the Use, Stockpiling, Production and Transfer of Anti-Personnel Mines and on Their Destruction, Sept. 18, 1997, 2056 U.N.T.S. 211.
[54] Nicaragua Merits Judgment, *supra* note 6.
[55] *Id.* ¶¶ 191–92.

Court relied primarily upon the U.N. General Assembly's Declaration on Principles of Friendly Relations.[56] In particular, it adopted the following:

> Every State has the duty to refrain from the threat or use of force to violate the existing international boundaries of another State or as a means of solving international disputes, including territorial disputes and problems concerning frontiers of States. . . .
>
> States have a duty to refrain from acts of reprisal involving the use of force.
>
> Every State has the duty to refrain from any forcible action which deprives peoples . . . of their right to self-determination and freedom and independence.
>
> Every State has the duty to refrain from organizing or encouraging the organization of irregular forces or armed bands including mercenaries, for incursion into the territory of another State.
>
> Every State has the duty to refrain from organizing, instigating, assisting or participating in acts of civil strife or terrorist acts in another State or acquiescing in organized activities within its territory directed towards the commission of such acts, when the acts referred to in the present paragraph involve a threat or use of force.[57]

The Court additionally considered that the prohibition to "organize, assist, foment, finance, incite or tolerate subversive, terrorist or armed activities"[58] directed to overthrow another State's government and to interfere in foreign civil strife contained in the Declaration's elaboration of the principle of non-intervention was applicable in determining what conduct was a prohibited use of force.[59]

In practice, this has enabled the Court to hold that certain examples of state armed conduct amount to prohibited uses of force. In *Military and Paramilitary Activities*, the Court approached the question whether conduct was prohibited by first testing if the conduct could be shown to be attributable to the United States, and subsequently considering its lawfulness.[60] The Court held that the mining of Nicaraguan harbors by U.S. actors constituted a

---

[56] *Id.* ¶ 191 (citing G.A. Res. 2625 (XXV), annex, Declaration on Principles of International Law Concerning Friendly Relations and Co-operation Among States in Accordance with the Charter of the United Nations, U.N. Doc. A/RES/2625(XXV) (Oct. 24, 1970) [hereinafter Declaration on Friendly Relations].

[57] *Id.* (quoting Declaration on Friendly Relations, *supra* note 56).

[58] Declaration on Friendly Relations, *supra* note 56.

[59] Nicaragua Merits Judgment, *supra* note 6, ¶ 192.

[60] *See generally id.* ¶¶ 77–122.

prohibited use of force.[61] The Court also determined that the various attacks on oil industry facilities and military bases amounted to a prohibited use of force.[62] Finally, the Court held that the United States additionally violated the prohibition through its recruitment, training, supplying, and encouragement of the Contra rebels.[63] In the *Armed Activities* case, the military conduct in question was more straightforwardly a use of force.[64] In that case, Ugandan forces "traversed vast areas of the DRC" and "engaged in military operations in a multitude of locations."[65] These included clashes with Rwandan forces hundreds of kilometers into Congolese territory.[66] The Court held that these constituted "grave violations of Article 2, paragraph 4."[67] Finally, the Court held that Uganda had violated the prohibition through its training and military support to *Mouvement de libération du Congo* rebels.[68]

The Court has occasionally dealt with claims regarding the use of force in the context of boundary disputes. In such cases, the Court has shown circumspection in its treatment of claims of the unlawful use of force, subordinating its detailed consideration to the interest of stability. In *Land and Maritime Boundary (Cameroon v. Nigeria: Equatorial Guinea intervening)*, Cameroon claimed that various Nigerian "invasion[s]" of disputed territory held to be Cameroonian amounted to a violation of Article 2(4) of the Charter.[69] In respect of these, Cameroon requested reparations for material and moral injuries and assurances of non-repetition.[70] The Court did not respond directly to Cameroon's claim that the principle of the non-use of force was violated. However, it rejected both Cameroon's claims for damages and assurances, noting that the binding determination of the boundary eliminated any confusion that could lead to repetition[71] and that through "the very fact of the present Judgment and of the evacuation of the Cameroonian territory occupied by Nigeria, the injury suffered by Cameroon by reason of the

---

[61] *Id.* ¶¶ 80, 227.

[62] *Id.* ¶¶ 81–86, 227.

[63] *Id.* ¶ 228.

[64] *See* Armed Activities Judgment, *supra* note 6, ¶¶ 72–91.

[65] *Id.* ¶ 153.

[66] *Id.* ¶ 154. The separate Congolese case against Rwanda failed, as noted above, on jurisdictional grounds. *See supra* note 35 and accompanying text.

[67] *Id.* ¶ 153.

[68] *Id.* ¶ 160.

[69] Land and Maritime Boundary Between Cameroon and Nigeria (Cameroon v. Nigeria: Eq. Guinea intervening), Merits Judgment, 2002 I.C.J. 303, ¶ 310 (Oct. 10) [hereinafter Land and Maritime Boundary Merits Judgment].

[70] *Id.* ¶¶ 310, 318.

[71] *Id.* ¶ 318.

occupation of its territory will in all events have been sufficiently addressed."[72] This is consistent with the Court's past practice on the question.[73]

C. *Threats of Force*

In the *Nuclear Weapons* Advisory Opinion, the Court had the opportunity to elaborate on the notion of a "threat" of force.[74] Article 2(4) of the Charter prohibits both the threat and the use of force.[75] The Court's analysis identifies both types of conduct that can amount to a threat and what consequences must be threatened. On the first question, the Court used several synonyms for "threat,"[76] including "signalled intention," "stated readiness," and "declared readiness."[77] Each of these implies a degree of explicit pronouncement, a suggestion that in order to make a threat, a State must express its readiness to use force. The Court further refined its analysis in response to the arguments of several States that the possession of nuclear weapons itself is an unlawful threat because it suggests the possibility of use in response to an attack.[78] The Court reasoned:

> Possession of nuclear weapons may indeed justify an inference of prepared-
> ness to use them. In order to be effective, the policy of deterrence, by which
> those States possessing or under the umbrella of nuclear weapons seek to
> discourage military aggression by demonstrating that it will serve no purpose,
> necessitates that the intention to use nuclear weapons be credible.[79]

From this, one can deduce the Court's position: that messages inferred from conduct can amount to threats just as can words.

On the question whether a particular threat amounts to a prohibited threat of force, the Court recognized the link between the concepts of threat and use made in the text of Article 2(4).[80] The Court reasoned that "the notions of 'threat' and 'use' of force under Article 2, paragraph 4, of the Charter stand

---

[72] *Id.* ¶ 319.
[73] *See* Temple of Preah Vihear (Cambodia v. Thai.), Merits Judgment, 1962 I.C.J 6, 37 (June 15) (holding that "Thailand is under an obligation to withdraw any military or police forces . . . on Cambodian territory").
[74] Nuclear Weapons Advisory Opinion, *supra* note 45, ¶¶ 47–49.
[75] U.N. Charter art. 2(4).
[76] Nuclear Weapons Advisory Opinion, *supra* note 45, ¶ 47.
[77] *Id.*
[78] *Id.* ¶ 48.
[79] *Id.*
[80] *Id.* ¶ 47.

together."[81] Thus, if a particular use of force itself would be unlawful, the threat of such force is also unlawful.[82] The Court noted that in the *Nuclear Weapons* advisory proceeding, no State participating in the proceeding had claimed otherwise.[83]

D. *The Principle of Non-Use of Force in Customary International Law*

A major doctrinal contribution of the Court has been its confirmation that the principle of the non-use of force exists in customary international law. The Court has only explicitly considered the direct application of Article 2(4) in two cases, the *Nuclear Weapons* Advisory Opinion and the *Armed Activities* case. As noted above, in the *Military and Paramilitary Activities* case, the Court did not have jurisdiction over disputes concerning the application of the Charter, but it could apply customary international law. The Court confirmed that, even if a customary rule and Article 2(4) share identical content, they exist independently and can be applied separately from each other.[84]

Having established this, the Court turned to the question of the content of the customary rules governing the use of force.[85] In this regard, the Court noted that Nicaragua and the United States seemed to share the positon that customary international law had identical content to Article 2(4) of the Charter.[86] The Court was not satisfied with the agreement of the parties and instead examined for itself whether any *opinio juris* existed that could prove a customary rule.[87] To determine this, the Court considered States', and especially the parties', attitudes regarding various resolutions of international organizations purporting to restate customary international law.[88] In this particular regard, the Court relied heavily on the Declaration on Principles of International Law Concerning Friendly Relations,[89] both for establishing the existence of the customary norm and its content.[90] As a consequence, the Court reinforced the status of the principle of the non-use of force in customary international law.

---

[81] *Id.*
[82] *Id.*
[83] *Id.*
[84] Nicaragua Merits Judgment, *supra* note 6, ¶ 179.
[85] *Id.* ¶ 187.
[86] *Id.*
[87] *Id.* ¶ 188.
[88] *Id.* ¶¶ 188–90.
[89] Declaration on Friendly Relations, *supra* note 56.
[90] *Id.* ¶¶ 190–91.

E. *Self-Defense*

Much of the Court's doctrinal contribution on the use of force concerns the right of self-defense. This is unsurprising considering that, as the Court suggested in *Armed Activities*, self-defense is one of only three justifications for an otherwise unlawful use of force between States (the others being consent and authorization by the Security Council).[91] The Court has recognized that the right of self-defense forms part of customary international law.[92] This is a consequence of the text of the Charter. Article 51 of the Charter provides:

> Nothing in the present Charter shall impair the inherent right of individual or collective self-defence if an armed attack occurs against a Member of the United Nations, until the Security Council has taken measures necessary to maintain international peace and security.[93]

The Court reasoned "that Article 51 of the Charter is only meaningful on the basis that there is a 'natural' or 'inherent' right of self-defence, and it is hard to see how this can be other than of a customary nature."[94] Continuing, the Court noted that the Charter neither defines the notion of armed attack nor specifies the contours of the right of self-defense, implying that customary international law must exist to supply these answers.[95] In other words, "the Charter itself testifies to the existence" of the right to both individual and collective self-defense in customary international law.[96]

The relative frequency with which the Court has considered self-defense claims has allowed it to expound on each of the conditions for its lawful exercise, primarily the existence of an armed attack, the criteria of necessity and proportionality, and the requirement of Security Council notification. Each of these will be considered in turn.

1. Existence of an Armed Attack

The Court has elaborated on the meaning of the armed attack precondition of Article 51 of the Charter on several occasions.[97] As a consequence, the Court

---

91 *See* Armed Activities Judgment, *supra* note 6, ¶ 144; Nuclear Weapons Advisory Opinion, *supra* note 45, ¶ 38.
92 Nicaragua Merits Judgment, *supra* note 6, ¶ 176.
93 U.N. Charter art. 51.
94 Nicaragua Merits Judgment, *supra* note 6, ¶ 176.
95 *Id.*
96 *Id.*
97 *See* U.N. Charter art. 51.

has established a line of jurisprudence delimiting a narrow definition of armed attacks sufficient to justify the use of force.

As the Court noted in *Military and Paramilitary Activities*, "self-defence presupposes that an armed attack has occurred."[98] In the case of individual self-defense, the Court has held that this requires an armed attack directed at the State purporting to act in self-defense.[99] Consequently, when the United States claimed to act in individual, but not collective, self-defense in *Oil Platforms*, whether certain actions were directed at the United States became a decisive question.[100] In the case of collective self-defense, the Court has held that there must be a victim State on whose behalf the State acting in self-defense acts.[101] That victim State must itself "form and declare the view" that it has suffered an armed attack; a third State's own assessment is not sufficient.[102] Additionally, the victim State must request assistance in collective self-defense.[103]

In multiple cases, the Court has considered the range of conduct that can constitute an armed attack. The Court clarified in *Military and Paramilitary Activities* that the armed attack is "the most grave" form of the use of force.[104] It continued to explain that armed attacks can include action both by regular armed forces and by "armed bands, groups, irregulars or mercenaries," drawing upon the General Assembly's Resolution on the Definition of Aggression.[105] The distinctive characteristic of an armed attack, the Court explained, is not that it was committed by regular forces but rather its "scale and effects."[106] Additionally, the Court specifically excluded the provision of assistance to rebels in the form of weapons, logistical, or other support from the category of armed attack.[107]

The Court has had several opportunities to put this definition into practice. Thus, in *Military and Paramilitary Activities*, it held that the provision of arms to Salvadorian rebels by Nicaragua could not amount to an armed attack against El Salvador.[108] The Court rejected the U.S. argument that Honduras and Costa Rica each suffered an attack that justified a response because

---

[98] Nicaragua Merits Judgment, *supra* note 6, ¶ 232.
[99] Oil Platforms Merits Judgment, *supra* note 10, ¶ 51.
[100] *Id.* ¶ 64.
[101] Nicaragua Merits Judgment, *supra* note 6, ¶ 195.
[102] *Id.*
[103] *Id.*
[104] *Id.* ¶ 191.
[105] *Id.* ¶ 195 (citing G.A. Res. 3314 (XXIX), annex, art. 3(g), Definition of Aggression, U.N. Doc. A/RES/3314(XXIX) (Dec. 14, 1974)).
[106] *Id.*
[107] *Id.*
[108] *Id.* ¶ 230.

neither had requested U.S. assistance.[109] In *Oil Platforms*, the Court focused on the attribution, gravity, and targeting criteria to dismiss U.S. claims that various actions constituted armed attacks. The attack on the U.S.-flagged *Sea Isle City* tanker was dismissed because it was not proven to be attributable to Iran nor aimed at a particular U.S. target.[110] Attacks on some oil tankers were dismissed because those tankers were not U.S.-flagged and the United States was not claiming to act in collective self-defense.[111] Claims regarding some attacks by marine mines were dismissed as not targeted against the United States.[112] The mining of the USS *Samuel B. Roberts* in particular was rejected as an attack because the United States could not conclusively link the mine to Iran.[113] The Court additionally suggested that none of these examples reached the gravity threshold it recited in *Military and Paramilitary Activities*.[114]

On two occasions, the Court has held that the right of self-defense does not arise in response to non-state actors.[115] First, in the *Wall* Advisory Opinion, the Court considered Israel's argument that the construction of its separation barrier in the West Bank was justified by its right of self-defense.[116] The Court rejected this claim because it found that Israel was not facing an armed attack attributable to another State.[117] Interpreting Article 51 of the U.N. Charter, the Court reasoned that the provision "recognizes the existence of an inherent right of self-defence in the case of an armed attack by one State against another State."[118] Applying this, the Court rejected Israel's position because Israel did not claim it was defending itself from another State and because Israel was the State in control of the territory from which its threats emanated.[119]

In the *Armed Activities* case, the Court reaffirmed this position.[120] Responding to the Congolese claim that Uganda was unlawfully using force on Congolese territory, Uganda claimed it acted in response to attacks from non-state armed groups operating from Congolese territory and that this was consistent with its right of self-defense.[121] The Court was clear that unless the armed attacks

---

[109] *Id.* ¶ 234.
[110] Oil Platforms Merits Judgment, *supra* note 10, ¶¶ 61, 64.
[111] *Id.* ¶ 64.
[112] *Id.* ¶ 64.
[113] *Id.* ¶ 71.
[114] *Id.* ¶¶ 64, 72.
[115] Wall Advisory Opinion, *supra* note 44, ¶ 139; Armed Activities Judgment, *supra* note 6, ¶ 146.
[116] Wall Advisory Opinion, *supra* note 44, ¶ 138.
[117] *Id.* ¶ 139.
[118] *Id.*
[119] *Id.* ¶¶ 139–40.
[120] Armed Activities Judgment, *supra* note 6, ¶¶ 146–47.
[121] *Id.* ¶ 146.

were attributable to the Democratic Republic of the Congo, they could not justify Ugandan self-defense actions on Congolese territory.[122] In light of these two consistent decisions, the Court's position that self-defense may only be exercised in response to an armed attack from a State seems well established.[123]

2. Necessity and Proportionality

The Court has recognized that customary international law imposes two conditions on the exercise of the right of self-defense: necessity and proportionality.[124] These conditions apply equally to self-defense under customary international law and considered in the light of Article 51 of the Charter.[125] The Court considered the necessity criterion in the *Oil Platforms* case.[126] Commenting generally on the necessity requirement and rejecting the U.S. contention that it has a self-judging character, the Court explained that the requirement is "strict and objective, leaving no room for any 'measure of discretion.'"[127] Turning to the facts at hand, the Court did not consider the United States to have proven that its actions were necessary.[128] It reached this conclusion considering both that the U.S. action would not have been sufficient to stop Iranian attacks and that the United States had never complained to Iran about the use of oil platforms to attack neutral shipping.[129] The Court's analysis suggests that, in order to plead self-defense, a State should be prepared to demonstrate how its actions relate to ending the armed attack.

The Court has considered the proportionality criterion in two cases. The *Nuclear Weapons* Advisory Opinion gave the Court occasion to dwell upon the nature of the proportionality criterion.[130] In that proceeding, several States argued that the use of nuclear weapons in self-defense is inherently disproportionate.[131] The Court did not answer, instead emphasizing the particular risks

---

[122] *Id.* ¶¶ 146–47.
[123] The Court's position on this question, however, remains controversial among both States and scholars. While this debate is beyond the scope of this Chapter, for more on the evolution of the legal positions in this regard, *see* Jennifer Trahan, *The Crime of Aggression and the International Criminal Court*, in this volume, notes 137–42 and accompanying text.
[124] Nuclear Weapons Advisory Opinion, *supra* note 45, ¶ 41; Nicaragua Merits Judgment, *supra* note 6, ¶ 176.
[125] Nuclear Weapons Advisory Opinion, *supra* note 45, ¶ 41.
[126] Oil Platforms Merits Judgment, *supra* note 10, ¶¶ 73–76.
[127] *Id.* ¶ 73.
[128] *Id.* ¶ 76.
[129] *Id.*
[130] Nuclear Weapons Advisory Opinion, *supra* note 45, ¶¶ 42–43.
[131] *Id.* ¶ 43.

of escalation and devastating damage posed by the use of nuclear weapons and the relevance of these risks to a proportionality analysis.[132] The Court addressed proportionality more concretely in the *Oil Platforms* case.[133] The Court was faced with a situation in which the United States claimed it was acting in self-defense by destroying several Iranian oil platforms, naval vessels and aircraft in response to a mine explosion that damaged a U.S. warship.[134] The Court considered this response to be disproportionate, which it added to the list of reasons why the U.S. action was not within its right of self-defense.[135]

3. Self-Defense as a Pretext

The Court has also considered the related question whether motives beyond self-defense can impact the lawfulness of the use of force. In *Military and Paramilitary Activities*, Nicaragua challenged the U.S. claim that it was acting in collective self-defense of Nicaragua's neighbors, arguing instead that the United States' involvement was aimed at coercing Nicaraguan policy decisions.[136] The Court rejected the formal legal relevance of U.S. motives beyond collective self-defense, reasoning that

> if Nicaragua has been giving support to the armed opposition in El Salvador, and if this constitutes an armed attack on El Salvador and the other appropriate conditions are met, collective self-defence could be legally invoked by the United States. . . . The existence of an additional motive, other than that officially proclaimed by the United States, could not deprive the latter of its right to resort to collective self-defence.[137]

However, the Court did take Nicaragua's allegations as grounds for "special caution" in considering whether the United States had legitimately acted in self-defense.[138]

4. Notification

Finally, the Court has also commented on the notification requirement imposed by the Charter on those acting in self-defense. Article 51(2) imposes

---

[132] *Id.*
[133] Oil Platforms Merits Judgment, *supra* note 10, ¶ 77.
[134] *Id.*
[135] *Id.* ¶¶ 77–78.
[136] Nicaragua Merits Judgment, *supra* note 6, ¶ 127.
[137] *Id.*
[138] *Id.*

a duty upon States acting in self-defense to immediately notify the Security Council of their actions.[139] The Court has noted that this requirement applies to all actions taken in self-defense governed by the U.N. Charter.[140] When considering whether this rule had a customary nature in *Military and Paramilitary Activities*, however, the Court noted that it was "clear" that it did not.[141] However, the Court nevertheless determined that the decision of a State acting in self-defense whether to notify could be taken to indicate "whether the State in question was itself convinced that it was acting in self-defence" when evaluating the State's compliance with customary international law.[142] Thus the Court took into account a U.S. failure to notify the Security Council in determining that its actions were not in self-defense.[143] This position was reinforced when the Court similarly took into account Uganda's failure to notify the Security Council in determining that it had not acted in self-defense in the *Armed Activities* case.[144]

F. Consent to the Use of Force

The Court has accepted consent as a potential justification for the use of force by one State on the territory of another.[145] In *Armed Activities*, the Court was faced with Uganda's claim that it was present on Congolese territory with consent pursuant to accords providing a timetable for Ugandan withdrawal.[146] Uganda argued that the accords legitimized its troops' presence on Congolese territory.[147] The Court rejected this argument by focusing on the text of the Lusaka Agreement and determining that "[i]t carries no implication as to the Ugandan military presence being accepted as lawful."[148] The Court considered that the Agreement only established a Congolese willingness to tolerate an orderly withdrawal, not a recognition of the legality of Ugandan presence.[149]

---

[139] U.N. Charter art. 51.
[140] Nuclear Weapons Advisory Opinion, *supra* note 45, ¶ 44.
[141] Nicaragua Merits Judgment, *supra* note 6, ¶ 200.
[142] *Id.*
[143] *Id.* ¶ 235.
[144] Armed Activities Judgment, *supra* note 6, ¶ 145.
[145] *See id.* ¶ 105.
[146] *Id.* ¶ 92.
[147] *Id.* ¶ 94.
[148] *Id.* ¶ 97.
[149] *Id.* ¶ 99.

G. *The Inadmissibility of Territorial Acquisition by Force*

An additional contribution of the Court has been its clarification that the acquisition of territory by force is now inadmissible under customary international law. Before the twentieth century, international law generally permitted States to gain territory by force, either by conquest and subjugation[150] or by cession in peace treaties, in which the possessor of a territory at the time of conclusion was presumed to keep that territory.[151] Today, such acquisition of territory is generally considered to be prohibited.[152]

   This rule faces the limitation that an explicit prohibition on the acquisition of territory by force, rather than the use of force, is not present in the text of the Charter. The conclusion that territorial acquisition through subjugation is inadmissible can be reached through the law of state responsibility, particularly through the obligation to cease and make reparations for internationally wrongful acts and the obligation of third States not to recognize the consequences of serious violations of international law. Such logic is perhaps unsatisfying. Should such a core principle of friendly relations between States find its source in secondary rules of international law? In the *Wall* Advisory Opinion and citing the Declaration on Friendly Relations, the Court forged a direct path to the prohibition and confirmed the sense of the General Assembly that the prohibition of territorial acquisition by force is part of customary international law.[153]

H. *Due Diligence with Respect to Non-State Actors*

The Court has also had the opportunity to offer its views on the obligations of States to suppress the armed activities of non-state actors on their territories. In *Armed Activities*, Uganda raised a counterclaim against the Democratic Republic of the Congo alleging that it offered support for anti-Ugandan armed groups operating from Congolese territory[154] and, in any event, had failed in "a duty of vigilance" to ensure that its territory was not being used for "subversive or terrorist activities against another State."[155] In considering the claim, the

---

[150] OPPENHEIM, WAR, *supra* note 4, § 264.

[151] *Id.* § 273.

[152] *See, e.g.,* JAMES CRAWFORD, BROWNLIE'S PRINCIPLES OF PUBLIC INTERNATIONAL LAW 242–43 (8th ed. 2012).

[153] Wall Advisory Opinion, *supra* note 44, ¶ 87.

[154] Armed Activities Judgment, *supra* note 6, ¶¶ 276–77.

[155] *Id.* ¶ 277.

Court once again recalled the Declaration on Friendly Relations.[156] In its elaboration of the principle of the non-use of force, the Declaration provides:

> Every State has the duty to refrain from . . . acquiescing in organized activities within its territory directed towards the commission of such acts, when the acts referred to in the present paragraph involve a threat or use of force.[157]

Expounding on the duty of non-intervention, the Declaration adds:

> [N]o State shall . . . tolerate subversive, terrorist or armed activities directed towards the violent overthrow of the regime of another State, or interfere in civil strife in another State.[158]

The Court stated its view that both of these provisions are "declaratory of customary international law"[159] consistent with its general attitude toward the Declaration.

The Court ultimately rejected Uganda's claims on factual grounds.[160] The Court concluded that, for periods when the Democratic Republic of the Congo was not either fighting rebels that threatened Uganda or entitled to use force in self-defense against Uganda, Uganda had not proven that Congolese reticence amounted to the "tolerating" or "acquiescence" necessary to constitute a violation of international law.[161] Uganda had argued that rebels were able to "operate unimpeded" in light of "its mountainous terrain, its remoteness from Kinshasa . . . and the complete absence of central government presence or authority in the region."[162] The Court interpreted this as a lack of ability to control, rather than a lack of will, reasoning that "[n]either Zaire[163] nor Uganda were in a position to put an end to [rebel] activities."[164] Thus, what seems to have been dispositive for the Court was the lack of government control over the relevant territory.[165]

---

[156] *Id.* ¶ 300.

[157] Declaration on Friendly Relations, *supra* note 56, princ. 1, ¶ 9.

[158] *Id.* princ. 3, ¶ 2.

[159] Armed Activities Judgment, *supra* note 6, ¶ 300.

[160] *Id.* ¶¶ 300–05.

[161] *Id.*

[162] *Id.* ¶ 301.

[163] The relevant time period was before the fall of the Mobutu government in 1997. *Id.* ¶ 292.

[164] *Id.* ¶ 301.

[165] *Id.*

IV. THE PRINCIPLE OF NON-USE OF FORCE AS AN
INTERPRETIVE PRINCIPLE

As discussed above, the Court more often than not finds itself confronted with
cases concerning the use of force in which the U.N. Charter is outside its
subject-matter jurisdiction. In such cases, the Court has nevertheless turned to
it as a guide for the interpretation of other sources of international legal
regulation of the use of force. This has taken two forms. The first, discussed
above, is the use of the Charter to determine the content of parallel norms in
customary international law. Thus, in *Military and Paramilitary Activities*,
the Court took the Charter "into account in ascertaining the content of the
customary international law" at issue and within the Court's competence.[166]

The second has been the use of the U.N. Charter to interpret other treaties.
In *Oil Platforms*, the Court considered the use of force in a case in which its
jurisdiction was based solely on the compromissory clause in a seemingly
unrelated treaty.[167] The legal basis for such interpretation is found in the law
of treaty interpretation. Article 31(3)(c) of the Vienna Convention on the
Law of Treaties directs that, when a treaty is to be interpreted, "[t]here shall
be taken into account ... [a]ny relevant rules of international law applicable
in the relations between the parties."[168] The Court has expressed its view many
times that this provision reflects the customary international rule governing
treaty interpretation.[169]

In *Oil Platforms*, Iran brought proceedings against the United States under
the 1955 Treaty of Amity, Economic Relations, and Consular Rights between
the United States and Iran (Treaty)[170] in respect of U.S. military action that
damaged or destroyed several oil platforms in the Gulf.[171] Finding that Iran's
application pled violations of the Treaty, the Court affirmed its jurisdiction[172]
and proceeded to its merits phase. In the merits proceedings, the United States

---

[166] Nicaragua Merits Judgment, *supra* note 6, ¶ 183.

[167] *See generally* Oil Platforms Merits Judgment, *supra* note 10. A similar treaty was also
considered and provided a basis for jurisdiction in the *Military and Paramilitary Activities* case,
but Nicaragua's claim under the treaty did not involve the use of force. Nicaragua Merits
Judgment, *supra* note 6, ¶¶ 270–82.

[168] Vienna Convention on the Law of Treaties art. 31(3)(c), May 23, 1969, 1155 U.N.T.S. 331.

[169] ANTHONY AUST, MODERN TREATY LAW AND PRACTICE 207 (3d ed. 2013). Aust cites examples:
Territorial Dispute (Libya/Chad), Judgment, 1994 I.C.J. 6, ¶ 21 (Feb. 3); Kasikili/Sedudu Island
(Bots./Namib.), Judgment, 1999 I.C.J. 1045, ¶ 18 (Dec. 13) [hereinafter Kasikili/Sedudu
Island Judgment].

[170] Treaty of Amity, Economic Relations, and Consular Rights, *supra* note 31.

[171] Oil Platforms Preliminary Objections, *supra* note 32, ¶ 9.

[172] *Id.* ¶ 16.

raised the defense established in Article XX of the Treaty. Article XX provides that the Treaty "shall not preclude the application of measures . . . necessary to protect [a Party's] essential security interests."[173] The United States argued that this provision excluded its measures from the scope of the treaty and that it stood alone from the international law on the use of force.[174] The Court, however, considered that Article XX could not have been "intended to operate wholly independently of the relevant rules of international law on the use of force."[175] Thus, the question of the lawfulness of a use of force under international law generally was relevant to the determination of the applicability of Article XX.[176] In making this determination, the Court offered an interpretation of the 1955 Treaty of Amity, Economic Relations, and Consular Rights that incorporated the U.N. Charter paradigm and gave it a central role in a harmonized international law against the use of force.

V. THE INTERNATIONAL COURT OF JUSTICE AND THE PREVENTION OF ARMED CONFLICT

The Court's role in preventing armed conflict is much greater than its doctrinal contributions. The Court is "the principal judicial organ of the United Nations."[177] In this capacity, it is part of a system whose ultimate goal, in the eloquent words of the U.N. Charter, has been "to save succeeding generations from the scourge of war."[178] While not explicitly demanded by the Charter, its use is suggested by Article 33(1) of the Charter, which obligates U.N. Member States to seek to resolve disputes peacefully.[179] Among the categories of international disputes, the ones most historically likely to lead States to resort to force have been boundary disputes. The prevalence of border wars is reflected in the Charter and the Declaration on Friendly Relations, both of which list territorial integrity first as an interest protected by the principle of the non-use of force.[180]

Since the establishment of the United Nations and the Court, however, border wars have markedly declined. This is reflected in a decrease in territorial changes resulting from military conflict. According to the Correlates

---

[173] Treaty of Amity, Economic Relations, and Consular Rights, *supra* note 31, art. XX.
[174] Oil Platforms Merits Judgment, *supra* note 10, ¶¶ 32, 39.
[175] *Id.* ¶ 42.
[176] *Id.*
[177] U.N. Charter art. 92.
[178] *Id.* pmbl.
[179] *Id.* art. 33(1).
[180] *Id.* art. 2(4); Declaration on Friendly Relations, *supra* note 56, princ. 1.

of War Territorial Changes dataset, roughly thirty percent of territorial changes from 1850–1899 involved military conflict.[181] Between 1900 and the entry into force of the Charter, roughly thirty-six percent did.[182] Since the entry into force of the Charter, fewer than seventeen percent of territorial changes involved military conflict.[183] This trend is remarkable for two reasons. First, over the course of the twentieth century, the number of States has roughly quadrupled. Writing in 1912, Oppenheim identified fifty entities he considered to be fully sovereign States.[184] Today there are 197.[185] A proportionate increase in border wars could reasonably be expected from such a proliferation of States. Second, the number of kinds of boundaries has also increased. The extension of the breadth of territorial waters and the creation of Exclusive Economic Zones and continental shelves as additional maritime spaces subject to States' jurisdiction have put millions of additional square kilometers of oceanic natural resources up for grabs. Indeed, at the time the international community was debating these additions, several observers expressed their concern that the further division of the oceans would create new incentives for armed conflict.[186]

Despite the potential for conflict these changes might have created, the Court has found a role in the peaceful settlement of boundary disputes. Indeed, for the Court, territorial and maritime disputes have become "classical issues."[187] This trend extends to regions historically less open to judicial

---

[181] *See* Jaroslav Tir, Philip Schafer, Paul F. Diehl & Gary Goertz, *Territorial Changes, 1816–1996: Procedures and Data*, 16 CONFLICT MGMT. & PEACE SCI. 89 (1998). For this Chapter, Version 5 of the dataset, dated March 21, 2015, and *available at* www.correlatesofwar.org/data-sets/territorial-change, was used. In creating the dataset, a territorial change was identified when control of a territory moved from a losing country (not necessarily a State) to a gaining country. *Territorial Change v.5 Coding Manual*, CORRELATES OF WAR PROJECT, at 2, *available at* www.correlatesofwar.org/data-sets/territorial-change (download "Territorial Change data"). A territorial change involved military conflict when it involved "organized forces of both sides." *Id.* at 4.

[182] *See id.*

[183] *See id.*

[184] 1 L. OPPENHEIM, INTERNATIONAL LAW: A TREATISE: PEACE §§ 108–11 (2d ed. 1912).

[185] The members of the United Nations, Cook Islands, Niue, Palestine and Vatican City.

[186] *See, e.g.,* U.N. GAOR, 1st Comm., 22d Sess., 1515th mtg., U.N. Doc. A/C.1/PV.1515 (Nov. 1, 1967) (Statement of Malta) and U.N. GAOR, 1st Comm., 22d Sess., 1516th mtg., U.N. Doc. A/C.1/PV.1516 (Nov. 1, 1967) (Statement of Malta); WOLFGANG FRIEDMANN, THE FUTURE OF THE OCEANS (1971).

[187] H. E. Judge Hisashi Owada, President of the Int'l Court of Justice, Speech to the Sixty-Fourth Session of the General Assembly of the United Nations 1 (Oct. 29, 2009), *available at* http://www.securitycouncilreport.org/atf/cf/%7B65BFCF9B-6D27-4E9C-8CD3-CF6E4FF96FF9%7D/ICJ%20A%2064%20PV%2030.pdf.

dispute settlement, such as Africa[188] and Asia.[189] In some cases, the parties have even cited the desire to avoid armed conflict as a reason for turning to the Court for dispute resolution.[190] The Court can take at least some credit for the avoidance of conflict in these instances. As is often recited, "good fences make good neighbors."[191] The Court has proven itself to be a builder of fences worthy of States' consideration.[192]

VI. LOOKING FORWARD: REPARATIONS IN *ARMED ACTIVITIES*

Predicting the future of the Court's relationship to armed conflict is not easy. Much depends on the cases that States and the United Nations choose to submit to it. If the Court's avoidance of the question of the use of force in its judgment in *Certain Activities Carried out by Nicaragua in the Border Area (Costa Rica v. Nicaragua)* is any indication, the Court does not seem eager to handle this politically charged topic.[193] However, at the time of this writing, the Court is poised once again to touch upon the use of force in the context of the reparations phase of *Armed Activities on the Territory of the Congo (Democratic Republic of the Congo v. Uganda)*.

In its merits judgment in *Armed Activities*, the Court, upon finding that Uganda violated the principle of the non-use of force and principles of human rights and humanitarian law, decided that "failing agreement between the Parties, the question of reparation due to the Democratic Republic of the

---

[188] E.g., Frontier Dispute (Burk. Faso/Niger), Judgment, 2013 I.C.J. 44 (Apr. 16); Frontier Dispute (Benin/Niger), Judgment, 2005 I.C.J. 90 (July 12); Kasikili/Sedudu Island Judgment, *supra* note 169; Land and Maritime Boundary Merits Judgment, *supra* note 69.

[189] Sovereignty over Pedra Branca/Pulau Batu Puteh, Middle Rocks and South Ledge (Malay./Sing.), Judgment, 2008 I.C.J. 12 (May 23); Sovereignty over Pulau Ligitan and Pulau Sipadan (Indon./Malay.), Merits Judgment, 2002 I.C.J. 625 (Dec. 12); Maritime Delimitation and Territorial Questions Between Qatar and Bahrain (Qatar v. Bahr.), Merits Judgment, 2001 I.C.J. 40 (Mar. 16).

[190] E.g., Framework Agreement on the Peaceful Settlement of the Territorial Dispute Between the Great Socialist People's Libyan Arab Jamahiriya and the Republic of Chad art. 4, Libya-Chad, Aug. 31, 1989, 1545 U.N.T.S. 108.

[191] ROBERT FROST, *Mending Wall, in* NORTH OF BOSTON 7, 8 (1st ed. 1914).

[192] In a metaphorical sense. The question of physical barriers is beyond this contribution, but not beyond the Court. Wall Advisory Opinion, *supra* note 44.

[193] Certain Activities Carried out by Nicaragua in the Border Area (Costa Rica v. Nicar.) and Construction of a Road in Costa Rica Along the San Juan River (Nicar. v. Costa Rica), Judgment, 2015 I.C.J. 665, ¶ 97 (Dec. 16) (holding that the question of non-use of force need not be reached in light of a conclusion that the activities in question were otherwise unlawful); *but see id.* (separate opinion by Judge Robinson).

Congo shall be settled by the Court."[194] The negotiations have failed, and on July 1, 2015, the Court fixed time limits for the filing of written submissions on reparations.[195] The first round of submissions have been filed, and the parties' respective counter-memorials were due in February 2018.[196] These will be followed by oral submissions. Whatever the Court's judgment, it will likely contain guidance on the appropriate method for determining reparations for the unlawful use of force and related violations of international law.

This is new ground for the Court, as the only previous determination of reparations in the context of the use of force was limited to the damage caused by mines to British warships and naval personnel in the *Corfu Channel* case.[197] The former was determined by comparing expert appraisals to the actual costs borne by the United Kingdom.[198] The latter was determined according to the actual pension and grant costs the United Kingdom paid.[199] The injuries in *Armed Activities* are substantially more widespread and involve the "illegal use of force, violation of sovereignty and territorial integrity, military intervention, occupation of Ituri, violations of international human rights law and of international humanitarian law, looting, plunder and exploitation of DRC's natural resources."[200] As a consequence, it is likely the *Armed Activities* quantum phase will lead the Court to offer a much more detailed methodology to calculate the reparations due after armed conflict and thus a substantial contribution to the jurisprudence on the use of force.

---

[194] Armed Activities Judgment, *supra* note 6, ¶ 345. The Court decided that it would similarly determine reparations due to Uganda by the Democratic Republic of the Congo for violations of diplomatic law should negotiations fail. *Id.*

[195] Armed Activities on the Territory of the Congo (Dem. Rep. Congo v. Uganda), Order Fixing Time Limits, 2015 I.C.J. 580 (July 1).

[196] Armed Activities on the Territory of the Congo (Dem. Rep. Congo. v. Uganda), Order Fixing Time Limits (Dec. 6, 2016), *available at* http://www.icj-cij.org/files/case-related/116/116-20051219-JUD-01-00-EN.pdf.

[197] *See generally* Corfu Channel (U.K. v. Alb.), Reparations Judgment, 1949 I.C.J. 244 (Dec. 15).

[198] *Id.* at 249.

[199] *Id.* at 249–50.

[200] Armed Activities Judgment, *supra* note 6, ¶ 259.

9

The Other Enemy

Transnational Terrorists, Armed Attacks, and Armed Conflicts

CARRIE MCDOUGALL

I. INTRODUCTION

The Islamic State of Iraq and Syria (ISIS)[1] has emerged as an enemy like
no other in the post-Charter era. Its *modus operandi*, combined with its
extraordinary capability, has galvanized a broad Coalition of States to stand
up in opposition against it, although a much smaller number have been
prepared to engage in active combat. The Coalition's actions in Iraq and
more particularly, Syria, have raised a range of questions under the *jus ad
bellum* and the *jus in bello*. This Chapter argues that while the Coalition's
actions against ISIS in Syria illustrate that the *jus ad bellum* has adapted to
meet the challenges posed by sophisticated transnational organized armed
groups, lawyers are struggling to find answers to parallel challenges in the
jus in bello. I examine why this is so, and why it is important for States to
shrug off the shroud of secrecy in which they cloak their military operations
in order to engage with the law and ensure that it remains relevant to
modern challenges.[2] A failure to do so risks international counterterrorism
operations being conducted in a legal vacuum, which is contrary to the
interests of organized armed groups, States, and innocent civilians caught
in the cross fire.

II. ISIS: THE OTHER ENEMY

ISIS is an unprecedented enemy. Estimates of its total military force differ. Before
Coalition airstrikes began, its force strength was estimated at 19,000–31,000.

---

[1] ISIS is also known as ISIL, the Islamic State, and Daesh. This volume uses ISIS for consistency.
[2] This Chapter has been written in a personal capacity and does not necessarily reflect the views
of the Australian government.

In the first two and a half years of Coalition operations against ISIS, that number was relatively steady, demonstrating the organization's remarkable regenerating ability, reportedly based in large part on forced conscription and foreign terrorist fighters, lured to fight through ISIS's sophisticated media and public relations operations.[3] With the tide of operations in Syria and Iraq turning against them, the last estimate of the size of ISIS's military force in Iraq and Syria was 12,000–15,000 in March 2017.[4]

Despite the motley nature of its ranks, ISIS has demonstrated sophisticated military capabilities since it assumed control of Mosul in June 2014 – largely a result of the strict command and control exercised by the group's Military Council and the professional-grade covert and intelligence operations directed by its Security Council.[5] While ISIS has exhibited the tactics that characterize modern asymmetric insurgencies (including clustering in urban areas and integrating into civilian populations), in many ways ISIS's military wing more closely resembles a conventional army.[6]

The extremely violent tactics employed by ISIS are so brutal that even al-Qaeda has criticized its radicalism.[7] There is, however, little doubting the effectiveness of its strategies. Two years after the commencement of Coalition airstrikes, ISIS controlled large swathes of territory in Iraq and Syria.[8] In many

---

[3] United States intelligence sources estimate that more than 36,500 foreign fighters have travelled to Syria from more than 100 different countries since 2012. *See Worldwide Threat Assessment of the U.S. Intelligence Community: Hearing Before the S. Armed Services Comm.*, 114th Cong. 5 (2016) (statement of James R. Clapper, Director of National Intelligence), www.armed-services.senate.gov/imo/media/doc/Clapper_02-09-16.pdf.

[4] Press Briefing by U.S. Army Lt. Gen. Stephen Townsend, Commander, Combined Joint Task Force – Operation Inherent Resolve (Mar. 1, 2017), www.defense.gov/news/Transcripts/Transcript-view/Article/1099469/department-of-defense-press-briefing-by-gen-townsend-via-teleconference-from-ba/.

[5] Hassan Abu Haniyeh, *Daesh's Organisational Structure*, AL JAZEERA CTR. FOR STUD. (Dec. 4, 2014), http://studies.aljazeera.net/en/dossiers/decipheringdaeshoriginsimpactandfuture/2014/12/201412395930929444.html.

[6] Audrey Kurth Cronin, *ISIS is not a Terrorist Group*, FOREIGN AFF., Mar.–Apr. 2015.

[7] Motaz al-Khateeb, *Daesh's Intellectual Origins: From Jurisprudence to Realism*, AL JAZEERA CTR. FOR STUD. (Jan. 18, 2015), http://studies.aljazeera.net/en/dossiers/decipheringdaeshoriginsimpactandfuture/2014/12/2014123981882756.html.

[8] The tide of operations turned in the second half of 2016, resulting in ISIS losing, by June 2017, seventy percent of the territory it once controlled in Iraq, and over fifty percent of territory once controlled in Syria. *Daesh Areas of Influence – May 2017 Update*, GLOB. COALITION AGAINST DAESH (June 23, 2017), http://theglobalcoalition.org/en/maps_and_stats/daesh-areas-of-influence-may-2017-update/.

of those areas, including those devastated by years of Syria's civil war, ISIS restored order and managed the needs of the population.[9]

While now in a declining financial situation, ISIS is still effectively self-sufficient, controlling a flexible and diversified revenue-generating structure.[10] It controls a significant portion of Syria's and Iraq's oil, at its height bringing in an estimated revenue of USD$1–3 million a day.[11] It operates a range of natural resource and mining operations, and generates significant agricultural revenue. Its bank lootings reportedly amount to tens of millions of dollars; in addition it has plundered antiquities, jewelry, cars, and machinery to sell on the black market. It controls major transportation routes, allowing it to tax the movement of goods and charge tolls. It demands taxes and stipends from owners and producers in the territory under its control, bringing in revenue from everything from small family farms to major utilities. It demands enormous ransom payments. And it operates an effective fundraising network.[12]

ISIS's effectiveness at least in part accounts for its attractiveness to other extremist groups. According to the U.N. Secretary-General, by the end of 2015, thirty-four groups from all around the world had pledged allegiance to ISIS.[13] ISIS affiliates have carried out attacks in places including Egypt, Libya, Tunisia, Kuwait, Beirut, Paris, and Jakarta. As the U.N. Secretary-General concluded in his January 2016 report, ISIS "represents an unprecedented threat to international peace and security."[14]

The significance of the threat posed by ISIS has generated a robust response by States. After increasingly losing control of territory to ISIS, Iraqi authorities requested assistance from the international community. U.S. airstrikes on ISIS began on August 8, 2014. Over the following months, the United States built a Coalition to contribute to Operation Inherent Resolve. Realizing that the defeat of ISIS in Iraq would likely only mean pushing the group across the border, airstrikes against ISIS in Syria commenced on September 22, 2014. In parallel, efforts to train and supply

---

[9] al-Khateeb, *supra* note 7.

[10] U.N. Secretary-General, *Rep. of the Secretary-General on the threat posed by ISIL (Da'esh) to international peace and security and the range of United Nations efforts in support of Member States in countering the threat,* ¶ 4, U.N. Doc. S/2016/92 (Jan. 29, 2016) [hereinafter *Rep. of the Secretary-General on the threat posed by ISIL*].

[11] Zachary Laub, *CFR Backgrounders: The Islamic State,* COUNCIL ON FOREIGN REL., https://www.cfr.org/backgrounder/islamic-state.

[12] Cronin, *supra* note 6.

[13] *Rep. by the Secretary-General on the threat posed by ISIL, supra* note 10, ¶ 7.

[14] *Id.* ¶ 13.

moderate Syrian opposition groups have intensified in order to assist those groups in fighting ISIS.

The Coalition's fight against ISIS has raised a significant number of complex legal issues. This Chapter examines a selection of those issues for the purpose of demonstrating that while the *jus ad bellum* has the capacity to respond to new security threats, the *jus in bello* is struggling to adapt to conflicts of the sort being fought against ISIS.

III. A RESPONSIVE *JUS AD BELLUM*

While the legal basis for the Coalition's intervention in Iraq was straightforward (force was used against ISIS in Iraq at the Government of Iraq's invitation and with its consent),[15] the use of force against ISIS in Syria has generated more commentary – at least among scholars.

On September 20, 2014, the Iraqi Foreign Minister wrote to the U.N. Security Council (UNSC), affirming that ISIS's safe haven outside of Iraq was a direct threat to Iraq, and requesting that the United States lead international operations to strike ISIS targets.[16] In their letters to the Security Council, the United States,[17] the United Kingdom,[18]

---

[15] Iraq's request for assistance and consent to the use of force is well documented. Iraq appealed by letter to the U.N. Secretary-General on June 25, 2014, requesting assistance from the international community in countering ISIS. *See* Letter dated June 25, 2014, from the Permanent Rep. of Iraq to the United Nations addressed to the Secretary-General, U.N. Doc. S/2014/440 (June 25, 2014). This request was reiterated by Iraq at the Paris Conference on Peace and Security in Iraq on September 9, 2014, and through numerous requests for assistance made to the United States, confirmed with individual members of the Coalition at the political level and through processes such as obtaining diplomatic clearances for flights, and in arrangements concluded in relation to matters such as privileges and immunities.

[16] Letter dated Sept. 20, 2014, from the Permanent Rep. of Iraq to the United Nations addressed to the President of the Security Council, U.N. Doc. S/2014/691 (Sept. 22, 2014).

[17] Letter dated Sept. 23, 2014, from the Permanent Rep. of the United States of America to the United Nations addressed to the Secretary-General, U.N. Doc. S/2014/695 (Sept. 23, 2014). The United States also asserted that it is exercising individual self-defense in taking action against al-Qaeda elements in Syria known as the Khorasan Group.

[18] *See* Identical letters dated Nov. 25, 2014, from the Permanent Rep. of the United Kingdom of Great Britain and Northern Ireland to the United Nations addressed to the Secretary-General and the President of the Security Council, U.N. Doc. S/2014/851 (Nov. 26, 2014); Letter dated Sept. 7, 2015, from the Permanent Rep. of the United Kingdom of Great Britain and Northern Ireland to the United Nations addressed to the President of the Security Council, U.N. Doc. S/2015/688 (Sept. 8, 2015); Letter dated Dec. 3, 2015, from the Permanent Rep. of the United Kingdom of Great Britain and Northern Ireland to the United Nations addressed to the President of the Security Council, U.N. Doc. S/2015/928 (Dec. 3, 2015). The United Kingdom's second and third letters to the Council reference both individual and collective self-defense.

Canada,[19] Turkey,[20] France,[21] Australia,[22] Germany,[23] Denmark,[24] Norway,[25] and Belgium[26] all stated that their use of force against ISIS in Syria's territory is an exercise of the right of collective self-defense on Iraq's behalf, in addition, in some cases, to individual self-defense.[27]

Arguments in relation to the existence of the right to exercise self-defense against non-state actors in the territory of another State have been well ventilated, so I will recap them only briefly here. Others have put forward the plausible argument that the *Caroline* incident of 1837 (which is the basis of other key elements of customary international law on self-defense) demonstrates that the law permits the use of force against non-state actors on the territory of a third State without its consent.[28] Certainly at no point did Daniel Webster argue that the United Kingdom was denied the right to act in self-defense because the attacks on the United Kingdom were made by Canadian rebels (who were using U.S. territory as a staging ground). Rather, the dispute

[19] Letter dated Mar. 31, 2015, from the Chargé d'affaires a.i. of the Permanent Mission of Canada to the United Nations addressed to the President of the Security Council, U.N. Doc. S/2015/221 (Mar. 31, 2015).

[20] Letter dated July 24, 2015, from the Permanent Rep. of Turkey to the United Nations addressed to the President of the Security Council, U.N. Doc. S/2015/563 (July 24, 2015). Turkey's letter also refers to individual self-defense.

[21] Letter dated Sept. 8, 2015, from the Permanent Rep. of France to the United Nations addressed to the Secretary-General and the President of the Security Council, U.N. Doc. S/2015/745 (Sept. 9, 2015). France's letter implied that it is exercising both individual and collective self-defense.

[22] Letter dated Sept. 9, 2015, from the Permanent Rep. of Australia to the United Nations addressed to the President of the Security Council, U.N. Doc. S/2015/693 (Sept. 9, 2015).

[23] Letter dated Dec. 10, 2015, from the Chargé d'affaires a.i. of the Permanent Mission of Germany to the United Nations addressed to the President of the Security Council, U.N. Doc. S/2015/946 (Dec. 10, 2015).

[24] Letter dated Jan. 11, 2016, from the Permanent Rep. of Denmark to the United Nations addressed to the President of the Security Council, U.N. Doc. S/2016/34 (Jan. 13, 2016).

[25] Letter dated June 3, 2016, from the Permanent Rep. of Norway to the United Nations addressed to the President of the Security Council, U.N. Doc. S/2016/513 (June 3, 2016).

[26] Letter dated June 7, 2016, from the Permanent Rep. of Belgium to the United Nations addressed to the President of the Security Council, U.N. Doc. S/2016/523 (June 9, 2016).

[27] Jordan has also asserted a right to exercise individual self-defense against ISIS in Syria on the basis of the cross-border threat it faces.

[28] *See, e.g.,* Ashley S. Deeks, *"Unwilling or Unable": Toward a Normative Framework for Extraterritorial Self-Defense,* 52 VA. J. INT'L L. 483, 502 (2012); Abraham D. Soafer, *On the Necessity of Preemption,* 14 EUR. J. INT'L L. 209, 216–17 (2003); Sean D. Murphy, *Self-Defense and the Israeli Wall Advisory Opinion: An Ipse Dixit from the ICJ?,* 99 AM. J. INT'L L. 62, 65 (2005) [hereinafter Murphy, *Self-Defense and the Israeli Wall Advisory Opinion*]; Jordan J. Paust, *Self-Defense Targetings of Non-State Actors and Permissibility of U.S. Use of Drones in Pakistan,* 19 J. TRANSNAT'L & POL'Y 237, 241–42, 244 (2010) [hereinafter Paust, *Self-Defense Targetings of Non-State Actors*]; Christopher Greenwood, *International Law and Pre-emptive Use of Force: Afghanistan, Al-Qaida, and Iraq,* 4 SAN DIEGO INT'L L.J. 7, 17, 225 (2010).

between Webster and Ashburton focused on whether the United States had been delinquent in failing to take action against the rebels and whether the United Kingdom's acts in response had been necessary and proportionate.[29] Equally, Article 51 of the Charter of the United Nations (which is widely understood to have preserved the pre-existing right to exercise self-defense under customary international law) is not confined in its terms of reference to armed attacks carried out by, or imputed to, States – in contradistinction to the prohibition of the use of force in Article 2(4).[30]

The International Court of Justice's (ICJ) decision in *Nicaragua* is generally cited as holding that self-defense can only be exercised in response to armed attacks in which States have at least played a key role. In relevant part, the Court held that

> it may be considered to be agreed that an armed attack must be understood as including not merely action by regular armed forces across an international border, but also "the sending by or on behalf of a State of armed bands, groups, irregulars or mercenaries, which carry out acts of armed force against another State of such gravity as to amount to" (inter alia) an actual armed attack conducted by regular forces, "or its substantial involvement therein." This description, contained in Article 3, paragraph (g), of the Definition of Aggression annexed to General Assembly resolution 3314 (XXIX), may be taken to reflect customary international law. The Court sees no reason to deny that, in customary law, the prohibition of armed attacks may apply to the sending by a State of armed bands to the territory of another State, if such an operation, because of its scale and effects, would have been classified as an armed attack rather than as a mere frontier incident had it been carried out by regular armed forces.[31]

---

[29] Correspondence between Gr. Brit. and the U.S., respecting the Arrest and Imprisonment of Mr. McLeod, for the Destruction of the Steamboat Caroline, 29 BFSP 1126, 1138 (1841), https://babel.hathitrust.org/cgi/pt?id=mdp.39015019751299;view=1up;seq=1152.

[30] *See* YORAM DINSTEIN, WAR, AGGRESSION AND SELF-DEFENCE 224–25 (5th ed. 2011); Claus Kreß, *Some Reflections on the International Legal Framework Governing Transnational Armed Conflicts*, 15 J. CONFLICT & SEC. L. 245, 248 (2010); Murphy, *Self-Defense and the Israeli Wall Advisory Opinion*, *supra* note 28, at 64, 70; Sean D. Murphy, *Terrorism and the Concept of "Armed Attack" in Article 51 of the U.N. Charter*, 43 HARV. INT'L L.J. 41, 50 (2002) [hereinafter Murphy, *Terrorism and the Concept of "Armed Attack"*]; Paust, *Self-Defense Targetings of Non-State Actors*, *supra* note 28, at 249; Jordan J. Paust, *Use of Armed Force Against Terrorists in Afghanistan, Iraq, and Beyond*, 35 CORNELL INT'L L.J. 533, 534 (2002); Theresa Reinold, *State Weakness, Irregular Warfare, and the Right to Self-Defense Post-9/11*, 105 AM. J. INT'L L. 244, 248 (2011); Christian J. Tams, *The Use of Force Against Terrorists*, 20 EUR. J. INT'L L. 359, 369 (2009).

[31] Military and Paramilitary Activities in and Against Nicaragua (Nicar. v. U.S.), Merits Judgment, 1986 I.C.J. 14, ¶ 195 (June 27).

Contrary to others, I would argue that the Court held only that in addition to armed attacks carried out by state armed forces, sending non-state actors into the territory of another State to carry out an armed attack, or the substantial involvement of a State therein, amounts to an armed attack giving rise to the right of self-defense. In other words, the ICJ confined its judgment to the facts of the case and was silent on the question of whether the acts of non-state actors, absent state involvement, can trigger the right of self-defense.

This said, it is difficult to deny the fact that, at least before the events of September 11, 2001 (9/11), evidence of unambiguous state practice and *opinio juris* concerning the exercise of self-defense against non-state actors in the territory of another State, without that State's consent, was limited. As Ashley Deeks, Christian Tams, and Tom Ruys (among others) have documented, force was used against non-state actors in the territory of another State on the basis of self-defense on a number of occasions between 1945 and 2000: Portugal's attacks on anti-Portuguese rebels in Guinea-Bissau, Senegal, and Zambia between 1969 and 1971; South Africa's attacks on the camps of the South West Africa People's Organization in Angola, Lesotho, Swaziland, and Zambia between 1976 and 1985; Israel's strike on the Palestine Liberation Organization headquarters in Tunis in 1985; U.S. strikes in Sudan and Afghanistan in response to the al-Qaeda bombings of U.S. Embassies in Kenya and Tanzania in 1998; Turkey and Iran's incursions into Iraq in response to attacks by the Kurdistan Workers' Party (PKK) in the 1990s; and Iran's uses of force against the bases of the Mujahedin-e Khalq Organization in Iraq from the mid-1990s.[32]

While some of these acts attracted lukewarm support or muted reactions, others were condemned. In some cases, disapproval hinged on a view that the non-state actor's actions did not amount to an armed attack, or related to concerns that the use of force in self-defense was disproportionate or

---

[32] The Shultz Doctrine developed by the United States in 1984 following the 1983 suicide attacks on the U.S. Embassy in Lebanon and on U.S. marine barracks in Beirut provided that "A nation attacked by terrorists is permitted to use force to prevent or preempt future attacks, to seize terrorists, or to rescue its citizens when no other means is available … this nation has consistently affirmed the right of States to use force in exercise of their right of individual or collective self-defense." GEORGE SHULTZ, U.S. SEC'Y OF STATE, BUREAU OF PUBLIC AFFAIRS, U.S. DEP'T OF STATE, CURRENT POLICY NO. 783, LOW-INTENSITY WARFARE: THE CHALLENGE OF AMBIGUITY 3 (1986), https://babel.hathitrust.org/cgi/pt?id= umn.31951d00810526r;view=1up;seq=1 (*cited in* TOM RUYS, 'ARMED ATTACK' AND ARTICLE 51 OF THE UN CHARTER: EVOLUTIONS IN CUSTOMARY LAW AND PRACTICE 422–23 [2010]). *See also* RUYS, *supra* at 426–30.

unnecessary, or alternatively, that the use of force could be attributed to ideological divisions.[33] But many of these acts were controversial because of the impact on the sovereignty of the State on whose territory the non-state actors in question were targeted. Also notable is the fact that the key documents adopted by the U.N. General Assembly that spelled out States' interpretation of the *jus ad bellum* in this period (namely the Friendly Relations Declaration[34] and the Definition of Aggression[35]) are silent in relation to the exercise of self-defense against non-state actors. Indeed, the push in this period to adopt conventions addressing different types of terrorist activities indicates that terrorism was primarily seen as a law enforcement, rather than *jus ad bellum*, issue.[36] For this reason, it is difficult to sustain a conclusion that, prior to September 11, 2001, there existed an unambiguous right to exercise self-defense against non-state actors in the territory of another State – although some States were certainly of this view.

The growth of the terrorist threat, culminating in the 9/11 attacks, led to a changed landscape. The vulnerability of the United States to large-scale uses of force by a non-state actor made such threats very real for all States. It is therefore hardly surprising that UNSC Resolutions 1368 (2001) and 1373 (2001), adopted in the wake of the 9/11 attacks, recognized a right of self-defense against non-state actors[37] and that the Coalition of States that participated in Operation Enduring Freedom initially relied on the exercise of individual and collective self-defense in taking action against al-Qaeda in Afghanistan without the Taliban government's consent,[38] or that the

---

[33] *See* Jake William Rylatt, *An Evaluation of the U.S. Policy of "Targeted Killing" Under International Law: The Case of Anwar Al-Aulaqi*, 44 CAL. W. INT'L L.J. 39, 60–61 (2013); Tams, *supra* note 30, at 367.

[34] G.A. Res. 2625 (XXV), annex, Declaration on Principles of International Law Concerning Friendly Relations and Co-operation Among States in Accordance with the Charter of the United Nations, U.N. Doc. A/RES/2625(XXV) (Oct. 24, 1970).

[35] G.A. Res. 3314 (XXIX), annex, Definition of Aggression, U.N. Doc. A/RES/3314(XXIX) (Dec. 14, 1974).

[36] Tams, *supra* note 30, at 363–64.

[37] Preambulatory paragraph 3 of Resolution 1368 recognized "the inherent right of individual or collective self-defence in accordance with the Charter." S.C. Res. 1368, U.N. Doc. S/RES/1368, pmbl., ¶ 3, (2001). Preambulatory paragraph 4 of Resolution 1373 reaffirmed "the inherent right of individual or collective self-defence as recognized by the Charter of the United Nations as reiterated in resolution 1368 (2001)." S.C. Res. 1373, U.N. Doc. S/RES/1373, pmbl., ¶ 4, (2001).

[38] *See, e.g.*, Letter dated Oct. 7, 2001, from the Permanent Rep. of the United States of America to the United Nations addressed to the President of the Security Council, U.N. Doc. S/2001/946 (Oct. 7, 2001).

Coalition's actions won explicit approval from a broad cross section of the international community of States.[39]

Since the use of force against al-Qaeda in Afghanistan, reliance on the right to exercise self-defense against non-state actors in the territory of another State

---

[39] On October 8, 2001, the European Union, together with Bulgaria, the Czech Republic, Estonia, Hungary, Latvia, Lithuania, Poland, Romania, Slovakia, Slovenia, Cyprus, Malta, Turkey, Iceland, Liechtenstein, and Norway, declared their "wholehearted support for the action that is being taken in self-defense and in conformity with the UN Charter and the UNSCR 1368." Eur. Comm'n Press Release C/01/337 (Oct. 8–9, 2001), http://europa.eu/rapid/press-release_PRES-01-337_fr.htm. On September 12, 2001, the North Atlantic Council issued a statement declaring that if it was determined that "this attack was directed from abroad against the United States, it shall be regarded as an action covered by Article 5 of the Washington Treaty, which states that an armed attack against one or more of the Allies in Europe or North America shall be considered an attack against them all." On October 2, 2001, NATO's Secretary-General confirmed that the attacks had been directed from abroad and were regarded as an action covered by Article 5. See N. Atl. Treaty Org. Press Release (2001) 124, Statement by the North Atlantic Council (Sept. 12. 2001), https://www.nato.int/docu/pr/2001/p01-124e.htm; N. Atl. Treaty Org. Statement, Statement by NATO Secretary-General, Lord Robertson (Oct. 2, 2014), https://www.nato.int/docu/speech/2001/s011002a.htm. On September 14, 2001, the Australian government invoked the self-defense provisions in the ANZUS Treaty. Security Treaty Between the United States, Australia, and New Zealand (ANZUS), Sept. 1, 1951, 3 U.S.T.S. 3423 (entered into force Apr. 29, 1952). On September 21, 2001, the Organization of American States adopted the Resolution on Terrorist Threat to the Americas, which recalled the inherent right of States to act in self-defense in accordance with the U.N. Charter and the Inter-American Treaty of Reciprocal Assistance ("Rio Treaty"), and determined that the 9/11 attacks were "attacks against all American states" and that "all States Parties to the Rio Treaty shall provide effective reciprocal assistance to address such attacks and the threat of any similar attacks against any American state. . . ." Org. of Am. States, Terrorist Threat to the Americas, O.A.S. Doc. OEA/Ser.F/II.24/RC.24/RES.1/01 (Sept. 21, 2001), www.oas.org/oaspage/crisis/rc.24e.htm. China, Egypt, Georgia, Japan, Oman, Pakistan, Qatar, Russia, Saudi Arabia, Turkey, Uzbekistan, and many others expressed support for the Coalition's actions; indeed, ironically in light of current events, Iraq was one of only a handful of States that challenged the legality of the use of force. See Ruys, *supra* note 32, at 436–37; Christine Gray, International Law and the Use of Force 193 (3d ed. 2008); Murphy, *Terrorism and the Concept of "Armed Attack"*, *supra* note 30, at 49; Reinold, *supra* note 30, at 251–52. A significant number of leading *jus ad bellum* scholars support the view that the Coalition's actions amounted to a lawful exercise of self-defense. See Jane E. Stromseth, *New Paradigms for the Jus ad Bellum*, 38 Geo. Wash. Int'l L. Rev. 561, 566 (2006); Michael Wood, *The Law on the Use of Force: Current Challenges*, 11 Sing. Y.B. Int'l L. 1, 6 (2007); Dinstein, *supra* note 30, at 227; Monica Hakimi, *Defensive Force Against Non-State Actors: The State of Play*, 91 Int'l L. Stud. 1, 8 (2015); Michael P. Scharf, *Seizing the "Grotian Moment": Accelerated Formation of Customary International Law in Times of Fundamental Change*, 43 Cornell Int'l L.J. 439, 451 (2010); Tams, *supra* note 30, at 378; Greenwood, *supra* note 28, at 17. Al-Qaeda operatives were not sent by the Taliban, nor did the Taliban have any substantial involvement in the events of September 11, 2001, or have effective or overall control of al-Qaeda. See Dinstein, *supra* note 30, at 228; Ruys, *supra* note 32, at 439–40; Murphy, *Self-Defense and the Israeli Wall Advisory Opinion*, *supra* note 28, at 68.

without that State's consent has become more common.[40] Among other examples: since 2001 the United States has repeatedly struck al-Qaeda operatives in Pakistan, as well as in Somalia and Yemen; in 2002 and 2007, Russia asserted a right to defend itself against attacks by pro-Chechen rebels operating from Georgia; following attacks on nightclubs in Bali that killed more than eighty Australians, Australia's then–Prime Minister said that Australia should have the right to attack terrorist groups in neighboring countries where credible evidence existed that such groups were planning to attack Australia or Australian citizens abroad; Israel relied on self-defense in striking Islamic Jihad on Syrian territory in 2003 and in striking Hezbollah in Lebanon in 2006;[41] in 2004, Rwanda relied on the right in pursuing Hutu rebels into the Democratic Republic of the Congo (DRC); in 2008, Colombia relied on self-defense against a non-state actor in striking a Revolutionary Armed Forces of Colombia (FARC) camp in Ecuador; the same year, Turkey relied on self-defense in moving into Iraq to attack the PKK; and France relied on the exercise of self-defense against non-state actors in taking action against al-Qaeda in Mali in 2010. In addition, Article 1 of the African Union Non-Aggression and Common Defense Pact[42] includes non-state actors among those who can commit an act of aggression, which triggers obligations of mutual assistance and collective defense under Article 4 of the Pact. In 2004, the German government advised Parliament that it recognized that non-state actors can commit armed attacks, while the U.K. Attorney General advised the House of Lords that large-scale terrorist action could constitute an armed attack that will give rise to the right of self-defense, permitting force to be used against those who plan and perpetrate such acts and against those harboring them. The Netherlands' Defense Doctrine, adopted in 2005, and the 2006 French White Paper on Terrorism also acknowledge that terrorist acts can amount to armed attacks under certain circumstances.[43]

Admittedly, the International Court of Justice has been slow to reflect these developments. In the *Wall* Advisory Opinion, the Court noted that, in other contexts, Israel had argued that the construction of the security barrier in the West Bank was consistent with Article 51 of the U.N. Charter, its inherent

[40] *See* Reinold, *supra* note 30, at 257; Hakimi, *supra* note 39, at 19.
[41] Ruys notes that the applicability of Article 51 of the U.N. Charter was recognized by the G8, the European Union, the United States, Russia, Canada, Australia, Norway, Brazil, Argentina, Peru, Guatemala, and Ghana, although Israel's actions were condemned by the League of Arab States, China, Iran, Cuba, and Venezuela. RUYS, *supra* note 32.
[42] African Union Non-Aggression and Common Defense Pact, Jan. 31, 2005, 2656 U.N.T.S. 285 (entered into force Dec. 18, 2009).
[43] *See* RUYS, *supra* note 32, at 443–72; Hakimi, *supra* note 39, at 10–11; Tams, *supra* note 30, at 378–81; Reinold, *supra* note 32, at 251–84; Deeks, *supra* note 28, at 549–50; GRAY, *supra* note 39, at 215.

right to self-defense, and U.N. Security Council Resolutions 1368 (2001) and
1373 (2001). Addressing the issue briefly, the Court held, after quoting Article
51, that

> Article 51 of the Charter thus recognises the existence of an inherent right of
> self-defence in the case of armed attack by one State against another State.
> However, Israel does not claim that the attacks against it are imputable to a
> foreign State.

> The Court also notes that Israel exercises control in the Occupied Palestinian
> Territories and that, as Israel itself states, the threat which it regards as
> justifying the construction of the wall originates within, and not outside, that
> territory. The situation is thus different from that contemplated by Security
> Council resolutions 1368 (2001) and 1373 (2001), and therefore Israel could
> not in any event invoke those resolutions in support of its claim to be
> exercising a right of self-defence.[44]

A year later in the *Armed Activities* case, the Court held that Uganda could
not rely on self-defense to justify uses of force against the DRC given that the
armed attacks it suffered came from the Allied Democratic Forces and were
not attributable to the DRC.[45] The Court went on to hold that "accordingly"
it had "no need to respond to the contentions of the Parties as to whether and
under what conditions contemporary international law provides for a right of
self-defense against large-scale attacks by irregular forces."[46]

Thus, while on some readings the Court has implied that it favors a more
restrictive interpretation of the law, the reality is that the ICJ has doggedly
avoided expressing an explicit view on the question of whether a State can
lawfully use force in self-defense against a non-state actor in the territory
of another State, an approach that has drawn criticism from a number
of individual members of the ICJ bench,[47] as well as a large number of

---

[44] Legal Consequences of the Construction of a Wall in the Occupied Palestinian Territory,
Advisory Opinion, 2004 I.C.J. 136, ¶ 139 (July 9) [hereinafter Wall Advisory Opinion].

[45] Armed Activities on the Territory of the Congo (Dem. Rep. Congo v. Uganda), Judgment,
2005 I.C.J. 168, ¶ 146 (Dec. 19) [hereinafter Armed Activities Judgment].

[46] *Id.* ¶ 147.

[47] In the *Wall* Advisory Opinion, Judge Higgins, Judge Kooijmans, and Judge Buergenthal
questioned the Court's failure to recognize the right to exercise self-defense against non-state
actors in the territory of another State. *See* Wall Advisory Opinion, *supra* note 44 (separate
opinion by Judge Higgins, ¶ 33); *id.* (separate opinion by Judge Kooijmans, ¶ 35); *id.*
(declaration of Judge Buergenthal, ¶ 6). In the *Armed Activities* case, Judge Kooijmans was
critical of the Court's failure to take the opportunity to address the issue and held that "it would
be unreasonable to deny the attacked State the right to self-defence merely because there is no
attacker State, and the Charter does not so require." *See* Armed Activities Judgment, *supra* note
45 (separate opinion by Judge Kooijmans, ¶¶ 22–30). Judge Simma was equally critical of the

use-of-force experts.[48] As such, I would argue that consideration of the ICJ's case law provides little assistance in relation to the matter at hand.

Overall, before the use of force against ISIS in Syria, I consider that the better interpretation of the law permitted force to be used in self-defense against non-state actors in the territory of another State without that State's consent in at least some circumstances – a view shared by an influential group of commentators.[49] A number of academics assert a contrary view, mostly based on a denial of the existence of sufficient state practice and *opinio juris*.[50] In my opinion, however, the response to operations against ISIS in Syria makes the naysayers' position increasingly difficult to maintain.

Strikes against ISIS in Syria were commenced by the United States, Bahrain, Jordan, Saudi Arabia, Qatar, and the United Arab Emirates. Subsequently, Australia,[51] Belgium, Canada, Denmark, France, Morocco, The Netherlands,

---

Court's failure to clarify the state of the law, which he described as being marked by "great controversy and confusion," which, he said, the Court had "substantially contributed to" in its *Nicaragua* judgment. *See id.* (separate opinion by Judge Simma, ¶¶ 8–12). Pointing to more recent developments in state practice and *opinio juris*, including U.N. Security Council Resolutions 1368 (2001) and 1373 (2001), Judge Simma stated that he fully agreed with Judge Kooijmans's conclusion quoted above. *Id.*

[48] *See* Rylatt, *supra* note 33, at 60; Murphy, *Self-Defense and the Israeli* Wall *Advisory Opinion*, *supra* note 28, at 63; Wood, *supra* note 39, at 6.

[49] *See* DINSTEIN, *supra* note 30, at 227–28; Kreß, *supra* note 30, at 249; Deeks, *supra* note 28, at 486; Paust, *Self-Defense Targetings of Non-State Actors*, *supra* note 28, at 238–39; Reinold, *supra* note 30, at 245; Tams, *supra* note 30, at 384–85; Greenwood, *supra* note 28, at 16.

[50] *See* Mary Ellen O'Connell, *Dangerous Departures*, 107 AM. J. INT'L L. 380, *passim* (2013); Kevin Jon Heller, *Ashley Deeks' Problematic Defense of the "Unwilling or Unable" Test*, OPINIO JURIS (Dec. 15, 2011), www.opiniojuris.org/2011/12/15/ashley-deeks-failure-to-defend-the-unwilling-or-unable-test; Kevin Jon Heller, *Do Attacks on ISIS in Syria Justify the "Unwilling or Unable" Test?*, OPINIO JURIS (Dec. 13, 2014), www.opiniojuris.org/2014/12/13/attacks-ISIS-Syria-justify-unwilling-unable-test; Kevin Jon Heller, *The Absence of Practice Supporting the "Unwilling or Unable" Test*, OPINIO JURIS (Feb. 7, 2015), www.opiniojuris.org/2015/02/17/unable-unwilling-test-unstoppable-scholarly-imagination; Kevin Jon Heller, *The Seemingly Inexorable March of "Unable or Unwilling" Through the Academy*, OPINIO JURIS (Mar. 6, 2015), http://opiniojuris.org/2015/03/06/the-seemingly-inexorable-march-of-unwilling-or-unable-through-the-academy/. Ruys's position is somewhat equivocal, and finds that state practice supports a more permissive interpretation of Article 51, but at the same time concludes that "it appears to be premature to conclude that this shift in customary practice has crystallized in the unequivocal emergence of a new ratione personae threshold. . . ." Ruys, *supra* note 32, at 486–87. See also Hakimi's argument that "For now, the position that best captures the operational practice seems not to be generally accepted as law. And whatever position is widely accepted as an authoritative statement of law seems not to reflect operational practice." Hakimi, *supra* note 39, at 31.

[51] Earlier, in April 2015, Australia's Prime Minister publicly confirmed that Australian refuellers and radar planes were providing assistance in relation to operations in Syria. David Wroe, *Australia Sends 330 Extra Troops to Iraq, but Tony Abbott Won't Rule Out Future Syria Attack*,

Turkey, and the United Kingdom have also carried out strikes.[52] The use of force against ISIS in Syria was authorized by the German Parliament in December 2015. A number of other States have provided support to Coalition airstrikes: according to the United States, nineteen States have provided supporting aircraft, carrying out tasks such as transport, surveillance, and aerial refueling.[53] In addition, in June 2016, Poland announced the deployment of aircraft to conduct reconnaissance operations over Syrian territory.[54] Other States, including Egypt, have confirmed their support for the strikes.[55]

At the time airstrikes against ISIS in Syria were commenced, they were criticized by Russia and Iran on the basis that they were being undertaken in absence of Security Council authorization and without the consent of the Syrian government.[56] Both Russia and Iran have, however, claimed the right to exercise self-defense against non-state actors in the territory of another State

SYDNEY MORNING HERALD (Apr. 14, 2015), www.smh.com.au/federal-politics/political-news/
australia-sends-330-extra-troops-to-iraq-but-tony-abbott-wont-rule-out-future-syria-attacks-
20150414-1mkoyo.html. In August 2015, Australia's Defense Minister confirmed that, in
addition, Australian Defense Force personnel were embedded in the U.S. Air Force and
were responsible for operating unmanned aircraft that support Coalition operations in
Syria as well as Iraq. Interview by Rafael Epstein with the Hon. Kevin Andrews, Austl.
M.P., in Austl. (Aug. 14, 2015), http://kevinandrews.com.au/abc-774-radio-interview-with-
rafael-epstein/.

[52] For more information on Coalition operations see Operation Inherent Resolve,
U.S. DEP'T OF DEF., www.defense.gov/OIR/ and the GLOB. COALITION AGAINST DAESH,
www.theglobalcoalition.org.

[53] Office of the Press Sec'y, *Fact Sheet: Maintaining the Momentum in the Fight Against ISIL*,
WHITE HOUSE (Jan. 15, 2016), www.whitehouse.gov/the-press-office/2016/01/15/fact-sheet-
maintaining-momentum-fight-against-isil.

[54] *Carter Lauds Poland's Expansion, New Zealand's Extension of Counter-ISIL Roles*, U.S. DEP'T
OF DEF. (Jun. 21, 2016), www.defense.gov/-News-Article-View/Article/805642/carter-lauds-
polands-expansion-new-zealands-extension-of-counter-isil-roles.

[55] Carol Morello & Anne Gearan, *Around the World, Mixed Reactions to U.S.-led Airstrikes in
Syria*, WASH. POST (Sept. 23, 2015), www.washingtonpost.com/world/national-security/around-
the-world-mixed-reaction-to-us-led-airstrikes-in-syria/2014/09-23/16985bb6-4352-11e4-9a15-
137aa0153527_story.html; *Middle East Updates US: 12,000–15,000 Syrian Rebels Needed to
Retake Eastern Syria*, HAARETZ (Sept. 27, 2014), www.haaretz.com/middle-east-news/1.617772;
and the misleadingly titled Ryan Goodman, *Australia, France, Netherlands Express Legal
Reservations About Airstrikes in Syria [Updated]*, JUST SEC. (Sept. 25, 2014), www.justsecurity
.org/15545/australia-france-netherlands-express-legal-reservations-airstrikes-syria/.

[56] *See Russia Slams U.S. Airstrikes Against Islamic State in Syria*, MOSCOW TIMES (Sept. 24,
2014), www.themoscowtimes.com/news/article/russia-slams-u-s-air-strikes-against-islamic-state-
in-syria/507661.html; Cristina Silva, *US Airstrikes in Syria: Russia Says Bombings Will
'Exacerbate Tensions'*, INT'L BUS. TIMES (Sept. 23, 2014), www.ibtimes.com/us-airstrikes-syria-
russia-says-bombings-will-exacerbate-tensions-1693464; *Iran's President Condemns 'Illegal' US
Airstrikes in Syria*, BUS. INSIDER (Sept. 23, 2014), www.businessinsider.com/hassan-rouhani-
illegal-us-airstrikes-in-syria-2014-9.

in other contexts, which suggests that their criticism was politically motivated, rather than an unambiguous statement on their interpretation of the law.[57] Syria did not object to Coalition airstrikes against ISIS on its territory between September 2014 and September 2015. Indeed, several Syrian government statements initially welcomed the strikes.[58] This changed when Russia commenced airstrikes on Syrian territory to assist the Assad regime's defeat of the opposition groups ranged against it, including ISIS. Even so, Syria is clearly still being given advance warning of strikes, with air operations being coordinated, evidencing a degree of Syrian government complicity in Coalition operations. Importantly, no other States have publically queried the legal justification of the Coalition's operations.

Of course, the merits of the military operation have been contested. Rather than demonstrating concerns about the legality of the operation, however, this reflects the geopolitical complexities of the situation in Syria, and the fact that many States are concerned that striking ISIS has strengthened the hand of Bashar al-Assad and/or extremist groups such as al-Nusra, or entrenched the Coalition in a conflict that has no end in sight and risks embroiling the region in an even larger conflagration.

Indeed, what I believe the Coalition's operations against ISIS in Syria illustrate is that there now clearly exists a right to exercise self-defense against non-state actors in the territory of another State without that State's consent – at least in the eyes of States, who are, after all, the makers of both conventional and customary international law.[59] I would argue that the available state practice and *opinio juris* is sufficient to meet any articulation of the test for the formation of customary international law. But at any rate, I think it would

[57] Hakimi, *supra* note 39, at 24–25 (citing Heather Saul, *Syria Air Strikes: Iran 'Says US Attacks on ISIS are Illegal'*, INDEP. [Sept. 23, 2014], www.independent.co.uk/news/world/middle-east/syria-air-strikes-iran-says-us-attacks-on-isis-are-illegal-9751245.html).

[58] *See* Interview by Jeremy Bowen, BBC News, with Syrian President Bashar al-Assad (Feb. 10, 2015), www.bbc.com/news/world-middle-east-31327153.

[59] On the legality of strikes on ISIS in Syria specifically, see Marc Weller, *Islamic State Crisis: What Force Does International Law Allow?*, BBC NEWS (Sept. 25, 2014), www.bbc.com/news/world-middle-east-29283286; Ranj Alaadin & Bilal Khan, *Airstrikes on ISIS Targets in Syria and Iraq are Legal Under International Law*, LONDON SCH. ECONS. U.S. CTR.: U.S. POL. & POL'Y BLOG (Oct. 1, 2014), http://blogs.lse.ac.uk/usappblog/2014/10/01/airstrikes-on-isis-targets-in-syria-and-iraq-are-legal-under-international-law/; Jennifer Daskal, Ashley Deeks & Ryan Goodman, *Strikes in Syria: The International Law Framework*, JUST SEC. (Sept. 24, 2014), www.justsecurity.org/15479/strikes-syria-international-law-framework-daskal-deeks-goodman/#more-15479; Claus Kreß, *The Fine Line Between Collective Self-Defense and Intervention by Invitation: Reflections on the Use of Force Against 'IS' in Syria*, JUST SEC. (Feb. 15, 2015), www.justsecurity.org/20118/claus-kreb-force-isil-syria/.

be exceedingly difficult to deny that there has been a "general toleration" of the exercise of self-defense against non-state actors in the territory of another State, or at least an acquiescence of specially affected States.[60]

Of course, this begs the question of the content of that right. Australia's letter to the Security Council, advising of its exercise of self-defense, was more detailed than that of other States, providing that

> States must be able to act in self-defence when the Government of the State where the threat is located is unwilling or unable to prevent attacks originating from its territory. The Government of Syria has, by its failure to constrain attacks upon Iraqi territory originating from ISIL bases within Syria, demonstrated that it is unwilling or unable to prevent those attacks.[61]

In a speech at the American Society of International Law, Stephen Preston (then–General Counsel of the U.S. Department of Defense), similarly argued that

> The inherent right of self-defense is not restricted to threats posed by states, and over the past two centuries states have repeatedly invoked the right of self-defense in response to attacks by non-state actors. . . . the Syrian government has shown that it cannot and will not confront these terrorist groups effectively itself.[62]

Similar approaches are reflected in the Chatham House Principles of International Law on the Use of Force in Self-Defence,[63] the Grotius Centre for

---

[60] Anglo-Norwegian Fisheries (U.K. v. Nor.), Judgment, 1951 I.C.J. 116, 139–40 (Dec. 18); Lotus Case (Fr. v. Turk.), Judgment, 1927 P.C.I.J. (ser. A) No. 10, at 23, 29. *See also* RUYS, *supra* note 32, at 38.

[61] Letter dated Sept. 9, 2015, from the Permanent Rep. of Australia, *supra* note 22. *See also* Letter from the Dutch Foreign Ministers of Def. and Foreign Trade and Dev. Cooperation to the President of the House of Representatives (Jun. 19, 2015), https://zoek.officielebekendmakingen.nl/dossier/27925/kst-27925–539?resultIndex=60&sorttype=1&sortorder=4. *See also* Letter from the Dutch Foreign Ministers of Def. and Foreign Trade and Dev. Cooperation to the President of the House of Representatives (Jan. 29, 2016), https://zoek.officielebekendmakingen.nl/dossier/27925/kst-27925–570?resultIndex=21&sorttype=1&sortorder=4.

[62] Stephen W. Preston, Gen. Counsel, U.S. Dep't of Def., The Legal Framework for the United States' Use of Military Force Since 9/11, Address Before the Annual Meeting of the American Society of International Law (Apr. 10, 2015), www.defense.gov/Speeches/Speech.aspx?SpeechID=1931.

[63] Elizabeth Wilmshurst, *The Chatham House Principles of International Law on the Use of Force in Self-Defence*, 55 INT'L & COMP. L.Q. 963 (2006). Principle F provides that

> Article 51 is not confined to self-defence in response to attacks by States. The right of self-defence may apply also to attacks by non-state actors. In such a case the attack must be large scale. If the right of self-defence in such a case is to be exercised in the territory of another State, it must be evident that that State is unable or unwilling to deal with the non-state actors itself, and that it is necessary to use force from outside to deal with the threat in

International Legal Studies' Leiden Policy Recommendations on Counter-
Terrorism and International Law,[64] an interesting article by Ashley Deeks,[65]
and the particularly illuminating principles articulated by Sir Daniel Bethlehem, former Foreign and Commonwealth Office Legal Adviser, whose efforts
were "informed by detailed discussions over recent years with foreign ministry,
defense ministry, and military legal advisers from a number of states who have
operational experience in these matters."[66]

Analyzing the contours of the right to exercise self-defense against non-state
actors is beyond the scope of this Chapter. What can be observed briefly is that
there appears to be broad support for the proposition that it is a prerequisite
that the State hosting the non-state actor in question must be either unwilling
or unable to restrain the non-state actor effectively, such as to leave the State
that needs to act in self-defense with no other reasonably available effective
means of defending itself against armed attacks.

It is also clear that an appropriate deference must be extended to the State
in which the non-state actor in question is located, especially where it is
unable rather than unwilling. Thus, as suggested by Bethlehem, where inability is relied upon, there must also be a strong, reasonable, and objective basis
for concluding that the seeking of consent would be likely to materially
undermine the effectiveness of action in self-defense. It also seems uncontroversial that the legality of an exercise of a use of force in self-defense against a
non-state actor in the territory of another State must be assessed by the same
standards used to judge an exercise of self-defense against a State: in other
words, the exercise of self-defense must be a response to an actual or imminent
armed attack; the force used must be limited to what is necessary to address the
attack; and the force used must be proportionate to the threat faced.[67]

> circumstances where the consent of the territorial state cannot be obtained. Force in self-
> defence directed against the Government of the State in which the attacker is found may be
> justified only in so far as it is necessary to avert or end the attack, but not otherwise.

Id. at 969.

[64] Nico Schrijver & Larissa van den Herik, *Leiden Policy Recommendations on Counter-Terrorism and International Law*, Grotius Ctr. for Int'l Legal Stud. (Apr. 1, 2010), www.uni-koeln.de/jur-fak/kress/Materialien/Chef/HP882010/LeidenPolicyRecommendations1April2010.pdf.

[65] Deeks, *supra* note 28, at 506.

[66] Daniel Bethlehem, *Principles Relevant to the Scope of a State's Right of Self-Defense Against an Imminent or Actual Armed Attack by Nonstate Actors*, 106 Am. J. Int'l L. 1, 4 (2012).

[67] Thus, most commentators have expressed concern over the United States' assertion, as articulated by the Bush Administration, that the necessity of an exercise of self-defense in response to the 9/11 attacks justified the use of force against al-Qaeda wherever it might be operating, for as long as it continues to operate. Many also have been concerned by the United States' interpretation of imminence, under which it has asserted that the United States is not required "to have clear evidence that a specific attack on US persons and interests will take

Importantly, the fact that the content of the right is still subject to much discussion is not evidence of the non-existence of the right. Many well-established rules of international law, the existence of which no one would deny, are subject to hotly contested interpretive debates.

What is critical to observe for the purpose of the current Chapter is that recent international counterterrorism military operations demonstrate that States have seen a need to ensure that the *jus ad bellum* meets new security threats and changes in geopolitical realities. I for one consider this to be a good thing. The *jus ad bellum* is fundamental to the maintenance of an international rules-based order. To greater and lesser degrees, States rely on respect for the *jus ad bellum* for their national security. In this context, it is critical that a certain degree of flexibility be built in to the interpretation of the *jus ad bellum*'s rules. A failure to do so runs the risk of the law being seen as inconsistent with national security interests, and the limits of the law being less frequently respected by political decision makers.

IV. THE *JUS IN BELLO*'S FAILURE TO RESPOND

In contrast to the *jus ad bellum*, the *jus in bello* has been relatively unresponsive to the threat posed by ISIS as well as its forerunners. Operations against ISIS have raised a range of legal issues that do not have ready answers under international humanitarian law (IHL) as it currently stands.

First is the question of whether all Coalition airstrikes in Iraq and Syria are part of an armed conflict and, if so, the proper characterization of that conflict. There is little doubt that ISIS meets the definition of an organized armed group and that there has been protracted armed violence between it and the Government of Iraq.[68] While there have been some claims that ISIS has

---

place in the immediate future," such that the unpredictable and sporadic nature of terrorist activities supports the conclusion that the criterion of imminence can be fulfilled where an individual is "an operational leader of al-Qaeda or an associated force and is personally and continually involved in planning terrorist attacks against the United States." U.S. DEP'T OF JUSTICE, WHITE PAPER ON THE LAWFULNESS OF A LETHAL OPERATION DIRECTED AGAINST A U.S. CITIZEN WHO IS A SENIOR OPERATIONAL LEADER OF AL QA'IDA OR AN ASSOCIATED FORCE 7–8 (2011), www.justice.gov/oip/docs/dept-white-paper.pdf. For completeness, it is noted that it is of concern that the United States has justified individual targeted killings on the basis of a *jus ad bellum* analysis, without consideration of the lawfulness of that killing under international human rights law or, where it is applicable, international humanitarian law.

[68] The *Tadić* case defined a non-international armed conflict as existing whenever there is "protracted armed violence between governmental authorities and organized armed groups or between such groups within a State." Prosecutor v. Duško Tadić, Case No. IT-94-1-1A, Appeals Decision on Defence Motion for Interlocutory Appeal on Jurisdiction, ¶ 70 (Oct. 2, 1995) [hereinafter Tadić Interlocutory Appeal Decision]. This definition is widely

certain support from within the Gulf States, available evidence points to individual, rather than state, support. Similarly, while Iran's backing of Shia militias in Iraq may need to be kept under review, Iran's intervention currently has Iraqi government consent, as illustrated by the military pact signed by the Iran and Iraq Defense Ministers in December 2014. As such, one can conclude with some confidence that there currently exists a non-international armed conflict (NIAC) in Iraq between the government of Iraq and ISIS, in which third States have intervened in support of the Iraqi government.

That conflict, however, has obviously not been contained within Iraq's borders. ISIS is readily able to cross back and forth between Iraq and Syria. Despite the implications that the application of IHL is geographically bound in the case law of the International Criminal Tribunals for the former Yugoslavia[69] and Rwanda,[70] it is now largely uncontroversial to assert that NIACs can cross state borders.[71] In this context, it seems correct to conclude

understood to represent the definition of non-international armed conflict under customary international law.

[69] "[I]nternational humanitarian law continues to apply in the whole territory of the warring States or, in the case of internal conflicts, the whole territory under the control of a party, whether or not actual combat takes place there." *Id.*

[70] *See* Prosecutor v. Akayesu, Case No. ICTR-96-4-T, Trial Judgment, ¶¶ 635–36 (Sept. 2, 1998) (international humanitarian law "must be applied to the whole territory of the state engaged in the conflict"); Prosecutor v. Rutaganda, Case No. ICTR-96-3, Trial Chamber Judgment, ¶ 102 (Dec. 6, 1999) (international humanitarian law "extends throughout the territory of the State where the hostilities are occurring").

[71] *See* Int'l Comm. of the Red Cross, International Humanitarian Law and the Challenges of Contemporary Armed Conflicts 9–10 (2011), https://www.icrc.org/en/document/international-humanitarian-law-and-challenges-contemporary-armed-conflicts; Noam Lubell & Nathan Derejko, *A Global Battlefield? Drones and the Geographical Scope of Armed Conflict*, 11 J. Int'l Crim. Just. 65, *passim* (2013); Michael N. Schmitt, *Charting the Legal Geography of Non-International Armed Conflict*, 90 Int'l L. Stud. 1, 11 (2014) [hereinafter Schmitt, *Charting the Legal Geography*]; Michael N. Schmitt, *Extraterritorial Lethal Targeting: Deconstructing the Logic of International Law*, 52 Colum. J. Transnat'l L. 77, 97 (2013) [hereinafter Schmitt, *Extraterritorial Lethal Targeting*]; Marco Sassòli, *Transnational Armed Groups and International Humanitarian Law* 9 (Harvard University Program on Humanitarian Policy and Conflict Research, Occasional Paper Series, Paper No. 6, 2006), http://www.uio.no/studier/emner/jus/humanrights/HUMR5503/h09/undervisningsmateriale/sassoli_transnational_armed_groups_and_ihl.pdf; Lydwien Toonstra, The 'Complexity' of the Geographical Scope of International Humanitarian Law: An Issue Highlighted by the Use of Drones in Pakistan, Yemen and Somalia, at 15 (Dec. 9, 2013) (unpublished M.A. thesis, Amsterdam Law School), http://scriptiesonline.uba.uva.nl/scriptie/463392; Jennifer Daskal, *The Geography of the Battlefield: A Framework for Detention and Targeting Outside the "Hot" Conflict Zone*, 161 U. Pa. L. Rev. 1165, 1189 (2013); Geoffrey S. Corn, *Geography of Armed Conflict: Why It Is a Mistake to Fish for the Red Herring*, 89 Int'l L. Stud. 77, 88 (2013); Sasha Radin, *Global Armed Conflict? The Threshold of Extraterritorial Non-International Armed Conflicts*, 89 Int'l L. Stud. 696, 719–20 (2013).

that at least some of the Coalition airstrikes against ISIS in Syria are best classified as part of the Iraq–ISIS NIAC, which has spilled over the border into Syria.

The prevailing view, however, is that the notion of a spillover or cross-border conflict cannot be stretched too far. Indeed, it is highly questionable whether all Coalition strikes on ISIS in Syria are properly characterized as part of the Iraq–ISIS NIAC. For example, the strikes launched by Jordan in February 2015 as part of Operation Martyr Moaz were explicitly aimed at avenging ISIS's execution of a Jordanian pilot rather than defending Iraqi sovereignty. U.S. strikes against the Khorasan Group and Turkish strikes against the PKK seem clearly to fall outside the Iraq–ISIS NIAC. A number of the Arab countries participating in strikes on ISIS in Syria have not participated in operations in Iraq, making it difficult to characterize their actions as being part of the Iraq–ISIS NIAC. Perhaps more significantly, the U.S. Department of Defense website provides regular updates of ISIS targets struck by U.S.-led airstrikes. The listed targets include many near al-Raqqa, Kobani, and Aleppo – all cities deep within Syria, far from the Iraqi border – and it seems unlikely that all individual targets have a demonstrable connection to ISIS's operations in Iraq.

The issues raised by Coalition airstrikes on ISIS in Syria are in some ways distinct from the question, much debated in the literature in recent years, as to whether individual al-Qaeda operatives or small cells could be considered to have "carried" the Afghanistan–al-Qaeda conflict with them to the territory of non-belligerent States[72] – but they are no less complicated. International humanitarian law provides little guidance as to how and where to draw the geographic boundaries of cross-border NIACs.[73] The dominant view is that military operations must have a nexus to the NIAC in question in order to be classified as part of that same conflict. The further the geographic distance between the target in Syria and the primary sphere of hostilities in Iraq, and the weaker the link between the target and the Iraq–ISIS NIAC, the less likely it can properly be concluded that an airstrike in Syria is part of the Iraq–ISIS NIAC.[74] But if it is accepted that not all Coalition airstrikes in Syria are part of the Iraq–ISIS NIAC, how are they properly characterized?

With the exception of the April 2017 U.S. strike on the Shayrat Airfield in Syria, which the United States said was aimed at preventing the further use of

---

[72] Schmitt, *Charting the Legal Geography, supra* note 71, at 15; Laurie R. Blank, *Defining the Battlefield in Contemporary Conflict and Counterterrorism: Understanding the Parameters of the Zone of Combat*, 39 GA. J. INT'L & COMP. L. 1, 26 (2010).

[73] Schmitt, *Extraterritorial Lethal Targeting, supra* note 71, at 99.

[74] Lubell & Derejko, *supra* note 71, *passim;* Toonstra, *supra* note 71, at 41.

chemical weapons, Coalition airstrikes in Syria have not been directed toward the Assad regime – indeed, Coalition airstrikes in Syria have clearly been carried out in coordination with the Syrian government as outlined above. Some authors maintain the view that, absent the consent of the State of residence of an armed group to the use of force by another State on its territory, an international armed conflict will exist, regardless of the object of a use of force. This approach, however, mistakenly conflates the *jus ad bellum* and *jus in bello*, and risks extending IHL's permissive rules to situations where this would be neither warranted nor desirable. Thus, while more ambiguous following the Shayrat Airfield strike, given the absence of an exchange of hostilities between Syria and the Coalition, the better view is that Coalition airstrikes have not given rise to an international armed conflict (IAC) between Syria and any member of the Coalition.[75]

This leads to the conclusion that at least some Coalition members, including the United States, are involved in a separate armed conflict with ISIS in Syria. And of course, the proper classification of an armed conflict with a transnational non-state actor in the territory of another State is what caused much hand-wringing in the context of U.S. operations against al-Qaeda.[76] In the wake of the 9/11 attacks, the United States asserted that it was in an armed conflict with al-Qaeda, but that it was neither an Article 2 (international) or Article 3 (non-international) armed conflict within the meaning of the Geneva Conventions, such that there was a lacuna in the law. However, in *Hamdan v. Rumsfeld*,[77] the U.S. Supreme Court held that a conflict between a nation and a transnational non-state actor, occurring outside the nation's territory, is an armed conflict "not of an international character" because it is not a "clash between nations." The *Hamdan* decision contains at least some counterintuitive elements, but the conclusion reached by most States and commentators examining these issues is that existing international humanitarian law offers no more appropriate means of classifying such hostilities.[78]

---

[75] Toonstra, *supra* note 71, at 12–13. Since 2012 there have been isolated border clashes between Syria and, at various times, Turkey, Jordan, Lebanon, and Israel, but at present there is no ongoing armed hostilities such as would lead to the conclusion that one or more of these States is at present in an international armed conflict with Syria.

[76] Sylvain Vité, *Typology of Armed Conflicts in International Humanitarian Law: Legal Concepts and Actual Situations*, 91 INT'L REV. RED CROSS 69, 90 (2009); Daskal, *supra* note 71, at 1175.

[77] Hamdan v. Rumsfeld, 548 U.S. 557, 628–31 (2006).

[78] Andreas Paulus & Mindia Vashakmadze, *Asymmetrical War and the Notion of Armed Conflict – A Tentative Conceptualization*, 91 INT'L REV. RED CROSS 95, 118–19 (2009); Dietrich Schindler, *International Humanitarian Law and Internationalized Internal Armed Conflicts*, 22 INT'L REV. RED CROSS 255 (1982).

Thus, the current manifestation of the War on Terror, just like its original incarnation, demonstrates the inadequacy of the taxonomy of the *jus in bello* in light of contemporary international counterterrorism military operations. This is of course part of a broader phenomenon that is being driven not only by the identity of our enemies, but also by the technologies employed in armed conflicts with them. As Lubell and Derejko have written:

> The very notion of armed conflict appears to be going through a process of shape-shifting whereby the use of new technologies such as drones or cyber operations are slowly erasing the crucial significance of geographical boundaries, truncating vast distances, and diminishing the need for boots on the ground.[79]

A second question is, which of the States in the Coalition are party to the Iraq–ISIS and/or U.S.–ISIS NIAC? The U.S. State Department website lists sixty-nine States as Coalition partners who "have committed themselves to the goals of eliminating the threat posed by ISIL and have already contributed in various capacities to the effort to combat ISIL in Iraq, the region and beyond."[80] And yet it is clear that the support of many of the listed States has come in the form of political statements, humanitarian assistance, or military supplies provided to the Iraqi government: only a small number of States have participated in hostilities.

Neither conventional nor customary IHL clearly articulates a test for when a State becomes (or for that matter, ceases to be) a party to an armed conflict. Some literature suggests that it is necessary to meet the organization and intensity criteria under Article 1 of Additional Protocol II (APII) (where applicable) or Common Article 3 or customary international law.[81] Given the non-applicability of APII in the current context, this would require evidence that the armed forces of a government are engaged in protracted

---

[79] Lubell & Derejko, *supra* note 71, at 66. *See also* Blank, *supra* note 72, at 4.

[80] Afghanistan, Albania, Australia, Austria, Bahrain, Belgium, Bosnia and Herzegovina, Bulgaria, Canada, Chad, Croatia, Cyprus, Czech Republic, Denmark, Djibouti, Egypt, Estonia, Ethiopia, Finland, France, Georgia, Germany, Greece, Hungary, Iceland, Iraq, Ireland, Italy, Japan, Jordan, Kosovo, Kuwait, Latvia, Lebanon, Lithuania, Libya, Luxembourg, Macedonia, Malaysia, Moldova, Montenegro, Morocco, The Netherlands, New Zealand, Niger, Nigeria, Norway, Oman, Panama, Poland, Portugal, Qatar, Romania, Saudi Arabia, Serbia, Singapore, Slovakia, Slovenia, Somalia, South Korea, Spain, Sweden, Taiwan, Tunisia, Turkey, Ukraine, United Arab Emirates, United Kingdom, and the United States. *See Partners*, GLOB. COALITION AGAINST DAESH, www.theglobalcoalition.org/en/partners (listing sixty-nine States as Coalition partners as of June 2017).

[81] Tristan Ferraro, *The Applicability and Application of International Humanitarian Law to Multinational Forces*, 95 INT'L REV. RED CROSS 561, 584 (2013).

armed violence with ISIS (which clearly satisfies the definition of an organized armed group).

But the factors that have been identified by international courts and tribunals to assist in case-by-case assessments of whether the intensity element of the definition of NIAC has been met (such as the number of attacks and clashes, the seriousness or intensity of individual attacks or confrontations, the distribution of weapons among the parties, the number of victims, and the extent of material destruction) seem to be a poor fit for assessing whether a State has become a party to a pre-existing NIAC. Putting aside issues such as the fact that the indicia identified by the tribunals provide almost no quantitative or qualitative guidance, it is quite clear that criteria developed for an *ex post facto* analysis of the existence of a NIAC are of very limited assistance in determining whether a Coalition partner's military contribution is sufficient to qualify it as a party to a pre-existing NIAC.

Tristan Ferraro has advocated a support-based approach, whereby the determinative question is whether a party undertakes actions related to the conduct of hostilities in support of a party to a pre-existing NIAC.[82] According to Ferraro:

> A general contribution to the war effort would not be sufficient, as it amounts to no more than loose, indirect involvement in the pre-existing armed conflict. War-sustaining activities such as financial support, or the delivery of weapons/ammunition to a party to the conflict, should be regarded as a form of indirect involvement in hostilities that has no effect on the ... [State's] status under IHL. A distinction must therefore be drawn between the provision of support that would have a direct impact on the opposing party's ability to conduct hostilities and more indirect forms of support which would allow the beneficiary only to build up its military capabilities.[83]

Ferraro continues:

> [M]ilitary operations which directly damage the party opposing the armed forces whom they support, or which are designed to directly undermine its military capabilities, are definitely included ... direct support also encompasses action that has an impact on the enemy *only in conjunction with* other acts undertaken by the supported party ... there must be a close link between the action undertaken by [the State] and the harm caused to one of the belligerents by specific military operations undertaken by the opponent. For example, transporting the supported state's armed forces to the front line or

---

[82] *Id.* at 584.
[83] *Id.* at 585.

providing planes for refueling jet fighters involved in aerial operations carried out by the supported state do implicate [state] forces in the collective conduct of hostilities and make them a party to the pre-existing NIAC.[84]

While Ferraro's theory is instructive in many ways, elements of it are bound to be controversial. Take the example of the provision of planes for refueling jet fighters involved in aerial operations carried out by the supported State: it is not at all clear that this conclusion would be accepted by States, which typically consider a greater degree of participation and more direct involvement in hostilities to be necessary for a State to be considered a party to a conflict.

Up to this point, I have considered only Coalition airstrikes. An added layer of complexity is the support that has been provided to the moderate opposition groups in Syria by a number of Coalition members. The issue of the degree and nature of a State's involvement in an armed conflict on another State's territory that is required for a conflict to be characterized as international was considered by the ICTY Appeals Chamber in *Tadić*.[85] While that decision has been criticized on the basis that the Tribunal inappropriately applied the law of state responsibility to resolve the IHL question before it (and misapplied the test for attribution under state responsibility set out in the ICJ's decision in *Nicaragua*), as the ICJ itself acknowledged in the *Bosnia Genocide* case, it may well be that the "overall control" test developed by *Tadić* is "applicable and suitable" for the purpose of determining whether or not an armed conflict is properly characterized as an international one.[86]

The *Tadić* Appeals Chamber held that a conflict will become international (or an IAC may come into existence alongside a NIAC) if "some of the participants in the internal armed conflict act on behalf of that other State."[87] Specifically, the Appeals Chamber held:

> [C]ontrol by a State over subordinate *armed forces or militias or paramilitary units* may be of an overall character (and must comprise more than the mere provision of financial assistance or military equipment or training). This requirement, however, does not go so far as to include the issuing of specific orders by the State, or its direction of each individual operation. Under international law it is by no means necessary that the controlling authorities

---

[84] *Id.* at 585–86.

[85] Prosecutor v. Duško Tadić, Case No. IT-94-1-1A, Appeals Judgment (July 15, 1999) [hereinafter Tadić Appeals Judgment].

[86] Application of the Convention on the Prevention and Punishment of the Crime of Genocide (Bosn. & Herz. v. Serb. & Montenegro), Merits Judgment, 2007 I.C.J. 43, ¶ 404 (Feb. 26).

[87] Tadić Appeals Judgment, *supra* note 85, ¶ 84.

should plan all the operations of the units dependent on them, choose their targets, or give specific instructions concerning the conduct of military operations and any alleged violations of international humanitarian law. The control required by international law may be deemed to exist when a State (or, in the context of an armed conflict, the Party to the conflict) *has a role in organizing, coordinating or planning the military actions* of the military group, in addition to the financing, training and equipping or providing operational support to that group.[88]

Commentators have complained that the *Tadić* criteria are "notoriously difficult to apply" as they give "little guidance as to the requisite level and type of intervention required by a State to categorise a conflict as international."[89] In the Syria context, as in many like situations, the assessment is complicated by the fact that much of the support provided has been clandestine. Even those States that have made their support for the moderate Syrian opposition public have been slow to provide details of the form that support takes.

Snippets of publicly available information indicate that since at least 2012, a number of Coalition partners, including the United States and France, have been providing lethal military equipment and funding to moderate Syrian opposition groups. While such support may amount to intervention in Syria's domestic affairs in breach of Article 2(7) of the U.N. Charter, it would not seem to be sufficient to meet the *Tadić* test for having internationalized one or more of the NIACs taking place in Syria. What may have crossed the line is the support provided by Saudi Arabia, Turkey, and Qatar. In late 2013, Saudi Arabia, allegedly the main financier and provider of arms to the Syrian opposition, was said to have appointed Prince Bandar bin Sultan to lead efforts to topple Assad through support of the rebels: in this role he reportedly played a part in covert command centers near the Syrian front. It has also been asserted that Qatar has brokered an alliance between Saudi Arabia and Turkey to bring down Assad, supposedly leading to the creation of an alliance of rebel groups, known as the "Army of Conquest" (which includes hardliners such as al-Nusra), which is controlled through a joint command center in the northeastern Syrian province of Idlib.[90] While publicly available information is

---

[88] *Id.* ¶ 137.

[89] Jed Odermatt, *Between Law and Reality: 'New Wars' and Internationalised Armed Conflict*, 5 AMSTERDAM L.F. 19, 22 (2013).

[90] Desmond Butler, *Turkey Officials Confirm Pact with Saudi Arabia to Help Rebels Fighting Syria's Assad*, WORLD POST (May 7, 2015), https://web.archive.org/web/20150509223547/http://www.huffingtonpost.com/2015/05/07/turkey-saudi-arabia-syria-rebels-pact_n_7232750.html?ncid=txtlnkusaolp00000592; David Ignatius, *Saudi Arabia, Qatar and Turkey are Getting Serious About Syria – and That Should Worry Assad*, BUS. INSIDER (May 13, 2015),

insufficient to draw conclusions, it is possible that such support could have internationalized the NIAC between such rebels and the Assad regime.

Of course the point is that a lack of clarity in the law and a lack of visibility of the facts make it very difficult for Coalition partners to determine how to properly classify the overlapping armed conflicts in Syria. In turn, an inability to identify with certainty who is a party to the relevant conflicts, and whether they are international or non-international in character, means there is a lack of clarity as to who exactly is bound by IHL and whether the rules being applied are those that apply in international or NIAC.

Most States and commentators agree that many of the Geneva Conventions' rules have become part of customary IHL applicable in NIAC, such that the rules are no longer "skeletal compared with those which apply to international conflicts."[91] This said, it is also clear that most States do not yet accept that the corpus of IHL applicable in IAC applies in NIAC. As the ICTY Appeals Chamber has held, "only a number of rules and principles governing international armed conflicts have gradually been extended to apply to internal conflicts" and "this extension has not taken place in the form of a full and mechanical transplant of those rules to internal conflicts; rather, the general essence of those rules, and not the detailed regulation they may contain, has become applicable to internal conflicts."[92]

The lack of clear agreement on exactly what rules of IHL apply in NIAC as a matter of customary international law raises two principal challenges: (1) a lack of certainty as to the obligations that must be met by ISIS and state armed forces (a particularly acute issue in the current context given neither Iraq nor Syria are party to APII, meaning that according to Article 1[1], APII does not apply to any parties engaged in any of the conflicts in question); and (2) interoperability difficulties caused by different States in the Coalition having different views on what rules have achieved customary status.

This raises a related issue. Members of organized armed groups party to a NIAC have never been afforded the combatant immunity enjoyed by belligerents in IAC.[93] Consistent with this distinction, Common Article 3 underlines that the application of its protections "shall not affect the legal status of the Parties to the conflict." However, IHL does not prohibit

---

www.businessinsider.com/saudi-arabia-qatar-and-turkey-are-getting-serious-about-syria–and-that-should-worry-assad-2015-5?IR=T.

[91] Christopher Greenwood, *International Humanitarian Law and United Nations Military Operations*, 1 Y.B. INT'L HUMANITARIAN L. 3, 9 (1998).

[92] *Tadić Interlocutory Appeal Decision*, *supra* note 68, ¶ 126.

[93] Jan Klabbers, *Rebel With a Cause? Terrorists and Humanitarian Law*, 14 EUR. J. INT'L L. 299, 303 (2003).

participation in NIAC, and Article 6(5) of APII requires authorities to endeavor "to grant the broadest possible amnesty to persons who have participated in the armed conflict, or those deprived of their liberty for reasons related to armed conflict." While Article 6(5) is not applicable to the conflicts in question, the rationale for the exhortation is nonetheless instructive: the intention, of course, is to create an incentive for organized armed groups to comply with IHL.

In the past there has been some recognition of the utility of carving out activities governed by IHL from the definition of terrorist conduct attracting criminal sanction. Article 20(2) of the much-contested Draft Comprehensive Convention Against International Terrorism excludes from the Convention's scope "the activities of armed forces during an armed conflict,"[94] mirroring the exemption provided in Article 19 of the 1998 Terrorist Bombings Convention.[95] The events of September 11, 2001, however, launched an "anti-terrorist legislative wildfire" at the national level.[96] The specter of ISIS has resulted in a second wave of such legislation, with security and intelligence agencies being given expanded powers, the rights of suspected terrorists further constrained, and additional criminal offenses created. This must cause one to wonder whether the harsh criminalization of all forms of terrorism risks undermining what little incentive there is for organized armed groups characterized as terrorists to comply with IHL, ironically increasing the threat posed by such organizations to both civilians and the members of armed forces deployed to defeat them.[97]

In a more practical sense, perhaps we should be thinking more about the type of enforcement action we take against members of terrorist organized armed groups. Prosecuting members of ISIS for war crimes (and crimes against humanity, possibly genocide) rather than for newly minted terrorist offenses would underscore that it is their method of fighting, rather than the fact that they are fighting, that attracts the greatest degree of reprobation. This

---

[94] Draft Comprehensive Convention Against International Terrorism, *in* Letter dated Aug. 3, 2005, from the Chairman of the Sixth Committee addressed to the President of the General Assembly, annex II, U.N. Doc. A/59/894 (Aug. 12, 2005). *See also* Klabbers, *supra* note 93, at 306.

[95] International Convention for the Suppression of Terrorist Bombing, *opened for signature* Dec. 15, 1997, 2149 U.N.T.S. 284 (entered into force May 23, 2001).

[96] Joan Fitzpatrick, *Speaking Law to Power: The War Against Terrorism and Human Rights*, 14 Eur. J. Int'l L. 241, 243 (2003) (citing Joshua D. Zelman, *Recent Developments in International law: Anti-Terrorism Legislation – Part One: An Overview*, 11 J. Transnat'l L. & Pol'y 183, 184 (2001).

[97] *See also* Geoffrey S. Corn, *Thinking the Unthinkable: Has the Time Come to Offer Combatant Immunity to Non-State Actors?*, 22 Stan. L. & Pol'y Rev. 253 (2011), who makes some compelling arguments for why combatant immunity should be offered to non-state armed actors that satisfy certain criteria.

would at least send an *ex post facto* message about the importance attached to IHL by the international community.

What I hope the foregoing illustrates is that the *jus in bello* is struggling to provide answers to some fundamental questions raised by Coalition operations against ISIS, in a way that might be contrasted with the *jus ad bellum*, which has demonstrated an ability to adapt without being weakened. To my mind, this inevitably raises the question of whether the *jus in bello* is becoming anachronistic and what the long-term implications of this are for the observance of IHL's obligations. I, for one, consider the rules that have been constructed to restrain the worst excesses of war too important for us to ignore these questions. And so in this last Section of this Chapter, I want to explore why the *jus ad bellum* has adapted to meet new challenges in the security space where the *jus in bello* has not, and what can be done to ensure that the *jus in bello* remains adaptive and thereby relevant.

V. RECLAIMING THE *JUS IN BELLO*

In some ways it is obvious that the *jus ad bellum* has adapted to meet emerging security challenges, in particular the threat posed by transnational non-state actors with sophisticated military capabilities, because state action in this space is highly visible. Compared with the *jus in bello*, which is often shrouded in operational secrecy and hidden behind the smoke of battle, it is difficult, in a media-saturated world, to use force (at least of the kinetic kind) in the territory of another State without the entire world knowing about it. This means both that state practice is usually readily available and that, at least in part because of that very visibility and the scrutiny it entails, States will often feel a need to make statements commenting on their own actions, or the actions of others, which can be a fertile field for *opinio juris*.

I would also argue that States attach a particular importance to the *jus ad bellum* as the keystone of the international rules-based order. This is, of course, not an uncontested view. Thomas Franck famously asked in 1970 who killed Article 2(4).[98] Franck's argument was that the evolution of the modes and means of interstate armed violence (which undid conventional thought about war and peace), combined with the exploitation of the "exceptions and ambiguities" in the U.N. Charter by States determined to act in their national interest, and the failure of the United Nations' collective security machinery,

---

[98] Thomas M. Franck, *Who Killed Article 2(4)? Or: Changing Norms Governing the Use of Force by States*, 64 AM. J. INT'L L. 809, 809 (1970).

had led to the erosion of the prohibition.[99] Perhaps more cynically, Michael Glennon argues that had States intended to make the prohibition binding "they would have made the costs of violation greater than the costs of compliance."[100]

I do not believe, however, that these are accurate descriptions of state behavior. As Louis Henkin notes, Franck judged "the vitality of the law by looking only at its failures": in fact, Article 2(4) has been "a norm of behavior" that has "deter[red] violations."[101] Indeed, "no government ... has been prepared or has wished to pronounce it dead."[102] And of course it is not merely that the prohibition has never been openly rejected by States: no State has invoked another's breach of Article 2(4) as a legal reason to repudiate Charter rules.[103]

More importantly, as noted above, States generally offer legal justifications for their armed violence.[104] This may sometimes be a self-serving exercise. Nonetheless, as Oscar Schachter notes, "the felt need of governments to advance a legal argument is itself a fact of some consequence."[105] As Yoram Dinstein puts it, "[t]here is a common denominator between those who try (even disingenuously) to take advantage of the refinements of the law, and those who rigorously abide by its letter and spirit. They all share a belief in the authority of the law."[106] Indeed, I would argue that a significant number of

---

[99] *Id. passim.*

[100] Michael J. Glennon, *Why the Security Council Failed*, FOREIGN AFF., May–June 2003, at 16, 23.

[101] *See* Louis Henkin, *The Reports of the Death of Article 2(4) Are Greatly Exaggerated*, 65 AM. J. INT'L L. 544, 544 (1971). Edward Gordon further suggests that "[t]he seeming frequency of discrepant behavior is evident largely because it is so much easier to itemize and recognize an overt incident of noncompliance than one that is compliant." Edward Gordon, *Article 2(4) in Historical Context*, 10 YALE J. INT'L L. 271, 272 n.2 (1985).

[102] Henkin, *supra* note 101, at 547. *See also* ANTHONY CLARK AREND & ROBERT J. BECK, INTERNATIONAL LAW AND THE USE OF FORCE: BEYOND THE UN CHARTER PARADIGM 180 (1993).

[103] Oscar Schachter, *In Defense of International Rules on the Use of Force*, 53 U. CHI. L. REV. 113, 129 (1986) [hereinafter Schachter, *In Defense of International Rules*].

[104] OSCAR SCHACHTER, INTERNATIONAL LAW IN THEORY AND PRACTICE 130–31 (1991); Gordon, *supra* note 101, at 272.

[105] Schachter, *In Defense of International Rules*, *supra* note 103, at 123.

[106] DINSTEIN, *supra* note 30, at 89–90. *See also* Constantine Antonopoulos, *The Unilateral Use of Force by States After the End of the Cold War*, 4 J. ARMED CONFLICT L. 117, 124 (1999); Mary Ellen O'Connell, *Enforcing the Prohibition on the Use of Force: The U.N.'s Response to Iraq's Invasion of Kuwait*, 15 S. ILL. U. L.J. 453, 468 (1991). *See also* Philippe Sands, *Lawless World: International Law After September 11, 2001 and Iraq*, 6 MELBOURNE J. INT'L L. 437 (2005); Mark A. Drumbl, *Self-Defense and the Use of Force: Breaking the Rules, Making the Rules, or Both?*, 4 INT'L STUD. PERSP. 409, 427 (2003).

States see the prohibition not as a shackle on their freedom but as a critical element of their national security. Few States are capable of defending themselves militarily from all modern threats. They thus rely on others' observance of the prohibition's obligations, and are motivated to reemphasize the importance of the prohibition continually.

Because States value the prohibition on the use of force, they need it to be, and to be seen to be, of ongoing relevance – it must be responsive to modern threats without being so open to flexible interpretation that the prohibition is stripped of its value. For the same reason, States also wish their actions in relation to the use of force to be considered legitimate. An assessment that a State's use of force is illegitimate does more than just inflict reputational harm or raise the prospect of the enforcement of the rules of state responsibility. It carries the risk that States will be seen as undermining the prohibition on the use of force, something that very few States are willing to embrace.

Why have States not been compelled to ensure that the *jus in bello* is reinterpreted or clarified in the same adaptive manner? There is a litany of reasons for the dearth of state practice and *opinio juris* on the record in relation to the *jus in bello*. First, there are sometimes genuine operational reasons why States do not make their military practices public. Disclosure of particular practices may expose armed forces to greater risk or give away operational or tactical advantages. States equally often refrain from discussing the practices of their adversaries because much of that information is gathered through the employment of intelligence, surveillance, and reconnaissance assets, and is classified due to the need to protect the nature and extent of such capabilities.[107]

The types of issues discussed in this Chapter are typically the subject of legal advice to senior officials, individual ministers, or governments. Legal professional privilege may attach to such advice, meaning that the content of the advice often cannot be disclosed – at least not without an express waiver by the recipients. Similarly, state views on *jus in bello* issues are often informed by conversations with allies and other like-minded States. Joint views or positions are sometimes confidential and cannot be disclosed without the agreement of all relevant parties. Even if no confidentiality obligations strictly exist, there can be a sense that the disclosure of one State's views may inadvertently reveal the position of military partners in a way that might not be welcome.

States generally also adopt quite conservative positions when it comes to advancing legal views, especially in relation to unsettled or contested questions. Often States see little to be gained in promoting a particular view of the

---

[107] Michael N. Schmitt & Sean Watts, *The Decline of International Humanitarian Law* Opinio Juris *and the Law of Cyber Warfare*, 50 TEX. INT'L L.J. 189, 210 (2015).

law. States may, in principle, favor an interpretation of IHL that is restrictive, or which favors humanitarian considerations over military ones, but it can be difficult to dispel residual concerns that the position might be too constraining in unknown future scenarios, particularly in relation to emerging methods and means of warfare.

The mode of articulating such views is another relevant consideration. Many States will seek out the views of like-mindeds to inform and test their own positions. And yet the coordinated publication or expression of views can raise questions about motivations and can induce resistance and reactions that may be counterproductive.

It goes without saying that States have varying levels of capacity but the reality is that even in States with sophisticated bureaucracies, government legal advisers are often jacks of many trades. Government legal advisers tend to cover a wide range of subject matter areas, often have to produce advice in highly reactive circumstances, with limited time for broader study and reflection, and are not uniformly experts in every field. This can affect the will to make legal opinions public, especially if there is concern that criticisms may have implications for politicians. In many state systems, responsibility to provide international legal advice is also spread across different agencies, which can make it difficult to reach agreement.

Of course, the lack of willingness to have frank conversations on the public record about these types of unsettled IHL issues is not necessarily the product of benign considerations. I do not think it is unfair to say that States are generally reluctant to consider the development of new rules of IHL. Partly a product of the shape of modern conflict and non-state actors' failure (generally speaking) to comply with existing obligations, partly a sense that it is not appropriate for States, organizations, scholars, or other actors that have little (or no) operational experience to suggest new rules, and partly a product of wanting to have a free hand, States have quite deliberately resisted attempts to discuss new rules, as evidenced by States' rejection of any proposal to consider new rules in response to the International Committee of the Red Cross's (ICRC) 2010 report on *Strengthening Legal Protection for Victims of Armed Conflicts*.

Efforts have instead been focused on the development of interpretive guidance. The production of such guidance has only rarely been initiated by States.[108] Rather, what we have seen in recent years is a proliferation of

---

[108] An obvious exception being the Copenhagen Process on the Handling of Detainees in International Military Operations. COPENHAGEN PROCESS ON THE HANDLING OF DETAINEES IN INT'L MILITARY OPERATIONS, THE COPENHAGEN PROCESS: PRINCIPLES AND GUIDELINES (2012), http://um.dk/en/~/media/UM/English-site/Documents/Politics-and-diplomacy/Copenhangen%20Process%20Principles%20and%20Guidelines.pdf.

expert publications, in which States' views are often not even sought out. In an
astute article that examines this phenomenon, Michael Schmitt and Sean
Watts catalogue how other actors have filled the vacuum created by the dearth
of state practice and *opinio juris* in relation to the *jus in bello*.[109] They observe
that the ICRC is active in trying to address unsettled issues of international
law[110] and that scholars and other IHL experts have produced numerous legal
manuals.[111] Schmitt and Watts are particularly concerned by the "many
authors and pundits" who "boldly masquerade legal innovations as accepted
understandings of IHL," drawing particular attention to the IHL blogosphere
that has recently materialized, which "serves to conveniently highlight
emerging issues and provide a first glimpse of IHL analysis" but where
"bloggers are frequently unable to offer the depth of expertise called for by
complex IHL issues."[112]

Of particular note is the role played by international and hybrid criminal
courts and tribunals. In addition to developing the law themselves, in the
absence of ready access to the views of States on the state of the law, these
bodies are often reliant on the aforementioned guidance produced by non-state
actors. This is resulting in a certain cycle of influence: courts and tribunals draw
on these resources in making determinations about the content of customary
international law, and court and tribunal pronouncements about customary
IHL are relied on by States in forming their views (together, in many cases, with
the same resources relied upon by the courts and tribunals, which are often
useful reference points for busy governmental advisers). In this way, non-state
actor pronouncements on what the law is, or should be, are slowly coloring
state understandings of the law – and in the process likely becoming custom.

Marco Sassòli has expressed doubt as to "whether States can be duped by
experts, NGOs, and international criminal tribunals claiming that obligations
which those states rejected as treaty obligations are in any event part of
customary international law."[113] But I agree with Schmitt and Watts when
they say that "jurists, NGOs, scholars and other non-state actors presently have
greater influence on the interpretation and development of IHL than do
States"[114] by virtue of the fact that "non-State actors are outpacing and, in

---

[109] Schmitt & Watts, *supra* note 107.
[110] Consider, for example, Nils Melzer, Int'l Comm. of the Red Cross, Interpretive Guidance on the Notion of Direct Participation in Hostilities Under International Law (2009).
[111] Schmitt & Watts, *supra* note 107, at 192–95.
[112] *Id.* at 192.
[113] Sassòli, *supra* note 71, at 41–42.
[114] Schmitt & Watts, *supra* note 107, at 209.

some cases displacing, State action in both quantitative and qualitative terms."[115]

In other words, States' inability or reluctance to articulate their views on the content of the *jus in bello* has left gaps in the law, as my brief examination of operations against ISIS has illustrated by way of example. In time, I think it is inevitable that, for better or worse, these gaps will be filled by others if States maintain their silence.

VI. CONCLUSION

Like Schmitt and Watts, I think that ceding the development of the *jus in bello* to others has come at a cost.[116] As the authors note, reliance on the views of non-state actors does "not necessarily create 'bad' law" or even law that runs "contrary to States' interests or intentions."[117] But one's understanding of IHL is almost inevitably colored by one's function and mandate. While scholarly, and particularly humanitarian, input is crucial, it needs to be balanced against the perspective of States, particularly those experienced in military operations. As Schmitt and Watts put it, States have a unique understanding of "the operational challenges, demands, and limitations of combat so essential to fairly striking the delicate balance between military necessity and humanity that infuses IHL and informs its interpretation and evolution."[118]

While the reasons for States' silence identified above are not illegitimate or irrational, they are also not insurmountable. While there will always be a need for certain information to be withheld from the public domain for operational and security reasons, there is much that can be disclosed without compromising particular operations or broader national security interests. With a little imagination, States can readily articulate their views on legal issues in a manner that is divorced from specific operational settings. And legal issues can be expressed and discussed without the development of new rules *per se*. At the end of the day, this is ultimately a question of changing the ingrained thinking that the preservation of security necessarily requires secrecy.

The emergence of ISIS, like al-Qaeda before it, has thrown up a significant number of legal questions in relation to the *jus in bello* to which there are not ready answers – in contrast to the situation in relation to the *jus ad bellum*. States should try and explore questions like the ones identified in this Chapter

[115] *Id.* at 193.
[116] *Id.* at 212.
[117] *Id.* at 193.
[118] *Id.* at 210.

with a view to closing the gaps in the law. This is necessary to ensure that IHL continues to reflect the views of States and, consequently, is seen as relevant by States, which is of critical importance to maintaining and enhancing compliance with IHL's rules by both States and organized armed groups. Clarifying specific rules of IHL is also important for assessments about the legitimacy of actions against transnational non-state actors like ISIS. While ISIS may not have many defenders, meaning that the risks associated with stretching unsettled interpretations of the law may be low, the legitimacy of acts that lie in the law's gray zone is likely to be questioned. The clearer the rules, the more readily State actions against ISIS and actors like them will be able to be judged on an informed basis and, assuming State actions conform to those rules, the more likely they will be considered legitimate. ISIS's lawlessness lies at the heart of why so many States have lined up to degrade and defeat the organization. Victory may not be hollow, but it will never be resounding if States are perceived, rightly or wrongly, to have acted outside of the law to neutralize ISIS as a threat. ISIS arguably grew out of the invasion of Iraq in 2003 by many of the same States that now make up the anti-ISIS Coalition. That 2003 invasion was widely perceived as illegitimate. If for no other reason than ending self-sustaining cycles of radicalization and violence, States can, and should, reclaim the debate over modern challenges to the *jus in bello*.

10

Toward the Substantive Convergence of International Human Rights Law and the Laws of Armed Conflict

The Case of Hassan v. the United Kingdom

ROBIN GEIß

I. INTRODUCTION

The question of which legal rules should govern modern armed conflicts remains highly relevant and much discussed. As armed conflicts evolve it requires constant reconsideration. For years the focus has been on the clarification and dynamic interpretation of the laws of armed conflict and their enhanced implementation rather than any form of legislative norm development.[1] Ongoing discussions over the implementation of a new law of armed conflict monitoring mechanism,[2] the International Committee of the Red Cross's (ICRC) current project of updating the Commentaries on the Geneva Conventions and their Additional Protocols,[3] as well as an inflation of (non-binding) experts manuals, codes of conduct, and norm-clarification processes,[4] are all testament to this reality. Yet, ever since it has come to be accepted that international human rights law continues to apply in times of

---

[1] *But see* the International Committee of the Red Cross's (ICRC) current consultation process on the question of how to strengthen legal protection for persons deprived of their liberty in relation to non-international armed conflict. *Detention in Non-International Armed Conflict: The ICRC's Work on Strengthening Legal Protection*, INT'L COMM. RED CROSS (Apr. 21, 2015), www.icrc.org/eng/what-we-do/other-activities/development-ihl/strengthening-legal-protection-ihl-detention.htm.

[2] Peter Maurer, President, Int'l Comm. of the Red Cross, Strengthening Compliance with International Humanitarian Law, Speech at the Fourth Meeting of States on Strengthening Compliance with International Humanitarian Law (Apr. 23, 2015) (transcript *available at* www.icrc.org/en/document/fourth-meeting-states-strengthening-compliance-international-humanitarian-law).

[3] Interview by Int'l Comm. of the Red Cross with Jean-Marie Henckaerts, Legal Advisor, Int'l Comm. of the Red Cross, Bringing the Commentaries on the Geneva Conventions and their Additional Protocols into the 21st Century (July 12, 2012), www.icrc.org/eng/resources/documents/interview/2012/geneva-conventions-commentaries-interview-2012-07-12.htm.

[4] *See, e.g.*, the ICRC's clarification process on the notion of direct participation in hostilities. *ICRC Clarification Process on the Notion of Direct Participation Under International*

armed conflict,[5] the question of which legal rules should govern modern armed conflicts is also addressed in the guise of "clarifying" the relationship between the law of armed conflict and human rights law. This project, which in its scope and potential impact exceeds conventional clarification processes, largely falls on the judiciary – stretching the role of courts in terms of norm-modification and norm-development to its limits (and arguably beyond).

Of course, for as long as the focus was still primarily on the separation of the laws of war and the laws of peace there was not much of an issue. Even after the International Court of Justice's (ICJ) *Nuclear Weapons* Advisory Opinion it seemed as if the interplay between the law of armed conflict and human rights law could be determined in a rather straightforward manner and with near-arithmetic precision on the basis of a simple formula (*lex specialis*) that would help to keep the two legal regimes separate and to determine which of them prevails in a given case. Over time, however, the focus shifted from separation toward increasing complementarity and mutual reinforcement.[6] This necessitated more complex interpretive processes. As a result the *lex specialis* standard was increasingly criticized and its utility cast into doubt.[7] Gradually and subtly the original black-and-white approach of asking which of the two legal regimes (or individual provisions thereof) should prevail started to give way to interpretive approaches aimed at harmonization and even substantive convergence.

It is in this context that the European Court of Human Rights (ECtHR) Grand Chamber's judgment in *Hassan v. United Kingdom* may rightly be described as a landmark ruling.[8] After many years of controversy and

---

Humanitarian Law (Proceedings), INT'L COMM. RED CROSS (June 30, 2009), www.icrc.org/
eng/resources/documents/article/other/direct-participation-article-020709.htm; INT'L INST. OF
HUMANITARIAN LAW, MANUAL ON THE LAW OF NON-INTERNATIONAL ARMED CONFLICT WITH
COMMENTARY (2006), http://stage.iihl.org/wp-content/uploads/2015/12/Manual-on-the-Law-of-
NIAC.pdf; TALLINN MANUAL ON THE INTERNATIONAL LAW APPLICABLE TO CYBER WARFARE
(Michael N. Schmitt ed., 2009), https://ccdcoe.org/tallinn-manual.html; INT'L COMM. OF THE
RED CROSS & SWISS FED. DEP'T OF FOREIGN AFFAIRS, THE MONTREUX DOCUMENT (2008),
www.icrc.org/eng/assets/files/other/icrc_002_0996.pdf.

[5] Legality of the Threat or Use of Nuclear Weapons, Advisory Opinion, 1996 I.C.J. 226, ¶ 25
(July 8) [hereinafter Nuclear Weapons Advisory Opinion].

[6] Cordula Dröge, *The Interplay Between International Humanitarian Law and International
Human Rights Law in Situations of Armed Conflict*, 40 ISR. L. REV. 310 (2007) [hereinafter
Dröge, *Interplay*].

[7] Nancie Prud'homme, *Lex Specialis: Oversimplifying a More Complex and Multifaceted
Relationship?*, 40 ISR. L. REV. 356 (2007).

[8] Hassan v. United Kingdom, App. No. 29750/09, Eur. Ct. H.R. (2014), http://hudoc.echr.coe
.int/eng?i=001-146501 [hereinafter Hassan Grand Chamber Judgment]. *See* Lawrence
Hill-Cawthorne, *The Grand Chamber Judgment in Hassan*, EJIL: TALK! (Sept. 16, 2014),

judgments on the matter, it is now fairly settled that the European Convention on Human Rights (ECHR or European Convention) continues to apply in situations of armed conflict and in cases of extraterritorial detention.[9] Against this backdrop, in *Hassan* the European Court of Human Rights had the opportunity to turn to some of the more specific, follow-up questions regarding the interplay of the law of armed conflict and human rights law, particularly with respect to the right to liberty and in the context of an international armed conflict.[10]

The Grand Chamber had to decide whether the Convention requires a formal derogation as a "door-opener" to any consideration of law of armed conflict rules, and – once this door is opened – how much scope there is for interpretation and what methodology should be employed to work out the harmonious interaction of these two legal regimes. The *Hassan* judgment arguably presents as many new questions as it contains answers. Nonetheless, it consolidates the trend toward complementarity, mutual reinforcement, and substantive convergence and presents a new – albeit still rather rudimentary and yet to be fully developed – approach for the systemic integration of the law of armed conflict and human rights law.

II. THE INTERPLAY BETWEEN HUMAN RIGHTS LAW AND THE LAWS OF ARMED CONFLICT: THE DEBATE SO FAR

Since it has come to be accepted that human rights law continues to apply in times of armed conflict, and at least as far as Europe is concerned extraterritorially, the relationship between this legal regime and the laws of armed conflict has increasingly come into focus. The ICJ's tripartite formula accurately describes how these regimes may interact.[11] But apart from its references

---

www.ejiltalk.org/the-grand-chamber-judgment-in-hassan-v-uk/ [hereinafter Hill-Cawthorne, *Hassan*].

9   MARKO MILANOVIC, EXTRATERRITORIAL APPLICATION OF HUMAN RIGHTS TREATIES (2011).

10 *But see* Cyprus v. Turkey (Report of the Commission), App. Nos. 6780/74 and 6950/75, 4 Eur. H.R. Rep. 482 and 556 (1976).

11 In *Armed Activities on the Territory of the Congo*, the International Court of Justice observed, with reference to its Advisory Opinion concerning the *Legal Consequences of the Construction of a Wall in the Occupied Palestinian Territory*, that "[a]s regards the relationship between international humanitarian law and human rights law, there are thus three possible situations: some rights may be exclusively matters of international humanitarian law; others may be exclusively matters of human rights law; yet others may be matters of both these branches of international law." *See* Armed Activities on the Territory of the Congo (Dem. Rep. Congo v. Uganda), Judgment, 2005 I.C.J. 168, ¶ 216 (Dec. 18) [hereinafter Armed Activities Judgment].

to *lex specialis* in the *Nuclear Weapons* and *Wall* Advisory Opinions,[12] the ICJ never presented any further substantive guidance as to how to resolve those instances in which rights fall within the ambit "of both these branches of international law."[13]

Nevertheless, for a while the *lex specialis derogat legi generali* maxim seemed to be perceived as a panacea, i.e., a self-standing tool to resolve all instances that equally touch upon human rights law and the law of armed conflict.[14]

The maxim is appealing in its brevity and ostensible simplicity and because of its openness and resultant flexibility.[15] Unlike with respect to contemporary cases, which often focus on detention and the right to liberty, its application to the initial set of cases, which by and large dealt with the protection of the right to life during the conduct of hostilities, seemed relatively evident and straight-forward. The *lex specialis* maxim was and arguably still is favored by all those who like the United States (post–September 11, 2001), Israel, and the United Kingdom wish to accord preference to the laws of war and want to keep international human rights law out of armed conflict scenarios as much as possible.

But of course the idea that two separate legal regimes with hundreds of provisions, different historical backgrounds, and partially divergent premises, objectives, and addressees could be reconciled on the basis of a single, simple maxim was illusionary.[16] Over time the *lex specialis* maxim proved increasingly impracticable, and many perceived it as obfuscating the relationship between the two legal regimes rather than clarifying it.[17] Leaving aside those

---

[12] Marko Milanovic, *The Lost Origins of Lex Specialis: Rethinking the Relationship Between Human Rights and International Humanitarian Law*, in THEORETICAL BOUNDARIES OF ARMED CONFLICT AND HUMAN RIGHTS 78, at 82 (Jens David Ohlin ed., 2016) [hereinafter Milanovic, *Lost Origins*].

[13] Armed Activities Judgment, *supra* note 11, ¶ 216.

[14] On *lex specialis*, see generally Anja Lindroos, *Addressing Norm Conflicts in a Fragmented Legal System: The Doctrine of Lex Specialis*, 74 NORDIC J. INT 'L L. 27, 46 (2005); Prud'homme, *supra* note 7, at 356; Milanovic, *Lost Origins*, *supra* note 12; Nele Matz-Lück, *Treaties, Conflicts Between*, in MAX PLANCK ENCYCLOPEDIA OF PUB. INT'L LAW, http://opil.ouplaw.com/view/ 10.1093/law:epil/9780199231690/law-9780199231690-e1485?rskey=cSJOu5&result=1&prd= EPIL; Matthew Happold, *International Humanitarian Law and Human Rights Law*, in RESEARCH HANDBOOK ON INTERNATIONAL CONFLICT AND SECURITY LAW 444 (Nigel D. White & Christian Henderson eds., 2013).

[15] Prud'homme, *supra* note 7, at 356.

[16] With respect to the differences between law of armed conflict and human rights law, *see* Cordula Dröge, *Elective Affinities? Human Rights and Humanitarian Law*, 90 INT'L REV. RED CROSS 501, 521 (2008) [hereinafter Dröge, *Elective Affinities*]; Dröge, *Interplay*, *supra* note 6, at 336.

[17] Hill-Cawthorne, *Hassan*, *supra* note 8.

writers who always doubted the applicability of this (allegedly) domestic law maxim to the (allegedly) incoherent, fragmented system of international law – which, unlike the *lex posterior* rule finds no mentioning in the Vienna Convention on the Law of Treaties (Vienna Convention) – the maxim proved largely unworkable in its application to the relationship of the law of armed conflict and human rights law primarily for a lack of an agreed definition of the parameters defining *"specialis,"* diverging opinions regarding the maxim's effects (full-fledged regime displacement or situational, norm-specific displacement),[18] and controversy regarding its precise function as either a mechanism for norm-conflict resolution, or an interpretive tool for harmonization and norm-conflict avoidance, or both.[19] Without further clarification, the *lex specialis* maxim in its application to the relationship of the law of armed conflict and human rights law by and large remained an empty shell without normative content, incapable of indicating whether a norm is special or general.[20]

Indeed, in spite of a tremendous volume of legal scholarship on the issue, the question of what actually renders one legal regime more specific than the other has never been settled. Is it that one legal regime (or individual provisions thereof) better matches the factual circumstances of a specific case, or that one legal regime addresses a given situation in more detail, or because it offers more specific protections? Or should a legal regime be regarded as *lex specialis* because it offers fewer protections, thereby heeding the specificities of conducting hostilities in times of armed conflict and allowing the military the operational flexibility that military necessity requires? It has been stated – and this seems to reflect the most common view on the matter – that "[i]n determining which rule is the more specialized one, the most important indicators are the precision and clarity of a rule and its adaptation to the particular circumstances of the case."[21] But when is a rule of either the law of armed conflict or human rights law actually "better adapted to the circumstances" of a given case? After all, it could always be argued that the law of armed conflict, precisely because it intentionally omits some of the more

---

[18] Oona A. Hathaway et al., *Which Law Governs During Armed Conflict? The Relationship Between International Humanitarian Law and Human Rights Law in Armed Conflict*, 96 MINN. L. REV. 1883, 1886 (2012).

[19] Marko Milanovic, *A Norm Conflict Perspective on the Relationship Between International Humanitarian Law and Human Rights Law*, 14 J. CONFLICT & SEC. L. 459, 473–76 (2009) [hereinafter Milanovic, *Norm Conflict Perspective*]; Matthew Happold, *supra* note 14, at 459–63.

[20] Prud'homme, *supra* note 7, at 394.

[21] Dröge, *Elective Affinities?*, *supra* note 16, at 524; *see also* Hathaway et al., *supra* note 18, at 1887.

protective details of international human rights law and leaves some discretion to military commanders, is more specific and therefore *per se* better adapted to the reality of armed conflict.[22] Conversely, it could just as easily be argued that because of greater specificity, precision, detail, and resultant higher standards of protection, human rights law should typically prevail. In the absence of any further substantive guidance beyond mere references to the *lex specialis* maxim and the general tenet to accord preference to the rule that is "better adapted to the circumstances," the answer chosen depends primarily on the interpreter's perspective and policy choice. It is for this reason that it has rightly been argued that the maxim allows for arbitrary and in fact diametrically opposed arguments.[23]

What is more, choosing which legal regime or specific provision is better adapted to the circumstances of a given case is further blurred by the fact that the spectrum of situations that fall within the ambit of the notion of armed conflict (and that are hence regulated by both armed conflict and human rights law) has broadened significantly over recent years, encompassing large-scale combat operations between sophisticated military actors, extraterritorial military operations, as well as highly asymmetric constellations that may be more akin to or resemble elements of peacetime policing and law enforcement operations.

Against this backdrop and in light of such complexity, the *lex specialis* maxim increasingly appeared like a "straitjacket." In other words, it became increasingly doubtful whether the intricate, context-specific relationship between the law of armed conflict and human rights law could be resolved merely on the basis of asking which of the two regimes (or individual provisions thereof) is more specific.

This development went hand in hand with a change of perception of the *lex specialis* maxim's nature and function and a general – albeit not entirely uncontroversial – trend toward complementarity and harmony in the relationship of the law of armed conflict and human rights law. Thus, initially, based on an "aggressive reading" of the ICJ's *Nuclear Weapons* Advisory Opinion,[24] the *lex specialis* maxim was widely understood as a principle for norm-conflict resolution with the effect of full-fledged regime displacement, whereby in times of armed conflict the law of armed conflict was understood to operate at

---

[22] The ICJ's earlier and rather sweeping assumption expressed in the *Nuclear Weapons* Advisory Opinion that considered the law of armed conflict to be the applicable *lex specialis* precisely because it "is designed to regulate the conduct of hostilities" seemed to point in this direction. Nuclear Weapons Advisory Opinion, *supra* note 5, ¶ 25.

[23] Prud'homme, *supra* note 7, at 394.

[24] Hathaway et al., *supra* note 18, at 1895.

the exclusion of international human rights law.[25] Although it came in a different guise and used different terminology, this approach largely resembled the classical divide between the law of war and the law of peace and placed strong emphasis on the divergences of the law of armed conflict and human rights law.[26] Over time this approach lost support. Today, the emphasis lies on complementarity, harmony, and mutual cross-fertilization.[27]

This trend toward complementary and arguably even substantive convergence has become manifest in various – sometimes diffuse – ways. Examples are the jurisprudential development of what could be called a regime of "wartime human rights."[28] Thus, the European Court of Human Rights has repeatedly considered genuine law of armed conflict considerations within the framework of human rights law, namely but not exclusively in its Chechnya cases.[29] Conversely, the infamous Chapter IX of the ICRC's *Interpretive Guidance on the Notion of Direct Participation in Hostilities* is widely seen to reflect an attempt to introduce human rights concepts into the heart of the law of armed conflict, i.e., into the core rules on the conduct of hostilities.[30] The Copenhagen Principles on the Handling of Detainees in International Military Operations may be seen to reflect yet another approach whereby law of armed conflict and human rights law considerations are (arguably) being merged more evenly.[31]

What is more, some recent international treaties and instruments incorporate or draw from both human rights and international humanitarian law provisions. As listed by Dröge, this is the case for the Convention on the Rights of the Child, the Rome Statute of the International Criminal Court, the Optional Protocol to the Convention on the Rights of the Child on the Involvement of Children in Armed Conflict, the Basic Principles and Guidelines on the Right to a Remedy and Reparation for Victims of Gross Violations of International Human Rights Law and Serious Violations of International

[25] Milanovic, *Norm Conflict Perspective, supra* note 19, at 464.
[26] Milanovic, *Lost Origins, supra* note 12, at 23–24.
[27] Dröge, *Interplay, supra* note 6, at 355.
[28] *See* Dröge, *Elective Affinities, supra* note 16, at 507.
[29] William Abresch, *A Human Rights Law of Internal Armed Conflict: The European Court of Human Rights in Chechnya*, 16 Eur. J. Int'l L. 741 (2005).
[30] W. Hays Parks, *Part IX of the ICRC "Direct Participation in Hostilities" Study: No Mandate, No Expertise, and Legally Incorrect*, 42 N.Y.U. J. Int'l L. & Pol. 769 (2010); Nils Melzer, *Keeping the Balance Between Military Necessity and Humanity: A Response to Four Critiques of the ICRC's Interpretive Guidance on the Notion of Direct Participation in Hostilities*, 42 N.Y.U. J. Int'l L. & Pol. 831 (2010).
[31] Hill-Cawthorne, *The Copenhagen Principles on the Handling of Detainees: Implications for the Procedural Regulation of Internment*, 18 J. Conflict & Sec. L. 481, 481–84 (2013).

Humanitarian Law and most recently the Convention on the Rights of Persons with Disabilities.[32]

In line with the general trend toward harmonious interpretation, the focus has shifted to Article 31(3)(c) of the Vienna Convention on the Law of Treaties as a starting point for working out the interplay between the law of armed conflict and human rights law. Article 31(3)(c) of the Vienna Convention requires that "any relevant rules of international law applicable in the relations between the parties" be taken into account for purposes of interpretation.[33] As far as the *lex specialis* maxim is concerned, which is increasingly understood as a multi-functional principle,[34] the focus has shifted from the maxim's function as a principle of norm-conflict resolution, which in cases of genuine norm conflicts (cases where the application of these provision leads to incompatible results) determines which rule prevails over the other, to its function as a principle of interpretation that provides guidance in cases in which a specific provision is generally in harmony with an equally applicable general rule.[35] In this latter sense, i.e., in its incarnation as a principle of norm interpretation, the *lex specialis* maxim corresponds to Article 31(3)(c) of the Vienna Convention and should be understood as a subprinciple thereof.

Against this backdrop of increasing emphasis on complementarity and harmonization (in Europe), the preconditions for harmonious interpretation, namely the question where and how to draw the line between areas that allow for harmonious interpretation and those areas in which genuine norm conflict remains and what interpretive methods (in addition to or instead of *lex specialis* as an interpretive tool) to employ to interpret the law of armed conflict and human rights law harmoniously, have increasingly come into focus. It is precisely in this context that *Hassan* brings fresh impetus, indicating – at least as far as Europe is concerned – the way forward to further

---

[32] Dröge, *Interplay*, *supra* note 6 at 317.

[33] Oliver Dörr, *General Rule of Interpretation*, *in* THE VIENNA CONVENTION ON THE LAW OF TREATIES: A COMMENTARY 521, 521–70, ¶ 99–104 (Oliver Dörr & Kirsten Schmalenbach eds., 2012).

[34] Milanovic, *Lost Origins*, *supra* note 12, at 103–14.

[35] *See* Int'l Law Comm'n, Rep. on Fragmentation of International Law: Difficulties Arising from the Diversification and Expansion of International Law, ¶¶ 56–57, U.N. Doc. A/CN4./L.682 (Apr. 13, 2006) ("[i.] where the specific rule should be read and understood within the confines or against the background of the general standard, typically as an elaboration, updating or a technical specification of the latter," or more narrowly, [ii.] "where two legal provisions that are both valid and applicable, are in no express hierarchical relationship, and provide incompatible direction on how to deal with the same set of facts ... instead of the (general) rule, one should apply the (specific) exception.")

consolidate the general trend toward greater complementary and mutual reinforcement of the law of armed conflict and human rights law.

III. THE *HASSAN* CASE

In the course of the international armed conflict in Iraq, British forces found Tarek Hassan armed and on the roof of his brother's house together with other objects of military value.[36] Tarek Hassan was arrested and briefly detained at Camp Bucca but after two screening processes was cleared for release within a few days of having been brought to the Camp. The European Court of Human Rights found that "United Kingdom authorities had reason to believe" that Tarek Hassan could be detained either "as a prisoner of war" or as a civilian "for imperative reasons of security" and that his capture and detention therefore was "consistent with the powers available to the United Kingdom under the Third and Fourth Geneva Conventions."[37] The Court found that in the case of Hassan the applicable humanitarian law limits Article 5(1) of the European Convention on Human Rights to its fundamental purpose, namely "to protect the individual from arbitrariness."[38] It further found that Hassan's detention was not arbitrary, as he was released from the Camp shortly after it was found that he did not pose a threat to security.

But whereas preventive security detention is an inevitable and accepted feature of the laws of armed conflict, it is prohibited under human rights law. As the Grand Chamber pointed out in *Hassan*, "[i]t has long been established that the list of grounds of permissible detention in Article 5 §1 does not include internment or preventive detention where there is no intention to bring criminal charges within a reasonable time."[39] The central question before the Court therefore was whether and, if so, how law of armed conflict conforming security detention could somehow be reconciled with the requirements of the European Convention on Human Rights.

The issue was brought to the fore because the United Kingdom had not lodged a formal derogation in accordance with Article 15 of the European Convention. *Prima facie*, the high protective level granted by Article 5 of the Convention, therefore remained fully intact.[40] Yet, notwithstanding the

---

[36] Hassan Grand Chamber Judgment, *supra* note 8, ¶¶ 47–58.

[37] *Id.* ¶¶ 109–10.

[38] *Id.* ¶ 105.

[39] *Id.* ¶ 97 (citations omitted).

[40] "Article 5 § 1 of the Convention, however, sets out the general rule that '[e]veryone has the right to liberty and security of the person' and that '[n]o one shall be deprived of his liberty' except in one of the circumstances set out in sub-paragraphs (a) to (f)." *Id.* ¶ 96.

limited grounds of permissible detention contained in Article 5, the Grand
Chamber reconciled the seemingly irreconcilable requirements of the law of
armed conflict and the European Convention by bringing both legal regimes
to bear side by side. In doing so the Court did not take the easy way out but
seized the opportunity to tackle the problem head on. Thus, in line with its
earlier jurisprudence, which had consistently required a narrow interpretation
of Article 5, the Court rejected the U.K. government's proposal to evade the
problem on the basis of an expansive reading of Article 5(1)(c),[41] which would
have simply brought wartime detention within the ambit of this provision.[42]
Instead, the Court focused on the issue of extraterritorial derogations in the
context of international armed conflicts and, in light of a uniform state
practice not to derogate in times of international armed conflict, saw no need
for such a formal derogation to be lodged.[43] Secondly, the Grand Chamber
looked into how seemingly conflicting law of armed conflict requirements
could nevertheless be reconciled with those of the European Convention and
shed light on what harmonious interpretation actually means in the view of
the European Court of Human Rights.[44]

IV. EXTRATERRITORIAL DEROGATION IN TIMES OF INTERNATIONAL ARMED CONFLICT

As far as international armed conflicts are concerned, the Court in *Hassan* did
not require a formal derogation to lower the protective standards of the
European Convention and to expand the list of permissible grounds of
detention.[45] Nor, however, did it exclude the possibility of a formal derogation
in times of international armed conflicts. Relying on Article 31(3)(b) of the
Vienna Convention and pointing out that in its view consistent practice could
modify the text of the Convention,[46] the Court found that "[t]he practice of
the High Contracting Parties *is not to derogate* from their obligations under
Article 5 in order to detain persons on the basis of the Third and Fourth
Geneva Conventions during international armed conflicts," and that in spite
of numerous (extraterritorial) military missions, "no State has ever made a

---

[41] *Id.* ¶¶ 88–90.
[42] *Id.* ¶ 97 ("there does not need to be any correlation between security internment and suspicion of having committed an offence or risk of the commission of a criminal offence.").
[43] *See infra* Section IV.
[44] *See infra* Section V.
[45] Hassan Grand Chamber Judgment, *supra* note 8, ¶ 103.
[46] *Id.* ¶ 101.

derogation pursuant to Article 15 of the Convention in respect of these activities."[47]

There is certainly a good case to be made in favor of requiring the lodging of formal derogations also in extraterritorial contexts and in the course of international armed conflicts. Indeed, apart from ensuring transparency as to the applicable legal rules, it would only appear logical that the reach of Article 15 should follow the Convention's scope of extraterritorial application and neither the wording nor the context militate against extraterritorial derogations.[48] But there are also arguments against the requirement of extraterritorial derogations in the context of international armed conflicts.[49] The wording of Article 15 is open to interpretation but can be read to exclude derogations in extraterritorial settings.[50] Such derogations could easily be abused, however. Thus far, no State has ever lodged a formal derogation in an extraterritorial context (either under the European Convention or under any other human

---

[47] *Id.* (emphasis added). Nor has any State made a derogation pursuant to Article 4 of the International Covenant on Civil and Political Rights (ICCPR).

[48] Thus, as was rightly stated in the partly dissenting opinion of Judge Spano, joined by Judges Nicolaou, Bianku, and Kalaydjieva, "[t]he extra-jurisdictional reach of the Convention under Article 1 must necessarily go hand in hand with the scope of Article 15." *Id.* (partly dissenting opinion of Judge Spano, ¶ 8). In *Bankovič*, the court held that "Article 15 itself is to be read subject to the 'jurisdiction' limitation enumerated in Article 1 of the Convention." Bankovič v. Belgium, Admissibility Decision, App. No. 52207/99, 2001-XII Eur. Ct. H.R. 333, ¶ 62. See also *Serdar Mohammed v. Ministry of Defence*, where Justice Leggat argued that

> Now that the Convention has been interpreted, however, as having such extraterritorial effect, it seems to me that Article 15 must be interpreted in a way which reflects this. It cannot be right to interpret jurisdiction under Article 1 as encompassing the exercise of power and control by a state on the territory of another state, as the European Court did in the Al-Skeini case, unless at the same time Article 15 is interpreted in a way which is consonant with that position and permits derogation to the extent that it is strictly required by the exigencies of the situation.
> Article 15, like other provisions of the Convention, can and it seems to me must be "tailored" to such extraterritorial jurisdiction. This can readily be achieved without any undue violence to the language of Article 15 by interpreting the phrase "war or other public emergency threatening the life of the nation" as including, in the context of an international peacekeeping operation, a war or other emergency threatening the life of the nation on whose territory the relevant acts take place.

Serdar Mohammed v. Ministry of Defence [2014] EWHC (QB) 1369, [155]-[156]. See also Heike Krieger, *After Al-Jedda: Detention, Derogation, and an Enduring Dilemma*, 50 MIL. L. & L. WAR REV. 419, 436 (2011) ("Although the wording of Article 15 para. 1 ECHR refers to the life of the nation seeking to derogate, it is not so strictly formulated that it could not allow for a more dynamic interpretation, so to include unstable foreign territories where the Member State in question would operate.").

[49] See generally Marko Milanovic, *Extraterritorial Derogations from Human Rights Treaties in Armed Conflict, in* THE FRONTIERS OF HUMAN RIGHTS 55 (Nehal Bhuta ed., 2016).

[50] R (Al-Jedda) v. Secretary of State for Defence [2007] UKHL 58, [2008] 1 AC (HL) 332.

rights treaty). Lastly, insisting on a formal derogation – apart from the obvious political repercussions – would have complicated the Court's task of working out the interplay between the law of armed conflict and human rights law in future cases. After all, derogations are context specific and all derogation clauses place limits on the possibility of derogations by allowing States to take only such measures as are *"strictly required by the exigencies of the situation."*[51] Thus, depending on the circumstances of each case, a derogation would not necessarily extinguish the protections granted by Article 5 in full and in each case the Court's task of working out the relationship between the law of armed conflict and human rights law would likely be complicated by the additional assessment of what the exigencies of the specific situation required. By leaving derogations aside and by turning directly to the law of armed conflict, the Court omitted a case-specific assessment of the prevailing exigencies and instead – in a more sweeping manner – resorted to the law of armed conflict with its already built-in (albeit more generic and categorical) considerations of the exigencies of armed conflict.

Against this backdrop, a detailed explanation as to why the Court did not insist on formal derogations in the context of international armed conflicts would of course have been highly desirable. The Court, however, decided the issue exclusively on the basis of a formal argument, namely by relying on subsequent state practice. Apart from the lost opportunity to shed more light on the issue of extraterritorial derogations, the methodology adopted by the Court has already been criticized.[52] In particular, the conclusiveness of the practice chosen by the Court is questionable. As has rightly been pointed out already, States may refrain from lodging derogations for a number of reasons,[53] most importantly in the case of the European Convention because they did not/do not want to concede its extraterritorial applicability in the first place.[54] What is more, for purposes of the interpretation of the European Convention, references to subsequent practice under the International Covenant on Civil and Political Rights (ICCPR) qualify as a use of supplementary means of interpretation in the sense of Article 32 of the Vienna Convention rather than

---

[51] International Covenant on Civil and Political Rights art. 4, Dec. 16, 1966, 99 U.N.T.S. 171; Convention for the Protection of Human Rights and Fundamental Freedoms art. 15, Nov. 4, 1950, 213 U.N.T.S. 222; American Convention on Human Rights art. 27, Nov. 22, 1969, 1144 U.N.T.S. 123 (emphasis added).

[52] Hill-Cawthorne, *Hassan, supra* note 8.

[53] Marko Milanovic, *A Few Thoughts on Hassan vs. United Kingdom*, EJIL: TALK! (October 22, 2014), www.ejiltalk.org/a-few-thoughts-on-hassan-v-united-kingdom/ [hereinafter Milanovic, *A Few Thoughts*].

[54] Hassan Grand Chamber Judgment, *supra* note 8 (partly dissenting opinion of Judge Spano, ¶ 12).

recourse to subsequent practice in the sense of Article 31.[55] In any case, the Court's assumption of such a pronounced modifying effect – without more – cannot normally be attached to subsequent practice.[56] As the International Law Commission's Special Rapporteur Georg Nolte recently pointed out:

> while there are indications in international jurisprudence that, absent indications in the treaty to the contrary, the agreed subsequent practice of the parties may lead to certain *limited modifications* of a treaty, *the actual occurrence of that effect is not to be presumed.* Instead, States and courts should make every effort to conceive an agreed subsequent practice of the parties as an effort to interpret the treaty in a particular way.[57]

Thus, whereas even proponents of extraterritorial derogations must concede that the result reached by the Court is neither wholly implausible nor indefensible, the way in which the Court reached its conclusion is not fully convincing. Finally, in order to partially compensate the transparency deficit caused by its approach the Grand Chamber required that "the provisions of Article 5 will be interpreted and applied in the light of the relevant provisions of international humanitarian law *only* where this is specifically pleaded by the respondent State."[58]

V. HARMONIOUS INTERPRETATION: ARTICLE 31(3)(C) OF THE VIENNA CONVENTION

With regard to the question whether and, if so, how the law of armed conflict prescriptions could be reconciled with those of the Convention in the absence of a formal derogation, the Court opted for harmonious interpretation/systemic integration on the basis of Article 31(3)(c) of the Vienna Convention.[59] Specifically, the Court argued that

---

[55] Luigi Crema, *Subsequent Practice in Hassan v United Kingdom: When Things Seem to Go Wrong in the Life of a Living Instrument*, 15 QUESTIONS INT'L L., ZOOM-IN 3, 8–13 (2015), www.qil-qdi.org/wp-content/uploads/2015/05/02_Hassan_CREMA_FIN.pdf.

[56] Hill-Cawthorne, *Hassan*, *supra* note 8.

[57] Georg Nolte (Special Rapporteur on Subsequent Agreements and Subsequent Practice in Relation to the Interpretation of Treaties), *Second Rep. on Subsequent Agreements and Subsequent Practice in Relation to Treaty Interpretation*, ¶ 142, U.N. Doc. A/CN.4/671 (Mar. 26, 2014) (emphasis added).

[58] Hassan Grand Chamber Judgment, *supra* note 8, ¶ 107 (emphasis added). It is further stated that "It is not for the Court to assume that a State intends to modify the commitments which it has undertaken by ratifying the Convention in the absence of a clear indication to that effect." *Id.*

[59] Campbell McLachlan, *The Principle of Systemic Integration and Article 31(3)(C) of the Vienna Convention*, 54 INT'L & COMP. L.Q. 279 (2005); Int'l Law Comm'n, Rep. of the Study

By reason of the co-existence of the safeguards provided by international humanitarian law and by the Convention in time of armed conflict, the grounds of permitted deprivation of liberty set out in subparagraphs (a) to (f) of that provision should be *accommodated, as far as possible*, with the taking of prisoners of war and the detention of civilians who pose a risk to security under the Third and Fourth Geneva Conventions.[60]

Accommodation in this sense may be seen as synonymous for harmonious interpretation, which is in line with Article 31(3)(c).

A. How Much Scope Is There for Harmonious Interpretation Between International Human Rights Law and the Law of Armed Conflict?

What is striking, however, is that the Court assumes a broad scope for harmonious interpretation in a case, which many observers would have regarded as a paradigmatic example of genuine norm conflict.[61] As has rightly been observed elsewhere, "if two treaty norms contradict each other in clear terms there is strictly speaking no room for systemic integration based upon interpretation."[62] Thus, the partly dissenting opinion of Judge Spano, joined by Judges Nicolaou, Bianku, and Kalaydjieva, while conceding that the Convention must of course be interpreted in harmony with other rules of international law, criticizes that "the doctrine of consistent interpretation of the Convention with other norms of international law has its limits"[63] and that "[t]here is simply no available scope to 'accommodate,' ... the powers of internment under international humanitarian law within, inherently or alongside Article 5 § 1."[64]

Indeed, on the basis of the Grand Chamber's ruling one may wonder whether – as the use of the phrase "as far as possible" in the above-cited passage seems to imply – the Court actually still sees any potential for genuine

Group on Fragmentation of International Law: Difficulties Arising from Diversification and Expansion of International Law, ¶ 27, U.N. Doc. A/CN.4/L.676 (July 29, 2005). *See also* Philippe Sands, *Treaty, Custom and the Cross-fertilization of International Law*, 1 YALE HUM. RTS. & DEV. L.J. 85, 95 (1998).

[60] Hassan Grand Chamber Judgment, *supra* note 8, ¶ 104 (emphasis added).
[61] *See, e.g.*, Hathaway et al., *supra* note 18, at 1901. The authors observe that there are some circumstances in which it may not be possible to reconcile conflicts between the two bodies of law through interpretation: "One example is the treatment of persons captured during armed conflict: humanitarian law specifies that "combatants" be held as POWs until the end of hostilities (and then returned), while human rights law specifies that detainees be tried for their offenses." *Id.*
[62] Matz-Lück, *supra* note 14, ¶ 23.
[63] Hassan Grand Chamber Judgment, *supra* note 8 (partly dissenting opinion of Judge Spano, ¶ 16).
[64] *Id.*

norm conflict between the law of armed conflict and human rights law or whether in the Court's view it is all "just" a matter of interpretation. It could be argued that the Court's reasoning is methodologically flawed because although the Court frames its ruling as an application of harmonious interpretation, it actually much closer resembles the application of the *lex specialis* principle in its function as a rule of norm conflict resolution whereby law of armed conflict prescriptions prevail.[65] After all, as the partly dissenting judges point out, "indefinite and preventive internment in wartime *flatly contradict*[]" the permitted grounds of detention in Article 5 of the European Convention on Human Rights.[66] Such an approach of overriding European Convention requirements in the guise of interpretation is arguably not without precedent in the European Court's case law. In *Al-Adsani*, the Court also "interpreted" the Convention in harmony with international rules on state immunity but in essence simply decided not to apply Article 6 of the Convention to facts it clearly covered by its ordinary meaning.[67]

The majority in *Hassan* argued that because these additional grounds of detention or internment are "*accepted features* of international humanitarian law" and "*only* in cases of international armed conflict ... Article 5 could be interpreted as permitting the exercise of such broad powers."[68] Thus, at least implicitly, the majority readily concedes that in times of peace, indefinite and preventive internment "flatly contradict" the wording of Article 5. But implicitly the majority also presumes that this is not necessarily the case in wartime because originally the continuous application of the Convention during armed conflict was unclear or not envisaged by the drafters.

This reasoning is hardly convincing. Recall the wording of Article 15, which explicitly envisages derogations in times of war. But whether on the basis of

---

[65] In the partly dissenting opinion of Judge Spano joined by Judges Nicolaou, Bianku, and Kalaydjieva, the judges wrote, "this novel method of *accommodation* cannot be implemented in such a manner as to have effectively the same legal effects as *disapplication* [on the basis of derogation]." *Id.* (partly dissenting opinion of Judge Spano, ¶ 18). It is telling that in *Serdar Mohammed*, although the Court of Appeal did not expressly equate the approach adopted in *Hassan* with an application of the *lex specialis* principle, it nevertheless discussed *Hassan* under the general heading of the relationship between international human rights law and international humanitarian law, recognized that international humanitarian law constituted the *lex specialis*, and accepted that this *lex specialis* could lead to the modification of international human rights law. Serdar Mohammed v. Ministry of Defence [2015] EWCA (Civ) 843 [82], [108] [hereinafter Serdar Mohammed Appeals Judgment].

[66] Hassan Grand Chamber Judgment, *supra* note 8 (partly dissenting opinion of Judge Spano, ¶ 17) (emphasis added).

[67] 40 YEARS OF THE VIENNA CONVENTION ON THE LAW OF TREATIES 146 (Alexander Orakhelashvili & Sarah Williams eds., 2010).

[68] Hassan Grand Chamber Judgment, *supra* note 8, ¶ 104.

the majority's method of "accommodation" or based on the minority's assumption of a genuine norm conflict and the resultant displacement of more protective human rights standards in line with the *lex specialis* maxim as a principle of norm-conflict resolution, the end result is the same: the detention of Tarek Hassan did not violate the European Convention.

B. *A New Interpretive Approach for Harmonizing the Law of Armed Conflict and Human Rights Law*

In the *Hassan* opinion, the Court refrained from even mentioning the *lex specialis derogat legi generali* maxim in its attempt to work out the interplay between the law of armed conflict and human rights law. Instead it adopted a more flexible – albeit yet to be further explained and clarified – approach for reconciling the two legal regimes. Article 31(3)(c) of the Vienna Convention provides that "there shall be taken into account, together with the context, [a]ny relevant rules of international law applicable in the relations between the parties."[69] While this provision gives expression to the idea of international law as a coherent system,[70] it does not stipulate how these other rules within the normative environment of a given provision are actually "to be taken into account." *Lex specialis* – in its function as a principle of interpretation – reflects the complementary approach contained in Article 31(3)(c) and is one way to consider treaty-extrinsic elements in the sense of the Vienna Convention.

But there is no indication that Article 31(3)(c) is in any way limited to harmonization based on the ill-defined notion of "specialty."[71] The consideration of extrinsic elements – just like the consideration of treaty-intrinsic elements ("context") envisaged by Article 31(1) – is a complex, comparative exercise. Without reference to the intention of the parties, the systemic integration envisaged by Article 31(3)(c) can hardly be implemented.[72] And whereas resort to *lex specialis* may in some instances accurately express the intention of the parties regarding the accommodation of a given rule within its wider normative environment, this need not be the case in all instances.[73] It is thus to be welcomed – and in line with the International Court of Justice's

---

[69] Vienna Convention on the Law of Treaties art. 31(3)(c), May 23, 1969, 1155 U.N.T.S. 331 (entered into force Jan. 27, 1980).

[70] Dörr, *supra* note 33, ¶ 91.

[71] Hill-Cawthorne, *Hassan, supra* note 8.

[72] Panos Merkouris, Article 31(3)(c) VCLT and the Principle of Systemic Integration: Normative Shadows in Plato's Cave 217–20 (2015).

[73] Rep. on Fragmentation of International Law, U.N. Doc. A/CN4./L.682, *supra* note 35, ¶ 58 (arguing that *lex specialis* can work in two ways).

judgment in *Armed Activities on the Territory of the Congo* – that in *Hassan* the Court suggests that complementarity between the law of armed conflict and human rights law should be worked out on the basis of a broader range of factors and need not be "arbitrarily" limited just to the *lex specialis* maxim.

While it is regrettable that the Court refrained from providing a more detailed explanation of its application of Article 31(3)(c), the critique in the partly dissenting opinion that "[t]his method of *accommodation* of Convention rights is a novelty in the Court's case-law. Its scope is ambiguous and its content wholly uncertain, at least as a legitimate method of *interpretation* of a legal text,"[74] appears exaggerated. "Accommodation" may be a novel term but it is an accurate description of and indeed synonymous with the harmonious interpretation envisaged by Article 31(3)(c) of the Vienna Convention. And while there is certainly still a significant degree of ambiguity and uncertainty, this is in large part due to the vagueness surrounding Article 31(3)(c) and the fact that in international jurisprudence explanations as to the application of this provision have only been provided very sporadically.[75]

C. Toward Substantive Convergence

Finally, as far as procedural safeguards are concerned, the Court opted for substantive convergence between international human rights law and the law of armed conflict. Thus, the Court confirms the continuous application of Article 5(2) and (4) of the European Convention in times of armed conflict. And although these human rights law prescriptions are to be interpreted "against the background of the provisions of international humanitarian law,"[76] central elements of these human-rights-based protections continue to operate in the background to ensure that the overarching object and purpose of Article 5, namely to forestall arbitrariness, is ensured. This approach can accurately be described as one of genuine cross-fertilization.

Thus, on the one hand the Court conceded that in the course of an international armed conflict "it might not be practicable ... for the legality of detention to be determined by an independent 'court' in the sense generally required by Article 5 § 4 [ECHR]."[77] On the other hand it required that the "competent body" required by Articles 43 and 78 of the Fourth Geneva

---

[74] Hassan Grand Chamber Judgment, *supra* note 8 (partly dissenting opinion of Judge Spano, ¶ 18).

[75] MERKOURIS, *supra* note 72, at 41–51.

[76] Hassan Grand Chamber Judgment, *supra* note 8, ¶ 104.

[77] *Id.* ¶ 106.

Convention[78] "should provide sufficient guarantees of impartiality and fair procedure to protect against arbitrariness," i.e., elements that cannot necessarily be deduced from the law of armed conflict alone.[79] Similarly, with respect to the review procedure, the Court added certain protective qualifiers, requiring the first review to take place "shortly" after the person is taken into detention – whereas the wording of Article 43 of the Fourth Geneva Convention requires the first review to take place "as soon as possible," which is weaker. It also found that subsequent reviews should take place "at frequent intervals"[80] and not merely, as is required by the law of armed conflict, "if possible every six months"[81] or "periodically, and at least twice yearly."[82]

In terms of substance, the actual "substantive convergence" achieved is rather marginal and should not be overstated. At least some of the additional human rights law protections against arbitrariness formulated by the Grand Chamber could arguably also have been deduced on the basis of a progressive reading and dynamic interpretation of the relevant law of armed conflict provisions. Still, the fact that the Court framed its approach as one of substantive convergence and cross-fertilization is important. It underlines that the Court rejected any notion of "displacement," whether partial or generic, and that, in its view, systemic integration under the Vienna Convention may entail substantive convergence of the rules from both legal regimes.

VI. *QUO VADIS*: IMPLICATIONS OF THE EUROPEAN COURT OF HUMAN RIGHTS' RULING BEYOND *HASSAN*

Hassan, like most judgments, can of course be read in different ways. A pessimistic reading would emphasize that the Grand Chamber adopted a genuine *lex specialis* approach in the (hardly convincing) guise of harmonious interpretation. *Prima facie*, this may perhaps help to appease the human rights community, but in terms of substance the Court simply displaced Article 15 of the European Convention as well as the more protective standards of Article 5. In the same vein, it could be argued that the law of armed conflict/human

---

[78] Geneva Convention Relative to the Protection of Civilian Persons in Time of War art. 43, 78, Aug. 12, 1949, 75 U.N.T.S. 287 [hereinafter Fourth Geneva Convention]. Article 43 of the Fourth Geneva Convention speaks of an "appropriate court or administrative board designated by the Detaining Power for that purpose"; Article 78 speaks of a "competent body set up by the said Power."

[79] Hassan Grand Chamber Judgment, *supra* note 8, ¶ 106.

[80] *Id.* ¶ 106.

[81] Fourth Geneva Convention, *supra* note 78, art. 78.

[82] *Id.* art. 43.

rights law symbiosis it suggests with respect to procedural safeguards is mere window dressing. The few human-rights-based protective specifications that the Court added could arguably also have been deduced on the basis of a progressive reading of the Geneva Conventions and without any reference to the European Convention.

Conversely, a more optimistic reading – and the one preferred by this author – would be that *Hassan* is a logical follow-on decision to the Court's previous case law regarding the European Convention's continuous application in times of armed conflict and extraterritorially. Strictly speaking, the Grand Chamber therefore has not lowered any of the protections granted by the Convention but adjusted its applicability to a situation not originally envisaged by its drafters.[83] Even though the result of *Hassan* could arguably also have been achieved on the basis of the *lex specialis* maxim, it is still to be welcomed that the Court presents a different approach, which – although it requires further clarification and refinement – has significant potential and will influence and shape the Court's future jurisprudence on the matter. Thus, by omitting any reference to the *lex specialis*, the Court opened the door for a more holistic interpretive approach on the basis of the Vienna Convention. This approach allows interpreters to resort more broadly to the tools of treaty interpretation and is thus better suited to work out the intricate interplay between the law of armed conflict and human rights law than the *lex specialis* maxim.[84] While it is unclear whether the omission of *lex specialis* in the *Armed Activities* case was based on similar considerations, *Hassan* is fully in line with the Human Rights Committee's approach, which has also continuously avoided the use of the *lex specialis* formulation and instead stresses the complementary nature of the legal regimes of the law of armed conflict and human rights law.[85] *Hassan* thus confirms that in spite of significant differences between the law of armed conflict and human rights law, the two regimes are by and large compatible and that their interaction and mutual relationship ("coexistence") can hence typically be determined by means of interpretation rather than mechanisms of norm-conflict solution. *Hassan,*

[83] Crema, *supra* note 55, at 22.
[84] The Grand Chamber refrained from using *lex specialis* as an interpretatory tool, but it cannot be excluded that when dealing with a genuine collision of norms in the interrelationship of the law of armed conflict and human rights law the Court will revert to *lex specialis* as a principle for norm-conflict resolution.
[85] The Human Rights Committee held that "both spheres of law are complementary, not mutually exclusive." U.N. Human Rights Comm., Gen. Comment No. 31 [80]: The Nature of the General Legal Obligation Imposed on States Parties to the Covenant, ¶11, U.N. Doc. CCPR/C/21/Rev.1/Add.13 (Mar. 29, 2004).

because it adopts such a generous approach toward harmonious interpretation, is thus not only fully in line with the overall trend toward complementarity but arguably takes this trend to the next level of substantive
convergence. After all, instead of merely asking which of the two legal regimes
is better adapted to the circumstances of a given case (*specialis*), the Grand
Chamber in Hassan is asking which synergetic mix of rules derived from both
legal regimes *is optimally* tailored to the circumstances of modern armed
conflicts. Such a far-reaching approach naturally raises concerns as to the
Court's role and competencies. Nevertheless, it seems the best approach to
find pragmatic answers to the overarching question of which legal rules
should govern modern armed conflicts.

With respect to the broader implications of *Hassan*, the Court's reliance on
Article 31(3)(c) of the Vienna Convention and thereby on European
Convention–extrinsic elements (in this case those derived from the Third
and Fourth Geneva Conventions), implies two things. First of all, if permissible grounds of detention may – as the Court in *Hassan* argues – be
"imported" from the law of armed conflict, there is at least *prima facie* no
compelling reason why equally clear grounds of detention derived from other
sources, namely U.N. Security Council resolutions or possibly bilateral agreements or even diplomatic notes,[86] should not also be "importable" to the
European Convention.[87] And if there is indeed such a broad scope for
harmonious interpretation as the Grand Chamber in *Hassan* assumes, in
the future when extrinsic, "importable" grounds of detention are available,
there will be no need to resort to rules of norm-conflict resolution such as *lex
specialis* or Article 103 of the U.N. Charter.

Secondly, because of the Grand Chamber's reliance on extrinsic rules of
the law of armed conflict, conflict qualification remains centrally important.[88]
Thus, as the Court argued:

> *It can only be in cases of international armed conflict*, where the taking of
> prisoners of war and the detention of civilians who pose a threat to security
> are accepted features of international humanitarian law, that Article 5 could
> be interpreted as permitting the exercise of such broad powers.[89]

Against this backdrop, *Hassan* contains only limited guidance as to how the
European Court of Human Rights will decide similar cases in the course of

---

[86] With regard to the latter, *see* Medvedyev v. France, App. No. 3394/03, 2010-III Eur. Ct. H.R. 61,
at 99, ¶¶ 94, 96, 98 (2010).
[87] Milanovic, *A Few Thoughts, supra* note 53.
[88] Hill-Cawthorne, *Hassan, supra* note 8.
[89] Hassan Grand Chamber Judgment, *supra* note 8, ¶ 104.

non-international armed conflicts.[90] Should the Court agree that the laws of
war pertaining to non-international armed conflicts do not contain a sufficiently clear and detailed permission to intern or detain[91] – and it seems quite
likely that it would – lawful detention under Article 5 of the European
Convention in the course of a non-international armed conflict would only
be possible after a formal derogation has been issued.[92] Given that – as
explained above – a derogation does not give *carte blanche* to a detaining
power and that in spite of a derogation a substantial number of human rights
protections may remain in place (depending on what the exigencies of the
specific situation require), the ruling in *Hassan* does not prevent the European Court of Human Rights from a much stronger reliance on substantive
human rights law when faced with situations of non-international armed
conflicts and from insisting on extraterritorial derogations.

[90]   Milanovic, *A Few Thoughts, supra* note 53.
[91]   Serdar Mohammed Appeals Judgment, *supra* note 65, at [219], [242].
[92]   Hill-Cawthorne, *Hassan, supra* note 8.

11

International Law on the Use of Force

Current Challenges

SERGEY SAYAPIN

I. INTRODUCTION

According to St. Malachy's *Prophecy of the Popes*,[1] Pope Francis's reign (from 2013 onward) should be the time of "many tribulations." It appears that some key events of the period in question do match the prophecy indeed: the rise of the Islamic State and the ongoing armed conflict in Syria,[2] the annexation of Crimea by the Russian Federation in March 2014,[3] its subsequent provision of support to separatists in Eastern Ukraine,[4] and the downing of the MH17 plane in July 2014 are just a few tragic events currently filling the international agenda. The military, political, and humanitarian implications of these developments are immense. They also challenge international law in a number of ways, and this law has to evolve in order to withstand these challenges of indeed universal gravity and scale. Important figures in international politics time and again refer to these events (many of which are interconnected) as the Third World War[5]   and if it is one, international law seems to be quite unprepared for it. Some important deficiencies in the applicable law were

---

[1] *See* JOHN HOGUE, THE LAST POPE: THE DECLINE AND FALL OF THE CHURCH OF ROME: THE PROPHECIES OF SAINT MALACHY FOR THE NEW MILLENNIUM *passim* (1998).

[2] *See* МАЙКЛ ВАЙС & ХАСАН ХАСАН, ИСЛАМСКОЕ ГОСУДАРСТВО: АРМИЯ ТЕРРОРА [MICHAEL WEISS & HASSAN HASSAN, ISIS: INSIDE THE ARMY OF TERROR] *passim* (2016).

[3] *See* Sergey Sayapin, *The United Nations General Assembly Resolution 68/262 in the Context of General International Law*, 2 EUR. POL. & L. DISCOURSE, issue 1, 2015, at 19; УКРАЇНСЬКА РЕВОЛЮЦІЯ ГІДНОСТІ І МІЖНАРОДНЕ ПРАВО [Ukrans'ka revoliutsīia gīdnostī ī mīzhnarodne pravo] 513–651 (О. Задорожній [O. Zadorozhnīĭ] ed., 2014).

[4] УКРАЇНСЬКА РЕВОЛЮЦІЯ ГІДНОСТІ І МІЖНАРОДНЕ ПРАВО [Ukrans'ka revoliutsīia gīdnostī ī mīzhnarodne pravo], *supra* note 3, at 745–845.

[5] *See* Reuters, *Jordan's King Abdullah: We Are Facing a Third World War*, JERUSALEM POST (Nov. 17, 2015), www.jpost.com/Middle-East/ISIS-Threat/Jordans-King-Abdullah-We-are-facing-a-Third-World-War-434408; Melik Kaylan, *Putin Threatens World War Again, This Time Over Syria: Will Turks and Saudis Call His Bluff?*, FORBES (Feb. 16, 2016),

revealed already after September 11, 2001, as the "war against terrorism" started unfolding,[6] but these deficiencies turned out to be more numerous and far-reaching in the years to come. Whereas the "war against terrorism" – itself a doubly untimely term[7] – affected, above all, the law of armed conflict and international human rights law, subsequent challenges reached to the very core of modern international law: the law of international security. This Chapter examines some of these challenges – especially as far as the international legal regulation of the use of force is concerned – and makes proposals for the progressive development of international law.

II. THE THREAT OF THE ISLAMIC STATE

The Islamic State of Iraq and Syria (ISIS, also known as Daesh) is among the most important threats to international peace and security – not only in terms of the actual dangers it poses to international peace and security and the well-being of identifiable (ethnic or religious) groups of individuals, but also due to the fact that *existing international law is somewhat helpless against it* because it does not fit within the Islamic State's quasi-religious ideology. Historically, international law was a product of European civilization,[8] which fact, by definition, makes "Christian" international law a phenomenon "alien" and *a priori* unacceptable to the Islamic State. Moreover, general international law is essentially secular, which is, from the point of view of the Islamic State's theocrats, arguably even worse than international law's "Christian legacy" because, to such theocrats, "secular" necessarily implies "godless" or worse, "anti-God." It is submitted that no meaningful dialogue with the Islamic State would be feasible on the basis of international law, because, to affiliates of the Islamic State, general international law itself is an embodiment of values of the enemy, the very order over which they seek to prevail. The civilized world should make no illusions regarding the Islamic State's compliance with international law: its affiliates are committing international crimes[9] including genocide, crimes against humanity, and war

---

www.forbes.com/sites/melikkaylan/2016/02/16/putin-threatens-world-war-again-this-time-over-syria-will-turks-and-saudis-call-his-bluff/#56f314995e53.

[6] *See* HELEN DUFFY, THE 'WAR ON TERROR' AND THE FRAMEWORK OF INTERNATIONAL LAW *passim* (2005).

[7] The terminological construct "war against terrorism" is referred to as a "doubly untimely term" because the term "war" has by now been largely outdated, and the term "terrorism" has not yet been uniformly defined as a matter of international law. This makes the entire construct a terminological fiction.

[8] *See* STEPHEN C. NEFF, JUSTICE AMONG NATIONS: A HISTORY OF INTERNATIONAL LAW 137–213 (2014).

[9] For the concept of crimes under international law, *see* GERHARD WERLE & FLORIAN JESSBERGER, PRINCIPLES OF INTERNATIONAL CRIMINAL LAW 32–33 (3d ed. 2014).

crimes – not because they are ignorant of the content of the law but because, by violating international law, they are challenging the ideological foundations of the adversary. The goals of ISIS are very clear: to extend, as far as possible, into the *Dar-al-Garb*, and to enforce what it considers the right version of Islam and Islamic law on territories under its control.[10] The civilized world's struggle against ISIS is and will be asymmetrical in that the former is bound to comply with international law – in particular, with international humanitarian, human rights, and criminal law – and this circumstance has a restrictive effect upon the methods and means to be used against ISIS, whereas the latter defies international law and has its hands untied.

Precisely because the ongoing struggle against ISIS is not only one of arms but also one of ideologies, it has been suggested to consider establishing a mechanism in order to hold ISIS affiliates who have committed crimes under international law liable *under Islamic international criminal law*.[11] It appears that the International Criminal Court (ICC) is not able to do the job, because the provisions of the Rome Statute are not appropriately reflective of Islamic international criminal law, which may be one reason for the low number of theocratic Islamic States among States Parties to the Statute.[12] The mechanism in question could be an internationalized ("hybrid") tribunal[13] whose legal basis would combine elements of the national substantive and procedural criminal laws of States affected by ISIS crimes, of Islamic international criminal law, and of general international criminal law and procedure. Such an approach could show that, as a matter of fact, Islamic law *is* compatible with general international law, and that Islamic States are not excluded from current trends in international criminal law. It goes without saying that the tribunal would only be credible if it involved objective and impartial judges with professional knowledge of Islamic law and representative of Islamic States in addition to judges representative of other legal traditions.

III. THE ARMED CONFLICT IN SYRIA

The armed conflict in Syria is a humanitarian disaster. According to credible reports, the conflict – originally non-international, but subsequently

---

[10] See a comprehensive overview of ISIS policies in Graeme Wood, *What ISIS Really Wants*, ATLANTIC (Mar. 2015), www.theatlantic.com/magazine/archive/2015/03/what-isis-really-wants/384980/.

[11] *See generally* FARHARD MALEKIAN, PRINCIPLES OF ISLAMIC INTERNATIONAL CRIMINAL LAW: A COMPARATIVE SEARCH (2d ed. 2011).

[12] For a list of States Parties to the Rome Statute, *see The States Parties to the Rome Statute*, INT'L CRIMINAL COURT, https://asp.icc-cpi.int/en_menus/asp/states%20parties/Pages/the%20states%20parties%20to%20the%20rome%20statute.aspx.

[13] On internationalized ("hybrid") tribunals, *see* WERLE & JESSBERGER, *supra* note 9, at 121–28.

internationalized – has already taken about 470,000 lives.[14] But what is more, the conflict is affecting the entire architecture of international security – as noted by Dr. Peter Maurer, President of the International Committee of the Red Cross (ICRC), in an important and unambiguous statement in this respect in an interview to *The Guardian* in July 2015.[15] Having noted at the outset that the ICRC budget has risen by almost 50 percent within only three years – an extraordinary development – Dr. Maurer further elaborated upon current trends in international relations in a style that, in this writer's view, was quite atypical for the ICRC as a traditionally neutral institution. He observed that the ICRC was spending more than 1.5 billion Swiss francs (£1bn) a year as it – and other humanitarian organizations – tried to "plug the gaps" in the global response to ongoing violence in Ukraine, the Middle East, and sub-Saharan Africa, concluding:

> *The international system is having difficulty getting to grips with those conflicts*; countries have difficulty moving to consensus on how to deal with those crises.

> That seems to open spaces for disorder and conflict and we have those dynamics – which may be distinct and different in each and every country – but together they nevertheless refer us to *an international system that does not seem to have international institutions with the ability to negotiate solutions* to conflicts or to the big, increasing and accelerating impact of crises.[16]

This statement was atypical in that ICRC officials at all levels usually refrain from making public pronouncements on political issues, for reasons of neutrality, and when making such statements, they are very cautious about choosing vocabulary. Here, though, the statement was quite direct and politically colored: it was openly critical of the international system's inability to deal with large-scale crises, and of the absence of potent "international institutions" that could "negotiate solutions to conflicts." A subsequent passage brings in more clarity regarding which institutions are meant here:

> Isn't it a bit of a symbol that high-quality negotiators have not been able to move anything significant in the Syrian context?

> We had Kofi Annan and Lakhdar Brahimi and now we have Staffan de Mistura at the present moment, and they have tried bottom-down, top-up approaches,

[14] *See* Ian Black, *Report on Syria Conflict Finds 11.5% of Population Killed or Injured*, Guardian (Feb. 11, 2016), www.theguardian.com/world/2016/feb/11/report-on-syria-conflict-finds-115-of-population-killed-or-injured.

[15] *See* Sam Jones, *Spread of Global Conflict Transforming Humanitarian Work, Says Red Cross Chief*, Guardian (July 8, 2015), www.theguardian.com/global-development/2015/jul/08/conflict-humanitarian-assistance-red-cross-chief-peter-maurer.

[16] *Id.* (emphasis added).

combinations of top-down and bottom-up; they have tried quiet, they have tried public; they have tried pressure, they have tried good will, and somehow there doesn't seem to be any political process that will turn the tide.[17]

Without naming the United Nations explicitly, Dr. Maurer named top U.N. officials who had been involved in attempts to settle the Syrian conflict at its various stages – and failed. It goes without saying that professional failures of high-ranking U.N. officials referred to above are regarded as the U.N.'s institutional failure to maintain international peace and security. The gravity of this failure is so extreme that approaches toward humanitarian action should be fundamentally reassessed, so that the many millions of victims of armed violence (a record 59.5 million displaced by war, violence, and persecution)[18] may have a better level of protection. In the words of Dr. Maurer:

> We will certainly have to do a sober assessment in order to retain what is critical for our basic operation. I wouldn't immediately give up and say, "This is just much too political and we will never do it, or we will never have a partnership with someone who does it."

> While conflicts have expanded and deepened and transformed, actors have transformed and humanitarian assistance is transforming. . . . Protection work is transforming and taking on another character.[19]

Undoubtedly, the ongoing armed conflicts in the Middle East, Ukraine, and elsewhere will continue to test the U.N.'s institutional capacity. If the global organization is to stand the test of time, it has to transform. The United Nations has to become quicker in reacting, more objective and resolute in responding to violations of international law (especially the prohibition of the use of force), and more trustworthy in terms of training and supervising its peacekeeping personnel.[20] Further, as the Rome Statute's amendments on the crime of aggression (Articles 8*bis*, 15*bis*, and 15*ter*) are about to enter into force in the foreseeable future, the role of the U.N. Security Council in making possible criminal prosecutions for aggressive uses of force in international relations will be critical. Under Article 15*ter* of the Rome Statute, the Security Council would have the power to refer situations in which one or multiple crimes of aggression would appear to have been committed to the ICC in a simplified fashion:

---

[17] *Id.*

[18] *Id.*

[19] *Id.*

[20] *See* Joanne Mariner, *UN Peacekeepers Who Rape and Abuse Are Criminals – So Treat Them as Such*, Guardian (Aug. 20, 2015), www.theguardian.com/global-development/2015/aug/20/un-peacekeepers-rape-sexual-abuse-criminals-car-ban-ki-moon.

[T]he jurisdictional modus operandi under Article 15 ter does differ from that established by Article 15 bis, by virtue of the absence in Article 15 ter of several procedural provisions, which are present in Article 15 bis. The most obvious differences are: (1) the irrelevance of the non-recognition of amendments to the Rome Statute contained in Articles 8 bis . . . 15 bis . . . and 15 ter by States Parties; (2) the irrelevance of opt-out declarations made by States Parties under Article 15 bis (4) . . .; (3) the irrelevance of a State's non-participation in the Statute . . .; and (4) a different procedure to be followed by the Prosecutor. . . . In other words, in the case of a Security Council referral, the ICC *would* have jurisdiction with respect to an alleged crime of aggression irrespective of the circumstances referred to in the first three points, by virtue of the Council's acting under Chapter VII of the Charter of the United Nations, and the States concerned would have to comply with the Security Council's referral as Members of the United Nations. . . . As far as the applicable procedure is concerned, clearly, no notification of the Secretary-General of the situation before the Court . . . and no authorisation on the part of the Pre-Trial Chamber . . . would be required, and the Prosecutor would have to proceed in accordance with Article 53 of the Statute.[21]

This new mechanism would be a chance for the U.N. Security Council to significantly improve the quality of its performance and, indeed, to start a new era in maintaining international peace and security. Let us hope this important chance will not be missed.

IV. THE ARMED CONFLICT IN UKRAINE

Russia's continued use of force against Ukraine since February 2014 is a flagrant violation of international law. The annexation of Crimea and subsequent provision of support to separatists in Eastern Ukraine constitute breaches of the Charter of the United Nations;[22] the 1974 U.N. Definition of Aggression;[23] the 1975 Helsinki Final Act;[24] the 1991 Alma-Ata Declaration;[25] the 1993 Statute of the Commonwealth of Independent States;[26] the

---

[21] *See* SERGEY SAYAPIN, THE CRIME OF AGGRESSION IN INTERNATIONAL CRIMINAL LAW: HISTORICAL DEVELOPMENT, COMPARATIVE ANALYSIS AND PRESENT STATE 311–12 (2014) [hereinafter SAYAPIN, CRIME OF AGGRESSION] (emphasis in original).

[22] *See* U.N. Charter art. 2(4).

[23] *See* G.A. Res. 3314 (XXIX), Definition of Aggression, U.N. Doc. A/RES/3314(XXIX) (Dec. 14, 1974).

[24] *See* Final Act of the Conference on Security and Co-operation in Europe (Helsinki Final Act), Aug. 1, 1975, 14 I.L.M. 1292.

[25] *See* Alma-Ata Declaration, pmbl. ¶ 3, Dec. 21, 1991, 31 I.L.M. 148.

[26] In accordance with Article 3 of the Statute, Commonwealth of Independent States (CIS) Member States should respect the territorial integrity of other States and refrain from "illegal acquisitions of territory" as well as from the "threat or use of force against the political

1994 Budapest Memorandum;[27] the 1997 Treaty on Friendship, Cooperation, and Partnership between Ukraine and the Russian Federation;[28] the 1997 Treaty on the Status and Conditions of Stationing the Russian Federation's Black Sea Fleet in the Territory of Ukraine;[29] and of Russia's obligations under the Shanghai Cooperation Organization's Charter.[30] These breaches made possible further numerous violations of individual and collective human rights, *inter alia*, killings, persecutions, deprivations of the right to a fair trial and unlawful imprisonments,[31] and ultimately led to Russia's officially questioning the authority of international law altogether.[32] Given Russia's military power and political influence as a Permanent Member of the U.N. Security Council and a major regional actor in Eurasia, Russia's internationally wrongful acts reach far beyond Ukraine's internationally recognized borders, and affect the international legal order as a whole.

In Crimea, the Russian Federation violated, at least, subparagraphs (d) and (e) of Article 3 of the 1974 U.N. Definition of Aggression. There have been reports of Russian troops blocking Ukrainian military units, suggesting that Ukrainian servicemen surrender,[33] and sinking Ukrainian military ships.[34] As concerns subparagraph (e), in accordance with Article 6(1) of the

---

independence of a member State." Charter of the Commonwealth of Independent States art. 3, Jan. 22, 1993, 1819 U.N.T.S. 58.

[27] *See generally* Memorandum on Security Assurances in Connection with Ukraine's Accession to the Treaty on the Non-Proliferation of Nuclear Weapons, Dec. 5, 1994, *in* Letter dated Dec. 7, 1994, from the Permanent Reps. of the Russian Federation, Ukraine, the United Kingdom of Great Britain and Northern Ireland, and the United States of America to the United Nations addressed to the Secretary-General, U.N. Doc. A/49/765 & S/1994/1399 (Dec. 19, 1994).

[28] Treaty on Friendship, Cooperation, and Partnership Between Ukraine and the Russian Federation, Russ.-Ukr., May 31, 1997, BMD 1999, No. 7 (Russ.). *See id.* arts. 2, 3.

[29] Partition Treaty on the Status and Conditions of Stationing the Russian Federation's Black Sea Fleet in the Territory of Ukraine, Russ.-Ukr., May 28, 1997, BMD 1999, No. 10 (Russ.).

[30] Charter of the Shanghai Cooperation Organization, June 7, 2002, U.N.T.S. Registration No. 50517. *See id.* arts. 1, 2.

[31] *See Crimea: One Year on from Annexation; Critics Harassed, Attacked and Silenced*, AMNESTY INT'L (Mar. 18, 2015), https://www.amnesty.org/en/latest/news/2015/03/crimea-annexation-critics-attacked-and-silenced/; AMNESTY INT'L, INTERNATIONAL REPORT 2015/2016, at 378–82 (2016), https://www.amnesty.org/download/Documents/POL1025522016ENGLISH.PDF.

[32] *See Бастрыкин предложил убрать международное право из Конституции* [Bastrykin predlozhil ubrat' mezhdunarodnoe pravo iz Konstitutsii], BBC RUSSIAN SERV. (July 24, 2015), www.bbc.com/russian/rolling_news/2015/07/150724_rn_bastrykin_law.

[33] *See* Александр Коц & Дмитрий Стешин, *Украинские военные части в Крыму блокируют без единого выстрела*, КОМСОМОЛЬСКАЯ ПРАВАА [Aleksandr Koch & Dmitriĭ Steshin, *Ukrainskie voennye chasti v Krymu blokiruiut bez edinogo vyctrela*, KOMSOMOL'SKAIA PRAVAA] (Mar. 2, 2014), www.kp.ru/daily/26201.7/3087658/.

[34] *See* Российские военные затопили в Крыму уже четвертый корабль [*Rossiĭskie voennye zatopili v Krymu uzhe chetvertyĭ korabl'*], BIGMIR.NET (Mar. 13, 2014), http://news.bigmir.net/ukraine/800672-Rossiiskie-voennie-zatopili-v-Krimy-yje-chetvertii-korabl.

Treaty on the Status and Conditions of Stationing the Russian Federation's Black Sea Fleet in the Territory of Ukraine, Russian troops should have complied with Ukraine's legislation and refrained from interfering in Ukraine's domestic affairs. They started moving, however, without permission from Ukrainian authorities, throughout the peninsula in late February 2014 and were subsequently employed in the use of force against Ukrainian servicemen, in exercising pressure upon members of Crimea's Supreme Council,[35] and in ensuring "security" in relation to the so-called "referendum" of March 16, 2014 – a fact that was later admitted by President Putin.[36]

However, it is submitted that the gravity of Russia's use of force against Ukraine exceeds that of aggression in the sense of the 1974 U.N. Definition of Aggression, because Russia used military force in order not just to overpower Ukraine politically, but indeed in order to distort Ukraine's very statehood. This author has elsewhere termed this phenomenon as *patriacide* – an extreme form of aggression aimed at destroying a State's constitutional, political, economic, or technical organization.[37] With the annexation of Crimea, Ukraine lost *de facto* control over a significant part of its territory, about two million of its nationals acquired the citizenship of another State, alternative political authorities were established on the occupied territory, and that territory's ability to effectively participate in international relations became significantly limited. Thus, all elements of Ukraine's statehood in the sense of Article 1 of the 1933 Montevideo Convention on the Rights and Duties of States have been affected adversely in the context of Crimea alone.

Yet, Russia went on practicing *patriacide* by insisting on a constitutional reform in Ukraine (in favor of a "federalization" of the State),[38] creating

---

[35] *See* interview with Russian GRU (Chief Intelligence Department) agent I. Girkin at Valerii Galagan, *Признание Гиркина (Стрелкова) в организации военного переворота в Крыму* [*Priznanie Girkina (Strelkova) v organizatsii voennogo perevorota v Krymu*], YouTube (Jan. 24, 2015), www.youtube.com/watch?v=ICgazA79a2g.

[36] *See Путин признал, что "зеленые человечки" в Крыму были россиянами*, Лига.Новости [*Putin priznal, chto "zelenye chelovechki" v Krymu byli rossiianami*, Liga.Novosti] (Apr. 17, 2014), http://news.liga.net/news/politics/1396095-putin_opravdal_deystviya_zelenykh_chelovechkov_v_krymu.htm.

[37] *See Сергей Саяпин, Патриацид. Преступление против Украины*, ГЛАВКОМ [Sergey Sayapin, *Patriatsid. Prestuplenie protiv Ukrainy*, GLABKOM] (Sept. 2, 2014), http://glavcom.ua/articles/22090.html; *Сергей Саяпин, Территориальная целостность Украины в свете Резолюции 68/262 Генеральной Ассамблеи ООН* [Sergey Sayapin, *Territorial'naia Tselostnost' Ukrainy v svete Rezoliutsii 68/262 General'noi Assamblei OOH*], 5 J. Const. & Hum. Rts., no. 1–2, 2014, at 66.

[38] *See Бриджет Кендалл, Федерализация Украины в вопросах и ответах* [Bridzhet Kendall, *Federalizatsiya Ukrainy v Voprosakh i Otvetakh*], BBC Russian Serv. (Apr. 2, 2014), www.bbc.com/russian/international/2014/04/140402_ukraine_federation_q_and_a.

favorable conditions for military intrusions from its territory into Ukraine, and providing support to separatists in Eastern Ukraine.[39] Following repeated denials of Russian involvement in Ukraine's Donetsk and Luhansk regions, President Putin finally admitted in a press conference on December 17, 2015, that Russia "never said there [in Eastern Ukraine] were not people there who carried out certain tasks including in the military sphere."[40] For the purpose of international law, it is immaterial that President Putin "insisted this was not the same as regular Russian troops,"[41] because under subparagraph (g) of Article 3 of the 1974 Definition of Aggression, aggression is also constituted by a State's *substantial involvement* in "[t]he sending by or on behalf of a State of armed bands, groups, irregulars or mercenaries, which carry out acts of armed force against another State." It is submitted that Russia's "substantial involvement" in the commission of aggression against Ukraine under subparagraph (g) of Article 3 of the 1974 Definition of Aggression consisted of Russia, on May 5, 2014, effectively decriminalizing Russian nationals' participation in military units in the territory of a foreign State, which are not provided for in the legislation of that State, where the aims of such participation would not contradict the interests of the Russian Federation,[42] and thus legitimized, under Russia's domestic law, the involvement of thousands of Russian "volunteers" in the armed conflict in Eastern Ukraine. Since this protracted involvement amounts to aggression in the sense of applicable international law, there is a ground for invoking Russia's responsibility under international law.

Despite that both Ukraine and Russia criminalize aggression under their domestic law, prospects for holding the authors of aggression (including *patriacide*) criminally responsible are close to zero – not only for procedural reasons (mutual legal assistance, immunities, etc.) but, above all, for those of substantive law. Both Criminal Codes are reflective of the so-called "Nuremberg and Tokyo model" of the criminalization of aggression,[43] which implies that the international armed conflict in question must be massive, protracted, and involving very significant human and technical resources. International

[39] See a report based upon data collected by B. Nemtsov: Путин. Война (Илья Яшин & Ольга Шорина Редакторы, 2015). [Putin. Voyna (Ilyia Yashin & Olga Shorina eds., 2015)], www.putin-itogi.ru/cp/wp-content/uploads/2015/05/Putin.Voina_.pdf (English version *available at* http://4freerussia.org/putin.war/Putin.War-Eng.pdf).

[40] *See* Shaun Walker, *Putin Admits Russian Military Presence in Ukraine for First Time*, GUARDIAN (Dec. 17, 2015), www.theguardian.com/world/2015/dec/17/vladimir-putin-admits-russian-military-presence-ukraine.

[41] *Id.*

[42] *See* UGOLOVNYY KODEKS ROSSIYSKOY FEDERATSII [UK RF] [Criminal Code of the Russian Federation] art. 208(2) ("Organization of an Illegal Armed Formation, or Participation in It").

[43] *See* SAYAPIN, CRIME OF AGGRESSION, *supra* note 21, at 202–07.

armed conflicts of a lesser scale and intensity are not covered by this model. It is recommended that Ukraine consider amending its Criminal Code, with a view to introducing the "objective war model" of criminal responsibility for aggression.[44] This model provides for criminal liability for virtually *any* use of military force in international relations, including for "hybrid warfare"[45] – and therefore appears to offer a better level of legal protection to potential victim States.

V. CONCLUSION

International law is now enduring significant challenges, which are likely to reshape it, to some extent, in the foreseeable future. In order for international law to become a more efficient tool, it should continually absorb and be reflective of values of various legal traditions and cultures. Much of international law is essentially about war and peace – and because religious, philosophical, political, and legal ideas of war and peace differ considerably between cultures, international lawyers hailing from these various cultures have to make a decisive collective effort to reduce those differences, which may themselves become sources of conflict, and to promote ideals of peace and mutual understanding.

At the same time, criminal liability for internationally unlawful uses of force should be reinforced at the national and international levels alike. Only a minority of States have criminalized aggression domestically,[46] and the ICC does not yet exercise its jurisdiction with respect to the crime. As the Kampala Amendments on the crime of aggression are about to become operational, sometime in 2017, the ICC should be prepared to start considering the first cases involving the crime of aggression. Although these cases are not likely to involve defendants from any major military powers,[47] they would still be a novelty in the Court's case law – and, more generally, in international criminal law (since there have been no trials on charges of aggression since the conclusion of the Nuremberg follow-up trials under the Control Council Law No. 10).[48] Such measures are indispensable if the world is serious about making progress toward a lasting peace.

---

[44] *Id.* at 212–17.

[45] For the concept of "hybrid warfare," *see* Евгений Магда, Гибридная война: выжить и победить [Evgeniy Magda, Gibridnaya Voyna: Vyzhit' i Pobedit'] (2015).

[46] *See* Sayapin, Crime of Aggression, *supra* note 21, at 200–02.

[47] *Id.* at 324.

[48] *Id.* at 148–49.

PART III

The Illegal Use of Force and the Prosecution of International Crimes

12

The Crime of Aggression under Customary International Law

YORAM DINSTEIN

I. INTRODUCTION

The crime of aggression in international law is an extrapolation of an earlier concept of crimes against peace. Whatever designation is preferred, the gravamen is the same: individual penal accountability for acts committed on behalf of a State. In terms of the sphere of application of the crime of aggression and crimes against peace, this Chapter will show that – while the semantics have changed – the difference between them is more apparent than real.

II. THE NUREMBERG LEGACY

Crimes against peace entered the international legal vocabulary, for the first time,[1] in the Charter of the International Military Tribunal (annexed to an Agreement done in London in 1945) for the prosecution of the major German criminals in World War II.[2] Article 6(a) of the Charter defines crimes against peace as follows: "planning, preparation, initiation or waging of a war of aggression, or a war in violation of international treaties, agreements or assurances, or participation in a common plan or conspiracy for the accomplishment of any of the foregoing."[3] The London Agreement originally had as Contracting Parties the four principal Allied Powers in the War – the United States, the

---

[1] On the process leading to this milestone, see KIRSTEN SELLARS, 'CRIMES AGAINST PEACE' AND INTERNATIONAL LAW 84–112 (2013).

[2] Charter of the International Military Tribunal – Annex to the Agreement for the Prosecution and Punishment of the Major War Criminals of the European Axis, Aug. 8, 1945, 82 U.N.T.S. 279, 284 [hereinafter London Charter].

[3] *Id.* art 6(a).

Union of Soviet Socialist Republics, the United Kingdom, and France – but later it was adhered to by nineteen additional Allied States.[4]

The London Charter served as the foundation for the Nuremberg trial before the International Military Tribunal. The nucleus of Article 6(a) was soon reiterated, with some variations, in Article II(1) of Control Council Law No. 10 (forming the legal basis of the so-called subsequent proceedings at Nuremberg, in which lower-level German criminals were tried by American military tribunals),[5] and in Article 5 of the Charter of the International Military Tribunal for the Far East (issued in a Proclamation by General Douglas MacArthur, in his capacity as Supreme Commander of the Allied Powers in the region, and designed for the trial of the major Japanese criminals in World War II).[6]

In its Judgment of 1946, the International Military Tribunal at Nuremberg held that the text of Article 6(a) of the London Charter expressed modern international law, which regarded a war of aggression as a grave crime.[7] Hence, the Tribunal rejected the argument that the provision amounted to *ex post facto* criminalization of the acts of the defendants in breach of the *nullum crimen sine lege* principle.[8] The Tribunal relied heavily on the renunciation of war in the Kellogg–Briand Pact of 1928.[9] The Pact had rendered unlawful war undertaken as an instrument of national policy,[10] and from that the Judgment inferred that "those who plan and wage such a war, with its inevitable and terrible consequences, are committing a crime in so doing."[11]

The International Military Tribunal conceded that the Kellogg–Briand Pact had neither expressly promulgated that aggressive war was a crime nor set up courts to try offenders.[12] But it pointed out that this was also true of the

---

[4] Agreement for the Prosecution and Punishment of the Major War Criminals of the European Axis, Aug. 8, 1945, 82 U.N.T.S. 279, 281 [hereinafter London Agreement].

[5] Allied Control Council Law No. 10, Punishment of Persons Guilty of War Crimes, Crimes Against Peace and Against Humanity art. II(1), Dec. 20, 1945, *reprinted in* 1 TRIALS OF WAR CRIMINALS BEFORE THE NUERNBERG MILITARY TRIBUNALS UNDER CONTROL COUNCIL LAW No. 10, at XVI, XVII (1949).

[6] Charter of the International Military Tribunal for the Far East art. 5, Jan. 19, 1946, *amended* Apr. 26, 1946, T.I.A.S. No. 1589 [hereinafter Tokyo Charter].

[7] 1 TRIAL OF MAJOR WAR CRIMINALS BEFORE THE INTERNATIONAL MILITARY TRIBUNAL, NUREMBERG, 14 NOVEMBER – 1 OCTOBER 1946, Judgment, at 171, 219–23 (1947), *available at* www.loc.gov/rr/frd/Military_Law/pdf/NT_Vol-I.pdf [hereinafter IMT JUDGMENT].

[8] *Id.* at 219.

[9] *Id.* at 219–20.

[10] General Treaty for Renunciation of War as an Instrument of National Policy (Kellogg–Briand Pact), Aug. 27, 1928, 94 L.N.T.S. 57, 63.

[11] IMT JUDGMENT, *supra* note 7, at 220.

[12] *Id.*

Hague Convention (IV) of 1907, which – through its Regulations – prohibits certain practices in the conduct of warfare.[13] Since 1907, these forbidden acts have been viewed as war crimes, notwithstanding the fact that the Hague Convention does not designate them as criminal and does not attach penal sanctions to them.[14] The Tribunal considered the criminality of war as analogous and even more compelling.[15] The Judgment further adduced diverse non-binding instruments (like the unratified 1924 Geneva Protocol on the Pacific Settlement of International Disputes, which enunciated that "a war of aggression constitutes ... an international crime"),[16] finding in them evidence for the dynamic development of customary international law.[17] The kernel of the Tribunal's position was, "Crimes against international law are committed by men, not by abstract entities, and only by punishing individuals who commit such crimes can the provisions of international law be enforced."[18] In other words, the banning of war is devoid of any practical significance unless international law is prepared to mete out real penalties to flesh-and-blood offenders acting on behalf of the artificial legal person that is the State.

When delivered, the Nuremberg decision concerning crimes against peace gave rise to some harsh criticism,[19] which cannot be easily dismissed. No doubt, the weakest link in the chain constructed by the International Military Tribunal is the certitude that the illegality of war (under the Kellogg–Briand Pact) ineluctably leads to its criminality.[20] International law brands many acts of State as unlawful, yet in most instances that does not mean that the forbidden behavior becomes a crime (entailing individual penal accountability). Why is the injunction against war different from other international legal prohibitions? A reply to the question may be gleaned in another section of the Judgment:

> War is essentially an evil thing. Its consequences are not confined to the belligerent States alone, but affect the whole world.

---

[13] *Id.*

[14] *Id.* at 220–21.

[15] *Id.* at 221.

[16] Protocol on the Pacific Settlement of International Disputes, *opened for signature* Oct. 2, 1924, 1008 L.N.O.J. 1521 (1925) (never entered into force), *available at* www.wdl.org/en/item/11582/view/1/1/.

[17] IMT JUDGMENT, *supra* note 7, at 221–22.

[18] *Id.* at 223.

[19] *See, e.g.,* F. B. Schick, *The Nuremberg Trial and the International Law of the Future*, 41 AM. J. INT'L L. 770, 783–84 (1947).

[20] *See* C. A. POMPE, AGGRESSIVE WAR: AN INTERNATIONAL CRIME 245 (1953).

> To initiate a war of aggression, therefore, is not only an international crime; it is the supreme international crime differing only from other war crimes in that it contains within itself the accumulated evil of the whole.[21]

The decisive point is that war is a cataclysmic event. There is no way in which war can be carried on as if it were a chess game. In the nature of things, blood and fire, suffering and pain, are the concomitants of war. As a result, war simply must be a crime.

The stand taken on this topic by the International Military Tribunal at Nuremberg is not invulnerable. If wars by their very nature (by dint of the devastation associated with them) are viewed as *mala in se*,[22] it is incomprehensible how they could have remained lawful in the centuries preceding the Kellogg–Briand Pact.[23] If, for most of its duration, international law managed to adapt itself to the legality of war, surely the proscription of war may be deemed an achievement that is sufficient unto itself. Why are criminal sanctions, directed against the individual organs of the State, assumed to be *sine qua non* to such an extent that they have to be looked upon as implicit in the Pact?

These and other difficulties were hotly debated in the late 1940s. It seems only fair to observe that when the London Charter was concluded, the criminalization of crimes against peace was not really declaratory of pre-existing customary international law.[24] The Nuremberg judgment was actually innovative when it ingested the criminality of war into general international law.[25] However, the issue is no longer of great importance today. Whatever the state of the law was before the midpoint of the twentieth century, it cannot be contested that the international law of the twenty-first century is perfectly in accord with the Nuremberg judgment.

The Nuremberg criminalization of aggressive war was upheld, in 1948, by the International Military Tribunal for the Far East at Tokyo.[26] It was also endorsed in trials of the lesser Nazi criminals of World War II, most

---

[21] IMT JUDGMENT, *supra* note 7, at 186. This well-known dictum is based on a passage from Lord Wright, *War Crimes Under International Law*, 62 L.Q. REV. 40, 47 (1946).

[22] *See* Quincy Wright, *The Law of the Nuremberg Trial*, 41 AM. J. INT'L L. 38, 63 (1947).

[23] *See* YORAM DINSTEIN, WAR, AGGRESSION AND SELF-DEFENCE 80–81 (6th ed. 2017).

[24] *See* Leo Gross, *The Criminality of Aggressive War*, 41 AM. POL. SCI. REV. 205, 218–20 (1947).

[25] *See* George A. Finch, *The Nuremberg Trial and International Law*, 41 AM. J. INT'L L. 20, 33–34 (1947).

[26] *"Tokyo trial," In re Hirota and Others*, International Military Tribunal for the Far East, *in* 1 THE TOKYO JUDGMENT: THE INTERNATIONAL MILITARY TRIBUNAL FOR THE FAR EAST, (I.M.T.F.E.) 29 APRIL 1946–12 NOVEMBER 1948, Judgment, 15, at 28 (B.V.A. Röling & C.F. Rütor eds., 1977).

conspicuously in the 1949 *Ministries* trial (the last of the subsequent proceedings at Nuremberg).[27]

Over the decades subsequent to the Nuremberg Judgment, its legacy has found support in a string of consensus United Nations General Assembly resolutions complemented by studies undertaken by the International Law Commission. As early as 1946, the General Assembly unanimously affirmed the principles of international law recognized by the London Charter and the Judgment of the International Military Tribunal.[28] In 1947, the General Assembly instructed the International Law Commission to formulate these principles and also to prepare a Draft Code of Offenses against the Peace and Security of Mankind.[29] The Commission composed the "Nürnberg Principles" in 1950: the text recites the Charter's definition of crimes against peace, accentuating that offenders bear responsibility for such crimes and are liable to punishment.[30]

As for the Draft Code, after long delays (caused by controversies surrounding the definition of aggression), the International Law Commission's work on the subject was concluded in 1996. The final text of the Draft Code of Crimes against the Peace and Security of Mankind (the term Crimes having replaced Offenses) refers to the crime of aggression in Article 16: "An individual who, as leader or organizer, actively participates in or orders the planning, preparation, initiation or waging of aggression committed by a State shall be responsible for a crime of aggression."[31] In the commentary, the Commission stressed that the stigmatization of aggression as a crime against the peace and security of mankind is drawn from the London Charter as interpreted and applied by the International Military Tribunal.[32]

---

[27] "*Ministries Case*," *Military Tribunal No. IV, Case 11, United States v. Von Weizsaecker et al.*, in 14 Trials of War Criminals Before the Nuernberg Military Tribunals Under Control Council Law No. 10, Judgment, 314, 318–22 (1972), *available at* www.loc.gov/rr/frd/ Military_Law/pdf/NT_war-criminals_Vol-XIV.pdf.

[28] G.A. Res. 95 (I), Affirmation of the Principles of International Law Recognized by the Charter of the Nürnberg Tribunal, U.N. Doc. A/RES/95(I) (Dec. 11, 1946).

[29] G.A. Res. 177 (II), Formulation of the Principles Recognized in the Charter of the Nürnberg Tribunal and in the Judgment of the Tribunal, U.N. Doc. A/RES/177(II) (Nov. 21, 1947).

[30] *Principles of International Law Recognized in the Charter of the Nürnberg Tribunal and in the Judgment of the Tribunal*, Rep. of the Int'l Law Comm'n to the Gen. Assembly, U.N. Doc. A/ 1316 (1950), *reprinted in* [1950] 2 Y.B. Int'l L. Comm'n 364, 374, 376, U.N. Doc. A/CN.4/ SER.A/1950/Add.1[hereinafter Nürnberg Principles].

[31] *Draft Code of Crimes Against the Peace and Security of Mankind*, Rep. of the Int'l Law Comm'n to the Gen. Assembly, U.N. Doc. A/51/10, *reprinted in* [1996] 2 Y.B. Int'l L. Comm'n 17, 42–43, U.N. Doc. A/CN.4/SER.A/1996/Add.1 (Part 2) [hereinafter 1996 Draft Code of Crimes].

[32] *Id.* at 43.

Yoram Dinstein

Irrespective of the codification undertaken by the International Law Commission, the General Assembly – in the 1970 consensus Declaration on Principles of International Law Concerning Friendly Relations and Co-operation Among States in Accordance with the Charter of the United Nations – proclaimed that "war of aggression constitutes a crime against peace, for which there is responsibility under international law."[33] It is noteworthy that the Friendly Relations Declaration was relied upon by the International Court of Justice, in the *Nicaragua* judgment of 1986, as evidence of the emergence of customary international law relative to the prohibition of the use of force.[34]

Admittedly, no indictments for crimes against peace have followed any of the multiple international armed conflicts waged in the post–World War II era.[35] Moreover, the initial failure of the drafters of the Statute of the International Criminal Court to define the crime of aggression, as noted below, raised some doubts as to the durability of the Nuremberg legacy in this respect. It is, therefore, enlightening to quote what the United Kingdom House of Lords (per Lord Bingham) had to say about such doubts in the *Jones* case of 2006:

> It was suggested, on behalf of the Crown, that the crime of aggression lacked the certainty of definition required of any criminal offence, particularly a crime of this gravity. This submission was based on the requirement in article 5(2) of the Rome statute that the crime of aggression be the subject of definition before the international court exercised jurisdiction to try persons accused of that offence. This was an argument which found some favour with the Court of Appeal. . . . I would not for my part accept it. It is true that some states parties to the Rome statute have sought an extended and more specific definition of aggression. It is also true that there has been protracted discussion of whether a finding of aggression against a state by the Security Council should be a necessary precondition of the court's exercise of jurisdiction to try a national of that state accused of committing the crime. I do not, however, think that either of these points undermines the appellants' essential proposition that the core elements of the crime of aggression have been understood, at least since 1945, with sufficient

---

[33] G.A. Res. 2625 (XXV), annex, Declaration on Principles of International Law Concerning Friendly Relations and Co-operation Among States in Accordance with the Charter of the United Nations, U.N. Doc. A/RES/2625(XXV) (Oct. 24, 1970).

[34] Military and Paramilitary Activities in and Against Nicaragua (Nicar. v. U.S.), Merits Judgment, 1986 I.C.J. 14, 99 (June 27) [hereinafter Nicaragua Merits Judgment].

[35] *See* John F. Murphy, *Crimes Against Peace at the Nuremberg Trial, in* THE NUREMBERG TRIAL AND INTERNATIONAL LAW 141, 153 (George Ginsburgs & V. N. Kudriavtsev eds., 1990).

clarity to permit the lawful trial (and, on conviction, punishment) of those accused of this most serious crime. It is unhistorical to suppose that the elements of the crime were clear in 1945 but have since become in any way obscure.[36]

This is the right conclusion: notwithstanding disagreements relating to its precise range, the "core elements of the crime of aggression" have entrenched themselves since Nuremberg as part and parcel of international law.

III. THE GENERAL ASSEMBLY DEFINITION OF AGGRESSION

In 1974, the General Assembly adopted by consensus a Definition of Aggression, Article 5(2) of which sets forth: "A war of aggression is a crime against international peace. Aggression gives rise to international responsibility."[37]

Despite this reference to a crime against international peace, the definition as a whole is not engrossed in the criminal ramifications of aggression. General Assembly Resolution 3314 (XXIX), to which the Definition of Aggression is annexed, makes it plain that the primary intention of the framers was to recommend the text as a guide to the Security Council when the latter is called upon to determine (pursuant to its collective security mandate under the Charter of the United Nations) the existence of an act of aggression.[38] That said, it must be discerned that – in the more than four decades that have elapsed since 1974 – the Security Council has never cited the Definition of Aggression: indeed, the definition has had no visible impact on the Council's deliberations.[39]

Although unsuccessful in its original aim of serving as a guide for the Security Council, the Definition of Aggression has come to the forefront in a totally different sphere of international relations. This is the domain of international criminal law, where an acute need arose to fill a legal vacuum created by the Statute of the International Criminal Court as crafted in Rome in 1998. Article 5(1) of the Rome Statute lists "[t]he crime of aggression" – together with genocide, crimes against humanity, and war crimes – among "the most serious crimes of concern to the international community as a whole," with respect to which subject-matter jurisdiction is conferred on the

---

[36] R. v. Jones [2006] UKHL 16, [2007] 1 AC (HL) 136, at 157–58.

[37] G.A. Res. 3314 (XXIX), Definition of Aggression, U.N. Doc. A/RES/3314(XXIX) (Dec. 14, 1974).

[38] *Id.* ¶ 4.

[39] *See* M. Cherif Bassiouni & Benjamin B. Ferencz, *The Crime Against Peace and Aggression: From Its Origins to the ICC, in* 1 INTERNATIONAL CRIMINAL LAW: SOURCES, SUBJECTS AND CONTENTS 207, 227 (M. Cherif Bassiouni ed., 3d ed. 2008).

newly established Court.[40] However, in contrast to the other crimes coming within the Court's jurisdiction, the crime of aggression was not defined in Rome. Article 5(2) expressly deferred the exercise of jurisdiction by the Court over this crime until a definition is adopted.[41]

In searching for an authoritative definition of the crime of aggression, the States Parties to the Rome Statute – gathered in a Review Conference held in Kampala in 2010 – reached the conclusion that the optimal course of action was to rely on the text of the General Assembly definition (although the actual exercise of the Court's jurisdiction over the crime of aggression was still deferred until further steps are taken at a date not earlier than January 1, 2017).[42] The criminal reorientation of the General Assembly definition should not come as a real surprise. Indeed, well before the adoption of the Rome Statute,[43] the present author has argued that the main potential value of the definition lies in the setting of international criminal law, rather than in the asserted (non-productive) goal of providing a guide to the Security Council.

The Kampala definition of the crime of aggression appears in a new Article 8*bis*, added to the Statute of the International Criminal Court. It is comprised of two parts. One part (paragraph 2) spells out the contours of acts of aggression:

> 2. For the purpose of paragraph 1, "act of aggression" means the use of armed force by a State against the sovereignty, territorial integrity or political independence of another State, or in any other manner inconsistent with the Charter of the United Nations. Any of the following acts, regardless of a declaration of war, shall, in accordance with United Nations General Assembly resolution 3314 (XXIX) of 14 December 1974, qualify as an act of aggression:
>
> (a) The invasion or attack by the armed forces of a State of the territory of another State, or any military occupation, however temporary, resulting from such invasion or attack, or any annexation by the use of force of the territory of another State or part thereof;

---

[40] Rome Statute of the International Criminal Court art. 5(1), *adopted on* July 17, 1998, 2187 U.N.T.S. 91 (entered into force July 1, 2002) [hereinafter Rome Statute].

[41] *Id.* art. 5(2).

[42] Review Conference of the Rome Statute of the International Criminal Court, *The Crime of Aggression*, Res. RC/Res.6, annex I (June 11, 2010), *available at* https://asp.icc-cpi.int/iccdocs/asp_docs/Resolutions/RC-Res.6-ENG.pdf [hereinafter Res. RC/Res.6]. On December 14, 2017, the crime of aggression was activated by the Assembly of States Parties. Res. ICC-ASP/16/Res.5, Activation of the jurisdiction of the Court over the crime of aggression (Dec. 14, 2017).

[43] *See* YORAM DINSTEIN, WAR, AGGRESSION AND SELF-DEFENCE 120 (1988).

(b) Bombardment by the armed forces of a State against the territory of another State or the use of any weapons by a State against the territory of another State;

(c) The blockade of the ports or coasts of a State by the armed forces of another State;

(d) An attack by the armed forces of a State on the land, sea or air forces, or marine and air fleets of another State;

(e) The use of armed forces of one State which are within the territory of another State with the agreement of the receiving State, in contravention of the conditions provided for in the agreement or any extension of their presence in such territory beyond the termination of the agreement;

(f) The action of a State in allowing its territory, which it has placed at the disposal of another State, to be used by that other State for perpetrating an act of aggression against a third State;

(g) The sending by or on behalf of a State of armed bands, groups, irregulars or mercenaries, which carry out acts of armed force against another State of such gravity as to amount to the acts listed above, or its substantial involvement therein.[44]

As the *chapeau* shows, the framers made no bones about the source of subparagraphs (a) to (g). These are lifted word-for-word from Article 3 of the General Assembly Definition of Aggression. Originally, the seven subparagraphs were preceded by a briefer *chapeau*: "Any of the following acts, regardless of a declaration of war, shall, subject to and in accordance with the provisions of article 2, qualify as an act of aggression."[45] The key phrase "regardless of a declaration of war" is repeated in the second sentence of the *chapeau* of Article 8*bis*(2).

The replication of paragraphs (a) to (g) of Article 3 of the General Assembly Definition of Aggression as subparagraphs in Article 8*bis*(2) suggests that each of the seven clauses may have been reckoned by the Kampala Conference to be declaratory of customary international law. However, thus far, only subparagraph (g) has gained that standing by pronouncement of the International Court of Justice, which held in the *Nicaragua* judgment that it "reflect[s] customary international law."[46] As for the other subparagraphs, there are critics who regard their language as both "overinclusive" and "underinclusive."[47] For instance, the words "marine and air fleets" in subparagraph

---

[44] Res. RC/Res.6, *supra* note 42, annex I.

[45] G.A. Res. 3314 (XXIX), *supra* note 37, annex, art. 3 intro.

[46] Nicaragua Merits Judgment, *supra* note 34, at 103.

[47] Harold Hongju Koh & Todd F. Buchwald, *The Crime of Aggression: The United States Perspective*, 109 Am. J. Int'l L. 257, 267 (2015).

(d) – which seem to remove from consideration any attack against a single merchant ship or aircraft – may go too far[48] (although it is plainly justified to exclude police action against, say, foreign vessels fishing within the territorial sea of a coastal State).[49] Irrespective of such question marks, it is not easy to refute the customary nature of the gist of the text. Most conspicuously, no State today would challenge the proposition that – in harmony with customary law – an outright invasion (covered by subparagraph [a]) amounts to an act of aggression. This is strongly supported by the separate opinion of Judge Bruno Simma in the *Armed Activities* case.[50]

The words "in accordance with United Nations General Assembly Resolution 3314 (XXIX) of 14 December 1974," appearing in the *chapeau* of Article 8*bis*(2), may imply more than a mere citation of its source. After all, Article 3 of the General Assembly Definition of Aggression – the fount of Article 8*bis*(2) – is explicitly subjected to Article 2 of the definition.[51] The latter stipulation specifies that "[t]he first use of armed force by a State in contravention of the Charter shall constitute *prima facie* evidence of an act of aggression," but the commission of an act of aggression may be determined otherwise "in the light of other relevant circumstances, including the fact that the acts concerned or their consequences are not of sufficient gravity."[52] The demand for "sufficient gravity" is now encapsulated in the "character, gravity and scale" conditions set up by Article 8*bis*(1) (discussed below). Still, it is necessary to pay particular heed to the allusion to the *prima facie* – i.e., non-conclusive – probative value of the "first use of armed force." This caveat may have immense practical import. What it means is that the opening of fire only creates a rebuttable presumption of the commission of an act of aggression.[53] When all the facts are weighed carefully, they may lead to the deduction that the State which has refrained from opening fire is nonetheless the perpetrator of an act of aggression. Subparagraph (e) provides a vivid example of an act of aggression being committed (by the armed forces of State A overstaying their welcome in State B) without a single shot being fired.

[48] *See* George K. Walker, *The Tanker War, 1980–88: Law and Policy*, 74 INT'L L. STUD. 118, 120 (2000).
[49] *See* Bengt Broms, *The Definition of Aggression*, 154 RECUEIL DES COURS 299, 351 (1977).
[50] Armed Activities on the Territory of the Congo (Dem. Rep. Congo v. Uganda), Judgment, 2005 I.C.J. 334, 334–35 (Dec. 19) (separate opinion by Judge Simma).
[51] G.A. Res. 3314 (XXIX), *supra* note 37, annex, art. 3 intro.
[52] *Id.* annex, art. 2.
[53] *See* Patrick Rambaud, *La Définition de l'Agression par l'Organisation des Nations Unies*, 80 REV. GÉN. DE DROIT INT'L PUB. 835, 872 (1976).

This is not to say that all the composites of the General Assembly Definition of Aggression can be read into Article 8*bis*(2). Plainly, in the criminal field there can be no effect to Article 4 of the General Assembly definition, which enunciates that the acts inscribed in Article 3 do not exhaust the scope of the definition and that the Security Council may determine other acts to be tantamount to aggression.[54] Nobody can deny that the Security Council is free, for its own purposes, to categorize as aggression acts falling outside the spectrum of Article 3. Yet, a new constellation of aggression – emerging in future practice of the Council but not included in Article 3 and, therefore, not engraved in Article 8*bis*(2) – cannot be categorized as an act of aggression over which the International Criminal Court is vested with jurisdiction.[55] In criminal matters, the governing principle is *nullum crimen sine lege*, and in the language of Article 22(2) of the original Rome Statute "[t]he definition of a crime shall be strictly construed and shall not be extended by analogy."[56]

IV. AGGRESSIVE WAR AND ACTS OF AGGRESSION

The text of Article 5(2) of the General Assembly Definition of Aggression differentiates between aggression as such (which only "gives rise to international responsibility") and a war of aggression (which is "a crime against international peace").[57] The authors of the definition thereby signaled clearly that not every act of aggression constitutes a crime against peace: only aggressive war does.[58] That is to say, an act of aggression "short of war" – as distinct from a war of aggression – would not result in individual criminal accountability,[59] although it would lay the ground for responsive measures against the acting State.

As noted earlier, Article 16 of the Draft Code penned by the International Law Commission alludes in a sweeping manner to "a crime of aggression." This coinage was endorsed by Article 5 of the 1998 Rome Statute of the International Criminal Court, which speaks about "[t]he crime of aggression"

---

[54] G.A. Res. 3314 (XXIX), *supra* note 37, annex, art. 4.

[55] *See* Karl M. Fletcher, *Defining the Crime of Aggression: Is There an Answer to the International Criminal Court's Dilemma?*, 65 A.F. L. REV. 229, 260 (2010).

[56] Rome Statute, *supra* note 40, art. 22(2).

[57] *See* Geoff Gilbert, *The Criminal Responsibility of States*, 39 INT'L & COMP. L.Q. 345, 360 (1990).

[58] *See* Broms, *supra* note 49, at 357.

[59] *See* Justin Hogan-Doran & Bibi T. van Ginkel, *Aggression as a Crime Under International Law and the Prosecution of Individuals by the Proposed International Criminal Court*, 43 NETH. INT'L L. REV. 321, 335 (1996).

generically. When the elaboration of the crime was finally accomplished as
an amendment to the Statute in the 2010 Review Conference in Kampala, the
"crime of aggression" vocabulary remained intact.[60]

The fact that the Kampala Amendments retain the broad "crime of aggres-
sion" mode of expression is ostensibly inconsistent with the narrower conceptual underpinning of "crimes against peace" in line with the precedent of the
London Charter and Nuremberg judgment. Furthermore, the Kampala
Amendments might give the impression of being at odds with the General
Assembly Definition of Aggression, which – like the London Charter and
Nuremberg Judgment – regards only a war of aggression as a crime under
international law. A departure from the General Assembly Definition of Aggression would be an embarrassing paradox, bearing in mind that Article 8*bis*(2),
as prescribed in Kampala, incorporates verbatim the language of Article 3 of
the definition, as noted above.

However, in fact, there is less disparity than meets the eye. One must
carefully analyze the overall structure of Article 8*bis*, as forged on the road to
Kampala.[61] As indicated earlier, the Kampala definition of aggression contains
two parts. Article 8*bis*(2) does not define the crime of aggression as such but only
itemizes acts of aggression. It must be underscored that, by themselves, these
acts are not tantamount to a crime of aggression.[62] For the crime of aggression
to materialize, it is not enough to consult the roster of acts of aggression in
paragraph 2. No crime is committed in accordance with Article 8*bis*(1) unless
certain indispensable requirements are satisfied:

> 1. For the purpose of this Statute, "crime of aggression" means the planning,
> preparation, initiation or execution, by a person in a position effectively to
> exercise control over or to direct the political or military action of a State, of
> an act of aggression which, by its character, gravity and scale, constitutes a
> manifest violation of the Charter of the United Nations.[63]

The center of attention should be the latter part of this passage. What it tells us
is that, to qualify as a crime subject to the jurisdiction of the International
Criminal Court, an act of aggression (set out in paragraph 2) must "by its
character, gravity and scale" constitute a "manifest violation" of the United

---

[60] Res. RC/Res.6, *supra* note 42, annex I.

[61] On the road to Kampala in this respect, *see* CARRIE McDOUGALL, THE CRIME OF AGGRESSION
UNDER THE ROME STATUTE OF THE INTERNATIONAL CRIMINAL COURT 13–16 (2013).

[62] *See* Jennifer Trahan, *The Rome Statute's Amendment on the Crime of Aggression: Negotiations
at the Kampala Review Conference*, 11 INT'L CRIM. L. REV. 49, 59 (2011).

[63] Res. RC/Res.6, *supra* note 42, annex I, ¶ 2.

Nations Charter. The formulation creates a high threshold that needs to be crossed if individual culpability for an act of aggression is to be generated.[64]

What would be perceived as a "manifest violation" of the United Nations Charter? The Elements of Crimes, as appended in Kampala for Article 8*bis*, state the obvious by pointing out that the term "manifest" is "an objective qualification."[65] The Kampala Review Conference also added an "Understanding" to the effect that

> in establishing whether an act of aggression constitutes a manifest violation of the Charter of the United Nations, the three components of character, gravity and scale must be sufficient to justify a "manifest" determination. No one component can be significant enough to satisfy the manifest standard by itself.[66]

Although the legal status of the Understanding is ambiguous,[67] it does no more than underline the conjunctive nature of the three conditions of "character, gravity and scale." The suggestion has been made that the rejection in the Understanding of the admissibility of "one component" – as "enough to satisfy the manifest standard by itself" – may open the door to the possibility that "two of those components are already sufficient."[68] But, actually, the connective word "and" in the formula "character, gravity and scale" rules out such an interpretation of the text.[69] Although the three conditions "need not all be present to the same degree,"[70] they must interlock if an act of aggression is to be branded as a manifest violation of the Charter and a crime of aggression.

The three conditions tackle acts of aggression from three different angles: their intrinsic nature ("character"), seriousness ("gravity"), and magnitude ("scale"). By itself, each of the three expressions is somewhat open-ended, yet their amalgamation should give an accurate idea of what the thrust of Article 8*bis*(1) is. Some commentators are censorious of the phraseology used, arguing in particular that the term "character" is "so indeterminate that it is

---

[64] *See* Fletcher, *supra* note 55, at 257.

[65] Res. RC/Res.6, *supra* note 42, annex II.

[66] Res. RC/Res.6, *supra* note 42, annex III.

[67] *See* Kevin Jon Heller, *The Uncertain Legal Status of the Aggression Understandings*, 10 J. Int'l Crim. Just. 229, 229–48 (2012).

[68] *See* Robert Heinsch, *The Crime of Aggression After Kampala: Success or Burden for the Future?*, 2 Goettingen J. Int'l L. 713, 729 (2010).

[69] *See* Marina Mancini, *A Brand New Definition for the Crime of Aggression: The Kampala Outcome*, 81 Nordic J. Int'l L. 227, 236–37 (2012).

[70] *See* Claus Kreß & Leonie von Holtzendorff, *The Kampala Compromise on the Crime of Aggression*, 8 J. Int'l Crim. Just. 1179, 1207 (2010).

almost meaningless."[71] However, there is nothing wrong with the framers' choice of words. "Gravity" and "scale" have their roots in dicta of the International Court of Justice in the *Nicaragua* case.[72] As for the idiom "character," it is worthwhile mentioning that Common Article 3 of the four Geneva Conventions of 1949 famously refers (in a correlative context) to an "armed conflict not of an international character."[73]

Unequivocally, Article 8*bis*(1) goes beyond Article 2 of the Definition of Aggression, which speaks only of "sufficient gravity" and thus lays down a *de minimis* requirement. The triple cumulative conditions of "character, gravity and scale" tangibly raise the bar for penal purposes. The level contemplated for a crime of aggression, entailing individual accountability, is significantly above a *de minimis* use of force.

Given the three higher-tier conditions registered in Article 8*bis*(1), aggressive use of force that is "short of war" would *ex hypothesi* fail to qualify as criminal. Only a full-fledged aggressive war could conceivably fit the joint requirements of "character, gravity and scale." *Ergo*, the pith of the Nuremberg legacy of "crimes against peace" is preserved notwithstanding the dissimilar outer linguistic crust of a "crime of aggression" preferred by the States Parties to the Rome Statute and the Kampala Amendment.

This is more than a nuance. Some of the concrete acts of aggression catalogued in Article 8*bis*(2) – following in the footsteps of the General Assembly Definition of Aggression – lend themselves to classification as incidents "short of war." This includes an isolated use of weapons across the territorial border (see subparagraph [b]). Even though explicitly mentioned in the text, such an act of aggression has no criminal repercussions. As accentuated, for a crime of aggression to consolidate, the combined conditions of "character, gravity and scale" (articulated in paragraph 1 of Article 8*bis*) must be grafted onto any of the acts listed in paragraph 2. A minor *act* of aggression – enumerated in paragraph 2 – would not pass muster as a *crime* of aggression since it would not satisfy the three conditions established in paragraph 1.

---

[71] Andreas Paulus, *Second Thoughts on the Crime of Aggression*, 20 EUR. J. INT'L L. 1117, 1121 (2009).

[72] Nicaragua Merits Judgment, *supra* note 34, at 103.

[73] Geneva Convention (I) for the Amelioration of the Condition of the Wounded and Sick in Armed Forces in the Field art. 3, Aug. 12, 1949, 75 U.N.T.S. 31; Geneva Convention (II) for the Amelioration of the Condition of Wounded, Sick and Shipwrecked Members of Armed Forces at Sea art. 3, Aug. 12, 1949, 75 U.N.T.S. 85; Geneva Convention (III) Relative to the Treatment of Prisoners of War art. 3, Aug. 12, 1949, 75 U.N.T.S. 135; Geneva Convention (IV) Relative to the Protection of Civilian Persons in Time of War art. 3, Aug. 12, 1949, 75 U.N.T.S. 287.

The issue of a manifest violation of the Charter of the United Nations has another aspect. The crux of the prohibition of the use of force appears in the Charter in Article 2(4).[74] The first sentence of the *chapeau* of Article 8*bis*(2) echoes the language of this central clause of the Charter. Still, two deviations from the matrix of Article 2(4) stand out.

First, Article 8*bis* speaks about inconsistency with the United Nations Charter as a whole, as distinct from the Purposes of the United Nations (as per Article 2[4]). The wider reference to the Charter contributes to a better appreciation that an interstate use of force that is in conformity with the Charter – either by fiat of the Security Council (in conformity with Article 39 *et seq.*[75]) or in exercise of the right of individual or collective self-defense (consistent with Article 51[76]) – cannot possibly be labeled a crime of aggression.

Second, a threat of force, included in Article 2(4), is excluded from the ambit of Article 8*bis*. It ensues that a mere threat of aggression is not subject to the jurisdiction of the International Criminal Court. This is perhaps regrettable in exceptional circumstances, such as when a small State is so intimidated by a threat of massive force emanating from a major Power that it prefers "capitulation without a fight."[77] Yet, from a more holistic perspective, the omission is welcome. It would be remiss to turn a blind eye to the reality that hollow threats of force are regularly exchanged in the international marketplace. The crime of aggression might consequently be trivialized if every threat of force were to be a ground for triggering penal proceedings.

V. AGGRESSION AS A LEADERSHIP CRIME

Who can commit the crime of aggression? Article 8*bis*(1) focuses on "a person in a position effectively to exercise control over or to direct the political or military action of a State." No doubt, this is a leadership crime.[78] A footnote appended to the Elements of Crimes explains that more than one person may meet these criteria.[79]

There is an obvious need to not inflate the numbers of persons who are indictable for the crime of aggression. If all those who execute acts of war

---

[74] U.N. Charter art. 2(4).

[75] *Id.* art. 39.

[76] *Id.* art. 51.

[77] *See* Benjamin B. Ferencz, *The United Nations Consensus Definition of Aggression: Sieve or Substance*, 10 J. INT'L L. & ECON. 701, 713 (1975).

[78] *See* Roger S. Clark, *Negotiating Provisions Defining the Crime of Aggression, Its Elements and the Conditions for ICC Exercise of Jurisdiction Over It*, 20 EUR. J. INT'L L. 1103, 1105 (2009).

[79] Res. RC/Res.6, *supra* note 42, annex II.

could be arraigned, all combatants in the armed forces of an aggressor State would automatically be liable to become criminals (and the rosters of those subject to criminal charges could also embrace many civilians). This was one of the primary charges levelled against the London Charter and the Nuremberg trial by their detractors.[80] The criticism cannot be entirely brushed aside, inasmuch as a broad interpretation of the Charter term "waging" was subscribed to in a separate opinion by the President of the International Military Tribunal for the Far East (W. F. Webb) in the Tokyo trial.[81] Yet, this is not part of the Nuremberg legacy.

The principal Nuremberg trial, before the International Military Tribunal, affected only major criminals. But even in the subsequent proceedings at Nuremberg, it became apparent that not everyone could be indicted for crimes against peace. In the *High Command* trial of 1948, an American Military Tribunal held that the criminality of aggressive war attaches only to "individuals at the policy-making level," whereas those acting as mere instruments of the policymakers "cannot be punished for the crimes of others."[82] In parallel proceedings of the same year, in the *I. G. Farben* trial, the Tribunal declared that only those persons in the political, military or industrial spheres who bear responsibility for the formulation and execution of policies are accountable for crimes against peace (adding that otherwise the results would be incongruous: the entire population could become culpable, including the private soldier on the battlefield, the farmer who supplied the armed forces with foodstuffs, and even the housewife who conserved commodities for the military industry).[83]

Pace some dicta weakening it, the general principle that can be derived from the subsequent proceedings at Nuremberg is that criminal liability for wars of aggression is limited to the policymaking level.[84] The International Law Commission, too, arrived in 1950 at the conclusion that only "high-ranking military personnel and high State officials" can be guilty of waging

---

[80] *See* VISCOUNT MAUGHAM, U.N.O. AND WAR CRIMES 18–39, 52–58 (1951).

[81] *Separate Opinion by the President*, International Military Tribunal for the Far East, *in* THE TOKYO JUDGMENT, *supra* note 26, at 469, 475.

[82] "High Command Trial," *Military Tribunal V, Case No. 12, United States v. Von Leeb et al., in* 11 TRIALS OF WAR CRIMINALS BEFORE THE NUERNBERG MILITARY TRIBUNALS UNDER CONTROL COUNCIL LAW NO. 10, Judgment, 462, 486, 489 (1950), *available at* http://loc.gov/rr/frd/ Military_Law/pdf/NT_war-criminals_Vol-XI.pdf [hereinafter High Command Judgment].

[83] "I.G. Farben trial," *Military Tribunal VI, Case No. 6, United States v. Krauch et al., in* 8 TRIALS OF WAR CRIMINALS BEFORE THE NUREMBERG MILITARY TRIBUNALS UNDER CONTROL COUNCIL LAW NO. 10, Judgment, 1081, 1124–1125 (1948), *available at* http://loc.gov/rr/frd/ Military_Law/pdf/NT_war-criminals_Vol-VIII.pdf.

[84] *See* George Brand, *The War Crimes Trials and the Laws of War*, 26 BRIT. Y.B. INT'L L. 414, 420–21 (1949).

a war of aggression.[85] In Article 16 of its 1996 Draft Code, the Commission strictly defined the crime of aggression as limited to leaders or organizers.[86] The United Kingdom House of Lords in the *Jones* case (per Lord Bingham) pronounced that Article 16 clearly indicates that "aggression is a leadership crime; it cannot be committed by minions and footsoldiers."[87]

Of course, even in a dictatorship, more than a few individuals placed at the pinnacle of power would bear the brunt of responsibility for the crime of aggression. As the Tribunal in the *High Command* trial rightly observed: "No matter how absolute his authority, Hitler alone could not formulate a policy of aggressive war and alone implement that policy by preparing, planning and waging such a war."[88] The challenge is to know where to draw the line. Insofar as the military hierarchy is concerned, the *High Command* Tribunal declined to set a fixed rank, somewhere between the private soldier and the Commander-in-Chief, at which criminal liability for a war of aggression begins.[89] The Tribunal did say that criminality hinges on the actual power of an individual to "shape or influence" the war policy of his country.[90]

The phrase "shape or influence" is fairly elastic. Some critics regard it as "too broad in that, especially in democracies, an excessively large group of people would be covered."[91] At Kampala, a different formula, which considerably restricts the range of policy-level decision makers,[92] was adopted in Article 8*bis*(1). The same formula is reiterated in a new paragraph 3*bis*, inserted in Article 25 of the Rome Statute (dealing with individual criminal responsibility): "In respect of the crime of aggression, the provisions of this article shall apply only to persons in a position effectively to exercise control over or to direct the political or military action of a State."[93] It is obvious that only "an inner circle steering the politico-military conduct of the State" is implicated.[94]

---

[85] Nürnberg Principles, *supra* note 30, at 376.
[86] 1996 Draft Code of Crimes, *supra* note 31, art. 16.
[87] R. v. Jones [2006], *supra* note 36, at 157.
[88] High Command Judgment, *supra* note 82, at 486.
[89] *Id.* at 486–87.
[90] *Id.* at 488–89.
[91] Kai Ambos, *The Crime of Aggression After Kampala*, 53 Ger. Y.B. Int'l L. 463, 490 (2010).
[92] *See* Kevin Jon Heller, *Retreat from Nuremberg: The Leadership Requirement in the Crime of Aggression*, 18 Eur. J. Int'l L. 477, 488 (2007).
[93] Res. RC/Res.6, *supra* note 42, annex I.
[94] *See* Tom Ruys, *Defining the Crime of Aggression: The Kampala Consensus*, 49 Mil. L. & L. War Rev. 97, 112 (2010).

Whatever criterion is employed, relevant leadership echelons capable of committing acts of aggression are not circumscribed to the military: the crime of aggression can be committed by civilians no less than military personnel. The most conspicuous example relates to members of the cabinet or senior government officials whose input is apt, at times, to outweigh that of generals and admirals.[95]

VI. CONCLUSION

Seven decades after the Nuremberg trial, it is safe to say that *en principe* aggressive war – or an act of aggression committed in circumstances where its "character, gravity and scale" constitutes a manifest violation of the Charter of the United Nations – is a crime under customary international law. Put differently, there are penal consequences for those in leadership echelons who are responsible for the crime.

Although the customary law status of the crime of aggression is unquestionable, there is no unanimity of views as to its exact scope.[96] Only criminal courts can shed light, in concrete cases, on what may otherwise be looked at as amorphous general law. At the time of writing, the International Criminal Court is still on the cusp of exercising jurisdiction to prosecute the crime of aggression and it is not quite there yet. All the same, the precedent set at Nuremberg is an historical fact. The *opinio juris* of the international community – as expressed time and again in consensus resolutions of the General Assembly and as evinced in Kampala – shows that the crime of aggression is now firmly embedded in contemporary international law.

---

[95] The International Military Tribunal convicted several high-ranking civilians of crimes against peace. *See* Yoram Dinstein, *The International Military Tribunal at Nuremberg*, 37 ISR. Y.B. ON HUM. RTS. 1, 10 (2007).

[96] *See* Bing Bing Jia, *The Crime of Aggression as Custom and the Mechanisms for Determining Acts of Aggression*, 109 AM. J. INT'L L. 569, 571 (2015).

13

The Crime of Aggression and the International Criminal Court

JENNIFER TRAHAN

I. INTRODUCTION

At the Review Conference on the International Criminal Court's Rome Statute, held in Kampala, Uganda, from May 31 to June 11, 2010 (Review Conference), States Parties to the Rome Statute[1] achieved a significant and historic result. They adopted, by consensus, a definition of the crime of aggression and conditions for the exercise of its jurisdiction for purposes of the International Criminal Court (ICC).[2] Not all States were completely satisfied with the outcome – some desiring a stronger jurisdictional regime, others desiring only Security Council referrals, and others disagreeing with the amendment process.[3] Further disagreements surfaced after the Kampala negotiations as to the crime's jurisdictional reach. Nonetheless, States Parties have now seemingly resolved these disagreements, and have taken the second historic step, to activate the crime's jurisdiction effective July 17, 2018. The commencement of jurisdiction has potential to change State practice with regard to uses of force, as well as the development of international criminal law.

---

[1] Rome Statute of the International Criminal Court, *adopted on* July 17, 1998, 2187 U.N.T.S. 91 (entered into force July 1, 2002) [hereinafter Rome Statute].

[2] Review Conference of the Rome Statute of the International Criminal Court, *The Crime of Aggression*, Res. RC/Res.6 (June 11, 2010), https://asp.icc-cpi.int/iccdocs/asp_docs/Resolutions/RC-Res.6-ENG.pdf [hereinafter Res. RC/Res.6].

[3] That non-States Parties are exempt from State Party referral and *proprio motu* initiation (discussed later in this Chapter) was not seen as ideal to many States Parties. On the other hand, Permanent Members of the U.N. Security Council – throughout the course of negotiations – tended to prefer referrals only by the U.N. Security Council. Japan, by contrast, had concerns about the integrity of the amendment process. These are the observations of the author at the Review Conference and prior negotiations.

This Chapter provides a brief overview of the negotiations leading up to the Review Conference.[4] It then discusses key features[5] of the amendment package adopted in Kampala, including the definition of the crime, the conditions for the ICC's exercise of jurisdiction over the crime, the elements of the crime, and certain understandings. It also discusses the crime's jurisdictional reach – both the competing views that existed, as well as the result apparently concluded in the activation decision at the December 4–14, 2017, meetings of the ICC's Assembly of States Parties (ASP). The Chapter finishes with suggestions of how commencement of the exercise of ICC crime of aggression jurisdiction could impact state decisions regarding uses of force as well as the ICC's docket.

II. OVERVIEW OF THE NEGOTIATIONS OF THE CRIME OF AGGRESSION

The concept of aggression as a crime is hardly new. The international community envisioned a world in which States would arbitrate their disputes without recourse to war when, in 1899, they founded the Permanent Court of Arbitration (PCA), and, in 1913, opened the Peace Palace in The Hague (*Vredespaleis*) to house it.[6] This vision failed with the advent of both World Wars I and II. But after World War II, the Allied Powers made the crime of waging aggressive war (crimes against peace) central to prosecutions before the International Military Tribunal at Nuremberg, and the International Military Tribunal for the Far East (Tokyo).[7] Indeed, at Nuremberg, the crime was held to constitute

---

[4] For a more extensive discussion of the negotiations, *see* Jennifer Trahan, *The Rome Statute's Amendment on the Crime of Aggression: Negotiations at the Kampala Review Conference*, 11 INT'L CRIM. L. REV. 49 (2011) [hereinafter Trahan, *Kampala Negotiations*].

[5] There are now entire books on the negotiations leading up to the Review Conference, discussions held there, and the outcome. *See, e.g.*, CRIME OF AGGRESSION LIBRARY: THE TRAVAUX PRÉPARATOIRES OF THE CRIME OF AGGRESSION (Stefan Barriga & Claus Kreß eds., 2012) [hereinafter CRIME OF AGGRESSION LIBRARY]; THE PRINCETON PROCESS ON THE CRIME OF AGGRESSION: MATERIALS OF THE SPECIAL WORKING GROUP ON THE CRIME OF AGGRESSION (Stefan Barriga, Wolfgang Danspeckgruber & Christian Wenaweser eds., 2009) [hereinafter THE PRINCETON PROCESS]; Christian Wenaweser & Stefan Barriga, *Forks in the Road: Personal Reflections on Negotiating the Kampala Amendments on the Crime of Aggression, in* FOR THE SAKE OF PRESENT AND FUTURE GENERATIONS: ESSAYS ON INTERNATIONAL LAW, CRIME AND JUSTICE IN HONOUR OF ROGER S. CLARK 281 (Suzannah Linton, Gerry Simpson, & William A. Schabas eds., 2015).

[6] *History*, PERMANENT CT. OF ARB., https://pca-cpa.org/en/about/introduction/history/. The Peace Palace came to house the Permanent Court of International Justice, later replaced by the International Court of Justice. The Peace Palace also houses The Hague Academy of International Law, the Carnegie Foundation (Netherlands), and the Peace Palace Library.

[7] The Nuremberg Tribunal was originally established by the United States, United Kingdom, France, and the Union of Soviet Socialist Republics in the London Charter of the

"the supreme international crime, differing only from other war crimes in that it contains within itself the accumulated evil of the whole."[8] The Nuremberg Tribunal, importantly, recognized that it was not sufficient that the law condemn *States* for committing aggression, but that "crimes against international law are committed by men, not by abstract entities, and only by punishing individuals who commit such crimes can the provisions of international law be enforced."[9] Indeed, crimes against peace[10] were the central focus of both the Nuremberg and Tokyo trials.[11] Genocide, formalized only after the 1945–46 Nuremberg trial in the 1948 Convention on the Prevention and Punishment of the Crime of Genocide,[12] was not prosecuted there.[13]

International Military Tribunal, August 8, 1945. Charter of the International Military Tribunal – Annex to the Agreement for the Prosecution and Punishment of the Major War Criminals of the European Axis, Aug. 8, 1945, 82 U.N.T.S. 279 [hereinafter London Charter]. *See generally* MICHAEL R. MARRUS, THE NUREMBERG WAR CRIMES TRIAL 1945–46: A DOCUMENTARY HISTORY (1997). The Tokyo Tribunal was created by Special Proclamation of U.S. General Douglas MacArthur. *See* Elizabeth S. Kopelman, *Ideology and International Law: The Dissenting of the Indian Justice at the Tokyo War Crimes Trial*, 23 N.Y.U. J. INT'L L. & POL. 373, 388 (1991). The judges were from eleven countries. *See* R. John Pritchard, *The International Military Tribunal for the Far East and its Contemporary Resonances*, 149 MIL. L. REV. 25, 27 (1995); *see also* Maria Hsia Chang & Robert P. Baker, *Victor's Justice & Japan's Amnesia: The Tokyo War Crimes Trial Reconsidered*, in THE SEARCH FOR JUSTICE: JAPANESE WAR CRIMES 33, 37–38 (Peter Li ed., 2003).

8   22 TRIAL OF THE MAJOR WAR CRIMINALS BEFORE THE INTERNATIONAL MILITARY TRIBUNAL, NUREMBERG, 14 NOVEMBER 1945 – 1 OCTOBER 1946, at 427 (1948), www.loc.gov/rr/frd/ Military_Law/pdf/NT_Vol-XXII.pdf.

9   *Id.* at 466. In an ignominious achievement, women now have also been convicted as high-level perpetrators. Former President of Republika Srpska, Biljana Plavšić, pled guilty before the International Criminal Tribunal for the former Yugoslavia (ICTY) to persecution as a crime against humanity. Prosecutor v. Plavšić, Case No. IT-0039 & 40/1, Sentencing Judgment, ¶ 5 (Feb. 27, 2003). The International Criminal Tribunal for Rwanda (ICTR) convicted former Rwandan Minister for Family Welfare and the Advancement of Women, Pauline Nyiramasuhuko, including for genocide, conspiracy to commit genocide, and crimes against humanity. Prosecutor v. Nyiramasuhuko et al., Case No. ICTR-98-42-T, Judgment and Sentence, ¶ 6186 (June 24, 2011) (the "Butare case").

10 *See* London Charter, *supra* note 7, art. 6(a).

11 *United States et al. v. Araki et al.*, International Military Tribunal for the Far East, Indictment (Apr. 29, 1946), www.legal-tools.org/uploads/tx_ltpdb/ArakietalIndictment.pdf (most of the counts of the indictment addressed aggressive war); Jack Curtis, *Nuremberg Lessons Still Fresh 70 Years Later*, BOS. GLOBE (Nov. 15, 2015), https://www.bostonglobe.com/ideas/2015/11/15/ nuremberg-lessons-still-fresh-years-later/Yz7HFD5BHjhfI3oCZO6zOJ/story.html.

12 *See* Convention on the Prevention and Punishment of the Crime of Genocide, Dec. 9, 1948, 78 U.N.T.S. 277.

13 For discussion of Raphael Lemkin's decades-long work relating to the crime of genocide, *see* SAMANTHA POWER, A PROBLEM FROM HELL: AMERICA AND THE AGE OF GENOCIDE (2002).

Accompanying this strong start for prosecuting the crime is the centrality of the ban on aggressive use of force enshrined in 1945 in Article 2(4) of the U.N. Charter.[14] As one scholar explains:

> The United Nations Charter has been the centerpiece of the international legal framework governing the use of force since 1945. The Charter represents an effort to construct effective barriers against aggression and to subject intervention to agreed upon international rules – an effort that stands out against the larger swath of human history during which states were largely free to resort to war as a matter of state policy.[15]

The prohibition on aggressive use of force in fact rises to the level of a *jus cogens* norm.[16] As to why this norm is so central to the U.N. System, scholar James A. Green reminds us:

> It is always worth remembering when considering the *jus ad bellum* that the use of military force usually involves the systematic killing of human beings, often on a vast scale. Forcible action is also obviously prone to

---

[14] The Preamble to the U.N. Charter makes clear that one of the fundamental aims of the United Nations is "to save succeeding generations from the scourge of war." U.N. Charter pmbl. "It is incontrovertible that the prohibition of the unilateral use of force is a fundamental aspect of the United Nations (U.N.) era system for governing the relations between states." James A. Green, *Questioning the Peremptory Status of the Prohibition of the Use of Force*, 32 Mich. J. Int'l L. 215, 215 (2011). *See also* Louis Henkin, *The Use of Force: Law and U.S. Policy, in* Right v. Might: International Law and the Use of Force 37, 38 (Louis Henkin et al. eds., 1991).

[15] Jane Stromseth, Can Might Make Rights?: Building the Rule of Law After Military Interventions 21 (2006); *see also* U.N. Charter art. 2(4); J. M. Spectar, *Beyond the Rubicon: Presidential Leadership, International Law & the Use of Force in the Long Hard Slog*, 22 Conn. J. Int'l L. 47, 47 (2006) (describing Article 2(4) as being "[a]t the heart of the post World War II order").

[16] "[A] peremptory norm of general international law is a norm accepted and recognized by the international community of States as a whole as a norm from which no derogation is permitted and which can be modified only by a subsequent norm of general international law having the same character." Vienna Convention on the Law of Treaties art. 53, May 23, 1969, 1155 U.N.T.S. 331.

Many authors cite to Article 2(4) as embodying the *jus cogens* norm. *See, e.g.*, Steven R. Ratner, Jus Ad Bellum *and* Jus in Bello *After September 11*, 96 Am. J. Int'l. L. 905, 914 (2002); Spectar, *supra* note 15, at 47–48; Military and Paramilitary Activities in and Against Nicaragua (Nicar. v. U.S.), Merits Judgment, 1986 I.C.J. 14, ¶ 190 (June 27) (citing Article 2(4) as "customary international law" and "having the character of *jus cogens* "); *Commentary on Draft Article 50*, Rep. of the Int'l Law Comm'n on the Work of Its Eighteenth Session, U.N. Doc. A/6309/Rev.1, *reprinted in* [1966] 2 Y.B. Int'l Law Comm'n 172, at 247, U.N. Doc. A/CN.4/SER.A/1966/Add.1. James Green observes that others "have taken the more nuanced view that it is the prohibition of the use of force" (and not the language of Article 2(4) *per se*) "that has the character of *jus cogens*." Green, *supra* note 14, at 227–28. He concludes serious difficulties exist in framing exactly what is encompassed by the so-called peremptory norm and therefore questions "whether the rule has, in fact, been accepted as *jus cogens* by states at all." *Id.* at 241.

causing regional and global instability and inherent damage to international peace, security, and order.[17]

Yet, after Nuremberg and Tokyo, prosecution of the crime languished – along
with the field of international justice generally – during the polarized climate
of the Cold War.[18]

The current revival of the crime of aggression commenced with the decision, in 1998, at the Rome Diplomatic Conference for the Establishment of an
International Criminal Court (Rome Conference), to include the crime in
the Rome Statute. Rome Statute Article 5(1) and Article 12(1) provide that the
crime of aggression *is* a crime over which the Court has jurisdiction – but
Article 5(2) provided that the crime still needed to be defined and conditions
for the exercise of jurisdiction agreed upon before that jurisdiction could be
"exercised" by the Court.[19] This has lent some to characterize the crime as
reflected in the 1998 Rome Statute as in the unique position of being "half-in"
and "half-out" of the Statute.[20]

The drafting process to agree upon the definition and conditions for the
exercise of jurisdiction thereafter continued[21] at Preparatory Commission

---

[17] Green, *supra* note 14, at 221.

[18] *See* David Donat-Cattin, *Intervention of Humanity or the Use of Force to Protect Civilians, the
Peremptory Prohibition of Aggression and the Interplay Between* Jus ad Bellum, Jus in Bello *and
Individual Criminal Responsibility on the Crime of Aggression, in* INTERNATIONAL LAW AND THE
PROTECTION OF HUMANITY: ESSAYS IN HONOR OF FLAVIA LATTANZI 353–96 (Pia Acconci,
David Donat-Cattin, Antonio Marchesi, Giuseppe Palmisano, & Valeria Santori eds., 2017).
See also Michael Walzer, *The Crime of Aggressive War*, 6 WASH. U. GLOBAL STUD. L. REV. 635
(2007) ("Since Nuremberg, no government officials have actually been taken to court and
charged with aggressive war."). Meanwhile, the U.N. General Assembly affirmed the principles
of the Nuremberg Charter and judgment in Resolution 95 (I), and versions of the Nuremberg
crime were incorporated into various domestic criminal codes. *See* G.A. Res. 95 (I), Affirmation
of the Principles of International Law Recognized by the Charter of the Nürnberg Tribunal,
U.N. Doc. A/RES/95(I) (Dec. 11, 1946); Astrid Reisinger Coracini, *National Legislation on
Individual Responsibility for Conduct Amounting to Aggression, in* INTERNATIONAL CRIMINAL
JUSTICE: LAW AND PRACTICE FROM THE ROME STATUTE TO ITS REVIEW 547, 551 n.29 (Roberto
Bellelli ed., 2010).

[19] Article 5(2) stated: "The Court shall exercise jurisdiction over the crime of aggression once a
provision is adopted in accordance with articles 121 and 123 defining the crime and setting out
the conditions under which the Court shall exercise jurisdiction with respect to this crime.
Such a provision shall be consistent with the relevant provisions of the Charter of the United
Nations." Rome Statute, *supra* note 1, art. 5(2). With adoption of the crime of aggression
amendment, it was also agreed at the Review Conference to delete Article 5(2) from the Rome
Statute. *See* Res. RC/Res.6, *supra* note 2, annex I, ¶ 1 ("Article 5, paragraph 2, of the Statute is
deleted").

[20] Wenaweser & Barriga, *supra* note 5, at 292.

[21] Drafting work, not in the ICC context, actually commenced far earlier, with the work of the
International Law Commission. *See* Draft Code of Offences Against the Peace and Security of

sessions held from 1999 to 2002,[22] and before the Special Working Group on the Crime of Aggression from 2003 to 2009.[23] The work culminated with general agreement of participants[24] on the definition of the crime, as well as the elements of the crime, but not yet on the conditions for the exercise of jurisdiction or the process for activation of what would become the amendment.[25] These last two items, as well as certain Understandings, were only concluded at the Review Conference. There, after two weeks of intensive negotiations – shared by certain sessions devoted to a "stocktaking" of the field of international justice[26] – consensus agreement was reached, adopting the crime of aggression amendment as well as an amendment on war crimes.[27]

The crime of aggression amendment also included a delay mechanism whereby for the ICC to be able to exercise jurisdiction there first needed to be

Mankind, art. 2, U.N. Doc. A/CN.4/44, *reprinted in* [1951] 2 Y.B. Int'l. L. Comm'n 44, at 58, U.N. Doc. A/CN.4/SER.A/1951/Add.1. For a compilation of the drafting work on the crime of aggression, from the International Law Commission, Preparatory Committee (pre-Rome Conference), Preparatory Commission (post-Rome Conference), and Special Working Group on the Crime of Aggression, through the Review Conference, *see* CRIME OF AGGRESSION LIBRARY, *supra* note 5.

[22] *See Preparatory Commission for the International Criminal Court*, UNITED NATIONS, http://legal.un.org/icc/prepcomm/prepfra.htm. The Preparatory Commission was created by Resolution F of the Final Act of the United Nations Diplomatic Conference of Plenipotentiaries on the Establishment of an International Criminal Court, U.N. Doc. A/CONF.183/10 (July 17, 1998). Key documents from the Preparatory Commission's work are reproduced in CRIME OF AGGRESSION LIBRARY, *supra* note 5, at 333–414.

[23] Once the Special Working Group's mandate ended, discussion on the crime continued at the Eighth Session of the ASP (held in November 2009 in The Hague), and the Resumed Eighth Session (held in March 2010 at the United Nations). Key documents from the Special Working Group are reproduced in CRIME OF AGGRESSION LIBRARY, *supra* note 5, at 421–708.

[24] Because the work of the Special Working Group coincided with the Bush Administration's term in office, the United States chose not to attend the negotiations, even though other non-States Parties did participate. Thus, the United States missed the opportunity to participate in drafting the definition and elements of the crime. By the time the United States started participating in ICC meetings during the Obama Administration, the definition and elements had been agreed upon, and States Parties were unwilling to revisit the negotiations already concluded.

[25] "[W]e came to an agreement on the definition of the crime of aggression, which was adopted at the last session of the Special Working Group in February 2009." Wenaweser & Barriga, *supra* note 5, at 286.

[26] These "stocktaking" sessions covered four topics: the impact of the Rome Statute system on victims and affected communities, peace and justice, complementarity, and cooperation.

[27] For a more detailed discussion of the negotiations, *see* Trahan, *Kampala Negotiations*, *supra* note 4. For the text of the war crimes amendment, *see* Review Conference of the Rome Statute of the International Criminal Court Res. RC/Res.5 (June 10, 2010), https://asp.icc-cpi.int/iccdocs/asp_docs/Resolutions/RC-Res.5-ENG.pdf. An additional war crimes amendment has also recently been adopted. Res. ICC-ASP/16/Res.4, Resolution on amendments to article 8 of the Rome Statute of the International Criminal Court (Dec. 14, 2017).

thirty ratifications of the amendment, one year's passage after the thirtieth ratification, and a decision after January 1, 2017, by "the same majority of States Parties as is required for the adoption of an amendment to the Statute" – that is, two-thirds or consensus.[28] The ratifications have now been achieved,[29] and ICC States Parties agreed in December 2017 by consensus to activate ICC jurisdiction over the crime to start July 17, 2018.[30]

III. THE KAMPALA AMENDMENTS ON THE CRIME OF AGGRESSION

A. *The Definition of the Crime*

The definition of the crime consists of two parts. Article 8*bis*(1) contains the definition of the crime that an individual commits. Article 8*bis*(2) contains the definition of the state act of aggression, which the State commits. Much is often made of the fact that the crime of aggression – because of these two component parts – is essentially different from the other ICC crimes due to the requirement of state action. Yet, it is hard to imagine genocide, war crimes, or crime against humanity occurring without state involvement or at least involvement of a significant non-state actor; each of these crimes also requires individual action, or non-action, by a perpetrator, and then a larger context in which the crime occurs.[31]

The crime of aggression is defined in Article 8*bis*(1):

> For the purpose of this Statute, "crime of aggression" means the planning, preparation, initiation or execution, by a person in a position effectively to exercise control over or to direct the political or military action of a State, of

---

[28] Rome Statute, *supra* note 1, art. 15*bis*(2)-(3), art. 15*ter*(2)-(3). *See also id.* art. 121(3) ("The adoption of an amendment at a meeting of the Assembly of States Parties or at a Review Conference on which consensus cannot be reached shall require a two-thirds majority of States Parties.").

[29] As of December 8, 2017, there are thirty-five ratifications. *See Status of Ratification and Implementation of the Kampala Amendments on the Crime of Aggression, Update No. 28,* CRIME OF AGGRESSION http://crimeofaggression.info/the-role-of-states/status-of-ratification-and-implementation/.

[30] *See* Res. ICC-ASP/16/Res.5, Activation of the jurisdiction of the Court over the crime of aggression (Dec. 14, 2017).

[31] Genocide requires large-scale destruction – namely, destruction "in whole or in part" of a "national, ethnical, racial, or religious group" "as such." Rome Statute, *supra* note 1, art. 6. Crimes against humanity require a "widespread or systematic attack" "directed against any civilian population" "pursuant to or in furtherance of a State or organizational policy." *Id.* art. 7 (1), art. 7(2)(a). Whereas war crimes could entail more limited criminality (subject to the gravity requirement), they are criminalized "in particular when committed as part of a plan or policy or as part of a large-scale commission of such crimes." *Id.* art. 8(1).

an act of aggression which, by its character, gravity and scale, constitutes a manifest violation of the Charter of the United Nations.[32]

There are at least four noteworthy aspects to this definition. First, we have the nouns "planning, preparation, initiation or execution"; these are based on the historic precedent of the London Charter of the Nuremberg Tribunal, which covered "planning, preparation, initiation or waging of a war of aggression."[33] Second, the crime is a "leadership crime," in that it only covers "a person in a position effectively to exercise control over or to direct the political or military action of a State."[34] It thereby would never cover an ordinary soldier or even a mid-level commander.[35] A footnote to Element 2 of the Elements of the Crime of Aggression (discussed below) further clarifies that "more than one person may be in a position that meets these criteria."[36] Third, we see that the crime requires the occurrence of a state "act of aggression," and thereby covers uses of force that fall short of a full-scale "war" of aggression, subject to the qualifications set forth below.[37]

Fourth, we see that any act of aggression must also constitute "by its character, gravity and scale ... a *manifest* violation of the Charter of the United Nations."[38] These qualifications would exclude state action that is

---

[32] *Id.* art. 8*bis*(1).

[33] *See* London Charter, *supra* note 7, art. 6(a). It is not clear how this provision will interrelate with Article 25 of the Rome Statute (individual criminal responsibility). For one such discussion, *see* Nicolaos Strapatsas, *Is Article 25(3) of the ICC Statute Compatible with the "Crime of Aggression"?*, 19 FLA. J. INT'L L. 155 (2007).

[34] Rome Statute, *supra* note 1, art. 8*bis*(1).

[35] For discussion of the leadership clause, *see* Stefan Barriga, *Against the Odds: The Results of the Special Working Group on the Crime of Aggression, in* THE PRINCETON PROCESS, *supra* note 5, at 1, 7–8; Roger S. Clark, *The Crime of Aggression from the Trial of Takashi Sakai, August 1946, to the Kampala Review Conference on the ICC in 2010, in* THE HIDDEN HISTORIES OF WAR CRIMES TRIALS 387 (Kevin Jon Heller & Gerry Simpson eds., 2013).

[36] Res. RC/Res.6, *supra* note 2, annex II, Amendments to the Elements of Crimes, element 2 n.1.

[37] The London Charter covered "planning, preparation, initiation or waging of a war of aggression, or a war in violation of international treaties, agreements or assurances, or participation in a common plan or conspiracy for the accomplishment of any of the foregoing." London Charter, *supra* note 7, art. 6(a). *See also* Charter of the International Military Tribunal for the Far East art. 5(a), Jan. 19, 1946, *amended* Apr. 26, 1946, T.I.A.S. No. 1589 [hereinafter Tokyo Charter] (adding that the war could be declared or undeclared); *see also* Allied Control Council Law No. 10, Punishment of Persons Guilty of War Crimes, Crimes Against Peace and Against Humanity art. II(1)(a), Dec. 20, 1945, *reprinted in* 3 Official Gazette of the Control Council for Germany at 50–55 (1946) (covering "initiation of invasions" and not limiting the forms of responsibility to planning, preparation, initiation or waging).

[38] Rome Statute, *supra* note 1, art. 8*bis* (1) (emphasis added).

de minimis (not having the proper "gravity" or "scale").[39] They would also exclude anything unclear or in a "grey area" in terms of its legality.[40] By excluding anything unclear or in a "grey area" in terms of its legality, the crime also would not cover leaders who pursue *bona fide* humanitarian intervention – which, if properly conducted, would not have the required "character" for prosecution, nor, arguably, the required gravity.[41] The "manifest" requirement also would presumably exclude from the crime's ambit leaders who pursue debatable (but at least arguably legal) cases of self-defense.[42] Certain of the Understandings, also agreed upon in Kampala (discussed further below), reinforce these conclusions.[43]

Thus, although the crime covers acts short of full-scale "war" (the third point above), by having the "manifest" qualifier, which acts as a "threshold clause,"[44] the definition of "act of aggression" is limited to ensure that

---

[39] *See* YORAM DINSTEIN, WAR, AGGRESSION AND SELF-DEFENCE 136 (5th ed. 2011) (there is "no doubt that minor acts of aggression – even if enumerated in Paragraph 2 [of Article 8*bis*] – would not pass muster as crimes within the jurisdiction of the Court").

[40] *Informal Inter-Sessional Meeting on the Crime of Aggression (June 2009 – ICC-ASP/8/INF.2), in* THE PRINCETON PROCESS, *supra* note 5, at 28, ¶ 24 (the manifest threshold "would exclude situations that could fall within a legal grey area"); *Report of the Special Working Group on the Crime of Aggression (June 2008 – ICC-ASP/6/20/Add.1, Annex II), in* THE PRINCETON PROCESS, *supra* note 5, at 87, ¶ 68 ("Delegations supporting this [manifest] threshold clause noted that it would appropriately limit the Court's jurisdiction to the most serious acts of aggression under customary international law, thus excluding cases of insufficient gravity and falling within a grey area"); Claus Kreβ & Leonie von Holtzendorff, *The Kampala Compromise on the Crime of Aggression*, 8 J. INT'L CRIM. JUST. 1179, 1200 (2010) (the "requirement of manifest illegality ... has the effect of excluding from the state conduct element any use of armed force that falls into the 'grey area' of the prohibition on the use of force"). One sees reference to a "grey zone of ambiguity" regarding NATO's 1999 Kosovo intervention. *See* INDEP. INT'L COMM'N ON KOSOVO, THE KOSOVO REPORT 164 (2000).

[41] This Chapter uses the term "humanitarian intervention" to mean an intervention whether unilateral or multilateral, for *bona fide* humanitarian purposes, that is not authorized by the U.N. Security Council. For discussion of criteria for evaluation of whether humanitarian intervention is *bona fide, see* Jennifer Trahan, *Defining the "Grey Area" Where Humanitarian Intervention May Not Be Fully Legal, but Is Not the Crime of Aggression*, 2 J. ON USE FORCE & INT'L L. 42, sec. IV.iv (a)-(b) (2015) [hereinafter Trahan, *Grey Area*].

[42] Ratner, *supra* note 16, at 914 ("Article 51 can be viewed as ... quite imprecise ... in that it leaves the decision maker with significant discretion as to its meaning").

[43] For discussion of the Understandings, *see infra* notes 100–109 and accompanying text.

[44] *See Informal Inter-Sessional Meeting of the Special Working Group on the Crime of Aggression (June 2006 – ICC-ASP/5/SWGCA/INF.1.), in* THE PRINCETON PROCESS, *supra* note 5, at 143–44, ¶ 18 ("the idea of a threshold was inherent in the limitation of the jurisdiction of the Court under article 1 of the Rome Statute [to the] 'most serious crimes of international concern'"); Barriga, *supra* note 35, at 8 (the threshold of a "manifest violation" "has been referred to as the 'threshold clause'").

the ICC takes up only serious cases.[45] That conclusion is in line with the mandate of the ICC to prosecute only "the most serious crimes of concerns to the international community as a whole"[46] as well as the ICC's gravity threshold.[47]

B. *The Definition of the Act of Aggression*

Article 8*bis*(2) then defines the state "act of aggression." An individual cannot commit the crime of aggression without there also being this necessary element of the state act of aggression. Article 8*bis*(2) states:

> For the purpose of paragraph 1, "act of aggression" means the use of armed force by a State against the sovereignty, territorial integrity or political independence of another State, or in any other manner inconsistent with the Charter of the United Nations. Any of the following acts, regardless of a declaration of war, shall, in accordance with United Nations General Assembly resolution 3314 (XXIX) of 14 December 1974, qualify as an act of aggression[.][48]

A list of acts then follows.[49]

There are various noteworthy aspects to this paragraph. First, this paragraph addresses state acts of aggression only "for purpose of paragraph 1" and paragraph 1 is only for "the purpose of this Statute."[50] Certain authors have asserted that the crime of aggression amendment interferes with the U.N. Security Council's power under the U.N. Charter.[51] That conclusion is misdirected, as States Parties have no power to alter anything under the U.N. Charter, and Article 8*bis* will only apply to adjudications of individual criminal responsibility before the ICC, and not elsewhere.[52] It certainly will

---

[45] "The threshold clause ensures that only *very serious and unambiguously illegal* instances of a use of force by a State can give rise to individual criminal responsibility of a leader of that State under the Statute." HANDBOOK: RATIFICATION AND IMPLEMENTATION OF THE KAMPALA AMENDMENTS TO THE ROME STATUTE OF THE ICC: CRIME OF AGGRESSION, WAR CRIMES 8 (2013), http://crimeofaggression.info/documents/1/handbook.pdf [hereinafter HANDBOOK] (emphasis added). *See also* Alain Pellet, *Response to Koh and Buchwald's Article: Don Quixote and Sancho Panza Tilt at Windmills*, 109 AM. J. INT'L L. 557, 559 (2015).

[46] Rome Statute, *supra* note 1, pmbl.

[47] *Id.* art. 53(1)(c).

[48] *Id.* art. 8*bis*(2).

[49] *Id.* art. 8*bis*(2)(a)-(g).

[50] *Id.* art. 8*bis*(1)-(2).

[51] *See* Bing Bing Jia, *The Crime of Aggression as Custom and the Mechanisms for Determining Acts of Aggression*, 109 AM. J. INT'L L. 569, 570 (2015).

[52] Separately, the language in Article 8*bis* could be incorporated into domestic criminal laws, and then domestic courts could apply it – but States were always free to incorporate a

not limit anything the Security Council may or may not do in making determinations as to international peace and security. To suggest otherwise misunderstands the relationship of the Security Council and the ICC: Security Council power stems from the U.N. Charter, which the Rome Statute, States Parties, and ICC judges are powerless to alter.[53]

Second, as with the first paragraph's quotations of the London Charter, the second paragraph is even more historically derived. The first sentence is nearly a verbatim quote of Article 2(4) of the U.N. Charter,[54] and the second sentence quotes language directly from General Assembly Resolution 3314.[55] Thus, far from being innovative, the crime of aggression amendment is in significant part derived from earlier sources. In fact, the crime of aggression amendment is now being criticized as too historically based in covering only individual action in the context of a "state" act of aggression, and not aggression by a non-state actor.[56]

Third, the list appears to be illustrative (an open-ended list) in that each of the listed acts "qualify" as an act of aggression as long as they also meet paragraph 1's requirement of a "manifest" Charter violation. In this way, and due to the first sentence of paragraph 2, the list is also "closed."[57] No doubt a defense lawyer would vigorously fight any attempted prosecution based on an act not expressly listed as violating the principle of *nullum crimen sine lege* (no crime without law), but given that "other inhumane acts" has survived as a crime against humanity at the international criminal tribunals without more delineation as to what it covers,[58] the listed acts may not necessarily

---

crime of aggression into their domestic criminal codes, and some already had such a crime prior to the ICC Review Conference. *See* Reisinger Coracini, *supra* note 18 (compiling domestic crime of aggression legislation).

[53] For background, *see* Jennifer Trahan, *The Relationship Between the International Criminal Court and the U.N. Security Council: Parameters and Best Practices*, 24 CRIM. L.F. 417 (2013).

[54] *See* U.N. Charter art. 2(4).

[55] *See* G.A. Res. 3314 (XXIX), Definition of Aggression, U.N. Doc. A/RES/3314(XXIX) (Dec. 14, 1974). Resolution 3314 was intended as "guidance" for the U.N. Security Council. *Id.* ¶ 4.

[56] *See, e.g.*, Pellet, *supra* note 45, at 561 (lamenting "the exclusion of non-state actors as potential authors of acts of aggression"). Note that Article 8*bis*(2)(g) provides some coverage – where a State sends "armed bands, groups, irregulars or mercenaries," but it does not cover attacks by the non-state actors *per se*.

[57] The list can also be described as "semi-open" or "semi-closed." Barriga, *supra* note 35, at 11.

[58] "Other inhumane acts" must be of comparable gravity to the acts expressly enumerated as underlying crimes against humanity in order to be prosecuted. *See* JENNIFER TRAHAN, HUMAN RIGHTS WATCH, GENOCIDE, WAR CRIMES AND CRIMES AGAINST HUMANITY: A DIGEST OF THE CASE LAW OF THE INTERNATIONAL CRIMINAL TRIBUNAL FOR RWANDA 142–46 (2010) (citing cases).

preclude other acts from being covered, providing they meet all other statutory requirements.[59]

Fourth, the list of covered acts, as noted above, quotes language adopted in 1974, and thereby does not include more recent challenges such as cyberattacks and as previously noted, attacks by non-state actors, which perhaps must await a future amendment of the crime of aggression amendment. Some might argue a cyberattack could be covered by the current definition, although this author does not see how it would constitute a "use of armed force."[60] Given repeated references in Article 8*bis* to action "of a State," it seems impossible to fit attacks by non-state actors into the current definition, although in using force a non-state actor certainly may commit other Rome Statute crimes.

C. *Conditions for the Exercise of Jurisdiction*

There are two different articles regarding the exercise of jurisdiction – Article 15*bis*, covering State Party referrals and *proprio motu* initiation by the Prosecutor, and Article 15*ter*, covering Security Council referrals.

As to Security Council referrals, under Article 15*ter*, the most significant features are that first, the ICC may receive Security Council referrals – as it may with the other Rome Statute crimes;[61] second, a delay mechanism was applicable (as under Article 15*bis*) and before the Court could exercise its crime of aggression jurisdiction, there needed to be (1) thirty ratifications of the crime of aggression amendment, (2) one year's delay from the thirtieth ratification, and (3) an ASP decision after January 1, 2017, by consensus or two-thirds.[62] As noted above, the required ratifications have since been obtained, and the ICC States Parties have decided to activate the crime's jurisdiction,

---

[59] *But see* Donat-Cattin, *supra* note 18 (taking the contrary position that the list is "exhaustive," as it would otherwise fail the principle of legality).

[60] *See* Green, *supra* note 14, at 239 (cyberattacks "are now becoming an increasing feature of inter-state relations," but noting no "consensus as to whether cyber-attacks are, or should be, considered a use of 'force' as prohibited by Article 2[4]").

[61] Rome Statute, *supra* note 1, art. 13(b). The U.N. Security Council has made two such referrals – the situations in Darfur, Sudan, and Libya. *See* S.C. Res. 1593, U.N. Doc. S/RES/1593 (Mar. 31, 2015); S.C. Res. 1970, U.N. Doc. S/RES/1970 (Feb. 26, 2011).

[62] Rome Statute, *supra* note 1, art. 15*ter*(2)-(3). Of course, the U.N. Security Council could attempt an aggression referral even earlier, as its power emanates from the U.N. Charter, and those powers are quite broad. *See* Prosecutor v. Tadić, Case No. IT-94-1, Decision on the Defense Motion for Interlocutory Appeal on Jurisdiction (Oct. 2, 1995), www.icty.org/x/cases/tadic/acdec/en/51002.htm. But the Court would be unable to address the referral, since its power derives from the Rome Statute and amendments thereto.

effective July 17, 2018; accordingly, as of that date the ICC may receive Security Council referrals that include the crime of aggression.

Significantly, any determination that the Security Council makes would not prejudice or bind the ICC's own determination. This last conclusion is made clear in paragraph 4 of article 15*ter*, which states: "A determination of an act of aggression by an organ outside the Court shall be without prejudice to the Court's own findings under this Statute."[63] Thus, another body – whether the International Court of Justice (ICJ), the U.N. General Assembly, or the U.N. Security Council – could make some form of determination as to a State's actions, but that would not bind the ICC's determination of individual criminal responsibility. This necessarily must be the case, as the ICC is an "independent . . . judicial institution"[64] and would need to make its own determination that all of the elements of the crime have been met. The ICJ, by contrast, could make findings regarding state actions in the process of a contentious case or advisory opinion, and the Security Council and General Assembly could take up issues of international peace and security, but neither would be making determinations of individual criminal responsibility. Thus, each body has its own area of competence. Admittedly, there is some risk of overlapping or inconsistent decisions, but this is a general risk that the international legal system runs by virtue of its diffuse nature. For instance, both the International Criminal Tribunal for the former Yugoslavia (ICTY) and the ICJ could make findings on genocide, the former for purposes of individual criminal responsibility and the latter for purposes of state responsibility;[65] if they make inconsistent rulings, there is no appellate mechanism to harmonize their decisions.[66]

---

[63] Rome Statute, *supra* note 1, art. 15*ter*(4).

[64] Negotiated Relationship Agreement between the International Criminal Court and the United Nations, art. 2(1), U.N. Doc. ICC-ASP/3/Res.1, www.icc-cpi.int/NR/rdonlyres/916FC6A2-7846-4177-A5EA-5AA9B6D1E96C/0/ICCASP3Res1_English.pdf ("The United Nations recognizes the Court as an independent permanent judicial institution.")

[65] Prosecutor v. Krstić, Case No. IT-98-33, Trial Judgment (Aug. 2, 2001), *aff'd on appeal*, Case No. IT-98-33-A, Appeals Judgment (Apr. 19, 2004); Application of the Convention on the Prevention and Punishment of the Crime of Genocide (Bosn. and Herz. v. Serb. and Montenegro.), Merits Judgment, 2007 I.C.J. 43 (Feb. 26); Application of the Convention on the Prevention and Punishment of the Crime of Genocide (Croat. v. Serb.), Merits Judgment, 2015 I.C.J. 3 (Feb. 3).

[66] Alain Pellet writes that the ICC making a determination inconsistent with one of the U.N. Security Council as to aggression would "run afoul of Article 103 of the Charter." Pellet, *supra* note 45, at 563. But that is comparing apples and oranges: if the U.N. Security Council finds that some act constitutes aggression, while that would seem highly persuasive, it would not bind the Court. First, the Security Council binds U.N. Member States, and not the ICC or its judges. Second, the Security Council would be making a determination regarding

As to State Party referrals and *proprio motu* exercise of the Prosecutor's powers, under Article 15*bis*, two significant features are, first, that a non-State Party is completely exempt, and, second, that even a State Party can avoid these triggers by lodging an "opt-out" declaration with the ICC Registrar.[67] These provisions – to the dismay of some States, but the approval of others – do indeed make State Party referrals and *proprio motu* initiation something of an optional regime, or, put more positively, a "consent-based jurisdictional regime."[68]

Specifically, as to non-States Parties, the fifth paragraph of Article 15*bis* provides: "In respect of a State that is not a party to the Statute, the Court shall not exercise its jurisdiction over the crime of aggression when committed by that State's nationals or on its territory."[69] Significantly, this is a different jurisdictional regime than is established for the Rome Statute's other three core crimes, as to which the nationals of a non-State Party could be subject to ICC jurisdiction if they commit a Rome Statute crime in the territory of a State Party.[70]

Under the fourth paragraph of Article 15*bis*, States Parties may "opt out" of Article 15*bis* by "lodging a declaration with the Registrar" declaring that they "[do] not accept such jurisdiction [under Article 15*bis*]."[71] "The withdrawal of such a declaration may be effected at any time and shall be considered by the State Party within three years."[72] Thus, a State Party may "opt out" of crime of aggression jurisdiction (somewhat similarly to the seven-year war crimes opt-out created under Article 124, which States Parties have now agreed to delete).[73] An interesting question might be *when* the State Party would need to file such an opt-out declaration to fully cover its nationals. Given that "planning" and "preparation" are covered under Article 8*bis*, it might be necessary to file such a declaration rather early. On the other hand, Article 8*bis* makes clear that the crime cannot occur without the required state act of aggression,

---

international peace and security, but the ICC would be adjudicating individual criminal responsibility. Third, Article 103 is not implicated, as it governs a conflict between the obligations of *States* under a treaty regime and the obligations of *States* under the U.N. Charter. Fourth, it is easy to imagine the ICC judges making an inconsistent decision, but it might rest on wholly different reasons – for instance, that the use of force was not "manifest" – a criterion that the U.N. Security Council does not apply.

[67] Rome Statute, *supra* note 1, art. 15*bis*(4)-(5).
[68] HANDBOOK, *supra* note 45, at 9.
[69] Rome Statute, *supra* note 1, art. 15*bis*(5).
[70] *Id.* art. 12(2)(a).
[71] *Id.* art. 15*bis*(4).
[72] *Id.*
[73] *Id.* art. 124; Assembly of States Parties Res. ICC-ASP/14/Res.2 (Nov. 26, 2015) (States Parties agreeing to delete Article 124, although the amendment still requires ratification by seven-eighths of States Parties).

so if an "opt-out" declaration is filed after the commencement of planning and preparation but before the State's act of aggression, it could be argued that the Court lacks jurisdiction over part of the crime and could not proceed. The language about "considering" the declaration "within three years"[74] – rather awkwardly drafted – suggests the State Party should consider after three years, or earlier, whether they could withdraw the declaration.

Two other significant features of Article 15*bis* include the Prosecutor's obligation to notify the Secretary-General if Article 15*bis* is used (and provide the Security Council six months to make its own determination as to whether the concerned State committed an act of aggression if it has not made one),[75] and, if the Security Council has not made such a determination, the requirement that there must be Pre-Trial Division authorization (not just Pre-Trial Chamber authorization) for both State Party referrals and *proprio motu* initiation by the Prosecutor.[76]

Finally, again, we see that "a determination of an act of aggression by an organ outside the Court shall be without prejudice to the Court's own findings under this Statute."[77] As discussed above, this necessarily preserves the Court's judicial independence.

D. *Entry into Force and the Exercise of Jurisdiction*

As noted above, both Articles 15*ter* and 15*bis* have a delay mechanism built into them. Both state: "The Court may exercise jurisdiction only with respect to crimes of aggression committed one year after the ratification or acceptance of the amendments by thirty States Parties," and that "[t]he Court shall exercise jurisdiction over the crime of aggression in accordance with this article, subject to a decision to be taken after 1 January 2017 by the same majority of States Parties as is required for the adoption of an amendment to the Statute."[78] As described more fully below, these events have now transpired, so the Court will be able to exercise jurisdiction over the crime of aggression as of July 17, 2018.

By contrast, "entry into force" of the amendment is a different matter. Article 121(5), first sentence, provides: "Any amendment to articles 5, 6, 7 and 8 of this Statute shall *enter into force* for those States Parties which have accepted the amendment *one year after the deposit* of their instruments of

---

[74] Rome Statute, *supra* note 1, art. 15*bis*(4).
[75] *Id.* art. 15*bis*(6)-(8).
[76] *Id.* art. 15*bis*(8).
[77] *Id.* art. 15*bis*(9).
[78] *Id.* arts. 15*bis*(2)-(3), 15*ter*(2)-(3).

ratification or acceptance."[79] (Somewhat problematically, of course, the crime of aggression amendment amends, or, maybe more accurately, inserts, articles after Articles 8 and 15.) Assuming this sentence is applicable – i.e., that Articles 8*bis*, 15*bis*, and 15*ter* are, in effect, amending Articles 5 and/or 8 – then, for example, for Liechtenstein, which deposited its instrument of ratification on May 8, 2012,[80] the crime of aggression amendment entered into force one year later, on May 8, 2013.

However, even for such an early ratifier of the crime of aggression amendment, there still will be no retroactive application of jurisdiction. Understanding 3 makes this clear. It states, for purposes of State Party referrals and *proprio motu* exercise of the Prosecutor's power:

> It is understood that in case of article 13, paragraphs (a) or (c), the Court may exercise its jurisdiction only with respect to crimes of aggression *committed after* a decision in accordance with article 15*bis*, paragraph 3, is taken, and one year after the ratification or acceptance of the amendments by thirty States Parties, whichever is later.[81]

The same is true for U.N. Security Council referrals. While any State could be subject to U.N. Security Council referral after activation of jurisdiction – whether or not the State has ratified or acceded to the amendment, and whether or not that State is a Rome Statute State Party – there also will be no retroactive application of jurisdiction.[82]

---

[79] *Id.* art. 121(5) (emphasis added).

[80] *Status of Ratification and Implementation of the Kampala Amendments on the Crime of Aggression, supra* note 29.

[81] Res. RC/Res.6, *supra* note 2, annex III, understanding 3 (emphasis added). *See also* HANDBOOK, *supra* note 45, at 13 ("Understanding 3 ... confirms that ... in cases of State referrals and *proprio motu* investigations, there is no retroactive effect. Only crimes committed after the full activation of the Court's jurisdiction can be investigated.").

[82] Understanding 1 states:

> It is understood that the Court may exercise jurisdiction on the basis of a Security Council referral in accordance with article 13, paragraph (b), of the Statute only with respect to crimes of aggression *committed after* a decision in accordance with article 15*ter*, paragraph 3, is taken, and one year after the ratification or acceptance of the amendments by thirty States Parties, whoever is later.

Res. RC/Res.6, *supra* note 2, annex III, understanding 1 (emphasis added). *See also* HANDBOOK, *supra* note 45, at 13 (Understanding 1 makes clear there is no retroactive application). *See also supra* note 62 (discussing the possibility of earlier U.N. Security Council referral, but concluding the Court could not exercise jurisdiction). The same would be true for a post-activation U.N. Security Council referral that purports to cover a pre-activation crime of aggression: the Court would not be able to exercise jurisdiction.

A lively debate developed since adoption of the crime of aggression amendment as to how many States Parties would be subject to the ICC crime of
aggression's jurisdiction after the date of activation for purposes of Article 15*bis*
(State Party referral and *proprio motu* initiation). One reading (let us call it the
French/British reading) was that even after activation, only States Parties that
had actively ratified the crime of aggression amendment could be covered by
jurisdiction for purposes of Article 15*bis*, presumably meaning that both the
"aggressor" State Party *and* the "victim" State Party needed to actively ratify
the amendment. Another reading (let us call it the Liechtenstein/Swiss/major-
ity reading) was that after activation, *all* States Parties could be covered by
crime of aggression jurisdiction for purposes of Article 15*bis*, as long as either
the "aggressor" or the "victim" State Party had actively ratified.[83]

Indeed, the Resolution adopted in Kampala states that the crime of aggression amendment "shall enter into force in accordance with article 121(5),"[84]
and Article 121(5), second sentence, states: "In respect of a State Party which
has not accepted the amendment, the Court shall not exercise its jurisdiction
regarding a crime covered by the amendment when committed by that State
Party's nationals or on its territory."[85] A superficial reading of the second
sentence tended to support the French/British interpretation.

However, the alternative reading – that appears to have been more widely
held – was that this general rule contained in the second sentence did not
apply to the crime of aggression, as it stands in tension with two other relevant
provisions of the Rome Statute, namely Articles 12(1) and 5(2), as well as with
the very concept of an opt-out mechanism (described above).[86] Specifically,

---

[83] The International Criminal Court and the Crime of Aggression, Panel at the German Mission
to the U.N. (Feb. 23, 2016) (discussion following the panel, citing France, Denmark, and the
United Kingdom as taking the former position, and most other States taking the latter position).
One State Party present expressed concern that in any given situation it is not always clear
which is the "aggressor" and which the "victim" State. A response given was that the ICC will
proceed only in clear cases; thus, it should be clear which is the "aggressor" and which the
"victim" State. Observations of the Author (Feb. 23, 2016).

[84] Res. RC/Res.6, *supra* note 2.

[85] Rome Statute, *supra* note 1, art. 121(5).

[86] *See, e.g.,* HANDBOOK, *supra* note 45, at 9–10 ("[p]assive consent in the form of abstention from
opting-out of the Court's exercise of jurisdiction suffices" as long as the amendment has "been
ratified by and entered into force for at least one of the States Parties involved – be it the
presumed aggressor or the victim State"). When this issue was voted on at the Resumed Eighth
Session of the ASP, twenty States voted that the "aggressor" State had to ratify, and thirty-two
voted that the victim State had to ratify in cases without U.N. Security Council referral,
meaning that a total of fifty-two States voted for "aggressor" *or* "victim" State ratification
without U.N. Security Council referral. An additional eleven States voted for either "aggressor"
or "victim" State ratification, with U.N. Security Council referral (nine voting for "aggressor"
State ratification and two voting for "victim" State ratification). *See* Chart reproduced in

under the Liechtenstein/Swiss/majority reading, States Parties had already, at least in principle, accepted the Court's jurisdiction over the crime of aggression under Article 12(1).[87] The Resolution adopted in Kampala only referred to Article 121(5) insofar as it regulated the entry into force of the amendment, and thus only the first sentence of Article 121(5).[88] The second sentence of Article 121(5), by contrast, "does not speak about entry into force but about the exercise of jurisdiction."[89] But, for the crime of aggression only, Article 5(2) provided that States could negotiate conditions for the exercise of jurisdiction, meaning States Parties could adopt a jurisdictional regime different from the one governing the other three core crimes in the Rome Statute, or other future amendments. In other words, Article 5(2) allowed States Parties to create a *sui generis* regime[90] on conditions for the exercise of jurisdiction, for the crime of aggression only, because of its unique status of being half-in

Trahan, *Kampala Negotiations, supra* note 4, at 63. There was no vote on the "aggressor" *and* "victim" State needing to ratify, nor was such a vote requested. And, there was certainly no agreement that the "aggressor" State needed to ratify – with votes roughly split between the two positions (twenty-nine for "aggressor" State ratification; thirty-four for "victim" State ratification). *Id.; see also* Stefan Barriga & Niels Blokker, *Conditions for the Exercise of Jurisdiction Based on State Referrals and* Proprio Motu *Investigations* (forthcoming) (manuscript on file with author) ("Roughly half of the delegations preferred such a consent-based regime [of "aggressor" State ratification], whereas the other half preferred a more protective regime that would not depend on such consent, since such [aggressor State] consent was unlikely to be forthcoming in real situations, and since such consent was not required under the existing jurisdictional regime of article 12.").

[87] "Since article 5(1) includes the crime of aggression, the ordinary meaning of [article 12(1)] is that parties to the 1998 Rome Statue have already accepted the Court's jurisdiction over the crime of aggression." Barriga & Blokker, *supra* note 86. *See* Rome Statute, *supra* note 1, art. 12 (1) ("A State which becomes a Party to this Statue thereby accepts the jurisdiction of the Court with respect to the crimes referred to in article 5").

[88] *See* Barriga & Blokker, *supra* note 86 ("the operative paragraph only states that the amendments 'enter into force' in accordance with article 121(5). . . . [H]owever, only the first sentence of that paragraph addresses questions of entry into force"). Barriga and Blokker also explain: "[t]he possibility for an alleged aggressor State Party to opt-out only makes sense if the Court can indeed exercise jurisdiction in the absence of an opt-out declaration – namely on the basis of the ratification of the other State Party involved [the victim State]." *Id. See also* Wenaweser & Barriga, *supra* note 5, at 292 ("Of course an opt-out clause only makes sense if the default positon is 'in'! Otherwise, the system would first require States Parties to opt in, and then allow them to opt out – an entirely absurd approach in this context, and one that no delegation ever advocated for during and prior to Kampala."); Jutta F. Bertram-Nothnagel, *A Seed of World Peace Growing in Africa: The Kampala Amendments on the Crime of Aggression and the Monsoon of Malabo, in* THE INTERNATIONAL CRIMINAL COURT AND AFRICA: ONE DECADE ON (Evelyn A. Ankumah ed., 2016) ("This observer does not recall that States ever argued for an arrangement that would require opt-in and permit opt-out by the same State.")

[89] Bertram-Nothnagel, *supra* note 88, at n.35.

[90] *See* HANDBOOK, *supra* note 45, at 10.

and half-out of the Rome Statute.[91] A day-by-day narrative of the Kampala negotiations – authored by individuals who were probably *the most central participants* to the negotiations – supports this second reading, highlighting in particular that having an opt-out mechanism makes sense primarily if the default position is "in."[92]

After a year-long "facilitation" process in 2017 attempted to reconcile these competing readings of the Kampala crime of aggression amendment, the issue was taken up at the December 4–14, 2017, ASP meeting, when States Parties agreed to activate ICC crime of aggression jurisdiction effective July 17, 2018. Specifically, States Parties, by resolution adopted by consensus, appear to have agreed upon the French/British reading of jurisdiction. The activating resolution reads in relevant part that the ASP:

1. *Decides* to activate the Court's jurisdiction over the crime of aggression as of 17 July 2018;
2. *Confirms* that, . . . in the case of a State referral or *propio motu* investigation the Court shall not exercise its jurisdiction regarding a crime of aggression when committed by a national or on the territory of a State Party that has not ratified or accepted these amendments;
3. *Reaffirms* paragraph 1 of article 40 and paragraph 1 of article 119 of the Rome Statute in relation to the judicial independence of the judges of the Court;
4. *Renews* its call upon all States Parties which have not yet done so to ratify or accept the amendments to the Rome Statute on the crime of aggression.[93]

Thus, the plain language of the second paragraph above could suggest that *both* the "aggressor" and "victim" State Party need to have actively ratified the crime of aggression amendment before the ICC may exercise jurisdiction over the crime for purposes of Article 15*bis* (State Party referrals and *proprio motu* initiation). This would *very significantly* cut down on the number of States Parties that would be subject to crime of aggression jurisdiction for purposes of Article 15*bis*, and was an outcome strenuously fought at the recent negotiations by many States Parties – who much preferred the reading that after activation, *all* States Partes could be subject to crime of aggression jurisdiction for purposes of Article 15*bis*, absent lodging an "opt out" declaration, as long as either the "aggressor" or "victim" State Party had ratified. The language in

---

[91] *See supra* note 21 and accompanying text.
[92] *See* Wenaweser & Barriga, *supra* note 5.
[93] Res. ICC-ASP/16/Res.5, *supra* note 30.

paragraph 3 appears to be a nod toward those unhappy States Parties who would have preferred the Liechtenstein/Swiss/majority reading – and suggests that the ICC judges are always free to revisit the issue of jurisdiction. A resolution adopted by the ASP ought to have less interpretative weight than the actual text of the crime of aggression amendment.

E. *The Elements of the Crime*

At the Review Conference, States Parties also adopted Elements of the Crime of Aggression.

There are a few items of note regarding the Elements. First, "elements" undoubtedly have lesser weight than statutory provisions, so in the event of inconsistency, it is the Statute that would govern. On the other hand, elements do have some interpretive weight.[94]

Second, Element 3 requires that the act of aggression be "committed."[95] This raises the question how to read Element 3, given that under Article 25(3)(f), "attempt" is a mode of individual criminal responsibility. One might ask whether "attempt" or "planning" or "preparation" of an act of aggression that never occurs is a Rome Statute crime or not. The Elements here are probably not conclusive, because all of the Elements of the Rome Statute are phrased as if the person at issue "committed" the crime, yet "attempt" is also a form of individual criminal responsibility as to genocide, war crimes, and crimes against humanity.[96] These are the type of intellectual debates academics ponder, but, in practicality, probably matter little. The best reading might be that "attempt" is a covered form of individual criminal responsibility (for all four core crimes). If one "attempts" the crime of aggression, and the act of aggression occurs, that would be the completed crime. If one "attempts" the crime of aggression and the act of aggression never occurs, even if technically covered, it is just not the type of situation with which the ICC should be filling

---

[94] Rome Statute, *supra* note 1, art. 21(1) ("The Court shall apply: (a) In the first place, this Statute, Elements of Crimes and its Rules of Procedure and Evidence.").

[95] "The act of aggression – the use of armed force by a State against the sovereignty, territorial integrity or political independence of another State, or in any other manner inconsistent with the Charter of the United Nations – was committed." Res. RC/Res.6, *supra* note 2, annex II, Amendments to the Elements of Crimes, element 3.

[96] Roger Clark – who has chronicled the negotiating history of the interface between Article 8*bis* and the general parts of the Rome Statute – explains: the drafting convention for the crimes in articles 6, 7, and 8 is that the definition and Elements set out the simple case where there is one lone perpetrator who succeeds; other parties and attempts are left to be dealt with under Article 25. E-mail exchange between Clark and the author (Feb. 25, 2015) (on file with author).

its docket.[97] The same would be true for "attempt" at genocide, war crimes, or crimes against humanity where the crime never occurs. The alternative reading is also possible, that whereas "attempt" is covered as a form of individual criminal responsibility, Article 8*bis* also requires the state act of aggression, and if the state act fails to occur, there is no crime. Both readings get one to the same result: weak cases do not get prosecuted.

Third, the Elements may be significant when considering mistake of law, particularly as to what may or may not constitute a "manifest" Charter violation. Introduction paragraph 3 provides that "[t]he term 'manifest' is an objective qualification." This suggests what matters is an *objective* measurement of the "manifest" Charter violation, and not the perpetrator's subjective state of mind. This is reinforced by Element 5, which provides: "The act of aggression, by its character, gravity and scale, constituted a manifest violation of the Charter of the United Nations." This makes clear there must actually *be* a manifest Charter violation (also reinforced by the text of Article 8*bis*). One might then ask how to read this, given the "mistake of law" provision of the Rome Statute, which states that mistake of law could negate *mens rea*.[98] Perhaps the best reading is that a reasonable belief that something is not a "manifest" Charter violation (even if erroneous) should insulate the individual accused, whereas a belief that something is not a "manifest" Charter violation that is unreasonable should not. The law should encourage reasonable behavior, and if someone reasonably believes one's actions are legal, or is so advised, then prosecutions should not occur; however, reliance on advice of counsel that is patently defective and hence unreasonable to rely upon, should, by contrast, provide no such protection from exposure.[99]

---

[97] *See* Rome Statute, *supra* note 1, art. 1 (the Court shall have "jurisdiction over persons for the most serious crimes of international concern"); *id.* pmbl (similar).

[98] *See id.* art. 32(2).

[99] *See* Trahan, *Grey Area*, *supra* note 41, at sec. IV.iv (c) (examining this question in more depth). Note also that the United States' proposed understanding on humanitarian intervention (discussed below) also would require the State to act in "good faith." *See infra* text accompanying note 110. *See also Informal Inter-Sessional Meeting on the Crime of Aggression (June 2009), in* THE PRINCETON PROCESS, *supra* note 5, at 28, ¶ 25 (as to the "manifest" qualifier being "objective," it "was submitted that the Court's determination as to whether the act of aggression constituted, by its character, gravity and scale a 'manifest' violation would be decisive, rather than the perpetrator's legal assessment. It was suggested that the Court would apply the standard of a 'reasonable leader,' similar to the standard of the 'reasonable soldier' that was embodied in the concept of manifestly unlawful orders in article 33 of the Rome Statute.").

F. *The Understandings*

At the Review Conference, States Parties also adopted various Understandings to accompany the crime of aggression. Understandings are clearly of lesser interpretative weight than the Statute or Elements, and, while they have some weight, it is arguably not that much.[100]

The most interesting Understandings are probably Understandings 4 and 5 (on domestic jurisdiction) and 6 and 7. Understandings 4 and 5 provide:

Domestic jurisdiction over the crime of aggression

4. It is understood that the amendments that address the definition of the act of aggression and the crime of aggression do so for the purpose of this Statute only. The amendments shall, in accordance with article 10 of the Rome Statute, not be interpreted as limiting or prejudicing in any way existing or developing rules of international law for purposes other than this Statute.

5. It is understood that the amendments shall not be interpreted as creating the right or obligation to exercise domestic jurisdiction with respect to an act of aggression committed by another State.

While there is another Chapter in this book devoted to the development of the crime of aggression under customary international law, Understanding 4 seems to be hinting at the fact that what was previously accepted as customary international law (indeed, a *jus cogens* norm) has been the Nuremberg definition of the crime (requiring a full "war" of aggression).[101] Perhaps the crime of aggression amendment's definition may come to be regarded as customary international law, but Understanding 4 suggests that adoption of the amendment says nothing as to whether or not this status has been achieved.[102]

Understanding 5 states that the crime of aggression amendment creates no right or obligation to prosecute aggression *committed by another State* under domestic criminal law. While thus seemingly discouraging the exercise of domestic jurisdiction in relation to other States, Understanding 5 does not prohibit such exercise of jurisdiction either. In any event, Understanding

---

[100] *See* Kevin Jon Heller, *The Uncertain Legal Status of the Aggression Understandings*, 10 J. Int'l Crim. Just. 229 (2012).

[101] *See supra* note 37 (quoting the London Charter); *supra* note 16 (discussing the *jus cogens* norm). For an article that challenges the view that the prohibition of the use of force is part of *jus cogens*, without challenging that it is customary international law, see Green, *supra* note 14.

[102] Understanding 4 also parallels text already found in Article 10 of the Rome Statute that "[n]othing in this Part shall be interpreted as limiting or prejudicing in any way existing or developing rules of international law for purposes other than this Statute." Rome Statute, *supra* note 1, art. 10.

5 does not affect the Statute's existing rules regarding complementarity, which fully apply to the crime of aggression.[103]

Understandings 6 and 7 provide:

Other understandings

    6. It is understood that aggression is the most serious and dangerous form of the illegal use of force; and that a determination whether an act of aggression has been committed requires consideration of all the circumstances of each particular case, including the gravity of the acts concerned and their consequences, in accordance with the Charter of the United Nations.

    7. It is understood that in establishing whether an act of aggression constitutes a manifest violation of the Charter of the United Nations, the three components of character, gravity and scale must be sufficient to justify a "manifest" determination. No one component can be significant enough to satisfy the manifest standard by itself.

Understandings 6 and 7 reinforce several of the conclusions already articulated as to the requirement of a "manifest" Charter violation.[104] Above, the author noted that anything *de minimis* or unclear in terms of legality would not be prosecutable.[105] This is reinforced by Understanding 6 that "aggression is the most serious and dangerous form of the illegal use of force" (language taken from the Preamble of General Assembly Resolution 3314).[106] Similarly, the author, as have many others, has concluded that *bona fide* humanitarian intervention would not be prosecutable as it would not have the right "character" to constitute a "manifest" Charter violation.[107] This is reinforced by Understanding 6 that one must consider the "gravity" of the acts "and their consequences."[108] As Beth Van Schaak explains: "The focus on 'consequences' in the Understandings allows for an opening to argue that a military operation that may have violated Article 2(4) of the U.N. Charter as a technical matter might not be deemed to constitute an act of aggression by virtue of the fact that it ultimately improved the situation on the ground by protecting civilians and

---

[103] *See also* HANDBOOK, *supra* note 45, at 13–14 (Understanding 5 "confirms that the Rome Statute, while built on the principle of complementarity, does not regulate under what conditions States may or must exercise domestic jurisdiction over international crimes, but merely regulates under which conditions the ICC may exercise jurisdiction.").
[104] *See supra* notes 38 & 41 and accompanying text.
[105] *See supra* notes 40–41 and accompanying text.
[106] *See* G.A. Res. 3314 (XXIX), *supra* note 55, annex, pmbl.
[107] *See supra* note 41 and accompanying text (humanitarian intervention not covered); Trahan, *Grey Area, supra* note 41, at 60 nn.124–26.
[108] This language as to "consequences" is also found in Resolution 3314. *See* G.A. Res. 3314 (XXIX), *supra* note 55, annex, art.2.

vulnerable groups from further attack."[109] Understanding 7 is probably unnecessary, as Article 8*bis* already states that there must be a manifest Charter violation by its "character, gravity *and* scale," so there already is an "and" – meaning the Statute already requires that all three items be considered.

G. *Absence of an Understanding on Humanitarian Intervention*

The U.S. delegation at the Review Conference had proposed an understanding stating:

> It is understood that, for purposes of the Statute, an act cannot be considered to be a manifest violation of the United Nations Charter unless it would be objectively evident to any State conducting itself in the matter in accordance with normal practice and in good faith, and thus an act undertaken in connection with an effort to prevent the commission of any of the crimes contained in Articles 6, 7 or 8 of the Statute would not constitute an act of aggression.[110]

While not necessarily endorsing this precise drafting,[111] this author has some sympathy for the U.S. proposal. While the Understanding should be unnecessary, since anything that is not a "manifest" Charter violation by its "character" should not carry exposure,[112] some type of Understanding of the variety the United States proposed could have lent clarification. States are not "lining up" to help with *bona fide* humanitarian intervention, and their nationals certainly should not be prosecuted or risk prosecution if the intervention is both properly motivated and properly conducted, especially if endorsed by a multilateral regional organization – in fact, the ICC Prosecutor would probably risk looking distinctly foolish if she were to prosecute in such a situation.[113]

The author is aware that many States and some authors would take the position that, subsequent to the development of the doctrine of the

---

[109] Beth Van Schaack, *The Crime of Aggression and Humanitarian Intervention on Behalf of Women*, 11 INT'L CRIM. L. REV. 477, 485 (2011).

[110] 2010 Non-Paper by the United States, *reproduced in* CRIME OF AGGRESSION LIBRARY, *supra* note 5, at 751, 751–52.

[111] For arguments why the proposed language by the United States was overbroad, *see* Trahan, *Kampala Negotiations, supra* note 4, at 75.

[112] *See supra* note 41 and accompanying text (humanitarian intervention not covered).

[113] For more extensive discussion, *see, for example,* Trahan, *Grey Area, supra* note 41, at sec. III.iii (listing many different reasons why a *bona fide* humanitarian intervention would not make a strong ICC case, including potential affirmative defenses and mitigating factors).

"Responsibility to Protect" (R2P),[114] there is no doctrine of "humanitarian intervention." Yet, because forceful intervention under R2P (often referred to as "pillar 3")[115] requires U.N. Security Council authorization,[116] and the U.N. Security Council often fails to exercise its responsibilities in the face of mass atrocity crimes,[117] at least some States, and this author, contend that there *is* still need for a doctrine of humanitarian intervention notwithstanding the development of R2P.[118] Yet, it is true that most States remain deeply wary of

---

[114] *See, e.g.,* INT'L COMM. ON INTERVENTION AND STATE SOVEREIGNTY, THE RESPONSIBILITY TO PROTECT (2001) [hereinafter ICISS Report]; U.N. Secretary-General's High-Level Panel on Threats, Challenges and Change, *A More Secure World: Our Shared Responsibility*, U.N. Doc. A/59/565 (Dec. 2, 2004) [hereinafter 2004 High-Level Panel Report]; G.A. Res. 60/1, 2005 World Summit Outcome, U.N. Doc. A/RES/60/1 (Sept. 16, 2005) [hereinafter 2005 World Summit Outcome]; U.N. Secretary-General, *Implementing the Responsibility to Protect*, U.N. Doc. A/63/677 (Jan. 12, 2009) [hereinafter 2009 Report].

[115] The 2009 R2P Report introduces the terminology of the three "pillars" of R2P. *See* 2009 Report, *supra* note 114.

[116] *See, e.g.,* 2004 High-Level Panel Report, *supra* note 114, ¶ 203; 2005 World Summit Outcome, *supra* note 114, ¶ 139; 2009 Report, *supra* note 114, ¶ 11(c) (requiring U.N.S.C. authorization for forceful intervention). The initial ICISS formulation would have been more permissive. *See* ICISS Report, *supra* note 114, at XIII, ¶ 3(F).

[117] For example, between 2011 and April 2017, the Russian Federation, supported by China (except on the October 8, 2016, vote to end the bombing of Aleppo), vetoed and threatened a veto to impede Security Council action at least seven times related to Syria. *See, e.g.,* Julian Borger & Bastien Inzaurralde, *Russian Vetoes Are Putting UN Security Council's Legitimacy at Risk, Says US*, GUARDIAN (Sept. 23, 2015), www.theguardian.com/world/2015/sep/23/russian-vetoes-putting-un-security-council-legitimacy-at-risk-says-us ("Russia has used its veto powers four times to block resolutions on Syria."); *Security Council – Veto List*, UNITED NATIONS, http://research.un.org/en/docs/sc/quick.

[118] The United Kingdom, United States, and Denmark have all invoked humanitarian intervention subsequent to the development of R2P. *See* PRIME MINISTER'S OFFICE, POLICY PAPER: CHEMICAL WEAPON USE BY SYRIAN REGIME: UK GOVERNMENT LEGAL POSITION (2013), www.gov.uk/government/uploads/system/uploads/attachment_data/file/235098/Chemical-weapon-use-by-Syrian-regime-UK-government-legal-position.pdf (concerning the possibility of intervening in Syria) [hereinafter U.K. POLICY PAPER]. The United Kingdom cites a legal basis of humanitarian intervention where three conditions are met:

> (1) there is convincing evidence, generally accepted by the international community as a whole, of extreme humanitarian distress on a large scale, requiring immediate and urgent relief; (2) it must be objectively clear that there is no practicable alternative to the use of force if lives are to be saved; and (3) the proposed use of force must be necessary and proportionate to the aim of relief of humanitarian need and must be strictly limited in time and scope to this aim (i.e. the minimum necessary to achieve that end and for no other purpose).

Id. See also President Barack H. Obama, Nobel Lecture: A Just and Lasting Peace (Dec. 10, 2009) ("I believe that force can be justified on humanitarian grounds, as it was in the Balkans."); *Denmark Stands Firm to Support Interventions in Syria Outside the UN*, SCANOMARK.COM (Aug. 29, 2013), www.scancomark.com/Political-economy/Denmark-stands-

the concept of humanitarian intervention, due to the risk of overbroad and pretextual use, and prefer only to endorse the more limited concept of R2P, which requires Security Council authorization for forceful action.[119]

Helpful initiatives aimed at limiting such harmful use of the veto include the Accountability Coherence and Transparency (ACT) Group's *Code of Conduct regarding Security Council action against genocide, crimes against humanity or war crimes* and the French/Mexican initiative to restrain use of the veto in cases of mass atrocity crimes.[120] When the U.N. Security Council lives up to its responsibilities and acts in the face of mass atrocity crimes and all Permanent Members endorse these initiatives, one will not need to still endorse a penumbral doctrine of humanitarian intervention. But we are not at such a stage. Thus, it cannot be ruled out that, in dire enough circumstances, the international community might still need to engage in a *bona fide* humanitarian intervention even absent U.N. Security Council approval, and individual States certainly should not be prosecuted for doing so.

In the absence of an understanding on humanitarian intervention, a State Party with legitimate question as to the legality of a future *bona fide* humanitarian intervention is of course free to exercise an opt-out declaration if it has ratified the crime of aggression amendment (or – pursuant to the 2017 ASP

---

firm-to-supports-interventions-in-Syria-outside-the-UN-231029082013. Any doctrine of humanitarian intervention must be narrowly defined, and carefully limited to exclude pretextual or overbroad application. *See* Trahan, *Grey Area, supra* note 41, at sec. IV.iv (a)-(b) (suggesting criteria for defining *bona fide* humanitarian intervention); Donat-Cattin, *supra* note 18 (calling for intervention that is "genuinely humanitarian" in that it meets the legal principles of necessity, proportionality, and good faith, but expressing profound skepticism that genuine humanitarian intervention can be accomplished through airstrikes alone).

[119] *See, e.g.*, Gelijn Molier, *Humanitarian Intervention and the Responsibility to Protect After 9/11*, 53 NETH. INT'L L. REV. 37, 44 (2006). ("The main argument against the legality of humanitarian intervention was that powerful states will abuse this doctrine for geopolitical reasons, as long as there are no clear, and generally accepted criteria which specify under which circumstances a humanitarian intervention is called for.") *Compare International Law Discussion Group Summary – Syria and International Law: Use of Force and State Responsibility*, CHATHAM HOUSE 3 (Sept. 30, 2013), www.chathamhouse.org/sites/files/ chathamhouse/public/Research/International%20Law/300913summary.pdf (suggesting that by using stringent conditions with a high threshold there would be "no carte blanche for humanitarian intervention").

[120] *See List of Supporters of the Code of Conduct Regarding Security Council Action Against Genocide, Crimes Against Humanity and War Crimes*, GLOBAL CTR. RESPONSIBILITY TO PROTECT (June 10, 2016), www.globalr2p.org/media/files/list-of-signatories-to-the-act-code-of-conduct.pdf (listing 115 States and two Observer States supporting the Code of Conduct); *List of Supporters of the Political Declaration on Suspension of Veto Powers in Cases of Mass Atrocity*, GLOBAL CTR. RESPONSIBILITY TO PROTECT (June 15, 2016), www.globalr2p.org/ media/files/veto-list.pdf (listing ninety-six States supporting the French/Mexican initiative).

activating resolution – not to ratify the amendment in the first place), and a non-State Party would in any case be exempt from jurisdiction initiated by State Party referral or *proprio motu*.[121] Alternatives to a full opt-out include a limited opt-out only regarding humanitarian intervention,[122] or an explanatory memorandum deposited with ratification of the Kampala Amendment.[123] Thus the crime of aggression amendment provides no reason not to conduct a *bona fide*[124] humanitarian intervention, nor should a would-be humanitarian interventionist State fear the ICC's ability to exercise jurisdiction over the crime of aggression.

IV. POTENTIAL IMPLICATIONS OF THE ICC'S ABILITY TO EXERCISE CRIME OF AGGRESSION JURISDICTION

A. *Will It Lessen Aggressive Uses of Force?*

The ICC's ability to exercise jurisdiction over the crime of aggression could be something of a "game-changer" on the international stage.[125] While, as already noted, the prohibition on aggressive use of force is central to the U.N. Charter, there are sometimes consequences that flow from a breach of Article 2(4) and sometimes not, in part dependent on the actions of the U.N. Security Council, a political body. Activation of the ICC crime takes the seriousness of enforcement to a wholly different level, closer to where the crime was thought to be – at the apex of crimes – before the Nuremberg Tribunal.[126]

Whether state behavior is concomitantly influenced depends on a variety of factors. As explained above, there are significant limitations to the ICC

---

[121] There is no similar opt-out provision or exemption from jurisdiction from Security Council referrals under Article 15*ter*.

[122] A question might exist as to whether such a limited opt-out would be valid, since Article 15*bis* only provides for a full opt-out. Yet, it seems preferable to have States opt out of less than the full crime, so a limited opt-out should be preferable and construed as valid.

[123] Germany deposited such a memorandum when it ratified the crime of aggression amendment. Author conversation with Claus Kreβ, Director, Institute of International Peace and Security Law, University of Cologne (Feb. 25, 2016). The advantage of a memorandum is that it suggests there is nothing to opt out "from" – that humanitarian intervention is not covered by the crime at all. *Id.* But, alternatively, perhaps an opt-out could be formulated in a nuanced way, so as not to suggest that the State opting out necessarily believes humanitarian intervention is covered.

[124] For discussion of what constitutes a *bona fide* humanitarian intervention, *see* Trahan, *Grey Area*, *supra* note 41, at sec. IV.iv (a)–(b) (discussing criteria of legitimacy for a humanitarian intervention and urging further crystallization of such criteria); U.K. POLICY PAPER, *supra* note 118 (setting forth criteria); Donat-Cattin, *supra* note 18.

[125] Noah Weisbord, Op-Ed., *Who Started the Fight?*, N.Y. TIMES (May 3, 2010), www.nytimes .com/2010/05/04/opinion/04iht-edweisbord.html?_r=0.

[126] *See supra* text accompanying note 8.

crime of aggression's jurisdictional regime (limitations that appear to be broadened under the 2017 ASP activating resolution). For example, non-States Parties are completely exempt from State Party referral and *proprio motu* initiation by the Prosecutor. Thus, will a future hypothetical Russian leader be influenced against committing incursions, such as the ones into Eastern Ukraine and annexation of Crimea? Probably not. Russia will be exempt from Article 15*bis* referrals, and, as a Permanent Member of the U.N. Security Council, could veto its own referral under Article 15*ter*. Also, if a non-State Party does not rely on building coalition support for its actions, then that non-State Party also will not be impacted by potential concerns of would-be coalition partners.

Will smaller States thinking of invading their neighbor, or sending military incursions into their neighbor's territory be deterred? Here, there is real potential. Again, whether a potential aggressor State Party and potential victim State Party have ratified the amendment will be significant for purposes of Article 15*bis* referrals,[127] but unless the potential aggressor State is a Permanent Member of the U.N. Security Council, the State (whether a State Party or not) cannot be sure it will not have its nationals or crimes committed on its territory be subject to U.N. Security Council referral under Article 15*ter*, and, there-fore, could potentially be deterred. This is a good result.

Will it be harder to form a coalition of willing States for the use of force in situations where the legality of the use of force is debatable? Yes, potentially, and this also is a good result. The United Kingdom very nearly did not join the U.S.-led coalition that supported the 2003 intervention in Iraq (Gulf War II or Operation Iraqi Freedom). High-level U.K. legal advisers had divergent views of the legality of the war, some openly taking the position that it was illegal.[128] With activation of the crime of aggression, one can easily imagine

---

[127] *See supra* note 86 and accompanying text (recent text of resolution could suggest both the aggressor State Party and victim State Party must actively ratify the amendment to be covered by jurisdiction for purposes of Article 15*bis*).

[128] *See, e.g.,* Letter of resignation from Elizabeth Wilmshurst, U.K. Deputy Legal Adviser to Michael Wood, U.K. Legal Adviser (Mar. 18, 2003), *reproduced at Wilmshurst Resignation Letter,* BBC News (Mar. 24, 2005), http://news.bbc.co.uk/2/hi/uk_news/politics/4377605.stm. ("I regret that I cannot agree that it is lawful to use force against Iraq without a second Security Council resolution."). *See also* Spectar, *supra* note 15, at 47 (describing the U.S. position in launching Gulf War II as done "in the absence of substantial legal justification" and showing a "worrisomely lax interpretation of the rules governing the appropriate use of force"). The United States has an (attenuated) argument for legality that relies upon open-ended use of force mandates related to Gulf War I that, it is argued, "revive" with the later breach of the U.N. Security Council–imposed inspections regime imposed in the lead-up to Gulf War II. John B. Bellinger III, *Authority for Use of Force by the United States against Iraq under*

such a debate, in the face of legitimate doubt as to legality, playing out quite differently. Yes, the United Kingdom (in a future scenario) could either (relying on the 2017 ASP activating resolution) never ratify the crime of aggression amendment, or execute an "opt-out" declaration. But note that not all "opt-outs" will be the same. One can imagine an opt-out exercised prior to a well-intended and well-planned *bona fide*[129] humanitarian intervention, with the opt-out executed because, while there are very good arguments why a *bona fide* humanitarian intervention should not be prosecuted before the ICC,[130] the legal adviser desires 100 percent certainty. One can also imagine an opt-out proposed because there is serious concern about whether the endeavor is legal at all – and simply making the argument for the need for an opt-out in the face of a potentially illegal war could provide the required circumspection for the State Party not to join in the use of force. Again, even a use of armed force only bordering on the illegal would not make a strong ICC case, but the uncertainty associated with whether it would or would not be prosecutable could provide helpful circumspection and restraint in the face of a potentially illegal war. The recent 2017 ASP activating resolution that appears to adopt a more limited understanding of the reach of jurisdiction under Article 15*bis*, unfortunately, may cut down on any such potential deterrent impact.

B. *Will There Be ICC Crime of Aggression Cases?*

The ICC's ability to exercise jurisdiction over the crime of aggression may not cause much of an impact on the Court's docket. One of the key goals of international criminal law is to deter crimes. As Louis Henkin has famously written: "The effective legal system, it should be clear, is not the one which punishes the most violators, but rather that which has few violations to punish because the law deters potential violators."[131] The goal of the crime of aggression is not to generate ICC cases, but to deter unwarranted uses of force.

The above analysis also suggests that it may be difficult for there to be crime of aggression cases. First is the issue of jurisdiction; as discussed above, there are many scenarios that simply will not be covered. Second, while the crime covers uses of force short of full-scale "war" it still requires a "manifest"

International Law, Council on Foreign Rel. (Apr. 10, 2003), http://www.cfr.org/world/authority-use-force-united-states-against-iraq-under-international-law/p5862.

[129] *See supra* note 41 (discussing *bona fide*).

[130] *See supra* notes 41 (humanitarian intervention not covered), 113 (affirmative defenses and mitigating factors).

[131] Louis Henkin, How Nations Behave 93 (2d ed. 1979).

Charter violation.[132] Thus, as explained above, anything *de minimis*[133] or unclear in terms of legality[134] will not be encompassed. This is also in line with the purposes of the ICC to prosecute the most serious crimes,[135] as well as the ICC's gravity threshold.[136] Third, the "act of aggression" relies on language agreed upon in 1974, which does not cover cyberwarfare nor attacks by non-state actors (nor any number of untold ways of using force that will be devised in the future).[137] Finally, if the U.N. Security Council maintains that ICC proceedings threaten international peace and security, it may defer the case for twelve-month renewable periods under Rome Statute Article 16.[138]

Yet, the result that there may not be crime of aggression cases is hardly troubling. As noted above, the point is not to prosecute the crime, but that the risk of possible prosecution will have a sufficient cautionary impact to deter state behavior as to illegal, or likely illegal, uses of force. (However, the text of the 2017 ASP activating resolution appears to cut down on such potential deterrent impact, as it would significantly limit the crime's jurisdictional reach).

C. *How Can the Crime of Aggression Accommodate Rapidly Accelerated Developments in* Jus ad Bellum *Norms?*

We currently seem to be in a period where use of force norms have been undergoing rapidly accelerated development, particularly regarding the acceptability of a military response to the armed attack of a non-state actor.[139] Can the ICC crime of aggression accommodate this rapid evolution in these norms?

As noted above, the "manifest" qualifier excludes anything debatable or in a grey area of legality from being prosecuted.[140] By including this "grey area," the crime permits developments in *jus ad bellum* norms to be mirrored in the definition of the crime. For example, as to the acceptability of the use of force in response to the armed attack of a non-state actor, there is support that it

---

[132] *See supra* note 40 (discussing manifest).
[133] *See supra* note 39 (discussing *de minimis*).
[134] *See supra* note 40 (nothing debatable).
[135] *See supra* note 97 (only the most serious crimes).
[136] *See* Rome Statute, *supra* note 1, art. 53(1)(c) (gravity).
[137] *See supra* notes 60 (no cybercrimes), 56 (no crimes by non-state actors). *But see supra* note 57 (whether the list of acts is open-ended).
[138] *See* Rome Statute, *supra* note 1, art. 16.
[139] *See infra* notes 141–44 and accompanying text (discussing current accelerated development of *jus ad bellum* norms).
[140] *See supra* note 40 (nothing debatable).

can be acceptable to respond through individual or collective self-defense.[141] This started with broad endorsement of September 11, 2001, as an "armed attack" that warranted self-defense, even though the attack was perpetrated by a non-state actor.[142] It has continued with the response to armed attacks by the so-called "Islamic State" (also known as ISIL, ISIS, or Daesh), with several countries invoking the doctrine that the government of the country where the threat is located (Syria) is "unwilling or unable" to prevent the use of its territory for such attacks.[143]

Thus, as our understanding of the permissible uses of force changes through the development of the law, the crime of aggression can similarly adapt. What is today's "grey area" may become tomorrow's accepted norm.[144]

---

[141] *See* Green, *supra* note 14, at 237–38 ("changes in state practice have suggested that there may be the beginnings of a paradigm shift in the customary international law toward allowing forcible actions taken in self-defense against non-state actors").

[142] The Security Council "in its first resolutions on the events of September 11, 'recognized the inherent right of individual or collective self-defence in accordance with the Charter.'" Ratner, *supra* note 16, at 909, quoting S.C. Res. 1368, U.N. Doc. S/RES/1368 (Sept. 12, 2001); Pellet, *supra* note 45, at 562 (similar). "[T]he U.S. military intervention in Afghanistan in 2001 ["Operation Enduring Freedom"] was widely viewed as lawful self-defense." STROMSETH, *supra* note 15, at 19. *See also* S.C. Res. 1368, *supra*; S.C. Res. 1373, U.N. Doc. S/RES/1373 (Sept. 28, 2001) (invoking the right of self-defense, thereby implicitly recognizing 9/11 as an "armed attack" although launched by a non-state actor). The ICJ, by contrast, seems distinctly behind the times on this issue. *See* Legal Consequences of the Construction of a Wall in the Occupied Palestinian Territory, Advisory Opinion, 2004 I.C.J. 136, ¶ 139 (July 9) (the inherent right of self-defense only applies "in the case of armed attack by one State against another State."); *but see* Douglas Pivnichny, *The International Court of Justice and the Use of Force*, in this volume.

[143] *See, e.g.*, Letter dated Sept. 23, 2014, from the Permanent Representative of the United States of America to the United Nations addressed to the Secretary-General, U.N. Doc. S/2014/695 (Sept. 23, 2014) (citing Iraq's letter to the U.N. Security Council requesting self-defense from continuing attacks by ISIS operating out of safe havens in Syria, and the U.S. invoking the right to collective self-defense, to assist Iraq, where "the government of the State where the threat is located is unwilling or unable to prevent the use of its territory for such attacks"). There are similar letters from Germany, Australia, Canada, and Turkey. While numerous countries are participating in the air campaign against ISIL, not all endorse the "unwilling or unable" doctrine. *See* Olivier Corten, *The 'Unwilling or Unable' Test: Has It Been, and Could It Be, Accepted?*, 29 LEIDEN J. INT'L L. 777 (2016).

[144] As the Nuremberg judgment states: "This law is not static, but by continual adaption follows the needs of a changing world." 1 TRIAL OF MAJOR WAR CRIMINALS BEFORE THE INTERNATIONAL MILITARY TRIBUNAL, NUREMBERG, 14 NOVEMBER – 1 OCTOBER 1946, Judgment, at 221 (1947), www.loc.gov/rr/frd/Military_Law/pdf/NT_Vol-I.pdf. *See also* Green, *supra* note 14, at 225 ("[J]us ad bellum develops in a dynamic and flexible manner in practice"), 237 ("the system as it stands allows for the legal elasticity required to adapt to the changing world of security threats and forcible action"), 240 ("one can make a strong argument that the rules of the *jus ad bellum* should be free to develop to deal with our changing world").

Thus, while some might argue that use of force in response to an "armed attack" by a non-state actor that the host State is "unwilling or unable" to control is legally acceptable, and some might argue it is not, the result is the same for the crime of aggression – in the face of legitimate uncertainty as to the state of the law, it should not be prosecuted. The "manifest" qualifier thus ensures that nothing that is arguably permissible under use of force norms ends up on the ICC's docket.

D. *Will Ratification of the Crime of Aggression Amendment Influence the Development of Domestic Practice?*

Will States implement the crime of aggression definition into their national laws? A number already have done so.[145] As more States Parties ratify the amendment, they may do so as well. With such ratifications and implementation, it becomes more likely that the crime of aggression amendment adopted in Kampala will come to be recognized as customary international law.[146] Whether there will actually be domestic cases that result is hard to know, because it depends on what the jurisdictional reach will be under the domestic laws, and what forms of aggression will occur in the future.

Would it be good to have a proliferation of crime of aggression cases in domestic courts? This author – who has argued for the adoption of a primacy regime regarding the ICC crime of aggression[147] – maintains that it might be preferable to concentrate expertise in this highly technical area of *jus ad bellum* law before one international court, the ICC, and not risk potentially vengeful national prosecutions. Others appear to agree that the ICC is the best forum.[148]

On the other hand, there is also interesting potential to deter, for example, the actions of a non-State Party that would otherwise be outside the jurisdictional regime of the ICC crime of aggression (e.g., Russia or other States), through domestic criminalization of aggression. It is perhaps not coincidental that early ratifiers of the crime of aggression amendment include Estonia, Lativa,

---

[145] *Status of Ratification and Implementation of the Kampala Amendments on the Crime of Aggression, Update No. 28, supra* note 29.
[146] *But see supra* text accompanying notes 104–109 (discussing Understanding 6).
[147] *See* Jennifer Trahan, *Is Complementarity the Right Approach for the International Criminal Court's Crime of Aggression? Considering the Problem of "Overzealous" National Court Prosecutions*, 45 CORNELL INT'L L.J. 569 (2012); *see also* Trahan, *Kampala Negotiations, supra* note 4, at 89 ("It is conceivable that a botched and/or biased national prosecution or two will make the ICC look like *the preferred forum* for adjudications as to the crime of aggression").
[148] *See* HANDBOOK, *supra* note 45, at 18 (the ICC "is better placed than a single State to exercise the *jus puniendi* of the international community over a crime of aggression").

and Lithuania, and that all three States already had pre-existing domestic laws criminalizing aggression.[149]

E. *Will the ICC's Ability to Exercise Jurisdiction over the Crime of Aggression Jeopardize Humanitarian Intervention?*

As noted above, because of the ability of a State Party that is in doubt about the legality of a proposed use of force to exercise an opt-out declaration – or a partial opt-out declaration, or file an explanatory memorandum upon ratification[150] – or (relying on the recent 2017 ASP activating resolution) to simply never ratify the crime of aggression amendment, there is no reason for a would-be humanitarian intervenor State to refrain from undertaking a *bona fide* humanitarian intervention, which, in any event, would not be prosecutable before the ICC due to the "manifest" qualifier.[151] A non-State Party need have no such concerns regarding the ICC, as it will be exempt from the ICC's crime of aggression jurisdiction, at least under Article 15*bis*.

The Responsibility to Protect, which requires U.N. Security Council authorization for any forceful (pillar 3) intervention,[152] is entirely consonant with the U.N. Charter, and would not constitute the crime of aggression. Only if the actual use of force clearly exceeds the scope of the force authorization could that perhaps be covered; use of force that only arguably exceeds its force authorization would not constitute a "manifest" Charter violation.[153]

V. CONCLUSION

The crime of aggression amendment is an historic accomplishment, building upon the foundations of the early peace movement – centered at the "Peace Palace" (*Vredespaleis*) in The Hague – and the work of the Nuremberg Tribunal. Despite the central role of the prohibition on the aggressive use of force found in Article 2(4) of the U.N. Charter, the world is, and has been,

---

[149] *Status of Ratification and Implementation of the Kampala Amendments on the Crime of Aggression, Update No. 28, supra* note 29.

[150] *See supra* notes 122–123 and accompanying text (partial opt-out or explanatory memorandum).

[151] *See supra* notes 41 and accompanying text (humanitarian intervention not covered), 113 (affirmative defenses and mitigating factors).

[152] *See supra* note 116 and accompanying text.

[153] For added discussion, *see* Trahan, *Grey Area, supra* note 41, text accompanying nn.171, 174. For example, it is sometimes questioned whether NATO's use of force in Libya pursuant to U.N. Security Council Resolution 1973 exceeded the terms of the force authorization.

perpetually at war in one place or another, for time immemorial. Although the use of force can be justifiable under international law, many times it is not, and there are almost inevitably large numbers of victims, "collateral damage," and combatants who suffer even when the laws of war are not violated. While there are limitations to what the rule of law can achieve, activation of the ICC's crime of aggression jurisdiction has the potential to make it somewhat harder to illegally use aggressive force in that it may give some would-be-perpetrators pause about the possibility of being prosecuted, something that has not happened since Nuremberg. And perhaps the limited jurisdictional reach of the crime that appears to be reflected in the 2017 ASP activating resolution can be broadened in future years by added States Parties ratifying the crime of aggression amendment, or in some other way.

While at least one Non-State Party in the past suggested that the ICC crime of aggression jurisdiction should not be activated because the crime criminalizes humanitarian intervention, that arguably distorts the purposes behind the crime of aggression amendment, the negotiating history that requires a "manifest" Charter violation, and a myriad of added arguments why a *bona fide* humanitarian intervention would not make a strong ICC case.

For better or worse, there are actually many conservative features built into the definition of the crime of aggression. The definition is nearly entirely historically derived from earlier texts, meaning the latest *jus ad bellum* challenges are not covered (cyberattacks and attacks by non-state actors). The crime is also hard to trigger, for example, with the "manifest" qualifier requiring clear cases. Yet, that limitation seems entirely appropriate, as the ICC is only charged with prosecuting the worst crimes. Because there now appear to be extensive limitations to the ICC crime of aggression jurisdiction for purposes of Article 15*bis*, there also will be situations in which activation of jurisdiction over the crime at the ICC may not influence State behavior; yet, here domestic incorporation of the definition into national criminal codes has potential to do so, and Security Council referral under Article 15*ter* could also potentially provide some deterrent impact. This author, however, has concerns about the ability of national courts to try high-level crime of aggression cases through impartial trials – and would prefer to concentrate crime of aggression expertise at the ICC. Due to the difficulty of satisfying all of the requirements necessary to bring an ICC crime of aggression case, the ICC's docket will hardly be flooded with cases. Yet, if the ICC's ability to exercise jurisdiction over this crime is able to deter even one launching of illegal force (that is, neither Security Council authorized, individual or collective self-defense, consensual, nor humanitarian), then the crime of aggression amendment will have fulfilled its historic purpose.

14

Prosecuting Aggression Through Other Universal Core Crimes at the International Criminal Court

TERJE EINARSEN

I. INTRODUCTION

One act may constitute several different crimes in "ideal concurrence," because different crime types contain different material elements and protect different legal interests. This feature of domestic criminal law also applies to international criminal law, and for the different crime categories under the Rome Statute of the permanent International Criminal Court (ICC): genocide, crimes against humanity, war crimes, and the crime of aggression.[1] The content of these four crimes are defined in Articles 6–8*bis* respectively. Hence, the ICC Prosecutor and Court may use multiple legal frameworks to address one particular act, or very closely related acts.

This Chapter discusses to what extent it is feasible, and desirable, to prosecute crimes of aggression through the more familiar legal frameworks of crimes against humanity, war crimes, and genocide. How this might be possible is explained subsequently. In the following, "prosecution" is understood in a broad, non-technical sense. It encompasses the work of the Prosecutor and the Court generally by including all the different stages in prosecutorial decision-making from the start of preliminary examinations of situations, to the opening of investigations and charging of individual suspects, the confirmation of charges by the Pre-Trial Chamber, and further on to trial proceedings before the Court, including sentencing.[2]

---

[1] *See* Rome Statute of the International Criminal Court art. 5, *adopted on* July 17, 1998, 2187 U.N.T.S. 91 (entered into force July 1, 2002) [hereinafter Rome Statute].

[2] The concept of prosecution is defined in more narrow terms under some provisions of the Rome Statute, as different from "investigation" and "preliminary examination." *See, e.g.,* Rome Statute *supra* note 1, arts. 15, 53.

Despite the International Military Tribunal (IMT) at Nuremburg proclaiming the initiation of a war of aggression as the "supreme international crime,"[3] no other subsequent international criminal tribunal has been vested with the power to prosecute individuals for aggression. In essence, the definition of a crime of aggression, according to the Rome Statute, Article 8*bis*, consists of three cumulative elements: an *act of aggression* as one of several enumerated types of the use of armed force by a State against another State (i.e., attack by armed forces, invasion, occupation, or blockade), which by its character, gravity, and scale constitutes *a manifest violation of the Charter of the United Nations*, and which has been *planned, prepared, initiated, or executed at the leadership level* by individuals in a position effectively to exercise control over or to direct the political or military action of the aggressive State. However, aggression will most likely remain difficult to prosecute directly in the foreseeable future, because of the *sui generis* jurisdictional regime for the formal prosecution of aggression under the Rome Statute of the ICC.[4]

The question is whether additional prosecutorial strategies should be developed in order to gradually end impunity for the crime of aggression. According to recent strategic planning documents, the ICC Prosecutor has not explicitly addressed this issue.[5] This Chapter nevertheless explores the possibility of taking aggression into account when utilizing the existing legal framework of the ICC as a whole, and in effect, if not formally, *de facto* prosecuting aggression despite lack of explicit and direct *de jure* jurisdiction to investigate, indict, and convict persons with respect to the distinct crime of

---

[3] 1 Trial of Major War Criminals before the International Military Tribunal, Nuremberg, 14 November – 1 October 1946, Judgment, at 186 (1947), www.loc .gov/rr/frd/Military_Law/pdf/NT_Vol-I.pdf [hereinafter IMT Judgment].

[4] The specific jurisdictional regime for the crime of aggression is complicated and its details are beyond the scope of this article. For a useful introduction, *see* Handbook: Ratification and Implementation of the Kampala Amendments to the Rome Statute of the ICC: Crime of Aggression, War Crimes (2013), http://crimeofaggression.info/documents/1/ handbook.pdf.

[5] *See* Office of the Prosecutor, Int'l Criminal Court, Strategic Plan June 2012–2015, at 11 (2013), www.icc-cpi.int/iccdocs/otp/OTP-Strategic-Plan-2013.pdf [hereinafter OTP Strategic Plan 2012–2015]; Office of the Prosecutor, Int'l Criminal Court, Strategic Plan 2016–2018 (2015), www.icc-cpi.int/iccdocs/otp/070715-OTP_Strategic_Plan_ 2016-2018.pdf [hereinafter OTP Strategic Plan 2016–2018]. The term "aggression" does not occur in these documents. It is however noteworthy that the OTP has a strategic goal of developing coordinated international efforts to address other "ancillary crimes" to the core crimes of genocide, crimes against humanity, and war crimes, namely other instances of criminality closely associated with atrocity crimes, such as organized crimes, transnational crimes, financial crimes, and terrorism, which the OTP can only address indirectly to the extent that the perpetrators also commit crimes falling within the ICC's jurisdiction. *See supra* OTP Strategic Plan 2016–2018, at 31–32.

aggression. The thesis is that by actively and systematically focusing on aggression while prosecuting other international crimes, it might be possible for the ICC Prosecutor and the Office of the Prosecutor (OTP) to integrate actual crimes of aggression at all stages of prosecution.

While this Chapter primarily focuses on crimes against humanity, it also includes the other core crimes in order to suggest a more complete prosecutorial strategy that might prove useful for those cases in which crimes against humanity is less suitable. The Chapter proceeds on the assumption that aggression can be lawfully prosecuted in such an indirect way at the ICC without the specific jurisdiction provided for in Articles 15*bis* and 15*ter*, i.e., that such prosecution would be lawful and not constitute an unlawful circumvention of those provisions.

This Chapter is divided into nine Sections. Section II provides a brief contextual background to the prosecution of aggression. Section III clarifies issues relating to the legality principle, while Section IV provides a structured overview of the possible integration of aggression at all stages of prosecution. Section V discusses the illegal use of force as a relevant factor when selecting and prioritizing situations and concrete cases for prosecution. Legal issues when utilizing crimes against humanity, war crimes, and genocide to prosecute aggression are analyzed in Section VI, and in Section VII with respect to modes of liability. Section VIII discusses aggression as an aggravating factor at the sentencing stage upon conviction for a different crime, before a few concluding remarks are offered in Section IX.

II. CONTEXTUAL BACKGROUND

The crime of aggression was prosecuted for the first time under the heading of crimes against peace at Nuremberg and Tokyo in the aftermath of World War II.[6] While it might be questionable whether waging a war of aggression as a matter of international law constituted a crime entailing individual responsibility at the time it was perpetrated, and whether convictions for crimes against peace thus represented an *ex post facto* application of the law,[7] the Nuremberg Tribunal reasoned that if the principle *nullum crimen sine lege* was a principle

---

[6]   *See* Charter of the International Military Tribunal – Annex to the Agreement for the Prosecution and Punishment of the Major War Criminals of the European Axis art. 6(a), Aug. 8, 1945, 82 U.N.T.S. 279 [hereinafter London Charter]. Charter of the International Military Tribunal for the Far East art. 5(a), Jan. 19, 1946, amended Apr. 26, 1946, T.I.A.S. No. 1589 [hereinafter Tokyo Charter].

[7]   Antonio Cassese et al., Cassese's International Criminal Law 25 (3d ed. 2013).

of justice, the unjust response would be to let the acts go unpunished.[8]
By means of the U.N. General Assembly's adoption of Resolution 95(I),[9]
recognizing the principles of international law as defined in the Charter of
the International Military Tribunal at Nuremberg and the Nuremberg jurisprudence, the international community reaffirmed illegal wars as an international crime and its determination to put an end to impunity for aggression
and the atrocities associated with it. This has not stopped States and others
from resorting to the use of military force against other States or against
enemies within States in turmoil or during a state of civil war, and a wide
range of armed conflicts have taken place since 1945.[10] During these international and non-international armed conflicts, in which a crime of aggression under international law may or may not have been committed at some
stage, a substantial number of other serious international crimes have surely
been committed.

International crimes[11] can also be referred to as "universal crimes," essentially because of their inherent gravity and violation of a universal value or
interest.[12] They typically constitute serious transgressions of various social and
moral norms, including human rights. As stated in the Preamble of the Rome
Statute, they are acts that "shock the conscience of humanity," and, furthermore, "threaten the peace, security and well-being of the world." Apart from
aggression, these crimes include, but are not necessarily limited to, genocide,

---

[8] *See* IMT JUDGMENT, *supra* note 3, at 219.

[9] *See* G.A. Res. 95 (I), Affirmation of the Principles of International Law Recognized by the
    Charter of the Nürnberg Tribunal, U.N. Doc. A/RES/1/95(I) (Dec. 11, 1946).

[10] *See, e.g.,* Christine Gray, *The Charter Limitations on the Use of Force: Theory and Practice, in*
    THE UNITED NATIONS SECURITY COUNCIL AND WAR: THE EVOLUTION OF THOUGHTS AND
    PRACTICE SINCE 1945, at 86, 87 (Vaughan Lowe, Adam Roberts & Jenifer Welsh eds., 2008)
    ("[T]here have been over 100 major conflicts since 1945.") *See also id.* app. 7.

[11] The term "international crimes" has been the prevailing concept used to express the special
    character of crimes for which there are individual liability directly under international law,
    which in turn has a number of repercussions. For discussions of the term "international
    crimes," *see, e.g.,* 2 KAI AMBOS, TREATISE ON INTERNATIONAL CRIMINAL LAW: THE CRIMES AND
    SENTENCING 226–45 (2014); M. CHERIF BASSIOUNI, INTRODUCTION TO INTERNATIONAL
    CRIMINAL LAW 137–284 (2d ed. 2013); ROBERT J. CURRIE & JOSEPH RIKHOF, INTERNATIONAL &
    TRANSNATIONAL CRIMINAL LAW 13–22, 107–66, 290–324 (2d ed. 2013) (distinguishing
    "international crimes" from "transnational crimes").

[12] For a discussion of the concepts "international crimes" and "universal crimes" and the criteria
    used to identify proper "universal crimes" under international law, *see generally* TERJE
    EINARSEN, THE CONCEPT OF UNIVERSAL CRIMES IN INTERNATIONAL LAW, (2012) [hereinafter
    EINARSEN, THE CONCEPT OF UNIVERSAL CRIMES]. *See also* Terje Einarsen, *New Frontiers of
    International Criminal Law: Towards a Concept of Universal Crimes,* 1 BERGEN J. CRIM. L. &
    CRIM. JUST. 1 (2013).

crimes against humanity, and war crimes.[13] For the purpose of this Chapter, however, the relevant crimes are confined to the universal core crimes, "the most serious crimes of concern to the international community as a whole."

The legal basis for the crime of aggression had, prior to the Rome Statute, rested on customary international law, general principles of international law, or a combination of both sources. Jurisdiction over the crime of aggression was thus neither included in the Statutes of the *ad hoc* tribunals for the former Yugoslavia (ICTY) and Rwanda (ICTR), nor in the Statutes of the Special Court for Sierra Leone (SCSL), the Special Tribunal for Lebanon (STL), or the Extraordinary Chambers in the Courts of Cambodia (ECCC).

As is evident from the negotiations at the Rome Conference in 1998, the main problems have been related to agreeing upon a definition and jurisdictional prerequisites for the crime of aggression.[14] While the U.N. General Assembly in 1974 managed to adopt a definition of aggression at the interstate level in Resolution 3314,[15] with respect to individual criminal liability the Rome Conference opted to postpone the question to a later date by simply stipulating the future adoption of a definition.[16] This intention was followed up at the Kampala Review Conference where the States Parties adopted a definition of the crime of aggression by consensus, which is now found in Article 8*bis*.

However, this achievement was only possible by once again postponing the Court's ability to exercise jurisdiction over the crime until at the earliest 2017, conditioned on a minimum of thirty state ratifications and adoption by consensus or by a two-thirds majority of the States Parties deciding to activate

---

[13] Different actors and authors of international criminal law have promoted different lists of international crimes at different times. For a comprehensive list of universal crimes *lex lata* and *lex ferenda*, see EINARSEN, THE CONCEPT OF UNIVERSAL CRIMES, *supra* note 12, at 319–28.

[14] *See* Matthew Gillett, *The Anatomy of an International Crime: Aggression at the International Criminal Court*, 13 INT'L CRIM. L. REV. 829, 830 (2013).

[15] G.A. Res. 3314 (XXIX), Definition of Aggression, U.N. Doc. A/RES/29/3314(XXIX) (Dec. 14, 1974). This definition was later integrated into the definition adopted for the Rome Statute at the Kampala Review Conference in 2010.

[16] Rome Statute, *supra* note 1, art. 5, as originally provided for prior to the Kampala Review Conference in 2010. One close observer of the treaty process stated that the compromise solution saved the proposal for the ICC from collapsing, but that it left the crime of aggression in limbo. *See The Prosecutor: Interview with Benjamin Ferencz, in* HEIKELINA VERRIJN STUART & MARLISE SIMONS, THE PROSECUTOR AND THE JUDGE: BENJAMIN FERENCZ AND ANTONIO CASSESE: INTERVIEWS AND WRITINGS 13, 43 (2009) ("That's what they did; they said aggression is in but it's out. Hocus pocus. It's in, but the court can't act on it unless you stand on your head and do all kinds of impossible things").

jurisdiction for the crime.[17] Due to other jurisdictional loopholes and obstacles created by Articles 15*bis* (state referral and *proprio motu*) and 15*ter* (Security Council referral) and the political nature of the matter, effective enforcement of the crime of aggression may be difficult even after the activation of jurisdiction from July 17, 2018 (decided December 14, 2017).[18]

In particular, absent a Security Council referral, nationals of non-States Parties enjoy complete immunity through Article 15*bis*(5),[19] contrary to the jurisdictional regime for the other core universal crimes with respect to crimes committed on the territory of a State Party. It means, for example, that Finland, by ratifying the Kampala Amendments in 2015, will not necessarily in the future enjoy direct legal protection by the ICC against invasion and occupation by a non-State Party.[20] Finland does, however, enjoy protection against simultaneous or subsequent crimes against humanity, war crimes, or genocide, committed by those nationals on Finnish territory.

An additional limitation and issue of interpretation is furthermore caused by Article 121(5), second sentence, read in conjunction with Article 15*bis*(4), which to a larger or lesser degree may provide *de facto* immunity from prosecution of aggression for nationals of States Parties to the Rome Statute that have not accepted the Kampala Amendments.[21]

---

[17] *See* Rome Statute, *supra* note 1, arts. 15*bis* (2)–(3) & 15*ter* (2)–(3); *See also* U.N. Secretary-General, *Depositary Notification*, C.N.651.2010.TREATIES-8 (Nov. 29, 2010), https://treaties .un.org/doc/Publication/CN/2010/CN.651.2010-Eng.pdf (with references also to Rome Statute Articles 121 and 123). As of June 2017, thirty-four States had ratified the amendments on the crime of aggression. *Status of Ratification and Implementation of the Kampala Amendments on the Crime of Aggression, Update No. 27*, CRIME OF AGGRESSION (May 1, 2017), http:// crimeofaggression.info/the-role-of-states/status-of-ratification-and-implementation/.

[18] *See, e.g.*, Donald M. Ferencz, *Aggression in Legal Limbo: A Gap in the Law that Needs Closing*, 12 WASH. U. GLOBAL STUD. L. REV. 507, 511 (2013). For a thorough account, see Claus Kreß & Leonie von Holtzendorff, *The Kampala Compromise on the Crime of Aggression*, 8 J. INT'L CRIM. JUST. 1179 (2010). On activation, *see* Res. ICC-ASP/16/Res.5, Activation of the jurisdiction of the Court over the crime of aggression (Dec. 14, 2017).

[19] This provision states: "In respect of a State that is not a party to this Statute, the Court shall not exercise its jurisdiction over the crime of aggression when committed by that State's nationals or on its territory." Rome Statute, *supra* note 1, art. 15*bis*(5).

[20] It should however be expected that Article 15*bis*(5), which was a political compromise that is legally unnecessary, will be attempted to be deleted when a substantial number of States Parties have ratified the Kampala Amendments because it would be in their interest to be protected by the ICC against non–State Party aggression.

[21] The interpretation of Article 121(5) on amendments' entry into force and consequences for non-accepting States is somewhat unclear. *See* Kreß & Holtzendorff, *supra* note 18, at 1194–99, 1212–16. *See*, however, Res. ICC-ASP/16/Res.5, *supra* note 18, ¶ 2.

It has been noted that the present state of affairs leaves a substantial lacuna in the law,[22] resulting in likely impunity for individuals responsible for breaching international peace and security and causing widespread suffering to the victims of illegal armed force. The best, although small, chance of seeing formal prosecutions for the crime of aggression is presumably by way of a Security Council referral involving an alleged crime of aggression committed by the leaders of a State that is not an ally of any Permanent Member of the U.N. Security Council.[23] The Kampala Amendments may thus represent another stalemate in the current development of international criminal law.[24]

Even though the use of force as a state act is prohibited by Article 2(4) of the U.N. Charter, with the exceptions of the Security Council acting under Chapter VII or in self-defense pursuant to Article 51, it is vital, as noted by the Nuremberg Tribunal, that "crimes against international law are committed by men, not by abstract entities, and only by punishing individuals who commit such crimes can the provisions of international law be enforced."[25] In other words, it is primarily through effective individual criminal responsibility that the crime of aggression can be deterred.

In light of the contemporary status of aggression as a distinct crime, where a clear definition now exists for the purpose of prosecutions at the ICC, while specific indictments and convictions for that particular crime at the same time might be prevented for a long time due to jurisdictional issues, there is arguably a pressing need to develop alternative prosecutorial strategies in order to end impunity. This need is compounded by the fact that waging a war of aggression not only poses a threat to the territorial integrity and autonomy of the victim State, but also jeopardizes international peace and security.

Furthermore, acts of aggression, whether amounting to crimes of aggression or not, create a general context of conflict and unease under which war crimes, crimes against humanity, and even genocide are more likely to occur.[26] It is partly this consequential aspect of aggression that elevates its gravity and led the International Military Tribunal at Nuremberg to label war as "essentially an evil thing" and to initiate a war of aggression "the supreme international crime" and "the accumulated evil of the whole."[27]

---

[22] Donald M. Ferencz, *Aggression in Legal Limbo, supra* note 18, at 507.

[23] *See* Jennifer Trahan, *Defining the "Grey Area" Where Humanitarian Intervention May Not Be Fully Legal, but Is Not the Crime of Aggression*, 2 J. ON USE FORCE & INT'L L. 42, 77–78 (2015).

[24] *See* Benjamin B. Ferencz, *Ending Impunity for the Crime of Aggression*, 41 CASE W. RES. J. INT'L L. 281, 290 (2009).

[25] *See* IMT JUDGMENT, *supra* note 3, at 223.

[26] *See* Gillett, *supra* note 14, at 832.

[27] *See* IMT JUDGMENT, *supra* note 3, at 186.

Although it could be argued that the particularly aggressive and "total" wars waged by the political, industrial, and military leaders of the Nazi government put them in a separate sociological category from other wars, the language of the judgment is not so confined in legal terms. One example of this is the assessment of the invasion and occupation of Norway from 1940 to 1945, discussed *infra* in Section III, which was brutal, but comparatively speaking probably no worse than most other wars, occupations, and individual crimes of aggression outside the World War II context.

Generally, there are different ways of taking aggression into account at the ICC. First, the broader context of aggression may be taken into account as a relevant factor in the gravity assessment for the purpose of selecting or prioritizing which situations and, later, which specific cases are to be investigated and prosecuted before the ICC as alleged crimes against humanity, war crimes or genocide.

Second, the factual matrix required for the elements of the crime of aggression under Article 8*bis* of the Rome Statute to some degree overlap with those of crimes against humanity, making it possible to focus systematically on prosecuting factual instances of aggression through the vehicle of crimes against humanity. In this respect, utilizing co-perpetration as a mode of liability may be a suitable approach to expand liability for foreseeable crimes against humanity to those high-ranking leaders responsible for the initial waging of aggression, although other modes of liability might be applicable as well. Under certain conditions, it might also be possible to utilize war crimes and genocide in a similar vein.

Third, aggression may be taken into account as an aggravating factor in sentencing for the most responsible perpetrators, after a conviction of other universal crimes under the present sentencing framework – for example if it could be established that subsequent crimes against humanity perpetrated at lower levels in a power structure followed as a consequence of a wider plan of aggression at the top. Including the latter as an aggravating factor would then better capture the overall blameworthiness or gravity of the entire criminal enterprise.

III. CLARIFICATIONS RELATING TO THE LEGALITY PRINCIPLE

In developing the strategies for dealing with the crime of aggression in this Chapter, it is necessary to stress that the analysis must be undertaken in compliance with the principle of legality (*nullum crimen nulla poene sine lege*). This entails three aspects: (1) individual criminal liability may not be imposed for acts that did not constitute a crime at the time of their commission; (2) the law must be strictly construed and not extended by analogy; and (3) in case of ambiguities the law shall be interpreted in favor of the accused.[28] At the same time, under general principles of treaty interpretation, the object and purpose of a treaty is a relevant factor when interpreting and applying the law in accordance with Article 31(1) of the Vienna Convention on the Law of Treaties.[29] While the strategies developed must be compatible with the existing legal framework in force at the present time, the object and purpose of the Rome Statute of enhancing "effective prosecution" of "the most serious crimes" – including the crime of aggression – supports innovative approaches within that framework "to put an end to impunity for the perpetrators of these crimes and thus to contribute to the prevention of such crimes."[30]

Partly in order to preserve a reasonable level of foreseeability in securing the best possible adherence to the principle of legality and partly due to the fact that the ICC is the only international criminal court with any prospect of being able to prosecute aggression as a separate crime in the near future, this Chapter limits the analysis to the definition of aggression in Article 8*bis* of the Rome Statute.[31] In order for the use of force by non-state actors to fall within the purview of the ICC Article 8*bis*, the use of force must thus be committed against a relevant state entity and the acts must at least be attributable to a State.[32] Hence Article 8*bis*(2)(g) on non-state actors is limited to the "sending by or on behalf of a State," or "its substantial involvement therein," of armed bands, groups, irregulars, or mercenaries, which carry out acts of armed force against another State of such gravity as to amount to the same acts otherwise defined as acts of aggression. Acts of a fully independent organization, e.g., a terrorist organization independent from any State, thus fall outside the scope

---

[28] *See* Rome Statute, *supra* note 1, art. 22.

[29] *See* Vienna Convention on the Law of Treaties, May 23, 1969, 1155 U.N.T.S. 331. The Court has confirmed "that the interpretation of the statutory provisions is governed by the 1969 Vienna Convention on the Law of Treaties," in particular by Articles 31 and 32. *See* Prosecutor v. Bemba Gombo *et al.*, Case No. ICC-01/05–01/13, Judgment Pursuant to Article 74 of the Statute, ¶ 17 (Oct. 19, 2016), www.icc-cpi.int/CourtRecords/CR2016_18527.PDF [hereinafter Bemba Trial Judgment].

[30] Rome Statute, *supra* note 1, pmbl., ¶¶ 4–5.

[31] While it is possible that this definition may deviate from an arguably somewhat broader definition with respect to perpetrators and/or protected (victim) interests applicable under customary law, this complex issue is not analyzed here. *See* CASSESE, *supra* note 7, at 139–42 (revised by Mary Fan) (arguing that under customary law criminal liability for aggression may also apply for non-state organizations or other organized entities); *see also* LARRY MAY, AGGRESSION AND CRIMES AGAINST PEACE 297–318 (2008) (discussing "Terrorist Aggression" under international law).

[32] *See, e.g.*, Gillett, *supra* note 14, at 840.

of Article 8*bis*. It should be noted, however, that for the purpose of sentencing, it might in principle be possible to take into account crimes other than the core crimes as strictly defined in Articles 6–8*bis* of the Rome Statute, as long as these crimes are substantive crimes under general international law and have also been proven and attributed to the defendant beyond a reasonable doubt at the main trial or sentencing stage (see Section VIII, *infra*).

Thus, in order for aggression to be utilized for the proposed prosecutorial strategies under the current legal framework, the elements, both objective and mental, as defined in Article 8*bis* must be established beyond a reasonable doubt. It must be established that the perpetrator intentionally and knowingly participated in the "planning, preparation, initiation or execution" of an act of aggression while occupying a position "effectively to exercise control over or to direct the political or military action of a State."[33] Liability for the individual further requires that a state "act of aggression," as defined in Article 8*bis*(2), in fact took place, i.e., that a State used armed force against the sovereignty, territorial integrity, or political independence of another State or in any other way inconsistent with the U.N. Charter. The enumerated underlying acts are intended to constitute an act of aggression;[34] however, whether a particular use of force is inconsistent with the U.N. Charter depends on the circumstances. While the starting point is that any use of force against another State not executed in either self-defense or authorized by the U.N. Security Council is illegal,[35] there are many gray areas under international law – it suffices to mention instances of humanitarian intervention, consent by authorities of the territorial (attacked) State, and attacks meant to constitute preemptive self-defense. Another contested issue concerns extraterritorial self-defense by a State against non-state actors (typically terrorist groups) operating from within the territory of a State that is considered "unwilling or unable" to prevent their aggressive acts.[36]

Given that any *act of aggression*, in order to qualify as a *crime of aggression* under Article 8*bis*(1), must satisfy the threshold of a "manifest violation" of the

---

[33] *See* Rome Statute, *supra* note 1, art. 8*bis* read in conjunction with art. 30.
[34] *See* Int'l Criminal Court, *Elements of Crimes*, art. 8*bis*, intro., ¶ 1 (2011) [hereinafter *Elements of Crimes*]. While not further explored in this Chapter, it should be mentioned that it is somewhat contested whether the list of enumerated acts is exhaustive. *Compare* Gillett, *supra* note 14, at 844–45 (arguing that the list should be considered non-exhaustive) *with* Ambos, *supra* note 11, at 202 (holding the principle of legality to require the list to be exhaustive).
[35] *See* U.N. Charter art. 2(4) read in conjunction with arts. 39, 42, 51.
[36] *See* Cassese, *supra* note 7, at 139 (stating that these gray areas are partly what "rendered the criminalization of aggression problematic"). For an in-depth discussion of various legal issues concerned with the legal characterization of the use of force, *see* Christine Gray, International Law and the Use of Force (3d ed. 2008).

U.N. Charter based on its "character, gravity and scale," it would be possible to take the position that all uses of substantial military force not clearly in self-defense or authorized by the Security Council constitute *prima facie*, an act of aggression,[37] and rather assess all the various gray areas under the "manifest" threshold. As for the mental element, the perpetrator need only know the factual circumstances establishing the manifest inconsistency with the U.N. Charter.[38]

It is however also possible to argue that because of its "character," *a genuine humanitarian intervention* can hardly constitute a crime of aggression despite lack of Security Council authorization.[39] A lawful humanitarian intervention may require the use of armed force by one or several States *for the legitimate purpose of defending a civilian population* of another State against crimes against humanity or other grave crimes, carried out *as a last resort and with proportionate means*, and *upon careful consideration of the consequences* of the intervention so that the humanitarian consequences are not likely to be worse than inaction. In principle, these requirements follow by implication from the general rules on self-defense under customary international law; that self-defense must be necessary and proportionate.[40] Under the legality principle of the Rome Statute, Article 22(2), the definition of the crime of aggression shall be strictly construed, and in case of ambiguity be interpreted in favor of the accused. As long as a reasonable doubt exists with respect to the lawfulness of a proclaimed humanitarian intervention, including armed interventions based

[37] This position has been indicated by the International Court of Justice (ICJ) on several occasions. *See, e.g.,* Military and Paramilitary Activities in and Against Nicaragua (Nicar. v. U.S.), Judgment, 1986 I.C.J. 14, ¶ 268 (June 27); Armed Activities on the Territory of the Congo (Dem. Rep. Congo v. Uganda), Judgment, 2005 I.C.J. 126, ¶ 152 (Dec. 19).; Legality of the Threat or Use of Nuclear Weapons, Advisory Opinion, 1996 I.C.J. 95 (July 8).

[38] *See Elements of Crimes, supra* note 34, art. 8*bis*, intro., ¶¶ 2, 4, elements 4, 6.

[39] *See also* Trahan, *supra* note 23, at 69–73. As a matter of principle, any Security Council resolution authorizing use of military force should provide or be followed by clearly stated reasons why intervention is considered to be a last resort, why it is necessary, and why it is likely to produce consequences no worse than inaction, as well as limits with respect to the proportionate means to be employed during the operations if no additional Security Council authorization is later provided.

[40] On the core of self-defense and "that necessity and proportionality are limits on all self-defence, individually or collectively," *see* GRAY; *supra* note 36, 148–55 (especially 150), with reference *inter alia* to several cases before the ICJ. To defend another (third) person (or a group of persons) in a manner proportionate to the degree of danger to that person against an imminent and unlawful use of force constitutes a ground for excluding criminal responsibility. Rome Statute, *supra* note 2, art. 31(1)(c). When a State uses armed force for the humanitarian purpose to defend a civilian group in another State, without being under attack itself, it is logical that the intervention must be required not to lead to worse humanitarian consequences in the ordinary course of events.

on the doctrine of the "Responsibility to Protect" (R2P), individual criminal responsibility for the political and military leaders planning or executing the intervention would be ruled out. Hence, if crimes against humanity or genocide were ongoing or an imminent threat against a civilian population existed, factual and legal doubt existing upon examination as to whether the conditions for a humanitarian intervention were fulfilled should bar any criminal responsibility.

With respect to *proclaimed self-defense* constituting an act of aggression, i.e., an attack by the armed forces of the territory of another State, a thorough investigation into its rationale, the necessity, and the proportionality of the means employed, may on the other hand be required in order to meaningfully assess its lawfulness and possibly criminal nature. In such cases, the "character" of the act might well be criminal by nature. As stated by the International Military Tribunal with respect to the German attack on Norway in 1940:

> It must be remembered that preventive action in foreign territory is justified only in case of "an instant and overwhelming necessity for self-defence, leaving no choice of means, and no moment of deliberation (The Caroline Case, *Moore's Digest of International Law*, II, 412.)."[41]

The strict criteria for the legal use of force are noteworthy, including the "overwhelming necessity" standard. In addition, the importance of the purpose and the time factor – the preventing of an *imminent* attack – was further highlighted by the International Military Tribunal:

> From all this it is clear that when the plans for an attack on Norway were being made, they were not made for the purpose of forestalling an imminent Allied landing, but, at the most, that they might prevent an Allied occupation at some future date.[42]

The formula adopted by the Tribunal might be applicable to contemporary international law also in cases where the government of a State during a national emergency or threatening security situation is consenting to an armed intervention by another State, or where the government is "unwilling or unable" to prevent an organization or a party to a civil war in that country from constituting a threat to vital interests of another State. The point is that the use of force in all cases of individual state or collective state self-defense

---

[41] IMT JUDGMENT, *supra* note 3, at 207.

[42] *Id.* The International Military Tribunal concluded that the invasion of Norway, along with the invasion of Denmark, "were acts of aggressive war," not defensive operations. *Id.* at 209. The defendants had not argued that there was "any plan by any belligerent other than Germany, to occupy Denmark." *Id.* at 208.

must be lawful under the U.N. Charter and must not by itself constitute aggression or result in other serious international crimes.

However, situations involving a combination of a prior attack by an adversary State, or by a non-state power structure, i.e., in the form of a terrorist attack, and retaliation or proclaimed preventive action against that State or non-state actor, in order to preempt new imminent attacks, are more difficult to assess with respect to lawfulness. Such acts may thus – in light of the legality principle – not so easily lead to any individual criminal liability for the leaders of the responding State or States. Again, the military action undertaken under these circumstances may not have the "character" of aggression, as long as the responding State is not taking advantage of the prior attack for other self-interested purposes. But in these situations as well, the means employed must be proportionate to any legitimate aim pursued, in particular with respect to damage to civilians and civilian objects.

Limiting the analysis to the definition in Article 8*bis* inevitably entails that some situations will be excluded from proposed prosecutorial strategies to deal with aggression. In particular, since Article 8*bis*(2) limits the definition of an act of aggression to the "use of armed force *by a State* against the sovereignty, territorial integrity or political independence of *another State*" (emphasis added), it effectively excludes most situations of civil war, and terrorist acts or other aggressive attacks committed by independent non-state actors.[43] This might actually be seen as a weakness of Article 8*bis* in the sense that it is more accommodated to classic interstate armed conflicts, whereas civil wars and acts of aggression or terrorism by non-state actors are more common today. However, aggression clearly within the parameters of Article 8*bis* has not completely disappeared, and may become more frequent again. Furthermore, there will be certain gray areas, including instances in which the legal characteristics of an armed conflict or the parties involved may change during the course of the conflict. An example is where an initial civil war leads to the breakup of the original territory into separate entities, as was the case in the former Yugoslavia during the wars there in 1992–95. Another relevant situation is the current one in the Middle East, where for instance the uncertain status of Palestine as an independent State causes some doubts as to the applicability

---

[43] With respect to terrorist attacks presumably planned or facilitated by the leadership of a non-state organization, such as the September 11, 2001, attacks on the United States and the more recent attacks on France in 2015, the question may however arise whether such attacks may constitute crimes of aggression under *customary international law* and as such could be taken into account in the future by the ICC Prosecutor and Court when prosecuting the same leaders for other core crimes.

of Article 8*bis* to the Israel/Palestine conflict.[44] Similar types of situations will have to be resolved by the Court on a case-by-case basis.

Although war crimes and the crime of aggression both contain an inherent element of armed force, their general fields of application to war-like situations do not completely overlap. Hence there are certain situations where the act of aggression may constitute a "manifest violation" of the U.N. Charter,[45] while at the same time not meeting the general threshold for an "armed conflict" required for war crimes under Article 8 of the Statute.[46] Following established case law, an armed conflict "exists whenever there is a resort to armed force between States or protracted armed violence between governmental authorities and organized armed groups or between such groups within a State,"[47] and where in particular the intensity of the conflict and the level of organization of the conflicting parties are important criteria in establishing that the threshold is met.[48] Thus, for example, an invasion of the territory of another State by military forces may constitute a manifest violation of the U.N. Charter;[49] however, if little or no organized resistance meets the invasion, the general threshold for armed conflict might not be satisfied. Similarly, if initial armed resistance of the victim State has ceased and the situation has turned into a prolonged unlawful occupation, there may still be an ongoing crime of aggression, although there is no longer any protracted armed violence.

Despite these points of departure, important exceptions apply that bring the two sets of rules back on the same track. For instance, a military occupation of another State both constitutes and continues an international armed conflict. The war crimes provisions of Article 8(2)(a) and (b) of the Rome Statute thus

---

[44] Given that Palestine recently has been accepted as a State Party to the Rome Statute, it seems however logical that this State Party must be considered a "State" also for the purpose of Article 8*bis*.

[45] *See* Rome Statute, *supra* note 1, art. 8*bis*(1).

[46] With respect to certain acts of occupation and blockade, *see infra*.

[47] Prosecutor v. Tadić, Case No. IT-94-1, Decision on the Defence Motion for Interlocutory Appeal on Jurisdiction, ¶ 70 (Oct. 2, 1995), www.icty.org/x/cases/tadic/acdec/en/51002.htm [hereinafter Tadić Decision on Interlocutory Appeal]. *See also* Prosecutor v. Lubanga, ICC-01/04-01/06-2842, Judgment Pursuant to Art. 74 of the Statute, ¶¶ 531-33 (Mar. 14, 2012) [hereinafter Lubanga Trial Judgment]; Prosecutor v. Katanga, ICC-01/04-01/07-3436, Judgment Pursuant to Art. 74 of the Statute, ¶ 1173 (Mar. 7, 2014) [hereinafter Katanga Trial Judgment] (both judgments citing the *Tadić* decision with respect to the threshold for armed conflict under Article 8 of the Rome Statute).

[48] *See* Prosecutor v. Boškoski, Case No. IT-04-82-A, Appeals Judgment, ¶ 21 (May 19, 2010) (drawing upon the *Tadić* decision and with reference to internal armed conflicts) [hereinafter Boškoski Appeals Judgment].

[49] Rome Statute, *supra* note 1, art. 8*bis* (1)-(2)(a).

also apply under military occupation according to a reasonable interpretation of the Rome Statute, taking into account also the Elements of Crimes,[50] regardless of the general threshold for armed conflict.[51] Whether a blockade by armed force under Article 8*bis*(2)(c) is also included in the term "international armed conflict" in Article 8(2) is not made clear in the Elements of Crimes. However, it is difficult to see why a blockade by armed forces should not be included as well if the blockade constitutes a manifest violation of the U.N. Charter.[52]

In other situations, where the threshold of protracted violence or the conditions for an international armed conflict are not met, the only prosecutorial possibility to address an initial crime of aggression would presumably be through the vehicle of crimes against humanity. If, on the other hand, the threshold for armed conflict is met, and possibly also the conditions for a crime of aggression, while the main focus of the prosecution is rather on prosecuting one or more of the other core universal crimes, this Chapter will also suggest a possibility for integrating the initial crime of aggression into the prosecution of one particular type of war crime.[53]

Finally, although possible from a practical and prosecutorial point of view, as further discussed below, are the Court and the Prosecutor *prohibited* from taking crimes of aggression into account in their respective future work before all the formal jurisdictional requirements are met? Would any such step by the Prosecutor violate the legality principle, or the Rome Statute as a whole? What is absolutely clear is that the Prosecutor cannot indict any person before all the necessary jurisdictional requirements are met, and the Court obviously cannot convict a defendant for a crime without an indictment. But are there also further legal limitations flowing from the current jurisdictional regime in Articles 15*bis* and *ter*?

The first five paragraphs of Article 15*bis* are addressed to the Court, whereas the next three are addressed to the Prosecutor. Paragraph 6 concerns the situation where "the Prosecutor concludes that there is a reasonable basis to

---

[50] *See* Rome Statute, *supra* note 1, art. 21(1) (on the legal status of the Elements of Crimes as a source of interpretation).

[51] *See Elements of Crimes*, *supra* note 34, art. 8(2)(a)(i), element 4 n.34 ("The term 'international armed conflict' includes military occupation. This footnote also applies to the corresponding element in each crime under article 8(2)(a).") Why an explicit reference to Article 8(2)(b) is not made in the same footnote, or in a different footnote is not explained. There is however no reason to make a principled distinction between letter (a) and letter (b) in this regard. The absence of a reference to letter (b) might be due to the fact that the crimes under (b) in most cases only occur during protracted armed violence.

[52] *See* Rome Statute, *supra* note 2, art. 8*bis*(1).

[53] *See infra* Section VI(B).

proceed with an investigation in respect of a crime of aggression." If so, the Prosecutor must take certain steps and notify the Secretary-General of the U.N. "of the situation before the Court, including any relevant information and documents." The provision presupposes that the Court may eventually exercise jurisdiction "over the crime of aggression in accordance with Article 13, paragraphs (a) and (c)," subject to the provisions of Article 15*bis*.[54] These provisions, however, are concerned with the formal jurisdiction to investigate, indict, and eventually convict a person at the ICC for the specific crime of aggression, and only as such fall within the scope of Articles 15*bis* and *ter*, and the legality principle of Article 22.

In other words, Articles 15*bis* and *ter* should not be construed as prohibiting the Prosecutor and eventually the Court from taking aggression *into account* in their decision-making. Otherwise prosecutorial and judicial powers of discretion would now and in the future be actually more limited than before the Kampala Amendments were adopted, since the crime of aggression was included already in Article 5 the Rome Statute of 1998 and no doubt was a universal crime before 2010.[55]

IV. INTEGRATING AGGRESSION AT ALL STAGES OF THE PROSECUTION

The main object of this Chapter is to suggest possible prosecutorial strategies where the factual matrix of aggression could systematically be incorporated into all stages of investigation and prosecution of other crimes over which the ICC clearly has jurisdiction, in particular, focusing on crimes against humanity.

Prosecuting international crimes at the ICC in general involves four different stages:

(1) preliminary examination of situations,
(2) investigation of alleged concrete crimes,
(3) selection of cases and accused individuals for court prosecution,
(4) trial proceedings including eventual sentencing.

---

[54] *See* Rome Statute, *supra* note 2, art. 15*bis*(1).
[55] In the words of the former British senior law lord Lord Thomas Bingham of Cornhill in a case before the U.K. Supreme Court (then House of Lords) in 2006, "the core elements of the crime of aggression have been understood, at least since 1945, with sufficient clarity to permit the lawful trial (and, on conviction, punishment) of those accused of this most serious crime." R. v. Jones [2006] UKHL 16 [19].

Prosecuting international crimes before the ICC starts with steps toward the initiation of an investigation, in the form of a *preliminary examination* into a particular situation as to whether there are grounds to proceed with further procedural steps.[56] Once a situation has been identified, Article 53(1)(a)–(c) establishes the legal framework. At this first stage the Office of the Prosecutor (OTP) does not enjoy investigative powers, and its findings are preliminary in nature. The purpose of the examination is to decide whether the information available to the Prosecutor provides "a reasonable basis to believe that a crime within the jurisdiction of the Court has been or is being committed."[57]

The Prosecutor is obliged to initiate an investigation and move to the second stage unless it is determined that there "is no reasonable basis to proceed" under the Rome Statute.[58] This decision may warrant assessments of *jurisdiction* (material, temporal, and either territorial or personal jurisdiction),[59] whether *the evidentiary threshold* is met,[60] *admissibility* (complementarity, double jeopardy, and gravity thresholds),[61] and whether an investigation would not serve the *interests of justice*.[62] The point for our purpose is that a possible formal prosecution of, e.g., crimes against humanity, in the form of a preliminary examination, must satisfy these requirements.

In assessing whether to proceed to the investigative stage, the OTP has developed a filtering process comprising *four consecutive phases*.[63] In phase one, the OTP conducts an initial assessment of all information collected or received on alleged crimes and filters out information on crimes that are outside the jurisdiction of the Court. Since the crime of aggression is within the subject-matter jurisdiction of the Court under Article 5(d) of the Rome Statute, information on this crime should not be immediately filtered out. Phase two represents the formal commencement of a preliminary examination with a focus on the preconditions of jurisdiction and a thorough factual

---

[56] OFFICE OF THE PROSECUTOR, INT'L CRIMINAL COURT, POLICY PAPER ON PRELIMINARY EXAMINATIONS (2013), www.icc-cpi.int/iccdocs/otp/OTP-Policy_Paper_Preliminary_ Examinations_2013-ENG.pdf [hereinafter 2013 OTP POLICY PAPER ON PRELIMINARY EXAMINATIONS]; *see also* OFFICE OF THE PROSECUTOR, INT'L CRIMINAL COURT, REPORT ON PRELIMINARY EXAMINATION ACTIVITIES (2015), www.icc-cpi.int/iccdocs/otp/OTP-PE-rep-2015-Eng.pdf [hereinafter 2015 OTP REPORT ON PRELIMINARY EXAMINATION ACTIVITIES].
[57] Rome Statute, *supra* note 1, art. 53(1)(a). On the reasonable basis standard, *see* 2015 OTP REPORT ON PRELIMINARY EXAMINATION ACTIVITIES, *supra* note 56, at 3–4.
[58] Rome Statute, *supra* note 1, art. 53(1).
[59] *Id.* art. 53(1)(a).
[60] *Id.*
[61] *Id.* art. 53(1)(b) read in conjunction with art. 17(a)–(d).
[62] *Id.* art. 53(1)(c). *See also* 2015 OTP REPORT ON PRELIMINARY EXAMINATION ACTIVITIES, *supra* note 56, at 2–5.
[63] 2015 OTP REPORT ON PRELIMINARY EXAMINATION ACTIVITIES, *supra* note 56, at 4–5.

and legal assessment of the alleged crimes with a view to identifying potential cases falling within the formal jurisdiction of the Court for a possible conviction. The alleged crimes for our purpose must be crimes against humanity (or war crimes or genocide).

Phase three focuses on the admissibility of potential cases in terms of complementarity and gravity. *Complementarity* involves an examination of the existence of relevant national proceedings in relation to the potential cases considered for investigation by the OTP, bearing in mind its general prosecutorial strategy of investigating and prosecuting (in a technical sense) those "most responsible for the most serious crimes."[64] This strategy implies investigating military and political leaders if they are suspected of being criminally involved in crimes against humanity. It is also very much compatible with taking aggression into account, since the group of responsible leaders might be the same in both respects and because national prosecutions of political and military leaders would usually not be realistic. *Gravity* includes an assessment of the scale, nature, manner of commission of the crimes, and their impact, bearing in mind the potential cases that would likely arise from an investigation of the situation.[65] While mid-level leaders and notorious low-level perpetrators might be the most responsible for the commission of crimes against humanity at particular crime scenes, it is when the leaders at the top of the relevant power structures are involved as planners, decision makers, or commanders that the most grave crimes are typically committed. This implies that possible crimes of aggression committed at the leadership level should be a relevant consideration with regard to assessment of gravity as well as complementarity. In this third phase the OTP will continue to collect information on subject-matter jurisdiction, when new or ongoing crimes are alleged to have been committed within the situation.[66] If some or all of the alleged crimes are committed within a context of aggression, or are closely connected to – or may simultaneously constitute – acts of aggression, this may impact the gravity assessment as a possible aggravating factor.

Finally, then, phase four examines the "interests of justice" consideration in order to formulate the final recommendation to the Prosecutor on whether there is a reasonable basis to initiate an investigation. It is hard to imagine from a "justice" point of view that a context of aggression might

[64] *Id.* at 2–3. *See also* OTP STRATEGIC PLAN 2012–2015, *supra* note 5.
[65] *See, e.g.,* Rome Statute, *supra* note 1, art. 53(1)(c); Office of the Prosecutor, Int'l Criminal Court, *Regulations of the Office of the Prosecutor*, Regulation 29(2) (Apr. 23, 2009) [hereinafter OTP, *Regulations of the Office of the Prosecutor*]. *See also* 2015 OTP REPORT ON PRELIMINARY EXAMINATION ACTIVITIES, *supra* note 56, at 3.
[66] 2015 OTP REPORT ON PRELIMINARY EXAMINATION ACTIVITIES, *supra* note 56, at 5.

weigh against prosecution of crimes against humanity. To the contrary, a context of aggression likely weighs in favor of investigation and prosecution considering the interests of victims and the increased gravity of the crimes, although in some cases where, for instance, a peace process that may include genuine justice mechanisms as a critical part of sustainable peace is ongoing, perhaps further prosecutorial steps should be at least temporarily deferred until the provisions of the agreement have been carefully reviewed.[67]

If an investigation is eventually opened and the process thus moves to the second stage, and it is, upon investigation, concluded that relevant crimes have been committed, decisions on the selection and prioritization of particular cases of crimes against humanity and identification of individual suspects that are to be indicted and sought to be prosecuted before the Court have to be made (the third stage). In this respect, too, the gravity of the crime(s) is a central factor in that it is a criterion in the Pre-Trial Chamber's ensuing assessment of the admissibility of a specific case under Article 17(1)(d). The factors that guide the Court's as well as the OTP's assessment of gravity include both quantitative and qualitative considerations, typically relating to the scale, nature, manner of commission, and impact of the crimes.[68] However, given that many cases might potentially be admissible under Article 17, the OTP may apply a stricter test when assessing gravity for the purposes of case selection than that which is legally required for the admissibility test under Article 17.[69] A context of aggression might thus in theory be important for the assessment.

The fourth and last stage is prosecuting the selected cases and individuals before the Court and, if the Court returns a guilty verdict, to decide on the appropriate sentence for the crime in question. In this respect, too, gravity constitutes an integral part of the assessment of the overall blameworthiness of the accused's conduct by the Prosecutor, defense lawyers, and the judges, ranging from considering the role and contribution of the accused, including the appropriate mode of perpetration, to sentencing.[70]

---

[67] *Id.* at 38–39, ¶¶ 163, 167 (with respect to the peace process in Colombia).

[68] *See* OFFICE OF THE PROSECUTOR, INT'L CRIMINAL COURT, POLICY PAPER ON CASE SELECTION AND PRIORITISATION (2016), www.icc-cpi.int/itemsDocuments/20160915_OTP-Policy_Case-Selection_Eng.pdf [hereinafter 2016 OTP CASE SELECTION POLICY], at 12–13, ¶¶ 32, 37; Situation in the Democratic Republic of the Congo, No. ICC-01/04-169, Judgment on the Prosecutor's Appeal Against the Decision of Pre-Trial Chamber I entitled "Decision on the Prosecutor's Application for Warrants of Arrest, Article 58", ¶¶ 69–79 (July 13, 2006).

[69] 2016 OTP CASE SELECTION POLICY, at 13, ¶ 36.

[70] *See* Rome Statute, *supra* note 1, art. 78(1); Prosecutor v. Lubanga, ICC-01/04-01/06, Decision on Sentence Pursuant to Article 76 of the Statute, ¶ 36 (July 10, 2012), www.icc-cpi.int/CourtRecords/CR2012_07409.PDF (listing gravity as one of the main factors in sentencing, held as "one of the principle factors") [hereinafter Lubanga Sentencing Decision].

At this point it suffices to note that the notion of gravity forms an integral part of all stages of prosecuting international crimes before the ICC. The notion of gravity is also central when possibly integrating the crime of aggression in the different stages of prosecuting other crimes as part of a future prosecutorial strategy. In general, the core legal considerations underlying such a policy would be that the illegal use of force may serve to aggravate the gravity of the whole crime complex. In the next Section, the potential and problematic aspects of such a strategy are discussed in more detail.

V. SELECTING AND PRIORITIZING SITUATIONS AND CASES

Following the Preamble and the jurisdictional limitation expressed in Article 5 of the Rome Statute, the ICC was intended to focus on the "most serious crimes of concern to the international community as a whole." In order to make sure that the situations and cases actually investigated and prosecuted are limited to these most serious crimes, both the OTP and the Court are required to assess given situations and specific cases as to whether they entail sufficient gravity to justify further attention.[71] As noted above, this includes assessing the scale, nature, and the manner of commission and impact of the crimes.[72] With respect to the criteria of manner and impact, these are further elaborated in the 2013 OTP Policy Paper on Preliminary Examinations, as follows:

> The manner of commission of the crimes may be assessed in light of, *inter alia*, the means employed to execute the crime, the degree of participation and intent of the perpetrator (if discernible at this stage), the extent to which the crimes were systematic or result from a plan or organised policy or otherwise resulted from the abuse of power or official capacity, and elements of particular cruelty, including the vulnerability of the victims, any motives involving discrimination, or the use of rape and sexual violence as a means of destroying groups. . . .
>
> The impact of crimes may be assessed in light of, *inter alia*, the sufferings endured by the victims and their increased vulnerability; the terror subsequently instilled, or the social, economic and environmental damage inflicted on the affected communities.[73]

---

[71] Rome Statute, *supra* note 1, arts. 53(1),17(1)(d).
[72] *See* OTP, *Regulations of the Office of the Prosecutor, supra* note 65, regulation 29(2), at 9; 2016 OTP CASE SELECTION POLICY, *supra* note 68, at 13.
[73] *See* 2013 OTP POLICY PAPER ON PRELIMINARY EXAMINATIONS, *supra* note 56, ¶¶ 64–65.

For the purpose of our analysis it is interesting to note that in the 2016 OTP Policy Paper on Case Selection and Prioritisation, "the destruction of the environment" is also mentioned with respect to *the manner of commission*, and that the element of the social, economic, and environmental damage with respect to *impact* is further elaborated.[74] Hence the OTP "will give particular consideration to prosecuting Rome Statute crimes that are committed by means of, or that result in, *inter alia*, the destruction of the environment, the illegal exploitation of natural resources or the illegal dispossession of land."[75] Although references are made to Articles 8(2)(b)(ix) and 8(2)(e)(iv) of the Rome Statute,[76] on attacks against certain buildings and places that should not be attacked intentionally, it is clear that these provisions do not concern destruction of the environment, illegal exploitation of natural resources, or illegal dispossession of land, as such. The OTP, therefore, seems to suggest that such other, possibly distinct, international crimes under customary international law, which in the future may also include, e.g., serious acts of governmental corruption or embezzlement,[77] may provide a context of increased gravity when assessing war crimes or crimes against humanity for case selection. Hence a context of aggression should be considered relevant as well by the OTP for this purpose.

With respect to possible leadership crimes, it is noteworthy that included among other factors potentially relevant to assessment of aggression are "the degree of participation and intent of the perpetrator" and the extent to which the crimes are resulting "from the abuse of power or official capacity."[78] In the 2016 OTP Policy Paper on Case Selection and Prioritisation, the degree of responsibility of the alleged perpetrators is even more emphasized, in particular with respect to those persons who appear to be the most responsible for the identified crimes.[79] Typically, but not necessarily, this will include the persons at the leadership level of a state or non-state organization (power structure) involved in the crimes being committed.[80] Furthermore, the responsibility of commanders and other superiors under Article 28 of the Rome Statute offers a

---

[74] *See* 2016 OTP CASE SELECTION POLICY, *supra* note 68, at 14.

[75] *Id.*

[76] *Id.* at 14 n.40.

[77] In EINARSEN, THE CONCEPT OF UNIVERSAL CRIMES, *supra* note 12, at 328, serious acts of willful damage to the environment, serious acts of pillaging of natural resources, or destruction or pillage of national treasuries, and serious acts of governmental corruption, theft, or embezzlement, when committed, organized, or tolerated at the leadership level of the relevant power structure, are listed as universal crimes *lex ferenda* that later on might be elevated to *lex lata* status under customary international law, depending on legal developments.

[78] *See* 2013 OTP POLICY PAPER ON PRELIMINARY EXAMINATIONS, *supra* note 56.

[79] *See* 2016 OTP CASE SELECTION POLICY, *supra* note 68, at 14.

[80] *Id.*

critical tool to ensure the principle of responsible command, and thereby end impunity for crimes and contribute toward their prevention.[81]

Thus, it is evident that in assessing gravity the existing framework allows for taking into account a wide range of factors. This is also reflected in the Court's jurisprudence, which has rejected formalistic approaches to admissibility.[82] Rather, the Court has favored a flexible approach assessing the entirety of the situation, taking into account a wide range of both quantitative and qualitative factors.[83] The Court has accepted that aggravating circumstances intended for sentencing are equally relevant for admissibility. Pre-Trial Chamber II stated that

> In making its assessment, the Chamber considers that gravity may be examined following a quantitative as well as a qualitative approach. Regarding the qualitative dimension, it is not the number of victims that matter but rather the existence of some aggravating or qualitative factors attached to the commission of crimes, which makes it grave. When considering the gravity of the crime(s), several factors concerning sentencing as reflected in rule 145(1)(c) and (2)(b)(iv) of the Rules, could provide useful guidance in such an examination. These factors could be summarized as: (i) the scale of the alleged crimes (including assessment of geographical and temporal intensity); (ii) the nature of the unlawful behavior or of the crimes allegedly committed; (iii) the employed means for the execution of the crimes (i.e., the manner of their commission); and (iv) the impact of the crimes and the harm caused to victims and their families. In this respect, the victims' representations will be of significant guidance for the Chamber's assessment.[84]

It is under this flexible approach to the gravity assessment that the existence of aggression may be utilized by the OTP as the first part of a prosecutorial strategy for integrating the crime into the existing legal framework. In

---

[81] *Id.* at 15.

[82] *See* Situation in the Democratic Republic of the Congo, No. ICC-01/04, Decision on the Prosecutor's Application for Warrants of Arrests, ¶¶ 73–79 (July 13, 2006), www.icc-cpi.int/CourtRecords/CR2006_01807.PDF.

[83] *See, e.g.*, Situation in the Republic of Kenya, No. ICC-01/09, Decision on the Authorization of an Investigation, ¶ 62 (Mar. 31, 2010), https://www.icc-cpi.int/Pages/record.aspx?docNo=ICC-01/09-19-Corr [hereinafter Kenya Authorization of Investigation]; Prosecutor v. Abu Garda, Case No. ICC-02/05–02/09, Decision on the Confirmation of Charges, ¶ 31 (Feb. 8, 2010), www.icc-cpi.int/CourtRecords/CR2010_00753.PDF [hereinafter Abu Garda Confirmation of Charges]. For a more elaborated account, *see* Margaret M. DeGuzman, *The International Criminal Court's Gravity Jurisprudence at Ten*, 12 WASH. U. GLOBAL STUD. L. REV. 475 (2013).

[84] Kenya Authorization of Investigation, *supra* note 83, ¶ 62 (internal citations omitted). *See also* Abu Garda Confirmation of Charges, *supra* note 83, ¶ 32; Prosecutor v. Muthaura, Case No. ICC-01/09–02/11, Decision on the Confirmation of Charges, ¶ 50 (Jan. 23, 2012), www.icc-cpi.int/CourtRecords/CR2012_01006.PDF.

performing its preliminary investigation, the OTP, in addition to investigating possible crimes against humanity, war crimes, or genocide, may also systematically focus attention on establishing whether the factual situation satisfies the elements of aggression as provided in Article 8*bis*. This includes considering acts of aggression as well as the threshold of a manifest violation of the U.N. Charter. If it could be established that the crimes within the full jurisdiction of the ICC may have taken place within a wider context of aggression, this extraterritorial aspect could be viewed as elevating the gravity of the situation and thus constitute an argument justifying further investigation. In respect of war crimes this seems particularly relevant in that Article 8(1) states that "[t]he Court shall have jurisdiction in respect of war crimes in particular when committed as part of a plan or policy or as part of a large-scale commission of such crimes." Although this is usually taken to refer to the planning and amount of war crimes as such (*jus in bello*), it is hard to see why acts of war crimes committed as an integral part of a plan to attack another State within the meaning of Article 8*bis* (*jus ad bellum*) should not also be relevant for the jurisdiction of the Court *in particular* with respect to such war crimes, or to the Prosecutor when considering the gravity of a situation as a whole or when selecting specific cases for investigation and prosecution.

Consequently, the presence of aggression in a situation could inform its gravity through several of the explicitly mentioned factors, i.e., misuse of official power or capacity, geographical intensity of the crime complex in the form of its extraterritorial aspect, and the fact that the crimes in question were a foreseeable result of the conditions created by the aggression and, thus, formed part of a wider criminal plan or organized policy. If it is quite clear that an *act of aggression* was committed as part of a criminal enterprise entailing sufficient evidence of war crimes or crimes against humanity, and there are grounds to believe that a *crime of aggression* has been committed as well, it would be justifiable to include aggression in the overall gravity analysis at the preliminary examination stage with a view to a possible investigation of the relevant core crimes.

A recent ICC Pre-Trial Chamber decision in the *Mavi Marmara* case lends some support to this line of reasoning. The Pre-Trial Chamber had been requested by the Union of the Comoros to review a decision by the Prosecutor not to initiate an investigation into the situation earlier referred to the Prosecutor by the Comoros "with respect to the 31 May 2010 Israeli raid on the Humanitarian Aid Flotilla bound for Gaza Strip."[85] It is noteworthy that the

---

[85] Situation on the Registered Vessels of the Union of the Comoros, the Hellenic Republic and the Kingdom of Cambodia, No. ICC-01/13, Decision on the Request of the Union of the

Prosecutor, in her decision not to investigate for lack of sufficient gravity for all potential cases within the situation, had determined that there was a reasonable basis to believe that some war crimes had been committed by Israeli forces during the event, and that "if the blockade of Gaza by Israel is to be deemed unlawful, also intentionally directing an attack against civilian objects under article 8(2)(b)(ii)" would have been committed in the context of the referred situation.[86] In other words, the possible illegality of the blockade and thus possible aggression seems to have been considered by the Prosecutor only as a *liability condition* for one particular war crime, and not as an *aggravating factor* with respect to the other possible war crimes identified by the Prosecutor. The approach to the gravity assessment by the Trial Chamber was broader in this regard, by emphasizing especially the "international concern" caused by the events at issue. It underlined that several international fact-finding missions had been established in response, including by the U.N. Human Rights Council and the U.N. Secretary-General. It also agreed with the Comoros in pointing out the clear message sent by the commission of the identified crimes on the Comoros vessel *Mavi Marmara* "to the people in Gaza (and beyond) that the blockade of Gaza was in full force and that even the delivery of humanitarian aid would be controlled and supervised by the Israeli authorities."[87] The decision was later appealed by the Prosecutor, but dismissed (3–2) by the Appeals Chamber as inadmissible without consideration of the merits of the appeal.[88]

In later selecting the specific cases to be prosecuted after having investigated a situation, the OTP could focus on those individuals that participated in the planning, preparation, initiation or execution of the initial use of force who also have criminal responsibility for other universal core crimes within the

---

Comoros to Review the Prosecutor's Decision Not to Initiate an Investigation, ¶¶ 1–7 (July 16, 2015), www.icc-cpi.int/CourtRecords/CR2015_13139.PDF.

[86] *Id.* ¶ 2.

[87] *Id.* ¶ 48. In this particular case, the attack on the *Mavi Marmara* also constituted *prima facie* an act of aggression against the Comoros since the ship was registered in the Comoros and thus was part of the territory of the Comoros as the flag State. *See* Rome Statute, *supra* note 2, art. 8*bis*(2)(a) ("attack by the armed forces of a State against the territory of another State"). The concept of "territory" in this provision must presumably be interpreted to include a civilian vessel or aircraft registered in the relevant State Party, consistent with Article 12(2)(a). Article 8*bis*(2)(d) covers attack on military ships and aircrafts.

[88] Situation on the Registered Vessels of the Union of the Comoros, the Hellenic Republic and the Kingdom of Cambodia, No. ICC-01/13, Decision on the Admissibility of the Prosecutor's Appeal Against the "Decision on the Request of the Union of Comoros to Review the Prosecutor's Decision Not to Initiate an Investigation", (Nov. 6, 2015), www.icc-cpi.int/CourtRecords/CR2015_20965.PDF.

Court's formal jurisdiction at the present time.[89] The logic would be that these individuals bear the greatest responsibility for the crimes due to their high-ranking position and their role in the initial aggression that created the conditions that later lead to the occurrence of other crimes. Of course, this presupposes that liability for those other crimes – crimes against humanity, war crimes, or genocide – could be attributed to these individuals. As is further explored in the next Section, this could possibly be achieved in several ways, in particular by exploiting co-perpetration as a mode of liability to extend liability to high-ranking officials for crimes that were foreseeable in the ordinary course of events, as well as command responsibility as a key form of liability at the leadership level.

The usefulness of this strategy is modeled below:[90]

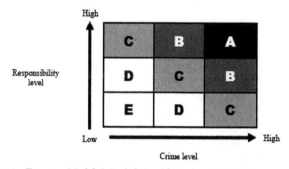

FIGURE 1: Gravity Function Model © Torkel Opsahl Academic EPublisher.

Since the definition of aggression in Article 8*bis* in effect limits the scope of liability for the crime to those occupying a *high-level position* in the power structure by requiring the perpetrator to be in a position "effectively to exercise control over or to direct the political or military action of a State,"[91] taking the factual matrix of aggression into account would typically secure a high score on the responsibility-level axis, i.e., a "high" (C), (B), or (A) in the model. Simultaneously, the "manifest violation" threshold for aggression makes sure that *crimes* of aggression will typically amount to a "high" (B) or (A). If taken into consideration when selecting cases of other core crimes to be prosecuted,

---

[89] *See* 2016 OTP CASE SELECTION POLICY, *supra* note 68, at 14, and the discussion *supra* on the analogous relationship between war crimes and crimes against humanity in a context of the destruction of the environment, the illegal exploitation of natural resources, the illegal dispossession of land, and governmental corruption, theft, or embezzlement.

[90] See further analysis in EINARSEN, THE CONCEPT OF UNIVERSAL CRIMES, *supra* note 12, at 73–82.

[91] Rome Statute, *supra* note 1, arts. 8*bis*(1) & 25(3*bis*).

it contributes to further elevating the sufficient crime level of the selected situation or case to the most responsible persons, which might include trusted subordinates at the mid-responsibility level. Combined, therefore, this strategy is consistent with the Prosecutor's current focus on those cases potentially positioned at the upper right corners of the model – (A) and (B) – namely those of the highest overall gravity and thus most suited for further attention by the Court. It must be underlined, however, that this strategy for integrating aggression would always constitute only one – although an important – *part* of an overall prosecutorial policy at the ICC. In many situations there would simply not have been any act of aggression committed within the meaning of Article 8*bis*. Furthermore, the suggested strategy does not preclude implementing, when deemed appropriate, "a building-upwards strategy by first investigating and prosecuting a limited number of mid- and high-level perpetrators in order to ultimately have a reasonable prospect of conviction for the most responsible,"[92] or, by a more recent formulation, "to ultimately build the evidentiary foundations for case(s) against those most responsible."[93] Lower-level perpetrators may however be assigned responsibility above their hierarchical status, "where their conduct has been particularly grave or notorious."[94]

It could be argued that all cases of crimes against humanity, war crimes, and genocide are in themselves of such gravity that all should be prosecuted, rather than excluding some situations or cases on account of the presence of aggression relative to others. However, it is a fact that the ICC's capacity to prosecute is limited, and that priorities must be made. Given that, as noted earlier, waging a war of aggression often creates a context that increases the likelihood for the occurrence of other international crimes, focusing systematically on aggression when selecting situations for investigation and cases for formal prosecution may have a positive effect on the overall deterrence of crimes, one of the primary purposes of the functioning of the ICC.

---

[92] OTP STRATEGIC PLAN 2016–2018, *supra* note 5, ¶ 34.
[93] *See* 2016 OTP CASE SELECTION POLICY, *supra* note 68, at 14.
[94] *Id. See also* EINARSEN, THE CONCEPT OF UNIVERSAL CRIMES, *supra* note 12, at 79 ("Determining the level of responsibility requires a principal focus on the rank and role of the primary leader allegedly responsible and of other high-ranking personnel, and their concrete modes of participation. However, the most notorious offenders positioned at the intermediate or low levels of the power structure may also, by the scale and cruelty of their involvement, be assigned a high level of responsibility.").

VI. PROSECUTING AGGRESSION THROUGH THE VEHICLE OF OTHER UNIVERSAL CRIMES

A. *Utilizing Crimes Against Humanity to Prosecute Aggression*

Crimes against humanity, as provided in Article 7 of the Rome Statute, can be perpetrated both in times of peace and war.[95] Historically, however, the notion of crimes against humanity required a direct link to acts of war. As noted by Cassese, the jurisdiction requirement in Article 6(c) of the Charter of the Nuremburg Tribunal that crimes against humanity had to be perpetrated "in execution of or in connexion with any crimes within the jurisdiction of the Tribunal" meant that crimes against humanity in effect required a context of armed conflict or waging of aggression.[96]

While this legal connection has disappeared, sufficient similarities between the factual matrix required for crimes against humanity and the crime of aggression can be identified, thus allowing for crimes against humanity to be used as a vehicle for alleviating the current state of impunity for aggression. This Subsection explores how this overlapping factual matrix could be utilized systematically in order for aggression to be prosecuted through crimes against humanity in the absence of ICC jurisdiction over the former as a distinct crime.

In adhering to the principle of legality, in order for the factual matrix of aggression to be prosecuted as a crime against humanity, the OTP would have to demonstrate that both the *actus reus* and *mens rea* of crimes against humanity are satisfied. In other words, all the elements of crimes against humanity as provided under Article 7 must be proven beyond a reasonable doubt – this includes the elements of at least one of the underlying crimes, the contextual element of a widespread or systematic attack on a civilian population furthering a state or organizational policy, and the corresponding mental elements for both.

With respect to the underlying crimes, there are in theory two possible ways to establish a sufficient legal basis for prosecution – either by establishing that the factual matrix of aggression may simultaneously constitute one of the underlying acts of crimes against humanity enumerated in Article 7(1)(a)–(j),

---

[95] Although Article 5 of the ICTY Statute links crimes against humanity to "armed conflict," the ICTY Appeals Chamber early on rejected such a nexus as a legal requirement under customary law. *See* Tadić Decision on Interlocutory Appeal, *supra* note 47, ¶ 141.

[96] CASSESE, *supra* note 7, at 86.

                         Terje Einarsen

or by establishing that aggression as a crime may constitute an "other inhumane act[]" under Article 7(1)(k).

A preliminary problem that arises with respect to both approaches is that the underlying crimes of crimes against humanity and aggression, as prescribed in Article 7(1)(a)–(k) and Article 8*bis*(2)(a)–(g) respectively, are of a different nature in that they are intended to protect different interests. While the underlying crimes of crimes against humanity are directly connected to a human rights perspective, the immediate interests protected by the underlying crimes of aggression are the territorial and/or political integrity of a State.[97] However, these two interests are also closely linked because the use of armed force of a certain scale against another State's territory regularly, and inevitably, carries with it grave consequences for the inhabitants of that State.[98] What at the outset may appear as irreconcilable differences between the underlying crimes of crimes against humanity and aggressive acts, can thus be seen as reflecting a different level of generality, or two sides of the same coin.

Ultimately, both crime categories protect the fundamental interests and values of human beings and their societies that are devastated when crimes against humanity and/or crimes of aggression are being committed.[99] Certain types of underlying acts of crimes against humanity may therefore be conceived as an implicit part of the protective scope of the various acts of aggression. By following the chain of events as they flow from the initial use of force, the more abstract underlying acts of aggression may be concretized down to specific underlying acts of crimes against humanity. Thus, what is required of the Prosecutor is simply to demonstrate how these concrete consequences for the civilian populations followed from the initial act of aggression.

If one accepts this logic, establishing that the factual matrix of aggression may simultaneously satisfy one of the underlying acts of Article 7(1)(a)–(j)

---

[97] *See* Rome Statute, *supra* note 1, art. 8*bis*(2) (requiring armed force against "the sovereignty, territorial integrity or political independence of another State").

[98] Exceptions in this respect may be those types of acts described in Article 8*bis*(d)–(e), which are less likely to cause direct civilian casualties. *See also* Benjamin B. Ferencz, *A New Approach to Deterring Illegal Wars, appended to* Donald M. Ferencz, *Aggression in Legal Limbo, supra* note 18, at 519 ("The illegal use of force almost invariably results in actions that should qualify as crimes against humanity.") [hereinafter Ferencz, *A New Approach*].

[99] This thought seems to be in line with a basic premise of liberal political theory. *See* Robert D. Sloane, *The Cost of Conflation: Preserving the Dualism of* Jus ad Bellum *and* Jus in Bello *in Contemporary Law of War*, 34 YALE J. INT'L L. 47, 54 (2009) ("I take for granted a premise . . . that only human beings, not abstractions like states, merit *foundational* moral weight.")

would often be quite easy. As already established elsewhere,[100] an invasion, attack, or bombardment would often satisfy the elements of "murder" under Article 7(1)(a)[101] if civilian casualties resulted directly from the attack, and those high-ranking leaders who planned or executed the initial act of aggression either intended or knew that civilians would be killed in the ordinary course of events.[102] Sufficient knowledge would often be present, for example, if an attack were deliberately launched at an inhabited area, and civilian deaths would be unavoidable consequences in the ordinary course of events.[103] Similarly, a blockade under Article 8*bis*(2)(c) may cause the "extermination" of a population under Article 7(1)(b)[104] if the blockade was intended to inflict conditions of life on the civilian population calculated to bring about its partial destruction[105] as a means of pressure against the leadership of the victim State.[106]

For consequences not fitting within any of the enumerated acts in Article 7(1)(a)–(j), the question has been asked whether the illegal use of force (aggression) may constitute "other inhumane acts" under Article 7(1)(k).[107] To hold that this would generally be the case would constitute an expansive interpretation of this provision, in conflict with the legality principle (see Section III, *supra*). That it *could* be the case, depending on the concrete circumstances, is another matter. This question is complicated, insofar as the precise content of "other inhumane acts" is inherently unclear. According to the full text, the relevant acts must be of "a similar character" and must "intentionally cause great suffering, or serious injury to body or to mental or physical health." The words "similar character" entails that the relevant acts must be established on the basis of the *ejusdem generis* principle following the

---

[100] *See* Chet Tan, *Punishing Aggression as a Crime Against Humanity: A Noble but Inadequate Measure to Safeguard International Peace and Security*, 29 Am. U. Int'l L. Rev. 145, 155–64 (2013).

[101] *See Elements of Crimes, supra* note 34, art. 7(1)(a), element 1 n.7 ("The term 'killed' is interchangeable with the term 'caused death.'").

[102] *See* Rome Statute, *supra* note 1, art. 30(2)(b) (providing the mental element of a consequence element).

[103] In these situations the established standard according to the case law of "virtual certainty" (*see infra* Section VII) of the outcome in the ordinary course of events would normally be satisfied.

[104] *Cf.*, Rome Statute, *supra* note 2, art. 7(2)(b).

[105] *Id.* "Extermination" includes the destruction of "part of a population."

[106] Tan, *supra* note 100, at 157.

[107] Ferencz, *A New Approach, supra* note 98, at 520.

explicitly enumerated acts in Article 7(1)(a)–(j), and in this respect the "nature and gravity of the act" constitute the primary factors.[108]

In the opinion of the Pre-Trial Chamber – while underlining that Article 7(1)(k) has a somewhat narrower scope than the antecedents in the Nuremberg Charter and *ad hoc* tribunal Statutes, "inhumane acts are to be considered as serious violations of international customary law and the basic rights pertaining to human beings, drawn from the norms of international human rights law, which are of a similar nature and gravity to the acts referred to in article 7(1) of the Statute."[109] The Chamber further added that the word "other" entails that "none of the acts constituting crimes against humanity according to article 7(1)(a) to (j) can be simultaneously considered as another inhumane act encompassed by article 7(1)(k) of the Statute."[110]

International criminal law jurisprudence has found that a number of acts fall under the category of "other inhumane acts," including physical or mental injuries short of murder,[111] forced undressing of women and marching them in public, beatings, humiliation, harassment, psychological abuse, confinement in inhumane conditions, etc.[112] The wide range of acts presumably falling within the term "other inhumane acts," and the purpose of Article 7 to protect civilians from severe violence and suffering,[113] jointly support the view that the illegal use of armed force may not be categorically excluded from its scope. Serious suffering inflicted upon civilians is a regular and often inevitable consequence of the illegal use of armed force.[114] Instances of aggression that could be prosecuted as "other inhumane acts" are those attacks that can be proven to have caused similar, but yet different, "great [civilian] suffering." This includes any physical injuries short of murder, or mental damages, under the condition that the injuries are of sufficient severity to elevate the suffering

---

[108] *See Elements of Crimes, supra* note 34, art. 7(1)(k), element 2 n.30. The third element of Article 7(1)(k) clarifies as to the mental element that the perpetrator only needs to be aware of the "factual circumstances that established the character of the act." *Id.* element 3.

[109] Prosecutor v. Katanga, Case No. ICC-01/04–01/07, Confirmation of Charges, ¶¶ 448, 450 (Sept. 30, 2008) [hereinafter Katanga Confirmation of Charges]. *See also* Prosecutor v. Kupreškić, Case No. IT-96–16-T, Trial Judgment, ¶ 566 (Jan. 14, 2000).

[110] Katanga Confirmation of Charges, *supra* note 109, ¶ 452.

[111] Prosecutor v. Blaškić, Case No. IT-95–14-T, Trial Judgment, ¶ 239 (Mar. 3, 2000) [hereinafter Blaškić Trial Judgment].

[112] *See, e.g.,* Prosecutor v. Brima, Case No. SCSL-2004–16-A, Appeals Judgment, ¶ 184 (Feb. 22, 2008).

[113] *See* Vienna Convention on the Law of Treaties, *supra* note 29, art. 31(1) ("A treaty shall be interpreted in good faith in accordance with the ordinary meaning to be given to the terms of the treaty in their context and in light of its object and purpose.").

[114] *See, e.g.,* CASSESE, *supra* note 7, at 98, 157–58 (arguing that "other inhumane acts" may also include acts of terrorism).

to the required gravity of the inhumane. A crime of aggression might thus simultaneously constitute "other inhumane acts." Under this line of reasoning, however, there is no need to draw a somewhat artificial distinction between, on the one hand, Article 7(1)(a)–(j) and, on the other hand, Article 7(1)(k), since most cases would fall under the former provisions. If so, there is no need for an expansive interpretation of subparagraph (k) that might provoke unnecessary opposition to the idea that certain acts of illegal use of armed force may *concurrently* constitute a possible crime of aggression *and* crimes against humanity by reference to murder and other enumerated acts clearly within the parameters of Article 7.[115] In other words, the point should not be that Article 7(1)(k) as such can be transformed into a crime of aggression provision, but rather that Article 7 may, depending on the concrete circumstances, apply in concurrence with Article 8*bis*. Hence the same act can be prosecuted as a crime against humanity independent of formal jurisdiction to prosecute the concurrent crime of aggression.

While the factual matrix of aggression may thus simultaneously satisfy the elements of the underlying crimes of Article 7(1)(a)–(k), in order to secure a conviction for crimes against humanity the context elements must be met as well. Thus, the proscribed acts must form part of "a widespread or systematic attack directed against any civilian population," in furtherance of a state or organizational policy, and those responsible for the waging of aggression must have knowledge in this respect.[116]

As noted by Ventura and Gillett, the elements of the crime of aggression are of such a nature that they will often by definition satisfy certain of these contextual elements.[117] A "systematic" attack refers to the "organised nature of the acts of violence and the improbability of their random occurrence."[118] Given that the leadership clause in Article 8*bis*(1)[119] in effect requires the act of

---

[115] Another question is whether Article 7(1)(k) might be more relevant with respect to the use of force that falls outside the scope of Article 8*bis*. An attack by a foreign non-state actor, typically an organization that carries out a terrorist attack, may however be sufficiently and better covered by some other provisions of Article 7(1). Systematic or large-scale attacks on a civilian group by the government or by a domestic non-state actor, which spark a non-international armed conflict within the State, could perhaps more digestively constitute a particular subcategory of "other inhumane acts." On the other hand, again, "first strike" as a possibly aggravating factor to the crimes against humanity committed might also be accommodated through application of some other provisions of Article 7(1).

[116] Rome Statute, *supra* note 1, art. 7(1)–(2)(a).

[117] Manuel J. Ventura & Matthew Gillett, *The Fog of War: Prosecuting Illegal Uses of Force as Crimes Against Humanity*, 12 WASH. U. GLOBAL STUD. L. REV. 523, 526–27 (2013).

[118] Katanga Trial Judgment, *supra* note 47, ¶ 1123.

[119] *See also* Rome Statute, *supra* note 1, art. 25(3*bis*).

aggression to be organized and executed at the highest state level, the contextual elements of a systematic attack pursuant to a state policy would be satisfied under Article 7.[120] The requirement of knowledge of such an attack would further be satisfied if the civilian casualties were a virtually certain outcome of the organized act of aggression in the ordinary course of events.

The crux of the matter thus becomes the requirement that the attack be "directed against any civilian population." This entails that the population be "the 'primary object of the attack,' and not just an incidental victim."[121] Generally, if those who orchestrated the aggression were fully aware that mass-scale civilian casualties would result from the attack, then the execution of the plan would also entail an intentional attack on a civilian population. This element is not necessarily negated by the presence of non-civilians among the victims.[122] Some of the victims of the underlying acts may thus be military personnel, as long as the offenses form part of a general attack on a civilian population.[123] However, proving this contextual element becomes more difficult where the civilian casualties could be argued to be mere collateral damage of an attack on a military target. The next Section addresses this particular issue.

B. *Utilizing War Crimes to Prosecute Aggression*

When civilian casualties are claimed to be collateral damage of attacks on legitimate military targets, it will often be difficult to satisfy the "directed

---

[120] Katanga Confirmation of Charges, *supra* note 109, ¶ 396 (according to the Pre-Trial Chamber the policy requirement is fulfilled if an attack is "planned, directed or organized").

[121] WILLIAM A. SCHABAS, THE INTERNATIONAL CRIMINAL COURT: A COMMENTARY ON THE ROME STATUTE 153 (2010) (quoting Prosecutor v. Bemba, Case No. ICC-01/05–01/08, Decision on the Confirmation of Charges against Jean-Pierre Bemba Gombo, ¶ 75 (June 15, 2009) [hereinafter Bemba Confirmation of Charges]).

[122] *See, e.g.*, Prosecutor v. Kordić *et al.*, Case No. IT-95–14/2-T, Trial Judgment, ¶ 180 (Feb. 26, 2001); Blaškić, *supra* note 111, ¶ 214. Despite some conflicting views on "civilian population" in the jurisprudence and scholarly literature, the conclusion of Kai Ambos is noteworthy:

> Thus, in sum, every individual, regardless of that person's formal status as a member of an armed force, must be regarded as a civilian unless the forces are hostile towards the perpetrator [through a hostile armed force] and the individual has not laid down his or her arms or, ultimately, been placed *hors de combat*.

AMBOS, *supra* note 11, at 66–67.

[123] *See, e.g.*, CASSESE, *supra* note 7, at 102; Elizabeth Santella Vargas, *Military or Civilian Jurisdiction for International Crimes? An Approach from Self-Interest in Accountability of Armed Forces in International Law*, *in* MILITARY SELF-INTEREST IN ACCOUNTABILITY FOR CORE INTERNATIONAL CRIMES 401, 409–10 (Morten Bergsmo & Song Tianying eds., 2015), www.legal-tools.org/uploads/tx_ltpdb/FICHL_PS_25_web.pdf.

against any civilian population" requirement of Article 7. This problem could prove to be a fatal blow to prosecuting even clear instances of aggression through crimes against humanity. For example, if military facilities within a city close to the border of a neighboring State are bombed in alleged self-defense by the neighboring State as a preemptive first military strike, while the attack is also targeting hospitals, schools, some close-by residential areas, and some other civilian objects because the strategy was also to force people to leave that city and thus civilians had to be targeted as well, the latter purpose could be difficult to prove beyond a reasonable doubt within a crimes against humanity framework.

Ventura and Gillett suggest a possible solution in that the presence of illegal use of force may negate the *legitimacy* of the military target, thus transforming the civilian casualties from collateral damage to attacks on the civilian population prosecutable as crimes against humanity.[124] This approach infringes on the traditional distinction between the *jus ad bellum* and the *jus in bello*.[125] The internal structure of the Rome Statute also shows that the drafters clearly intended that the illegality of a war and the legality of actions in armed conflict be separate matters addressed by separate provisions.[126] This does not mean that the doctrine of "one act, several crimes" (ideal concurrence) may not apply also across the said distinction. To the contrary, there is no reason why an aggressive attack on another State of a certain scale and with certain purposes in principle cannot simultaneously constitute war crimes, crimes against humanity and even genocide, as well. If the legitimacy of all military targets were to be cancelled out due to the presence of an initial aggression, however, the effect could be the undermining of established rules on proportionality and military necessity in times of armed conflict.[127] This would be counterproductive from a humanitarian perspective since there would be no incentive anymore for the aggressor State to exercise restraint during the war.

An interpretation of the Statute, presumably more in line with recognized principles of treaty interpretation,[128] thus might require the suggestion of an alternative prosecutorial approach. For those instances where the factual matrix of aggression also reaches the threshold of armed conflict under Article 8, it may function as a secondary, back-up prosecutorial strategy for alleviating the

---

[124] Ventura & Gillett, *supra* note 117, at 528.

[125] *See, e.g.*, Prosecutor v. Fofana, Case No. SCSL-04-14-T, Sentencing Judgment, ¶¶ 529–30, 534 (Oct. 9, 2007). *See also* Boškoski Appeals Judgment, *supra* note 48, ¶ 44.

[126] More generally, strong arguments have been advanced for preserving the distinction between the *jus ad bellum* and *jus in bello*, also for analytical purposes. *See* Sloane, *supra* note 99.

[127] *See* Rome Statute, *supra* note 1, art. 8(2)(b)(iv), (xiii).

[128] *Id.* arts. 21–24; Vienna Convention on the Law of Treaties, *supra* note 29, art. 31(1).

impunity for aggression in situations where it cannot be established that the attack was "directed against any civilian population" under Article 7.

Under Article 8(2)(b)(iv), it is a war crime to intentionally launch an attack knowing it will cause incidental loss of life or injury to civilians, civilian objects or the natural environment if this damage is "clearly excessive in relation to the concrete and direct overall military advantage anticipated." Thus, in assessing the legitimacy of civilian "collateral damage," the test is whether the military target was of sufficient concrete and direct strategic military importance relative to the damage caused by the specific attack with respect to loss of civilian life, injury to civilians, damage to civilian objects, or a combination thereof.[129] The proportionality of the different strikes during the collective attack can then be distinguished and assessed separately. Such a proportionality analysis *jus in bello* would be different from the proportionality analysis of the armed attack on another State as such, as an act of aggression *jus ad bellum*.[130]

To investigate and formally prosecute crimes falling under Article 8(2)(b)(iv) would be unproblematic under the Rome Statute. The principal point is, therefore, that by systematically prioritizing prosecuting the singular war crimes committed in concurrence with or closely related to a possible crime of aggression, one may achieve not only accountability for the war crimes but also general preventive effects with respect to aggression. In addition, if the material conditions for a crime of aggression were established for sentencing purposes, this would further contribute to accountability under international law, as discussed in Section IX, below.

Lex ferenda, would it potentially also be possible for the OTP to integrate the illegal nature of the use of force into the proportionality assessment, thus raising the threshold for the civilian casualties to be accepted as legitimate collateral damage? The logic would be that since the initial use of force is in itself illegal, the claim of military necessity with respect to civilian casualties and injuries must meet a higher threshold to succeed. Since the illegality of the use of force is only taken into account as a factor in the assessment, this approach does not collapse the distinction between the *jus in bello* and the *jus ad bellum*. Furthermore, raising the threshold for justification based on

---

[129] This is not to say that the application of the formula is simple. To the contrary, a consistent and principled interpretation and application of this important legal norm is urgently called for. *See, e.g.,* Sloan, *supra* note 99, at 111.

[130] *Ad bellum* proportionality basically seeks to limit the quantum of force used in any resort to force. *Id.* at 108–10. The relevant concept is not, as *in bello* proportionality, "collateral damage," but instead whether the use of force was clearly necessary and proportional to the aim of self-defense or defense of a third party.

aggression does not imply that the limiting principles of distinction and proportionality do not apply or that the threshold should be lowered in other instances. Amending the Elements of Crimes[131] to the Rome Statute seems like the best way to change the law *lex lata* in this respect, taking into account the legality principle,[132] as well as the need for a brief explanation in the Elements (2–3) to Article 8(2)(b)(iv).[133]

The idea of applying a differentiated threshold based on the prevailing circumstances is not unknown in international law. In the context of the prohibition of inhumane or degrading treatment under Article 3 of the European Convention on Human Rights (ECHR), for instance, the European Court of Human Rights (ECtHR) has applied a higher threshold for considering deportation of foreigners with serious diseases to countries with insufficient health care as inhumane or degrading, as compared to deportation entailing a real risk of persecution or inhumane treatment inflicted by state authorities or non-state actors.[134] And in expulsion cases under Article 8, the European Court of Human Rights has applied different thresholds for proportionality assessments depending on whether the persons were to be considered lawfully "settled migrants" at the time of their expulsion by national authorities.[135] Thus, while concerning completely different matters, the notion of differentiated thresholds should be possible to adopt also within international criminal law if good reasons exist.

Such an approach would, subject to the legality principle,[136] permit the prosecution of high-level leaders also for war crimes of foreseeable excessive civilian casualties in the ordinary course of implementing the common plan to wage the initial aggression. By investigating both crimes against humanity and war crimes in these cases, and eventually maybe only prosecuting for war crimes if crimes against humanity is too difficult to prove,[137] the OTP could

---

[131] *See supra* note 34.

[132] *See* Rome Statute, *supra* note 2, art. 22, *cf.* art. 21(1)(a).

[133] This could be done by adding that the "clearly excessive" standard does not apply to the initial aggressive acts that are deemed to have started the international armed conflict and that *also* caused incidental death, injury, or damage to civilians, civilian objects, or long-term and severe damage to the natural environment.

[134] *See, e.g.,* D. v. United Kingdom, App. No. 30240/96, 1997-III Eur. Ct. H.R. 777, ¶¶ 46–54; N. v. United Kingdom, App. No. 26565/05, 2008-III Eur. Ct. H.R. 227, ¶¶ 42–51.

[135] *See, e.g.,* Butt v. Norway, App. No. 47017/09, 2012 Eur. Ct. H.R. ¶¶ 78–80, http://hudoc.echr.coe.int/fre?i=001-115012#{%22itemid%22:[%22001-115012%22]}.

[136] *See supra* Section III.

[137] Indicting for both is fully possible because they contain material elements distinct from each other. *See* Prosecutor v. Musema, Case No. ICTR-96-13-A, Appeals Judgment, ¶¶ 369–70 (Nov. 16, 2001).

thus increase the chances of securing at least a conviction for war crimes in cases where the leadership of an aggressive State cannot be prosecuted and convicted for the crime of aggression for jurisdictional reasons.

C. *Utilizing the Crime of Genocide to Prosecute Aggression*

While the main focus of this Chapter is on utilizing crimes against humanity as a legal framework for prosecuting aggression, it should briefly be noted that a strategy to prosecute the factual matrix of aggression might also include the crime of genocide under Article 6 of the Rome Statute. However, due to the nature of genocide, *inter alia* the legal requirement of specific genocidal intent, this complementary strategy would presumably be limited to extraordinary situations. On the other hand, since genocide is not limited to destruction of a "civilian population," an aggressive armed attack on another State *with* the required genocidal intent will typically constitute genocide as well.

With respect to the underlying crimes of genocide, the same logic as described for crimes against humanity would apply. The factual matrix of the underlying acts of aggression will often simultaneously satisfy the underlying crimes of genocide in that the more abstract act of aggression can be concretized down to specific underlying acts of the former in the form of its consequences. For example, to start a large-scale bombardment of another State's territory inhabited by a particular national, ethnical, or religious group satisfies the elements of "killing" or "causing serious bodily or mental harm" to members of the protected group, if those responsible for the waging of aggression either intended or were aware such a group of persons would be killed or seriously injured in the ordinary course of events.[138]

What limits the use of the crime of genocide is that it must also be established that the destruction of a protected group, "in whole or in part," was a specific purpose of the initial aggression, or, in the case of invasion and occupation, a specific purpose of the ongoing act of aggression.[139]

This, however, is not unimaginable, and the historical link to the Nuremberg jurisprudence is obvious. The main reason that genocide was not provided for as a distinct crime within the Nuremberg Charter is that it was not sufficiently developed as a legal concept, and not strictly necessary in addition

---

[138] *See* Rome Statute, *supra* note 1, arts. 8*bis*(2)(a)–(b) & 6(a)–(b) read in conjunction with art. 30.
[139] Rome Statute, *supra* note 1, art. 6 (requires the underlying acts to be "committed with intent to destroy, in whole or in part, a national, ethnical, racial or religious group, as such").

to war crimes and crimes against humanity.[140] The systematic genocide in the form of extermination of perceived "national, racial, or religious groups, particularly Jews, Poles and Gypsies and others,"[141] was formally prosecuted and judged under the heading of "War Crimes and Crimes against Humanity," which in the Nuremberg judgment included subheadings on "Slave Labour Policy" and "Persecution of the Jews."[142] In the charges of the "Major War Criminals" at Nuremberg and in the subsequent Nuremberg trials, however, the notion of genocide was explicitly used for descriptive purposes in the context of illegal use of force and occupation.[143] For instance in *Greifelt et al.*, the Tribunal found that a "systematic program of genocide" was "part of the Nazi doctrine of total warfare, war waged against populations rather than against states and armed forces."[144] Here we see that the separation of the *jus ad bellum* and the *jus in bello* is not legally clear-cut, but rather is affected by the concrete circumstances whereby the subsequent crimes shed light on the planning, preparation, and execution of aggression, while at the same time the crime and context of aggression adds aggravating factors to the resulting genocide and crimes against humanity. The same act or closely related acts, constituted, in certain cases, both a crime against peace (aggression) and crimes against humanity (genocide).

In other words, concurrent application of *ad bellum* crimes and *in bello* crimes does not collapse the analytical and legal distinction between them. Thus, although limited to the more extreme cases, it is legally possible to effectively prosecute the factual matrix of aggression under the heading of genocide where it can be proven that such a genocidal policy and perpetration

---

[140] On the conceptual development facilitated by the Nuremberg trials with respect to genocide, *see* David Cohen, *The Historiography of the Historical Foundations of Theories of Responsibility in International Criminal Law*, in 1 HISTORICAL ORIGINS OF INTERNATIONAL CRIMINAL LAW 23, 33–34 (Morten Bergsmo, Cheah Wui Ling & Yi Ping eds., 2014), www.fichl .org/fileadmin/fichl/FICHL_PS_20_web.pdf.; EINARSEN, THE CONCEPT OF UNIVERSAL CRIMES, *supra* note 12, at 48–50.

[141] IMT JUDGMENT, *supra* note 3, at 44.

[142] *Id.* at 243, 247; *see also* CASSESE, *supra* note 7, at 109.

[143] In the indictment at the International Military Tribunal, the word genocide was indeed used, and "systematic genocide" defined: "Throughout the period of their occupation of territories overrun by their armed forces the defendants, for the purpose of systematically terrorizing the inhabitants, murdered and tortured civilians, and ill-treated them, and imprisoned them without legal process.... They conducted deliberate and systematic genocide, viz., the extermination of racial and national groups ... particularly Jews, Poles, and Gypsies and others." *See* IMT JUDGMENT, *supra* note 3, at 43–44.

[144] *See* "*The RuSHA Case*," *Military Tribunal No. I, Case 8, United States of America v. Ulrich Greifelt*, in 4 TRIALS OF WAR CRIMINALS BEFORE THE NUERNBERG MILITARY TRIBUNALS UNDER CONTROL COUNCIL LAW NO. 10, Judgment, 597, at 622, 701 (1948), www.loc.gov/rr/frd/ Military_Law/pdf/NT_war-criminals_Vol-IV.pdf.

of crimes against a protected group can be linked to the initial plan of aggression or to ongoing aggression, *inter alia* an unlawful occupation, for which persons at the military or political leadership level are responsible.

VII. UTILIZING MODES OF LIABILITY

A. *Prosecuting Aggression Through Crimes Against Humanity Under the Doctrine of Co-Perpetration*

Underlying crimes of crimes against humanity are often committed by personnel at the intermediate and low levels of the relevant power structure. This creates a possible lacuna in the suggested strategy to prosecute aggression through crimes against humanity. It will often be difficult to prove sufficient involvement of the high-ranking leaders in various crimes against humanity, each committed at a particular crime scene. When this *is* possible, for instance, through singular *ordering* or by means of *direct perpetration through another* as the applicable modes of liability,[145] the issues discussed in the following might not be necessary to analyze further in any specific case since the gravity of the crimes might then be adequately expressed through more limited investigation and prosecution (sufficient crime level and a high level of responsibility can be proven).[146]

The premise is further that despite the leaders being responsible for a crime of aggression under general international law, a *conviction* for aggression at the ICC would be impossible because of lacking formal jurisdiction under Articles 15*bis* and *ter*. In order to attach liability to the high-level planners and executors through a *conviction for concurrent or subsequent crimes against humanity*, it could however in some cases be possible to move the time frame backward to the planning and execution stages of the initial aggression. While the following primarily focuses on crimes against humanity, it should be noted that in those instances, as described above, war crimes and genocide may similarly be suitable for integrating aggression in prosecuting these crimes.

---

[145] *See* Rome Statute, *supra* note 1, art. 25(3)(a)–(b).

[146] This Chapter does not aim at being exhaustive on the applicability of modes of liability and the mental elements. Co-perpetration and command responsibility discussed in Section VII are exemplary, chosen mostly for their assumed practical applicability. On modes of liability applicable to the leadership level in theory and practice more generally, *see* Joseph Rikhof, *Prosecution of International Crimes – a Historical and Empirical Overview*, 2 BERGEN J. CRIM. L. & CRIM. JUST. 108 (2014).

A prosecutorial strategy that involves utilizing the common plan element of co-perpetration (or indirect co-perpetration) as a mode of liability[147] has already been suggested by Ventura and Gillett,[148] which may also be suitable in resolving this particular problem and thus expand the effectiveness of the prosecutorial strategy outlined above. The main focus of Ventura and Gillett's contribution seems, however, to be on exploiting the common plan element of co-perpetration to establish the factual matrix of aggression, and by that enable the ICC to utilize it for sentencing purposes. While this certainly seems to be a fruitful approach, limiting its practical usefulness to the sentencing stage is an understatement of the potential significance of co-perpetration as a mode of liability in integrating aggression in prosecuting other universal crimes.

With respect to the main elements of co-perpetration, the ICC has required the existence of a mutual agreement between two or more individuals in the form of a common plan with acceptance of the crimes and the consequences flowing from it. These latter mental elements are precarious to our subject matter, and they are further discussed in the following sections. The planning does not have to be "specifically directed at the commission of a crime," rather it suffices for it to contain a "critical element of criminality" in that the execution of the plan would result in the commission of crimes.[149] Thus, while aggression at the time being does not constitute a distinct crime for which the ICC has jurisdiction, the common plan as an element of co-perpetration may take the form of an organized plan to wage aggression.[150]

Utilizing co-perpetration as a mode of liability may in fact also function to expand the reach of an indictment for crimes against humanity, or under the circumstances other universal crimes, to those high-ranking leaders responsible for the initial aggression that would otherwise be out of prosecutorial reach due to the difficulties in proving a sufficient causal link with the subsequent crimes committed by actors at lower levels of the power structure. Making use of the common plan element in co-perpetration might enable the Prosecutor to move the relevant time frame backward even to the early criminal planning stages, thereby extending provable liability higher up in the power structure and to the leadership level for clearly foreseeable crimes against humanity occurring in the ordinary course of executing the common plan to wage aggression.

---

[147] *See* Rome Statute, *supra* note 1, art. 25(3)(a).

[148] Ventura & Gillett, *supra* note 117, at 530–33.

[149] *See, e.g.*, Prosecutor v. Lubanga, Case No. ICC-01/04-01/06, Appeals Judgment, ¶ 445–51 (Dec. 1, 2014) [hereinafter Lubanga Appeals Judgment].

[150] *See, e.g.*, Ventura & Gillett, *supra* note 117, at 532–33.

This is an important aspect of any strategy attempting to integrate aggression in prosecuting other crimes, in that the degree to which liability may be expanded to those high-level leaders varies depending on different types of situations – more precisely on the different underlying acts of aggression. With respect to the objective side, the Court has held that under co-perpetration any accused must have made an "essential contribution" to the crime's occurrence.[151] Thus, the crux of the matter becomes that in adhering to the principle of legality, it would be necessary to establish a causal connection between the initial plan of aggression and the subsequent occurring crimes in order to expand liability to those leaders operating at the planning stage.

In situations where an armed attack on the territory of another State leads to prolonged occupation,[152] the crime of aggression would be ongoing for the entire duration of the occupation, which would make it possible to establish a sufficient link from the subsequent foreseeable crimes back to the high-level leaders as flowing from one single initial plan of aggression. As for underlying acts consisting of several more or less independent acts of aggression, such as sequential bombardment of another State's territory,[153] or others kinds of distinguishable serial attacks, the task is more challenging. In these cases it is possible to imagine an initial plan of aggression consisting of one instance of bombardment that did not cause consequences constituting a crime of aggression, while later another and more forceful act of bombardment does in fact result in a crime of aggression as well as the commission of crimes against humanity in its ordinary course of events. Since these two acts of bombardment in fact follow from two different plans of aggression, and may involve different high-level actors involved in the initiation, planning, preparation, and/or execution of the two attacks, the time frame for liability for the subsequent crimes against humanity may only be moved back as far as the second planning is concerned. For the first act of bombardment it would not be feasible to utilize other crimes as a vehicle to *de facto* prosecute those responsible for the initial aggression, since there is not a sufficient link between this particular act of aggression and the subsequent crimes.

For those cases where a sufficient causal link can be established between the initial plan of aggression and the subsequent crimes, the decisive matter becomes the scope of *mens rea*. In order to attach liability for specific acts of

---

[151] Lubanga Appeals Judgment, *supra* note 149, ¶ 473 (The "essential contribution" entails that the accused had the ability to frustrate the commission of the crime by not carrying out his/her contribution.); *see also* Lubanga Trial Judgment, *supra* note 47, ¶¶ 989–1006.

[152] *See, e.g.*, Rome Statute, *supra* note 1, art. 8*bis*(2)(a).

[153] *See, e.g., id.* art. 8*bis*(2)(b).

crimes against humanity, or other universal crimes, committed by lower-level perpetrators to those high-ranking leaders who planned and executed the initial act of aggression, what needs to be proven is that these crimes were a sufficiently foreseeable consequence of the execution of the common plan of aggression.

The Trial Chamber in the *Lubanga* case appeared to introduce a "risk" standard in this respect. However, the Appeals Chamber rejected "risk" as the correct notion, holding that the wording of Article 30(2)(b) and (3) entails that the "standard for the foreseeability of events is *virtual* certainty."[154] This does not require absolute certainty, rather awareness that in the ordinary course of events the execution of the common plan "will necessarily bring about the consequence . . . barring an unforeseen or unexpected intervention or event to prevent its occurrence."[155] The virtual certainty standard has been confirmed, e.g., by the Trial Chamber in *Bemba et al.*[156]

Therefore, the decisive question is whether the regular occurrence of widespread civilian casualties in armed conflict is sufficient to satisfy a virtual certainty standard.[157] In instances of large-scale military attacks on civilian inhabited areas, mass civilian casualties are an unavoidable result, and therefore also a virtually certain outcome of the decision to initiate the plan of aggression. On the other side, the standard would exclude acts committed by individuals or groups of foot soldiers acting unpredictably and outside the agreed operational plan or code of conduct in the execution of the common plan. For the gray areas between these two extremes, no general answer can be given in that it must be assessed on a case-by-case basis.

Thus, in principle it would be feasible to prosecute those responsible for the planning and execution of aggression for foreseeable other core crimes ensuing from the execution of the common plan to wage aggression.

B. *Prosecuting Aggression Through Crimes Against Humanity Under the Doctrine of Command Responsibility*

In those cases where establishing that subsequent crimes were a foreseeable outcome of the initial aggression, an alternative strategy might be to utilize

---

[154] Lubanga Appeals Judgment, *supra* note 149, ¶ 447; *see also* Katanga Trial Judgment, *supra* note 47, ¶ 776.
[155] Katanga Trial Judgment, *supra* note 47, ¶ 777; *see also* Bemba Confirmation of Charges, *supra* note 121, ¶¶ 352–69.
[156] *See* Bemba Trial Judgment, *supra* note 29, ¶ 29.
[157] Donald M. Ferencz, *Aggression in Legal Limbo*, *supra* note 18, at 515–16.

command responsibility as a mode of perpetration to prosecute those responsible for the initial aggression for failure to prevent the ensuing crimes against humanity, or war crimes. While the *mens rea* for co-perpetration follows from the general rule on *mens rea* in Article 30, command responsibility in Article 28 requires a deviating *mens rea* standard as *lex specialis*.

The ICC Trial Chamber in the *Bemba* case has summarized the elements to be proven for command responsibility as follows:

> The Chamber finds that, for an accused to be found guilty and convicted as a military commander or person effectively acting as a military commander under Article 28(a), the following elements must be fulfilled: (a) the crimes within the jurisdiction of the Court must have been committed by forces; (b) the accused must have been either a military commander or a person effectively acting as a military commander; (c) the accused must have had effective command and control, or effective authority and control, over the forces that committed the crimes; (d) the accused either knew or, owing to the circumstances at the time, should have known that the forces were committing or about to commit such crimes; and (e) the accused must have failed to take all necessary and reasonable measures within his power to prevent or repress the commission of such crimes or to submit the matter to the competent authorities for investigation and prosecution; and (f) the crimes committed by the forces must have been a result of the failure of the accused to exercise control properly over them.[158]

While this statement directly concerns only *command responsibility* for commanders under Article 28(a), it is, with an exception for the mental element stated by the Court in (d), presumably applicable also to *superior responsibility* under Article 28(b) regarding civilian leaders who are not military commanders but still exercise effective authority and control over subordinates to the same effect.[159] Since Article 8*bis* limits the scope of individual liability to those "in a position effectively to exercise control over or to direct the political or military action of a State," those responsible for the initial aggression would often satisfy the element of being a military commander or "effectively acting as a military commander" under Article 28(a), or being a superior under Article 28(b). A possible limitation is that it must be demonstrated that the accused exercised "effective control" or "effective authority"

---

[158] Bemba Trial Judgment, *supra* note 29, ¶ 170.
[159] The mental element of superior responsibility under the Rome Statute, *supra* note 1, art. 28(b), differs in that the "should have known" standard of commanders has been substituted with the more demanding standard of having "consciously disregarded information" that "clearly indicated" that the subordinates were committing or about to commit such crimes.

over those forces or subordinates committing the actual crimes in the form of a material ability to prevent them from committing the crimes.[160] However, existing jurisprudence suggests that it is not necessary that the direct subordinates physically commit the crimes themselves, but may perpetrate the crimes through most other modes of perpetration.[161] Thus, it would be sufficient for establishing criminal liability for crimes against humanity or war crimes that those high-level leaders responsible for planning or waging aggression had effective control over military leaders at the intermediate level that planned or initiated the concrete crimes, even if they again perpetrated the crimes through lower-level foot soldiers.[162]

As for the mental element, Article 28(a)(i) requires either that the accused knew or should have known owing to the circumstances. The ICC has viewed the "should have known" standard as a form of negligence that also imposes positive duties on a commander. In the words of the Pre-Trial Chamber:

> Thus, it is the Chamber's view that the "should have known" standard requires more of an active duty on the part of the superior to take the necessary measures to secure knowledge of the conduct of his troops and to inquire, regardless of the availability of information at the time on the commission of the crime. The drafting history of this provision reveals that it was the intent of the drafters to take a more stringent approach towards commanders and military-like commanders compared to other superiors that fall within the parameters of article 28(b) of the Statute. This is justified by the nature and type of responsibility assigned to this category of superiors.[163]

Thus, high-ranking leaders responsible for planning and initiating the initial plan of aggression have an active duty to secure knowledge of the conduct of their subordinates in executing the plan of aggression. If the OTP could prove that those responsible for the aggression failed to adhere to this duty, and that they otherwise could have acquired knowledge making it possible to prevent the subsequent crimes against humanity or war crimes, it

---

[160] See Bemba Trial Judgment, *supra* note 29, ¶ 183. *See also* Bemba Confirmation of Charges, *supra* note 121, ¶ 415. *See also* Prosecutor v. Delalić *et al.*, Case No. IT-96-21-A, Appeals Judgment, ¶ 256 (Feb. 20, 2001) [hereinafter Delalić Appeals Judgment].

[161] *See* Bemba Trial Judgment, *supra* note 29, ¶ 184 ("Whether or not there are intermediary subordinates between the commander and the forces which committed the crimes is immaterial; the question is simply whether or not the commander had effective control over the relevant forces."). *See also, e.g.,* Prosecutor v. Orić, Case No. IT-03-68-T, Trial Judgment, ¶ 297–306 (June 30, 2006) (referring to Prosecutor v. Boškoski, Case No. IT-04-82-PT, Decision on Prosecution's Motion to Amend the Indictment, ¶¶ 18–48 [May 26, 2006]).

[162] That is by way of "indirect co-perpetration," i.e., perpetration "jointly with another" and perpetration "through another person." Rome Statute, *supra* note 1, art. 25(3)(a).

[163] Bemba Confirmation of Charges, *supra* note 121, ¶ 433 (internal citations omitted).

might be possible to extend criminal liability to these high-ranking leaders.[164]
The point is that individuals at the leadership level, although they cannot
formally be prosecuted for the crime of aggression, could be prosecuted for
subsequent crimes against humanity or war crimes planned or organized by
their subordinates even in those instances where these crimes were not
virtually certain outcomes of executing the plan of aggression at the planning
stage of its commission.

VIII. AGGRESSION AS AN AGGRAVATING FACTOR IN SENTENCING

Since this Chapter sets out to analyze how aggression could be integrated at
all stages of ICC procedure, this final Section concerns sentencing. The
possibility of reaching this stage is also the principal argument for incorpor-
ating the factual matrix of aggression in the prosecutorial strategies at the
ICC independent of the *sui generis* jurisdictional requirements.

The concept of gravity forms an integral part of ICC proceedings, and the
sentencing stage is no exception. A person at a leadership level convicted for
crimes against humanity, who simultaneously satisfies all material requirements of criminal responsibility for a crime of aggression, deserves a longer
prison sentence than another person at a leadership level who is only responsible for similar crimes against humanity. The crime of aggression may thus
inform the gravity of the crime complex as a whole for the convicted person,
which should be reflected in the sentence imposed.

There is no substantive provision in the Rome Statute stating the purpose
of punishment. However, the Preamble refers to ending impunity and the
prevention of the most serious crimes,[165] thus indicating retribution and
general deterrence as two primary objectives of the Court.[166] Since, as already
noted, aggression creates a context in which other crimes are more likely
to occur, the primary objectives, in particular effective deterrence of all
international crimes, support taking aggression into account in sentencing.

---

[164] Whether the stricter mental standard for superior responsibility under Article 28(b)(i), with
respect to acquiring the necessary information on the ensuing crimes, would be factually and
legally applicable at the leadership level of a State for non-military leaders taking part in the
planning, preparation, initiation, or execution of aggression that results in other prosecutable
core crimes, seems doubtful. This alternative is clearly not envisaged for situations where the
superior intentionally and simultaneously participates in a crime of aggression.
[165] Rome Statute, *supra* note 1, pmbl., ¶ 5.
[166] *See* Lubanga Sentencing Decision, *supra* note 70, ¶ 16. *See also* Prosecutor v. Stakić, Case No.
IT-97-24-T, Trial Judgment, ¶ 900 (July 31, 2003). *See also* MARK A. DRUMBL, ATROCITY,
PUNISHMENT, AND INTERNATIONAL LAW 60 (2007) (holding retribution and general deterrence
to be the main rationale of punishment within the field of international criminal law).

In addition, proportionality is a fundamental principle underlying sentencing in international criminal law;[167] any sentence imposed should as accurately as possible reflect the overall blameworthiness of the convicted individual. This arguably presupposes taking into account not only the attributes of the specific crime but also the wider context and circumstances of its commission.

Taking such a wide approach in establishing the blameworthiness of the convicted person seems possible under the substantive provisions on sentencing, as the Statute opens for a wide range of factors to be taken into account as relevant when determining the appropriate sentence. Article 78(1) of the Statute states that the main factors in determining the sentence are "the gravity of the crime and the individual circumstances of the convicted person."[168] The prominence of gravity as the fundamental factor at sentencing is also clearly evident from the jurisprudence of the ICC and other international criminal tribunals, it being referred to as the litmus test.[169] The overall gravity of a crime is further informed by the non-exhaustive list of relevant aggravating and mitigating circumstances listed in the Rules of Procedure and Evidence (RPE) Rule 145. The factual matrix of aggression may in fact inform the overall gravity of the crime through several of these factors, such as the nature of the unlawful behavior and the means employed to execute the crime, abuse of official capacity and other circumstances by virtue of their nature similar to those explicitly enumerated.[170]

Thus, as noted by Ventura and Gillett,[171] both the superior factor of gravity and the different aggravating factors are wide enough to include the factual matrix of aggression. If the Prosecutor could demonstrate that the convicted person for crimes against humanity also satisfied the material elements of aggression, both objective and mental elements, it could serve to elevate the gravity of the crime in forming part of the larger crime complex and by that

---

[167] *See* Prosecutor v. Akayesu, Case No. ICTR-96-4-T, Sentence, ¶ 40 (Oct. 2, 1998). *See also* Rome Statute, *supra* note 1, art. 81(2)(a); Lubanga Sentencing Decision, *supra* note 70, ¶ 36.

[168] The same factors are also listed in Article 24(2) of the Statute of the International Criminal Tribunal for the former Yugoslavia and in Article 23(2) of the Statute of the International Tribunal for Rwanda. U.N. Security Council, Statute of the International Criminal Tribunal for the former Yugoslavia art. 24(2) (as amended on July 7, 2009), S.C. Res. 827, U.N. Doc. S/RES/827 (May 25, 1993); U.N. Security Council, Statute of the International Criminal Tribunal for Rwanda art. 23(2) (as amended on Dec. 16, 2009), S.C. Res. 955, U.N. Doc. S/RES/955 (Nov. 8, 1994).

[169] *See, e.g.,* Prosecutor v. Aleksovski, Case No. IT-95-14/1-A, Appeals Judgment, ¶ 182 (Mar. 24, 2000); Delalić Appeals Judgment, *supra* note 160, ¶ 731. Lubanga Sentencing Decision, *supra* note 70, ¶ 36 (holding the "gravity of the crime as one of the principle factors" in sentencing).

[170] *See* Int'l Criminal Court, *Rules of Procedure and Evidence*, r. 145(1)(c), (2)(b)(ii), (2)(b)(vi) (2012).

[171] Ventura & Gillett, *supra* note 117, at 534.

justify a longer sentence. The presence of aggression as part of the whole crime complex might potentially even justify raising the maximum sentence to life imprisonment.[172]

Existing jurisprudence supports such an expansive approach to sentencing, in the form of a general openness to exploit the wide discretion granted to the international criminal tribunals in this regard. The ICTY Appeals Chamber has remarked that the Court may "exercise a considerable amount of discretion ... in determining an appropriate sentencing [sic]," and that this "is largely because of the overriding obligation to individualize a penalty to fit the individual circumstances of the accused and the gravity of the crime."[173] As noted by Drumbl, the existing jurisprudence demonstrates the willingness of the judges to take into account factors beyond those provided in the Statutes in order to secure justice at sentencing.[174]

Although the Rome Statute offers more positive guidance with respect to sentencing than the *ad hoc* Statutes, the ICC has likewise taken a broad approach regarding which factors may be taken into account at sentencing. In *Lubanga* the Trial Chamber accepted incidents of rape and sexual violence as aggravating factors irrespective of whether they formed part of the indictment or not.[175] Interestingly, the SCSL in *Taylor* took this discretion as far as taking into account as an aggravating factor that Taylor, in perpetrating the crimes, was also individually engaged as a head of state in acts contrary to the customary principle of non-intervention under public international law.[176] Upon appeal, the Appeals Chamber considered the reference to public international law unnecessary, but accepted the general relevance of the "extraterritorial aspect" – in reality aggression – which was not a crime within the jurisdiction of the SCSL:

> The Appeals Chamber considers that it was unnecessary for the Trial Chamber to refer to public international law in order to take into consideration the extraterritorial nature and consequences of Taylor's acts and conduct.... . The Appeals Chamber concludes that it was proper for the Trial Chamber to consider the different aspects of Taylor's acts and conduct in assessing

[172] *See* Rome Statute, *supra* note 1, art. 77(1)(b); *Rules of Procedure and Evidence*, *supra* note 170, r. 145(3).
[173] Delalić Appeals Judgment, *supra* note 160, ¶ 717.
[174] *See* DRUMBL, *supra* note 166, at 59. *See also* Prosecutor v. Kayishema, Case No. ICTR-95-1-T, Sentence, ¶ 4 (May 21, 1999); Delalić Appeals Judgment, *supra* note 160, ¶ 718.
[175] *See* Lubanga Sentencing Decision, *supra* note 70, ¶¶ 67–68 (July 10, 2012). The problem in this respect was that insufficient evidence was provided linking these acts to the accused. *Id.* ¶ 75.
[176] Prosecutor v. Taylor, Case No. SCSL-03-01-T, Sentencing Judgment, ¶ 27 (May 30, 2012).

the gravity of the totality of Taylor's culpable conduct, and that the Trial Chamber did not impermissibly double-count the same factor.[177]

Considering that the Rome Statute provides jurisdiction over the crime of aggression and a definition of individual criminal liability for this crime, it should be even more legitimate for the ICC to utilize its discretion offered with respect to sentencing, and take into account that an individual convicted for other crimes under the Statute, related to the commission of these offenses, simultaneously satisfied the definition of a crime of aggression under Article 8*bis*. As asserted by Ventura and Gillett,[178] it would be perfectly possible to include aggression even if the lack of jurisdiction prevents it from being formally prosecuted as a distinct crime. In fact, it is only by taking into account that a convicted person for crimes against humanity, war crimes, or genocide also participated in a concurrent or closely linked crime of aggression that it would be possible to capture the overall blameworthiness of the criminal conduct and to mete out a sentence proportional to the circumstances of the specific case.

But in order to adhere to the principle of personal culpability and the legality principle, taking aggression into account as an aggravating factor at sentencing in assessing the overall gravity of the collective crime complex requires that the Prosecutor has been able to establish that the accused person fulfills the material and mental elements under Article 8*bis*. These elements would have to be proven beyond a reasonable doubt.[179] There are in principle different ways in which the OTP could establish the required factual matrix in this respect. First, the above strategy of utilizing co-perpetration in order to extend liability for the subsequent crimes against humanity or war crimes to those high-ranking leaders responsible for the initial aggression may have already served to establish the factual matrix of aggression by revealing the whole common plan.[180] Second, in accordance with Article 77(2) of the Rome Statue, the Prosecutor may demand the Court hold a hearing to present additional evidence relevant to sentencing, since the issue had earlier not been sufficiently elucidated and examined. Thus, if all the material and mental elements of aggression are then finally established with respect to the accused, this crime under general international law can be taken into account as an aggravating factor.

[177] Prosecutor v. Taylor, Case No. SCSL-03-01-A, Appeals Judgment, ¶¶ 683, 687 (Sep. 26, 2013).
[178] Ventura & Gillett, *supra* note 117, at 535.
[179] Lubanga Sentencing Decision, *supra* note 70, ¶ 33 (stating that "[s]ince any aggravating factors ... may have a significant effect on the overall length of the sentence ... it is necessary that they are established to the criminal standard of proof, namely 'beyond a reasonable doubt.'").
[180] Ventura & Gillett, *supra* note 117, at 533–35.

A possible counterargument against this prosecutorial strategy relates to its practical effectiveness. As the ICTR has held, "on account of their extreme gravity, crimes against humanity and genocide must be punished appropriately."[181] Adding the factual matrix of aggression at the sentencing stage may in some cases not lead to any significant increase in the final sentence. However, even in such cases one would still at least include the aggression aspect in the judgment, and by that, reinforce and authoritatively communicate the unacceptable nature of such conduct under international law. Even this would be a significant improvement compared to the current status of total impunity for the crime of aggression.

IX. CONCLUSION

This Chapter has analyzed the feasibility of making recourse to alternative prosecutorial strategies in order to alleviate the current state of impunity for the crime of aggression, due to the ICC's lack of full jurisdiction over this crime under the Rome Statute.

It has been argued that the illegal use of force as a crime of aggression can be lawfully utilized as a relevant factor in the gravity assessment in selecting situations and cases. Furthermore, aggression may be prosecuted through the vehicle of other core universal crimes. It would in some cases be possible to take aggression into account as an aggravating circumstance at sentencing if a military or political leader has been formally convicted of crimes against humanity, war crimes, or even genocide. Consequently, aggression, in the form of the factual matrix required to satisfy the elements of Article 8*bis*, could thus be integrated at all prosecutorial stages at the ICC.

While the different parts of such a prosecutorial strategy have their respective limitations, the combined effect may prove successful. By utilizing the existing legal framework and systematically focusing on aggression when relevant in the prosecution of other universal crimes, in particular crimes against humanity and some war crimes, the Prosecutor, and, eventually, the Court, could contribute to deterring future occurrences of illegal war. If political and military leaders around the world get the message that the ICC Prosecutor will scrutinize their acts whenever they may resort to illegal use of force, including with a view to possible criminal responsibility for concurrent or subsequent crimes against humanity, it seems likely that this consequence will be considered a substantial cost and liability at the planning and

[181] Prosecutor v. Kambanda, Case No. ICTR-97-23-S, Judgment and Sentence, ¶ 17 (Sep. 4, 1998).

preparatory stages of future military operations. Hence, important preventive effects should be expected, since most potential perpetrators at the leadership level are rational and self-interested human beings who do not want the attention of international prosecutors and criminal courts.

A related and unexplored question is whether it would be desirable and legitimate for the OTP to make use of the strategies suggested. Given the fact that the Assembly of States Parties at the Kampala Review Conference in 2010 decided not to grant the ICC full and unconditioned jurisdiction over the crime of aggression at this time, subject only to the same limitations as other crimes within the Rome Statute, an argument could be made that it would not be faithful to the Parties' intentions to integrate the factual matrix of aggression when prosecuting other universal crimes and that the Prosecutor and the Court should therefore refrain from doing so. Applying the suggested prosecutorial strategies may increase the opposition among States Parties and non-State Parties with respect to the overall functioning of the ICC, which might be problematic in the long run for an institution still in the process of consolidating its position in the international community. In response, however, it must be underlined that the proposed strategies fit well within the existing legal frameworks of the Rome Statute. Applying these strategies would legally fall clearly within the mandate granted and encouraged generally by States Parties. If the ICC's organs were to be more focused on making decisions and assessments of a political character for fear of offending state leaders, rather than strictly and without discrimination applying the existing legal frameworks in order to prosecute the gravest criminal behavior, that would arguably serve to undermine the legitimacy of the ICC more severely.

Finally, the prosecutorial strategies suggested are flexible and might be implemented gradually. They should be seen as another important tool in the ICC toolbox rather than a threat to independent and future effective prosecution of core crimes. The "ultimate step in avoiding periodic wars," to borrow a phrase from the U.S. Chief Prosecutor Robert H. Jackson in his opening statement at Nuremberg, "is to make statesmen responsible to law," while the law universally "must condemn aggression."[182] This may require actors with courage, as well as the practical means of prudent step-by-step enforcement of international criminal law.

---

[182] Robert H. Jackson, *Opening Statement Before the International Military Tribunal, in* 2 Trial of Major War Criminals Before the International Military Tribunal, Nuremberg, 14 November – 1 October 1946, Proceedings, at 154 (1947), www.loc.gov/rr/frd/Military_Law/pdf/NT_Vol-II.pdf.

15

The Illegal Use of Force (Other Inhumane Act) as a Crime Against Humanity

An Assessment of the Case for a New Crime at the International Criminal Court

MANUEL J. VENTURA

I remind you that 23 members of the United Nations have bound themselves by the Charter of the Nuremberg Tribunal to the principle that planning, initiating or waging a war of aggression is a crime against humanity for which individuals as well as states shall be tried before the bar of international justice.

– *United States President Harry S. Truman*[1]

I. INTRODUCTION

The law makes a fundamental distinction between peace and war. During times of war, the extensive peacetime constraints on the exercise of violence are relaxed and give way to the far more permissible rules of international humanitarian law (IHL) as informed and influenced by human rights law.[2] As a result, we would like to think that in our modern world, unlike in times gone by, war is no longer a free-for-all in which victory is put above any law, morality, or humanity – the famous Martens Clause can be cited as evidence of this mentality.[3] Yet, crimes inevitably occur in armed conflict – one would

---

[1] Harry S. Truman, Address to the Opening Session of the United Nations General Assembly (Oct. 23, 1946), *available at* http://trumanlibrary.org/publicpapers/viewpapers.php?pid=914.

[2] *See generally* Human Rights Comm., General Comment No. 31: The Nature of the General Legal Obligation Imposed on States Parties to the Covenant, U.N. Doc. CCPR/C/21/Rev.1/Add.13, ¶ 11 (May 26, 2004); Legal Consequences of the Construction of a Wall in the Occupied Palestinian Territory, Advisory Opinion, 2004 I.C.J. 178, ¶ 106 (July 9); Case Concerning Armed Activities on the Territory of the Congo (Dem. Rep. Congo v. Uganda), Judgment, 2005 I.C.J. 168, 242–43, ¶ 216 (Dec. 19).

[3] *See* Convention (II) with Respect to the Laws and Customs of War on Land pmbl., ¶ 9, July 29, 1899, 32 Stat. 1803, T.S. No. 403:

> Until a more complete code of the laws of war is issued, the High Contracting Parties think it right to declare that in cases not included in the Regulations adopted by them, populations and belligerents remain under the protection and empire of the principles of

be hard-pressed naming a war that was completely bereft of criminal activity. Indeed, if one were to speak to anyone who has actually lived through and fought in wars – rather than only having read about them – they will attest to the horrors, bloodshed, and anguish that they entail. The effects of war do not end when the firing stops. Even where international humanitarian law is generally respected, mentally, if not psychically, the men and women who experience war firsthand soon realize that they are no longer the same person. War has a way of fundamentally changing all those involved – and not necessarily for the better. It is thus not surprising when, during remembrance services around the world every year, mature men and women who lived through the effects of armed conflicts that ended many decades ago still vividly remember their experiences. So much so that it brings many of them to tears.

This is perhaps why the International Military Tribunal (IMT) at Nuremberg was of the opinion, as far back as 1947, that "[w]ar is essentially an evil thing."[4] It also helps to explain why there now exists the crime of aggression under the Rome Statute of the International Criminal Court that awaits ratification and activation.[5] In a perfect world, this crime would reach all those who illegally take a nation or the world out of peace and plunge it into war. But we do not reside in a perfect world. As this Chapter will demonstrate, the crime of aggression, as defined under the Kampala Amendments of 2010, leaves a number of significant gaps and loopholes – enough to justify a different approach. One such approach has been recently advanced by the last surviving Nuremberg-era prosecutor (specifically, of the *Einsatzgruppen* case[6]), Ben Ferencz. He posits that the illegal use of (armed) force should be prosecuted as a crime against humanity, namely, other inhumane acts, along the following lines:

> [A]ny person responsible for the illegal use of armed force in violation of the UN Charter, which unavoidably and inevitably results in the death of large

---

international law, as they result from the usages established between civilized nations, from the laws of humanity, and the requirements of the public conscience.

[4]   1 Trial of Major War Criminals Before the International Military Tribunal, Nuremberg, 14 November – 1 October 1946, Judgment, at 186 (1947), *available at* www.loc.gov/rr/frd/Military_Law/pdf/NT_Vol-I.pdf [hereinafter IMT Judgment].

[5]   *See* Rome Statute of the International Criminal Court arts. 8*bis*, 15*bis*(2)–(3), 15*ter*(2)–(3), *adopted on* July 17, 1998, 2187 U.N.T.S. 91 (entered into force July 1, 2002) [hereinafter Rome Statute].

[6]   *See* "The Einsatzgruppen Case," *Military Tribunal No. II, Case 9, United States of America v. Ohlendorf et al.*, Judgment, *in* 4 Trials of War Criminals Before the Nuernberg Military Tribunals Under Control Council Law No. 10, at 411 (1948), *available at* www.loc.gov/rr/frd/Military_Law/pdf/NT_war-criminals_Vol-IV.pdf.

numbers of civilians, should be subject to punishment for his individual criminal responsibility in the perpetration of a crime against humanity.[7]

Yet, as he himself concedes, this idea "would have to be more explicitly defined and explained."[8] This Chapter is an attempt to do just that. In fact, as we will see below, the formulation proposed by Ben Ferencz does not, arguably, go far enough. Thus, a slightly more nuanced position – though with the same underlying vision in mind – will be explored vis-à-vis the requirements of other inhumane acts pursuant to Article 7(1)(k) of the Rome Statute. It concludes that where in an armed conflict crimes (e.g., murders, rapes, etc.) are committed as part of a widespread or systematic attack against a civilian population, and if the initiation of that war – whether international or non-international – had no legal justification, had civilians as its target, and was part of that attack on the civilian population, then those responsible for initiating the war could be guilty of the illegal use of force as a crime against humanity (other inhumane act) along the lines proposed by Ben Ferencz. This Chapter will further argue that such an offense would be both wider and narrower than the present definition of aggression and could potentially be prosecuted before the International Criminal Court (ICC) without the need to engage with the problematic clauses contained in the Kampala Amendments. However, it will also posit that such a crime brings with it certain issues that could render its prosecution an unattractive proposition for ICC prosecutors and its recognition problematic for ICC judges.

II. THE GAPS AND LOOPHOLES IN THE DEFINITION OF AGGRESSION IN THE KAMPALA AMENDMENTS OF 2010

There was an understandable atmosphere of celebration and rejoicing in Kampala, Uganda, during the early hours of June 12, 2010, when States Parties to the Rome Statute agreed to a definition of aggression. It marked the culmination of a long and arduous process that had begun in the aftermath of World War II and beyond. It was an important legal milestone. And yet, while not downplaying its importance, upon a close reading of the definition and accompanying provisions, one quickly realizes that the amendments were the result of political compromises that left much to be desired. While this is not the place to enter into an exhaustive discussion of all the finer points of the

---

[7]   Benjamin B. Ferencz, *The Illegal Use of Armed Force as a Crime Against Humanity*, 2 J. ON USE FORCE & INT'L L. 187, at 195 (2015).

[8]   *Id.* at 193.

definition of aggression,[9] this is the place to highlight the numerous deficiencies that justify the consideration of a different approach to the prosecution of those who end peace by illegally initiating war.

First, the Kampala definition defines an act of aggression as "the use of armed force *by a State* against the sovereignty, territorial integrity or political independence of *another State*."[10] This wording only captures international armed conflicts. The proposition advanced by Ben Ferencz, by tying itself down to the U.N. Charter,[11] suffers from the same deficiency, since Article 2 (4) contains no prohibition on the initiation of civil war and instead only prohibits the use of force between States.[12] In doing so, the most prominent type of armed conflict that currently exists in the world today is excluded: those of a non-international character. Indeed, a recent study found that in 2012 at least thirty-seven armed conflicts took place and of these only one was an "active international armed conflict ... narrowly defined" while "belligerent occupations continued [in] parts of nine states and territories."[13] In 2013, the same study found that the total number of armed conflicts had risen to thirty-nine, with two active international armed conflicts and the number of belligerent occupations remaining unchanged.[14] As such, the initiation of war by non-state armed groups against a State or against other non-state armed groups simply cannot be prosecuted before the ICC under the Kampala definition[15] or under the proposal by Ben Ferencz, despite the fact that they outnumber international armed conflicts by a significant margin.

---

[9] *See, e.g.,* CARRIE MCDOUGALL, THE CRIME OF AGGRESSION UNDER THE ROME STATUTE OF THE INTERNATIONAL CRIMINAL COURT (2013); Matthew Gillett, *The Anatomy of an International Crime: Aggression at the International Criminal Court*, 13 INT'L CRIM. L. REV. 829 (2013); SERGEY SAYAPIN, THE CRIME OF AGGRESSION IN INTERNATIONAL CRIMINAL LAW: HISTORICAL DEVELOPMENT, COMPARATIVE ANALYSIS AND PRESENT STATE 253–320 (2014).

[10] Rome Statute, *supra* note 5, art. 8*bis*(2) (emphasis added).

[11] *See* Ferencz, *supra* note 7.

[12] However, Ben Ferencz may perhaps also be open to the idea of outlawing the illegal use of force in a civil war context, since, in his view, his proposal "might induce *militant extremist groups* or states to pause and desist from causing great suffering to large numbers of blameless civilians." Ferencz, *supra* note 7, at 193 (emphasis added). *See also* Eliav Lieblich, Internal *Jus Ad Bellum*, 67 HASTINGS L.J. 687 (2016) (where the author recognizes that Article 2[4] only applies between States and proposes a novel theory of *jus ad bellum*, which would apply *within* a State – both to governments as well as non-state armed groups).

[13] Stuart Casey-Maslen, *Armed Conflicts in 2012 and Their Impacts*, in THE WAR REPORT: 2012, at 3–4 (Stuart Casey-Maslen ed., 2013) [hereinafter 2012 WAR REPORT].

[14] Stuart Casey-Maslen, *Armed Conflicts in 2013 and Their Impacts*, in THE WAR REPORT: ARMED CONFLICT IN 2013, at 27–29 (Stuart Casey-Maslen ed., 2014).

[15] This is not to say that the actions of non-state armed groups could *never* fall within the definition of aggression. Article 8*bis*(2)(g) specifically refers to the actions "of armed bands, groups, irregulars or mercenaries" against a State provided that they are of sufficient gravity and

Second, as per Article 8*bis*(1), only "person[s] in a position effectively to exercise control over or to direct the political or military action of a State" are liable to criminal prosecution for the crime of aggression. This is commonly referred to as aggression's "leadership element." The idea that the common foot soldier should not be held criminally responsible for aggression originates from the first prosecutions for crimes against peace (as aggression was then called) and the jurisprudence of the IMT at Nuremberg and the International Military Tribunal for the Far East (IMTFE) at Tokyo.[16] The drafters of the Kampala Amendments broadly agreed; the leadership element "seemed to be the only issue on which there was agreement in principle."[17] However, in formulating the "control or direct" standard, "many delegations often invoked the Nuremberg precedent ... [but] only a few questioned whether the clause did in fact reflect that precedent."[18] In fact, a closer look reveals that the Kampala Amendments' aggression leadership element does not align with World War II–era case law. Instead, it *narrows* the class of persons who could be criminally liable for aggression, since a number of defendants were convicted after World War II not on the basis that they controlled or directed the political or military action of their respective States, but instead that they were in a position to *shape or influence* such action – a less restrictive standard.[19] In other words, the scope of criminal responsibility for aggression under customary international law[20] is wider than that at the ICC. The few explanations for

were "sen[t] by or on behalf of a *State*" or a *State* was "substantial[ly] involve[d] therein." In other words, unless the actions of a non-state armed group can be attributed to a State or a State can be proved to be substantially involved in them, they would stand to be excluded from the Kampala definition of aggression. See Rome Statute, *supra* note 5, art. 8*bis*(2)(g).

[16] *See, e.g.,* "The I.G. Farben Case," *Military Tribunal No. VI, Case 6, United States of America v. Krauch et al., in* 8 TRIALS OF WAR CRIMINALS BEFORE THE NUERNBERG MILITARY TRIBUNALS UNDER CONTROL COUNCIL LAW No. 10, Judgment, at 1126 (1948), *available at* www.loc.gov/rr/frd/Military_Law/pdf/NT_war-criminals_Vol-VIII.pdf ("[I]ndividuals who plan and lead a nation into and in an aggressive war should be held guilty of crimes against peace, but not those who merely follow the leaders.").

[17] Stefan Barriga, *Negotiating the Amendments on the Crime of Aggression, in* THE TRAVAUX PRÉPARATOIRES OF THE CRIME OF AGGRESSION 3, 10 (Stefan Barriga & Claus Kreß eds., 2012).

[18] *Id.* at 22.

[19] For a detailed account of the relevant jurisprudence, *see* Kevin Jon Heller, *Retreat from Nuremberg: The Leadership Requirement in the Crime of Aggression,* 18 EUR. J. INT'L L. 477 (2007). *See also* MCDOUGALL, *supra* note 9, at 182 ("A comparison between the definition of a potential perpetrator under Article 8 *bis*[1] and the range of persons prosecuted by the post-war Tribunals shows that Heller was right to conclude that the decision to adopt the control or direct standard 'represents a significant *retreat* from the Nuremberg principles – not their codification.'").

[20] As various international criminal tribunals have held on numerous occasions, World War II–era jurisprudence is "indicative of customary international law." Prosecutor v. Taylor,

this anomaly found in the *travaux préparatoires* are that "the responsibility of persons beyond the direct leaders would be difficult to prove";[21] that the shape or influence standard is "too broad in defining potential perpetrators of the crime of aggression";[22] and that "especially in relation to democracies ... a very large circle of persons could be said to 'shape or influence' the State's action."[23]

Third, Article 15*bis*(4)[24] permits the opting out of the Kampala Amendments by States Parties[25] that commit acts of aggression in instances where the ICC Prosecutor acts *proprio motu* or there is a State referral as per Article 13(a) and (c) of the Rome Statute. There are elegant ways of explaining what this provision was intended to accomplish. One view was articulated by the former President of the ICC Assembly of States Parties, who, when introducing the text of what became Article 15*bis*(4), explained that "this would not constitute an 'opt out' of the amendment, much rather it would be a declaration that would affect a State Party's acceptance already given under article 12(1)."[26] But another way to articulate what was achieved is to simply say this: States Parties were given explicit permission to reserve to themselves the right to commit aggression and not face any criminal consequences – immunity for the crime of aggression. Imagine if States Parties could do this with respect to the other crimes under the ICC's jurisdiction: crimes against humanity, genocide, or war crimes. This would be an odd – if not nonsensical – situation.[27] That is

---

Case No. SCSL-03-01-A, Appeals Judgment, ¶ 417 (Sept. 26, 2013) (and the case law cited therein). *See also* Prosecutor v. Šainović, Case No. IT-05-87-A, Appeals Judgment, ¶¶ 1626–27 (Jan. 23, 2014) [hereinafter Šainović Appeals Judgment].

[21] 2007 *Princeton Report*, in THE TRAVAUX PRÉPARATOIRES OF THE CRIME OF AGGRESSION, *supra* note 17, at 561, ¶ 12.

[22] 1997 *Proposal by Germany (February)*, in THE TRAVAUX PRÉPARATOIRES OF THE CRIME OF AGGRESSION, *supra* note 17, at 224.

[23] Barriga, *supra* note 17, at 22 (citing 2007 *Princeton Report*, *supra* note 21, at 561, ¶ 12).

[24] Rome Statute, *supra* note 5, art. 15*bis*(4):

The Court may, in accordance with article 12, exercise jurisdiction over a crime of aggression, arising from an act of aggression committed by a State Party, unless that State Party has previously declared that it does not accept such jurisdiction by lodging a declaration with the Registrar. The withdrawal of such a declaration may be effected at any time and shall be considered by the State Party within three years.

[25] There is some debate in the literature as to whether, *inter alia*, this provision was intended to apply to *all* States Parties (including those who have not ratified the Kampala Amendments on aggression) or whether it applies to States Parties who ratify the amendments. *See* MCDOUGALL, *supra* note 9, at 249–60. For the purposes of the present discussion, nothing hinges on which view is right.

[26] Christian Wenaweser, 2010 *Introductory Remarks by the President (10 June, 11:00 a.m.)*, in THE TRAVAUX PRÉPARATOIRES OF THE CRIME OF AGGRESSION, *supra* note 17, at 780.

[27] Nevertheless, one could point to Article 124 of the Rome Statute. That provision allowed a State, upon becoming a State Party to the ICC, to declare that it does not accept the ICC's

why the drafters of the original Rome Statute included Article 120 which provides in the clearest of terms that "[n]o reservations may be made to this Statute." Yet, the practical effect of Article 15*bis*(4), particularly for new States that join the Statute after the aggression amendments are activated, is to allow the entering of reservations with respect to the crime of aggression in all but name. Indeed, in such cases, Article 15*bis*(4) is the very *definition* of a reservation as per the Vienna Convention on the Law of Treaties:

> "Reservation" means a unilateral statement, however phrased or named, made by a State, when signing, ratifying, accepting, approving or acceding to a treaty, whereby it purports to exclude or to modify the legal effect of certain provisions of the treaty in their application to that State[.][28]

As such, it is difficult to reconcile Article 15*bis*(4) with Article 120 of the Rome Statute.

Finally, Article 15*bis*(5) provides that "[i]n respect of a State that is not a party to th[e] [Rome] Statute, the Court shall not exercise its jurisdiction over the crime of aggression when committed by that State's nationals or on its territory."[29] This marks a significant shift away from Article 12(2)(a)–(b) whereby the ICC has jurisdiction over crimes committed by nationals of a State Party (regardless of where the crime is physically committed), or when committed on the territory of a State Party (regardless of the nationality of the person(s) who commit them). In contrast, when it comes to aggression, the ICC would not have jurisdiction when it is committed on the territory of a State Party by the nationals of a State that is not a party to the Rome Statute. In such circumstances the ICC would be in the awkward position of being able to prosecute crimes against humanity, genocide, and war crimes

---

jurisdiction over war crimes for a period of seven years after the entry into force of the Statute on July 1, 2002. Rome Statute, *supra* note 5, art. 124. However, as its title makes clear, it was a "[t]ransitional provision" that was never intended to be permanent, it could only be exercised once (upon joining the Rome Statute), and it was open to mandatory (deletion) review by the ICC Assembly of States Parties (ASP) at Kampala, Uganda, in 2010 (States Parties agreed not to delete Article 124 at that time). However, in November 2015 in The Hague, The Netherlands, an amendment on its deletion was passed by the ICC ASP: Resolution ICC-ASP/14/Res.2, annex, (Nov. 26, 2015), (pursuant to Article 121[4] of the Rome Statute, the amendment will enter into force one year after seven-eighths of ICC States Parties have ratified or accepted it). None of these elements are present with respect to the opt-out clause contained in Article 15*bis*(4).

[28] Vienna Convention on the Law of Treaties art. 2(1)(d), May 23, 1969, 1155 U.N.T.S. 331.

[29] However, it should be noted that this provision does not affect the U.N. Security Council's power to refer a situation where aggression was suspected of having been committed to the ICC pursuant to Article 13(b) of the Rome Statute – regardless of the State in which it occurred and the nationality of the perpetrator(s). *See* Rome Statute, *supra* note 5, art. 15*ter*.

committed on the territory of the State Party, but being unable to prosecute the aggressive war that facilitated the commission of these crimes in the first place. Similarly, the ICC would not have jurisdiction over aggression where the nationals of a State Party commit the crime on the territory of a State that is not a State Party to the Rome Statute. Thus, this odd enforcement model signifies and codifies an unequal application of the law. It requires, in effect, a "double ratification": the ICC can only exercise its jurisdiction over aggression where the State of nationality of the person(s) who commit the crime *and* the State on which the crime takes place have both ratified the amendments (unless the U.N. Security Council, acting under Chapter VII of the U.N. Charter, refers the matter to the ICC pursuant to Article 13(b) and Article 15*ter*).

In summary, both the aggression amendments and the Ben Ferencz proposal exclude the most common armed conflicts that are presently waged today: non-international armed conflicts. Instead, they focus solely on international armed conflicts that, in our contemporary times, are smaller in number. Further, the class of persons who can be held criminally responsible for aggression is narrower than it was historically by virtue of the "control or direct" (rather than the "shape and influence") standard for the leadership element. These realities already serve to significantly limit the ability of the ICC to prosecute those who illegally initiate war. To make matters worse, of those already limited number of conflicts and persons, Article 15*bis*(4)–(5) narrows them even further by allowing States Parties to opt out and then requiring a "double ratification" of the amendments. When each of these are viewed cumulatively, it becomes apparent that it is highly unlikely that an aggression case will come before the ICC in the foreseeable future in the absence of a U.N. Security Council referral, even if we discard other potential barriers that are found in the Rome Statute.[30]

For these reasons, exploring an alternative for criminalizing aggression, like the one proposed by Ben Ferencz, is not completely unjustified. But, rather than prosecuting such actions as a crime in and of itself (i.e., aggression), is it legally viable for it to fit within the architecture of, and be prosecuted as, "other inhumane acts" as a crime against humanity as per Article 7(1)(k) of the Rome Statute? To that analysis, this Chapter now turns.

---

[30] *See, e.g.*, Rome Statute, *supra* note 5, art. 16 (whereby the U.N. Security Council, acting under Chapter VII of the U.N. Charter, can defer an ICC investigation for a renewable period of twelve months).

III. ILLEGAL USE OF FORCE (OTHER INHUMANE ACT) AS A CRIME AGAINST HUMANITY UNDER THE ROME STATUTE

A. *Historical Pedigree of Other Inhumane Acts as a Crime Against Humanity*

"Other inhumane acts" as a crime against humanity was born, from a positivist perspective,[31] in the aftermath of World War II and can be found for the first time in the IMT Charter as a crime over which the IMT had jurisdiction:

> CRIMES AGAINST HUMANITY: namely, murder, extermination, enslave-
> ment, deportation, and *other inhumane acts* committed against any civilian
> population, before or during the war, or persecutions on political, racial or
> religious grounds in execution of or in connection with any crime within the
> jurisdiction of the Tribunal, whether or not in violation of the domestic law
> of the country where perpetrated.[32]

This definition of crimes against humanity, however, was subsequently held by the IMT to be intimately linked with war – as a matter of law, crimes against humanity could not take place without a nexus to armed conflict at that time.[33] This formulation was replicated in the IMTFE Charter[34] and Control Council Law No. 10,[35] although with respect to the latter the nexus to armed conflict was expressly removed. Similarly, the existence of "other inhumane acts" as a crime against humanity was also subsequently affirmed by the International Law Commission (ILC) in the Nuremberg Principles (albeit utilizing different wording)[36] and in the Draft

---

[31] This is not to say that crimes against humanity did not have prior historical origins. Indeed, one can trace its origins many years before the outbreak of World War II. *See generally* M. CHERIF BASSIOUNI, CRIMES AGAINST HUMANITY: HISTORICAL EVOLUTION AND CONTEMPORARY APPLICATION 86–111 (2011).

[32] Charter of the International Military Tribunal – Annex to the Agreement for the Prosecution and Punishment of the Major War Criminals of the European Axis art. 6(c), Aug. 8, 1945, 82 U.N.T.S. 279, *in* IMT JUDGMENT, *supra* note 4, at 11 (emphasis added).

[33] Indeed, as a result of this requirement, the IMT found that pre-1939 crimes could not constitute crimes against humanity under the IMT Charter. IMT JUDGMENT, *supra* note 4, at 254–55.

[34] Charter of the International Military Tribunal for the Far East art. 5(c), Jan. 19, 1946, *amended* Apr. 26, 1946, T.I.A.S. No. 1589 (utilizing the identical language of IMT Charter art. 6[c]).

[35] Allied Control Council Law No. 10, Punishment of Persons Guilty of War Crimes, Crimes Against Peace and Against Humanity art. II(1)(c), Dec. 20, 1945, *reprinted in* 3 Official Gazette of the Control Council for Germany at 50–55 (1946) (utilizing almost the identical language of IMT Charter art. 6[c]).

[36] Principles of International Law Recognized in the Charter of the Nürnberg Tribunals and in the Judgment of the Tribunal, princ. VI(c), *in* Int'l Law Comm'n, Rep. on the Work of Its Second Session, U.N. GAOR, 5th Sess., Supp. No. 12, U.N. Doc. A/1316, at 11–14 (1950) (emphasis added):

Code of Offences Against the Peace and Security of Mankind (while also removing the armed conflict nexus).[37]

However, as with much of international criminal law, the law on crimes against humanity lay relatively dormant until its revival with the advent of the wars in the former Yugoslavia in the 1990s and the genocide in Rwanda in 1994 and the creation by the U.N. Security Council of the International Criminal Tribunals for the former Yugoslavia (ICTY) and Rwanda (ICTR), respectively. Both of these Tribunals' Statutes included a specific provision on other inhumane acts as a crime against humanity. The ICTY Statute included it in Article 5[38] while in the ICTR Statute it can be found in Article 3,[39] although both of these definitions included what were later held to be additional jurisdictional elements not required under customary international law.[40] Thus, when it came time to draft the Rome Statute of

> The crimes hereinafter set out are punishable as crimes under international law: ...
> Crimes against peace: murder, extermination, enslavement, deportation and *other inhumane acts* done against any civilian population, or persecutions on political, racial or religious grounds, when such acts are done or such persecutions are carried on in execution of or in connection with any crimes against peace or any war crime.

[37] *Draft Code of Offences Against the Peace and Security of Mankind*, art. 2(11), [1954] 2 Y.B. Int'l L. Comm'n 112, U.N. Doc. A/CN.4/85 (emphasis added):

> The following acts are offences against the peace and security of mankind: ...
> *Inhuman acts* such as murder, extermination, enslavement, deportation or persecutions, committed against any civilian population on social, political, racial, religious or cultural grounds by the authorities of a State or by private individuals acting at the instigation or with the toleration of such authorities.

[38] *See* U.N. Security Council, Statute of the International Criminal Tribunal for the former Yugoslavia art. 5(i) (as amended on July 7, 2009), S.C. Res. 827, U.N. Doc. S/RES/827 (May 25, 1993) [hereinafter ICTY Statute]:

> The International Tribunal shall have the power to prosecute persons responsible for the following crimes when committed in armed conflict, whether international or internal in character, and directed against any civilian population: ...
> (i) other inhumane acts.

[39] *See* U.N. Security Council, Statute of the International Criminal Tribunal for Rwanda art. 3(i) (as amended on Dec. 16, 2009), S.C. Res. 955, U.N. Doc. S/RES/955 (Nov. 8, 1994) [hereinafter ICTR Statute]:

> The International Tribunal for Rwanda shall have the power to prosecute persons responsible for the following crimes when committed as part of a widespread or systematic attack against any civilian population on national, political, ethnic, racial or religious grounds: ...
> (i) other inhumane acts.

[40] *See* Prosecutor v. Tadić, Case No. IT-94-1-AR72, Decision on the Defence Motion for Interlocutory Appeal on Jurisdiction, ¶¶ 140–41 (Oct. 2, 1995) (in which the ICTY Appeals Chamber held that the requirement under Article 5[i] of the ICTY Statute that crimes

the ICC, there was general agreement as to its existence although some debate still ensued, particularly with respect to the armed conflict nexus. Nevertheless, the negotiations led to the definition currently found in Article 7:

1. For the purpose of this Statute, "crime against humanity" means any of the following acts when committed as part of a widespread or systematic attack directed against any civilian population, with knowledge of the attack: ...
    (k) Other inhumane acts of a similar character intentionally causing great suffering, or serious injury to body or to mental or physical health.
2. For the purpose of paragraph 1:
    (a) "Attack directed against any civilian population" means a course of conduct involving the multiple commission of acts referred to in paragraph 1 against any civilian population, pursuant to or in furtherance of a State or organizational policy to commit such attack[.]

Later, other inhumane acts as a crime against humanity was also included in the Special Court for Sierra Leone (SCSL) Statute[41] and the Extraordinary Chambers in the Courts of Cambodia (ECCC) Statute.[42]

On the basis of this extensive practice, there can be little doubt that other inhumane acts (as a crime against humanity) forms part of customary international law. Indeed, as the Trial Chamber in *Tadić* rightly put it, "since the Nürnberg [IMT] Charter, the customary status of the prohibition against crimes against humanity and the attribution of individual criminal responsibility for their commission have not been seriously

against humanity be "committed in armed conflict, whether international or internal in character" was not part of customary international law but merely jurisdictional in nature) [hereinafter Tadić Interlocutory Appeal on Jurisdiction]; Prosecutor v. Akayesu, Case No. ICTR-96-4-A, Appeals Judgment, ¶¶ 464–69 (June 1, 2001) (in which the ICTR Appeals Chamber held that the requirement under Article 3[i] of the ICTR Statute that crimes against humanity be against a civilian population "on national, political, ethnic, racial or religious grounds" was not part of customary international law but merely jurisdictional in nature).

[41] *See* Statute of the Special Court for Sierra Leone art. 2(i), Jan. 16, 2002, 2178 U.N.T.S. 137 (Jan. 16, 2002) [hereinafter SCSL Statute].
[42] *See* Law on the Establishment of the Extraordinary Chambers in the Courts of Cambodia for the Prosecution of Crimes Committed During the Period of Democratic Kampuchea art. 5, Oct. 27, 2004, NS/RKM/1004/006 [hereinafter ECCC Statute].

questioned."[43] The ICTY Appeals Chamber would later go on to state that "the notion of 'other inhumane acts' . . . cannot be regarded as a violation of the principle of *nullum crimen sine lege* as it forms part of customary international law."[44] This position has been most recently affirmed by the ECCC.[45]

Similarly, the First Report of the ILC's Special Rapporteur on crimes against humanity – tasked with the formulation of a treaty on the subject – similarly concluded, after a more thorough study of international and national practice, that "it is now well settled that, under customary international law, criminal responsibility attaches to an individual for committing crimes against humanity."[46] As a result, his proposed definition of crimes against humanity for inclusion in a future treaty includes "other inhumane acts" as a crime against humanity in Draft Article 2(1)(k).[47] There can be no doubt that this crime will be included in any final treaty on crimes against humanity.[48] In any event, the lack of objection or implicit acceptance or acquiescence by States and other concerned international subjects when the various international criminal tribunals have consistently convicted persons of such an offense could also arguably lead to the formation of a customary rule of international law.[49]

---

[43] Prosecutor v. Tadić, Case No. IT-94-1-T, Trial Judgment, ¶ 623 (May 7, 1997) [hereinafter Tadić Trial Judgment].

[44] Prosecutor v. Stakić, Case No. IT-97-24-A, Appeals Judgment, ¶ 315 (Mar. 22, 2006).

[45] *See* Co-Prosecutors v. Noun and Khieu, Case No. 002/19-09-2007/ECCC/TC/E313, Case 002/01 Trial Judgment, ¶¶ 435–36 (Aug. 7, 2014). *See also* Prosecutor v. Katanga and Ngudjolo, Case No. ICC-01/04-01/07-717, Decision on the Confirmation of Charges, ¶ 448 (Sept. 30, 2008) ("inhumane acts are to be considered as serious violations of international customary law and the basic rights pertaining to human beings").

[46] Sean D. Murphy (Special Rapporteur on Crimes Against Humanity), *First Report on Crimes Against Humanity*, ¶ 51, U.N. Doc. A/CN.4/680 (Feb. 17, 2015).

[47] *Id.* annex.

[48] For a further discussion on the lead-up to and the current ILC processes on the matter of a treaty for crimes against humanity, *see* Leila Nadya Sadat, *Towards a New Global Treaty on Crimes Against Humanity, in* FOR THE SAKE OF PRESENT AND FUTURE GENERATIONS: ESSAYS ON INTERNATIONAL LAW, CRIME AND JUSTICE IN HONOUR OF ROGER S. CLARK 311 (Suzannah Linton, Gerry Simpson & William A. Schabas eds., 2015).

[49] *See In re* El Sayed, Case No. CH/AC/2010/02, Decision on Appeal of Pre-Trial Judge's Order Regarding Jurisdiction and Standing, ¶ 47 (Nov. 10, 2010) (concerning the exercise of *compétence de la compétence* by various international criminal tribunals without any objections by States and other international subjects).

B. *Illegal Use of Force as an Other Inhumane Act and the Requisite Elements of a Crime Against Humanity Under the Rome Statute*

The underlying crime of the illegal use of force would involve the following: (1) the transformation of a situation of peace into a situation of war – whether international (between States) or non-international (between non-state armed groups or between States and non-state armed groups) – with no legal justification, where (2) civilians are the intended target. This substantively differs from the proposal by Ben Ferencz in that it is not linked to a violation of the U.N. Charter – it encompasses all armed conflicts. Such acts – what Ben Ferencz has called an "illegal use of armed force" – potentially meet the requisite elements of the underlying crime of other inhumane acts under Article 7(1)(k) of the Rome Statute and, when committed before or during the context of other crimes directed against the civilian population (murders, rapes, etc.), meets the *chapeau* elements of crimes against humanity set forth in Article 7(1) and Article 7(2)(a) of the Rome Statute. As demonstrated below, utilizing the rule of *ejusdem generis*, this respects the *nullum crimen sine lege* principle and in particular the requirement that "[t]he definition of a crime shall be strictly construed and shall not be extended by analogy."[50]

1. Chapeau Elements

A. PART OF A WIDESPREAD OR SYSTEMATIC ATTACK First, the underlying crime (in this case, the illegal use of force) must have been committed as part of a widespread or systematic attack. In this context, we must consider the words "part of [an] attack." On its face, the illegal use of force ought to be considered as an attack on its own – war is the most violent of all of humanity's activities. As the ICC Elements of Crimes points out, "the acts need not constitute a military attack,"[51] implicitly suggesting that a military attack could perhaps constitute an "attack." However, we must also inquire whether it is permissible for the crime (the illegal use of force) to *be* the attack, rather than simply forming *part of* an attack. In other words, is it permissible to prosecute the illegal use of force *only* when it is committed in the context of other attacks (such as murder, rapes, etc.), or is it enough for the illegal use of force itself to constitute the attack?

---

[50] Rome Statute, *supra* note 5, art. 22(2).
[51] Int'l Criminal Court, *Elements of Crimes*, art. 7, intro., ¶ 3 (2011) [hereinafter *Elements of Crimes*].

Here, the Rome Statute provides some guidance by stating that the "attack" requires "a course of conduct involving the multiple commission of acts" rather than a singular act.[52] The ICC has also held "that an attack may also be defined as a campaign or operation"[53] – which the illegal use of force inherently is – and that "the commission of the acts referred to in article 7 (1) of the Statute constitute the 'attack' itself and, beside the commission of the acts, no additional requirement of an 'attack' should be proven."[54] However, the jurisprudence of the *ad hoc* tribunals, the views of academics, and the International Law Commission might suggest something more nuanced, at least under customary international law. For example, Cryer, Friman, Robinson, and Wilmshurst assert that "[t]he act of the accused may also in itself *constitute* the attack, if it is of great magnitude,"[55] and since this is so, as Hall and Ambos note, "the acts could constitute the attack itself."[56] Indeed, as the ICTR pointed out early on, "[a]n attack ... like imposing a system of apartheid, which is declared a crime against humanity in Article 1 of the Apartheid Convention of 1973 ... may come under the purview of an attack, if orchestrated on a massive scale or in a systematic manner."[57] Similarly, the ICTY,

---

[52] Rome Statute, *supra* note 5, art. 7(2)(a). *See also* Prosecutor v. Ntaganda, Case No. ICC-01/04-02/06-309, Decision Pursuant to Article 61(7)(a) and (b) of the Rome Statute on the Charges of the Prosecutor Against Bosco Ntaganda, ¶ 23 (June 9, 2014) [hereinafter Ntaganda Confirmation of Charges]; Prosecutor v. Gbagbo, Case No. ICC-02/11-01/11-656-Red, Decision on the Confirmation of Charges Against Laurent Gbagbo, ¶ 208 (June 12, 2014) [hereinafter Gbagbo Confirmation of Charges]; Prosecutor v. Blé Goudé, Case No. ICC-02/11-02/11-186, Decision on the Confirmation of Charges Against Charles Blé Goudé, ¶ 125 (Dec. 11, 2014) [hereinafter Blé Goudé Confirmation of Charges].

[53] Prosecutor v. Ruto, Case No. ICC-01/09-01/11-373, Decision on the Confirmation of Charges Pursuant to Article 67(1)(a) and (b) of the Rome Statute, ¶ 164 (Jan. 23, 2012) [hereinafter Ruto Confirmation of Charges]. *See also* Situation in the Republic of Kenya, No. ICC-01/09-19-Corr, Decision Pursuant to Article 15 of the Rome Statute on the Authorization of an Investigation into the Situation in the Republic of Kenya, ¶ 80 (Mar. 31, 2010) [hereinafter Authorization of Kenya Investigation]; Situation in the Republic of Côte d'Ivoire, No. ICC-02/11-14-Corr, Corrigendum to "Decision Pursuant to Article 15 of the Rome Statute on the Authorisation of an Investigation into the Situation in the Republic of Côte d'Ivoire", ¶ 31 (Nov. 15, 2011) [hereinafter Authorization of Côte d'Ivoire Investigation].

[54] Prosecutor v. Bemba, Case No. ICC-01/05-01/08-424, Decision Pursuant to Article 61(7)(a) and (b) of the Rome Statute on the Charges of the Prosecutor Against Jean-Pierre Bemba Gombo, ¶ 75 (June 15, 2009) [hereinafter Bemba Confirmation of Charges].

[55] ROBERT CRYER ET AL., AN INTRODUCTION TO INTERNATIONAL CRIMINAL LAW AND PROCEDURE 243 (3d ed. 2014) (emphasis in original).

[56] Christopher K. Hall & Kai Ambos, *Article 7: Crimes Against Humanity – Section B(I)(1)(c)*, in THE ROME STATUTE OF THE INTERNATIONAL CRIMINAL COURT: A COMMENTARY 165 (Otto Triffterer & Kai Ambos eds., 3d ed. 2016).

[57] Prosecutor v. Akayesu, Case No. ICTR-96-4-T, Trial Judgment, ¶ 581 (Sept. 2, 1998) [hereinafter Akayesu Trial Judgment]. It is worth noting, however, that the ICC Elements of Crimes concerning apartheid as a crime against humanity requires that one or more inhumane

like the ILC, has been of the view that "[a] crime may be widespread or committed on a large scale by [...] the singular effect of an inhumane act of extraordinary magnitude."[58]

Regardless, in this discussion one must not lose sight of the realities of war: it is hard, if not impossible, to think of a war in which crimes were not committed – in a climate of such great violence, crimes often, unfortunately, result. Thus, where the illegal use of force – the initiation of war – is directed against a civilian population (this element is discussed in more detail in Section III[B][1][b]), the resulting and parallel crimes (murders, rapes, etc.) could constitute the "course of conduct involving the multiple commission of acts" referred to in Article 7(2)(a) of the Rome Statute – so long as they, too, targeted civilians. In other words, in the real world, the illegal use of force will not likely be a singular isolated act or event. This is all the more so when such violence is *directed* against civilians. In such a milieu, the commission of one or more of the enumerated acts contained in Article 7(1)(a)–(k) of the Rome Statute that constitute the underlying acts of crimes against humanity are all but guaranteed. In turn, this means that the illegal use of force would indeed form *part* of a larger attack directed against civilians. This would be consistent with ICC jurisprudence emphasizing that the relevant underlying crime must be related to the attack and not be isolated or random conduct.[59]

In the alternative, the illegal use of force could be viewed as taking place *before* the widespread or systematic attack – that is, the precursor to all the crimes that take place in the ensuing armed conflict. This would be consistent with the jurisprudence of the ICTY, which has held that "the acts of the accused ... need not be committed in the midst of the attack. A crime which is committed *before* ... the main attack against the civilian population or away

acts of the kind referred to in Article 7(1) of the Rome Statute be committed "in the context of an institutionalized regime of systematic oppression and domination by one racial group over any other racial group or groups" and that this conduct be committed as part of a widespread or systematic attack against a civilian population. *See, e.g., Elements of Crimes, supra* note 51, art. 7(1)(j), elements 4–5 (suggesting that apartheid itself cannot, on its own, constitute the relevant attack).

[58] Prosecutor v. Blaškić, Case No. IT-95-14-T, Trial Judgment, ¶ 206 (Mar. 3, 2000) (citing Int'l Law Comm'n, Rep. on the Work of Its Forty-Eighth Session, at 47, U.N. Doc. A/51/10, *available at* http://legal.un.org/ilc/texts/instruments/english/commentaries/7_4_1996.pdf).

[59] *See* Prosecutor v. Katanga, Case No. ICC-01/04-01/07-717, Decision on the Confirmation of Charges, ¶ 394 (Sep. 30, 2008) [hereinafter Katanga Confirmation of Charges]; Bemba Confirmation of Charges, *supra* note 54, ¶ 77; Prosecutor v. Katanga, Case No. ICC-01/04-01/07-3436-tENG, Judgment Pursuant to Article 74 of the Statute, ¶ 1101 (Mar. 7, 2014) [hereinafter Katanga Trial Judgment].

from it could still, if sufficiently connected, be part of that attack."[60] Viewed in this light, the illegal use of force would, in effect, be the crime that facilitates the commission of other crimes, or, as the IMT at Nuremberg put it, "it contains within itself the accumulated evil of the whole."[61]

With respect to the "widespread or systematic" criteria, these are clearly disjunctive – it is enough to prove one or the other, but not both.[62] The ICC has interpreted "widespread" to refer to the large-scale nature of the attack and the number of targeted persons, although "this assessment is not exclusively quantitative or geographical, but must be carried out on the basis of the individual facts."[63] "Systematic" has been held to pertain to the organized nature of the acts of violence and the improbability of their random occurrence, and "refers to the existence of 'patterns of crimes' reflected in the non-accidental repetition of similar criminal conduct on a regular basis."[64] However, it is important to remember that "only the attack, not the individual acts of the accused, must be widespread or systematic."[65] In other words, the underlying criminal offense – in this case the illegal use of force – need not, as a matter of law, be itself widespread or systematic.

Notwithstanding, where such actions are directed against a civilian population, more often than not, it will target a particular geographical location and a sizeable amount of civilians. It will also be an organized affair – armed

---

[60] Prosecutor v. Kunarac, Case No. IT-96-23 & IT-96-23/1-A, Appeals Judgment, ¶ 100 (June 12, 2002) (emphasis added) [hereinafter Kunarac Appeals Judgment]. *See also* Prosecutor v. Semanza, Case No. ICTR-97-20-T, Trial Judgment, ¶ 326 (May 15, 2003); Co-Prosecutors v. Kaing, Case No. 001/18-07-2007/ECCC/TC/E188, Trial Judgment, ¶ 318 (July 26, 2010) [hereinafter Kaing Trial Judgment]; Prosecutor v. Mrkšić, Case No. IT-95-13/1-A, Appeals Judgment, ¶ 41 (May 5, 2009) [hereinafter Mrkšić Appeals Judgment].

[61] IMT JUDGMENT, *supra* note 4, at 186.

[62] Katanga Confirmation of Charges, *supra* note 59, ¶ 448; Bemba Confirmation of Charges, *supra* note 54, ¶ 82. *See also* Prosecutor v. Limaj, Case No. IT-03-66-T, Trial Judgment, ¶¶ 210–11, 228 (Nov. 30, 2005) (in which the Chamber found that the relevant attack had been systematic but not widespread, but ultimately not directed against a civilian population).

[63] Gbagbo Confirmation of Charges, *supra* note 52, ¶ 222; Katanga Confirmation of Charges, *supra* note 59, ¶¶ 394–96; Bemba Confirmation of Charges, *supra* note 54, ¶ 83; Ruto Confirmation of Charges, *supra* note 53, ¶ 179; Katanga Trial Judgment, *supra* note 59, ¶¶ 176–78; Ntaganda Confirmation of Charges, *supra* note 52, ¶ 24; Blé Goudé Confirmation of Charges, *supra* note 52, ¶ 131.

[64] Katanga Trial Judgment, *supra* note 59, ¶ 1123. *See also* Katanga Confirmation of Charges, *supra* note 59, ¶¶ 397–98; Ruto Confirmation of Charges, *supra* note 53, ¶ 179; Ntaganda Confirmation of Charges, *supra* note 52, ¶ 24; Gbagbo Confirmation of Charges, *supra* note 52, ¶ 223; Blé Goudé Confirmation of Charges, *supra* note 52, ¶132.

[65] Kunarac Appeals Judgment, *supra* note 60, ¶ 96. *See also* Prosecutor v. Blaškić, Case No. IT-95-14-A, Appeals Judgment, ¶ 101 (July 29, 2004); Prosecutor v. Kordić, Case IT-95-14/2-A, Appeals Judgment, ¶ 94 (Dec. 17, 2004) [hereinafter Kordić Appeals Judgment].

Manuel J. Ventura

conflicts that target civilians do not generally break out by accident (discussed in more detail in Section III[B][1][c]). In addition, as aforementioned, the unfortunate nature of war means that, inevitably, crimes are committed in such a context. What this means in practice is that even if the illegal use of force itself is not widespread or systematic, then this element is still satisfied so long as it can instead be shown that the resulting crimes (murders, rapes, etc.) are widespread or systematic. This is not a tall (or unrealistic) order in an armed conflict that specifically targets the civilian population.

B. DIRECTED AGAINST ANY CIVILIAN POPULATION The ICC has interpreted "population" to mean a group of persons of any nationality, ethnicity, political affiliation, or other distinguishing features toward which the attack is directed against so that it cannot be characterized as directed against a limited or random selection of individuals.[66] As a corollary, it need not be proven that the entire population of the relevant geographical area was being targeted so long as they were sufficient in number or were targeted in a manner that reveals that they were effectively the intended targets. The words "directed against" mean that the relevant population must be the primary object of the attack and not merely incidental victims.[67] In addition, particularly because of the armed conflict backdrop, a "civilian" in our context "mean[s] any person who is not a member of either State or non-State armed forces"[68] and because of the word "any," the nationality (or lack thereof) of the civilians is irrelevant.[69]

It is here where an accused has the opportunity to stand his or her ground – "directed against any civilian population" is an important element that serves to distinguish armed conflicts that align with international humanitarian law

---

[66] Bemba Confirmation of Charges, *supra* note 54, ¶¶ 76–77; Ruto Confirmation of Charges, *supra* note 53, ¶ 164; Prosecutor v. Muthaura, Case No. ICC-01/09-02/11-382-Red, Decision on the Confirmation of Charges Pursuant to Article 67(1)(a) and (b) of the Rome Statute, ¶ 110 (Jan. 23, 2012) [hereinafter Muthaura Confirmation of Charges]; Gbagbo Confirmation of Charges, *supra* note 52, ¶ 209.

[67] Katanga Trial Judgment, *supra* note 59, ¶ 802; Bemba Confirmation of Charges, *supra* note 54, ¶¶ 76–77; Authorization of Kenya Investigation, *supra* note 53, ¶ 82; Authorization of Côte d'Ivoire Investigation, *supra* note 53, ¶ 33.

[68] Katanga Trial Judgment, *supra* note 59, ¶ 801; Bemba Confirmation of Charges, *supra* note 54, ¶ 78; Authorization of Kenya Investigation, *supra* note 53, ¶ 82; Authorization of Côte d'Ivoire Investigation, *supra* note 53, ¶ 33. However, one should bear in mind that, according to the jurisprudence of the ICTY, under the right conditions, the victims of crimes against humanity may include *hors de combat* within a civilian population. Prosecutor v. Martić, Case No, IT-95-11-A, Appeals Judgment, ¶¶ 303–14 (Oct. 8, 2008) [hereinafter Martić Appeals Judgment]; Mrkšić Appeals Judgment, *supra* note 60, ¶¶ 29–33.

[69] Katanga Trial Judgment, *supra* note 59, ¶ 1103; Bemba Confirmation of Charges, *supra* note 54, ¶ 76; Katanga Confirmation of Charges, *supra* note 59, ¶ 399.

(IHL) with those that do not. While the use of force certainly involves the use of violence and the transformation of a situation of peace into one of war, such actions need not – and indeed should never – be directed against civilians. If an accused charged with the illegal use of force as an other inhumane act can demonstrate that such actions were directed against either the armed forces of a State or a non-state armed group, and civilians were merely incidental and unfortunate victims, or can raise doubt as to the Prosecution's case that civilians were in fact the target, then the *chapeau* element for a crime against humanity will not be present. An acquittal for this crime must then follow. In other words, this requirement ensures that the initiation of armed conflict *per se* is not prohibited, but only armed conflict that has as its aim an attack against civilians. In fact, there is already precedent for this kind of analysis, and ultimately an acquittal on all counts: the ICTY's *Gotovina* case.

In *Gotovina*, the ICTY Prosecutor alleged that the accused were responsible for war crimes and crimes against humanity resulting from the launch by Croatia of "Operation Storm" on August 4, 1995, a military offensive to retake the Krajina region of the country that was at that time under the control of breakaway Croatian Serbs. At trial, the Chamber held that a joint criminal enterprise (JCE) had existed to remove the Croatian Serb population from the Krajina region and "was to a large extent achieved through ... unlawful attacks against civilians and civilian objects" (i.e., shelling) in various towns, and this promoted the goal of "forc[ing] the Krajina Serbs from their homes."[70] In other words, the military offensive, it was alleged, had been directed against the civilian population and formed the "touchstone of the Trial Chamber's analysis"[71] – "[t]he failure by members of the Croatian political and military leadership to make the distinction between the civilian population and the military [went] to the very core of th[e] case."[72] On appeal, however, the "200-metre standard" employed by the Trial Chamber to determine the existence or not of an unlawful artillery strike[73] was held to be

---

[70] Prosecutor v. Gotovina, Case No. IT-09-90-T, Trial Judgment, ¶¶ 2310–11 (Apr. 15, 2011) [hereinafter Gotovina Trial Judgment].

[71] Prosecutor v. Gotovina, Case No. IT-09-90-A, Appeals Judgment, ¶ 24 (Nov. 16, 2012) [hereinafter Gotovina Appeals Judgment].

[72] Gotovina Trial Judgment, *supra* note 70, ¶ 2309.

[73] Gotovina Appeals Judgment, *supra* note 71, ¶ 25 (citations omitted) ("The Trial Chamber's Impact Analysis was premised on its conclusion that 'a reasonable interpretation of the evidence' was that an artillery projectile fired by the Croatian Army which impacted within 200 metres of a legitimate target was deliberately fired at that target ('200 Metre Standard'). Using the 200 Metre Standard as a yardstick, the Trial Chamber found that all impact sites

erroneous.[74] As a result, having fatally undermined the conclusion that the artillery attacks were unlawful and not having found other sufficient evidence on the record to support such a determination, the holding on the existence of a JCE fell apart and the accused were acquitted on all counts.[75]

Although the above discussion and the (initial) convictions primarily centered on JCE – a mode of liability – and not crimes against humanity *per se* (although the accused had been charged with crimes against humanity and war crimes), the underlying analysis for the illegal use of force would have been the same. Had, for example, the accused in *Gotovina* been charged and tried for the crime envisaged by Ben Ferencz and this Chapter (and assuming peace existed beforehand), then the following defense would have been available: that the Prosecution did not prove beyond a reasonable doubt that the use of force was directed against the Croatian Serb civilian population of the Krajina region (rather than simply directed against the armed forces of the Croatian Serbs). As a result, an acquittal for this offense would follow.

C. PURSUANT TO OR IN FURTHERANCE OF A STATE OR ORGANIZATIONAL POLICY The "policy" element has been described by the ICC as referring to an "inten[tion] to carry out an attack against a civilian population, whether through action or deliberate failure to take action." Although it "does not preclude a design [being] adopted," "the statutory framework does not require that a formal design exist[] ... [but] the policy must always target a particular civilian population or part thereof."[76] Similarly, it has been held that this element

> [E]nsures that the attack ... must still be thoroughly organised and follow a regular pattern. It must also be conducted in furtherance of a common policy involving public or private resources.... [A]n attack which is planned,

---

located more than 200 metres from a target it deemed legitimate served as evidence of an unlawful artillery attack.").

[74] *Id.* ¶¶ 58–61.

[75] Gotovina Appeals Judgment, *supra* note 71, ¶¶ 64–68, 77–84, 89–98. This result, however, has been subject to academic discussion and disagreements. *See generally* Damien Scalia, *Jurisprudence in the Ad Hoc International Tribunals in 2012: Contributions and Controversy, in* 2012 WAR REPORT, *supra* note 13, at 464–72. For opposing perspectives, *see* Janine Natalya Clark, *Courting Controversy: The ICTY's Acquittal of Croatian Generals Gotovina and Markač,* 11 J. INT'L CRIM. JUST. 399 (2013) (critical of the decision), and Gary D. Solis, *The* Gotovina *Acquittal: A Sound Appellate Course Correction,* 215 MIL. L. REV. 78 (2013) (supportive of the decision).

[76] Katanga Trial Judgment, *supra* note 59, ¶ 802.

directed or organised – as opposed to spontaneous or isolated acts of violence – will satisfy this criterion.[77]

In addition, the policy can be "an ongoing process whose every aspect is not always predetermined before the operation or course of conduct pursued ... has commenced or even once it has started"; "in the majority of situations ... some aspects of the policy pursued ... will only crystallise and develop as actions are set in train and undertaken by the perpetrators."[78]

Further, the attack must be consistent with a policy pursued by a "State or organization" or the attack must further a policy of a "State or organization." "State" is fairly straightforward; little elaboration is required: it is sufficient for the policy to be attributed to persons who act as either *de jure* or *de facto* officials of a State or individuals whose actions can be attributable to a State or its organs.[79] Thus a state policy need not necessarily be conceived of or executed from the highest levels of the State; "a policy adopted by regional or even local organs of the State could satisfy the requirement."[80] Where controversy has arisen, however, is with respect to the interpretation of the term "organization."

Two views have arisen from the jurisprudence. The first sees this term as not being defined or limited by "the formal nature of the group and the level of its organization" (although this is relevant), but rather "on whether a group has the capability to perform acts which infringe on basic human values."[81] In other words, its "capacities for action, mutual agreement and coordination[] ... are essential features to defining an organisation that, by very reason of the means and resources it possesses and its membership,

---

[77] Katanga Confirmation of Charges, *supra* note 59, ¶ 396. *See* Bemba Confirmation of Charges, *supra* note 54, ¶ 81; Authorization of Kenya Investigation, *supra* note 53, ¶¶ 84, 86–88; Authorization of Côte d'Ivoire Investigation, *supra* note 53, ¶ 43; Ruto Confirmation of Charges, *supra* note 53, ¶ 210; Gbagbo Confirmation of Charges, *supra* note 52, ¶ 214; Prosecutor v. Bemba, Case No. ICC-01/05–01/08–3343, Judgment Pursuant to Article 74 of the Statute, ¶¶ 160–61 (Mar. 21, 2016).

[78] Katanga Trial Judgment, *supra* note 59, ¶ 1110.

[79] *See, e.g.,* Prosecutor v. Gaddafi, Case No. ICC-01/11–01/11–1, Decision on the "Prosecutor's Application Pursuant to Article 58 as to Muammar Mohammed Abu Minyar Gaddafi, Saif Al-Islam Gaddafi and Abdullah Al-Senussi," ¶¶ 17–31 (June 27, 2011) (noting that although Muammar Gaddafi was not a *de jure* head of state, he "organised and control[led] a State apparatus ... which was designed to ensure the endurance of his regime" and therefore he was considered to be the *de facto* head of state of Libya).

[80] Authorization of Kenya Investigation, *supra* note 53, ¶ 89; Authorization of Côte d'Ivoire Investigation, *supra* note 53, ¶ 45.

[81] Authorization of Kenya Investigation, *supra* note 53, ¶ 90; Authorization of Côte d'Ivoire Investigation, *supra* note 53, ¶ 46; Ruto Confirmation of Charges, *supra* note 53, ¶ 33; Muthaura Confirmation of Charges, *supra* note 66, ¶ 114.

allow an attack to be executed."[82] The late Judge Kaul, who insisted that the entity in question must possess State-like characteristics, has most succinctly expressed the second view. According to him, they must "partake of some characteristics of a State ... [which] eventually turn the private 'organization' into an entity which may act like a State or has quasi-State abilities"[83] in order to qualify as an "organisation" for the purposes of Article 7(2)(a).[84] The ICC Appeals Chamber has yet to definitively address the matter, although as Ambos has rightly pointed out, the criteria or characteristics outlined by both sides of the debate "as possible distinguishing features for the determination of an 'organisation' ... [shows that those] criteria are in large part identical ... and only differ substantially insofar as [Judge] Kaul regards them as indications of state-likeness."[85]

For our purposes, these requirements can be disposed of relatively easily. The initiation of war with no legal justification and directed against civilians (i.e., the illegal use of force as an other inhumane act) and the resulting crimes are not an accidental or freak occurrence – it is inherently the result of *organized* armed violence. As *Tadić* stated, in a now often repeated holding, "an armed conflict exists whenever there is a resort to armed force between States or protracted armed violence between governmental authorities and organized armed groups or between such groups within a State."[86]

---

[82] Katanga Trial Judgment, *supra* note 59, ¶ 1120.

[83] Authorization of Kenya Investigation, *supra* note 53 (dissenting opinion of Judge Kaul, ¶ 51). *See also* Prosecutor v. Ruto, Case No. ICC-01/09–01/11–2, Decision on the Prosecutor's Application for Summons to Appear for William Samoei Ruto, Henry Kiprono Kosgey and Joshua Arap Sang (Mar. 15, 2011) (dissenting opinion of Judge Kaul); Prosecutor v. Muthaura, Case No. ICC-01/09–02/11–3, Decision on the Prosecutor's Application for Summonses to Appear for Francis Kirimi Muthaura, Uhuru Muigai Kenyatta and Mohammed Hussein Ali (Mar. 15, 2011) (dissenting opinion of Judge Kaul); Ruto Confirmation of Charges, *supra* note 53 (dissenting opinion of Judge Kaul); Muthaura Confirmation of Charges, *supra* note 66 (dissenting opinion of Judge Kaul).

[84] *See generally* Authorization of Kenya Investigation, *supra* note 53 (dissenting opinion of Judge Kaul, ¶¶ 33–70).

[85] Kai Ambos, Treatise on International Criminal Law: The Crimes and Sentencing 74–75 (2014). *See also* Christopher K. Hall & Kai Ambos, *Article 7: Crimes against humanity – Section B(II)(1)(c)*, *in* The Rome Statute of the International Criminal Court: A Commentary, *supra* note 56, at 249.

[86] Tadić Interlocutory Appeal on Jurisdiction, *supra* note 40, ¶ 70. *See also* Prosecutor v. Lubanga, Case No. ICC-01/04–01/06–803-tEN, Decision on the Confirmation of Charges, ¶ 233 (Jan. 29, 2007) [hereinafter Lubanga Confirmation of Charges]; Katanga Confirmation of Charges, *supra* note 59, ¶ 381; Bemba Confirmation of Charges, *supra* note 54, ¶ 229; Prosecutor v. Lubanga, Case No. ICC-01/04–01/06–2842, Judgment Pursuant to Article 74 of the Statute, ¶ 533 (Mar. 14, 2012) [hereinafter Lubanga Trial Judgment]; Katanga Trial Judgment, *supra* note 59, ¶ 1173.

While it is true that the intensity level for an international armed conflict is generally considered to be lower than it is for a non-international armed conflict,[87] this does not detract from the fact that such actions would generally meet the requirement of a state or organizational policy. This is evident from the fact that armed hostilities between States, or other actors acting on their behalf,[88] would be a *purposeful* event (i.e., according to a policy) and especially so when it is directed against civilians – armed forces would not break out in such a spontaneous burst of violence without the approval of, or control by, the relevant State. On the other hand, in a non-international armed conflict, the armed group (i.e., an "organization") must possess "some degree of organisation and the ability to plan and carry out sustained military operations."[89] Planning and executing an illegal use of force in such a context would also not occur randomly – a policy would underlie such actions. In short, armed conflicts directed against civilians – whether international or non-international in nature – do not generally start by accident: they are coordinated, planned and executed either by States, or alternatively, by a group/organization with the capabilities of taking on the military forces of a State or another armed group. Either way, because of the circumstances, this criterion is likely to be inherently fulfilled. What would be more difficult, however, as recounted above, is proving that the illegal use of force, and the crimes committed in the resulting conflict, were part of a state or organizational policy *directed against any civilian population.*

D. KNOWLEDGE OF THE ATTACK AND NEXUS BETWEEN THE CONDUCT AND THE ATTACK With respect to this requirement, the ICC Elements of Crimes stipulates that the perpetrator must have known "that the conduct was part of or intended the conduct to be part of a widespread or systematic attack directed against a civilian population."[90] However, this does not "requir[e] proof that the perpetrator has knowledge of all characteristics of the attack or

---

[87] *See* Dapo Akande, *Classification of Armed Conflicts: Relevant Legal Concepts, in* INTERNATIONAL LAW AND THE CLASSIFICATION OF CONFLICTS 41–42, 52–53 (Elizabeth Wilmshurst ed., 2012); ANTHONY CULLEN, THE CONCEPT OF NON-INTERNATIONAL ARMED CONFLICT IN INTERNATIONAL HUMANITARIAN LAW 131–32 (2010).

[88] Katanga Trial Judgment, *supra* note 59, ¶ 1177; Lubanga Trial Judgment, *supra* note 86, ¶ 541.

[89] Lubanga Trial Judgment, *supra* note 86, ¶ 535. *See also* Lubanga Confirmation of Charges, *supra* note 86, ¶ 233; Prosecutor v. Mbarushimana, Case No. ICC-01/04–01/10–465-Red, Decision on the Confirmation of Charges, ¶ 103 (Dec. 16, 2011) [hereinafter Mbarushimana Confirmation of Charges]; Katanga Trial Judgment, *supra* note 59, ¶ 1186. *See also* SANDESH SIVAKUMURAN, THE LAW OF NON-INTERNATIONAL ARMED CONFLICT 170–74 (2012).

[90] *Elements of Crimes, supra* note 51, art. 7(1)(a)–(k).

the precise details of the plan or policy of the State or organization."[91] The ICC has explained, on the basis of the jurisprudence of the *ad hoc* tribunals, that this requires: (1) the perpetrator's knowledge of the existence of the widespread or systematic attack directed against a civilian population in general terms, and (2) that the perpetrator knew that his or her acts were part of that attack (nexus requirement).[92] The latter in particular ensures that the acts were committed "as part of" a civilian-orientated attack and involves consideration of the characteristics, aims, nature, or consequences of the conduct.[93] However, it is "not required that the perpetrator ... subscribed to the State or the organisation's criminal design" but that he or she "intended his or her acts to form part of the attack against the civilian population."[94] With respect to "knowledge," the ICTY has held that the accused "at least must have taken the risk that his acts were part thereof" of the widespread or systematic attack[95] – suggesting that recklessness is sufficient in this context. However, whether recklessness is sufficient at the ICC is an open question, particularly in light of the default *mens rea* standard contained in Article 30 of the Rome Statute and its definition of "knowledge"[96] together with ICC jurisprudence rejecting recklessness[97] or *dolus eventualis* (advertent recklessness).[98] Nevertheless, these requirements "may be inferred from

---

[91] *Id.* art. 7, intro., ¶ 2. *See also* Katanga Trial Judgment, *supra* note 59, ¶ 1125; Bemba Confirmation of Charges, *supra* note 54, ¶ 88; Gbagbo Confirmation of Charges, *supra* note 52, ¶ 214.

[92] *See* Katanga Confirmation of Charges, *supra* note 59, ¶ 401; Gbagbo Confirmation of Charges, *supra* note 52, ¶ 214.

[93] Bemba Confirmation of Charges, *supra* note 54, ¶¶ 84, 86; Authorization of Kenya Investigation, *supra* note 53, ¶¶ 97–98.

[94] Katanga Trial Judgment, *supra* note 59, ¶ 1125. Bemba Confirmation of Charges, *supra* note 54, ¶ 88.

[95] Šainović Appeals Judgment, *supra* note 20, ¶¶ 270–71. *See also* Kunarac Appeals Judgment, *supra* note 60, ¶ 102; Martić Appeals Judgment, *supra* note 68, ¶ 316.

[96] Rome Statute, *supra* note 5, art. 30(3) ("[f]or the purposes of this article, 'knowledge' means awareness that a circumstance exists or a consequence will occur in the ordinary course of events. 'Know' and 'knowingly' shall be construed accordingly.").

[97] *See* Lubanga Confirmation of Charges, *supra* note 86, ¶ 355 n.438; Lubanga Trial Judgment, *supra* note 86, ¶ 1011; Bemba Confirmation of Charges, *supra* note 54, ¶ 360; Ruto Confirmation of Charges, *supra* note 53, ¶¶ 335–36.

[98] Initially, *dolus eventualis* (advertent recklessness) was accepted by the Pre-Trial Chamber in *Lubanga* and *Katanga*, but these holdings were subsequently rejected by the respective Trial Chambers. Lubanga Confirmation of Charges, *supra* note 86, ¶¶ 352–54; Katanga Confirmation of Charges, *supra* note 59, ¶ 251, n.329; Lubanga Trial Judgment, *supra* note 86, ¶ 1101; Katanga Trial Judgment, *supra* note 59, ¶¶ 775–76. Although the ICC Appeals Chamber has yet to definitively reject *dolus eventualis* (advertent recklessness), it has nonetheless cautioned against the use of language such as "risk" when discussing the common plan requirement of co-perpetration. Prosecutor v. Lubanga,

circumstantial evidence" such as the accused's position, his or her important role in the criminal campaign, presence at the scene of the crime(s), references to the superiority of his or her group vis-à-vis other groups, and the general historical and/or political environment.[99]

In the present case, the Prosecution may plausibly claim that in an international armed conflict, at the very least, senior military and political officials must have had knowledge that the armed forces of the State, or other forces acting on their behalf, were engaging in a military campaign that targeted civilians. Such forces are generally integrated within a military command and control structure or are in communication with the political or military structures of a State. This makes it extremely unlikely that senior military or political authorities were completely unaware that an armed conflict was taking place right under their noses. Further, to feign ignorance of crimes (murders, rapes, etc.) committed in such a context when past experience shows that crimes inevitably result in situations of armed conflict is, on its face, rather implausible, and particularly so when a policy exists that denotes civilians as the primary object of the attack and not incidental victims. Something similar can be argued in a non-international armed conflict where the level of organization and sophistication reaches a point where a non-state armed group has the capability to attack not only the military forces of the State or of other non-state armed groups on a sustained basis and to a certain level of intensity, but also to simultaneously target civilians in the process. As aforementioned, such actions are not the result of an inadvertent endeavor or a totally unexpected series of events – the requirement of a state or organizational policy would make short work of any claim to the contrary.

As to the nexus requirement, one must recall that the crimes that would be alleged to constitute the attack directed against the civilian population (murders, rapes, etc.), of which the illegal use of force would form part, would not have been committed but for the existence of war. In other words, it is the illegal use of force that created the conditions and environment that facilitated and enabled the widespread or systematic attack directed against the civilian population. There is therefore an inherent link between the illegal use of force and the crimes that take place during the conflict. As a result, the requirement

---

Case No. ICC-01/04–01/06–3121-Red, Judgment on the Appeal of Mr Thomas Lubanga Dyilo Against his Conviction, ¶ 449 (Dec. 1, 2014). However, Ambos is of the view that the *chapeau* of Rome Statute Article 7 constitutes an additional *mens rea* requirement that is to be distinguished from the default *mens rea* of Rome Statute Article 30. Rome Statute, *supra* note 5, arts. 7, 30. In his view, the jurisprudence of the ICTY and its "risk" or recklessness approach is transposable at the ICC. *See* AMBOS, *supra* note 85, at 77–78.

[99] Katanga Confirmation of Charges, *supra* note 59, ¶ 402.

of a nexus between the acts of the accused (illegal use of force as an other inhumane act) and the attack would likely not be difficult to demonstrate.

2. Underlying Crime: Other Inhumane Acts

So far, the ICC Prosecutor has accused a number of individuals of other inhumane acts as a crime against humanity pursuant to Article 7(1)(k) of the Rome Statute. In doing so, various Chambers have had the opportunity to outline the ICC's understanding of this offense. To begin with, the ICC has noted that "the [Rome] Statute has given to 'other inhumane acts' a different scope than its antecedents like the Nuremberg Charter and the ICTR and ICTY Statutes"[100] in the sense that it has "define[d] these acts in a more precise way"[101] as will be outlined and discussed below. Further, they "are to be considered as serious violations of international customary law and the basic rights pertaining to human beings."[102] They constitute "a residual category within the system of article 7(1) of Statute" so that "if a conduct could be charged as another specific crime under this provision, its charging as other inhumane acts is impermissible."[103]

At the *ad hoc* and hybrid tribunals, this category has been utilized to recognize a variety of criminal actions as other inhumane acts when they have not been explicitly included in the crimes against humanity provision in their respective Statutes and when they meet the legal requirements under their jurisprudence. These have included acts such as forcible transfers,[104] forced marriages,[105] inhumane and degrading treatment,[106] the use of human shields,[107] mutilation,[108] beatings,[109] enforced

---

[100] *Id.* ¶ 450.

[101] AMBOS, *supra* note 85, at 115. *See also* BASSIOUNI, *supra* note 31, at 409. However, at least one Trial Chamber of the ICTY seemed to think otherwise, noting that Article 7(1)(k) "fail[ed] to provide an indication, even indirectly, of the legal standards which would allow us to identify the prohibited inhumane acts." Prosecutor v. Kupreškić, Case No. IT-95–16-T, Trial Judgment, ¶ 565 (Jan. 14, 2000) [hereinafter Kupreškić Trial Judgment].

[102] Katanga Confirmation of Charges, *supra* note 59, ¶ 448.

[103] Muthaura Confirmation of Charges, *supra* note 66, ¶ 269. *See also* Katanga Confirmation of Charges, *supra* note 59, ¶ 452.

[104] Prosecutor v. Blagojević, Case No. IT-02–60-T, Trial Judgment, ¶¶ 629–30 (Jan. 17, 2005) [hereinafter Blagojević Trial Judgment].

[105] Prosecutor v. Brima, Case No. SCSL-2004–16-A, Appeals Judgment, ¶¶ 200–02 (Feb. 22, 2008).

[106] Kupreškić Trial Judgment, *supra* note 101, ¶ 566.

[107] Prosecutor v. Naletilić, Case No. IT-98–34-T, Trial Judgment, ¶ 334 (Mar. 31, 2003).

[108] Prosecutor v. Kajelijeli, Case No. ICTR-98–44A-T, Trial Judgment, ¶¶ 934–36 (Dec. 1, 2003).

[109] Tadić Trial Judgment, *supra* note 43, ¶ 730.

disappearances,[110] humiliation,[111] forced undressing,[112] deliberate sniping and shelling of civilians,[113] the imposition of deplorable conditions of detention[114] and enforced prostitution.[115] However, while one Chamber at the ICC has been of the view that "this residual category . . . must be interpreted conservatively and must not be used to expand uncritically the scope of crimes against humanity,"[116] Schabas has opined that other inhumane acts under "the Rome Statute leaves the door open for some evolution,"[117] while Ben Ferencz has noted that the "[e]numeration of certain actions as 'crimes against humanity' in the ICC Statute . . . was never intended to be exhaustive or exclusive."[118] It is submitted below that the illegal use of force can potentially meet the criteria to qualify as an other inhumane act under the Rome Statute.

A. SIMILAR CHARACTER AS THE ENUMERATED ACTS The first requirement for an other inhumane act is that the act must be of a similar nature, scale, and gravity as the acts referred to in Article 7(1) of the Rome Statute.[119] In order to make this determination, all the factual circumstances of the conduct ought to be considered. While "guidance may be derived from norms prohibiting inhumane treatment under human rights law and international humanitarian law," "[u]ltimately, the similarity assessment under paragraph 1(k) involves a value judgment."[120] Notwithstanding, "[i]t is [also] necessary to inquire whether the conduct is already subsumed under any of the other existing 'inhumane acts,'" necessitating that the conduct should have at least

---

[110] Kupreškić Trial Judgment, *supra* note 101, ¶ 566.
[111] Prosecutor v. Kvočka, Case No. IT-98/30/1-T, Trial Judgment, ¶ 209 (Nov. 2, 2001).
[112] Akayesu Trial Judgment, *supra* note 57, ¶ 697.
[113] Prosecutor v. Galić, Case No. IT-98-29-A, Appeals Judgment, ¶ 158 (Nov. 30, 2006).
[114] Kaing Trial Judgment, *supra* note 60, ¶ 372.
[115] Kupreškić Trial Judgment, *supra* note 101, ¶ 566.
[116] Muthaura Confirmation of Charges, *supra* note 66, ¶ 269.
[117] WILLIAM A. SCHABAS, AN INTRODUCTION TO THE INTERNATIONAL CRIMINAL COURT 119 (4th ed. 2011).
[118] Ferencz, *supra* note 7, at 195.
[119] *Elements of Crimes*, *supra* note 51, art. 7(1)(k) n.30; Katanga Confirmation of Charges, *supra* note 59, ¶¶ 448, 451; Authorization of Côte d'Ivoire Investigation, *supra* note 53, ¶ 83; Muthaura Confirmation of Charges, *supra* note 66, ¶ 269; Blé Goudé Confirmation of Charges, *supra* note 52, ¶ 120.
[120] Christopher K. Hall & Carsten Stahn, *Article 7: Crimes against humanity – Section B(I)(2)(k) (aa)*, in THE ROME STATUTE OF THE INTERNATIONAL CRIMINAL COURT: A COMMENTARY, *supra* note 56, at 239.

one element that is materially distinct from those of other acts outlined in Article 7(1)(a)–(j) of the Rome Statute.[121]

There can be little doubt that the illegal use of force is a particularly (and inherently) grave event of the same, if not higher, level than the existing acts that qualify as crimes against humanity. Indeed, when one considers the various listed acts, one can appreciate that their prohibition and punishment "protect diverse interests and values ... including the right to life, health, liberty and human dignity."[122] It is the displacement or elimination of such protections that give the crimes their grave character. An illegal use of force that targets civilians accomplishes precisely this. We can see this quite vividly by the fact that in a time of armed conflict, international humanitarian law applies and serves to modify – or in some cases supersedes entirely – international human rights law. This is not to say that international human rights law is completely eliminated by IHL *per se* in armed conflict – it is overwhelmingly accepted that the two apply side-by-side[123] – or that war is a free-for-all. Rather, the prohibition on violence that normally serves to ensure that diverse human-rights-based interests and values are protected is relaxed and gives way to another set of norms where an interference with a person's right to life, health, liberty, and human dignity is far more likely. In fact, given that crimes appear to be an inherent part of armed conflict one might say that their violation is almost guaranteed. In other words, the illegal use of force has particularly grave consequences for the targeted civilian population.

Apart from this, in our context, if one looks closely at the variety of different acts that qualify as crimes against humanity under the Rome Statute, one quickly notices a certain pattern. Generally speaking, the listed crimes involve the commission of acts upon one or more persons so that the suffering or injury caused is individualized to a person or persons by virtue of those acts alone. This holds true of enslavement, deportation or forcible transfers, torture, rape, enforced disappearance, enforced sterilization, forced pregnancy, imprisonment or other severe deprivation of liberty, etc. (or what Hall and

---

[121] *Id.* at 237. *See also* Katanga Confirmation of Charges, *supra* note 59, ¶¶ 456–65 (holding that indiscriminate gunfire and machete blows that resulted in serious and life-threatening injuries committed with the intent to kill were to be characterized as attempted murder, which could not be charged simultaneously under Article 7(1)(a) and Article 7(1)(k) because "the clear intent to kill persons cannot be transformed into intent to severely injure persons by means of inhumane acts solely on the basis that the result of the conduct was different from that which was intended and pursued by the perpetrators").

[122] Hall & Stahn, *supra* note 120, at 237.

[123] *See supra* note 2.

Carsten refer to as the "murder" type of crimes).[124] This is not to say that the criminal acts cannot involve a large multitude of persons or victims (indeed, in many instances this will be the case), but that, ultimately, the crime itself is "brought home" to an identified person or persons. Thus, for example, it is the act of rape itself, or torture, or murder, that results in suffering or injury. However, there are some listed crimes that do not fit neatly within this general mold – these can and do involve a scale that sees a collective group being targeted, of which an identified person or persons happens to form part, through the commission of *other* crimes.

The crime against humanity of persecution, for example, involves, *inter alia*, the targeting of any identifiable group or collectivity of people based on their political, racial, national, ethnic, cultural, religious, or gender identity, or other grounds universally recognized as impermissible under international law.[125] However, it is in fact other underlying crimes (murder, rape, etc.) that are committed within such a context that ultimately result in suffering or injury being visited upon the victims. Thus, "persecution" is not in and of itself an "act" that is carried out against individuals, but rather, it requires the commission of other crimes so that the completed offense of persecution can occur. In other words, persecution is committed *through* other acts – persecution cannot exist alone and independently. That is why, for example, in the *Muthaura* and *Ruto* cases, it was held that there were substantial grounds to believe that persecution was committed *through* murder, deportation or forcible transfer, rape, serious physical injuries, and acts causing serious mental suffering.[126]

In addition, persecution requires an "intentional and severe deprivation of fundamental rights contrary to international law by reason of the identity of the group or collectivity."[127] Clearly the violent acts described above are encompassed by the words "severe deprivation of fundamental rights," but one must also remember that "it [also] contemplates racist or other discriminatory acts

[124] Hall & Stahn, *supra* note 120, at 237.
[125] *Elements of Crimes*, *supra* note 51, art.7(1)(h), elements 2–3; Muthaura Confirmation of Charges, *supra* note 66, ¶ 282; Mbarushimana Confirmation of Charges, *supra* note 89 (dissenting opinion of Judge Monageng, ¶ 34).
[126] Muthaura Confirmation of Charges, *supra* note 66, ¶ 283; Ruto Confirmation of Charges, *supra* note 53, ¶¶ 271–74. *See also* Ntaganda Confirmation of Charges, *supra* note 52, ¶ 58; Gbagbo Confirmation of Charges, *supra* note 52, ¶¶ 204–06; Blé Goudé Confirmation of Charges, *supra* note 52, ¶¶ 122–23.
[127] Rome Statute, *supra* note 5, art. 7(2)(g). *See also* Muthaura Confirmation of Charges, *supra* note 66, ¶ 282; Ruto Confirmation of Charges, *supra* note 53, ¶ 274; Ntaganda Confirmation of Charges, *supra* note 52, ¶ 58.

and policies of a State that may in fact be authorized by its legal regime."[128] This would include, for example, discriminatory orders, laws, decisions, or other regulations – i.e., a deliberate policy – put in place and executed by the apparatus of a State or an organization (non-state group).

Similarly, we should consider the particular characteristics of the crime of apartheid as a crime against humanity – Articles 7(1)(j) and 7(2)(h). Not only does apartheid have its own treaty – the Convention on the Suppression and Punishment of the Crime of Apartheid (1973), but, like persecution, its commission is accomplished *through* other acts. Specifically, Article 7(2)(h) clarifies that the crime, *inter alia*, "means inhumane acts of a character similar to those referred to in [Article 7] paragraph 1." The ICC Elements of Crimes further stipulates that "the perpetrator [must] commit[] an inhumane act" as "referred to in article 7, paragraph 1, of the Statute, or . . . an act of a character similar to any of those acts."[129] Because of the reference to "other inhumane acts," Article 7(2)(h) "seems to define this crime as a residual category for certain inhumane acts under specific circumstances when they do not other-wise fit within one of the other acts listed in Article 7 para. 1."[130] In practice, for apartheid to be committed "any of the offences specified in Article 7(1),"[131] such as murder, rape, deportation or forcible transfers, torture, and others (e.g., legislative or other measures designed to divide the population along racial lines, denial of the right to work or education, cruel, inhumane or degrading treatment or punishment) would suffice.[132]

In addition, these acts must occur within an "institutionalized regime of systematic oppression and domination by one racial group over any other racial group or groups."[133] In particular, the word "regime" "implies State involvement, whereas others cast the net wider so as to also cover *de facto* States and armed opposition groups."[134] Similarly, the word "institutionalized" "presupposes that the apartheid is anchored in domestic [State] laws"[135]

---

[128] William A. Schabas, The International Criminal Court: A Commentary on the Rome Statute 175 (2010).

[129] *Elements of Crimes, supra* note 51, art. 7(1)(j), elements 1–2.

[130] Christopher K. Hall & Larissa van den Herik, *Article 7: Crimes against humanity – Section B (II)(8)(a)–(b), in* The Rome Statute of the International Criminal Court: A Commentary, *supra* note 56, at 283.

[131] Christine Byron, War Crimes and Crimes Against Humanity in the Rome Statute of the International Criminal Court 242 (2009).

[132] Hall & van den Herik, *supra* note 130, at 283–84.

[133] Rome Statute, *supra* note 5, art. 7(2)(h).

[134] Hall & van den Herik, *supra* note 130, at 284.

[135] *Id.*

"but also by a *de facto* policy."[136] The latter position would permit apartheid being implemented and maintained by actors that are not States, such as armed opposition/non-state armed groups.[137] In short, the requirement of "institutionalized regime" "could be described as an established law or practice by a government or prevailing order."[138]

What we can take away from this discussion of the nature of both persecution and apartheid as crimes against humanity is that their commission is perpetrated *through* other crimes and they can (in the case of persecution) and do (in the case of apartheid) involve a State or an armed opposition/non-state armed group in the development and execution of a preconceived and deliberate policy.[139] We also see that entire groups of persons are targeted – a racial group (in the case of apartheid) or political, racial, national, ethnic, cultural, religious, or gender groups or on other grounds universally recognized as impermissible under international law (in the case of persecution). In the case of apartheid in particular, this also means that a sizeable amount of persons are on the receiving end; they are not generally small-scale endeavors.

When one considers these in the context of the present discussion, utilizing the rule of *ejusdem generis*, it is submitted that the illegal use of force could arguably align with the scale and nature of existing crimes under Article 7(1), namely apartheid and persecution. First, the nature of the illegal use of force means that it would, by definition, be perpetrated *through* other conduct or crimes that target civilians – those carried out by the military forces of a State (or others acting on their behalf) or the armed forces of a non-state armed group. And second, an illegal use of force, in which civilians are the targets, would generally involve the targeting of a sizeable number of persons (civilians) through the armed forces of a State or a non-state armed group. Therefore, for a successful prosecution, the similarities between the illegal use of force and crimes like persecution and apartheid ought to be emphasized and compared.[140]

---

[136] AMBOS, *supra* note 85, at 114.

[137] Although, as Hall and van den Herik point out, "a too liberal interpretation might be inconsistent with the understanding that it is precisely the fact that apartheid is a system created by law and enforced by legal institutions which renders it particularly offensive." Hall & van den Herik, *supra* note 130, at 284.

[138] BYRON, *supra* note 131, at 242.

[139] Although, as noted earlier, with respect to apartheid, this position is up for academic discussion. *See supra* notes 134–137.

[140] It suffices to say that the absence of apartheid as a crime against humanity in the Statutes of any of the *ad hoc* or hybrid tribunals would make the argument advanced in this Chapter before those courts difficult.

B. INTENTIONALLY CAUSING GREAT SUFFERING, OR SERIOUS INJURY TO
BODY OR TO MENTAL OR PHYSICAL HEALTH   The second requirement for an
inhumane act is that the act must intentionally cause particular results: namely,
"great suffering, or serious injury to body or to mental or physical health."
The requirement of intention is clarified in the ICC Elements of Crimes that
stipulates that the "perpetrator [must have been] aware of the factual circumstances that established the character of the act."[141] The ICC has interpreted this
to mean that the "offence encompasses, first and foremost, cases of *dolus
directus* of the first and second degree,"[142] in line with the default *mens rea* of
Article 30.[143] This is in contrast to (and more strict than) the jurisprudence of
the *ad hoc* tribunals where it has been held that it is sufficient for the perpetrator
to know that the relevant conduct was "likely to cause" such consequences.[144]

   With respect to the consequences – i.e., great suffering or serious injury to
body, mental or physical health – the ICC has yet to interpret this requirement to any significant extent, except to say (citing ICTY jurisprudence) that
"the degree of severity must be assessed on a case-by-case basis with due regard
for the individual circumstances."[145] While the Rome Statute and the ICC
Elements of Crimes do not define the words "serious injury" and "great
suffering," both are included in Article 8(2)(a)(iii) of the Rome Statute, as
well as Articles 2(c) of the ICTY Statute[146] ("wilfully causing great suffering, or
serious injury to body or health" as a grave breach of the Geneva Conventions[147]). In this context, according to ICTY jurisprudence, "great suffering"
denotes acts that are severe enough to be torture (albeit without a prohibited
purpose) and also includes moral suffering,[148] while "serious injury" refers to

---

[141] *Elements of Crimes, supra* note 51, art. 7(1)(k), element 3.
[142] Katanga Confirmation of Charges, *supra* note 59, ¶ 455.
[143] *See supra* notes 96–98.
[144] *See* Prosecutor v. Prlić, Case No. IT-04-74-T, Trial Judgment, Volume 1 of 6, ¶ 77(c) (May 29,
     2013); Prosecutor v. Tolimir, Case No. IT-05-88/2-T, Trial Judgment, ¶ 802 (Dec. 12, 2012);
     Prosecutor v. Lukić, Case No. IT-98-32/1-T, Trial Judgment, ¶ 962 (July 20, 2009) [hereinafter
     Lukić Trial Judgment]; Prosecutor v. D. Milošević, Case No. IT-98-29/1-T, Trial Judgment, ¶
     935 (Dec. 12, 2007); Prosecutor v. Galić, Case No. IT-98-29-T, Trial Judgment, ¶ 154 (Dec. 5,
     2003); Prosecutor v. Kayishema, Case No. ICTR-95-1-T, Trial Judgment, ¶ 153 (May 21, 1999).
[145] Katanga Confirmation of Charges, *supra* note 59, ¶ 454. *See also* Kordić Appeals Judgment,
     supra note 65, ¶ 117.
[146] *See also* ECCC Statute, *supra* note 42, art. 6.
[147] Convention (I) for the Amelioration of the Condition of the Wounded and Sick in Armed
     Forces in the Field art. 1, Aug. 12, 1949, 75 U.N.T.S. 311; Convention (II) for the Amelioration
     of the Condition of Wounded, Sick and Shipwrecked Members of Armed Forces at Sea art. 47,
     Aug. 12, 1949, 75 U.N.T.S. 85; Convention (III) Relative to the Treatment of Prisoners of War
     art. 13, Aug. 12, 1949, 75 U.N.T.S. 135; Convention (IV) Relative to the Protection of Civilian
     Persons in Time of War art. 33, Aug. 12, 1949, 75 U.N.T.S. 287.
[148] Prosecutor v. Delalić, Case No. IT-96-21-T, Trial Judgment, ¶¶ 506–10 (Nov. 16, 1998).

harm that is not permanent or irremediable, but more than "temporary unhappiness, embarrassment or humiliation."[149] Academics have been of the view that the "terms 'great' and 'serious' indicate that this war crime can also include conduct that falls short of the threshold ... required for the war crime of torture."[150] Further, in interpreting other inhumane acts, the ICTY has repeatedly stated that "[w]hile it is not necessary that the victim suffered long-term effects from the act, the fact that it has long-term effects can be relevant to an assessment of the seriousness of the act."[151]

This requirement should not be difficult to meet in the present case. Armed conflict – and particularly the illegal use of force – by its very nature inflicts great suffering to mental or physical health, and in many cases results in serious physical injury. Although not a legal requirement *per se*, it is worth remembering that such events have a long-lasting impact upon all the societies they touch – even when IHL is generally respected. The effects can last generations. These are the inevitable results of engaging in humankind's most destructive endeavors. However, when one adds to this mix the civilian population as the intended target, then the ensuing suffering and injury is amplified even further. Indeed, the mere experience of living through such violence and seeing the horrors that unfold would result in the infliction of the requisite injury and suffering. With respect to the perpetrators, where the illegal use of force targets civilians, then one must infer that the infliction was intentional – one cannot plausibly claim a total lack of awareness as to the results of unleashing such destruction and violence against civilians. Mental trauma, physical injury, death, and great suffering are the perfectly predictable – and inevitable – results of such criminal actions.

IV. THE DIFFERENCES AND SIMILARITIES BETWEEN AGGRESSION AND THE ILLEGAL USE OF FORCE (OTHER INHUMANE ACT) AS A CRIME AGAINST HUMANITY

At this point, regardless of the analysis conducted above, one might very well ask whether the illegal use of force as an other inhumane act is really all that different from aggression. After all, both crimes are intimately concerned with,

---

[149] Prosecutor v. Krstić, Case No. IT-98–33-T, Trial Judgment, ¶ 513 (Aug. 2, 2001).

[150] Knut Dörmann, *Article 8: War crimes – Part II(B)(II)(3)*, in THE ROME STATUTE OF THE INTERNATIONAL CRIMINAL COURT: A COMMENTARY, *supra* note 56, at 338.

[151] Lukić Trial Judgment, *supra* note 144, ¶ 961. *See also* Prosecutor v. Vasiljević, Case No. IT-98–32-T, Trial Judgment, ¶ 235 (Nov. 29, 2002); Prosecutor v. Krnojelac, Case No. IT-97–25-T, Trial Judgment, ¶ 144 (Mar. 15, 2002); Prosecutor v. Simić, Case No. IT-95–9-T, Trial Judgment, ¶ 75 (Oct. 17, 2003); Blagojević Trial Judgment, *supra* note 104, ¶ 627.

and connected to, the use of armed force. That is a perfectly legitimate concern and criticism. However, there are some important and substantive differences between the two that give an indication that we might be talking about two separate – though related and intertwined – criminal conducts.

The illegal use of force as an other inhumane act, as articulated in this Chapter, is, unlike aggression, not concerned with the classification of the armed conflict – it is irrelevant whether one classifies it as either international or non-international so long as one can prove that a state of war is in existence (in the spirit of Article 3 of the ICTY Statute[152]). In contrast, as we have seen earlier,[153] aggression as defined by the Kampala Amendments of 2010 and the proposed illegal use of force definition of Ben Ferencz requires hostilities between two States; the conflict must always be of an international character. This has an important practical effect. It means that the ambit of the illegal use of force as per this Chapter is *wider* than that of aggression and would capture a larger number of armed conflicts, since in the modern world, there are more non-international armed conflicts than there are international armed conflicts.[154]

However, the illegal use of force as an other inhumane act is also *narrower* than aggression, since it must have as its target the civilian population rather than combatants. This requirement is not necessary for the crime of aggression – from a prosecutorial perspective, this actually makes the illegal use of force harder to prove beyond a reasonable doubt. Indeed, this element denotes a crucial distinction between aggression and the illegal use of force as an other inhumane act. While it is certainly the case that both overlap in the sense that they are both linked to the use of armed force, aggression is more concerned with the *initiation* of war, whereas the latter can perhaps be more accurately described as concerned with the *conduct* of that war. This aligns with ICTY jurisprudence (albeit in a different legal context), which has emphasized that "whether an attack was ordered as pre-emptive, defensive or offensive is from a legal point of view irrelevant... The issue at hand is whether *the way the military action was carried out was criminal or not.*"[155]

This also raises another matter: the *jus ad bellum*. Article 31(1) of the Rome Statute lists various defenses that accused persons can invoke in order to

---

[152] When crimes are charged under Article 3 of the ICTY Statute, the ICTY "has jurisdiction ... regardless of whether they occurred within an internal or an international armed conflict." Tadić Interlocutory Appeal on Jurisdiction, *supra* note 40, ¶ 137.

[153] *See supra* Section II.

[154] *See supra* notes 13–14.

[155] Kordić Appeals Judgment, *supra* note 65, ¶ 812 (emphasis added). *See also* Prosecutor v. Boškoski, Case No. IT-04-82-A, Appeals Judgment, ¶ 44 (May 19, 2010).

absolve themselves of responsibility for charged crimes: mental disease/defect (Article 31[1][a]), intoxication (Article 31[1][b]), self-defense (Article 31[1][c]), and duress (Article 31[1][d]). But Article 31(3) also permits an accused to rely on, at trial, other defenses "where such a ground is derived from applicable law as set forth in article 21." In turn, Article 21(1)(b) of the Rome Statute commands the Court to apply, when the Rome Statute, ICC Elements of Crimes, and the Rules of Procedure do not provide an answer, "where appropriate, applicable treaties and the principles and rules of international law, including the established principles of the international law of armed conflict." The question, then, is whether an accused charged with the illegal use of force (other inhumane act) as a crime against humanity can rely on international law – whether treaty or customary international law – in order to defend his or her conduct before the ICC. Since we are concerned here with the use of armed force, an accused may well attempt to rely on the *jus ad bellum*.

In an international armed conflict, an accused can argue that his or her actions were consistent with the U.N. Charter by virtue of it being initiated on the basis of self-defense (Article 2[4] of the U.N. Charter), authorized by the U.N. Security Council (Article 42 of the U.N. Charter), or, perhaps, as an exercise of humanitarian intervention. This type of argument is hardwired into the definition of aggression as per the Kampala Amendments of 2010, although, noticeably, the threshold is higher since a "manifest violation" of the U.N. Charter is required (and not a mere violation).[156]

A non-international armed conflict scenario is, however, more interesting. Shaw for example, is of the view that "[t]here is no rule against rebellion in international law" although acknowledging that a "possible exception [could be] self-determination conflicts."[157] On the other hand, many scholars and States "have suggested that there is a general prohibition on military assistance to governments in a situation of civil war or international rebellion.... In short, on this view international law guarantees the right to rebel against the government."[158] In fact, the view that international law permits some form of remedial external self-determination when groups are oppressed or experience tyranny (i.e., the right of the group to challenge their place within a State) has been accepted by a minority of the International Court of Justice in the *Kosovo*

---

[156] *See* Rome Statute, *supra* note 5, art. 8*bis*(1).
[157] MALCOLM N. SHAW, INTERNATIONAL LAW 1148–49 (6th ed. 2008).
[158] Dapo Akande & Zachary Vermeer, *The Airstrikes Against Islamic State in Iraq and the Alleged Prohibition on Military Assistance to Governments in Civil Wars*, EJIL: TALK! (Feb. 2, 2015), *available at* www.ejiltalk.org/the-airstrikes-against-islamic-state-in-iraq-and-the-alleged-prohibition-on-military-assistance-to-governments-in-civil-wars/.

Advisory Opinion.[159] Furthermore, a number of States explicitly recognize the right of their people to resist or rebel in specific circumstances in their domestic law.[160] This is not the time or place to discuss this subject in detail, but suffice to say that this would be a fascinating matter for legal argumentation – and potentially for the advancement (or, regression, depending on one's point of view) of international law.

Lastly, but perhaps most obviously, the illegal use of force as an other inhumane act would not be beholden to any of the problematic and uniquely restrictive clauses included in the Kampala Amendments of 2010 concerning aggression.[161] It matters not that jurisdiction over the crime has not yet been activated,[162] whether both the victim State and the State of nationality of the

---

[159] See Accordance with International Law of the Unilateral Declaration of Independence in Respect of Kosovo, Advisory Opinion, 2010 I.C.J. 523 (July 22) (separate opinion by Judge Trindade, ¶¶ 173–76) [hereinafter Kosovo Advisory Opinion]; Kosovo Advisory Opinion, *supra* (separate opinion by Judge Yusuf, ¶¶ 7–17). *See also* G.A. Res. 217 (III) A, Universal Declaration of Human Rights, U.N. Doc. A/RES/217(III), pmbl., ¶ 3 (Dec. 10, 1948) ("Whereas it is essential, if man is not to be compelled to have recourse, as a last resort, to rebellion against tyranny and oppression, that human rights should be protected by the rule of law.").

[160] Such countries include Benin (*see* CONSTITUTION DE LA RÉPUBLIQUE DU BÉNIN art. 66), Burkina Faso (*see* CONSTITUTION DU BURKINA FASO art. 167), Chad (*see* CONSTITUTION DE LA RÉPUBLIQUE DU TCHAD pmbl. [Chad]), Cuba (*see* CONSTITUCIÓN DE LA REPÚBLICA DE CUBA art. 3), Czech Republic (*see* Listina základních práv a svobod [Czech Charter of Fundamental Rights and Freedoms] č. 2/1993 Sb. art. 23), Germany (*see* GRUNDGESETZ [GG] [BASIC LAW] art. 20[4], *translation at* www.gesetze-im-internet.de/englisch_gg/), the Democratic Republic of the Congo (*see* CONSTITUTION DE LA RÉPUBLIQUE DÉMOCRATIQUE DU CONGO art. 64), Ecuador (*see* CONSTITUCIÓN DE LA REPÚBLICA DEL ECUADOR art. 98), El Salvador (*see* CONSTITUCIÓN POLÍTICA DE LA REPÚBLICA DE EL SALVADOR arts. 87–88), Estonia (*see* EESTI VABARIIGI PÕHISEADUS [CONSTITUTION] art. 54 [Est.]), Greece (*see* 2001 SYNTAGMA [SYN.] [CONSTITUTION] art. 120[4] [Greece]), Honduras (*see* CONSTITUCIÓN POLÍTICA DE LA REPÚBLICA DE HONDURAS art. 3), Liberia (*see* CONSTITUTION OF THE REPUBLIC OF LIBERIA art. 1), Peru (*see* CONSTITUCIÓN POLÍTICA DEL PERÚ art. 46), Portugal (*see* CONSTITUIÇÃO DA REPÚBLICA PORTUGUESA arts. 7[3], 21), Slovakia (*see* ÚSTAVA SLOVENSKEJ REPUBLIKY [CONSTITUTION OF THE SLOVAK REPUBLIC] č. 460/1992 Zb. art. 32), Togo (*see* CONSTITUTION DE LA IVè RÉPUBLIQUE art. 45 [Togo]), and Venezuela (*see* CONSTITUCIÓN DE LA REPÚBLICA BOLIVARIANA DE VENEZUELA art. 350). *See also* Lieblich, *supra*, note 12 (where the author proposes a novel theory of *jus ad bellum* that would apply *within* a State – both to governments as well as non-state armed groups).

[161] *See supra* Section II.

[162] The earliest date at which the ICC could have exercised jurisdiction over aggression was January 1, 2017, provided that a decision had been made by ICC States Parties to activate the ICC's jurisdiction over the crime after at least one year had passed since thirty States Parties had ratified or accepted the amendments. *See* Rome Statute, *supra* note 5, art. 15*bis*(2)–(3), 15*ter*(2)–(3). While, as of July 2017, thirty-four States Parties have ratified or accepted the Kampala Amendments of 2010 (and more than a year has passed since the thirtieth) no decision has yet been made to activate the ICC's jurisdiction over aggression by the ICC Assembly of States Parties. *See Status of Amendments on the Crime of Aggression to the Rome Statute of the*

accused are both States Parties to the Rome Statute, and that no "opt-out" possibilities would be in play.[163] As a crime against humanity, its prosecution would, generally, be only prevented by the regular jurisdictional trigger mechanisms for the ICC, the Court's existing *ratione temporis, loci,* and *personae* jurisdiction as well as, admittedly, by prosecutorial conservatism.

V. PROBLEMATIC ISSUES WITH THE ILLEGAL USE OF FORCE (OTHER INHUMANE ACT) AS A CRIME AGAINST HUMANITY

There are at least two problems with the Ben Ferencz proposal explored in this Chapter. The first is that, frankly, it is a little "too easy." States would be more than a little surprised (to say the least) to discover overnight that acts that overlap significantly (though not entirely) with aggression could have been prosecuted the whole time at the ICC as a crime against humanity without the need for the Kampala Amendments of 2010. States will (and justifiably) wonder why they wasted their time, energy and political capital in coming up with a definition for the crime of aggression only to have the rug pulled from under them a few years later via the recognition of the illegal use of force as a crime against humanity (other inhumane act). Indeed, the close similarities with aggression are hard to put aside or to erase completely from the mind, even if substantive differences can be identified.[164] When the arguments are considered in their totality, concluding that the illegal use of force is simply an attempt to "dress up" aggression with another name or label is not a difficult mental step to take.

Therefore, there is a strong policy argument to be made that, whether we like it or not, States made conscious choices in defining aggression as they did, decisions that were the result of protracted negotiations, compromises, and diplomacy. To "undo" this long and arduous process and, with a legal sleight of hand, blindside States by revealing to them that their acceptance of "other inhumane acts" as a crime against humanity under the Rome Statute also meant accepting a modified version of aggression, would likely be counterproductive and not conducive to state cooperation with the ICC. States that

---

International Criminal Court, Kampala, 11 June 2010, U.N. Treaty Series (July 1, 2017), *available at* https://treaties.un.org/doc/Publication/MTDSG/Volume%20II/Chapter%20XVIII/XVIII-10-b.en.pdf.

[163] *But see* Rome Statute, *supra* note 5, art. 124 (a "transitional" provision that allows States to declare that, for a period of seven years, the State in question did not accept the ICC's jurisdiction over war crimes). An amendment on its deletion was recently passed by the ICC Assembly of States Parties. *See supra* note 27.

[164] *See supra* Section IV.

have yet to ratify the Rome Statute might wonder what other surprises will be in store should they decide to join. After all, if the crime of aggression – as politically sensitive as it is – is not safe, who knows what could be next. When the present political climate surrounding the ICC, particularly emanating from Africa,[165] is taken into account, then the recognition of the illegal use of force as a crime against humanity easily risks the creation of a lightning rod for anti-ICC sentiment. And in this case, the criticisms are unlikely to remain concentrated among African States.

Second, from a legal perspective, the illegal use of force as an other inhumane act creates an uncomfortable and serious anomaly. Historically, crimes against humanity required a nexus with armed conflict. Under the IMT Charter, the IMT at Nuremberg held that crimes against humanity could not occur unless they were linked to armed conflict.[166] Although there is judicial and academic disagreement as to whether this requirement was jurisdictional or substantive in nature,[167] the point is that in present times this nexus is no longer required for crimes against humanity. Indeed, Article 7(1) of the Rome Statute contains no such element, although the *travaux préparatoires* reveals that States certainly engaged in spirited discussions and debates on the subject during the process of its drafting.[168] Yet, as proposed by Ben Ferencz, the illegal use of force, as a crime against humanity, inherently requires the existence of armed conflict.

---

[165] *See* AFRICA AND THE INTERNATIONAL CRIMINAL COURT (Gerhard Werle, Lovell Fernandez & Moritz Vormbaum eds., 2014); THE INTERNATIONAL CRIMINAL COURT AND AFRICA: ONE DECADE ON (Evelyn A. Ankumah ed., 2016); Somini Sengupta, *As 3 African Nations Vow to Exit, International Court Faces Its Own Trial*, N.Y. TIMES (Oct. 26, 2016), *available at* www.nytimes.com/2016/10/27/world/africa/africa-international-criminal-court.html; *African Union Backs Mass Withdrawal from ICC*, BBC NEWS (Feb. 1, 2017), *available at* www.bbc .com/news/world-africa-38826073.

[166] *See supra* note 33.

[167] The ICTY Appeals Chamber and the U.K. House of Lords (as it then was) has opined that it was jurisdictional in nature. Tadić Interlocutory Appeal on Jurisdiction, *supra* note 40, ¶ 140; R v. Bow Street Metropolitan Stipendiary Magistrate, *ex parte* Pinoche Ugarte (No. 3) [2000] 1 AC 147 (HL) 272 (per Lord Millett). On the other hand, the Grand Chamber of the European Court of Human Rights and the late Professor Antonio Cassese appear of the view that it was substantive in nature. *See* Korbely v. Hungary, App. No. 9174/02, 50 Eur. H.R. Rep. 48, ¶ 82 (2008); Antonio Cassese, *Balancing the Prosecution of Crimes Against Humanity and Non-Retroactivity of Criminal Law: The* Kolk and Kislyiy v. Estonia *Case Before the ECHR*, 4 J. INT'L CRIM. JUST. 410 (2006). The ECCC Trial Chamber was of the opinion that there was no consistency in World War II–era jurisprudence to make a definitive determination either way. *See* Co-Prosecutors v. Nuon, Case No. 002/19-09-2007/ECCC/TC/E95/8, Decision on Co-Prosecutors' Request to Exclude Armed Conflict Nexus Requirement from the Definition of Crimes Against Humanity, ¶ 20 (Oct. 26, 2011).

[168] *See* SCHABAS, *supra* note 128, at 145–47.

In other words, what was once an increasingly irrelevant historical vestige would be potentially resurrected. The illegal use of force would therefore serve to relink crimes against humanity to armed conflict and potentially return to an antiquated notion that had been previously discarded by States to the benefit of international criminal law. As a corollary, and perhaps more importantly, if recognized, the illegal use of force (as an other inhumane act) would become the only underlying crime against humanity that could *not* occur during peacetime – it can only occur during times of war. This reality is truly an oddity and significantly undermines the argument that the crime is similar in character to the existing enumerated crimes listed in Article 7(1)(a)–(j) of the Rome Statute.[169] As such, the modern, orthodox notion that crimes against humanity can occur during peacetime would be challenged and perhaps rewritten. If so, rather than being a progressive development, the illegal use of force could in fact be *regressive* insofar as crimes against humanity are concerned.

VI. CONCLUSION

This Chapter has as its genesis the position advanced by Ben Ferencz: that the illegal use of force is an other inhumane act as a crime against humanity.[170] Building upon that idea, it has presented a slightly different proposition: that the use of force without legal justification that targets civilians could be considered as a crime against humanity. However, it is a notion that is still in its very infancy and further work to develop it and to iron out the associated policy and legal issues identified in this Chapter would still need to be undertaken.[171] Without this, it would likely be, and remain, an unpalatable proposition for ICC prosecutors and judges.

Nevertheless, this Chapter is cognizant of the reality that war is the most violent of all human activities and one in which we, as a species, have engaged

---

[169] *See supra* Section III(B)(2)(a). On the other hand, this would not be the first time that an underlying crime against humanity would be unique vis-à-vis other underlying crimes. For example, international criminal law accepts that only persecution as a crime against humanity requires discriminatory intent (*dolus specialis*). Ruto Confirmation of Charges, *supra* note 53, ¶¶ 280–81, 347; Prosecutor v. Al Bashir, Case No. ICC-02/05-01/09-3, Decision on the Prosecution's Application for a Warrant of Arrest Against Omar Hassan Ahmad Al Bashir, ¶ 141 (ii) (Mar. 4, 2009). Such intent is not required for any of the other underlying crimes that can constitute crimes against humanity.

[170] *See* Ferencz, *supra* note 7.

[171] Other areas worth exploring are modes of liability, Rome Statute, *supra* note 5, art. 25, and who can be held responsible for the illegal use of force (other inhumane act) as a crime against humanity, particularly in light of aggression's leadership element.

in far too often and far too readily throughout our collective history. Only with the advent of the twentieth century have we seen a transformation in this attitude. Before this, there existed an extended period of time in humanity's existence where the mere idea that a State was (or should be) prohibited from engaging in war with little to no limits seemed far-fetched and fanciful. War was commonplace. Now, we have come to recognize that peace should be the norm, and war the exception. Even then, it is still presently the case that, in particular circumstances, the use of force to settle disputes is permitted and can be voted upon.[172] One should pause and truly appreciate just how primitive this state of affairs is.

It is true that States have not given up on war entirely. But there is certainly cause to think that their populations are of a different mood. Whereas in the not too distant past, people enthusiastically cheered the outbreak of war (e.g., World War I in 1914), today people protest *against* war before a single shot is even fired. While it would be unrealistic and naïve to think that the recognition of the Ben Ferencz proposal would put an end to war through the law, it is perhaps yet another step toward that ultimate destination.

[172] *See* U.N. Charter art. 42.

16

Aggression, Atrocities, and Accountability

Building a Case in Iraq

JOHN HAGAN AND ANNA HANSON

I. INTRODUCTION

Justice Robert Jackson as Chief Prosecutor for the Nuremberg Tribunal presumably did not foresee the troublesome standard he set when he wrote with regard to the war of aggression that "we are not prepared to lay down a rule of criminal conduct against others which we would be unwilling to have invoked against us."[1] He could not have known that more than a half-century later former Nuremberg prosecutor Benjamin Ferencz would invoke this logic when he declared the American invasion of Iraq to be a war of aggression – what Jackson also called the "supreme international crime."[2] Yet few expect the prosecution of such a charge against military or political leaders of the United States or the country itself.

Jonathan Bush observes that public attention is typically concentrated more narrowly on atrocities of war.[3] A reliance on dry legal documents such as formal treaties is a barrier to successfully charging leaders or nations for committing wars of aggression and to investigating and collecting evidence of the atrocities involved. David Scheffer makes a similar point with regard to charges of genocide. He argues for applying the alternative concept of atrocity crime during the preliminary stages of building a case for charging genocide.[4] Scheffer's goal is to get investigations started that can later lead to the filing of charges and obtaining convictions.

---

[1] U.S. Dep't of State, Pub. No. 3880, International Conference on Military Trials 330 (1945).

[2] Benjamin B. Ferencz, Foreword to Michael Haas, George W. Bush, War Criminal?: The Bush Administration's Liability for 269 War Crimes xi, xii (2008).

[3] Jonathan A. Bush, "The Supreme ... Crime" and Its Origins: The Lost Legislative History of the Crime of Aggressive War, 102 Colum. L. Rev. 2324, 2331 (2002).

[4] David Scheffer, Genocide and Atrocity Crimes, 1 Genocide Stud. & Prevention 229 (2006).

This seems also to have been the logic of a famous American criminologist, Sheldon Glueck, who played an important role in plans for and debates about charging the Nazi leadership at Nuremberg with waging a war of aggression.[5] Bush writes that "Glueck is widely deemed one of the first and most significant American voices on the war crimes debate."[6] Justice Jackson observed of Glueck that "his original plan is substantially the system pursued throughout the Nuremberg trial."[7]

Bush notes that Jackson's "flattery" was primarily intended to help promote a book by his former subordinate.[8] Glueck had been a helpful ally in Justice Jackson's work at Nuremberg, although in an ambivalent way. Before working with Jackson in planning the trials, in 1944 Glueck had written against war of aggression charges for the Nazi leadership.[9] However, the following year brought a dramatic change.

President Roosevelt, shortly before his death and through an unusual set of circumstances involving seemingly chance combinations of contacts and influence, issued a memo that surprisingly brought war of aggression charges to center stage.[10] The presidential memo instructed that "the charges should include an indictment for waging aggressive warfare, in violation of the Kellogg Pact," adding that "[p]erhaps these and other charges might be joined in a conspiracy indictment."[11]

Glueck confronted a dilemma. He had been working on the issue of war crimes at least since the summer of 1942, when he was elected a "corresponding member" of the London International Assembly on the Trial of War Criminals. In February of 1945, Glueck had testified before a congressional committee about war crimes, purposefully omitting aggressive war from his definition of war crimes. He argued that "to include such categories will only confuse the much clearer legal basis of liability for atrocities and crimes committed during the conduct of war, whether it be deemed a 'legal' or 'just' war, or otherwise."[12]

---

[5]   Bush, *supra* note 3, at 2327.

[6]   *Id.* at 2343.

[7]   Robert H. Jackson, *Foreword* to SHELDON GLUECK, THE NUREMBERG TRIAL AND AGGRESSIVE WAR vii, vii (1st ed. 1946).

[8]   Bush, *supra* note 3, at 2345 n.60.

[9]   SHELDON GLUECK, WAR CRIMINALS: THEIR PROSECUTION AND PUNISHMENT (1944).

[10] Bush, *supra* note 3, at 2363.

[11] Bush traces President Roosevelt's memorandum to BRADLEY F. SMITH, THE AMERICAN ROAD TO NUREMBERG 92 (1982).

[12] *See* Sheldon Glueck, Professor, Harvard Law School, Statement in Regard to House Resolution No. 93, Concerning the Trial and Punishment of Axis War Criminals (Mar. 20, 1945), *in* Glueck Papers (on file with the Harvard Law School Library).

Policymakers in Roosevelt's War and Justice Departments quickly set to work implementing the President's directive. Bush reports that "even senior officials who had misgivings felt duty bound to follow the January 22 agreement, consoled perhaps by the thought that almost every Nazi who would be guilty of aggressive war-making would likely be guilty of other more traditional offenses." Then, in April, President Roosevelt died.

Within the month, President Truman selected Supreme Court Justice Robert Jackson to lead preparations for Nuremberg. Jackson made clear his enthusiasm for the charge of aggressive war. He wanted to emphasize through the war of aggression charge that the atrocities that were belatedly receiving increasing public attention were a part of an even larger "supreme international crime" – which Jackson saw as "the accumulated evil of the whole."[13]

Glueck soon found himself not only in the middle of the legal and theoretical debate about the charge of aggressive war, but also in a struggle between two dominant personalities in planning the trials: Justice Jackson and General James B. "Wild Bill" Donovan. Donovan was Head of the Office of Strategic Services (OSS) and Jackson appointed him as head of his Board of Strategy, perhaps not knowing that Donovan was skeptical of the war of aggression approach.

Donovan was in charge of the day-to-day planning of the coming trials.[14] While Jackson was insistent about formally documenting the aggression charge, Donovan was intent on presenting the more graphic photographic evidence of the atrocities of the Holocaust finally filtering back from Germany to the American public. Jackson observed that "the crimes of the Hitler regime were all a little remote to this country,"[15] and it would seem they were also remote to Jackson himself. Although Jackson had the position of higher authority in the planning process, it was Donovan who was more immediately involved in the on-the-ground collection and development of the evidence of atrocity crimes.

Glueck would subsequently write another book in 1946 that steered a cautious path between the positions of Jackson and Donovan, perhaps not only to preserve the favor of both, but possibly also because he actually had come to believe there was a time and place for both approaches. This latter

[13] 1 Trial of Major War Criminals Before the International Military Tribunal, Nuremberg, 14 November – 1 October 1946, Judgment, at 186 (1947), www.loc.gov/rr/frd/Military_Law/pdf/NT_Vol-I.pdf.

[14] *See* John Hagan & Scott Greer, *Making War Criminal*, 40 Criminology 231, 244–56 (2002).

[15] Harlan Phillips, Justice Robert Jackson's Oral History of Nuremberg 1282 (Feb. 1995) (unpublished manuscript) (on file with Columbia University's Butler Library) [hereinafter Jackson's Oral History].

possibility – combining initial attention to the collection of evidence of egregious atrocities with later attention to establishing cumulative account-ability for aggressive war – is the position we adopt below.

Thus while Glueck on the one hand wrote after the war in defense of using conspiracy and aggression arguments as Justice Jackson had favored, he also assigned priority to a grounded empirical strategy and method of investigation that he himself implemented in focusing more narrowly and concretely on Nazi atrocities. This was consistent with Glueck's empirical approach and his position as the leading criminologist of his era, as well as with his appointment as the Roscoe Pound Professor at Harvard Law School, which recognized his social science approach to legal realism. Furthermore, as a European Jewish immigrant, Glueck was fully aware of the Holocaust. For all these reasons, Glueck's imperative was to concentrate preparation for the Nuremberg trials on the collection of observational evidence of the full range of Nazi atrocities. General Donovan shared Glueck's prioritization of evidence about atrocities and appointed him as "Consultant Supervising Installation of the Control System" for the collection of this evidence.

The control system to which Glueck's title referred involved managing evidence collected in separately developed "Digest Forms" that summarized interrogation reports from witness interviews and were based on official documents. Standard information about source and content was included on the forms and the forms were then cross-referenced in terms of other proof and data required, the point of law or possible defense at issue, connected OSS or other study material, and an indication of the subheading of the count and instrument of accusation to which the evidence was linked. Finally, each Digest Form ended with an open prompt for "quotable material to be used by the prosecutor in summing up."[16]

The documentary material summarized in the Digest Forms was official and formal in its character and dry in its content. In contrast, the witness and interrogation testimony was shockingly vivid in its references to and depictions of atrocities. As a result, the non-documentary evidence prevailed in shifting the focus of the trial from the aggressive war charges favored by Jackson to crimes against humanity charges that more vividly captured the horror of the Holocaust. Glueck's systematic organization of the Digest Forms bore out Donovan's focus on atrocities, leading even Justice Jackson to later recall the inevitable outcome:

[16] *See* Shelden Glueck, Professor, Harvard Law School, Digest Forms for Interrogation Reports and Documentary Proof, *in* Glueck Papers (on file with the Harvard Law School Library).

General Donovan ... couldn't see that we were justified in making a documentary case. He argued that a witness was something the newspapers could see – there was some drama in oral testimony and cross-examination. If we put in a documentary case, it was going to be dead and dull. The papers wouldn't pay much attention to it. From that point of view he was undoubtedly correct.[17]

Donovan ultimately prevailed with a recommendation that much of the documentary evidence ("laws, decrees, regulations, historical facts, etc.") be entered into the trial record by judicial notice.[18]

This might be the end of a story about the struggle between documentary and non-documentary forms of evidence and charges of aggressive war if the nature of accessible documents were not so different in today's age of the Internet. The advent of the Internet has given us access to a much wider range of documents that include and much more fully depict government planning and conduct. We argue in this Chapter that such documentary as well as non-documentary evidence can be used to initially build a case of command responsibility for atrocity crimes by the American forces in Iraq – which were a central part of the war of aggression in Iraq – and which therefore in turn can set the foundation and increase the possibility for war of aggression charges against the United States.

The atrocity crimes that are the focus of this Chapter were concentrated during the American-led invasion and occupation of Iraq and consist of command responsibility for detention and torture. The Chapter first demonstrates the criminal intent of the administration of President George W. Bush. The Administration intentionally redefined torture as legal and then purposefully engaged in criminal acts of torture in the expectation of revealing suspected threats – such as the development of weapons of mass destruction – as justification for waging a preemptive war in Iraq. The Chapter then documents how a widespread detention policy was combined with the criminal use of torture by U.S. military forces and the new U.S.-supported Iraq Ministry of Interior security personnel. These operations prominently featured the use of torture authorized and enacted through the chain of command of the Bush Administration. We argue in conclusion that the investigation and development of evidence of these atrocity torture crimes can further set the foundation for war crimes charges, initiating a process that can lead ultimately to charges of aggressive war against the United States.

---

[17] Jackson's Oral History, *supra* note 15, at 1385.

[18] Memorandum, Progress Report on Preparation of Prosecution, Classified SECRET (May 30, 1945), *in* Glueck Papers (on file at Harvard Law School Library).

II. THE INTENT TO TORTURE

On August 1, 2002, in response to a request from White House Counsel
Alberto Gonzales, the Office of Legal Counsel (OLC) issued a memorandum
entitled *Standards of Conduct for Interrogation*, now commonly known as the
"Torture Memo." This memo was written by a Berkeley law professor then
working in the OLC, John Yoo, and signed by his OLC superior, Assistant
Attorney General Jay Bybee. As a legal matter, the purposes of an OLC memo
are to advise the President as to the state of the law and its interpretation.

Following the September 11 attacks, the Bush Administration declared a
"Global War on Terror," a central part of which became the war in Iraq. The
techniques and venues of interrogation became subjects of intense discussion
at the highest levels of the Administration, as a central part of this global war.
President Bush signed a statement on February 7, 2002, determining that
"none of the provisions of Geneva apply to our conflict with al-Qaeda in
Afghanistan or elsewhere throughout the world,"[19] thus reserving the right to
subsequently disregard the constraints of the Geneva Conventions.

Because of the importance then attributed to al-Qaeda in Iraq in the War
on Terror, the Administration sought further legal advice about the methods
CIA interrogators could use with al-Qaeda detainees. White House Counsel
Alberto Gonzales requested that Assistant Attorney General Jay Bybee and
John Yoo provide an opinion from OLC about the restrictions imposed by the
Convention Against Torture and Other Cruel, Inhuman, or Degrading Treat-
ment (CAT), as well as other binding agreements.

In the memo, Yoo argued:

> 18 U.S.C. section 2340A does not prohibit as "torture" merely cruel and
> inhuman interrogation techniques, but only those interrogation techniques
> that inflict pain akin in severity to death or organ failure.... But if we are
> wrong, to the extent 18 U.S.C. section 2340A prohibits interrogation tech-
> niques the President approved, the law would violate the American Consti-
> tution. This is because it is inherent in the Presidential office to determine
> what interrogation techniques shall be used, and neither Congress nor the
> Supreme Court has a greater power than the President on the subject.
> However, if the President's commands were found subject to 18 U.S.C.

---

[19] Memorandum from President George W. Bush to the Vice President, the Sec'y of State, the
Sec'y of Def., the Attorney Gen., Chief of Staff to the President, Dir. of Cent. Intelligence,
Assistant to the President for Nat'l Sec. Affairs, and Chairman of the Joint Chiefs of Staff, Subj:
Humane Treatment of Taliban and al Qaeda Detainees (Feb. 7, 2002), www.pegc.us/archive/
White_House/bush_memo_20020207_ed.pdf.

section 2340A without violating the Constitution, then, nevertheless, the President's endorsement of such interrogation techniques could still be justified as a matter of necessity and self-defense, being the moral choice of a lesser evil: harming an individual enemy combatant in order to prevent further Al Qaeda attacks upon the United States.[20]

Written in the aftermath of the September 11 attack on the United States, Yoo was first asserting that there was a legal distinction between torture and "merely" cruel and inhuman interrogation practices.

Torture, the Yoo memo therefore reasoned, referred only to those interrogation techniques that it specified as causing "pain similar to death or organ failure." According to Yoo, although the Convention Against Torture prohibits both "cruel, degrading, and inhuman treatment" as well as extreme torture, there is a distinction between the two. Yoo claimed that "certain acts may be cruel, inhuman, or degrading, but still not produce enough pain and suffering of the requisite intensity to fall within Section 2430(A)'s proscription against torture."[21]

Yoo then further claimed that the President of the United States had constitutional authority to determine which interrogation techniques shall be used as a matter of national necessity and self-defense against further al-Qaeda attacks.

Finally, Yoo argued for a legal distinction between protected prisoners of war and unlawful enemy combatants to justify the use of torture. He claimed that the Taliban and al-Qaeda prisoners were not entitled to prisoner-of-war status under the Geneva Conventions, which meant that U.S. personnel and officials were protected from being prosecuted under the War Crimes Act.

The intent of Yoo's memo was to nullify the legal scope and force of the Geneva Conventions and to place the final authority in the hands of the U.S. President to determine what torture meant broadly, and more specifically in the context of al-Qaeda in Iraq. Jack Goldsmith, Yoo's successor at the Office of Legal Counsel, writes that

> The message of the August 2, 2002, OLC opinion was indeed clear: violent acts aren't necessarily torture; if you do torture, you probably have a defense;

---

[20] Michael Hatfield, *Fear, Legal Indeterminacy, and the American Lawyering Culture*, 10 LEWIS & CLARK L. REV. 511, 514 (2006) (summarizing the reasoning in the "Torture Memo," Memorandum from Jay S. Bybee, Assistant Attorney Gen., Office of Legal Counsel, to Alberto R. Gonzales, Counsel to the President, Re: Standards of Conduct for Interrogation under 18 U.S.C. §§ 2340–2340A (August 1, 2002), http://nsarchive.gwu.edu/torturingdemocracy/documents/20020801-1.pdf [hereinafter Torture Memo]).

[21] Torture Memo, *supra* note 20, at 1.

and even if you don't have a defense, the torture law doesn't apply if you act under the color of presidential authority. CIA interrogators and their supervisors, under pressure to get information about the next attack, viewed the opinion as a golden shield, as one CIA official later called it, that provided enormous comfort.[22]

Goldsmith was asserting that the intention of the OLC opinion was to facilitate the use of torture in the Global War on Terror.

Goldsmith did not accept the Torture Memo's reasoning and he took the highly unusual step of withdrawing the Torture Memo in 2004. Goldsmith felt so strongly about the torture issue that he resigned from the Office of Legal Counsel simultaneously with his withdrawal of the Memo. A former White House lawyer has suggested that "if you line up 1,000 law professors, only six or seven would sign up to [the Torture Memo's viewpoint]."[23] Nonetheless, the new head of the Office of Legal Counsel, Daniel Levin, reaffirmed in subsequent opinions the interpretations of Yoo's earlier memo, again facilitating the continued use of torture in Iraq. In 2006, the Supreme Court finally agreed with internal dissenters inside the Administration that legal protections of the Geneva Conventions applied to al-Qaeda in *Hamdan v. Rumsfeld*.[24]

The importance of the Torture Memo was that despite internal dissent within the Bush Administration, it intentionally set the predicate for torture of detained suspects in the Global War on Terror and in Iraq. Following September 11, coercive interrogation techniques, based on the heretofore little-known Survival Evasion Resistance and Escape (SERE) program,[25] were authorized at the highest levels of the Administration. These techniques were overseen by Defense Secretary Donald Rumsfeld in conjunction with the then also little-known Joint Recovery Agency in the Department of Defense (DoD), and were communicated down the chain of command to prison guards and interrogators.

The Joint Personnel Recovery Agency (JPRA) is a part of the Department of Defense tasked with training captured military personnel in Survival Evasion Resistance and Escape (SERE) techniques. During SERE training, U.S. military personnel are subjected to physical and psychological measures

---

[22] JACK GOLDSMITH, THE TERROR PRESIDENCY 144 (2007).

[23] R. Jeffrey Smith, *Slim Legal Grounds for Torture Memos*, WASH. POST, July 4, 2004, at A12 (quoting David B. Rivkin Jr., a White House lawyer during the Reagan Administration), *cited in* Hatfield, *supra* note 20, at 516.

[24] Hamdan v. Rumsfeld, 548 U.S. 557 (2006).

[25] Jane Mayer, *The Experiment: The Military Trains People to Withstand Interrogation. Are Those Methods Being Misused at Guantánamo?*, NEW YORKER (July 11, 2005), www.newyorker.com/magazine/2005/07/11/the-experiment-3.

designed to replicate the conditions they might experience when taken prisoner by "enemies" that do not abide by the Geneva Conventions. As one JPRA instructor explained, SERE training is "based on illegal exploitation [under the Geneva Conventions] of prisoners over the last 50 years."[26] The techniques used in SERE training include techniques used by Chinese government interrogators during the Korean War to elicit false confessions, including stripping students of their clothing, placing them in stress positions, putting hoods over their heads, disrupting their sleep, subjecting them to loud music, flashing lights, extreme temperatures, and waterboarding.

It is important to note that SERE training is not designed to obtain reliable intelligence information from detainees. Rather, the job of the interrogators using SERE tactics is, as one instructor put it, to "train our personnel to resist providing reliable information to our enemies . . . 'the expertise of JPRA lies in training personnel how to respond and resist interrogations – not in how to conduct interrogations.'"[27] Notwithstanding this important difference of purpose, in 2002 high-ranking officials within the Bush Administration were already investigating the possibility of utilizing SERE tactics for interrogations in the War on Terror.

In the summer of 2002, William "Jim" Haynes II and Richard Shiffrin, Department of Defense General and Deputy Counsel for Intelligence, contacted the Joint Personnel Recovery Agency requesting information on the SERE physical pressures and interrogation techniques that had been used against Americans. The Joint Personnel Recovery Agency provided the General Counsel's office with several documents including excerpts from SERE lesson plans, a list of psychological and physical pressures used in resistance training, and a memo from a psychologist assessing the long-term effects of SERE training. Richard Shiffrin later confirmed in a Senate report investigating the abuse of detainees that the purpose of this request was to "reverse engineer" the techniques.[28]

By September 2002, a group of interrogators and behavioral scientists from Guantanamo Bay travelled to Fort Bragg in order to attend a training session conducted by the instructors from JPRA's SERE school. Just days after the interrogators returned to Cuba, a delegation of senior Administration lawyers visited Guantanamo Bay. On October 11, 2002, two behavioral scientists that

---

[26] *Id.*

[27] COMM. ON ARMED SERVICES, 110TH CONG., INQUIRY INTO THE TREATMENT OF DETAINEES IN U.S. CUSTODY xiii (Comm. Print 2008), http://documents.nytimes.com/report-by-the-senate-armed-services-committee-on-detainee-treatment.

[28] *Id.* at x.

had attended the SERE training session drafted a memo proposing new interrogation techniques for use at Guantanamo. This memo was then sent to General James Hill, the Commander of U.S. Southern Command, for approval. According to one of those scientists, by early October 2002, there was "increasing pressure to get 'tougher' with detainee interrogations." He further stated that "if the interrogation policy memo did not contain coercive techniques then it wasn't going to go very far."[29]

By November 2002, Jim Haynes sent Donald Rumsfeld a one-page memo recommending that he approve all but three of the eighteen techniques in the Guantanamo request.[30] Haynes's memo indicates that he had discussed the request with Deputy Secretary of Defense Paul Wolfowitz, Under Secretary of Defense for Policy Doug Feith, and Chairman of the Joint Chiefs of Staff General Richard Myers, all of whom agreed with his recommendation. On December 2, 2002, Rumsfeld signed the recommendation, adding a handwritten note that referred to the limits proposed in the memo on the use of stress positions: "I stand for 8–10 hours a day. Why is standing limited to 4?"[31]

Following Rumsfeld's authorization, senior staff at Guantanamo began drafting a Standard Operating Procedure (SOP) specifically for the use of SERE techniques in interrogations. The SOP stated that "The premise behind this is that the interrogation tactics used at U.S. military SERE schools are appropriate for use in real-world interrogations. These tactics and techniques are used at SERE school to 'break' SERE detainees. The same tactics and techniques can be used to break real detainees during interrogation."[32]

In January 2003, Secretary of Defense Donald Rumsfeld formed a working group to further study the interrogation techniques based on the SERE program. Much of the language of the Torture Memo was incorporated in the resulting report.[33] The report itself was an historic form of what Daniel

[29] *Id.* at xvii.
[30] Memorandum from William J. Haynes II, Gen. Counsel of the Dep't of Def., to the Sec'y of Defense, Subj: Counter-Resistance Techniques (Nov. 27, 2002), www.gwu.edu/~nsarchiv/NSAEBB/NSAEBB127/02.12.02.pdf.
[31] *Id.* Rumsfeld's order stated: "Should you determine that particular techniques in either of these categories are warranted in an individual case, you should forward that request to me. Such a request should include a thorough justification for the employment of those techniques and a detailed plan for the use of such techniques." Memorandum from Donald Rumsfeld, Sec'y of Def., to Commander, U.S. S. Command (Jan. 15, 2003), http://nsarchive.gwu.edu/NSAEBB/NSAEBB127/03.01.15.pdf.
[32] JTF GTMO "SERE" Interrogation Standard Operating Procedure (Dec. 10, 2002), https://file.wikileaks.org/file/us-jtfgtmo-sere-2002.pdf.
[33] WORKING GROUP REPORT ON DETAINEE INTERROGATIONS IN THE GLOBAL WAR ON TERRORISM: ASSESSMENT OF LEGAL, HISTORICAL, POLICY, AND OPERATIONAL

Patrick Moynihan called "defining deviance down."[34] It identified forms of torture that were redefined as "enhanced interrogation." Rumsfeld subsequently developed a list of twenty-four aggressive interrogation procedures to be used at Guantanamo Bay,[35] and as indicated in the Taguba Report discussed next, the use of these SERE techniques as well as instructors from the JPRA SERE unit reappeared in Iraq.[36] In August of 2003, this included the advisory role at Abu Ghraib of Geoffrey Miller, the Commander at Guantanamo Bay.

III. DETENTION AND TORTURE PRACTICES IN IRAQ

As it became increasingly apparent that the decision to invade Iraq was premised on false intelligence, and as the challenges of bringing peace and security to Iraq became clear, the occupying U.S.-led Coalition became preoccupied with acquiring new intelligence about an increasingly violent opposition to the presence of Coalition forces in Iraq and to the new Iraqi government formed under the terms of the occupation. Torture was practiced at detention facilities operated by both the U.S. government and the new Ministry of Interior installed by the U.S.-led and Coalition-guided Iraqi government.

While the extent of Iraqi detentions and internments are unknown but are assumed to be extensive, the U.S. numbers alone are believed to have peaked during the Surge in the tens of thousands.[37] The U.N. Assistance Mission for Iraq used the term "mass detention" to express its concerns in its September 2005 *Human Rights Report* about U.S.-led Coalition detention practices. The Mission's reports noted that "[m]ass detentions of persons without warrants continue to be used in military operations by MNF-I [Multi-National Force – Iraq]. Reports of arbitrary arrest and detention continue to be reported," and

---

CONSIDERATIONS (2003), *reprinted in* THE TORTURE PAPERS: THE ROAD TO ABU GHRAIB 286 (Karen J. Greenberg & Joshua L. Dratel eds., 2005).

[34] Daniel Patrick Moynihan, *Defining Deviancy Down: How We've Become Accustomed to Alarming Levels of Crime and Destructive Behavior*, 62 AM. SCHOLAR 17 (1993).

[35] Memorandum from Donald Rumsfeld, Sec'y of Def., to Commander, U.S. S. Command 1–3 (Apr. 16, 2003), http://nsarchive.gwu.edu/NSAEBB/NSAEBB127/03.04.16.pdf.

[36] ANTONIO M. TAGUBA, ARTICLE 15–6 INVESTIGATION OF THE 800TH MILITARY POLICE BRIGADE (2004), https://fas.org/irp/agency/dod/taguba.pdf (classification markings are omitted throughout this Chapter) [hereinafter TAGUBA REPORT].

[37] Jeffrey Azarva, *Is U.S. Detention Policy in Iraq Working?*, 16 MIDDLE E.Q. 5 (2009), www.meforum.org/2040/is-us-detention-policy-in-iraq-working.

that there was "an urgent need to provide remedy to lengthy internment for reasons of security without adequate judicial oversight."[38]

The two largest U.S.-run prisons in Iraq were by their very names, Abu Ghraib and Camp Bucca, a vengeful mix of American and Iraqi practices of mass incarceration. Abu Ghraib Prison was the site of the Saddam Hussein regime's most notorious human rights abuses, holding more than 50,000 inmates and imposing weekly executions. Iraqis literally tore Abu Ghraib apart after the fall of Hussein, only to see it rebuilt by the Americans as the site of new human rights abuses. Additional detainees were held in brigade and division facilities across the country.

Abu Ghraib was rebuilt to hold 4,000 persons, but housed as many as 7,000 detainees, a level of overcrowding similar to what the U.S. Supreme Court held in the California case of *Brown v. Plata*[39] was a violation of the U.S. Eighth Amendment clause on cruel and unusual punishment. The Taguba Report discussed below included a description of conditions at the two largest U.S.-run prisons in Iraq that read like a passage from the Supreme Court majority opinion describing mass incarceration in California:

> The Abu Ghraib and Camp Bucca detention facilities are significantly over their intended maximum capacity while the guard force is undermanned and under resourced. This imbalance has contributed to the poor living conditions, escapes, and accountability lapses at the various facilities. The overcrowding of the facilities also limits the ability to identify and segregate leaders in the detainee population who may be organizing escapes and riots within the facility.[40]

The report speculated that the overcrowding was also intensified in a way analogous to prisons in the United States: by slowness in releasing a majority of detainees who "are of no intelligence value and no longer pose a significant threat to Coalition forces."[41]

Camp Bucca was larger than Abu Ghraib and named for an American victim of the attack on the World Trade Center – a New York City Fire Marshall, Ronald Bucca – underlining the false link drawn between the

[38] United Nations Assistance Mission for Iraq (UNAMI), Human Rights Report, 1 July – 31 August 2005, ¶ 10 (2005), www.ohchr.org/Documents/Countries/Jul-Aug05_en.pdf; United Nations Assistance Mission for Iraq (UNAMI), Human Rights Report, 1 September – 31 October 2005, ¶ 6 (2005), www.ohchr.org/Documents/Countries/Sep-Oct05_en.pdf.

[39] Brown v. Plata, 565 U.S. 493 (2011).

[40] Taguba Report, *supra* note 36, at 25.

[41] *Id.*

former Iraq regime and September 11. Both Abu Bakr al-Baghdadi, who became the leader of ISIS, and Ayman al-Zawahiri, who became the leader of al-Qaeda in Iraq, are known to have been incarcerated at Camp Bucca.

At least six Pentagon investigations addressed the treatment of detainees in U.S. custody.[42] The best-known[43] and most revealing of these investigations was of the 800th Military Police Brigade and was conducted by Major General Antonio Taguba. The introduction of the Taguba Report made clear that the investigation was undertaken in response to a January 2004 request of Lieutenant General Ricardo Sanchez, Commander of the Forces in Iraq. Sanchez requested Taguba's investigation in response to mounting reports of detainee abuse and accountability problems in 2003 at a number of U.S. prisons operated by the 800th Brigade, including Camp Bucca, Camp Ashraf, Abu Ghraib, and the High Value Detainee Complex/Camp Cropper.

Taguba's investigation included a review of the then-recent September 2003 investigation by Major General Geoffrey Miller, Commander at Guantanamo (GTMO), who had been tasked with assessing the "ability to rapidly exploit internees for actionable intelligence" in U.S. military prisons in Iraq.

Geoffrey Miller is a crucial link in the chain of command that connected the enhanced interrogation/torture techniques developed under Donald Rumsfeld at the Department of Defense in Washington to their implementation at Guantanamo and their migration to Abu Ghraib Prison. Use of the enhanced interrogation/torture techniques during Miller's command at Guantanamo was widely reported to be excessive, with FBI documents indicating that "in late 2002 and continuing into mid-2003, the Behavioral Analysis Unit raised concerns over interrogation tactics being employed by the U.S. Military."[44]

Lieutenant General Randall Schmidt and Brigadier General John Furlow led an investigation of the application of these techniques during Miller's

---

[42] GEORGE R. FAY, INVESTIGATION OF INTELLIGENCE ACTIVITIES AT ABU GHRAIB (2004); DONALD J. RYDER, REPORT ON DETENTION AND CORRECTIONS OPERATIONS IN IRAQ (2003); GEOFFREY D. MILLER, ASSESSMENT OF DoD COUNTER-TERRORISM INTERROGATION AND DETENTION OPERATIONS IN IRAQ (2003); TAGUBA REPORT, *supra* note 36; FINAL REPORT OF THE INDEPENDENT PANEL TO REVIEW DoD DETENTION OPERATIONS (2004); ALBERT T. CHURCH III, EXECUTIVE SUMMARY OF REPORT ON DEPARTMENT OF DEFENSE DETENTION OPERATIONS AND DETAINEE INTERROGATION TECHNIQUES (2005).

[43] Journalist Seymour Hersh gained access to Taguba's report before it became public, leading to several articles in the *New Yorker* magazine and his book, CHAIN OF COMMAND: THE ROAD FROM 9/11 TO ABU GHRAIB (2004). True to the "first draft of history" tradition, the book contains no citations based on the report itself. While the report itself is more opaque in its prose, it importantly provides an official government presentation of the facts of torture in U.S. detention facilities in Iraq.

[44] Fed. Bureau of Investigation, Detainee Interviews (Abusive Interrogation Issues) ¶1 (May 6, 2004), www.aclu.org/sites/default/files/torturefoia/released/FBI.121504.4194.pdf.

command at Guantanamo.[45] FBI agents had alleged the use of the following interrogation techniques:

a. That military interrogators improperly used military working dogs during interrogation sessions to threaten detainees, or for some other purpose;

b. That military interrogators improperly used duct tape to cover a detainee's mouth and head;

c. That DoD interrogators improperly impersonated FBI agents and Department of State officers during the interrogation of detainees;

d. That, on several occasions, DoD interrogators improperly played loud music and yelled loudly at detainees;

e. That military personnel improperly interfered with FBI interrogators in the performance of their FBI duties;

f. That military interrogators improperly used sleep deprivation against detainees;

g. That military interrogators improperly chained detainees and placed them in a fetal position on the floor, and denied them food and water for long periods of time;

h. That military interrogators improperly used extremes of heat and cold during their interrogation of detainees.[46]

The investigation did not review the legal validity of the interrogation techniques approved by Secretary of Defense Rumsfeld and then in use at Guantanamo.[47] This is crucial because the investigation revealed, for example, in "Finding 16K," that "[o]n seventeen occasions, between 13 Dec 02 and 14 Jan 03, interrogators, during interrogations, poured water over the subject of the first Special Interrogation Plan head."[48]

The Special Interrogation Plan was authorized for use at Guantanamo by Secretary of Defense Rumsfeld and implemented under the command of Geoffrey Miller. The treatment of the detainee identified in Finding 16K is further detailed:

> The techniques used against [the detainee who was] the subject of the first Special Interrogation Plan were done in an effort to establish complete control and create the perception of futility and reduce his resistance to

[45] INVESTIGATION INTO FBI ALLEGATIONS OF DETAINEE ABUSE AT GUANTANAMO BAY, CUBA DETENTION FACILITY (2005), www.thetorturedatabase.org/files/foia_subsite/pdfs/schmidt_ furlow_report.pdf [hereinafter SCHMIDT-FURLOW REPORT].

[46] *Id.* at 2.

[47] *Id.* at 4.

[48] *Id.* at 19.

interrogation. For example, this included the use of strip searches, the control of prayer, the forced wearing of a woman's bra, and other techniques noted above. It is clear based upon the completeness of the interrogation logs that the interrogation team believed that they were acting within existing guidance. Despite the fact that the AR 15–6 concluded that every technique employed against [the detainee who was] the subject of the first Special Interrogation Plan was legally permissible under the existing guidance, the AR 15–6 finds that the creative, aggressive, and persistent interrogation of [the detainee who was] the subject of the first Special Interrogation Plan resulted in the cumulative effect being degrading and abusive treatment. Particularly troubling is the combined impact of the 160 days of segregation from other detainees, 48 of 54 consecutive days of 18 to 20-hour interrogations, and the creative application of authorized interrogation techniques. Requiring [the detainee who was] the subject of the first Special Interrogation Plan to be led around by a leash tied to his chains, placing a thong on his head, wearing a bra, insulting his mother and sister, being forced to stand naked in front of a female interrogator for five minutes, and using strip searches as an interrogation technique the AR 15–6 found to be abusive and degrading, particularly when done in the context of the 48 days of intense and long interrogations.[49]

By the tendentious reasoning of the Schmidt–Furlow investigation, which excluded consideration of the legal validity of the techniques applied, this treatment was found to be abusive and degrading but nonetheless humane and within legal limits of acceptability.[50]

A key part of the investigation related directly to procedures and practices that Taguba reported Miller, through his recommendations, subsequently introduced at Abu Ghraib. These procedures and practices had led in the earlier Schmidt–Furlow investigation at Guantanamo to "Recommendation #26." This recommendation indicated the necessity of "a policy-level determination on role of Military Police in 'setting the conditions' for intelligence gathering and interrogation of detainees at both the tactical level and strategic level facilities."[51] When Lieutenant General Schmidt was interviewed by journalist Seymour Hersh, he observed regarding these conditions that "for lack of a camera, you could have seen in Guantanamo what was seen at Abu Ghraib."[52]

---

[49] *Id.* at 20.

[50] *Id.*

[51] *Id.* at 29.

[52] Seymour M. Hersh, *The General's Report*, NEW YORKER (June 27, 2005), www.newyorker.com/ magazine/2007/06/25/the-generals-report.

The Taguba Report also reviewed a November 2003 investigation of detention and corrections operations directed by Major General Donald Ryder. Although similarly conducted only months earlier and in the same settings, neither the Miller nor Ryder Reports addressed issues of torture with the clarity of the Taguba Report.

When Taguba first addressed the Miller Report, he observed that "Miller's team recognized that they were using JTF-GTMO operational procedures and interrogation authorities as baselines for its ... recommendations."[53] This has been widely referred to as "Gitmoizing" the use of enhanced interrogation/torture in Iraq and raises chain-of-command issues since Miller reported to the deputies of Secretary of Defense Donald Rumsfeld, who oversaw development of these techniques and their implementation at Guantanamo. Taguba's emphasized that Guantanamo and Iraq detainees were presumably quite different, with the latter including many if not mostly suspected criminals rather than terrorists or members of terrorist organizations.[54]

Taguba further observed that Miller's report had explicitly recommended that "the 'guard force' be actively engaged in setting the conditions for successful exploitation of internees." Taguba emphasized that military guards are not trained in the same way as military interrogators and are thus not permitted by military regulations to engage in "setting the conditions for successful exploitation of internees."[55]

The Taguba Report then further reviewed the results of the November 2003 investigation headed by Major General Ryder. Taguba emphasized that an explicit recommendation of the Ryder Report – to stop the practice of having guards "set the conditions" for the interrogators – was not implemented. He wrote that "the systemic problems that surfaced during MG Ryder's Team's assessment are the very same issues that are the subject of this investigation."[56]

Taguba then emphatically took issue with the Ryder Report's conclusion that guards had not been instructed (following Miller's September 2003 recommendations) to "set the conditions" for interrogations. Taguba wrote that "I disagree with the conclusion of MG Ryder's Team in one critical aspect, that being its conclusion that the 800th MP Brigade had not been asked to change its facility procedures to set the conditions for MI interviews."[57] This conclusion was critical because it underlined the link between the development of interrogation

[53] TAGUBA REPORT, *supra* note 36, at 7.
[54] *Id.* at 8.
[55] *Id.* at 9.
[56] *Id.* at 12.
[57] *Id.*

practices under Secretary of Defense Rumsfeld, the implementation of these practices by Major General Miller in his command role at Guantanamo, and the migration of these practices to Iraq through Miller's recommendations.

The latter recommendations resulted in interrogators being sent to Iraq from Guantanamo, where witnesses reported that they encouraged guards to "set the conditions" for interrogations. "It is obvious from a review of comprehensive CID interviews of suspects and witnesses," Taguba wrote, "that this was done at lower levels." He reported, "Military Intelligence (MI) interrogators and Other US Government Agency's (OGA) interrogators actively requested that MP guards set physical and mental conditions for favorable interrogation of witnesses."[58]

Taguba then went on to identify in detail how guards "set the conditions" for interrogators, beginning with references to numerous photos that were withheld from the report, most of which at this writing have not yet been declassified. "We reviewed numerous photos and videos," he reported, "which are now in control of the US Army Criminal Investigation Command and the CJTF-7 prosecution team."[59] Some of the photos were soon placed on the *New Yorker* magazine website and shown on the CBS network show *60 Minutes*. The decision not to release some 1,800 photos continued into the Obama Administration after earlier promises to release them, and appears to remain the policy of the Trump Administration, which is a reflection of their presumably provocative and probative content, and is an echo of the powerful potential impact of visual evidence dating to Nuremberg.

In lieu of photos, the report includes an extensive itemization of observed forms of "intentional abuse of detainees by military police," including the following:

    a. Punching, slapping, and kicking detainees; jumping on their naked feet;
    b. Videotaping and photographing naked male and female detainees;
    c. Forcibly arranging detainees in various sexually explicit positions for photographing;
    d. Forcing detainees to remove their clothing and keeping them naked for several days at a time;
    e. Forcing naked male detainees to wear women's underwear;
    f. Forcing groups of male detainees to masturbate themselves while being photographed and videotaped;

[58] *Id.* at 18.
[59] *Id.* at 12.

g. Arranging naked male detainees in a pile and then jumping on them;

h. Positioning a naked detainee on a MRE Box, with a sandbag on his head, and attaching wires to his fingers, toes, and penis to simulate electric torture;

i. Writing "I am a Rapest" (sic) on the leg of a detainee alleged to have forcibly raped a 15-year-old fellow detainee, and then photographing him naked;

j. Placing a dog chain or strap around a naked detainee's neck and having a female Soldier pose for a picture;

k. A male MP guard having sex with a female detainee;

l. Using military working dogs (without muzzles) to intimidate and frighten detainees, and in at least one case biting and severely injuring a detainee;

m. Taking photographs of dead Iraqi detainees.[60]

In addition, the report includes credible witness descriptions of further detainee abuse by military police, including the following:

a. Breaking chemical lights and pouring the phosphoric liquid on detainees;

b. Threatening detainees with a charged 9mm pistol;

c. Pouring cold water on naked detainees;

d. Beating detainees with a broom handle and a chair;

e. Threatening male detainees with rape;

f. Allowing a military police guard to stitch the wound of a detainee who was injured after being slammed against the wall in his cell;

g. Sodomizing a detainee with a chemical light and perhaps a broom stick;

h. Using military working dogs to frighten and intimidate detainees with threats of attack, and in one instance actually biting a detainee.[61]

These described abuses were accompanied by named witnesses who testified about the role of military interrogators in encouraging these practices by military police.

The report further indicates that the military police at Abu Ghraib were untrained and uninformed about detention/internee operations and the applicable rules of the Geneva Conventions. Taguba indicated that "I also find that very little instruction or training was provided to MP personnel on the applicable rules of the Geneva Convention Relative to the Treatment of

[60] *Id.* at 16–17.
[61] *Id.* at 17–18.

Prisoners of War ... Moreover, I find that few, if any, copies of the Geneva Conventions were ever made available to MP personnel or detainees."[62] More generally, the report concluded that "there was virtually a complete lack of detailed SOPs at any of the detention facilities."[63]

IV. RESPONSIBILITY FOR TORTURE BY COMMISSION AND OMISSION

Although Taguba's explosive report was submitted in March of 2004, a month later Geoffrey Miller was appointed Deputy Commander for Detainee Operations overseeing Abu Ghraib. His mission was presumably to correct the abuses that the Taguba Report had exposed in graphic detail – the same abuses the Taguba Report had attributed to practices recommended by Miller in his August 2003 report on Abu Ghraib. Although lower-level members of the military were prosecuted, there was no official investigation of higher chain of command responsibility.

With the installation of a new Iraqi government in June of 2004, the legal circumstances were somewhat changed. The conflict between the newly named but still U.S.-led Multi-National Force and a still-growing insurgency became legally non-international. This modified the application of the Geneva Conventions, but Common Article 3 of the four Geneva Conventions continued to require the humane treatment of those held in detention. Furthermore, the basic provisions for the protection of detainees in the International Covenant on Civil and Political Rights (ICCPR) continued in force, as the United States and Iraq are both parties to the Covenant.

The official change in the legal standing of the Iraq conflict in June 2006 coincided with a growing role of the Iraq Army and the Ministry of the Interior in the operation of its own detention facilities and in their relationship with and treatment by the U.S. military. Allegations of abuse and torture within these facilities became common, and the U.S. military, again with leadership from Secretary of Defense Rumsfeld, declined to take much public responsibility for operations within them. This conflicted with continued legal obligations under the Geneva Conventions and the ICCPR, particularly the scope of these obligations given that American force levels would increase through the Surge in 2007.

It is important to have a sense of how extensive Iraq detention operations became, although there are no precise numbers. Estimates based on the *Iraq War Logs* indicate 180,000 Iraqis were detained between 2004 and 2009,

---

[62] *Id.* at 19–20.
[63] *Id.* at 31.

which would be the equivalent of one in fifty of the male population.[64] The Pew Educational Trust estimates that one in one hundred adults are incarcerated in the United States.[65]

Knowledge of the abuse and torture of these detainees is equally uncertain, but there are several persuasive indications that the problem has been acute. Human Rights Watch interviewed ninety detainees in Iraqi facilities between July and October 2004, about three-quarters of whom reported that they had been tortured or ill-treated during their detention.[66] The report indicates a pattern in which torture occurred soon after detention and while the detainees were held in solitary confinement. If they were taken before an investigative judge, it was usually after the evidence of physical torture had disappeared.[67] About a quarter of the detainees reported they were held as a result of their political activities or suspected involvement with militia groups.

From November to December 2004, U.S. forces reported on several Iraq-run detention facilities in Baghdad where detainees showed signs of torture and ill-treatment. Amnesty International summarized what they found:

> US military forces raided one detention facility controlled by the Interior Ministry in the al-Jadiriyah district of Baghdad, where they reportedly found more than 170 detainees being held in appalling conditions, many of whom alleged that they had been tortured. On 8 December 2005, Iraqi authorities and US forces inspected another detention facility in Baghdad, also controlled by the Interior Ministry. At least 13 of the 625 detainees found there required medical treatment, including several reportedly as a result of torture or ill-treatment ... the US ambassador to Iraq, Zalmay Khalilzad, stated that "over 100" detainees found at the detention facility in al-Jadiriyah and 26 detainees at the other detention location had been abused.[68]

---

[64] *See* Angus Stickler & Chris Woods, *Iraq War Logs: US Troops Ordered Not to Investigate Iraqi Torture*, BUREAU INVESTIGATIVE JOURNALISM (May 23, 2011), www.thebureauinvestigates.com/2011/05/23/us-troops-ordered-not-to-investigate-iraqi-torture/.

[65] PEW CTR. ON THE STATES, ONE IN 100: BEHIND BARS IN AMERICA 2008, at 5 (2008), www.pewtrusts.org/~/media/legacy/uploadedfiles/wwwpewtrustsorg/reports/sentencing_and_corrections/onein100pdf.

[66] HUMAN RIGHTS WATCH, THE NEW IRAQ? TORTURE AND ILL-TREATMENT OF DETAINEES IN IRAQI CUSTODY 11 (2005), www.hrw.org/reports/2005/iraq0105/iraq0105.pdf.

[67] *Id.* at 74.

[68] AMNESTY INT'L, BEYOND ABU GHRAIB: DETENTION AND TORTURE IN IRAQ 4 (2006), www.amnestyinternational.be/IMG/pdf/MDE140012006_IRAK.pdf. *But cf.* Kirk Semple, *Iraqi Ministry Denies Captives Were Abused*, N.Y. TIMES (Dec. 13, 2005), www.nytimes.com/2005/12/13/world/middleeast/iraqi-ministry-denies-captives-were-abused.html?_r=0; John F. Burns, *To Halt Abuses, U.S. Will Inspect Jails Run by Iraq*, N.Y. TIMES (Dec. 14, 2005), www.nytimes.com/2005/12/14/world/middleeast/to-halt-abuses-us-will-inspect-jails-run-by-iraq.html.

Follow-up reporting confirmed that detainees in both sites indicated that they had received electric shocks and had finger nails pulled out.[69]

In the interval between these accounts of detention and associated torture in Iraq-run facilities, Secretary Donald Rumsfeld and the head of the National Security Council, General Peter Pace, held a press conference in Washington. Rumsfeld and Pace disagreed when asked the following question:

Q Sir ... I can give you actual examples from coalition forces who talked to me when I was over there – about excesses of the Interior Ministry, the Ministry of Defense, and that is in dealing with prisoners or in arresting people and how they're treated after they're arrested. What are the obligations and what are the rights of the U.S. military over there in dealing with that? ...

SEC. RUMSFELD: That's a fair question. I'll start, and Pete, you may want to finish. . . . Obviously, the United States does not have a responsibility when a sovereign country engages in something that they disapprove of; however, we do have a responsibility to say so and to make sure that the training is proper and to work with the sovereign officials so that they understand the damage that can be done to them in the event some of these allegations prove to be true.

Q And General Pace, what guidance do you have for your military commanders over there as to what to do if – like when General Horst found this Interior Ministry jail?

GEN. PACE: It is absolutely the responsibility of every U.S. service member, if they see inhumane treatment being conducted, to intervene to stop it. . . .

SEC. RUMSFELD: But I don't think you mean they have an obligation to physically stop it; it's to report it.

GEN. PACE: If they are physically present when inhumane treatment is taking place, Sir, they have an obligation to try to stop it.[70]

[69] Caroline Hawley, *Iraqi Detainees Tell of Torture*, BBC News (Nov. 24, 2005), http://news.bbc.co.uk/1/hi/world/middle_east/4465194.stm; Ellen Knickmeyer, *Abuse Cited in 2nd Jail Operated by Iraqi Ministry*, Wash. Post (Dec. 12, 2005), www.washingtonpost.com/wp-dyn/content/article/2005/12/11/AR2005121101002.html.

[70] News Briefing with Donald Rumsfeld, Sec'y of Def., and Gen. Peter Pace, Chairman, Joint Chiefs of Staff (Nov. 29, 2005), http://archive.defense.gov/Transcripts/Transcript.aspx?TranscriptID=1492.

General Pace's clear and concise answer was consistent with U.S. obligations under international law, but inconsistent with what American forces were mostly doing, while Secretary Rumsfeld's response was inconsistent with international law, but more consistent with what American forces were apparently mostly not doing – that is, they were apparently mostly not intervening when they encountered inhumane treatment in Iraqi facilities.

Much of what we know about Iraqi detention facilities is based on separate analyses by the *Guardian*[71] and the *Bureau of Investigative Journalism*[72] using the *Iraq War Logs*. The latter consist of nearly 400,000 reports by U.S. soldiers of "SIGACTS" (or significant actions) from 2004 through 2009 and released through WikiLeaks. While this data requires further validation and analysis, the two reviews of this data by the above media sources are consistent with one another, and the basic descriptive account they provide of what U.S. soldiers encountered and observed during the 2004–09 period has not been questioned. The Department of Defense responded in a statement published in the *New York Times* that "'significant activities' reports are initial, raw observations by tactical units. They are essentially snapshots of events, both tragic and mundane, and do not tell the whole story."[73]

The *Bureau of Investigative Journalism* reported that the *Iraq War Logs* included more than 1,300 cases of detainee abuse by Iraqi authorities reported by U.S. soldiers. However, even more revealing were references in many of these reports to two military orders that inform understanding of the above transcribed press conference exchange between General Pace and Secretary Rumsfeld.

Der Spiegel created its own annotated version of the *Iraq War Logs* and provided the following documentation of the first significant action report that referred to two interrelated "fragmentary" orders that initially required no intervention or reporting by U.S. soldiers of evidence of "Iraq on Iraq" abuse (FRAGO 242), and then required no intervention but the filing of a report (FRAGO 039):

IRAQI ON IRAQI (NO US FORCES PERSONNEL WERE INVOLVED) NOTE: MNCI FRAGO 039 DTD 29 APRIL 2005 HAS MODIFIED FRAGO 242 AND NOW REQUIRES REPORTS OF IRAQI ON IRAQI ABUSE BE REPORTED THROUGH OPERATIONAL CHANNELS.

[71] Nick Davies, *Iraq War Logs: Secret Order That Let US Ignore Abuse*, GUARDIAN (Oct. 22, 2010), www.theguardian.com/world/2010/oct/22/iraq-detainee-abuse-torture-saddam.

[72] Stickler & Woods, *supra* note 64.

[73] *The Defense Department's Response*, N.Y. TIMES (Oct. 22, 2010), www.nytimes.com/2010/10/23/world/middleeast/23response.html.

INCIDENTS OF DETAINEE ABUSE COMMITTED BY IRAQI
FORCES FALL WITH MNF-IS CCIR #8. REPORTING WILL BE
MADE USING THE FORMAT ATTACHED TO MNCI FRAGO 039.
PROVIDED THE INITIAL REPORT CONFIRMS US FORCES WERE
NOT INVOLVED IN THE DETAINEE ABUSE, NO FURTHER INVES-
TIGATION WILL BE CONDUCTED UNLESS DIRECTED BY HHQ.[74]

The files record a great deal of abuse in Iraqi detention facilities and there is
little indication in the files or in the Department of Defense response that
many of these "significant actions" were further investigated.

V. CONCLUSIONS

American authorities turned over control of Abu Ghraib Prison to the Iraqi
government in 2006. It was closed by the Iraqi government in 2014, ten years
after the photo-driven torture scandal broke. In the year before the 2006 turn-
over occurred, the State Department reported to Congress that ninety-two
new and unprosecuted cases of alleged detainee abuse were recognized as
"founded."[75] Despite prosecutions of lower-level participants for their involvement in torture at Abu Ghraib, no higher-level officials have been punished
beyond receiving military reprimands or demotions.

Although selecting a single starting event as the beginning of a war can be
arbitrary, an important part of the planning for a war of aggression in Iraq was
signaled by President George W. Bush's February 2002 determination in a
memo to Vice President Richard Cheney that protections of the Geneva
Conventions did not apply to al-Qaeda in Afghanistan or anywhere else. This
was a first step toward using torture to obtain false intelligence indicating
that Saddam Hussein's regime in Iraq possessed weapons of mass destruction –
the pretext for launching the Administration's preemptive war in Iraq.

We have argued that focusing on the atrocities resulting from torture in the
Bush Administration's War on Terror and in Iraq is a promising starting point
for building a case that can lead to charging military and political leaders for a
war of aggression in Iraq. Torture was a key part of what Justice Robert Jackson

---

[74] *The Global Intelligence Files: Re: Der Spiegel on Iraq War Logs*, WikiLeaks (Oct. 18, 2012),
https://wikileaks.org/gifiles/docs/16/1614401_re-der-spiegel-on-iraq-war-logs-.html.
[75] U.S., Update to Annex One of the Second Periodic Report of the United States of
America to the Committee Against Torture (2005), *reproduced at* www.state.gov/j/drl/rls/
55712.htm.

called "the supreme international crime" – the crime of the war of aggression – and an important part of what Jackson further called "the accumulation of evil" in such wars.

The intent to use torture in waging aggressive war in Iraq was advanced in August 2002 when John Yoo and John Bybee, through the Office of Legal Counsel of the Department of Justice, responded to a request for advice from the President. The resulting legal opinion became known as the Torture Memo. This memo advised – notwithstanding opinions to the contrary within the Administration and ultimately confirmed by the U.S. Supreme Court – that cruel, inhuman, or degrading acts during interrogations of al-Qaeda and other enemy combatants would not fall within legal proscriptions against torture unless they produced pain and suffering "akin" to death or failure of a bodily organ.

Also during the summer of 2002, the Department of Defense under Secretary Donald Rumsfeld adopted techniques that had been used to elicit false confessions by Chinese interrogators during the Korean War for use in the War on Terror and in Iraq. These techniques included stripping detainees of their clothing, placing them in stress positions, putting hoods over their heads, disrupting their sleep, and subjecting them to loud music, flashing lights, extreme temperatures, and waterboarding. Rumsfeld subsequently constructed a list of interrogation techniques including some of those used by the Chinese and authorized their use at Guantanamo Bay.

The Commander at Guantanamo Bay, Geoffrey Miller, was a crucial connecting figure. The FBI's Behavioral Analysis Unit alleged that torture techniques were being used at Guantanamo in late 2002 and continuing into mid-2003. Miller was in command at Guantanamo during the period when the torture techniques were authorized for use by Secretary Rumsfeld. A military investigation by Generals Schmidt and Furlow later found that prisoners were abused under Miller's command, although the report was not tasked with assessing the legal validity of the techniques applied. The report nonetheless further questioned the use of abusive techniques under Miller's command by military guards who "set conditions" for interrogators.

Miller was directed to conduct an investigation and report on Abu Ghraib Prison in September of 2003. His report included a key recommendation for Abu Ghraib Prison, as at Guantanamo, that military guards be employed in "setting the conditions" for "successful exploitation of internees." Soon after Miller's report and recommendations, accounts began to emerge of abuse and torture at Abu Ghraib Prison. A November 2003 investigation and report by Major General Ryder also questioned the use of military guards to "set conditions" for interrogations at Abu Ghraib.

When General Antonio Taguba was placed in charge of an investigation in early 2004, he came into possession of numerous photographs of flagrant abuse at Abu Ghraib. The visual meaning of "setting conditions" for interrogations was now inescapably clear. Taguba observed that Miller's team intentionally drew from operational procedures and interrogation authorizations at Guantanamo as the foundation for their recommendations that the military guard force at Abu Ghraib be used "in setting the conditions for successful exploitation of internees." Taguba emphasized that military guards were not trained in the same way as military interrogators and thus were not permitted by military regulations to do this.

Taguba's report was submitted in March 2004. In April 2004, just a month later, Geoffrey Miller was appointed Deputy Commander for Detainee Operations overseeing Abu Ghraib. His mission presumably was to correct the same abuses that his August 2003 report had recommended for Abu Ghraib. Furthermore, investigators who had already abused detainees at Guantanamo were now sent to initiate the same procedures involving guards in "setting conditions" for interrogations at Abu Ghraib.

Despite the evidence leading from the approval of torture in Washington, through the use of torture at Guantanamo, to the implementation of a similar torture regime at Abu Ghraib Prison – there was no official investigation and punishment of the chain of command figures that led to this outcome. Although the U.S.-led and renamed Multi-National Force did not reach peak troop levels until the 2007 Surge, official sovereign responsibility was passed in 2006 from the Coalition Provisional Authority to the new Government of Iraq. This included increased responsibility of the Iraqi government for detention facilities. Since U.S. forces were still operating alongside and training the Iraqi military throughout the country, the United States as well as the Iraqi government was still bound by international prohibitions against the use of torture. However, intervention was uncommon as a result of orders instructing U.S. soldiers not to take action beyond reporting it when they observed evidence of "Iraq on Iraq" torture.

Sufficient evidence exists in the form of graphic photographic and documentary evidence to warrant the further investigation and likely charging of U.S. chain of command responsibility for torture in Iraq. Torture was an important part of the planning and conduct of a war of aggression in Iraq. The investigation and prosecution of military and political leaders responsible for torture practices in Iraq can be an important step toward criminal accountability for the war of aggression in Iraq.

PART IV

Imagining a Better World

17

Rethinking the Relationship Between *Jus in Bello* and *Jus ad Bellum*

A *Dialogue Between Authors*

FEDERICA D'ALESSANDRA AND ROBERT HEINSCH

I. INTRODUCTION

The question of the relationship between the two bodies of law regulating the use of deadly force in armed conflict is complex, diversified, and highly relevant to the realities of modern warfare. Increasingly, in fact, the lawfulness or even legitimacy of a war or other recourse to deadly force[1] is invoked as a yardstick to determine the level of compliance with the laws of armed conflict. Claims that enemy combatants' lack of observance of religious percepts justifies gratuitous brutality toward them and the civilian populations under their control, unless they prove themselves worthy of compassion by forcefully converting to a distorted and offensive version of Islam, pervades the rhetoric and war ethos of ISIS fighters.[2] Similarly, violations of the laws of war, justified

---

[1] Deborah Pearlstein, *The Strike in Syria – Is the International Law Calculation Different Now Than in 2013?*, OPINIO JURIS (Apr. 6, 2017), http://opiniojuris.org/2017/04/06/the-strike-in-syria-is-the-international-law-calculation-different-now-than-in-2013/; Julian Ku, *The Syria Attacks: Haven't We Had These Debates Already?*, OPINIO JURIS (Apr. 5, 2017), http://opiniojuris.org/2017/04/05/why-trump-cant-legally-attack-assad-without-the-u-n-s-consent/; Deborah Pearlstein, *Re-Engaging on an ISIL AUMF*, OPINIO JURIS (Sept. 22, 2016), http://opiniojuris.org/2016/09/22/re-engaging-on-an-isil-aumf/; Myriam Feinberg, Guest Post: *'New Battlefields, Old Laws' – Debate on the Future of the 2001 AUMF*, OPINIO JURIS (Sept. 28, 2014), http://opiniojuris.org/2014/09/28/guest-post-new-battlefields-old-laws-debate-future-2001-aumf/; Dapo Akande, *When Does the Use of Force Against a Non-State Armed Group Trigger an International Armed Conflict and Why Does this Matter?*, EJIL: TALK! (Oct. 18, 2016), www.ejiltalk.org/when-does-the-use-of-force-against-a-non-state-armed-group-trigger-an-international-armed-conflict-and-why-does-this-matter/; Marc Weller, *Forcible Humanitarian Action in International Law – Part I and II*, EJIL: TALK! (May 17–18, 2017), www.ejiltalk.org/forcible-humanitarian-action-in-international-law-part-ii.

[2] Cole Bunzel, *From Paper State to Caliphate: The Ideology of the Islamic State*, CTR. FOR MIDDLE E. POL'Y, BROOKINGS INST. (Mar. 2015), www.brookings.edu/wp-content/uploads/2016/06/The-ideology-of-the-Islamic-State.pdf. *See also* Graeme Wood, *What ISIS Really Wants*, ATLANTIC (Mar. 2015), www.theatlantic.com/magazine/archive/2015/03/what-isis-really-wants/384980/P;

by considerations of state survival on one hand, and self-determination or military necessity on the other, are a daily occurrence in many international and non-international armed conflicts.[3] In the wake of the September 11th attacks, the United States advanced an alternative legal architecture to justify its treatment of detainees and its conduct of hostilities in the so-called "Global War on Terror."[4] Most recently, the reform of peacekeeping and the increase in mandates for the protection of civilians and atrocity prevention has raised the question of whether current rules of engagement should be revisited to accommodate the fundamentally different nature of these military operations.[5] Moreover, recent scholarship has questioned whether in the case of a war of aggression, proportionality and military necessity can ever be rightfully invoked by the aggressor, positing that force used in contravention

---

Peter Gilbert, *Kill Unto Others: ISIS and the Reciprocity of Modern Terrorism*, Ethos (Sept. 16, 2014), www.ethosreview.org/intellectual-spaces/isis-reciprocity-of-terrorism/; Robert Spencer, *Islamic State Beheads Four Children for Refusing to Convert to Islam*, Jihad Watch (Dec. 9, 2014), www.jihadwatch.org/2014/12/islamic-state-beheads-four-children-for-refusing-to-convert-to-islam.

[3] Human Rights Council, *Out of Sight, Out of Mind: Deaths in Detention in the Syrian Arab Republic*, U.N. Doc. A/HRC/31/CRP.1 (Feb. 3, 2016); G.A. Res. 67/262, The Situation in the Syrian Arab Republic, U.N. Doc. A/RES/67/262 (June 4, 2013); S.C. Res. 2268, U.N. Doc. S/RES/2268 (Feb. 26, 2016); *Syria Conflict: BBC Exclusive Interview with President Bashar al-Assad*, BBC News (Feb. 10, 2015), www.bbc.com/news/world-middle-east-31327153.

[4] Office of the Press Sec'y, White House Press Secretary announcement of President Bush's determination re legal status of Taliban and Al Qaeda detainees, U.S. Dep't State (Feb. 7, 2002), www.state.gov/s/l/38727.htm. Although it has been largely dismantled, and certainly discredited in the eyes of international law observers and of the international community, the post–9/11 U.S. legal architecture inflicted tremendous damages, most of which are still to be understood. *See* Douglas A. Johnson, Alberto Mora & Averell Schmidt, *The Strategic Costs of Torture: How "Enhanced Interrogation" Hurt America*, Foreign Aff., Sept.–Oct. 2016, https://www.foreignaffairs.com/articles/united-states/strategic-costs-torture. *See also* Alberto Mora, United States Naval Academy Stutt Lecture: American Cruelty and the Defense of the Constitution (Feb. 27, 2017), https://carrcenter.hks.harvard.edu/files/cchr/files/american_cruelty_and_the_defense_of_the_constitution.pdf; *Carr Center's Strategic Consequences of the U.S. Use of Torture – Conference Report*, Carr Ctr. For Hum. Rts. Pol'y, Harv. Kennedy Sch. (Oct. 20, 2016), https://carrcenter.hks.harvard.edu/news/carr-center%E2%80%99s-strategic-consequences-us-use-torture-%E2%80%93-conference-report.

[5] Sarah Sewall & Sally Chin, Carr Ctr. for Human Rights Policy, Harvard Kennedy Sch. of Gov't, & Dwight Raymond, U.S. Army Peacekeeping & Stability Operations Inst., Mass Atrocity Response Operations: A Military Planning Handbook (2010), http://pksoi.armywarcollege.edu/default/assets/File/MARO%20Workshop%20Report.pdf; Int'l Indep. Comm'n on Kosovo, The Kosovo Report (2000), http://reliefweb.int/sites/reliefweb.int/files/resources/6D26FF88119644CFC1256989005CD392-thekosovoreport.pdf; *see, e.g.*, Jeff McMahan, *Morality, Law, and the Relation Between* Jus ad Bellum *and* Jus in Bello, 100 Am. Soc'y Int'l L. Proc. 112 (2006); Walter Gary Sharp, Sr., *Revoking an Aggressor's License to Kill Military Forces Serving the United Nations: Making Deterrence Personal*, 22 Md. J. Int'l L. 1 (1998).

of modern *jus contra bellum* is in itself a violation of the law of armed conflict.[6] These positions, which sometimes inject *ad bellum* considerations into *in bello* discussions and vice versa, pose important theoretical and epistemic challenges to the discipline of *jus belli*. Moreover, these challenges have important consequences both in the battlefield (as the experience of combatants and civilians whose protection under humanitarian law has been arbitrarily removed attests), as well as in its aftermath. Scholars have in fact questioned what the consequences of the *ex injuria jus non oritur* principle are for *jus post bellum*,[7] and insofar as the issue of accountability for the illegal use of force is concerned, some authors have recently argued that wars of aggression should be prosecuted as either a war crime or a crime against humanity, and that the main obstacle to doing so would be the conventional dogma of separation in characterizing the relationship between *jus ad bellum* and *jus in bello*.[8]

This Chapter is meant to be a contribution to the divisive debate on the issue of the relationship between these two legal strands. It is written as a conversation between two authors, each bringing their perspective to the discussion. In Section II, we discuss the basic principles of the laws of war, and whether a common core between the law on the use of force and the law of armed conflict exists. In Section III, we discuss the historical contours of the debate, and recent authoritative scholarship and jurisprudence on the issue of the relationship. In Section IV, we engage in a dialogue in an attempt to find common ground on the issues of the relationship and separation between the law on the use of force and international humanitarian law. This Chapter should not be considered as having a strictly technical nature, and the arguments hereby presented are neither comprehensive nor exhaustive. Rather, this Chapter reflects upon different aspects of the discussion

---

[6] McMahan, *supra* note 5. *See also* 1 Jean-Marie Henckaerts & Louise Doswald-Beck, Customary International Humanitarian Law: Rules 3 (2005).

[7] Dieter Fleck, Jus Post Bellum *as a Partly Independent Legal Framework, in* Jus Post Bellum: Mapping the Normative Foundations 43 (Carsten Stahn et al. eds., 2014); David Rodin, *Two Emerging Issues of the* Jus Post Bellum: *War Termination and the Liability of Soldiers for Crimes of Aggression, in* Jus Post Bellum: Towards a Law of Transition From Conflict to Peace 53, 62 (Carsten Stahn & Jann K. Kleffner eds., 2008); Hersch Lauterpacht, *The Limits of the Operation of the Law of War*, 30 Brit. Y.B. Int'l L. 206 (1953) [hereinafter Lauterpacht, *Limits*].

[8] Benjamin B. Ferencz, *The Illegal Use of Armed Force as a Crime Against Humanity*, 2 J. on Use Force & Int'l L. 187 (2015), http://dx.doi.org/10.1080/20531702.2015.1092705. *See also* Rachel E. VanLandingham, *Criminally Disproportionate Warfare: Aggression as a Contextual War Crime*, 48 Case W. Res. J. Int'l L. 215, 218 (2016); Manuel J. Ventura & Matthew Gillett, *The Fog of War: Prosecuting Illegal Uses of Force as Crimes Against Humanity*, 12 Wash. U. Global Stud. L. Rev. 523 (2013).

surrounding the relationship between the two bodies of law, of which some
are considered more frequently, others less so. It has been written in the hope
that the conversation will continue beyond the scope of this volume, in a
manner that is informed, conscientious of the inviolability of civilians, and
receptive of the needs of warriors and the changing nature of the institution
they personify.

II. THE BASIC PRINCIPLES AND THE SCOPE OF *JUS IN BELLO* COMPARED TO *JUS AD BELLUM*

When examining the relationship between the *jus in bello* and the *jus ad
bellum*, and the question of whether considerations of one can influence the
other, a good place to start is the basic principles that govern these two areas of
law and that are essential for determining the legality of an act under either.
This is because looking at the exact role and content of these principles and
examining whether they correspond to each other, or whether there are
substantial differences, might give an indication of whether they have to be
applied differently in both areas of law, or rather have an inherent core that
is similar. Legality under the *jus in bello* is determined decisively by the
principle of distinction,[9] the principle of proportionality,[10] the principle of
military necessity,[11] and the principle of humanity,[12] whereas the principles of
necessity and proportionality regulate the use of force under the *jus ad
bellum*.[13] *Prima facie*, it might in fact appear that, insofar as the principles of
necessity and proportionality are concerned, common ground could exist
between the two disciplines. The prevailing view, however, is that these are
false equivalences, and that these principles have a different content within
each area of law. This reinforces the view that both areas of law ought to be
applied separately.[14] In this Section, we enter into the merits of this argument.

---

[9] Henckaerts & Doswald-Beck, *supra* note 6, at 3.
[10] *Id.* at 46.
[11] *See* ROBERT KOLB & RICHARD HYDE, AN INTRODUCTION TO THE INTERNATIONAL LAW OF ARMED CONFLICT 44 (2008).
[12] Henckaerts & Doswald-Beck, *supra* note 6, ch. 1. *See also* YORAM DINSTEIN, THE CONDUCT OF HOSTILITIES UNDER THE LAW OF INTERNATIONAL ARMED CONFLICT 4–9 (2010) [hereinafter DINSTEIN, CONDUCT OF HOSTILITIES]; KOLB & HYDE, *supra* note 11, at 43–51.
[13] Legality of the Threat or Use of Nuclear Weapons, Advisory Opinion, 1996 I.C.J. Rep. 226, ¶ 41 (July 8) [hereinafter Nuclear Weapons Advisory Opinion].
[14] As stated in the Tallinn Manual with regard to the newly emerging phenomenon of cyberwarfare, "[i]t is important to note that the concepts of necessity and proportionality in the *jus ad bellum* are distinct from the concept of military necessity and the rule of proportionality in the *jus in bello*." *See* TALLINN MANUAL ON THE INTERNATIONAL LAW APPLICABLE TO CYBER

Before doing so, however, we will lay down the authors' frame of reference by outlining the scope and origin of the basic principles of the laws of war.

A. Ex Injuria Jus Non Oritur *and the Universal Validity of the Principle of Distinction*

Whereas the principle of military necessity and the principle of humanity underlie most of the rules of international humanitarian law, the principle of distinction is the clearest pillar of the law of armed conflict. The obligation to always make a distinction between civilians and combatants,[15] and between civilian objects and military objectives,[16] is a non-negotiable principle of the conduct of hostilities.[17] Indeed, while parties to an armed conflict may target combatants or military objectives in order to progress toward victory,[18] an absolute prohibition exists against deliberately targeting civilian objects and the civilian population *as such*.[19] It is required that "[i]n order to ensure respect for and protection of the civilian population and civilian objects, the Parties to the conflict shall at all times distinguish between the civilian population and combatants and between civilian objects and military objectives and accordingly shall direct their operations only against military objectives."[20] This notion of distinction lies at the core of the doctrine of combatants' privileges and liabilities and, as highlighted in the first sentence

---

WARFARE 62 (Michael N. Schmitt ed., 2013). *See also, e.g.,* Marco Sassòli, Ius ad Bellum *and* Ius in Bello–*The Separation Between the Legality of the Use of Force and Humanitarian Rules to be Respected in Warfare: Crucial or Outdated?, in* INTERNATIONAL LAW AND ARMED CONFLICTS: EXPLORING THE FAULTLINES: ESSAYS IN HONOUR OF YORAM DINSTEIN 241, 249 (Michael N. Schmitt & Jelena Pejic eds., 2007); KEIICHIRO OKIMOTO, THE DISTINCTION AND RELATIONSHIP BETWEEN *JUS AD BELLUM* AND *JUS IN BELLO* 79 (2011).

[15] Henckaerts & Doswald-Beck, *supra* note 6, at 3.

[16] *Id.* at 25.

[17] Although, as we will see when discussing proportionality and necessity, civilians and civilian objects might at times become legitimate military targets when their use and status aligns with that of those participating in hostilities.

[18] *Id.* at 29. For the definition of a military objective, *see* Rule 8. *Id.* at 29–32 (objects offering a definite military advantage).

[19] *Id.* at 3, 25.

[20] 1977 Protocol Additional to the Geneva Conventions of 12 August 1949, and relating to the Protection of Victims of International Armed Conflicts (Protocol I) art. 48, June 8, 1977, 1125 U.N.T.S. 3 [hereinafter Additional Protocol I]. *See also* Henckaerts & Doswald-Beck, *supra* note 6, r. 1 & 7, at 3, 25. On the question whether humanitarian law grants belligerents rights, "including the right to shoot at the soldiers of an opposing army," *see* Adam Roberts, *The Equal Application of the Laws of War: A Principle Under Pressure*, 90 INT'L REV. RED CROSS 931, 935 (2008).

of Article 48 of Additional Protocol I,[21] lies at the heart of the idea of protecting the civilian population from the effects of war.

Some commentators have argued that the soldier of a State that has violated the prohibition against the use of force should not benefit from combatants' privileges and liabilities.[22] This is because, by virtue of the *ex injuria jus non oritur* principle, which affirms that no legal rights can be derived from an unlawful act, violating international law at the beginning of the conflict would compromise the legality of all further actions by the State's armed forces, and they should not be able to rely on the beneficial treatment otherwise granted by the laws of war to those participating in hostilities.[23] While this might instinctively seem reasonable, the proposition as it is seems to place an unfair burden on the war executioner (i.e., the soldier), rather than the war planner (the government or military official who plans and prepares the war, and instructs the military to execute it). With many armies in the world requiring mandatory military service, and little recognition being granted to selective conscientious objection,[24] penalizing those carrying out the conflict as opposed to those who arrange and advocate for it might in fact strengthen war planners' position of unaccountability. Furthermore, as some have argued,[25] this proposition might in certain ways even undermine the principle of distinction. If punishment were to be feared irrespective of whether an act was carried out under the prism of combatants' privileges (i.e., the killing of enemy soldiers), restraining from other forms of violence banned under the rules of armed conflict (e.g., deliberate violence against civilians, sexual and gender-based violence, pillaging, etc.) could also see a decline in compliance. In other words, if the soldier were to fear punishment irrespective of whether

---

[21] Additional Protocol I, *supra* note 20, art. 48.

[22] Sharp, *supra* note 5.

[23] *See, e.g.,* 1 L. OPPENHEIM, INTERNATIONAL LAW: A TREATISE: PEACE 141–42 (Hersch Lauterpacht ed., 8th ed. 1955); François Bugnion, *Just Wars, Wars of Aggression and International Humanitarian Law,* INT'L REV. RED CROSS, Sept. 2002, at 1, www.icrc.org/eng/assets/files/other/irrc-847-2002-bugnion-ang.pdf (originally published in French at 84 INT'L REV. RED CROSS 523 [2002]).

[24] *See* Rachel E. VanLandingham, *Duty, Disobedience, and the Law of Armed Conflict,* ASIL CABLES (Apr. 15, 2017), www.asil.org/blogs/duty-disobedience-and-law-armed-conflict; Keith Petty, *A Duty to Disobey?,* JUST SEC. (Nov. 28, 2016), www.justsecurity.org/34612/duty-disobey/; Keith A. Petty, *Duty and Disobedience: The Conflict of Conscience and Compliance in the Trump Era* (June 20, 2017), https://papers.ssrn.com/sol3/papers.cfm?abstract_id=2870548.

[25] *See also* Jasmine Moussa, *Can* Jus ad Bellum *Override* Jus in Bello? *Reaffirming the Separation of the Two Bodies of Law,* 90 INT'L REV. RED CROSS 963, 986 (2008); Hersch Lauterpacht, *Rules of Warfare in an Unlawful War, in* LAW AND POLITICS IN THE WORLD COMMUNITY: ESSAYS ON HANS KELSEN'S PURE THEORY AND RELATED PROBLEMS IN INTERNATIONAL LAW 89, 92 (George A. Lipsky ed., 1953).

the conduct would have otherwise been considered legal or illegal, this could diminish soldiers' overall incentives to abide by the laws of war, and civilians could become the targets of indiscriminate violence. The protection of civilians from the scourge of war lies at the heart of international humanitarian law, and any discussion concerning the question of its relationship to the law on the use of force cannot depart from this fundamental principle.

B. *Balancing Military Necessity and the Principle of Humanity*

The central idea behind the laws of war is to find a balance between two principles: the principle of military necessity and the principle of humanity. The principle of military necessity is originally linked to the Hague part of international humanitarian law, as it deals with (and encompasses the idea that) the use and choice of means and methods of warfare is not unlimited, but rather allows only what is necessary in order to achieve a party's military objectives in progressing toward victory. On the other hand, the principle of humanity is intrinsically linked to the Law of Geneva, protecting especially persons *hors de combat*. Apart from this general observation, it is in principle accepted that all humanitarian law rules are characterized by the effort to balance these two concepts.[26] Although one of the first codifications of the principle of necessity can be found in Articles 14–16 of the Lieber Code,[27] under contemporary *jus in bello* rules the principle of necessity is not explicitly codified in any of the current humanitarian law treaties. Rather, it finds expression in specific provisions of the respective conventions, such as the prohibition of the use of means and methods of warfare that are likely to cause unnecessary suffering[28] or the prohibition of the unnecessary destruction of property.[29] The principle of necessity prohibits "unnecessary or wanton

---

[26] *See, e.g.*, Michael N. Schmitt, *Military Necessity and Humanity in International Humanitarian Law: Preserving the Delicate Balance*, 50 VA. J. INT'L L. 795 (2010); DINSTEIN, CONDUCT OF HOSTILITIES, *supra* note 12, at 16; Declaration Renouncing the Use, in Time of War, of Explosive Projectiles Under 400 Grammes Weight, Dec. 11, 1868, *reprinted in* THE LAWS OF ARMED CONFLICTS: A COLLECTION OF CONVENTIONS, RESOLUTIONS AND OTHER DOCUMENTS 101 (Dietrich Schindler & Jiří Toman eds., 1988).

[27] THE LAWS OF ARMED CONFLICTS, *supra* note 26, at 3. For more details on the content and value of the Lieber Code, cf. Robert Heinsch, *Lieber Code, in* ATROCITIES, MASSACRES, AND WAR CRIMES: AN ENCYCLOPEDIA 414, 414–17 (Alexander Mikaberidze ed., 2013).

[28] Convention (IV) Respecting the Laws and Customs of War on Land art. 23(e), Oct. 18, 1907, 2277 U.N.T.S. 539 (entered into force Jan. 26, 1910) [hereinafter 1907 Hague Convention].

[29] *Id.* art. 23(g); *see also* Christopher Greenwood, *Historical Development and Legal Basis, in* THE HANDBOOK OF INTERNATIONAL HUMANITARIAN LAW 1, at 35, ¶ 131 (Dieter Fleck ed., 2007).

application of force,"[30] and requires that "a belligerent may apply only that amount and kind of force necessary to defeat the enemy."[31] Furthermore, humanitarian law presupposes that the principle of military necessity can only be used in order to justify a certain military behavior when it is *expressly* allowed by a respective international treaty or customary law provision.[32] The International Committee of the Red Cross (ICRC), with reference to consistent state practice, has confirmed that "[c]onsequently, a rule of the law of armed conflict cannot be derogated from by invoking military necessity unless this possibility is explicitly provided for by the rule in question."[33] While at times observers contended that the "necessities of war prevailed over legal considerations,"[34] jurisprudence has evolved in line with the ICRC position. For instance, the U.S. Military Tribunal in *United States v. List* ruled that "[m]ilitary necessity or expedience do not justify a violation of positive rules."[35] Likewise, the Martens Clause of the Preamble of the 1907 Hague Convention IV states:

> Until a more complete code of the laws of war has been issued, the High Contracting Parties deem it expedient to declare that, in cases not included in the Regulations adopted by them, the inhabitants and the belligerents remain under the protection and the rule of the principles of the law of nations, as they result from the usages established among civilized peoples, from the laws of humanity, and the dictates of the public conscience.[36]

---

[30] Greenwood, *supra* note 29, at 35, ¶ 131.

[31] *Id.*

[32] OKIMOTO, *supra* note 14, at 93.

[33] INT'L COMM. OF THE RED CROSS, COMMENTARY ON THE ADDITIONAL PROTOCOLS OF 8 JUNE 1977 TO THE GENEVA CONVENTIONS OF 12 AUGUST 1949 393 (Yves Sandoz et al. eds., 1987), https://ihl-databases.icrc.org/applic/ihl/ihl.nsf/Comment.xsp?action=openDocument& documentId=2F157A9C651F8B1DC12563CD0043256C.

[34] Greenwood, *supra* note 29, at 38, ¶ 133 & n.172.

[35] *"The Hostage Case," Military Tribunal No. V, Case 7, United States of America v. Wilhem List, in* 11 TRIALS OF WAR CRIMINALS BEFORE THE NUERNBERG MILITARY TRIBUNALS UNDER CONTROL COUNCIL LAW NO. 10, Judgment, 757, 1256 (1948), www.loc.gov/rr/frd/Military_Law/pdf/NT_war-criminals_Vol-XI.pdf. This principle was also confirmed by other war crimes trials, including *In re* von Lewinski (called von Manstein), 16 Ann. Dig. 509, 511–513 (British Military Ct. at Hamburg, 1949); Trial of Gunther Thiele & Georg Steinert, 3 LAW REPORTS OF TRIALS OF WAR CRIMINALS 56, 58–59 (U.S. Military Comm'n at Ausberg, 1945); Peleus Trial, 1 LAW REPORTS OF TRIALS OF WAR CRIMINALS 1, 15–16 (British Military Ct. at Hamburg, 1945).

[36] A slightly modified version of the Martens Clause is found in Article 1(2) of Additional Protocol I and the fourth paragraph of the Additional Protocol II Preamble. "Recalling that, in cases not covered by the law in force, the human person remains under the protection of the principles of humanity and the dictates of the public conscience." Protocol Additional to the Geneva Conventions of 12 August 1949, and Relating to the Protection of Victims on Non-International Armed Conflicts (Protocol II) pmbl., June 8, 1977, 1125 U.N.T.S. 609 [hereinafter Additional Protocol II]; *see also* Additional Protocol I, *supra* note 20, art. 1(2).

In other words, although perhaps epistemically difficult to implement, the counterbalancing of the principle of humanity with the principle of necessity is a stringent requirement of all military action under the law of armed conflict, and one that cannot be departed from either.

C. *The Principles of Necessity and Proportionality Under the* Jus in Bello

The principles of necessity and proportionality are common features of many legal regimes. They play a major role in balancing situations in which the freedoms, rights, or privileges of one person or entity infringe upon the rights of another. Only if the infringement of a certain right is necessary (i.e., to achieve a certain legitimate goal) are assessments concerning the proportionality of the measure (in relation to the infringed right) plausible.[37] This framework of analysis applies equally to human rights (the right to life, right to physical integrity, etc.) and state rights (e.g., the inviolability of the territory), as well as rights protected by the laws of armed conflict (e.g., the right of the civilian not to be attacked). While these principles are common to different areas of law, neither principle provides *absolute* guidance on how to balance the two conflicting interests. They are, in fact, inherently relative to the objective sought (principle of necessity), or the infringement to be expected (principle of proportionality). The same is true for their relationship to the objectives pursued under the laws of armed conflict. The principle of military necessity generally encompasses "measures which are actually necessary to accomplish a legitimate military purpose and are not otherwise prohibited by international humanitarian law."[38] From this limitation, important rules follow, such as the prohibition on measures that cause unnecessary suffering. The principle of necessity does not stand alone, but is limited by other humanitarian law principles, first and foremost by the principle of proportionality, which prohibits the taking of measures (even complying with military necessity) that cause excessive damage to civilians.

International humanitarian law treaties do not mention proportionality independently from other humanitarian rules, but connect it to additional core principles of the law of armed conflict. On one side, the principle is used to define indiscriminate attacks (which would violate the principle of distinction)

---

[37] *Cf.* Christopher Greenwood, *Self-Defence, in* OXFORD PUB. INT'L L., MAX PLANCK ENCYCLOPEDIA OF PUBLIC INTERNATIONAL LAW ¶¶ 26–28 (Apr. 2011), http://opil.ouplaw.com/view/10.1093/law:epil/9780199231690/law-9780199231690-e401?prd=EPIL (stressing that these two requirements have to be dealt with separately and sequentially).

[38] *Military Necessity,* INT'L COMM. RED CROSS (June 5, 2012), https://casebook.icrc.org/glossary/military-necessity.

as attacks "which may be expected to cause incidental loss of civilian life, injury to civilians, damage to civilian objects, or a combination thereof, which would be excessive in relation to the concrete and direct military advantage anticipated."[39] On the other side, the proportionality principle is used as one of the core principles of international humanitarian law to ensure effective protection of civilian objects and persons.[40] This requires the attacker to make an *ex ante* assessment of whether the expected collateral damage would be excessive with respect to the military advantage sought through the attack (i.e., he has to take "precautions in attack"). As we will see in the next Section, this is a fundamentally different calculus than the one required by proportionality under the *jus ad bellum*.

D. *The Principles of Necessity and Proportionality under the* Jus ad Bellum

Whereas it might appear that the principles of necessity and proportionality offer a common framework for understanding the law on the use of force[41] and international humanitarian law, it should not be assumed that their application is the same across both bodies of law. First and foremost, neither principle is explicitly mentioned or defined in treaty law relative to the *jus ad bellum*.[42] Neither Articles 2(4) and 51 of the U.N. Charter nor Chapter VII of the Charter mention the requirements that actions ought to be "necessary and proportional." Instead, the requirements of necessity and proportionality come from the "inherent" character[43] of the right to self-defense,[44]

---

[39] Additional Protocol I, *supra* note 20, art. 51(5)(b).

[40] *See* Military and Paramilitary Activities in and against Nicaragua (Nicar. v. U.S.), Merits Judgment, 1986 I.C.J. Rep. 14, ¶ 232 (June 27) [hereinafter Nicaragua Merits Judgment]; Oil Platforms (Iran v. U. S.), Merits Judgment, 2003 I.C.J. Rep. 161, ¶ 50 (Nov. 6) [hereinafter Oil Platforms Merits Judgment]; Armed Activities on the Territory of the Congo (Dem. Rep. Congo v. Uganda), Judgment, 2005 I.C.J. Rep. 168, ¶ 146 (Dec. 19) [hereinafter Armed Activities Judgment]. This is a rule of customary humanitarian law, as evidenced in Rule 14 of the ICRC Study on Customary Humanitarian Law. *See also* Henckaerts & Doswald-Beck, *supra* note 6, r. 14, at 46.

[41] For an overview of this issue, *compare* Yoram Dinstein, War, Aggression and Self-Defence 207–12 (3d ed. 2001); Christine Gray, International Law and the Use of Force 148–55 (3d ed. 2008); Thomas M. Franck, Recourse to Force: State Action Against Threats and Armed Attacks 45–51 (2002).

[42] *See* David Kretzmer, *The Inherent Right to Self-Defence and Proportionality in* Jus Ad Bellum, 24 Eur. J. Int'l L. 235, 239 (2013).

[43] *Id.*

[44] Nuclear Weapons Advisory Opinion, *supra* note 13, ¶ 41; Yoram Dinstein, War, Aggression and Self-Defence 187 (5th ed. 2011) [hereinafter Dinstein, War, Aggression and Self-Defence (5th ed. 2011)].

or the "lawfulness" of the enforcement measure of the Security Council under Chapter VII.[45]

The law on the use of force sets stringent limits on the notion of necessity. Whereas the concept of military necessity in international humanitarian law is dictated by the value that certain action brings from a military perspective, in the context of the *jus ad bellum* "necessity" means that "no alternative response [is] possible," not that a particular military action ought to contribute to a military advantage.[46] This notion of necessity in the law of the use of force has remained constant since the 1837 *Caroline* incident, in which a diplomatic note sent by Daniel Webster dealt with the conditions for a preemptive attack of the British armed forces against a group of Canadian rebels in order to counter an expected attack from the United States.[47] According to Webster, there must be a "necessity of self-defense, instant, overwhelming, leaving no choice of means and no moment of deliberation."[48] While some commentators have questioned whether this test can be transferred to the current *jus ad bellum*,[49] consistent jurisprudence has confirmed it can.[50] The most authoritative decision of the International Court of Justice (ICJ) on this issue is the *Nicaragua* case, in which the Court concluded that the United States could not rely upon the doctrine of necessity to justify military action against Nicaragua based upon Nicaragua's armed attack against El Salvador because it had taken place several months earlier.[51] The Court came to a similar conclusion with regard to the necessity of the actions in the *Oil Platforms* case.[52] This is a quintessentially different conception of necessity than the one existing in *jus in bello*.

---

[45] This has regularly been confirmed by the International Court of Justice's jurisprudence. *See* Nuclear Weapons Advisory Opinion, *supra* note 13, ¶ 41; DINSTEIN, WAR, AGGRESSION AND SELF-DEFENCE (5th ed. 2011), *supra* note 44, at 187; Nicaragua Merits Judgment, *supra* note 40, ¶ 186.

[46] GRAY, *supra* note 41, at 150.

[47] For more details, *see* R. Y. Jennings, *The Caroline and McLeod Cases*, 32 AM. J. INT'L L. 82, 86 (1938).

[48] Correspondence between Gr. Brit. and the U.S., respecting the Arrest and Imprisonment of Mr. McLeod, for the Destruction of the Steamboat Caroline, 29 BFSP 1126, 1138 (1841), https://babel.hathitrust.org/cgi/pt?id=mdp.39015019751299;view=1up;seq=1152.

[49] For further references, *see* GRAY, *supra* note 41, at 149 n.150.

[50] *See* Nicaragua Merits Judgment, *supra* note 40, ¶ 194; Nuclear Weapons Advisory Opinion, *supra* note 13, ¶ 141; Oil Platforms Merits Judgment, *supra* note 40, ¶ 43; Armed Activities Judgment, *supra* note 40, ¶ 147.

[51] Nicaragua Merits Judgment, *supra* note 40, ¶ 237.

[52] Oil Platforms Merits Judgment, *supra* note 40, ¶ 76.

The difference in scope is even clearer with regard to the principle of proportionality, which by definition puts two different values into relation with each other. Under the *jus ad bellum*, the proportionality of an action is not directly related to the civilian harm and military advantage expected (although the former is usually part of the *jus in bello* calculus), but is considered in relation to the original attack. As the ICJ stated in *Nicaragua*: "self-defence would warrant only measures which are proportional to the armed attack and necessary to respond to it."[53]

The criteria that determine proportionality *can* include the choice of target, the effects of the attack on civilians, or its geographical and temporal scope,[54] but this equation differs from the proportionality calculation carried out during target clearance under *jus in bello*. This approach to the principle of proportionality in the area of *jus ad bellum* is widely agreed upon.[55] Furthermore, proportionality differs from reciprocity in that the State acting in self-defense does not have to use the same means and methods of warfare as the attacker,[56] as long as the result is commensurate with the original attack and achieves no goal other than "defending itself and guaranteeing its future security."[57] The range of latitude concerning the scope of what constitutes proportionality is not unanimously agreed upon, however. Judge Ago of the ICJ, for example, put a slightly differentiated approach forward in the *Armed Activities* case, stating that proportionality requires balancing the armed attack of the aggressor with "the aim to halt and repel" it.[58] This interpretation, which recalls the argument advanced by the Republic of Korea with respect to the beginning of the 1950–53 Korean War,[59] has garnered support over the past decades, especially during the negotiations

---

[53] Nicaragua Merits Judgment, *supra* note 40, ¶ 176.

[54] OKIMOTO, *supra* note 14, at 59.

[55] *See, e.g.,* U.N. Secretary-General, *Question of Defining Aggression: Rep. of the Secretary-General,* ¶ 41, U.N. Doc. A/2211 (Oct. 3, 1952); ROSALYN HIGGINS, PROBLEMS AND PROCESS: INTERNATIONAL LAW AND HOW WE USE IT 231 (1993); Oscar Schachter, *International Law in Theory and Practice: General Course in Public International Law, in* 178 COLLECTED COURSES OF THE HAGUE ACADEMY OF INTERNATIONAL LAW 9, 155 (1982).

[56] OKIMOTO, *supra* note 14, at 60. *See also* Nuclear Weapons Advisory Opinion, *supra* note 13 (dissenting opinion by Judge Higgins, ¶ 5) ("[T]he concept of proportionality referred to was that which was proportionate to repelling the attack, and not a requirement of symmetry between the mode of the initial attack and the mode of response.").

[57] Greenwood, *supra* note 29, at 36, ¶ 131.

[58] Armed Activities Judgment, *supra* note 40, ¶ 304. *See also* OKIMOTO, *supra* note 14, at 60; Report of the Special Committee on the Question of Defining Aggression, 24 February – 3 April 1969, ¶ 73, U.N. Doc. A/7620 (1969).

[59] S.C. Res. 83, Complaint of Aggression upon the Republic of Korea, U.N. Doc. S/RES/83 (June 27, 1950).

on the Definition of the Crime of Aggression,[60] and in the dissenting or separate opinions of various ICJ judges.[61]

In conclusion, the current requirements associated with the principles of necessity and proportionality in the law on the use of force show that there are important differences in their meanings with regard to humanitarian law, because they involve different factual inquiries. While the principle of proportionality in the *jus in bello* only considers the factual circumstances of a particular military operation ("concrete and direct military advantage"), proportionality in the *jus ad bellum* context takes a more global approach and refers to the long-term aim of countering an armed attack. In other words, although it could superficially appear that proportionality and necessity are common traits of the *jus in bello* and *jus ad bellum*, their content and application is profoundly different in each context. This seems to support the idea that the two bodies of law should continue to be kept (and applied) separately. Challenges to the principle of separation, however, are regularly raised, and the next Section considers these arguments.

III. ON THE RELATIONSHIP BETWEEN THE *JUS AD BELLUM* AND THE *JUS IN BELLO*

The equal and symmetrical application of humanitarian law has become a staple of the principle of separation between the *jus in bello* and the *jus ad bellum* on the premise that "the legal status of conflicting parties under *jus ad bellum* does not affect the application of [humanitarian law]."[62] The corollary of this position is that "the application of [humanitarian law] does not legitimise the illegal use of force under *jus ad bellum*."[63] In other words, the legality of the initial use of force does not impact the application of humanitarian law in the course of hostilities, meaning that regardless of which side of the fight a combatant is on, the full body of the law of armed conflict, comprising of both privileges and liabilities, will apply. Most importantly, regardless of which side's control they fall under (that of the aggressor or victim State, that of the occupying power or that of the occupied State), civilians on all sides will benefit from the full protection of humanitarian law at all times, and in no circumstance should the fact that they will be

---

[60] Report of the Special Committee on the Question of Defining Aggression, *supra* note 58.

[61] Nicaragua Merits Judgment, *supra* note 40 (dissenting opinion by Judge Schwebel, ¶¶ 211–14); Nuclear Weapons Advisory Opinion, *supra* note 13 (dissenting opinion by Judge Higgins, ¶ 5); Armed Activities Judgment, *supra* note 40 (separate opinion by Judge Kooijmans, ¶¶ 33–34).

[62] OKIMOTO, *supra* note 14, at 14.

[63] *Id.*

interpreted as a license to wage war. This vision has been considered by the majority of scholars as the bedrock of the discipline,[64] and these rules have been widely recognized as the substratum of the *jus in bello* and the *jus ad bellum* relationship. The greater contours of this relationship, however, have been and continue to be the topic of lively exchanges in academic and practitioners' circles.[65] The principle of separation, for example, has been challenged by new threats posed by the evolution of armed conflict (the asymmetrical character of modern warfare, the emergence of humanitarian wars, and the global struggle against international terrorism), as well as by ethical and moral philosophy scholarship reflecting on the role of individual criminal liability in questions of the use of force.[66] This Section considers some of these challenges.

A. *The Genesis of the Principle of Separation and the Principle of Equal Application*

Some have argued that the principle of separation – that the law on the use of force and international humanitarian law are two distinct bodies of law – was introduced for the first time in the twentieth century in order to differentiate between two otherwise not separated classes of war acts (the beginning of a conflict and conduct within the conflict). Faced with increasingly destructive arsenals, nations mutually agreed on limitations on their ability to conduct themselves freely within the conflict, in exchange for the maintenance of the status quo vis-à-vis their sovereign belligerent privileges. In other words, they

---

[64] OKIMOTO, *supra* note 14, at 59.

[65] This is particularly true when the issue of the interplay of a third body of law, generally international criminal law or international human rights law, comes into question. *See* William Schabas, *A Human Right to Peace*, 58 HARV. INT'L L.J. ONLINE 28 (2017), www .harvardilj.org/2017/04/the-human-right-to-peace/; Frédéric Mégret, *State Responsibility for Aggression: A Human Rights Approach*, 58 HARV. INT'L L.J. ONLINE 62 (2017), www.harvardilj .org/2017/04/state-responsibility-for-aggression-a-human-rights-approach/; Leila Nadya Sadat, *Accountability for the Illegal Use of Force: Putting Peacetime First*, 58 HARV. INT'L L.J. ONLINE 74 (2017), www.harvardilj.org/2017/04/accountability-for-the-unlawful-use-of-force-putting-peacetime-first/; Federica D'Alessandra, *Accountability for Violations of the Prohibition Against the Use of Force at a Normative Crossroads*, 58 HARV. INT'L L.J. ONLINE 7 (2017), www .harvardilj.org/2017/04/accountability-for-violations-of-the-prohibition-against-the-use-of-force-at-a-normative-crossroads/ [hereinafter D'Alessandra, *Normative Crossroads*]; William A. Schabas, *Lex Specialis? Belt and Suspenders? The Parallel Operation of Human Rights Law and the Law of Armed Conflict, and the Conundrum of Jus ad Bellum*, 40 ISR. L. REV. 592 (2007); Federica D'Alessandra, *Israel's Associated Regime: Exceptionalism, Human Rights and Alternative Legality*, 30 UTRECHT J. INT'L & EUR. L. 30 (2014).

[66] *See, e.g.*, McMahan, *supra* note 5; Sharp, *supra* note 5; Rodin, *supra* note 7, at 53.

agreed to limit the scope and intensity of war, so to be able to continue to wage war.[67] It is arguably for this reason that the Hague Conventions versed far more ink on clarifying the permissible means and methods of warfare than on banning war altogether.[68] Given the war capabilities at stake, which gave rise to the need for the law itself, it was a matter of vital interest to all belligerents that the agreed limits on means and methods of warfare be respected by all.

Whatever the origins of the Hague Law, prior to the Covenant of the League of Nations it was generally believed that whatever may cause the war, and whether or not the cause of war be a so-called "just" cause, the same rules of law applied among belligerents, and between belligerents and neutrals, even if these were seldom applied consistently.[69] With the emergence of the *jus ad bellum*, however (particularly with the 1928 General Treaty for Renunciation of War as an Instrument of National Policy or Kellogg–Briand Pact), war was no longer "just" or "unjust," and with the question of *lawfulness* or *unlawfulness* of the war arising, so did the question of the *jus in bello* applicability.[70] In 1934, formulating Article 7 of the Articles of Interpretation of the Kellogg–Briand Pact, the International Law Association weighed in, writing that "The Pact does not affect such humanitarian obligations as are contained in … the Hague Conventions of 1899 and 1907, the Geneva Conventions of 1864 and 1906, and the International Convention relating to the Treatment of Prisoners of War, 1929."[71] In 1939, experts of the Harvard Research in International Law reiterated this point in Article 14 of the Draft Convention on Rights and Duties of States in Case of Aggression that they prepared, which read: "Nothing in this Convention shall be deemed to excuse

---

[67] *See* Heidi Matthews, From Aggression to Atrocity: Interrogating the *Jus in Bello* Turn in International Criminal Law (submitted in 2014) (unpublished S.J.D. dissertation, Harvard Law School). Until then, in fact, the regulation of soldiers' conduct in war was essentially a matter of domestic scrutiny.

[68] An alternative, authoritative, and non-conflicting explanation of why the *jus in bello* began being regulated before the *jus ad bellum* is that until the League of Nations, that is until a clear framework was laid out for the "legality" or "illegality" of a war, the lack of a central authority that could decide who was a "just" or "unjust" combatant made it impossible to limit the recourse to war to "just" wars, and it was thus in all belligerents' interest to ensure that their own combatants be treated humanely in battle, even if they were fighting for an "unjust" cause.

[69] 2 L. OPPENHEIM, INTERNATIONAL LAW: A TREATISE: DISPUTES, WAR AND NEUTRALITY 217 (Hersch Lauterpacht ed., 7th ed. 1952) [hereinafter OPPENHEIM, DISPUTES, WAR AND NEUTRALITY (7th ed.)]. *See also* DINSTEIN, WAR, AGGRESSION AND SELF-DEFENCE, *supra* note 41, at 156–62.

[70] *See supra* note 68.

[71] Int'l Law Ass'n, *Report on the Effect of the Briand–Kellogg Pact of Paris on International Law*, 38 INT'L L. ASS'N REP. CONF. 1, 68 (1934).

any State for a violation of the humanitarian rules concerning the conduct of hostilities."[72] This notion was crystallized in Common Article 1 of the 1949 Geneva Conventions and subsequent Additional Protocols, which underscored the application of the treaties "in all circumstances."[73] While both the International Law Association and the Harvard Research in International Law group concluded that nothing could excuse the application of humanitarian rules,[74] the International Law Association found that "signatories [to the Pact] could legally discriminate against an illegal aggressor,"[75] and an attached commentary to the Harvard Research's Draft Convention explained that "humanitarian provisions were maintained in a large part by the threat of reciprocity, and reflected the common interest of humanity and self-interest."[76] Based on the *ex injuria jus non oritur* principle, the Harvard group also found that "an aggressor does not have any of the rights which it would have if it were a belligerent,"[77] and the reason why neither of the two went beyond this limited proposition was not that they were trying to protect the principle of distinction, but that "[t]he Kellogg-Briand Pact was simply too sparse and toothless to argue that . . . far-reaching consequences flowed automatically from its provisions."[78] Quite simply, because the *jus in bello* (and the "deeply ingrained . . . social practice" of applying it equally) pre-existed, "their tradition of equal application drove the continued separation between the two fields."[79]

A few years later, prosecutors at the U.S. International Military Tribunals in Nuremberg, in the *Hostage* case, tried to argue on similar questions. Their argument was that the law of occupation (which is, of course, part of international humanitarian law) never became effective after Germany's occupation of Greece and Yugoslavia, because the occupation had taken place subsequent

---

[72] Harvard Research in Int'l Law, *Draft Convention on Rights and Duties of States in Case of Aggression* 33 Am. J. Int'l L. 827, 830 (Supp. 1939).

[73] Convention (I) for the Amelioration of the Condition of the Wounded and Sick in Armed Forces in the Field art. 1, Aug. 12, 1949, 75 U.N.T.S. 31 [hereinafter First Geneva Convention].

[74] *Id.*

[75] JHH Weiler & Abby Deshman, *Far Be It from Thee to Slay the Righteous with the Wicked: An Historical and Historiographical Sketch of the Bellicose Debate Concerning the Distinction Between* Jus ad Bellum *and* Jus in Bello, 24 Eur. J. Int'l L. 25, at 31 (2013) (citing Int'l Law Ass'n, *Briand–Kellogg Pact of Paris: Budapest Articles of Interpretation*, 20 Transactions Grotius Soc'y 205 [1934]).

[76] *Id.* at 31 (citing Harvard Research in Int'l Law, *supra* note 72).

[77] *Id.*

[78] Weiler & Deshman, *supra* note 75, at 31.

[79] *Id.*

to an "aggressive war" and was thus "unlawful,"[80] (another exposition of the *ex injuria jus non oritur* principle). The tribunal, however, responded:

> international law makes no distinction between a lawful and unlawful occupant dealing with the respective duties of occupants and population in occupied territory. There is no reciprocal connection between the manner of the military occupation of territory and the rights and duties of the occupant and population to each other after the relationship has in fact been established.[81]

On the same principle, Hersch Lauterpacht wrote in 1953 that

> any application to the actual conduct of war of the principle of *ex injuria jus non oritur* would transform the contest into a struggle which may be subjected to no regulation at all. The results would be the abandonment of most rules of warfare, including those which are of humanitarian character.[82]

Similarly, at the 1974–77 Conference on the Reaffirmation and Development of International Humanitarian Law Applicable in Armed Conflict, France, Romania, and Afghanistan[83] expressed concern that Article 51 of Additional Protocol I, prohibiting indiscriminate attacks against civilians, should not be seen as restricting the State's right to self-defense when faced with aggression. While in the end the argument was rejected, the Preamble to Additional Protocol I – which had been negotiated as a statement of the principle that "nothing in this Protocol or in the Geneva Conventions can be construed as legitimizing or authorizing any act of aggression or any other use of force inconsistent with the Charter of the United Nations"[84] – came to be read as a statement of the separation principle;[85] yet, it is reasonable to ask whether that reading simply intended to reject providing a *carte blanche* for fighting wars illegally. During the Vietnam War, a similar challenge to the principle of separation and equal application of humanitarian law was advanced when the Democratic Republic of Vietnam refused to apply the

---

[80] *"The Hostage Case," Military Tribunal No. V, Case 7, United States of America v. Wilhem List,* in 11 Trials of War Criminals Before the Nuernberg Military Tribunals Under Control Council Law No. 10, Judgment, 757, 1246–47 (1948), www.loc.gov/rr/frd/Military_Law/pdf/NT_war-criminals_Vol-XI.pdf [hereinafter Hostage Case Judgment].

[81] Okimoto, *supra* note 14, at 17 (citing the Hostage Case Judgment, *supra* note 80, at 1247).

[82] Lauterpacht, *Limits, supra* note 7, at 212.

[83] Summary Record of the Forty-First Plenary Meeting, Doc. CDDH/SR.41 (May 26, 1977), *in* 6 Official Recs. Dipl. Conf. on Reaffirmation & Dev. Int'l Humanitarian L. Applicable Armed Conflicts 141, at 162, 165, ¶¶ 111, 114, 126, & annex, 175, at 196–97 (1978), www.loc.gov/rr/frd/Military_Law/pdf/RC-records_Vol-6.pdf.

[84] Additional Protocol I, *supra* note 20, pmbl.

[85] Okimoto, *supra* note 14, at 22.

Third Geneva Convention Relative to the Treatment of Prisoners of War to U.S. soldiers captured in combat on the basis that, in its view, the United States had unlawfully waged a war of aggression.[86] Again, the *ex injuria jus non oritur* principle was summoned. To this argument, however, the Diplomatic Conference on the Reaffirmation and Development of International Humanitarian Law Applicable in Armed Conflict (in the context of which the 1977 Additional Protocols to the Geneva Conventions were being negotiated) replied that such a position would be "condemned not only by modern positive law but also by logic, intelligence, and morality."[87]

The most significant challenge to date to the concept of the equal application of humanitarian law, used as an excuse to deny the protection afforded by the law of armed conflict to detainees, has come in the guise of an armed conflict that escapes conventional classifications under international law, the "Global War on Terror."[88] In the aftermath of the September 11th attacks, the United States' response to the deadliest attack on U.S. soil since Pearl Harbor challenged the conventional understanding of both the *jus in bello*,[89] and the *jus ad bellum* (by arguing, for example, that "unlawful enemy combatants" were not entitled to Prisoner of War status in accordance with the Third Geneva Convention,[90] a claim based on an "inexistent" third category in humanitarian law clearly rejected by the ICRC and by the jurisprudence of the United Nations International Criminal Tribunal for the former Yugoslavia [ICTY],[91] among others, or by arguing that grounds for legitimate self-defense extended beyond the scope of traditional self-defense against an imminent armed attack by another State to include preventive wars, such as the campaign fought in Iraq, or – more successfully – by arguing it extended to non-state armed groups).[92] The U.S. position was met with harsh criticism and

---

[86] Weiler & Deshman, *supra* note 75.

[87] Summary Record of the Sixteenth Meeting, Doc. CDDH/III/SR.16 (Feb. 10, 1975), *in* 14 OFFICIAL RECS. DIPL. CONF. ON REAFFIRMATION & DEV. INT'L HUMANITARIAN L. APPLICABLE ARMED CONFLICTS 127, at 131, ¶ 21 (1979), www.loc.gov/rr/frd/Military_Law/pdf/RC-records_Vol-14.pdf.

[88] Office of the Press Sec'y, *supra* note 4.

[89] With its denial of the applicability of the Geneva Conventions to enemy combatants, its creation of a new legal category for jihadist fighters, and its "progressive interpretation" of targeting.

[90] *See* sources cited *supra* note 4.

[91] *See FAQ: The Relevance of IHL in the Context of Terrorism*, INT'L COMM. RED CROSS (Jan. 1, 2011), www.icrc.org/eng/resources/documents/faq/terrorism-ihl-210705.htm; Prosecutor v. Delalić et al., Case No. IT-96-21-T, Trial Judgment (Nov. 16, 1998).

[92] With Security Council Resolution 1368's recognition of the right of national and collective self-defense by States in the face of a terrorism threat – and the lowering of the threshold of attribution for terrorism to "harboring" or "supporting" perpetrators, organizers, or sponsors of

strong opposition. In the words of Bugnion: "The law of armed conflict was adopted to restrict violence in war and no argument can be advanced to justify repudiating it, no matter how serious the aggression suffered, no matter what the causes espoused by the parties to the conflict and their reasons for taking up arms."[93] On the same issue, Shearer wrote that

> the application of the *jus in bello* is not dependent upon the demonstration of a legal basis for the resort to armed force in the *jus ad bellum*. The law of armed conflict (which term I regard as including international humanitarian law) applies its protection equally to the just and the unjust sides to a conflict. This is an established and undoubted proposition.[94]

This should come as no surprise, given that the application of the law to both sides of the conflict comes not only from the specific terms of the Geneva Conventions, which explicitly provide for their application in "all circumstances,"[95] but from the cogency of the law itself.

A thorough review of state practice since 1945, which looked at the most controversial international armed conflicts to date, found that state practice supports the principle that "the legal status of the conflicting parties under *jus ad bellum* does not affect the application of international humanitarian law."[96] The separate opinion of Judge Kooijmans and the declaration of Judge Verhoeven in the *Armed Activities* case,[97] as well as the Arab League's statement in the *Wall* advisory proceedings,[98] can also be read as a confirmation that the lawfulness of a particular use of force does not affect the application of humanitarian law and principles. The protection of the law,

---

terror threats. S.C. Res. 1368, Threats to International Peace and Security Caused by Terrorist Acts, U.N. Doc. S/RES/1368, ¶ 3 (Sept. 12, 2001). Security Council Resolution 1373 recognition of international terrorism as a threat to international peace and security, and the subsequent – and unilateral – recognition of the doctrine of preemptive self-defense. S.C. Res. 1373, Threats to International Peace and Security Caused by Terrorist Acts, U.N. Doc. S/RES/1373 (Sept. 28, 2001).

[93] Bugnion, *supra* note 23, at 24.

[94] Ivan Shearer, *Rules of Conduct During Humanitarian Intervention, in* 78 INTERNATIONAL LAW STUDIES: LEGAL AND ETHICAL LESSONS OF NATO'S KOSOVO CAMPAIGN 71, 73 (Andru E. Wall ed., 2002).

[95] *See, e.g.*, First Geneva Convention, *supra* note 73, art. 1 ("The High Contracting Parties undertake to respect and to ensure respect for this convention in all circumstances.")

[96] OKIMOTO, *supra* note 14, at 19–22.

[97] Armed Activities Judgment, *supra* note 40 (separate opinion of Judge Kooijmans); *id.* (declaration of Judge *ad hoc* Verhoeven).

[98] Legal Consequences of the Construction of a Wall in the Occupied Palestinian Territory, Written Statement of the League of Arab States (Jan. 28, 2014), www.icj-cij.org/files/case-related/131/1545.pdf.

472 Federica D'Alessandra and Robert Heinsch

in other words, cannot be withdrawn neither from combatants nor from civilians, no matter their legal status.

B. *The Modern Understanding of the Principle of Separation of Humanitarian Law from the Law on the Use of Force*

The second axiom of the dichotomy characterizing modern understandings of the principle of separation between the *jus in bello* and *jus ad bellum* – that the application of humanitarian law does not legitimize the illegal use of force under the *jus ad bellum* – is also an incontestable proposition. Although, as mentioned above, some argue that humanitarian law was first codified to sanction "a reciprocity-based system of obligation where, in exchange for belligerent privilege, States agreed to be bound equally by *in bello* rules"[99] in order to "prevent . . . military annihilation,"[100] since the Law of Geneva was adopted its purpose has fundamentally changed,[101] and it is now widely understood as *primarily* protecting the victims of war. For this reason, the protection afforded by the *jus in bello* must remain separate from *ad bellum* questions. Delegates to the Diplomatic Conference on the Reaffirmation and Development of International Humanitarian Law Applicable in Armed Conflict championed this view in their primary outcome document stating, in the Preamble of Additional Protocol I, that "nothing in this Protocol or in the Geneva Convention(s) . . . can be construed as legitimizing or authorizing any act of aggression or any other use of force inconsistent with the Charter of the United Nations."[102] They then added, in Article 4, that "the application of the Conventions and of this Protocol, as well as the conclusion of the agreements provided for therein shall not affect the legal status of the Parties to the conflict."[103] Thus, when complying with international humanitarian law, an aggressor State, or a State using force illegally, is still subject to the full regime of sanctions and enforcement mechanisms envisioned by contemporary public international law. Commentators on the separation principle have argued that this, ironically, produces a situation in which the victim State is constrained by more legal provisions (*jus ad bellum* and *jus in bello*) than the aggressor (who, in plain disregard of the *jus ad bellum*, must nonetheless

---

[99] Matthews, *supra* note 67.
[100] Carl Schmitt, The *Nomos* of the Earth in the International Law of the *Jus Publicum Europaeum* 141 (G. L. Ulmen trans., 2006).
[101] Theodor Meron, *The Humanization of Humanitarian Law*, 94 Am. J. Int'l L. 239 (2000).
[102] Additional Protocol I, *supra* note 20, pmbl.
[103] Additional Protocol I, *supra* note 20, art. 4.

respect the *jus in bello*).[104] And while – as VanLandingham writes – "international criminal law partially rectifies this apparent injustice by criminalizing clear *jus ad bellum* violations,"[105] this rectification is incomplete. With the International Criminal Court's (ICC) rather limited regime of jurisdiction over the crime of aggression,[106] very little concrete possibility will continue to exist to hold the majority of individuals abusing their sovereign war powers to account. Thus, it should come as no surprise that some scholars have begun considering alternative means to impose individual liability for illegal wars.[107] While the application of humanitarian law clearly does not legitimize an otherwise illegal use of force, it is fair to ask whether the relative impunity of aggressors under the current system does not run counter to the protective scope of humanitarian law.[108]

C. *The ICJ* Nuclear Weapons *Advisory Opinion and the Principle of Separation*

While it has thoroughly and consistently endorsed the application of humanitarian law to all sides of the conflict regardless of their status under the law on the use of force, the ICJ has supplied the biggest challenge to the reading of the separation principle as preventing considerations of *jus ad bellum*

---

[104] *See generally* OKIMOTO, *supra* note 14. Even though there are reasons to believe that a casual approach to legality *of* an armed conflict might produce a casual approach to legality *in* an armed conflict. *See* Charles Garraway, *Comments on Illegal War and Illegal Conduct: Are the Two Related?*, 59 NETH. INT'L L. REV. 473 (2012).

[105] M. Cherif Bassiouni, *The History of Aggression in International Law, Its Culmination in the Kampala Amendments, and Its Future Legal Characterization*, 58 HARV. INT'L L.J. ONLINE 87 (2017), www.harvardilj.org/2017/04/the-history-of-aggression-in-international-law-its-culmination-in-the-kampala-amendments-and-its-future-legal-characterization/; Sanji Mmasenono Monageng, *The Crime of Aggression: Following the Needs of a Changing World?*, 58 HARV. INT'L L.J. ONLINE 79 (2017), www.harvardilj.org/2017/04/the-crime-of-aggression-following-the-needs-of-a-changing-world/; VanLandingham, *supra* note 8, at 218 (citing art. 8*bis* of the Rome Statute of the International Criminal Court).

[106] *See* Rome Statute of the International Criminal Court art. 15*bis*, *adopted on* July 17, 1998, 2187 U.N.T.S. 91 (entered into force July 1, 2002) [hereinafter Rome Statute].

[107] VanLandingham, *supra* note 8, at 218; Ventura & Gillett, *supra* note 8, at 523. *See also* Ferencz, *supra* note 8.

[108] On this question, see Symposium, *Accountability for the Illegal Use of Force*, 58 HARV. INT'L L.J. ONLINE 1 (2017), www.harvardilj.org/wp-content/uploads/ILJ_Online_2017_Symposium_FINAL-1.pdf, and particularly Rebecca F. Green, Federica D'Alessandra & Juan P. Calderon-Meza, *Accountability for the Illegal Use of Force – Will the Nuremberg Legacy Be Complete?*, 58 HARV. INT'L L.J. ONLINE 1 (2017), www.harvardilj.org/2017/04/accountability-for-the-illegal-use-of-force-will-the-nuremberg-legacy-be-complete/, and D'Alessandra, *Normative Crossroads*, *supra* note 65.

from influencing *jus in bello* to date. While some have observed that the ICJ's treatment of *jus in bello* and *jus ad bellum* questions separately in the *Nicaragua, Nuclear Weapons, Wall,* and *Armed Activities* decisions should be read as an implicit endorsement of the principle of separation,[109] the Court's response was much different the first time the Court had an opportunity to address directly both the *jus ad bellum* and the *jus in bello*. In reply to the question submitted by the U.N. General Assembly in the *Nuclear Weapons* advisory proceedings: "Is the threat or use of nuclear weapons in any circumstance permitted under international law?" the Court replied that "the threat or use of nuclear weapons would generally be contrary to the rule of international law applicable in armed conflict, and in particular the principles and rules of humanitarian law."[110] In a very controversial paragraph, the Advisory Opinion also read that

> in view of the current state of international law, and of the elements of fact at its disposal, the Court cannot conclude definitively whether the threat or use of nuclear weapons would be lawful or unlawful in an extreme circumstance of self-defense, in which the very survival of a State would be at stake.[111]

However, the fact that a State might possibly be acting in self-defense, or even that its survival might be at stake, should not justify any violation of humanitarian law rules by allowing the killing of more civilians (or soldiers *hors de combat*) or the use of an indiscriminate weapon such as a nuclear one. Thus, it is unfortunate that the Court indicated (and later in the *Oil Platforms* case) that in situations of "extreme self-defence" when the "survival of the State" is at stake, principles of humanitarian law might have to give way.[112] This could indeed lead to an expansive interpretation of the "survival of the State" criterion,[113] and it does not come as a surprise that this controversial statement has been heavily criticized as an "alarming precedent."[114]

---

[109] *Id.*

[110] Nuclear Weapons Advisory Opinion, *supra* note 13, ¶ 105(2)(E).

[111] *Id.*

[112] *Id. See also* Oil Platforms Merits Judgment, *supra* note 40, ¶ 51.

[113] Therefore, the ICJ Advisory Opinion has been heavily criticized in academic literature. *See* DINSTEIN, WAR, AGGRESSION AND SELF-DEFENCE (5th ed. 2011), *supra* note 44, at 172; Sassòli, *supra note 14, at 251;* Yoram Dinstein, *The Laws of Air, Missile and Nuclear Warfare,* 27 ISR. Y.B. ON HUM. RTS. 1, 12–13 (Yoram Dinstein & Fania Domb eds., 1997); Eric David, *The Opinion of the International Court of Justice on the Legality of the Use of Nuclear Weapons,* 37 INT'L REV. RED CROSS 21, 31 (1997); Louise Doswald-Beck, *International Humanitarian Law and the Advisory Opinion of the International Court of Justice on the Legality of the Threat or Use of Nuclear Weapons,* 37 INT'L REV. RED CROSS 35, 53 (1997).

[114] DINSTEIN, WAR, AGGRESSION AND SELF-DEFENCE (5th ed. 2011), *supra* note 44, at 172. *See also* Wil Verwey, *The International Court of Justice and the Legality of Nuclear Weapons: Some*

Whereas some judges have admitted that "this paragraph was unclear as to its meaning,"[115] the majority opinion in *Nuclear Weapons* signaled a significant jurisprudential development in the separation and mutually exclusive doctrines with significant intellectual leverage on the international legal discourse.[116] An analysis of the separate and dissenting opinions reveals the division of the Court on the issue. Judge Higgins's dissenting opinion, for example, provides some insight on the Court's rationalization that "proportionality in the strategic sense (*jus ad bellum*) can be reconciled with proportionality in the tactical sense (*jus in bello*) in circumstances of State survival."[117] The dissenting opinion submits that

> in order to meet the legal requirement that a military target may not be attacked if collateral civilian casualties would be excessive in relation to the military advantage, the "military advantage" must indeed be one related to the very survival of a State or the avoidance of infliction (whether by nuclear or other weapons of mass destruction) of vast and severe suffering on its own population: and that no other method of eliminating this military target be available.[118]

Similarly, Judge Weeramantry (speaking on the proportionality of civilian deaths in the aggressor State in the case of use of nuclear weapons justified by the survival of the attacked State), concluded that "one can measure only the measurable. With nuclear war, the quality of measurability ceases. Total destruction admits no scales of measurement. We are in territory where the principle of proportionality becomes void of any meaning."[119] Even more controversially, Judge Fleischhauer, in his separate opinion, determined *unequivocally* that the right to self-defense had priority over the dictates of the law of armed conflict.[120] While his opinion was a minority opinion, and one that the legal community strongly rejected based on the applicability

---

Observations, in INTERNATIONAL LAW: THEORY AND PRACTICE: ESSAYS IN HONOUR OF ERIC SUY 751, 760 (Karel Wellens ed., 1998).

[115] OKIMOTO, *supra* note 14, at 23.

[116] Nuclear Weapons Advisory Opinion, *supra* note 13.

[117] Dale Stephens, The Relationship Between the *Jus ad Bellum* and *Jus in Bello*, A Critique of Revisionist Developments that Threaten the Mutual Exclusivity of the *Jus ad Bellum* and *Jus in Bello* 26 (submitted in 2004) (unpublished LL.M. thesis, Harvard Law School).

[118] Nuclear Weapons Advisory Opinion, *supra* note 13 (dissenting opinion by Judge Higgins, ¶ 21).

[119] *Id.* (dissenting opinion by Judge Weeramantry).

[120] Even though the concept of "state survival" has been criticized by commentators as not a validly acknowledged concept within positivist conceptions of international law. *See* Marcelo G. Kohen, *The Notion of 'State Survival' in International Law, in* INTERNATIONAL LAW, THE INTERNATIONAL COURT OF JUSTICE AND NUCLEAR WEAPONS 293, 293 (Laurence Boisson de Chazournes & Philippe Sands eds., 1999).

of humanitarian law in every circumstance, the overall impact of the ICJ might have been to further erode, in a way, the compartmentalization of the relationship between the two legal strands.

D. *Independent or Concurrent Application?*

In the context of this discussion, an important middle-ground position ought to be noted. In reaction to the ICJ *Nuclear Weapons* Advisory Opinion, Sir Christopher Greenwood, Advocate for the U.K. government in the case, and later a Judge before the very same Court,[121] saw paragraph 105(2)(E) of the Court's opinion as a legitimization of the continued impact of *jus ad bellum* in *jus in bello*, as well as a testament to the harmonious relationship between the two streams of law, thus concluding that a "cumulative relationship" between the two legal regimes is what emerges from the apparent contradiction in the ICJ opinion. Other scholars have subsequently developed this thesis.[122] The most influential endorsement came from the ICJ itself when, in the *Nuclear Weapons* Advisory Opinion, it said: "a use of force that is proportionate under the law of self-defence, must, in order to be lawful, *also* meet the requirements of the law applicable in armed conflict which comprises in particular the principles and rules of humanitarian law."[123] Okimoto has posited that the concurrent application of the two legal strands has two legal implications: "1) *jus ad bellum* and *jus in bello* are applicable at the same time, and not one after the other; and 2) the two can be complementary, and not simply mutually exclusive, self-contained legal regimes that never have an intersection."[124] This is sensible: both the *jus ad bellum* and the *jus in bello* share the ultimate objective of minimizing human suffering. This goal "should not be obscured by the technicalities inherent in the two legal regimes,"[125] and when the principle of separation – whose *raison d'être* is to maximize the protection of the law for the sake of the principle of humanity – produces the opposite result, or stands in the way of accountability for violations of the *jus belli*, it should not be invoked as a dogmatic principle.

---

[121] *See* Christopher Greenwood, Jus ad Bellum *and* Jus in Bello *in the* Nuclear Weapons Advisory Opinion, *in* INTERNATIONAL LAW, THE INTERNATIONAL COURT OF JUSTICE AND NUCLEAR WEAPONS, *supra* note 120, at 247.

[122] *Id.* at 263–64. For further elaborations of this position see Iain Scobbie, *Words My Mother Never Taught Me: "In Defense of the International Court"*, 99 AM. J. INT'L L. 76 (2005); Werner Meng, *War, in* 4 ENCYCLOPEDIA OF PUBLIC INTERNATIONAL LAW 1334 (Rudolf Bernhardt ed., 2000); *see also* OKIMOTO, *supra* note 14, at 136.

[123] Nuclear Weapons Advisory Opinion, *supra* note 13, ¶ 42 (emphasis added).

[124] OKIMOTO, *supra* note 14, at 31.

[125] *Id.* at 10–11.

E. *Humanitarian Interventions and the Principle of Separation*

On the way paved by the ICJ Advisory Opinion on *Nuclear Weapons*, another separate challenge to the question of separation came with the 2000 report of the Independent International Commission on Kosovo. The Commission recommended that the International Committee of the Red Cross (or another qualified body) prepare a new legal convention for peacekeeping operations or humanitarian interventions in order to "impose more constraints on the use of force than are embodied in the law of war as now generally interpreted."[126] In the Commission's work, the question had arisen whether there was a need to hold humanitarian intervention and peacekeeping forces to a higher standard of accountability with respect to the use of force, given that their humanitarian missions would require these forces to take greater safety risks and tilt their targeting decisions and proportionality calculus more favorably toward the principle of humanity.[127]

More recently, a further dent in the separation principle, and the subsequent application of humanitarian rules, came with the question of whether both the enforcement nature of Chapter VII measures and the moral force of the international community's will as mobilized in these interventions could ever be invoked to justify suspending the equal application of humanitarian law to peacekeepers that become parties to a conflict.[128] As advanced by David Rodin, the argument goes that just as police officers do not forfeit their right not to be attacked by criminals when responding to a threat they pose to civilians, peacekeepers operating in the framework just described (just combatants in the very true sense of the definition) would not lose their right not to be attacked in the course of their missions.[129] This would mean that peacekeepers' adversaries would not enjoy the combatant's privilege to attack them, as they would be protected by virtue of some sort of "supra-national" authority

---

[126] *See* Int'l Indep. Comm'n on Kosovo, *supra* note 5, at 184. The Commission arguably acknowledged that "[a] less ambitious alternative, recommended by Amnesty International, would be to accept stricter adherence to the existing standards of international law, particularly as already embodied in Protocol I." *Id.*

[127] *Id.*

[128] *See, e.g.,* Stephens, *supra* note 117; Rodin, *supra* note 7; Of a much opposite view was Richard Baxter, *see* Humanizing the Laws of War: Selected Writings of Richard Baxter (Detlev F. Vagts, Theodor Meron, Stephen M. Schwebel & Charles Keever eds., 2013).

[129] Just and Unjust Warriors: The Moral and Legal Status of Soldiers (David Rodin & Henry Shue eds., 2008).

or immunity.[130] The approach taken and legal reasoning applied by the ICC in investigating and possibly judging crimes against peacekeepers in Georgia, Sudan, and the Democratic Republic of the Congo will be telling as to how the discourse may evolve in the future. With the reform of peacekeeping ongoing, and the status of peacekeepers under international law still not fully determined, however, the issue is still very much under discussion.

This sentiment for a "humanitarian project of renewal" of the discipline is endorsed by many scholars that regard the level of discretion enjoyed by military forces to determine issues of life and death as "excessive," as this discretion is seen as always favoring "military necessity" at the cost of humanitarian considerations.[131] Whether or not giving up the separation between the two bodies of law is dangerous or pioneering, and whether considerations on a reformative approach should target the whole or a part of the relationship should continue to be discussed, and no particular position is endorsed by these authors. It appears fair, however, to note that the principle of separation between *jus in bello* and *jus ad bellum* is not as static, and might not be as foundational as previously perceived, and that the issue of their relationship cannot be simplistically reduced to whether or not their governing principles are in fact applied in a similar manner.

IV. CRITICAL APPROACHES TO THE QUESTION OF THE RELATIONSHIP BETWEEN THE *JUS IN BELLO* AND THE *JUS AD BELLUM*: A TWO-VOICES DISCUSSION ON THE ISSUE OF SEPARATION

While none of the debates presented in the previous Section has been conclusive in crystallizing the precise nature of the relationship between the two legal strands, a picture has emerged that the relationship between the *jus in bello* and the *jus ad bellum* might not always be so linear. This Section, which has been written in the hopes of finding common ground on the question of their relationship, will take stock of some of the advantages and disadvantages of enforcing the separation between the two legal strands, and will enter into the merit of some of the criticisms that have been

---

[130] Stephens, *supra* note 117. Though this position has been criticized as compromising the integrity of the laws of war. *See* Christopher Greenwood, *Protection of Peacekeepers: The Legal Regime*, 7 DUKE J. COMP. & INT'L L. 185 (1996).

[131] *See* Chris af Jochnick & Roger Normand, *The Legitimation of Violence: A Critical History of the Laws of War*, 35 HARV. INT'L L.J. 49 (1994).

applied to existing formulations of their relationship, as well as important counterarguments.

A. Jus Belli *and Modern Warfare – Is There a Need for a New Approach?*

These developments in jurisprudence and academia appear against the background of a gradual change in the way in which wars are being fought. The first major changes were noted in the 1960s or 1970s, with a higher percentage of non-international armed conflicts taking place and the emphasis switching from interstate conflicts to intrastate conflicts. This tendency was further enhanced after the fall of the Berlin Wall and the end of the Cold War, with a higher number of ethnic wars occurring within previously rather stable countries (the former Yugoslavia being just one example). At the same time, international wars between States seem to have become more (officially or unofficially) of an international matter.

One new crucial aspect of modern warfare is the growing involvement of non-state actors.[132] The strengthening of international terrorist activities around the world has further blurred the line between situations of armed conflict and situations in which a law enforcement (i.e., a human-rights-dominated) paradigm should be applied.[133] The "fight against terrorism" has in fact given rise to some substantial questions regarding the issue of conduct and regulation of hostilities. This is due to the unprecedented nature of modern terrorist attacks, whose strength and intensity is sometimes tantamount to "armed attacks" in the traditional, warlike manner. This, in turn, has pushed the boundaries of traditional conceptions of self-defense to include counterterrorism measures,[134] and to justify a more lenient approach to the application of humanitarian law.[135] Of course, the growing ability of non-state

---

[132] *See* Marco Sassòli, *Taking Armed Groups Seriously: Ways to Improve Their Compliance with International Humanitarian Law*, 1 J. INT'L HUMANITARIAN LEGAL STUD. 5, 13–14 (2010); Sandesh Sivakumaran, *Implementing Humanitarian Norms Through Non-State Armed Groups, in* INDUCING COMPLIANCE WITH INTERNATIONAL HUMANITARIAN LAW: LESSONS FROM THE AFRICAN GREAT LAKES REGION 125, 125–133 (Heike Krieger ed., 2015).

[133] *See* Steven R. Ratner, Jus ad Bellum *and* Jus in Bello *After September 11*, 96 AM. J. INT'L L. 905 (2002); William K. Lietzau, *Old Laws, New Wars:* Jus ad Bellum *in an Age of Terrorism*, 8 MAX PLANCK Y.B. U.N. L. 383 (2004).

[134] *See* Asa Kasher & Amos Yadlin, *Military Ethics of Fighting Terror: An Israeli Perspective*, 4 J. MIL. ETHICS 3, 7 (2005); Asa Kasher, *The Principle of Distinction*, 6 J. MIL. ETHICS 152 (2007).

[135] This includes anything from a "progressive interpretation" of possible legitimate targets to the claim that civilian terrorist suspects are legitimate "self-defense" targets at all times. *See cf.* Kimberley Trapp, *Back to Basics: Necessity, Proportionality, and the Right of Self-Defence Against Non-State Terrorist Actors*, 56 INT'L & COMP. L.Q. 141, 142 (2007) (claims that "the International Court's jurisprudence need not be read as absolutely requiring that armed attacks

actors to act on an international level creates the need to find a legal regime that can deal with this phenomenon effectively. Perhaps, however, it should be asked whether the dichotomy between the *jus ad bellum* and the *jus in bello* is the correct answer to this question.[136] The legal regime dealing with the prohibition against the use of force was created to contain the use of force between sovereign States.[137] Although Article 51 of the U.N. Charter does not specify who the author of the "armed attack" should be, most scholars hold the view (confirmed by the ICJ) that the attack must be attributed to another State in order to trigger the right of self-defense.[138] Accordingly, it is still the prevalent view that a legitimate "self-defense" argument against terrorists exists only when their actions can be linked to a third party that is a State. At the same time, even when States have been the object of an armed attack in the sense of Article 51, not all counterterrorism measures fall under the scope of application of the laws of war. There will be situations in which the use of force will not meet the threshold of armed conflict required by either Common Article 2 (international armed conflict) or Common Article 3 (non-international armed conflict) of the Geneva Conventions. Especially in the latter situation, when the requirement of "protracted armed violence" is not fulfilled, a good argument exists that a law enforcement paradigm might be more appropriate to deal with this kind of situation. If existing rules and principles of law enforcement seem inadequate to deal with existing threats, further studies should be dedicated to how to make them more effective in responding to the peculiar challenges terrorism threats pose on the international level.

B. *Advantages of the Principle of Separation*

There are many other reasons to maintain, in general terms, the separation between the *jus in bello* and the *jus ad bellum*. The most crucial aspect is

be launched by (or attributable to) a State before the right to use force in self-defence is engaged.").

[136] Bassiouni, *supra* note 105; Monageng, *supra* note 105.

[137] U.N. Charter art. 2(4). *See also* D'Alessandra, *Normative Crossroads*, *supra* note 65, 117.

[138] Nicaragua Merits Judgment, *supra* note 40, ¶ 195; Michael N. Schmitt, *Responding to Transnational Terrorism under the* Jus ad Bellum: *A Normative Framework, in* INTERNATIONAL LAW AND ARMED CONFLICT: EXPLORING THE FAULTLINES, *supra* note 14, at 157, 167; Gilbert Guillaume, *Terrorism and International Law*, 53 INT'L & COMP. L.Q. 537, 546 (2004). *But see* Jennifer Trahan, *The Crime of Aggression and the International Criminal Court*, in this volume. *See also* TOM RUYS, 'ARMED ATTACK' AND ARTICLE 51 OF THE UN CHARTER: EVOLUTIONS IN CUSTOMARY LAW AND PRACTICE ch. 5 (2010); GRAY, *supra* note 41; OLIVIER CORTEN, THE LAW AGAINST WAR: THE PROHIBITION ON THE USE OF FORCE IN CONTEMPORARY INTERNATIONAL LAW (2012).

perhaps the preservation of the very ethos of the discipline of international humanitarian law, and particularly the protection of civilians and other persons *hors de combat* regardless of on which side of the conflict they fall.[139] While it might indeed seem counterintuitive that a party to a conflict that has illegally initiated a war could benefit from the protection of humanitarian law, the principle of humanity, upon which international humanitarian law rests, so requires. If international humanitarian law is not respected on one or both sides, it could lead to an enormous amount of civilian casualties. The high civilian toll of World War II was in fact one of the reasons why the Fourth Geneva Convention for the Protection of Civilians was negotiated in 1949 (four years after the incorporation of the prohibition of the use of force in Article 2[4] of the U.N. Charter).[140] If the drafters had in mind that an aggressor State was to be treated differently before the law insofar as the equal application principle was concerned, they would have included a provision to this end.[141] On the contrary, Common Article 1 to the Geneva Conventions is very clear that humanitarian law applies "in all circumstances."[142] This is reaffirmed clearly in the new commentary to the First Geneva Convention.[143] It was stated even more clearly in the 1977 Additional Protocol I to the 1949 Geneva Conventions, the Preamble of which provides

> that the provisions of the Geneva Conventions of 12 August 1949 and of this Protocol must be fully applied in all circumstances to all persons who are protected by those instruments, without any adverse distinction based on the

---

[139] This idea goes back to the foundational moment of humanitarian law and principles, to when Henry Dunant walked over the battlefields of Solferino, and realized that every human being is the same, no matter to which side he or she belongs. *See* HENRY DUNANT, A MEMORY OF SOLFERINO (INT'L COMM. RED CROSS 1986), www.icrc.org/eng/assets/files/publications/icrc-002-0361.pdf.

[140] On the history of the development of the 1949 Geneva Conventions, *see* Robert Heinsch, *The International Committee of the Red Cross and the Geneva Conventions of 1949, in* HUMANIZING THE LAWS OF WAR: THE RED CROSS AND THE DEVELOPMENT OF INTERNATIONAL HUMANITARIAN LAW 27 (Robin Geiß et al. eds, 2017).

[141] For the same observation *see* Roberts, *supra* note 20, at 937.

[142] *See, e.g.*, First Geneva Convention, *supra* note 73, art. 1.

[143] INT'L COMM. OF THE RED CROSS, COMMENTARY OF 2016 ¶ 186, https://ihl-databases.icrc.org/applic/ihl/ihl.nsf/Comment.xsp?action=openDocument&documentId=72239588AFA66200C1257F7D00367DBD ("The undertaking to respect and to ensure respect 'in all circumstances' also reaffirms the strict separation of *jus ad bellum* and *jus in bello* as one of the basic safeguards for compliance with the Conventions. In other words, the application of the Conventions does not depend on the legal justification for the conflict under the *jus ad bellum*.") [hereinafter ICRC COMMENTARY OF 2016].

nature or origin of the armed conflict or on the causes espoused by or attributed to the conflict.[144]

This same approach has been clearly laid down both in treaty law and customary international law.[145] It therefore should not come as a surprise that academic commentators refer to the separation of the *jus ad bellum* from *jus in bello* as a "fundamental distinction,"[146] an "absolute dogma,"[147] and even as "one of the oldest and best established *axiomata* of international law."[148]

Another reason for upholding the separation between the *jus in bello* and the *jus ad bellum* is to avoid limiting the incentives to observe humanitarian law on one or both sides. The so-called *si omnes* clause,[149] an explicit rule that the obligation of compliance with humanitarian law is actually dependent on the opposing side also being party to the respective *jus in bello* convention, was still contained in the 1906 Geneva Convention and in the 1907 Hague Conventions.[150] Nowadays, however, the obligation to respect and ensure humanitarian law rules does not depend on reciprocity, and this has been recognized as a customary law rule.[151] Nevertheless, there seems to be an expectation that if one side complies with humanitarian law, the other side will do the same.[152] The current situation in Syria demonstrates what might happen when one side believes it is not bound by the law of armed conflict. Since both government troops and non-state actors have shown a continued

---

[144] Additional Protocol I, *supra* note 20, pmbl. (emphasis added).

[145] Antoine Bouvier, *Assessing the Relationship Between* Jus in Bello *and* Jus ad Bellum: An *"Orthodox" View*, 100 AM. SOC'Y INT'L L. PROC. 109 (2006).

[146] 1 MARCO SASSÒLI ET AL., HOW DOES LAW PROTECT IN WAR? 14 (3d ed. 2011).

[147] Doswald-Beck, *supra* note 113, at 53.

[148] Terry Gill, *The Nuclear Weapons Advisory Opinion of the International Court of Justice and the Fundamental Distinction Between the* Jus ad Bellum *and the* Jus in Bello, 12 LEIDEN J. INT'L L. 613, 614 (1999).

[149] *See* Philippe Gautier, *General Participation Clause (Clausula si omnes)*, MAX PLANCK ENCYCLOPEDIA OF PUB. INT'L L. (Apr. 2006), http://opil.ouplaw.com/view/10.1093/law:epil/9780199231690/law-9780199231690-e1409.

[150] ICRC COMMENTARY OF 2016, *supra* note 143, ¶ 184 ("In 1929, the drafters felt that the participation of a State not party to the Conventions in a conflict should no longer affect the binding nature of the Conventions on those belligerents who were party to the Conventions.") "[T]o the effect that the Conventions were only applicable if all of the belligerents in a given conflict were party to it," referencing the wording of Article 24 of the 1906 Geneva Convention, "[t]he provisions of the present Convention are obligatory only on the Contracting Powers, in case of war between two or more of them. The said provisions shall cease to be obligatory if one of the belligerent Powers should not be signatory to the Convention." *Id.* at n.130.

[151] Henckaerts & Doswald-Beck, *supra* note 6, at 498. Rule 140 of the ICRC Study on Customary International Humanitarian Law clarifies that "The obligation to respect and ensure respect for international humanitarian law does not depend on reciprocity."

[152] Moussa, *supra* note 25, at 967.

disrespect for humanitarian law, the overall situation has deteriorated, resulting in extreme brutality, with more suffering for the civilian population and other persons not participating in hostilities.[153] It seems that, as anticipated earlier,[154] without reciprocity there is a tendency that neither party will respect the principles of humanitarian law, and as a consequence the protection usually ensured by humanitarian law will be significantly lowered.[155]

A similar observation can be drawn from one of the "old" measures of forcible self-help in international law, the concept of belligerent reprisal. Reprisals consist of the use of force against the opposing party to stop it from violating the law of armed conflict and are still partly seen as legitimate.[156] Both sides accuse the other of disrespecting the *jus in bello*, and continue with humanitarian law violations in order to halt the same behavior on the other side. Without stretching the imagination, it is possible to envision the cyclical violence reprisals produce, which is why belligerent reprisals are no longer allowed, but are indeed prohibited, *against protected persons.*[157] The ICTY has confirmed this prohibition of belligerent reprisals against protected persons in non-international armed conflicts.[158] There are in fact other (and more legitimate) ways to enforce compliance with humanitarian law (including Security Council resolutions under Chapter VII, proceedings before the ICJ, fact-finding commissions, and international criminal trials for the commission of war crimes).

A third advantage of maintaining the separation between the *jus ad bellum* and the *jus in bello* is that determinations concerning which side of the conflict was the original aggressor during hostilities may be impracticable.[159]

---

[153] *See, e.g.,* Human Rights Council, Rep. of the Ind. Int'l Comm'n of Inquiry on the Syrian Arab Republic, at 5–7, U.N. Doc. A/HRC/31/68 (Feb. 11, 2016) [hereinafter Syria Report].

[154] *See* discussion *supra* Section II(A).

[155] Moussa, *supra* note 25, at 964; *see also* Lauterpacht, *Rules of Warfare in an Unlawful War, supra,* note 25, at 89.

[156] *See* FRITS KALSHOVEN, BELLIGERENT REPRISALS (1971).

[157] First Geneva Convention, *supra* note 73, art. 46; Convention (II) for the Amelioration of the Condition of Wounded, Sick and Shipwrecked Members of Armed Forces at Sea art. 47, Aug. 12, 1949, 75 U.N.T.S. 85 [hereinafter Second Geneva Convention]; Convention (III) Relative to the Treatment of Prisoners of War art. 13, Aug. 12, 1949, 75 U.N.T.S. 135 [hereinafter Third Geneva Convention]; Convention (IV) Relative to the Protection of Civilian Persons in Time of War art. 33, Aug. 12, 1949, 75 U.N.T.S. 287 [hereinafter Fourth Geneva Convention]; Additional Protocol I, *supra* note 20, arts. 51–56; Henckaerts & Doswald-Beck, *supra* note 6, at 513–26; ANTONIO CASSESE, INTERNATIONAL LAW 371–73 (2d ed. 2005).

[158] Prosecutor v. Kupreškić, Case No. IT-95-16-T, Judgment, ¶¶ 529–36 (Jan. 14, 2000).

[159] *See* OPPENHEIM, DISPUTES, WAR AND NEUTRALITY (7th ed.), *supra* note 69.

This aspect should not be underestimated.[160] Unfortunately, the situation is often unclear at the beginning of (or even during) a conflict, and only in rare situations does an independent international body determine whether an aggression (or other violation of the *jus ad bellum*) has actually taken place. While the Security Council in theory is competent under Article 39 of the U.N. Charter to determine that an act of aggression has taken place, the Council has used this power only on very rare occasions.[161] The same is likely true for the ICC. Even given that the jurisdiction of the Court under Article 8*bis* has entered into force,[162] it is in the nature of the ICC that a possible determination of the crime of aggression would only be made long after the beginning of hostilities has taken place. The ICJ faces the same problems as the ICC.[163] Court proceedings by nature only take place *after* the underlying conflict occurs, even though the ICJ may grant provisional measures during a conflict that is ongoing.[164] However, this possibility has not led to timely determinations in the past. By the same token, the ICRC, bound by its neutrality and impartiality, would not take a position on the legality of the use of force against those who initiate hostilities.[165] Without some independent institution that could determine if a violation of the *jus ad bellum* took place, most situations will be difficult to assess. A few conflicts, like Iraq's

[160] Judith Gardam, *Proportionality and Force in International Law*, 87 Am. J. Int'l L. 391, 394 (1993).

[161] For a summary of Security Council practice with respect to aggression, see U.N. Secretariat, Historical Review of Developments Relating to Aggression, at 115–21, U.N. Doc. PCNICC/2002/WGCA/L.1 (2003), www.un.org/law/books/HistoricalReview-Aggression.pdf.

[162] Jennifer Trahan, *Historic Activation of the International Criminal Court's Crime of Aggression: The Assembly of States Parties Decides to Activate the ICC's 4th Crime*, International Judicial Monitor (2017), http://www.judicialmonitor.org/fall2017/specialreport1.html; Dapo Akande, *The International Criminal Court Gets Jurisdiction Over the Crime of Aggression*, EJIL: Talk! (Dec. 15, 2017), https://www.ejiltalk.org/the-international-criminal-court-gets-jurisdiction-over-the-crime-of-aggression/.

[163] *See* Dapo Akande & Antonios Tzanakopoulos, *The Crime of Aggression in the ICC and State Responsibility*, 58 Harv. Int'l L.J. Online 33 (2017), www.harvardilj.org/2017/04/the-crime-of-aggression-in-the-icc-and-state-responsibility/; Christopher Greenwood, *What the ICC Can Learn from the Jurisprudence of Other Tribunals*, 58 Harv. Int'l L.J. Online 71 (2017), www.harvardilj.org/2017/04/what-the-icc-can-learn-from-the-jurisprudence-of-other-tribunals/.

[164] *See* Statue of the International Court of Justice art. 41(1), June 26, 1945, 59 Stat. 1055, 3 Bevans 1179 ("The Court shall have the power to indicate ... any provisional measures which ought to be taken ..."); Application of the International Convention for the Suppression of the Financing of Terrorism and of the International Convention on the Elimination of All Forms of Racial Discrimination (Ukr. v. Russ.), Request for the Indication of Provisional Measures, 2017 I.C.J. No. 166 (Apr. 19).

[165] *Cf.* Statutes of the International Committee of the Red Cross art. 4(1)(a), adopted on Nov. 19, 2015; *see also The Fundamental Principles of the Red Cross and Red Crescent*, Int'l Comm. Red Cross (1996), www.icrc.org/eng/assets/files/other/icrc_002_0513.pdf.

attack against Kuwait in 1990, seem more or less clear cut.[166] In other situations, like the NATO intervention in Kosovo, the legality of the use of force is highly disputed.[167] These practical difficulties make it hard to imagine the basis for the unequal application of the law of armed conflict. Last but not least, an additional practical aspect to take into account is the burden that the unequal application of humanitarian law would put on the individual soldier.[168] This would require every army to provide training on two sets of humanitarian law rules: one applicable to the lawful opponent, and the other one to armies in violation of the prohibition against the use of force. In the heat of battle, this will lead to situations of confusion, to the detriment of the rights of protected persons.

C. *Disadvantages of the Principle of Separation*

Downsides to the principle of separation of the two legal regimes also exist. Disadvantages to the separation are often dismissed, when discussed, as the lesser of two evils.[169] However, whereas it might be true that upholding the separation has important advantages, especially from the pragmatic and tactical perspectives, there are considerations that escape this narrowly construed approach to the detriment of overall strategic, disciplinary, or even normative considerations. Take the example of wars of aggression, the most serious violation of the contemporary *jus ad bellum*.

Aggressive wars have been outlawed since the nineteenth century,[170] and – while their criminality was already being debated at the turn of the twentieth century – their status as crimes under international law crystallized, indisputably, with Nuremberg.[171] Because of the principle of separation, any acts conducted by the aggressor in pursuance of the initial act of aggression will be judged separately from any acts carried out, once the aggression starts, to achieve the military objective sought throughout the course of the aggression

---

[166] Panel Discussion, *The Relationship Between* Jus Ad Bellum *and* Jus In Bello: *Past, Present, Future*, 100 AM. SOC'Y INT'L L. PROC. 109 (2006).

[167] Moussa, *supra* note 25, at 964.

[168] See *supra* note 25 and accompanying text.

[169] *See, e.g.,* Julie Mertus, *The Danger of Conflating* Jus ad Bellum *and* Jus in Bello, 100 AM. SOC'Y INT'L L. PROC. 114 (2006); Robert D. Sloane, *The Cost of Conflation: Preserving the Dualism of* Jus ad Bellum *and* Jus in Bello *in the Contemporary Law of War*, 34 YALE J. INT'L L. 47 (2009).

[170] Kathryn Sikkink, Federica D'Alessandra & Aroop Mukharji, Memo: Has International Law Diminished the Illegal Use of Armed Force? (Carr Center for Human Rights Policy White Paper, unpublished).

[171] *Id.*

campaign. Thus, notwithstanding that the aggression itself runs counter to the *jus ad bellum*, any assessment of proportionality of the use of force *during* the aggressive campaign will be carried out, pursuant to the *jus in bello*, against the background of the tactical needs of each operation within the campaign.[172] This outcome is as incongruous as it is undesirable. It is incongruous because, again as demonstrated previously, it produces a situation in which only the victim State is bound by both the *jus ad bellum* and the *jus in bello*,[173] and it is undesirable because it creates a situation where, *de facto* (but, in most cases, also *de jure*), no concrete possibility exists to hold the aggressor to account. While some commentators have pointed out that the aggressor State is at the same time subject to various sanctions if one looks from a wider perspective of public international law, this does not impact the *de facto* paradox and conditions of unaccountability. It has been discussed above how the lack of accountability for initiating wars of aggression runs afoul of the primary purpose of humanitarian law, which is to protect civilians from wanton and criminal violence.[174]

Another important consequence, which is as common to wars of aggression as it is to other uses of force in violation of the *jus ad bellum*, is for targeting and proportionality assessments. Existing international humanitarian law envisions the lawfulness of civilian casualties as either proportional collateral damage to legitimate military targets, or as legitimate military targets when civilians directly participate in hostilities or civilian infrastructures are used for military purposes.[175] The underlying rationale of this proportionality calculus (particularly insofar as collateral damage is concerned) is that the loss of civilian life is a terrible but necessary evil to be endured in order to make progress toward the end of the war (i.e., victory and military defeat of the adversary). This can be true, however, only where the advantage derived from the targeting decision contributes to progress toward a lawful, or at least legitimate,[176] military goal. The question then arises as to how such determinations can be made when there is no legitimate cause against which to weigh the assessment and justify the loss of human life. If not from a moral perspective, the lawfulness of such action should be void because if no right exists to recur to force in the first place, how can assessments of what is a proportional (as opposed to wanton and criminal) loss of life be made? And while – as rightly pointed out above – assessments of this sort (when stretched to the

---

[172] *See* OKIMOTO, *supra* note 14, at 97.
[173] *Supra* note 104.
[174] *Supra* note 108.
[175] Additional Protocol I, *supra* note 20, art. 52; Rome Statute, *supra* note 106, art. 8.
[176] INT'L INDEP. COMM'N ON KOSOVO, *supra* note 5.

overall issue of "what rules of engagement to apply") might bear an unreasonable burden on the soldier in the heat of the battle, target clearance is generally removed from the battlefield (and it might at times be escalated through several levels up the chain of command). Those directing military operations, themselves often removed from battle, have the required knowledge and relevant information to make reasonable assessments concerning the lawfulness or legality of their overall military campaigns, and of actions required to make progress within them.

The effectiveness of this system was demonstrated, for example, by the NATO bombing campaign in Kosovo, which was found to be in compliance with international humanitarian law rules.[177] The high toll overall of civilian deaths, however, in a campaign that was mandated to protect them, should make us reflect on whether existing standards truly match the nature of some modern military operations. Critics of the Prosecutor of the ICTY[178] contended indeed that operators of the NATO aerial bombing campaign over Kosovo in 1999 should have been held to more restrictive legal standards regarding the foreseen but unintended civilian casualties and destruction of civilian property given the overall military campaign's humanitarian *raison d'être*.[179] They also charged that the humanitarian motive behind the overall military campaign inappropriately relaxed interpretations and assessments of the *jus in bello*, such as the calculus involved in the proportionality principle,

---

[177] Final Rep. to the Prosecutor by the Committee Established to Review the NATO Bombing Campaign Against the Federal Republic of Yugoslavia (June 8, 2000), *reprinted in* 39 I.L.M. 1257 (2000), www.icty.org/x/file/Press/nato061300.pdf; Press Release, Office of the Prosecutor for the Int'l Criminal Tribunal for the former Yugoslavia, Prosecutor's Report on the NATO Bombing Campaign, ICTY Doc. PR/P.I.S./510-e (June 13, 2000), www.icty.org/sid/7846 [hereinafter Office of the Prosecutor for the ICTY].

[178] *See, e.g.*, Anne-Sophie Massa, *NATO's Intervention in Kosovo and the Decision of the Prosecutor of the International Criminal Tribunal for the Former Yugoslavia Not to Investigate: An Abusive Exercise of Prosecutorial Discretion?*, 24 Berkeley J. Int'l L. 610, 618 (2006); *cf.* Office of the Prosecutor for the ICTY, *supra* note 177.

[179] *See, e.g.*, Michael Bothe, *The Protection of the Civilian Population and NATO Bombing in Yugoslavia: Comments on a Report to the Prosecutor of the ICTY*, 12 Eur. J. Int'l L. 531, 535 (2001) (suggesting a heightened proportionality targeting equation in humanitarian interventions); *cf.* Frédéric Mégret, Jus in Bello *and* Jus ad Bellum, 100 Am. Soc'y Int'l L. Proc. 121, 122 (2006) (describing a "tension between the rhetoric of a 'humanitarian' intervention, and taking advantage of all the still rather permissive elasticity of the laws of war"). There were also those that charged that the humanitarian nature of NATO's intervention caused the rules to be retroactively applied less rigorously. *See, e.g.*, Sloane, *supra* note 169, at 96 (suggesting that the humanitarian impetus behind NATO's intervention influenced the *ex post facto* assessments of proportionality by the ICTY Prosecutor, loosening the rules and thereby legally allowing greater civilian casualties and damage to civilian property than what the standard was supposed to allow).

to the detriment of civilians, because NATO-contributing countries were not willing to accept casualties among their contingents.[180]

As discussed, another (and broader) question relevant to the issue of the relationship between the two bodies of law is that of rules of engagement for and *against* peacekeepers, to better protect them in the delivery of their mandates. If Blue Helmets were subjected to the same level of danger (because subjected to the same liabilities and privileges) as regular combatants in missions with "aggressive mandates,"[181] we might soon face a situation in which States refuse to contribute troops to these types of unusual but nevertheless important missions because of the risks involved to their soldiers. Perhaps the question should be asked as to whether these "just" forces should be subjected to the same liabilities as other parties to that conflict, meaning whether a humanitarian or U.N. international peace and security enforcement exception should not be considered to the scope of humanitarian law application for U.N. contingent with aggressive mandates, *not* to the detriment of the protection of other parties to the conflict or protected persons or objects, but to strengthen the protection of U.N. or international contingents *from third parties' armed attacks*.[182] Perhaps, in

---

[180] This same dynamic was, per some scholars, also present earlier in the decade in the 1991 Gulf War, in which Iraq was forced out of Kuwait following Iraq's illegal invasion: *jus ad bellum*, it was maintained, inappropriately affected the interpretation of *jus in bello* proportionality, allowing greater civilian casualties because of the *jus ad bellum* propriety of the conflict itself. *See* Gardam, *supra* note 160, at 412 ("It seems unlikely that the international community would have tolerated the scale of civilian casualties in the conflict if it were not for the consensus that Iraq's action had no legal or moral basis").

[181] Aggressive mandates are conferred to peacekeeping contingents invested with the powers to enforce U.N. conditions of disarmaments, engaging resistance in battle when necessary. *See* John Bosco Nizeimana & Alfred G. Nhema, *United Nations (UN)-Sanctioned Aggressive Mandate and the Future of UN Peacekeeping Operations: The Case of the Democratic Republic of Congo (DRC)*, 5 INT'L J. HUMAN. & SOC. SCI., no. 8(1), at 37 (2015).

[182] To be clear, the conversation concerning whether the laws of war should apply or not to United Nations forces has already happened. *See, e.g.*, Frederic Kirgis, *International Law and the Report of the High-Level U.N. Panel on Threats, Challenges and Change*, 10 INT'L PEACEKEEPING: Y.B. INT'L PEACE OPERATIONS 163 (2006). The position advanced by a group of scholars that it should not was rebutted, and the view of those who like Richard Baxter insisted on the applicability of IHL to UN forces prevailed. See HUMANIZING THE LAWS OF WAR: SELECTED WRITINGS OF RICHARD BAXTER (Detlev F. Vagts, Theodor Meron, Stephen M. Schwebel & Charles Keever eds., 2013). On the same topic, *also see* FREDERIC KIRGIS, THE AMERICAN SOCIETY OF INTERNATIONAL LAW'S FIRST CENTURY: 1906–2006 248 (2006). *See* most recently, Dapo Akande & Emanuela-Chiara Gillard, *Oxford Guidance on the Law Relating to Humanitarian Relief Operations in Situations of Armed Conflict* (2016), https://docs.unocha.org/sites/dms/Documents/Oxford%20Guidance%20pdf.pdf. However, that conversation has mostly focused on the status of operations that are consent and neutrality based, and conducted without adverse distinction. By accounts of many, the adoption of resolution 2098 that invoked the aggressive mandate by the United Nations Security Council in 2013 was a development that signified a modification of the nature and form of United Nations (UN) peacekeeping operations. U.N. Doc. S/RES/2098 (Mar. 28, 2013).

fact, the Commission's recommendation that a peacekeeping convention outlining the privileges, immunities, and liabilities of peacekeepers (regardless of whether they serve under a U.N. flag) be drafted is not such a far-fetched idea.

On a different but related question, various legal scholars have made similar calls to incorporate *jus ad bellum* factors within the *jus in bello* proportionality analysis, particularly regarding asymmetric conflicts against non-state actors.[183] Some outline what they deem a "fuller" interpretation of proportionality that takes into account *jus ad bellum* propriety.[184] Historically, in fact, *jus ad bellum* considerations have been injected in debates surrounding the regulation of war to justify behavior usually not allowed under *jus in bello*[185] (a prime example has been the fight against terrorism).[186] It is usually problematic to determine whether there is a justification of self-defense in situations in which a State is taking military anti-terrorism measures against non-state actors on the territory of a third State;[187] or whether, under these circumstances, the proportionality balance should be weighted more toward the military advantage. Of course, such approaches tend to be reductionist and binary in that they fail to acknowledge the role played by other bodies of law, including international human rights law, in assessments of targeting and proportionality.

---

[183] Legal scholars have questioned the separation of *jus ad bellum* and *jus in bello* in other contexts as well, such as at the intersection of the principles of military necessity and distinction and the propriety of killing belligerents based on their status as such. *See, e.g.,* Gabriella Blum, *The Dispensable Lives of Soldiers,* 2 J. LEGAL ANALYSIS 115, 128 (2010). *See also* Eyal Benvenisti, *Rethinking the Divide Between* Jus ad Bellum *and* Jus in Bello *in Warfare Against Nonstate Actors,* 34 YALE J. INT'L L. 541, 547 (2009) (describing McMahan's moral objections to the concept of equal application of *jus in bello* standards regardless of *jus ad bellum* considerations).

[184] *See, e.g.,* Benvenisti, *supra* note 183, at 546 (describing a "fuller account of the *jus in bello* proportionality analysis" that takes into account "the legitimacy of the pursuit of the military goals"). *See also* Inger Österdahl, *Dangerous Liaison? The Disappearing Dichotomy Between* Jus ad Bellum *and in Bello,* 78 NORDIC J. INT'L L. 553, 553–66 (2010) (outlining existing points of contact between the legal frameworks); *see generally* Enzo Cannizzaro, *Contextualizing Proportionality:* Jus ad Bellum *and* Jus in Bello *in the Lebanese War,* 88 INT'L REV. RED CROSS 779 (2006) (suggesting that *jus ad bellum* consider *jus in bello* proportionality); *see also* Mégret, *supra* note 179, at 122 ("how about asking more of states in terms of *jus in bello* in certain cases on the basis of their *jus ad bellum* motivation for going to war?").

[185] Dealing with this recent phenomenon, *see* Adam Roberts, *The Equal Application of the Laws of War: A Principle Under Pressure,* 90 INT'L REV. RED CROSS 931, 933 (2008).

[186] Describing this kind of argumentation but opposing it strongly, *see* Geoffrey S. Corn, *Self-Defense Targeting: Blurring the Line Between the* Jus ad Bellum *and the* Jus in Bello, 88 INT'L L. STUD. 57 (2011) (referencing Kenneth Anderson, *Targeted Killing and Drone Warfare: How We Came to Debate Whether There Is a "Legal Geography of War"* [Am. U. WCL Research Paper No. 2011–16]).

[187] For more information on the topic, *see, e.g.,* Monica Hakimi, *Defensive Force Against Non-State Actors: The State of Play,* 91 INT'L L. STUD. 1 (2015); LINDSAY MOIR, REAPPRAISING THE RESORT TO FORCE: INTERNATIONAL LAW, JUS AD BELLUM AND THE WAR ON TERROR (2010); Christian J. Tams, *The Use of Force Against Terrorists,* 20 EUR. J. INT'L L. 359 (2009).

Given that the challenges posed by modern realities of warfare to the laws of armed conflict are real, a systematic study of the interplay of human rights law, humanitarian law, and the law on the use of force would be a welcome scholarly development.

To conclude, in societies in which responsibilities for war fighting are delegated to professional armies, it is essential to provide our soldiers with clear rules to guide them through battle. At the same time, especially in democratic societies where this delegation takes place through voluntary subscription to the highest social contract, it is a moral imperative to expect our sovereigns and armies to exercise this responsibility with utmost caution, and demand accountability when they manifestly fail to live up to their peoples' trust. As demonstrated by Garraway in fact,

> where the attitude of higher political and military command is that the law is irrelevant, that attitude will filter down to lower levels and it will therefore be difficult to instill in junior ranks any respect for the law of whatever kind. . . . This will have an inevitable effect on the conduct of operations.[188]

V. CONCLUSIONS

As this Chapter highlights, the question of the relationship between the law on the use of force and the law of armed conflict, and particularly the question of their separation, is complex and consequential. That both areas of law might in some way affect each other cannot be denied, since both the *jus ad bellum* and the *jus in bello* deal with constraining the waging of war acts. This Chapter has shown, however, that the two legal regimes have been established independently from each other, and that their basic principles (even when resembling a common core of values) are generally applied in an independent manner and seen as having different content. Furthermore, whatever the initial motivations behind the separation of the two legal regimes, the protection of both combatants and civilians, as well as persons *hors de combat*, is the most valued result, and one that absolutely cannot be departed from. The exact nature of this relationship, however, is still a topic of lively debate in both academic and practitioners' circles, especially against the background of new challenges posed by modern warfare in recent conflict situations. In this Chapter, we have tried to highlight the most salient aspects of this discussion, demonstrating how the basic principles of these two areas of law are usually

[188] Garraway, *supra* note 104, at 475.

applied, the theoretical and historical background for the principle of separation and equal application, and what the advantages and disadvantages of this approach might be vis-à-vis modern challenges and conflict situations. When discussing the core question of whether these challenges warrant a moderate reform of the understanding of the principle of separation, the authors found themselves holding a mix of different views on the subject, with a more traditional approach on the one hand, reflected in discussions concerning the reasons for continuing to uphold a strict separation between the *jus ad bellum* and the *jus in bello*, and a more progressive view on the other hand, reflected in the Chapter's discussions on the possibility of taking into account *jus ad bellum* considerations when dealing with some aspects of the *jus in bello*, at least under certain conditions and provided that the result is not detrimental to the existing protection afforded by the latter. A certain agreement existed regarding the need to look further into the question of a more extensive protection of peacekeepers, and the possibility that the humanitarian nature of certain types of operations might warrant proportionality to put a stronger emphasis on the possibility of further limiting a change in the collateral calculus in order to prevent further disadvantages to the civilian population. Agreement also existed on the need to further study and understand the role played by human rights law in situations of armed conflict, and how this body of law interacts with, and is applied alongside the laws of war and the law on the use of force. Disagreements, however, persisted on a number of issues. On the question of peacekeepers, for example, doubts remained as to whether a more progressive reading of the *jus in bello* (aimed at expanding peacekeepers' protection), or a completely different paradigm (that of law enforcement) might be the answer.

While it is indeed desirable that everything be done to prevent violations of Article 2(4) of the U.N. Charter, including bringing those responsible for aggressive wars to justice, doubts also still prevail on where the solution lies. Whereas it appears clear that the separation approach should not be taken for granted and be upheld simply for dogmatic reasons, legitimate doubts and a certain amount of anxiousness loom over the discussion of whether or not separation should be abandoned in favor of a more liberal approach to the issue of their relationship. A step forward from the complete separation of these legal strands is embedded in Greenwood's proposal of considering the relationship as "cumulative" rather than "linear"; how this would manifest itself in the case studies analyzed in this Chapter is, however, yet to be seen. Whereas we invite both scholars and practitioners to weigh in and further study what consequences such an approach might have, and whether it might respond suitably to some of the challenges posed by specific types of use of military force (such as humanitarian interventions and peacekeeping missions with mandates to protect civilians), we also evoke the potential for negative consequences that such an approach could have if embraced by those who seek to reduce the protection of the law rather than improve it. For example, we recognize that any approach that undercuts the equal application of international humanitarian law (geared for example toward greater protection for peacekeepers) runs the risk of being instrumentalized by those who seek to lessen the protection of combatants belonging to non-state armed groups. From these latter groups' perspective, it could even trigger discussions of whether international humanitarian law should be followed at all, to the great detriment of the rights and protection afforded to civilians. The law of armed conflict has been established to provide humanity with a minimum set of rules aimed at taming the damage and suffering inflicted by war. This is a non-negotiable outcome. The most important takeaway for us was that, even with this goal in mind, no single set of answers exists, and each issue might have to be dealt with separately. Many of these questions require separate study, but if this Chapter's discussion can in any way contribute to the further engagement of scholarship on the subject, we would find ourselves extremely satisfied.

18

Twenty-First Century Paradigms on Military Force for Humane Purposes

DAVID J. SCHEFFER AND ANGELA WALKER

I. INTRODUCTION

The international community has arrived at a crossroads in legitimizing the use of military force for humane purposes. Since 2005, a guiding principle for both national and international responses to certain kinds of assaults on civilian populations has been the much promoted "Responsibility to Protect" (R2P), which the United Nations General Assembly adopted unanimously as a procedural instrument for both non-military and military means of protecting civilians.[1] In reality, however, the military dimensions of R2P have constituted a well-intentioned sideshow for what actually has transpired throughout modern history and to the present day, namely, that it is national governments and organizations that determine when, how, and under what legal justification to intervene militarily across sovereign borders to confront the enemies of humankind. In the result, there is little coherence to what justifies the use of military force in the twenty-first century. Conventional international law, including the law of war, has become a time-warped body of law, projecting rules of behavior that either relate to a world that no longer exists or a fantasy world that is far too perfect for those who must seek peace and security amidst global chaos.

In this Chapter, we take a few modest steps toward piercing the veil of both R2P and the doctrine of humanitarian intervention to propose three paradigms for the future lawful application of military force in the service of humanitarian objectives.[2] Specifically, our objective is to strengthen the legal justifications and thus effective application of both doctrinal traditions – one (R2P) quite

---

[1] G.A. Res. 60/1, 2005 World Summit Outcome, U.N. Doc. A/RES/60/1, ¶¶ 138–40 (Oct. 24, 2005).

[2] The views expressed in this Chapter are strictly the personal views of these authors and should not be ascribed to any institution to which these authors are associated.

new and the other (humanitarian intervention) of considerable heritage – to confront a complex world of threats from state and non-state actors and the plight of civilians suffering in the midst of armed conflicts, international terrorism, and atrocity crimes. Our proposed paradigms challenge the intransigence and political resistance to effective and timely use of military force to protect civilian populations from large-scale assaults imperiling their survival.

The first paradigm examines four opportunities under U.N. Charter law that if utilized could provide stronger legal bases to respond to humanitarian crises. One of these would be to address the problems inherent with the use of veto power in the U.N. Security Council. We propose to influence the political behavior of Permanent Members of the Security Council by withholding the veto power under certain compelling circumstances. Other opportunities include the *Uniting for Peace* Resolution,[3] U.N. Charter Chapter VI options, and military standby forces under Article 43 of the U.N. Charter. Taken individually or collectively, these are readily available tools to change the dynamic of R2P or other humanitarian intervention initiatives.

The second paradigm adopts an expansive and pragmatic application of the right of self-defense, including collective self-defense, under the United Nations Charter and customary international law. We will explore how to use the right of self-defense in the context of twenty-first century realities.

The third paradigm introduces the "exhaustion" principle underlying R2P and humanitarian intervention and the acceptance of legal risks in the quest for morally justifiable and politically legitimate action to save lives. This paradigm may challenge conventional thinking the most, but it also reflects the fact that without its availability as a rationale for action, civilian populations will remain at dire risk.

We do not pretend to cover all possibilities or respond to all of the normative thinking that this subject elicits within the legal academy. An enormous amount of impressive scholarship has emerged recently that merits the attention of scholars and policymakers.[4] Within the limitations of this Chapter, we

---

[3] G.A. Res. 377 A (V), Uniting for Peace, U.N. Doc. A/RES/377(V) (Nov. 3, 1950).

[4] Some of the more recent scholarship includes, for example, Andrew M. Bell, *Using Force Against the "Weapons of the Weak": Examining A Chemical-Biological Weapons Usage Criterion for Unilateral Humanitarian Intervention Under the Responsibility to Protect*, 22 Cardozo J. Int'l & Comp. L. 261, 263 (2014); Sara Dillon, *Yes, No, Maybe: Why No Clear "Right" of the Ultra-Vulnerable to Protection via Humanitarian Intervention?*, 20 Mich. St. Int'l L. Rev. 179, 180 (2013); Jasmeet Gulati & Ivan Khosa, *Humanitarian Intervention: To Protect State Sovereignty*, 41 Denv. J. Int'l L. & Pol'y 397, 397 (2013); Mohamed S. Helal, *Justifying War and the Limits of Humanitarianism*, 37 Fordham Int'l L.J. 551, 559 (2014); Thomas H. Lee, *The Law of War and the Responsibility to Protect Civilians: A Reinterpretation*, 55 Harv. Int'l L.J. 251, 252 (2014); Robert A. Pape, *When Duty Calls: A Pragmatic Standard of*

concentrate on how to reach beyond the normative stagnation of current practice to a more pragmatic and adaptive methodology for the lawful use of military force, such that it more effectively and timely responds to humanitarian imperatives. Section II provides a background on R2P and humanitarian intervention by briefly describing their respective histories and modern-day shortcomings. Section III proposes three paradigms to strengthen the legal rationale underlying these doctrines such that the international community may better protect civilians exposed to disastrous and time-sensitive threats. Section IV offers a final cautionary note about the crime of aggression.

II. BACKGROUND

A. *A Fragile Responsibility to Protect*

The principle of R2P is set forth in the non-binding General Assembly Resolution 60/1 of October 24, 2005, known as the "World Summit Outcome Document." The principle's two provisions bear full recitation:

> 138. Each individual State has the responsibility to protect its populations from genocide, war crimes, ethnic cleansing and crimes against humanity. This responsibility entails the prevention of such crimes, including their incitement, through appropriate and necessary means. We accept that responsibility and will act in accordance with it. The international community should, as appropriate, encourage and help States to exercise this responsibility and support the United Nations in establishing an early warning capability.

> 139. The international community, through the United Nations, also has the responsibility to use appropriate diplomatic, humanitarian and other peaceful means, in accordance with Chapters VI and VIII of the Charter, to help to protect populations from genocide, war crimes, ethnic cleansing and crime against humanity. In this context, we are prepared to take collective action, in

Humanitarian Intervention, 37 INT'L SEC. 41 (2012); Neomi Rao, *The Choice to Protect: Rethinking Responsibility for Humanitarian Intervention*, 44 COLUM. HUM. RTS. L. REV. 697, 698 (2013); Anna Spain, *Deciding to Intervene*, 51 HOUS. L. REV. 847, 849 (2014); Jennifer Trahan, *Defining the 'Grey Area' Where Humanitarian Intervention May Not Be Fully Legal, But Is Not the Crime of Aggression*, 2 J. ON USE FORCE & INT'L L. 42 (2015). For further background, see, for example, SIMON CHESTERMAN, JUST WAR OR JUST PEACE?: HUMANITARIAN INTERVENTION AND INTERNATIONAL LAW (2001); SEAN D. MURPHY, HUMANITARIAN INTERVENTION: THE UNITED NATIONS IN AN EVOLVING WORLD ORDER (1996); FERNANDO R. TESÓN, HUMANITARIAN INTERVENTION: AN INQUIRY INTO LAW AND MORALITY (3d ed. 2005); NICHOLAS J. WHEELER, SAVING STRANGERS: HUMANITARIAN INTERVENTION IN INTERNATIONAL SOCIETY (2003).

a timely and decisive manner, through the Security Council, in accordance with the Charter, including Chapter VII, on a case-by-case basis and in cooperation with relevant regional organizations as appropriate, should peaceful means be inadequate and national authorities are manifestly failing to protect their populations from genocide, war crimes, ethnic cleansing and crimes against humanity. We also intend to commit ourselves, as necessary and appropriate, to helping States build capacity to protect their populations from genocide, war crimes, ethnic cleansing and crimes against humanity and to assisting those which are under stress before crises and conflicts break out.[5]

The Security Council embraced the R2P provisions in its own Resolution 1674 of April 28, 2006: "[The Security Council] *[r]eaffirms* the provisions of paragraphs 138 and 139 of the 2005 World Summit Outcome Document regarding the responsibility to protect populations from genocide, war crimes, ethnic cleansing and crimes against humanity."[6]

R2P is a principle that pertains only to the most egregious *criminal* assaults on populations in the form of genocide, crimes against humanity (which includes ethnic cleansing), and war crimes.[7] While it is exceptionally important to confront these atrocity crimes with duties of responsibility, action, and accountability, they can present challenges when the gravity of the crimes is initially unknown or held in question, where the determination of state or non-state actor responsibility remains uncertain, when effective military action awaits improbable approval, and the investigation of individual leadership perpetrators awaits another distant day. The R2P principle also is irrelevant for the survival of civilian populations arising from causes other than such particular atrocity crimes.[8]

Even if there was greater political will among national governments, particularly those of the five Permanent Members of the Security Council, the lack of an incentive to activate R2P under U.N. Chapter VII authority will

---

[5] G.A. Res. 60/1, *supra* note 1, ¶¶ 138–39.

[6] S.C. Res. 1674, U.N. Doc. S/RES/1674, ¶ 4 (Apr. 28, 2006). For the seventh, and most recent, iteration of R2P from the U.N. Secretary-General, see U.N. Secretary-General, A *Vital and Enduring Commitment: Implementing the Responsibility to Protect: Rep. of the Secretary-General*, U.N. Doc. A/69/981-S/2015/500 (July 13, 2015), www.un.org/en/ga/search/view_doc.asp?symbol=S/2015/500.

[7] David Scheffer, *Atrocity Crimes Framing the Responsibility to Protect, in* RESPONSIBILITY TO PROTECT: THE GLOBAL MORAL COMPACT FOR THE 21ST CENTURY 77, 77 (Richard H. Cooper & Juliette Voïnov Kohler eds., 2009); David Scheffer, *Atrocity Crimes Framing the Responsibility to Protect*, 40 CASE W. RES. J. INT'L L. 111 (2008).

[8] U.N. Secretary-General, *Implementing the Responsibility to Protect: Rep. of the Secretary-General*, ¶ 11(a), U.N. Doc. A/63/677 (Jan. 12, 2009) (States have the primary responsibility to protect their own populations "from genocide, war crimes, ethnic cleansing and crimes against humanity, and from their incitement").

continue to undermine this doctrine until its legal rationale is cemented. Currently, however, inaction far exceeds action for such situations.

Granted, there is rhetorical endorsement of R2P in an impressive number of Security Council resolutions and presidential statements since 2005,[9] as well as important civil society support behind implementation of the principle.[10] And there have been a couple of instances, such as Libya and Syria, where R2P clearly strengthened the rationale for significant Council action authorizing the use of force or the deployment of humanitarian convoys into an armed conflict area.[11] But actual Security Council action to unleash R2P in the way the World Summit Outcome Document contemplates has been so minimal as to call into question the sufficiency of the principle.

Because R2P addresses only particular atrocity crimes, it often fails to provide a legal rationale for protecting civilian populations threatened by non-state actors, including terrorists or terrorist organizations, who fight to overturn state authority and replace it with repressive, authoritarian rule. If the commission of atrocity crimes is anticipated or actually committed in the course of any such revolutionary conduct, then R2P would be relevant provided it is actually implemented.[12] But without atrocity crimes, or when they lag far behind the terrorist or rebel attack on state authority, R2P risks not gaining traction in time for any meaningful national or international response. For example, the Taliban, al-Qaeda, Boko Haram, and the so-called Islamic State are four movements imposing enormous danger to the freedom, well-being, and survival of various civilian populations, and yet in most instances R2P has not been used to justify action against any of them.[13]

---

[9] David Scheffer, *The Fate of R2P in the Age of Retrenchment, in* GLOBALIZATION AND ITS IMPACT ON THE FUTURE OF HUMAN RIGHTS AND INTERNATIONAL CRIMINAL JUSTICE 617, 619 (M. Cherif Bassiouni ed., 2015) [hereinafter Scheffer, *R2P in the Age of Retrenchment*]; GLOB. CTR. FOR THE RESPONSIBILITY TO PROTECT, R2P REFERENCES IN UNITED NATIONS SECURITY COUNCIL RESOLUTIONS AND PRESIDENTIAL STATEMENTS (2014), http://s156658.gridserver.com/media/files/unsc-resolutions-and-statements-with-r2p-table-as-of-may-2014.pdf.

[10] *See, e.g., Genocide Prevention,* STANLEY FOUND., www.stanleyfoundation.org/programs.cfm?id=27; GLOBAL CTR. RESPONSIBILITY TO PROTECT, www.globalr2p.org; INT'L COAL. RESPONSIBILITY TO PROTECT, www.responsibilitytoprotect.org/.

[11] Scheffer, *R2P in the Age of Retrenchment, supra* note 9, at 618–19.

[12] *See* Lianna Brinded, *British Politicians Found a Way to Force 127 Countries to Help Fight Against ISIS,* BUS. INSIDER (Dec. 21, 2015), www.businessinsider.com/david-camerons-use-of-un-article-ii-to-help-fight-isis-2015-12?r=UK&IR=T.

[13] Recently, however, Security Council members discussed how to treat non-state actors within the R2P paradigm, with Chile and Spain hosting an Arria-formula meeting to address the topic on December 14, 2015. *Arria-Formula Meeting: Responsibility to Protect and Non-State Actors,* WHAT'S IN BLUE (Dec. 10, 2015), www.whatsinblue.org/2015/12/arria-formula-meeting-responsibility-to-protect-and-non-state-actors.php#read-more.

The legal rationale currently underlying R2P also fails to protect civilian populations who have suffered through natural disasters and environmental catastrophes. If a national government is failing in its responsibility to protect or rescue its civilian populations from the catastrophic impact of a natural phenomenon, as Myanmar tragically demonstrated in 2008 when Cyclone Nargis hit the Irrawaddy Delta killing at least 138,000 people, then R2P, because of its narrow character, is irrelevant. Some other principle should rise to the challenge and legally underwrite an international intervention to save countless lives at risk when a national government is unable or unwilling to respond. Absent a Security Council resolution approving military intervention – which in any event would be improbable since the Council has jurisdictional authority only over threats to international peace and security – the international community's use of military intervention to prevent mass deaths, starvation, or other calamity arising from a natural disaster would be paralyzed. Another example would be a refugee invasion so significant that military action is required to discipline the process and ensure peace and security in the region even if the receiving nation refuses to request such assistance.

Paradoxically, R2P has the potential to shift international attention away from utilizing military intervention such that the humanitarian needs of civilian populations suffer more than if R2P did not exist. Despite R2P's goal of compelling the national government to protect its own population (paragraph 138) and its mandate to persuade other governments to use non-military measures to the same effect (paragraph 139), R2P can increase the suffering of civilian populations by acting as a "brake" on timely humanitarian intervention. The challenge of obtaining a veto-free Security Council resolution for military force under R2P and U.N. Charter law (a threat to international peace and security) and practice is such a daunting, political, and time-consuming process that R2P can have the effect of retarding rather than advancing the cause it purports to trumpet.

Significantly, the Security Council acted in late 2015 outside of Chapter VII in response to the threat from the so-called Islamic State following the attacks on Paris on November 13, 2015. In Resolution 2249, the Council unanimously called upon States to take action "in compliance with international law." The relevant section of the resolution reads:

> 5. Calls upon Member States that have the capacity to do so to take all necessary measures, in compliance with international law, in particular with the United Nations Charter, as well as international human rights, refugee and humanitarian law, on the territory under the control of ISIL also known

as Da'esh, in Syria and Iraq, to redouble and coordinate their efforts to prevent and suppress terrorist acts committed specifically by ISIL also known as Da'esh as well as ANF, and all other individuals, groups, undertakings, and entities associated with Al Qaeda, and other terrorist groups, as designated by the United Nations Security Council, and as may further be agreed by the International Syria Support Group (ISSG) and endorsed by the UN Security Council, pursuant to the Statement of the International Syria Support Group (ISSG) of 14 November, and to eradicate the safe haven they have established over significant parts of Iraq and Syria. . . . [14]

This resolution opens up intriguing opportunities for States to "take all necessary measures" with Security Council authorization falling short of Chapter VII enforcement power, and thus on a voluntary basis, provided international law is complied with in respect of such actions. One can begin to see in this formulation the return of a doctrine of humanitarian intervention that falls within the parameters of international law. The alternative to R2P that requires Chapter VII enforcement action by the Security Council would be military action based on the doctrine of humanitarian intervention – and yet encouraged by the Security Council as evidenced in Resolution 2249 – or possibly even further untethered from Security Council constraints. Unyielding allegiance to R2P, with its narrow substantive scope and procedural minefields, can result in putting more people at risk than would otherwise be the case if R2P were not such a restraining influence.

B. *The Resilience of Humanitarian Intervention*

A quarter-century ago one of us wrote a law review article entitled *Toward a Modern Doctrine of Humanitarian Intervention*.[15] This was published before the atrocity crimes of the 1990s occurred and before their influence on the creation ultimately of an alternative formulation that was endorsed as R2P in 2005. But in that article and in the scholarly works of others,[16] precedents of humanitarian intervention since the early 1800s have been examined and the international law that might justify such actions discussed.

---

[14] S.C. Res. 2249, U.N. Doc. S/RES/2249, ¶ 5 (Nov. 20, 2015).

[15] David J. Scheffer, *Toward a Modern Doctrine of Humanitarian Intervention*, 23 U. TOL. L. REV. 253, 253–93 (1992) [hereinafter Scheffer, *Modern Doctrine*].

[16] *See, e.g.*, ALEXIS HERACLIDES & ADA DIALLA, HUMANITARIAN INTERVENTION IN THE LONG NINETEENTH CENTURY: SETTING THE PRECEDENT (2015); MURPHY, *supra* note 4; Thomas M. Franck & Nigel S. Rodley, *After Bangladesh: The Law of Humanitarian Intervention by Military Force*, 67 AM. J. INT'L L. 275 (1973).

That article set forth the following basic tenets, which continue to resonate for contemporary analyses:

(1) There was a time prior to World War II when unilateral military intervention for strictly humanitarian purposes was regarded as legitimate by a large community of international law scholars and was arguably embodied in customary international law. Following World War II, the U.N. Charter's prohibition on the use of force except in cases of self-defense or at the direction of the Security Council had the effect of generally de-legitimizing humanitarian intervention in the view of many legal scholars.[17]
(2) Long-standing norms of respecting the sovereignty of nations and non-interference in the internal affairs of States, as well as U.N. Charter Article 2(4)'s prohibition on "the threat or use of force against the territorial integrity or political independence of any state, or in any manner inconsistent with the Purposes of the United Nations," challenge the legality of unilateral humanitarian intervention and of any collective action not expressly authorized by the U.N. Security Council.[18]
(3) A modern doctrine of humanitarian intervention should establish the legitimacy of certain types of non-forcible and forcible intervention undertaken without the express consent of the target country's government, but with collective authorization or, in some limited circumstances, unilaterally or multinationally for the purpose of defending or alleviating the mass suffering of people for whom no other alternative realistically exists.[19]
(4) Common sense and historical experience point toward the classification of large-scale humanitarian crises as *presumptive* threats to international peace and security, thus engaging the Security Council's jurisdiction and responsibility under the U.N. Charter.[20]
(5) The right of non-forcible humanitarian intervention for international aid agencies should arise under several well-defined conditions.[21]
(6) The right of forcible humanitarian intervention should arise under the same conditions as non-forcible intervention, including Security Council approval, but with the important caveat that in the absence of collective authorization, there arise a number of conditions which, if

---

[17] Scheffer, *Modern Doctrine, supra* note 15, at 258–59 (footnote omitted).
[18] *Id.* at 259–64 (quoting U.N. Charter art. 2, ¶ 4).
[19] *Id.* at 265 (wherein there is explanation of purposes justifying such intervention).
[20] *Id.* at 286–88.
[21] *Id.* at 288; S.C. Res. 2165, U.N. Doc. S/RES/2165 (July 14, 2014).

met, nonetheless should render the forcible intervention for humanitarian objectives as one meeting the test of legitimacy if not legality.[22]

While these tenets continue to apply today, what so vexes the entire debate
over humanitarian intervention under U.N. Charter rules is that the Security
Council may lack the jurisdiction to authorize forcible intervention. The
resulting dilemma of inaction has deeply influenced how one assesses the
legality of the use of force, particularly in light of contemporary world affairs.
Transforming the Security Council into a viable instrument for protecting
civilian populations remains a political challenge of the highest order and one
that may never be satisfactorily met so as to ensure effective action. It thus is
incumbent upon the legal academy to continue to explore ways to address the
problem, for the alternative is simply to leave the fate of civilians to the
collective political will of the Security Council and the ideological designs
of each Permanent Member. While the latter option may satisfy conventional-
ists who would articulate how the U.N. Charter protects sovereignty and
empowers the Security Council to enforce international peace and security,
those pillars of international law cannot support the realities of the modern
world alone.

A doctrine for the twenty-first century is required – one that recognizes the
reasoning of the constraints built into the U.N. Charter system of managing
international peace and security and other human affairs while also providing
a roadmap to confront the reality of humanitarian crises. The humanitarian
wedge into the fundamental principle of the non-use of force may strike some
as uncontrollable, unpredictable, dangerously undefined, and thus unwise to
pursue, but such an opinion is no solace to the countless numbers of human
beings whose very survival is threatened by forces beyond their control,
whether they be sourced among those who lead armies, militia, or terrorist
organizations, or among the forces of nature. No doctrine will be implemented perfectly, but there should be something more than R2P and conventional interpretations of the U.N. Charter to guide the future.

C. *Problems with Pursuing the Conventionalist Option*

The path of least resistance would be to continue to push the status quo in
terms of how military force is or should be authorized for humanitarian
objectives. This option would continue efforts to bolster the acceptability of
R2P and to leave the legal procedure for the use of force to the discretion of

---

[22] Scheffer, *Modern Doctrine, supra* note 15, at 289–93.

the Security Council. R2P would operate as advertised, with adherence to the procedural steps outlined in the World Summit Outcome Document. Situations would arise where popular pressure or other political imperatives might still trigger unilateral or multinational use of force, giving rise to legal challenges and rhetorical criticism because they lack firm footing in Security Council authorization. But those would be exceptions to the conventional methodology grounded in R2P and the U.N. Charter, and they would risk almost certain legal opprobrium, apathy, or both.

The significant shortcoming of the conventionalist option is exemplified in U.S. President Barack Obama's commencement address at West Point Military Academy on May 28, 2014,[23] which set forth the paradigm of limited American engagement in the face of humanitarian crises at issue in this study.[24] Of course, doctrines can change from one administration to another and that may well occur with R2P and how Washington seeks to implement or withdraw from it. But the Obama paradigm has deeply influenced contemporary policymaking and may reflect comparable views of other major military powers in the world. It thus merits brief scrutiny.

None of the four principles President Obama set forth at West Point explicitly embrace R2P. The first principle ties using military force to "when our core interests demand it: when our people are threatened; when our livelihoods are at stake; when the security of our allies is in danger. . . ." The Obama Doctrine requires that there be multilateral action or a higher threshold for military action when a typical R2P event occurs. The second principle sharply focuses on terrorism and essentially elevates it, along with its military responses, above atrocity crimes or other events devastating civilian populations of no direct relationship to the United States. The third principle essentially looks to peacekeeping operations, staffed by other nations, "to actually keep the peace so that we can prevent the type of killing we've seen in Congo and Sudan." Under the fourth principle, President Obama expresses "our willingness to act" to promote democratization and basic human rights, but this is a far cry from expressing the willingness to intervene *militarily* for humanitarian objectives. Perhaps implied in this last principle is the fact that the United States will respect international norms and turn to multilateral institutions for forcible action on atrocity crime situations relevant to R2P or other humanitarian debacles, but it is not explicitly stated.

---

[23] President Barack Obama, Remarks by the President at the United States Military Academy Commencement Ceremony (May 28, 2014), www.whitehouse.gov/the-press-office/2014/05/28/remarks-president-united-states-military-academy-commencement-ceremony.

[24] Scheffer, *R2P in the Age of Retrenchment, supra* note 9, at 621–28.

All of this reflects a conventionalist view of the problem, which represents a logical and defensible approach that respects the soundest principles of international law. But it does little to address the plight of civilian populations who remain on the international agenda with unacceptable frequency and gravity. Moreover, it may not even serve U.S. interests, as fifty-one State Department officials argued in respect of the situation in Syria in 2016.[25] For this reason, pursuing the status quo has proven to be an inadequate vehicle for addressing mass human suffering. Under the current framework, national governments fail to respond quickly enough to ensure the safety, health, and well-being of survivor populations in the immediate aftermath of armed conflicts, terrorist assaults, political tyranny or repression, or natural disasters. The following Section proposes three paradigms to strengthen the legal rationale behind the international community's military response to protect these populations and create overall coherence to what justifies the use of military force in the twenty-first century.

III. THREE TWENTY-FIRST CENTURY PARADIGMS ON MILITARY FORCE FOR HUMANE PURPOSES

A. *Paradigm #1: Four Charter Initiatives*

There are at least four concrete initiatives that could be pursued, either collectively or individually, in connection with the U.N. Charter and that could bolster the legality of authorizing and using military force in response to egregious humanitarian crises. We focus on these prospects because they should not require any amendment of the Charter or any unreasonable interpretation of the Charter.

1. Responsibility Not to Veto (RN2V)

The first initiative that we believe bears emphasizing as a politically and legally potent means of strengthening R2P – for a more assertive and timely use of military force in the name of humanitarian objectives – is the Responsibility Not to Veto, or RN2V, Movement. Between October 2011 and May 2014, the Security Council voted on four resolutions to hold those responsible for atrocities in Syria accountable, including, in the fourth resolution, referring

---

[25] Max Fisher, *The State Department's Dissent Memo on Syria: An Explanation*, N.Y. Times (June 22, 2016), www.nytimes.com/2016/06/23/world/middleeast/syria-assad-obama-diplomats-memo.html?_r=0.

the Syrian situation to the International Criminal Court for investigation.[26] Each such resolution was vetoed by both Russia and China.[27] That fact alone has spurred much interest in addressing the obvious failure of the Security Council to implement R2P with respect to the Syrian armed conflict and its humanitarian outrages.[28]

France, as a Permanent Member of the Security Council, has spearheaded RN2V in recent years, albeit unsuccessfully. At the Sixty-Eighth Session of the U.N. General Assembly in September 2013, French President François Hollande called upon the five Permanent Members of the Security Council to "collectively renounce their veto powers" in mass atrocity situations that are covered by R2P.[29] This would be a non-binding political agreement or code of conduct, in which the Permanent Five agree to suspend their veto powers in cases of mass atrocity. The idea was not a new one, as it had been proposed in 2001 by French Foreign Minister Vedrine and by the International Commission on Intervention and State Sovereignty.[30] But the Syrian situation presented the obvious crippling effect of the veto power on Security Council action, which is essential under R2P when non-military measures fail to accomplish the objective of protecting civilian populations.

[26] U.N. Doc. S/2014/348 (May 22, 2014); U.N. Doc. S/2012/538 (July 19, 2012); U.N. Doc. S/2012/77 (Feb. 4, 2012); U.N. Doc. S/2011/612 (Oct. 4, 2011). *See also UN Security Council Code of Conduct*, GLOBAL CTR. RESPONSIBILITY TO PROTECT, www.globalr2p.org/our_work/un_security_council_code_of_conduct.

[27] In total, the Union of Soviet Socialist Republics/Russia has cast 132 vetoes, the United States 83 vetoes, the United Kingdom 32 vetoes, France 18 vetoes, and China 11 vetoes. Not reflected in these statistics is the use of the "hidden" veto, which refers to instances in which the threat of veto by one or more Permanent Members thwarts draft resolutions. SEC. COUNCIL REPORT, RESEARCH REPORT: THE VETO 3 (2015), www.securitycouncilreport.org/special-research-report/the-veto.php.

[28] Lee, *supra* note 4, at 257; Rao, *supra* note 4, at 735–36; MEGAN PRICE ET AL., PRELIMINARY STATISTICAL ANALYSIS OF DOCUMENTATION OF KILLINGS IN THE SYRIAN ARAB REPUBLIC 1 (2013), www.ohchr.org/Documents/Countries/SY/PreliminaryStatAnalysisKillingsInSyria.pdf. *See also* SEC. COUNCIL REPORT, *supra* note 27, at 3 (reporting that 250,000 people had been killed and 11.7 million people had been displaced as of 2015).

[29] *See* François Hollande, President of France, Statement at the Opening of the 68th Session of the United Nations General Assembly (Sept. 24, 2013), http://gadebate.un.org/sites/default/files/gastatements/68/FR_en.pdf; *See also* Laurent Fabius, Op-Ed., *A Call for Self-Restraint at the U.N.*, N.Y. TIMES (Oct. 4, 2013), www.nytimes.com/2013/10/04/opinion/a-call-for-self-restraint-at-the-un.html?_r=0.

[30] Stewart M. Patrick, Senior Fellow & Dir., Int'l Insts. & Global Governance Program, Remarks Offered at a Sciences Po/PSIA Conference on Regulating the Use of the Veto at the U.N. Security Council in Case of Mass Atrocities: Limiting the Veto in Cases of Mass Atrocities: Is the Proposed Code of Conduct Workable? (Jan. 21, 2015).

Following the Russian and Chinese vetoes of a resolution on Syria in May 2014,[31] the RN2V proposal has been picking up steam. France and Mexico have co-hosted two ministerial-level meetings on the initiative, the most recent of which was held on September 30, 2015.[32] Thus far, it has received the support of eighty countries.[33] Gareth Evans, writing for Project Syndicate, described the moral argument as being that the veto should not be used in cases of mass atrocity crimes because the five Permanent Members of the Security Council have obligations under the U.N. Charter not to undermine international humanitarian law and human rights law through use of the veto in such situations.[34]

Although France is still refining the proposal,[35] it currently contains three key provisions. First, cases must be defined clearly and build upon well-established R2P language (hence, only atrocity crimes situations). Second, there must be a speedy and objective mechanism to determine when such cases actually arise. This could include a "double trigger," namely a U.N. Secretary-General certification to the Security Council that the case meets the R2P definitional requirements, and that at least fifty Member States request restraint on the use of the veto, including at least five nations from each recognized geographical grouping at the United Nations. Lastly, the initiative contains a provision allowing any Permanent Member of the Security Council to exercise the veto when it claims that a "vital national interest" is at stake.[36] Although the Security Council still retains significant authority under this initiative, the additional pressure of the "double trigger" function – from the Secretary-General as well as fifty Member States –

---

[31] Somini Sengupta, *China and Russia Block Referral of Syria to Court*, N.Y. Times (May 23, 2014), www.nytimes.com/2014/05/23/world/middleeast/syria-vote-in-security-council.html.

[32] Sec. Council Report, *supra* note 27, at 5. One year prior, on September 25, 2014, France and Mexico co-convened the ministerial-level side event on the margins of the General Assembly entitled "Regulating the veto in the event of mass atrocities." *See* Press Release, Security Council, Speakers Call for Voluntary Suspension of Veto Rights in Cases of Mass Atrocity Crimes, as Security Council Debates Working Methods, U.N. Press Release SC/11164 (Oct. 29, 2013), www.un.org/press/en/2013/sc11164.doc.htm. Over one hundred Member States reportedly attended the meeting, and thirty-two Member States spoke. *See* UN Security Council Veto Restraint, *supra* note 26.

[33] Sec. Council Report, *supra* note 27, at 5.

[34] Gareth Evans, *Limiting the Security Council Veto*, Project Syndicate (Feb. 4, 2015), www.project-syndicate.org/commentary/security-council-veto-limit-by-gareth-evans-2015-02.

[35] Sec. Council Report, *supra* note 27, at 5 ("For example, [France] recently announced that it favoured calling on permanent members to explain their vote when casting a veto. . . .").

[36] Evans, *supra* note 34.

ideally would restore greater trust in the Security Council by acting as a check on political decision-making.

The French proposal has yet to gain traction, however, with three Permanent Members of the Security Council: Russia, China, and the United States. The Russian and Chinese vetoes of the resolution on Syria in May 2014, which did not seek to authorize military enforcement under Chapter VII but rather judicial accountability by referral to the International Criminal Court, demonstrated how firmly entrenched the veto power remains and how difficult it is to blunt it in any way. Nonetheless, several other initiatives continue to make headway.

On October 23, 2015, in a meeting hosted by Liechtenstein on the day before the seventieth anniversary of the United Nations, the twenty-six-member Accountability, Coherence and Transparency (ACT) Group proposed a "Code of Conduct" that calls on Member States to "pledge to support timely and decisive action by the Security Council aimed at preventing or ending the commission of genocide, crimes against humanity or war crimes[.]"[37] The purpose of the Code is to increase political accountability at the United Nations. More than one hundred Member States, including nine members of the Security Council, signed on in 2015.[38] Permanent Members United Kingdom and France were among the supporters pledging not to use their respective vetoes in cases of mass atrocities and called on other Permanent Member States to pledge the same.[39]

Earlier, on February 7, 2015, a group of global leaders chaired by former U.N. Secretary-General Kofi Annan called on the Permanent Members to pledge "not to use, or threaten to use, their veto" in crises involving genocide or other mass atrocities "without explaining, clearly and in public, what

---

[37] Sec. Council Report, *supra* note 27, at 5 (quoting Accountability, Coherence, and Transparency Grp., Code of Conduct Regarding Security Council Action Against Genocide, Crimes Against Humanity or War Crimes ¶ 1 (2015), www.centerforunreform .org/sites/default/files/Final%202015-09-01%20SC%20Code%20of%20Conduct%20Atrocity .pdf); Press Release, The Elders, The Elders and Global Centre for the Responsibility to Protect Call Upon the Security Council to Act to Prevent Mass Atrocity Crimes (Sept. 26, 2015), http://theelders.org/article/elders-and-global-centre-responsibility-protect-call-upon-un-security-council-act-prevent; Jessica Kroenert, *ACT Group Formally Launches Security Council Code of Conduct*, Ctr. U.N. Reform Educ. (Oct. 26, 2015), www.centerforunreform.org/?q=node/679.

[38] As of February 12, 2018, the Code of Conduct has been signed by 115 Member States and two observers. Global Centre for the Responsibility to Protect, *UN Security Council Code of Conduct* (2018), http://www.globalr2p.org/our_work/un_security_council_code_of_conduct.

[39] Kroenert, *supra* note 37.

alternative course of action they propose, as a credible and efficient way to protect populations in question."[40]

These recent initiatives indicate that the RN2V proposal remains on the table and could influence, if only subconsciously, the decision-making of Permanent Members of the Security Council when future opportunities arise to act not only when atrocity crimes trigger R2P situations, but also when other humanitarian debacles merit immediate Security Council responses.

2. *Uniting for Peace* Resolution

The second initiative would entail re-invoking the U.N. General Assembly's *Uniting for Peace* Resolution, which was adopted on November 3, 1950.[41] A well-known relic of the early days of the Cold War, the *Uniting for Peace* Resolution was originally designed to overcome Permanent Members' use of the veto power to prevent authorization of military force under Chapter VII of the U.N. Charter to confront aggression or other threats to international peace and security. Two recent studies of the *Uniting for Peace* Resolution authored by Dominik Zaum and Andrew Carswell provide excellent critiques of how the Resolution has fared as a matter of law and practice and its relevance for the future.[42] Both scholars observe that it has been used sparingly in the past to address a small number of situations that are neither simple cases of aggression nor conventional threats to peace and security and leave open the possibility of future implementation of the *Uniting for Peace* Resolution for wider purposes. Zaum notes that the International Commission on Intervention and State Sovereignty's report on *The Responsibility to Protect*,[43] a precursor to the World Summit Outcome's endorsement of R2P,[44] raised the possibility of

---

[40] SEC. COUNCIL REPORT, *supra* note 27, at 5. The Elders co-hosted an event with the Global Centre for the Responsibility to Protect the following September, entitled "Preventing mass atrocity crimes: how can the UN Security Council do better?" to "urge[] the members of the UN Security Council to act more effectively to prevent mass atrocity crimes." Press Release, The Elders, *supra* note 37.

[41] G.A. Res. 377 A (V), *supra* note 3.

[42] Dominik Zaum, *The Security Council, the General Assembly, and War: The Uniting for Peace Resolution, in* THE UNITED NATIONS SECURITY COUNCIL AND WAR: THE EVOLUTION OF THOUGHT AND PRACTICE SINCE 1945, at 154, 154–74 (Vaughan Lowe et al. eds., 2008); Andrew J. Carswell, *Unblocking the UN Security Council: The Uniting for Peace Resolution*, 18 J. CONFLICT & SEC. L. 453 (2013).

[43] INT'L COMM'N ON INTERVENTION AND STATE SOVEREIGNTY, THE RESPONSIBILITY TO PROTECT (2001), http://responsibilitytoprotect.org/ICISS%20Report.pdf.

[44] G.A. Res. 60/1, *supra* note 1, ¶ 139.

using the *Uniting for Peace* Resolution to address major human rights violations or humanitarian emergencies.[45]

The *Uniting for Peace* Resolution was originally introduced by the United
States in 1950 to ensure that the United Nations would back U.S.-led military
actions in Korea once the Soviet Union returned to occupy its seat in the
Security Council, where it was expected to, and did, veto further actions in
Korea. More than five years later, the Resolution was successfully employed by
the General Assembly to establish peacekeeping operations during the Suez
Crisis of 1956 after French and British vetoes in the Security Council blocked
action by that body. In subsequent years, Member States used the Resolution for
purposes that sometimes ran contrary to American interests at the time (such as
complaints about Israel and the Occupied Territories) and American, French,
and British opposition to economic sanctions against South Africa in 1981.

The Resolution's relatively moribund status for many years suggests that its
utility has been spent on the world stage. The concerns of major powers,
particularly the Permanent Members of the Security Council, with respect to
Member States' use of the *Uniting for Peace* Resolution for objectives that
are only tenuously associated with international peace and security is a long-
standing dilemma that can render the Resolution extremely problematic in its
implementation and strain relations with the Permanent Members of the
Security Council.

But the *Uniting for Peace* Resolution could be employed, with the support
of the United States, France, and the United Kingdom, to authorize speedy
military action, including U.N. peacekeeping operations with or, in certain
circumstances such as the creation of safe zones in highly contested conflict
areas, without host country consent, in the face of severe assaults on civilian
populations. R2P and inexcusable Security Council inaction in the face of
humanitarian debacles, particularly those caused by warfare and unrestrained
atrocity crimes, begs for the logic of the *Uniting for Peace* Resolution in order
to authorize timely interventions that could save large numbers of lives. The
risk, of course, is creating an even greater breach with Russia and China not
only in the Security Council, but in world affairs. Political analysts and
theorists would weigh in heavily to oppose actions under the *Uniting for Peace*
Resolution that would increase tensions with these two major powers.

---

[45] Zaum, *supra* note 42 at 156, 173.

3. Peacekeeping Actions Under U.N. Charter Chapter VI

The World Summit Outcome Document points explicitly, albeit not exclusively, to U.N. Charter Chapter VII as the procedural means by which the Security Council should authorize military intervention when non-military means prove inadequate to protect civilian populations suffering from atrocity crimes.[46] Thus, much of the ongoing dialogue about R2P focuses on the Security Council's option to act under Chapter VII to authorize military enforcement. However, this particular focus encourages governments to rely increasingly only on Chapter VII as the legal vehicle for force deployment under U.N. authority.[47] They already are inclined to look to the Security Council to establish peacekeeping operations under Chapter VII authority rather than the authority derived from Chapter VI that has been the traditional legal pillar.[48] This can have the effect of transforming Chapter VII into a presumptive requirement for enforcement and peacekeeping authority by the Security Council even in situations that do not require it, particularly those where a peacekeeping force alone might suffice. Requiring a Chapter VII

---

[46] Chapter VII provides for "Action with Respect to Threats to the Peace, Breaches of the Peace, and Acts of Aggression" and authorizes the Security Council to "take such action by air, sea, or land forces as may be necessary to maintain or restore international peace and security." U.N. Charter art. 42. *See also* G.A. Res. 60/1, *supra* note 1, ¶ 139 (referencing Chapter VI [and Chapter VIII] of the U.N. Charter in the context of the international community having the responsibility to use "peaceful means" to protect populations from atrocity crimes). We do not examine possible methodologies under U.N. Charter Chapter VIII, which requires that any enforcement action by "regional arrangements or agencies" thereunder have Security Council authorization. That establishes a threshold for action that requires a thorough examination of what may be possible with regional bodies, a task outside the scope of this study. For a discussion of Chapter VIII in this respect, see Dan Sarooshi, *The Security Council's Authorization of Regional Arrangements to Use Force: The Case of NATO, in* THE UNITED NATIONS SECURITY COUNCIL AND WAR, *supra* note 42, at 226–47.

[47] Júlia Gifra Durall, *United Nations Peacekeeping Operations Under Chapter VII: Exception or Widespread Practice?*, REVISTA DEL INSTITUTO ESPAÑOL DE ESTUDIOS ESTRATÉGICOS, 2013, at 1, 9, dialnet.unirioja.es (stating that "the number of UN peacekeeping operations under Chapter VII of the Charter is steadily on the increase . . .").

[48] For example, in Bosnia, Kosovo, and Somalia, peacekeeping operations under Chapter VII authority were undertaken without the consent of the parties to the conflict and involved armed forces. *See Department of Peacekeeping Operations*, UNITED NATIONS PEACEKEEPING, www.un.org/en/peacekeeping/about/dpko/; *see also* Durall, *supra* note 47, at 9 (footnote omitted) ("Looked at globally, of the 68 deployed to date, half of these [peacekeeping operations] incorporate some humanitarian function in their mandates; in a further 22, the Security Council has adopted enforcement measures, in consideration of the provisions in Chapter VII of the Charter"). For a concise examination of the legal authority and practice of U.N. peacekeeping and the Security Council's role, see Mats Berdal, *The Security Council and Peacekeeping, in* THE UNITED NATIONS SECURITY COUNCIL AND WAR, *supra* note 42, at 175.

resolution may attract the kind of decision-making by Permanent Members under which the veto power comes prominently into play. A much broader perspective and interpretation of the U.N. Charter is required as humanitarian situations demand more effective and flexible responses.

Chapter VII remains the preferred legal authority where there is no state consent for intervention on that State's territory. But where state consent can be obtained, or where state consent is essentially an irrelevant issue, as we discuss below, R2P does not exclude other Charter authority, such as that which can be taken under "Chapter VI 1/2."[49] There are two provisions in Chapter VI that bear emphasizing and that can relate to the basic, albeit interpretative, authority for peacekeeping and humanitarian operations. Article 34 empowers the Security Council to "investigate any dispute, or any situation which might lead to international friction or give rise to a dispute, in order to determine whether the continuance of the dispute or situation is likely to endanger the maintenance of international peace and security." Article 36 empowers the Security Council to, "at any stage of a dispute [the continuance of which is likely to endanger the maintenance of international peace and security] *or of a situation of like nature*, recommend appropriate procedures or methods of adjustment."[50] These two Articles can be vehicles for R2P and other humanitarian action by the Security Council, as they can be interpreted to protect a civilian population from risks associated with armed conflicts, atrocity crimes, humanitarian catastrophes, or natural disasters.

Much of what is required to protect civilian populations at risk can be achieved legally without resorting to Chapter VII, whether it be approved by the Security Council or by the General Assembly acting under the procedures of the *Uniting for Peace* Resolution. The veto power is more likely to be invoked by a Permanent Member of the Security Council when a military enforcement action under Chapter VII is under consideration, and that situation usually implies either the lack of consent by the targeted State or an anticipated combat

---

[49] In the midst of the Congo Crisis, Secretary-General Dag Hammarskjöld coined the term "Chapter VI 1/2" to describe peacekeeping operations whose methods lie between resolving disputes peacefully and more forceful action. *See* U.N. Secretary-General, *Question Considered by the Security Council at its 749th and 750th Meetings held on 30 October 1956: Second and Final Rep. of the Secretary-General on the Plan for an Emergency International United Nations Force Requested in the Resolution Adopted by the General Assembly on 4 November 1956 (A/3276)*, U.N. Doc. A/ 3302 (Nov. 6, 1956); *Guide for Participants in Peace, Stability, and Relief Operations*, U.S. INST. PEACE, https://www.usip.org/guide-participants-peace-stability-and-relief-operations; *see also* Berdal, *supra* note 48, at 179–82; Durall, *supra* note 47, at 5.

[50] U.N. Charter art. 36 (emphasis added).

scenario requiring enforcement rather than peacekeeping action. In contrast, a U.N. peacekeeping operation authorized under "Chapter VI½" can defuse much of the political jeopardy a Permanent Member might face, particularly when the targeted country is an ally of the Permanent Member. Where host state consent can be obtained for the introduction of a peacekeeping operation, the central mission of which is the protection of civilians trapped in the middle of an actual or threatened armed conflict, then R2P can be a workable initiative under such Charter authority. The peacekeeping option therefore should be explored more proactively as an initial option in the context of R2P and humanitarian emergencies.

We recognize the disillusion, indeed despair, with U.N. peacekeeping that infused the Balkans conflict of the early 1990s and Rwanda in 1994. But we present this point in the belief that more pragmatic deployment of U.N. peacekeeping forces, including proactive rules of engagement that aim at effective defensive and protective measures, is possible.

Importantly, host state consent for the introduction of peacekeeping operations is not technically required under the U.N. Charter. The preference for state consent is a political condition that arose in the formulation of peacekeeping operations more than a half-century ago as it was being derived from Chapter VI authority.[51] Granted, one might interpret Article 2(7) of the U.N. Charter[52] as anticipating such consent if the military operation is not authorized as an enforcement action under Chapter VII, but that interpretation would require a further determination that atrocity crimes decimating a civilian population or some other humanitarian calamity endangering the lives of a large population remain strictly within the domestic jurisdiction of the relevant State. That would be a rebuttable determination,[53] thus enabling the Security Council or the General Assembly to authorize a peacekeeping operation under Chapter VI (if not an enforcement action under Chapter VII) designed strictly to address a humanitarian situation that is *not* solely within the domestic jurisdiction of the relevant State.

---

[51] U.S. INST. PEACE, *supra* note 49. *See also* Berdal, *supra* note 48, at 178–82; BRIAN D. LEPARD, RETHINKING HUMANITARIAN INTERVENTION: A FRESH LEGAL APPROACH BASED ON FUNDAMENTAL ETHICAL PRINCIPLES IN INTERNATIONAL LAW AND WORLD RELIGIONS (2002).

[52] U.N. Charter art. 2, ¶ 7 ("Nothing contained in the present Charter shall authorize the United Nations to intervene in matters which are essentially within the domestic jurisdiction of any state or shall require the Members to submit such matters to settlement under the present Charter; but this principle shall not prejudice the application of enforcement measures under Chapter VII.").

[53] For an analysis of what constitutes "domestic jurisdiction" under Article 2(7), *see* Kawser Ahmed, *The Domestic Jurisdiction Clause in the United Nations Charter: A Historical View*, 10 SING. Y.B. INT'L L. & CONTRIBUTORS 175 (2006).

Given the character of so many conflicts in modern times, where large segments of a State's territory may be under the control of one or more rebel or terrorist groups or the territory lacks effective governance in the wake of a natural disaster, the introduction of a U.N. peacekeeping force whose mission is strictly the protection of a civilian population should not necessarily require central government consent. Part of what would dissuade U.N. approval in the absence of state consent is the risk of subjecting U.N. peacekeepers to combat situations which they may not be adequately trained or equipped to repel and which would threaten their original R2P mission to protect the civilian population. By definition, however, such protection could involve defending against armed attacks on civilians. If peacekeeping forces are well trained and equipped for risky defensive operations and available in a timely manner for such missions authorized by the Security Council or the General Assembly, then some of the presumptions about limitations on peacekeeping operations may become less plausible. We discuss below how this could come to pass.

4. Article 43 Standby Forces

Ensuring that Member States of the Security Council or the General Assembly (acting under the *Uniting for Peace* Resolution) have the collective political will to act under either Chapter VI or Chapter VII authority to protect civilian populations can depend on whether suitable armed forces are available quickly enough to be deployed into the targeted territory and perform either as peacekeepers prepared for the defense of civilian populations or as combat forces prepared for offensive operations. The United Nations suffers from what might be described as "deployment fatigue" by the major military powers and many other governments, namely a resistance to committing well-equipped forces of sufficient number, talent, and training to undertake the necessary military operations of protective, defensive, or offensive character for the task at hand. Indeed, while the top five funders of peacekeeping operations in 2013–15 were the United States, Japan, France, Germany, and the United Kingdom, most of the operations were staffed by troops drawn from Bangladesh, India, and Pakistan.[54] There is no automaticity to the availability of forces. Officials, including the Secretary-General, in the U.N. Secretariat are reduced to telephoning and otherwise contacting prospective contributing governments for troops for each peacekeeping and

---

[54] Danielle Renwick, *Peace Operations in Africa: How are Peace Operations Staffed and Funded?*, COUNCIL ON FOREIGN REL. (May 15, 2015), https://www.cfr.org/backgrounder/peace-operations-africa.

peace enforcement operation and then awaiting highly problematic and often tardy responses from capitals. Meanwhile, a civilian population enduring atrocity crimes or terrorist assaults or a natural disaster suffers grievous hardship and losses, all because the United Nations cannot react quickly enough or with sufficient forces because Member States are unwilling or incapable of deploying military forces for the sake of U.N. objectives.[55]

The difficulties encountered in staffing U.N. peacekeeping and enforcement operations have a direct bearing on the legality of using force for humanitarian objectives. Without sufficient forces of properly trained and equipped soldiers for U.N. operations, nations may resort to unauthorized operations with their own forces or with coalition forces if there exists the political will. The legality of such operations will be called into question, and other legal rationales will seek to legitimize the use of armed force in connection with humanitarian imperatives. (Indeed, we will explore two of them shortly.) Since the legality of U.N. peacekeeping or enforcement actions should withstand scrutiny under international law, there would be added value in arranging affairs so that the prospects of timely U.N.-authorized actions are strengthened with highly trained and immediately deployable armed forces (as well as law enforcement personnel). That was the original intent of the framers of the U.N. Charter, namely that military forces be available on standby for U.N.-authorized operations.

The U.N. Charter explicitly provides for such force availability in Article 43, which still remains dormant seventy years later but, if activated, could energize the entire spectrum of R2P and humanitarian intervention theory and practice. Article 43 reads in full:

1. All Members of the United Nations, in order to contribute to the maintenance of international peace and security, undertake to make available to the Security Council, on its call and in accordance with a special agreement or agreements, armed forces, assistance, and facilities, including rights of passage, necessary for the purpose of maintaining international peace and security.
2. Such agreement or agreements shall govern the numbers and types of forces, their degree of readiness and general location, and the nature of the facilities and assistance to be provided.

---

[55] An early treatment of this issue and the efforts to build some standby capabilities at the United Nations appears in David J. Scheffer, *United Nations Peace Operations and Prospects for a Standby Force*, 28 CORNELL INT'L L.J. 649 (1995).

3. The agreement or agreements shall be negotiated as soon as possible on the initiative of the Security Council. They shall be concluded between the Security Council and Members or between the Security Council and groups of Members and shall be subject to ratification by the signatory states in accordance with their respective constitutional processes.

The requirement to negotiate agreements with Member States or groups of Member States provides for enormous latitude in how such armed forces are to be made available, particularly on short notice, to fulfill U.N. peacekeeping or enforcement requirements. Since no such agreement has ever been negotiated, the field is wide open to test the system and see if governments are willing to establish procedures and capabilities in advance of humanitarian emergencies, including those under R2P where atrocity crimes are committed against civilian populations, so that effective action can be taken under U.N. legal authority. Ideally, the Security Council would be able to enter into negotiations for such agreements with voting guided by U.N. Charter Article 27(2), which provides that, "Decisions of the Security Council on procedural matters shall be made by an affirmative vote of nine members." The initiation and conduct of negotiations, already sanctioned by Article 43, thus would be viewed as procedural in character and avoid the prospect of blockage by veto. We realize that the prospects of categorizing such a vote as being only procedural in nature would be slim.[56] But there is nothing to lose, and possibly much to gain, by testing the proposition.

The final conclusion of an Article 43 agreement between the Security Council and any Member State or group of Member States undoubtedly would be a substantive decision under Article 27(3) and thus subject to the veto power of the Permanent Members. It may make some difference that a Permanent Member of the Security Council need not enter into an Article 43 agreement itself with the Council, thus insulating such Permanent Member from any force commitments to peacekeeping or enforcement operations. Any negotiated Article 43 agreement involving a Permanent Member of the Security Council or any other U.N. Member State likely would leave to the discretion of the national government whether, in any particular situation or

---

[56] See 3 Repertory of Practice of United Nations Organs, art. 27 (Supp. Nos. 7–9, 1985–1988, 1995–1999), http://legal.un.org/repertory/art27.shtml (listing examples of procedural votes as being related to inserting, ordering, removing, or deferring items on the agenda and adjourning a meeting; and listing nonprocedural votes as those arising from matters considered by the Council under its responsibility for the maintenance of international peace and security).

request for force contributions by the U.N. Secretariat, that government would provide armed forces. For certain governments, the value of the Article 43 agreement might be no more than ensuring that planning has occurred to identify those military contingents, equipment stockpiles, or airlift capabilities that would be available for timely deployment or use if the government so determines, on a case-by-case basis, when a specific request is made.

If a meaningful number of Article 43 agreements could be negotiated and concluded with the Security Council, then the prospects would improve greatly for effective action once the Security Council or the General Assembly under the *Uniting for Peace* Resolution determines that a response is required under R2P or another humanitarian emergency. The negotiating initiative required by Article 43(3) could be triggered by one Security Council member seeking a (possibly procedural?) vote to launch the initiative and, like RN2V, it could be bolstered by an appeal for such action to Council members joined by a significant number of U.N. Member States. Such an initiative doubtless would take many years to implement but it could set the stage for more effective deployments of military forces under U.N. authorization, which itself would be incentivized because of the availability of standby forces, and for the use of such forces to meet humanitarian objectives arising from either atrocity crimes or other causes.

Each of the U.N. Charter initiatives described above could stand on its own as a means to undertake or facilitate the launching of lawful military interventions under U.N. authority, and to do so in a manner that improves upon the current situation whereby civilian populations remain at dire risk because of the failure of the Security Council and the General Assembly to exercise their Charter powers. Taken together, these four initiatives would provide a powerful basis for U.N.-authorized action when humanitarian crises arise.

B. *Paradigm #2: Expanding the Legal Theory of Collective Self-Defense*

The narrow and constrained character of R2P invites a new inquiry into the doctrine of humanitarian intervention. What could be a legitimate basis, still grounded in the U.N. Charter but also customary international law, to enable a more effective application of the use of military force in the face of humanitarian debacles, whether driven by atrocity crimes or by other repressive assaults or natural calamities? We examined the previously cited Article 2(7) of the U.N. Charter in this context. In our view, a reexamination of Articles 2(4) and 51 of the U.N. Charter also could point to a fresh understanding of how military force can be justified in the context of modern realities.

The conventional interpretation of Article 2(4) of the U.N. Charter typically envisages a cross-border armed attack by a foreign military force against the territory or political independence of a Member State. Article 2(4) reads: "All Members shall refrain in their international relations from the threat or use of force against the territorial integrity or political independence of any state, or in any other manner inconsistent with the Purposes of the United Nations." Is the use of force to rescue a civilian population at risk, to protect it from actual or near-certain atrocity crimes on a mass scale, to ensure its survival against all odds – considered to be a use of force *against* the territorial integrity or political independence of a State that is contrary to the "Purposes of the United Nations?" The use of force by one or more foreign powers might preserve the territorial integrity or political independence of a State by stabilizing the survival of a civilian population.

Indeed, any authentic humanitarian operation should be structured with the sole objective of responding to the threat to the civilian population, and thus not jeopardize a State's territorial integrity through permanent military occupation, annexation, or otherwise. Nor should the objective be to change or overthrow the government of the State where the civilian population is at risk in such a manner that would challenge the political independence of the State. The Libyan experience of 2011 notwithstanding, the law should be resilient enough to reinforce the humanitarian limitations of R2P for future implementation or, in the alternative, invite an interpretation of Article 2(4) that addresses the modern realities of what literally constitutes an armed attack, what exposes territorial integrity to the needs of humanity and the interest of the international community, and how humanitarian interventions need not be an armed attack on the political independence of a State.

Granted, these are difficult conditions to honor without raising deep suspicions about true political intent in launching a military intervention on a targeted State's territory solely to protect and even rescue a civilian population at severe risk. But the doctrine of humanitarian intervention has long been premised on a gamble, namely that the intention remains true to the sole objective of saving many lives in a manner that is limited, effective, focused, and implemented in accordance with the laws of war and international humanitarian law. Where the gamble implodes on the intervening power, and objectives and actions veer off course from the original intent of humanitarian rescue, the law remains available to condemn and, when possible, discipline the offending State. But if legal theorists are confined to rules and principles that only work by virtue of inaction – so as to avoid any risk of illegal conduct – then that may create a secure legal paradigm for state conduct but it ignores the reality of human suffering.

Humanitarian intervention based upon such a modern interpretation of Article 2(4) of the U.N. Charter need not stand alone, however. Article 51 of the Charter reads:

> Nothing in the present Charter shall impair the inherent right of individual or collective self-defence if an armed attack occurs against a Member of the United Nations, until the Security Council has taken measures necessary to maintain international peace and security. Measures taken by Members in the exercise of this right of self-defence shall be immediately reported to the Security Council and shall not in any way affect the authority and responsibility of the Security Council under the present Charter to take at any time such action as it deems necessary in order to maintain or restore international peace and security.[57]

Notably, no explicit distinction is made between an external or internal armed attack in the wording of Article 51. Nor is "armed attack" associated with the "State" even though a conventional understanding of "a Member of the United Nations" would point toward the "State." The admittedly unconventional reading would be to see in the "Member of the United Nations" its human dimension, namely a large civilian population that is the target of an "armed attack" either from within or outside the borders of the country. The *travaux préparatoires* of the Charter would not reveal such an interpretation of "a Member of the United Nations," but we suggest a more sophisticated understanding of the term as it relates to this core dimension of a Member State's identity – its civilian population within its borders.

Furthermore, circumstances can arise (indeed often have arisen) whereby a neighboring or nearby country is seriously impacted by a humanitarian situation that results in cross-border waves of tens or hundreds of thousands, or even millions, of refugees; the infiltration of foreign militia and terrorists; the introduction of epidemic diseases; and unsustainable stresses on the economic stability, food stocks, or fresh water supplies of the country.[58] If the source of such cross-border events is armed conflict directed against a civilian

---

[57] For background, see YORAM DINSTEIN, WAR, AGGRESSION AND SELF-DEFENCE (5th ed. 2011).

[58] Syrian refugees have fled to Lebanon (1,048,275), Turkey (over 3,000,000), Jordan (over 636,482), Iraq (245,022), Egypt & North Africa (117,658), and Greece. *ECHO FACTSHEET: SYRIA CRISIS*, HUMANITARIAN AID & CIVIL PROT., EUR. COMM'N (May 2016), http://ec .europa.eu/echo/files/aid/countries/factsheets/syria_en.pdf; P.J. Tobia, *The Worst Humanitarian Crisis Since World War II*, PBS NEWSHOUR (July 29, 2015), www.pbs.org/ newshour/updates/worst-humanitarian-crisis-since-world-war-ii/; *Greece: Humanitarian Crisis Mounts as Refugee Support System Pushed to Breaking Point*, AMNESTY INT'L (June 25, 2015), www.amnesty.org/en/latest/news/2015/06/greece-humanitarian-crisis-mounts-as-refugee-support-system-pushed-to-breaking-point/.

population on the target State's territory, whether that armed attack is generated from within or outside the State's borders, then that attack should be seen as an indirect but very real armed attack against the victim nation (assuming it is not the aggressor nation as well).

A civilian population forcibly displaced by atrocity crimes or just a straightforward armed attack on such civilians will project that armed attack onto foreign territory when the humanitarian crisis follows such refugees across the border. The country under such threats and pressures could invoke the right of individual self-defense under Article 51 of the U.N. Charter to take proportionate and critical measures to protect its own people and its own territory from such consequences of a humanitarian crisis. Such measures might include the need to militarily intervene on the foreign target territory to repel the perpetrating military force responsible for the armed attack on the civilian population. The purpose of such intervention would be to prevent further actions that would only exacerbate the humanitarian threat to both the civilian population of the target country and the security (in all its dimensions) of the victim State.

Thus, any such action in self-defense would have to address the core problem giving rise to the humanitarian crisis so that the civilian population under threat in the target country is not abandoned. If a nation uses the right of self-defense only to protect its own people and territory by intervening on foreign territory to end the threat, but then fails to protect the very civilian population whose plight is threatened on the territory of the target country, then there may well be nothing humanitarian in such an act of self-defense and it will have to rest on other legal principles of self-defense to be considered a legally justifiable action.

Another circumstance could arise whereby the victim nation seeks the aid of one or more other nations to undertake the type of humanitarian intervention described above. That possibility could arise as an act of collective self-defense under Article 51. This would enable the victim nation or nations to join in a coalition of nations whose military forces would be justified to intervene, jointly or individually, to end the armed attack giving rise to the humanitarian crisis. (It could be, of course, that the victim nation seeks assistance from only one other country which then might be the only nation launching the humanitarian intervention. This would still constitute a request under collective self-defense.) Consider for example Turkey, which is experiencing a massive flow of Syrian refugees who are fleeing from armed attacks in Syria. If Turkey were to request assistance under collective self-defense from its NATO allies or from other nations, then a humanitarian intervention onto Syrian territory under a coalition banner requested by

Turkey should satisfy Article 51 requirements. In reality, the call for collective self-defense has not yet occurred, but with Turkish consent, NATO (which includes Turkey) approved American and British air power being projected along with Turkish air power from Turkish territory against the Islamic State and other targets in Syria absent Security Council authorization.[59] Regardless of whether the Turkish government ever articulates the words "collective self-defense" in permitting such multinational military assistance, the point remains that the Turkish situation fits a model of collective self-defense that could be interpreted as legitimate under Article 51, although it would require a report to the Security Council.

One further application of collective self-defense would require a bolder interpretation of Article 51, but it merits some consideration. The armed attack identified in Article 51 is described as an armed attack against a "Member of the United Nations," which in reality is sometimes an armed attack against a portion of the civilian population of the Member State. Could such a civilian population that is under attack request assistance from other nations to come to its rescue and defense? Principles of self-defense, either individual or collective, should not be relegated only to governments, and certainly not to the benefit of an aggressor nation or one that is attacking its own civilian population. There are precedents for such pleas for survival assistance, including from the Kurds in northern Iraq during the Gulf War, the Tutsis during the Rwandan genocide of 1994, isolated Muslim populations in Bosnia and Herzegovina during the Balkans conflict of the early 1990s, the people of East Timor in 1999, the Kosovo-Albanian population in 1999, and the Muslim tribes of Darfur during the early 2000s.

It may appear unorthodox to view such pleas for military intervention to save civilian lives as "collective self-defense," but we would argue that is precisely what the situation becomes, namely, a significant component of the State (a portion of its civilian population) reaches out for assistance when it comes under attack by its own government, or by militia or rebels when the government cannot or will not come to its aid, to protect the population. Indeed, in the modern realities of multi-party state and non-state military engagements that are not necessarily, indeed rarely, interstate armed conflicts, Article 51 would be rendered mostly irrelevant if it were not interpreted to reflect those situations that truly require the right of self-defense in the twenty-

---

[59] Robin Emmott & Nick Tattersall, *NATO Backs Turkey on Islamic State, Some Urge Peace with Kurds*, REUTERS (July 28, 2015), www.reuters.com/article/2015/07/28/us-mideast-crisis-turkey-nato-idUSKCN0Q20RQ20150728. Of course, the use of Turkish air power against Kurdish militants in this context raises other disturbing questions.

first century. The inherent right of self-defense under customary international law likewise would become archaic if it did not evolve in this direction.

Applying the right of collective self-defense to the plight of civilian populations might well invite misuse by minority populations that should be seeking peaceful means to resolve disputes with the central government. But where the level of violence against the population reaches egregious levels, including when atrocity crimes are being inflicted upon the population, then the right under Article 51 should be available. It would be implausible to create a precise definition of when the line would be crossed into the realm of a legitimate appeal by a civilian population for collective self-defense, including who would be the rightful individual or group within that population to articulate such an appeal. But the U.N. Charter never was designed to answer those questions and should not be held to such a high standard of definitional character. We take the world as it is, and that includes the stark realities of civilian populations struggling for their own survival. Either the U.N. Charter can be relevant and implemented under those circumstances or its value will be greatly diminished.

C. *Paradigm #3: The Exhaustion Principle*

If one combines R2P procedures, what the U.N. Charter offers within its own codified provisions, and a modern interpretation of the right of self-defense – all examined above – there remains the final frontier of legal reasoning for the use of military force for humanitarian purposes of the most critical nature. As discussed in Scheffer's 1992 article, *Toward a Modern Doctrine of Humanitarian Intervention*, and by the bodies examining the issues of humanitarian intervention and R2P prior to the World Summit Outcome Document of 2005, the stage can be reached where no legal procedure or theory has been successfully used while tens or hundreds of thousands of civilians are in dire peril if not at the gates of their own extermination. We know from past experience that the inaction of the international community creates the worst possible outcome – Syria since 2011, Darfur in the early 2000s, Srebrenica in 1995, Rwanda in 1994, and Cambodia in the late 1970s. The world stands aside and the demise of a significant portion of a distinct population continues, unabated. The entire Genocide Prevention Movement, including the prevention of other atrocity crimes, of the last two decades seeks to conquer the risks of inaction.[60] So what is to be done?

---

[60] *See, e.g.*, Stephen Pomper, *Update on Atrocity Prevention Strategy Implementation*, WHITE HOUSE (May 1, 2013), www.whitehouse.gov/blog/2013/05/01/update-atrocity-prevention-strategy-

Timing is everything in human calamities, whether they are caused by armed attacks or by natural disasters. One can map out the procedural and institutional means of confronting such situations with great precision and in full compliance with longstanding principles of international law. But those procedures, and the limitations of the codified law, can fail in their implementation. They can take so long to comply with that the humanitarian consequences already will have occurred, making any legally proper action irrelevant to the needs of the population at risk.[61]

The proper adherence to procedural requirements under any of the theories set forth previously may be diligently followed at the Security Council among governments interested in protecting the population at risk. Such action may indeed result in effective responses to the crisis. Collective security might work. But that may not be the outcome. There may be an exhaustion of procedures that occurs without the kind of result that will save large numbers of human beings at risk of atrocity crimes, of direct armed attack, and/or of forcible displacement.

When that moment of definitive inaction arrives and the humanitarian situation has reached intolerable, indeed immoral, dimensions, then unilateral or multilateral military action to save a civilian population should find some justification in international law. We recognize that any nation taking military action under these circumstances runs a considerable risk that its intervention will be criticized as illegal because it has no codified basis in international law. But this would be a political decision only partly influenced by strict legality. If the doctrine of humanitarian intervention has any lasting content, it has to embrace the situation where procedural steps have been exhausted and unauthorized intervention has become the last resort. We call this the "exhaustion principle" that ideally should be rare in practice but nonetheless available to cover a situation of last resort. Realistically, given the potential for humanitarian crises to erupt rapidly, sometimes within hours or days, the exhaustion principle may arise within a short period of time. Any nation or group of nations acting upon the exhaustion principle would have to take the risk that its actions will be severely criticized and perhaps condemned as constituting a violation of international law. But there also would be the possibility, perhaps probability, that nations will be willing to acquiesce in

---

implementation; *Preventing Genocide*, UNITED TO END GENOCIDE, http://endgenocide.org/learn/preventing-future-genocides/; ENOUGH PROJECT: THE PROJECT TO END GENOCIDE AND CRIMES AGAINST HUMANITY (Mar. 2, 2016), www.enoughproject.org/.

[61] Syria is a prime example. *See* sources cited *supra* note 28.

favor of the moral imperative to save the civilian population from near certain injury and death.

The following factors should exist when the exhaustion principle has occurred and the political decision to act must happen quickly to save a population at risk:

(1) In a situation involving atrocity crimes, R2P principles, including non-military and military options, have been attempted, bearing in mind that the timeline required for action may make some R2P options, particularly non-military ones, implausible or futile. The effort under R2P to obtain Security Council authorization for a military intervention would have failed. In a situation not involving atrocity crimes but some other humanitarian calamity, every effort has been made to obtain Security Council authorization under Chapter VII of the U.N. Charter for a military intervention, and such efforts would have failed.

(2) No act of individual self-defense has arisen to solve the problem and no request for assistance under the Article 51 or customary law principle of collective self-defense has been made, or if made has not elicited any effective response.

(3) Efforts should be made to obtain regional or other multilateral organizational approval for the military intervention, time permitting, so that a coalition of nations responds to the humanitarian crisis rather than a unilateral response of one nation's military forces.

(4) There are credible grounds to believe that the military intervention will have a beneficial outcome for the population at risk, leaving the human rights, health, and habitable situation for that population in better condition than if no intervention were to be undertaken.

(5) The intervention remains narrowly focused on the plight of the civilian population at risk so that the political independence and territorial integrity of the targeted nation will be fully restored, if possible.[62]

(6) Once the safety and well-being of the civilian population is ensured and their security stabilized, foreign forces must be withdrawn as quickly as feasible.

All of these factors can and should be heavily caveated with political, economic, social, and military realities that assuredly arise with any such situation. For example, it may be that the tyranny of a particular regime unleashing atrocity crimes upon its own population, or significant portion thereof, will

---

[62] Scheffer, *Modern Doctrine, supra* note 15, at 290–92.

mean that a humanitarian intervention will have to confront the regime itself, with unpredictable consequences, if that population under attack is to survive. We do not underestimate the challenge these factors and realities pose for the rule of law in terms of the use of force for the survival of populations at risk.

All of this might suggest a fourth paradigm that clearly identifies the right of humanitarian intervention as modern customary international law super- seding conventional interpretations of the U.N. Charter. We refrain from reaching that conclusion even though we see sands shifting in that direction. Our hope is that the analysis in this Chapter invites dynamic and innovative thinking about how the U.N. Charter can be more pragmatically complied with in the context of twenty-first century realities, particularly the humanitar- ian crises driven by atrocity crimes.

IV. CONCLUSION AND A CAUTIONARY NOTE ABOUT THE CRIME OF AGGRESSION

Much further inquiry and discussion is required to sort out this normative challenge for international law. We do not underestimate the constitutional challenges that could arise in how the U.N. Charter is interpreted and followed if our views were to take hold. Nonetheless, if Security Council Resolution 2249 is any indication, the time appears ripe for giving rebirth to a doctrine of humanitarian intervention that falls within the parameters of international law. We must continue to make the effort because humanitarian crises demanding action will continue, and a methodology must exist that permits effective and normatively sound responses by the United Nations and concerned States. We have set forth several paradigms, two of which rest upon firm U.N. Charter principles for their implementation.

The first paradigm looks at four U.N. Charter provisions and practices – the possibility of a political agreement to effectively overcome the veto power held by the Permanent Members of the Security Council when humanitarian crises arise, reactivating the *Uniting for Peace* Resolution, resorting more frequently to U.N. peacekeeping forces and "Chapter VI½" authority for humanitarian action, and negotiating Article 43 standby force agreements between nations and the Security Council. The second paradigm explores a more pragmatic and hence expansive interpretation of the Article 51 and customary law right of individual and collective self-defense. Both offer the advantage of working within established U.N. Charter law and procedure and can build upon one another in various configurations of implementation.

The third paradigm reaches beyond conventional U.N. Charter theory to recognize what we term as the "exhaustion principle," namely a situation where U.N. Charter procedures are exhausted and the humanitarian situation remains dire. A military intervention, launched onto foreign territory where the humanitarian crisis is erupting but U.N. Charter authorization (literal or interpretative) remains absent, is a gamble under the law. It may, however, eventually find a basis in customary international law where human rights principles can influence the morality, if not legality, of the initiative, thereby leading to the acquiescence of other nations.

These paradigms may establish the basis for a new doctrine of humanitarian intervention in the twenty-first century. One can envisage all of them working together as a framework for action. Where one paradigm may fail in a particular situation, another paradigm might replace it depending on the circumstances of the humanitarian peril and the all-important question, "If not now, when?"[63]

We express, however, serious caution about how to advance the law in this area in light of the crime of aggression arising from the Rome Statute of the International Criminal Court (with its definitional and procedural factors agreed to in Kampala in 2010 and with the number of ratifications achieving the required number of thirty States Parties in 2016 for the crime to become operational for investigative and prosecutorial purposes).[64] The definitions for the crime of aggression and an act of aggression set forth in Article 8*bis* of the Rome Statute of the International Criminal Court do not envisage the legality of humanitarian interventions falling outside of Security Council authorization under Chapter VII unless one occurs squarely within the inherent right of self-defense without triggering a manifest violation of the U.N. Charter.[65]

---

[63] Primo Levi, If Not Now, When? (1995).

[64] Amendments to the Rome Statute of the International Criminal Court, Adoption of Amendments on the Crime of Aggression (Nov. 29, 2010), https://treaties.un.org/doc/Publication/CN/2010/CN.651.2010-Eng.pdf; Review Conference of the Rome Statute of the International Criminal Court, *The Crime of Aggression*, Res. RC/Res.6 (June 11, 2010), https://asp.icc-cpi.int/iccdocs/asp_docs/Resolutions/RC-Res.6-ENG.pdf; *see also* David Scheffer, *The Crime of Aggression, in* Beyond Kampala: Next Steps for U.S. Principled Engagement with the International Criminal Court 87 (Rachel Gore ed., 2010); David Scheffer, *The Complex Crime of Aggression Under the Rome Statute*, 23 Leiden J. Int'l L. 897 (2010); David Scheffer, *States Parties Approve New Crimes for International Criminal Court*, ASIL Insights (June 22, 2010), www.asil.org/insights/volume/14/issue/16/states-parties-approve-new-crimes-international-criminal-court.

[65] For an examination of the interface between humanitarian intervention and the crime of aggression, see Trahan, *supra* note 4, at 42–80; *see also* Davis Brown, *Why the Crime of Aggression Will Not Reduce the Practice of Aggression*, 51 Int'l Pol. 648 (2014) ("[N]o longer does a state assert a right to invade and annex other states without asserting good cause such as historical territorial claims and self-determination (or specious claims of self-defense or humanitarian intervention).").

The introduction of the crime of aggression to the Rome Statute thus may create a new and daunting disincentive for any nation considering how it might respond to a serious humanitarian situation that is a compelling one for military intervention. There will be some countries that will not be subject to the International Criminal Court's scrutiny of their leaders for the crime of aggression. They will be non-party States and States Parties that have opted out of liability for the crime. But for those countries that ratify the amendment for the crime of aggression and embrace its coverage, the prospect of persuading such governments to step up to the challenge of a military intervention for humanitarian purposes likely will be undercut by the Rome Statute's operational coverage of aggression.

One way to overcome this problem would be to amend the Rome Statute's definition of an "act of aggression" so that it explicitly excludes "acts that are in exercise of the right of self-defense under Article 51 of the Charter of the United Nations or of the responsibility to protect under United Nations General Assembly resolution 60/1 (XXIX)(¶¶ 138–139) of 24 October 2005."[66] Although this would not cover the exhaustion principle, at least it would undeniably recognize the legality of self-defense and R2P grounds for a forcible humanitarian intervention and thus exclude individual criminal responsibility from the normative framework of the crime of aggression when armed force is used for these purposes.[67]

---

[66] Of course, a legitimate act of self-defense under Article 51 of the U.N. Charter would not be a manifest violation of the U.N. Charter and thus should be a self-evident means under the Kampala Amendment on aggression to address a humanitarian crisis that merits self-defense. It would prove helpful, however, to explicitly state the right of self-defense in order to remove any ambiguity that could slow down effective responses constituting humanitarian interventions that are undertaken as genuine acts of self-defense.

[67] *See* David Scheffer, *Amending the Crime of Aggression Under the Rome Statute, in* THE CRIME OF AGGRESSION: A COMMENTARY 1480 (Claus Kreß & Stephan Barriga eds., 2017).

19

The Presumption of Peace

Illegal War, Human Rights, and Humanitarian Law

MARY ELLEN O'CONNELL

I. INTRODUCTION

On September 11, 2015, world headlines were focused on people fleeing war rather than the anniversary of terrorist attacks in the United States fourteen years earlier. In Europe, men, women, and children were drowning, suffocating, and freezing in desperate attempts to escape civil wars in Africa, the Middle East, and South Asia. No greater proof could be provided of the urgent need for peace. Yet, instead of seeking to enhance the capacity of law and diplomacy to prevent and end armed conflict, some experts in militarily powerful States were arguing for interpretations of law and moral principle permitting more war, not less. These experts sought relaxation of the rules restricting resort to military force or the right to follow wartime rules governing killing and detention to peacetime situations.[1] Their positions may well be based on a sincerely held belief that military force is the most effective way to respond to terrorism, dictatorial regimes, and other causes of insecurity. Prominent ethicists are making a similar case for expanding resort to war for similar reasons. Yet, in the words of a former British diplomat, "governments' failed attempts to impose order by force are themselves the source of disorder."[2]

In the search for bold action in the face of serious challenges, it can be overlooked that war is in fact the cause of tragedy not the solution. Protecting human lives and the natural environment from the ravages of war can best be accomplished by promoting restrictions on force and peaceful resolution of conflict. The contemporary civil wars in Syria, Iraq, Libya, Afghanistan,

---

[1] *See infra.*
[2] Ross Carne, *Chilcot Report: How Tony Blair Sold the War*, N.Y. TIMES (July 6, 2016), http://nyti.ms/29zllMg.

Congo, Burundi, and elsewhere are feeding the flood of migrants. These wars need resolution not escalation through foreign military intervention. It will be argued here that however understandable the calls for greater military force may be, war is rarely the answer. Fostering understanding and respect for law and even expanding restrictions to prohibit civil war hold greater promise. The recent trend toward interpreting the scope of peacetime human rights protections to apply more broadly is an important counterpoint to war-expansion arguments.[3] Expanding human rights follows the plan of the World War II generation to save succeeding generations from the scourge of war through law and moral suasion. In fact, the whole body of international law is structured to move toward eliminating war. International humanitarian law rules that apply in war are designed to apply exceptionally in short-term emergencies. It is the body of human rights law that applies normally, as a matter of presumption. In any case of doubt, international law requires erring on the side of peace and peacetime law.

II. THE CURRENT DEBATE

In the effort to save succeeding generations from the scourge of war, the drafters of the 1945 United Nations Charter included a general prohibition on the use of any force as the central legal principle of the new organization. The Charter contains only two express exceptions to the Article 2(4) prohibition,[4] and they are narrow. Under Article 51, force may be used in individual or collective self-defense "if an armed attack occurs."[5] Under Articles 39–42, the U.N. Security Council has the power to authorize force to "restore inter-national peace and security."[6] In addition to these Charter rules, international

---

[3] *See infra.*

[4] U.N. Charter art. 2(4) ("All Members shall refrain in their international relations from the threat or use of force against the territorial integrity or political independence of any state, or in any other manner inconsistent with the Purposes of the United Nations.").

[5] U.N. Charter art. 51 ("Nothing in the present Charter shall impair the inherent right of individual or collective self-defence if an armed attack occurs against a member of the United Nations, until the Security Council has taken measures necessary to maintain international peace and security. Measures taken by members in the exercise of this right of self-defence shall be immediately reported to the Security Council and shall not in any way affect the authority and responsibility of the Security Council under the present Charter to take at any time such action as it deems necessary in order to maintain or restore international peace and security.").

[6] U.N. Charter art. 39 ("The Security Council shall determine the existence of any threat to the peace, breach of the peace, or act of aggression and shall make recommendations, or decide what measures shall be taken in accordance with Articles 41 and 42, to maintain or restore international peace and security.").

law further restricts the resort to force through important rules of customary international law and general principles. The term *"jus ad bellum"* is given to the combined restrictions from all sources, and under the *jus ad bellum*, virtually every first use of force by a State is unlawful. Non-state actors are not bound directly by the U.N. Charter but are, along with States, obligated to respect human rights, environmental protections, and territorial integrity, to name some of the subsets of rules relevant to regulating the use of force.

The use of force is not the same as armed conflict. Armed conflict is a particular type of force. Whether a use of force amounts to armed conflict is significant because certain fundamental rules are modified within an armed conflict. The legal definition of armed conflict is understandably narrow, so the legal changes triggered should be a rare occurrence. The most important rule that changes within an armed conflict is the protection of the human right to life. Within the restricted space of armed conflict, lawful combatants – members of a State's regular armed forces or associated militias[7] – have the combatant's privilege to kill. This means they may not be prosecuted for the deaths they cause so long as they comply with international humanitarian law principles and practices, including, most importantly, the norms of distinction, necessity, proportionality, precautions, and humanity.[8] These rules,

---

U.N. Charter art. 41 ("The Security Council may decide what measures not involving the use of armed force are to be employed to give effect to its decisions, and it may call upon the Members of the United Nations to apply such measures. These may include complete or partial interruption of economic relations and of rail, sea, air, postal, telegraphic, radio, and other means of communication, and the severance of diplomatic relations.").

U.N. Charter art. 42 ("Should the Security Council consider that measures provided for in Article 41 would be inadequate or have proved to be inadequate, it may take such action by air, sea, or land forces as may be necessary to maintain or restore international peace and security. Such action may include demonstrations, blockade, and other operations by air, sea, or land forces of Members of the United Nations.").

7 *See* Geneva Convention Relative to the Treatment of Prisoners of War art. 4, Aug. 12, 1949, 75 U.N.T.S. 135 [hereinafter Third Geneva Convention]; *see also* Protocol Additional to the Geneva Conventions of 12 August 1949, and Relating to the Protection of Victims of International Armed Conflicts arts. 43, 44 & 51, June 8, 1977, 1125 U.N.T.S. 3 [hereinafter Protocol I].

8 These norms are often described as within the category of customary international law. The better characterization is that they are general principles. This is because they are procedural in nature in that they moderate the way action is conducted, and they are not subject to change in the way that customary international law rules are. *See* Mary Ellen O'Connell, *Jus Cogens: International Law's Higher Ethical Norms, in* THE ROLE OF ETHICS IN INTERNATIONAL LAW 78 (Donald Earl Childress III ed., 2011). The International Court of Justice (ICJ) has indicated that the principle of civilian distinction may well be *jus cogens*, meaning it is a peremptory norm not subject to change through treaty or customary international law, among other attributes. *See* Jurisdictional Immunities of the State (Ger. v. It.: Greece intervening), Judgment, 2012 I.C.J. 99, ¶ 92 (Feb. 3) ("Assuming for this purpose that the rules of the law of

together with other rules relevant to conduct of conflict including restrictions on the means and methods of war, the remainder of international humanitarian law, and certain rules of international human rights law, are still known collectively as the *jus in bello*. The *jus in bello* applies most completely to international armed conflict and, to a lesser extent, to non-international armed conflict. The conduct rules are the same for States, even a State that has violated the *jus ad bellum*.[9]

The philosopher Jeff McMahan, however, has tried to argue that (1) there is no viable law on resort to force given his view that the *jus ad bellum* "is crude and simplistic," and (2) troops of a party to a conflict fighting consistently with just war analysis should have a different, more advantageous set of rules applicable to them compared with opponents who do not comply. What plainly matters for him is just war analysis in the fields of philosophy and theology.[10] The human rights scholar Rosa Brooks takes a similarly provocative position respecting the prevailing legal regime. She argues that there is no longer such thing as peacetime, only war. This means there is nothing identifiable as an initial resort to war – war is pervasive.[11] Consequently, there is no need for the *jus ad bellum*. On the other hand, there is a need, in her view, to fundamentally rethink international humanitarian and human rights law because this law is based on the existence of a war/peace distinction.

armed conflict which prohibit the murder of civilians in occupied territory, the deportation of civilian inhabitants to slave labour and the deportation of prisoners of war to slave labour are rules of *jus cogens*, there is no conflict between those rules and the rules on State immunity.") [hereinafter Jurisdictional Immunities Judgment]. *See also* O'Connell, Jus Cogens: *International Law's Higher Ethical Norms, supra.*

9   *See* Karl Thomas Jayaram Dannenbaum, Inextricable Accomplices, The Meaning of Fighting in an Illegal War and International Law's Dissonant Treatment of the Soldiers Forced to Do It ch. 7 (Fall 2014) (unpublished Ph.D. thesis, Princeton University) (on file with the author); Mary Ellen O'Connell, *Historical Development and Legal Basis, in* THE HANDBOOK OF INTERNATIONAL HUMANITARIAN LAW 101, 101–51 (Dieter Fleck ed., 3d ed. 2013).

10 *See* Jeff McMahan, *Laws of War, in* THE PHILOSOPHY OF INTERNATIONAL LAW 493, 496 (Samantha Besson & John Tasioulas eds., 2010). McMahan also cites Ingrid Detter for the proposition that the rules of the *jus ad bellum* are "obsolete." He takes Detter's reference out of context. She is not referring to the post-U.N. Charter *jus ad bellum*, but to the pre-Charter *jus ad bellum*, much of which did become obsolete with the adoption of the Charter, such as the rules on neutrality. *Id.* at 496 (citing INGRID DETTER, THE LAW OF WAR 157–58 (2d ed. 2000)).

11 Rosa Brooks, *There is No Such Thing as Peacetime*, FOREIGN POL'Y (Mar. 13, 2015), http://foreignpolicy.com/2015/03/13/theres-no-such-thing-as-peacetime-forever-war-terror-civil-liberties/. *See also* ROSA BROOKS, HOW EVERYTHING BECAME WAR AND THE MILITARY BECAME EVERYTHING: TALES FROM THE PENTAGON (2016).

Brooks advocates reworking all human rights and international humanitarian law in light of her conclusion that there is no peace.[12]

Both positions are unpersuasive as a matter of fact, law, and morality. Yet, Brooks and McMahan have reached large audiences and their views require a response. No State in the world takes the position today that the U.N. Charter is not binding. Moreover, despite the number of serious armed conflicts at present, most of the world is at peace. Each armed conflict has a discernible beginning when a party either violated the U.N. Charter, the right to life, or other rules. In situations where it may be uncertain whether fighting has developed into an armed conflict, international law errs on the side of peace, so that the full array of peacetime human rights, environmental protections, and other obligations apply. The fact that even some international lawyers seem unaware of the default to peace may be related to their interest in interpreting international law to permit certain militarily powerful States to use force at times prohibited under classic legal interpretation. In addition, certain human rights advocates take the view that armed conflict to respond to humanitarian crises is, if not lawful, then "legitimate."[13] The evidence that will be reviewed below does not support the advocacy of using military force for promoting human rights, regime change, or countering terrorism. Rather, promoting the classic *jus ad bellum* and *jus in bello* provides the greatest opportunity for protecting the right to life and the natural world.[14] This understanding is embedded in the principle of defaulting to peacetime rules.

---

[12] Yet another perspective on illegal war, international humanitarian and human rights law was seen following NATO's intervention in Kosovo in 1999. Some advocates of that intervention wanted States like the United States to follow a more cautious set of *jus in bello* rules. *See, e.g.,* Ove Bring, *International Humanitarian Law After Kosovo: Is the Lex Lata Sufficient?*, 78 INT'L L. STUD. 257 (Andru Wall ed., 2002). Gabriella Blum delivers a heavy critique of this view in Gabriella Blum, *On a Differential Law of War*, 52 HARV. INT'L L.J. 164 (2011). Blum, however, overlooks that those suggesting a higher standard are often those who advocate for illegal war. Using military force for humanitarian causes or counterterrorism without Security Council authorization violates the *jus ad bellum*. In pushing for the unlawful resort to war, these advocates realize they are sacrificing some people's human rights protected under the *jus ad bellum* to promote the rights of others. Blum fails to account for the fact that calls for a higher standard are thought of as a way to mitigate undermining the *jus ad bellum*. Interest in this view seems to have faded and will not be pursued here.

[13] The concept that "legitimacy" is an acceptable substitute for legality began with attempts to justify NATO's 1999 intervention in the Kosovo crisis. *See* INDEP. INT'L COMM'N ON KOSOVO, THE KOSOVO REPORT: CONFLICT, INTERNATIONAL RESPONSE, LESSONS LEARNED (2000).

[14] *See* William Schabas, Lex Specialis? *Belt and Suspenders? The Parallel Operation of Human Rights Law and the Law of Armed Conflict, and the Conundrum of Jus ad Bellum*, 40 ISR. L. REV. 592, 593 (2007).

III. THE HISTORY, REALITY, AND MORALITY OF THE *JUS AD BELLUM*

McMahan acknowledges that today's moral and legal principles on the use of force have intertwined origins.[15] Yet, he criticizes the "tendency to conflate . . . the laws of war and moral principles governing war."[16] In his view, the two areas currently "diverge in fundamental ways," so he proposes creating "the greatest possible congruence between law and morality" through "rigorous moral analysis and innovations in the design of new international legal institutions."[17] A brief review of the history of religious and moral principles relevant to armed conflict compared with the current rules on the use of force reveals that the congruence already exists. [18]

Stephen Neff has written that early Christians along with Confucians developed the concept that peace is the normal condition of human life and war the abnormal.[19] The Christian insistence on "the existence of a residual or background condition of peace in world affairs" was owing to "a powerful strain of radical pacifism inherent in Christian doctrine. . . ."[20] St. Ambrose and St. Augustine initiated the teaching that moved Christians away from radical pacifism to a position of accepting as necessary the limited use of force.[21] Augustine wrote:

> Peace should be the object of your desire; war should be waged only as a necessity and waged only that God may by it deliver men from the necessity and preserve them peace. For peace is not sought in order to [be] the kindling of war, but war is waged in order that peace may be obtained.[22]

St. Thomas Aquinas, writing in the thirteenth century, systematized Christian teaching on war into a set of law-like principles that famously included a declaration by a right authority, a just cause, and the right

---

[15] McMahan, *supra* note 10, at 493. *See also* STEPHEN C. NEFF, WAR AND THE LAW OF NATIONS: A GENERAL HISTORY (2005); WILHELM G. GREWE, THE EPOCHS OF INTERNATIONAL LAW 108–11 (Michael Byers trans. & rev., 2000); ARTHUR NUSSBAUM, A CONCISE HISTORY OF THE LAW OF NATIONS 35 (rev. ed. 1962).

[16] McMahan, *supra* note 10, at 493.

[17] *Id.* at 493–94.

[18] Mary Ellen O'Connell, *The Just War Tradition and International Law Against War: The Myth of Discordant Doctrines*, 35 J. SOC'Y CHRISTIAN ETHICS 33 (2015).

[19] NEFF, *supra* note 15, at 31, 39.

[20] *Id.* at 39–40.

[21] *Id.*

[22] LEON FRIEDMAN, THE LAW OF WAR: A DOCUMENTARY HISTORY 7 (1972).

intention on the part of the authority.[23] Aquinas's restrictions on resort to war are part of his wider, general view of the importance of human law in the flourishing of humanity. As Cathleen Kaveny explains, "in considering human law, he shows how it can lead men and women to virtue in order to promote the common good."[24]

Hugo Grotius, the renowned Dutch Protestant legal scholar, theologian, and diplomat, argued strenuously for law as the substitute for the Pope and the emperor. Grotius rejected the thinking of those, like Alberico Gentili, who wanted to leave each prince supreme in his own realm, relying on his own conscience as to the just cause of war.[25] For Grotius, resort to war could be judged against objective standards as he argued in his seminal work, *On the Law of War and Peace*.[26] He wanted to help end the Thirty Years' War and mitigate its barbarism. He wanted to inspire greater humanity in the conduct of the war and encourage the establishment of a legal order superior to the warring factions after the war. A group of legally coequal sovereign States did in fact emerge in Western Europe under the treaties known as the Peace of Westphalia.[27]

In many accounts of the nineteenth and early twentieth centuries, it is thought that the rise of positivism and the concept of absolute state sovereignty meant the end of legal restraint on force.[28] This view is based on an understanding of the prevailing theory, not on the actual historic record of state practice. Scholars and government officials in Europe as well as North and South America continued to recognize the Just War Doctrine.[29] Few European governments ever failed to justify the use of force in terms of some lawful end. Natural law explained why just war principles bound sovereigns. Positive sources of law in the form of treaties and customary international law existed, but general principles of international law and international law's

---

[23] GREWE, *supra* note 15, at 109.

[24] CATHLEEN KAVENY, LAW'S VIRTUES: FOSTERING AUTONOMY AND SOLIDARITY IN AMERICAN SOCIETY 29 (2012).

[25] *See* MARY ELLEN O'CONNELL, THE POWER AND PURPOSE OF INTERNATIONAL LAW ch.1 (2008).

[26] For example, Grotius holds that a party may lawfully resort to war for only a short, concrete list of causes, most prominently, self-defense. HUGO GROTIUS, DE JURE BELI AC PACIS bk. II, ch. I (1625).

[27] *See generally* LEO GROSS, *The Peace of Westphalia 1648–1948, in* 1 ESSAYS ON INTERNATIONAL LAW AND ORGANIZATION 3 (1984).

[28] 2 L. OPPENHEIM, INTERNATIONAL LAW: A TREATISE: DISPUTES, WAR AND NEUTRALITY 55–56 (1st ed. 1906).

[29] JAMES TURNER JOHNSON, JUST WAR TRADITION AND THE RESTRAINT OF WAR: A MORAL AND HISTORICAL INQUIRY (2014); JUST WAR IN A COMPARATIVE PERSPECTIVE (Paul Robinson ed., 2003).

authority to bind continued to be described as based in natural law, much as Grotius had taught. While several prominent international law scholars in Britain and the United States began crusading for the elimination of natural law jurisprudence from the "science" of international law, natural law never disappeared.[30] Indeed, in recent years, new interest has emerged in understanding the place of natural law in the international legal system.[31]

The Austrian Hans Kelsen, reputed to be the greatest legal mind of the first half of the twentieth century by Harvard Law School's mid-century dean, Roscoe Pound, lent his considerable talent to the legal problem of war. He wrote that the contemporary Just War Doctrine was found in the Treaty of Versailles, the Covenant of the League of Nations, and the Kellogg–Briand Pact. He cited Augustine, Aquinas, and Grotius as the founders of the Doctrine and blamed nineteenth-century political theories of absolute state sovereignty as responsible for its decline. Kelsen argued against absolute state sovereignty as destructive, not just of the Just War Doctrine's limitations on war but of all of international law.[32] The United Nations Charter was finalized at a conference after the end of the Second World War in San Francisco.[33] The Charter remains the single most important normative restraint on resort to force in our multicultural world.

As mentioned above, the U.N. Charter generally prohibits the use of force in Article 2(4).[34] Only States are members of the United Nations, meaning that in treaty form, the rule applies only to States. The Charter's two exceptions are for force in self-defense to an armed attack and force authorized by the U.N. Security Council to restore international peace and security. The International Court of Justice (ICJ) in a series of decisions, including several as recently as the first years of the twenty-first century, has held that the armed attack requisite to trigger the right of self-defense must be significant.[35] This

---

[30] *See* 1 L. OPPENHEIM, INTERNATIONAL LAW: A TREATISE: PEACE (1st ed. 1905).

[31] *See, e.g.,* opinions of Judge Antonio Cançado Trindade, especially his dissenting opinion in Jurisdictional Immunities Judgment, *supra* note 8, at 179 (dissenting opinion of Judge Cançado Trindade). *See also* Mary Ellen O'Connell & Caleb Day, *Natural Law as Source of Normativity, in* THE OXFORD HANDBOOK OF THE SOURCES OF INTERNATIONAL LAW (Samantha Besson & Jean d'Aspremont eds., forthcoming).

[32] HANS KELSEN, GENERAL THEORY OF LAW AND STATE 336 (Anders Wedberg trans., 1943).

[33] *See generally* 1–22 DOCUMENTS OF THE UNITED NATIONS CONFERENCE ON INTERNATIONAL ORGANIZATION (United Nations Information Organizations 1945).

[34] For comprehensive treatments of the law governing resort to force, see YORAM DINSTEIN, WAR, AGGRESSION AND SELF-DEFENCE (5th ed. 2011); OLIVIER CORTEN, THE LAW AGAINST WAR: THE PROHIBITION ON THE USE OF FORCE IN CONTEMPORARY INTERNATIONAL LAW (2010); CHRISTINE GRAY, INTERNATIONAL LAW AND THE USE OF FORCE (3d ed. 2008).

[35] *See infra.*

interpretation is consistent with the plain terms and structure of the Charter, as well as its negotiating history, which all support the priority of peaceful settlement of disputes over permitting the use of force. In addition to the express ban on force, the Charter supports the realization of peace in other ways. It provides for alternatives to the use of force, and it supports respect for human rights and the achievement of economic development to eliminate the causes of conflict.

In this context, it is easy to understand why Article 2(4) was intended as a broad prohibition on force in international relations despite the rather clumsy formulation of the English version of the prohibition. The drafting history underscores that Article 2(4) prohibits all force between States except minimal forms. A member of the U.S. delegation in responding to a question by the Brazilian delegation on the scope of Article 2(4) said that the authors of the original text intended "to state in the broadest terms an absolute all-inclusive prohibition; the phrase 'or in any other manner' was designed to insure that there should be no loopholes."[36] Requiring an armed attack placed an important control on force that had not been authorized by the Security Council. The defending State could point to open, public evidence of the need to respond with force. The Charter exception is limited to cases where objective evidence of an emergency exists for the entire world to see, namely, evidence of an armed attack or an action amounting to an armed attack.[37] Other less tangible or immediate threats must be submitted to the collective scrutiny of the Security Council. The design relies on collective deliberation of the Council as a better process for determining threats to the peace than would the unilateral decision of the potential victim. Articles 39 and 42 provide for the Security Council to authorize force if necessary to restore international peace in the face of a "threat to the peace, breach of the peace, or act of aggression."[38]

The International Court of Justice has ruled that an armed attack triggering the right of self-defense must be significant – it must be more than a mere frontier incident. In addition, the ICJ has found that the reference in Article 51 to "the inherent right" of self-defense is to additional restrictive principles found in international law. The principles of necessity and proportionality require that any use of force in self-defense be undertaken only as a last resort and where there is a high likelihood that using military force will succeed in

---

[36] Summary Report of Eleventh Meeting of Committee I/1, Doc. 784, I/1/27 (June 4, 1945), *in* 6 DOCUMENTS OF THE UNITED NATIONS CONFERENCE ON INTERNATIONAL ORGANIZATION, *supra* note 33, at 331, 334–45.

[37] *See generally* Military and Paramilitary Activities in and Against Nicaragua (Nicar. v. U.S.), Merits Judgment, 1986 I.C.J. 14 (June 27) [hereinafter Nicaragua Merits Judgment].

[38] *See* U.N. Charter arts. 39, 42.

the legitimate objective of defense.[39] Even when these aspects of necessity are met, if military force in self-defense will impose a disproportionate cost on the State responsible for the armed attack compared with the injury to the defending State, the use of force is unlawful. Further, force may only be used on the territory of a foreign sovereign State where the government of that State is responsible for the wrongful armed attack. Some scholars have attempted to assert that attacking a single individual or armed group found on the territory of a State is somehow different than attacking the State itself.[40] That is an erroneous characterization under the law of state responsibility and the right of territorial integrity. This means, generally, that a State may not be attacked because of the presence of armed terrorist organizations uncontrolled by the State.[41] The territorial State may have failed to exercise due diligence with respect to controlling non-state actors. Failure of due diligence, however, does not give rise to the right to use force in self-defense.

Less clear is the right of an outside State to enter into a civil war at the invitation of a government. It is clear that States are barred from assisting rebels seeking to overthrow a government or to secede from a larger State unless the outside State receives Security Council authorization. Some also argue that the prohibition on the use of force in Article 2(4) extends to assisting a government in fighting rebels. The plain terms of Article 2(4) do indicate that assisting governments in suppressing internal rebellion is within the scope of the Article 2(4) prohibition.[42] Presumably, any such use of force would require, at a minimum, Security Council authorization to be lawful. Nevertheless, governments have regularly intervened in internal conflicts in former colonies, often where a puppet government has been instituted for the very purpose of making the invitation. Considering the record of intervention on the side of governments is one of consistent failure, it provides a powerful

---

[39] Oil Platforms (Iran v. U.S.), Merits Judgment, 2003 I.C.J. 161, 198 (Nov. 6).

[40] In the *Armed Activities* case, Judges Simma and Kooijmans argued in separate opinions that in responding to an armed attack by a non-state-actor armed group, a victim State need not be concerned about whether the State where the non-state actor is located bears any responsibility for the attack. Their position fails wholly to consider the rights of the State where a counterattacking State will wreak death, destruction, and injury. Armed Activities on the Territory of the Congo (Dem. Rep. Congo v. Uganda), Judgment, 2005 I.C.J. 334, 337 (Dec. 19) (separate opinion by Judge Simma, ¶ 12); *id.* at 314 (separate opinion by Judge Kooijmans, ¶ 30).

[41] *Id.* at 222–23, 268, ¶¶ 146, 301. *See also* James Thuo Gathii, *Irregular Forces and Self-Defense Under the UN Charter, in* WHAT IS WAR? AN INVESTIGATION IN THE WAKE OF 9/11, at 91, 97 (Mary Ellen O'Connell ed., 2012).

[42] *See, e.g.,* Mary Ellen O'Connell, *The True Meaning of Force,* AJIL UNBOUND (Aug. 3, 2014), www.asil.org/blogs/true-meaning-force.

policy basis for interpreting Article 2(4) as prohibiting outside intervention. France alone provides ample evidence of failure in its more than twenty interventions over forty years.[43] France sent troops to the Central African Republic in 2013, where they are implicated in child sex abuse but are not contributing significantly to stability.[44] The record of intervention on the side of governments is one of extending conflict and keeping authoritarian, unpopular leaders in power.

The International Court of Justice has supported a strict interpretation of the Charter rules on the use of force since it was first called upon to decide a case on the topic, the *Corfu Channel* case of 1949.[45] The ICJ's most important decision on the use of force is the *Nicaragua* judgment from 1986.[46] In addition to the ICJ, the U.N. Security Council, General Assembly, and official government statements repeatedly confirm the importance and binding nature of the Charter's rules and their meaning. Indeed, the international community has repeatedly affirmed its support for the regime of peace and the prohibition on the use of force. The most recent and significant reaffirmation came with the overwhelming vote of confidence in the Charter during the 2005 United Nations World Summit in New York. The World Summit Outcome Document contains these provisions:

78. We reiterate the importance of promoting and strengthening the multilateral process and of addressing international challenges and problems by strictly abiding by the Charter and the principles of international law, and further stress our commitment to multilateralism.

79. We reaffirm that the relevant provisions of the Charter are sufficient to address the full range of threats to international peace and security. We further reaffirm the authority of the Security Council to mandate coercive action to maintain and restore international peace and

---

[43] *See* Andrew Hansen, *Backgrounder: The French Military in Africa*, COUNCIL ON FOREIGN REL. (Feb. 8, 2008), https://www.cfr.org/backgrounder/french-military-africa. Since the report was issued, France undertook major interventions in Mali and the Central African Republic. For evidence and argument against the legality of intervention by invitation of a government, *see also* Louise Doswald-Beck, *The Legal Validity of Military Intervention by Invitation of the Government*, 56 BRIT. Y.B. INT'L L. 189, 191–92, 210 (1985).

[44] David Smith, *France's Poisoned Legacy in the Central African Republic*, GUARDIAN (Apr. 29, 2015), www.theguardian.com/world/2015/apr/29/france-poisoned-legacy-central-african-republic.

[45] Corfu Channel (U.K. v. Alb.), Merits Judgment, 1949 I.C.J. 4 (Apr. 9).

[46] Nicaragua Merits Judgment, *supra* note 37.

security. We stress the importance of acting in accordance with the purposes and principles of the Charter.[47]

Given that the international community so recently recommitted to these rules, they are obviously not "obsolete," despite McMahan's view.[48] Nor is he correct in concluding that the *jus ad bellum* conflicts with moral principles of the just war tradition. As discussed above, there is little divergence between the Just War Doctrine and U.N. Charter rules and other international law on the use of force. Moreover, even the brief discussion above should correct McMahan's description of the *jus ad bellum* as crude and simplistic. Finally, his views have no bearing on whether this law is binding. No government or major international organization leadership in the world denies that the rules of international law are binding and deserve respect.

IV. THE EXISTENCE OF WAR *AND* PEACE

Any significant first use of force by States not authorized by the Security Council will violate Article 2(4). Unlawful force becomes an armed conflict when organized armed groups engage in fighting of some intensity.[49] States frequently attack other States without the victim State counterattacking.[50] In these cases, the attacking State has likely violated the U.N. Charter prohibition on the use of force, but no armed conflict resulted because there was no counterattack. If a victim State counterattacks, triggering organized armed fighting of some intensity, then an armed conflict has begun. It may be recalled that the International Committee of the Red Cross confirmed the existence of an internal armed conflict in Syria in mid-July 2012, about a year after anti-government violence began. That violence did not have the characteristics of an armed conflict for many months.[51]

Brooks, however, argues:

Revolutionary technological changes have reduced the salience of state borders and physical territory and have increased the lethality and disruptive

---

[47] G.A. Res. 60/1, 2005 World Summit Outcome, U.N. Doc. A/RES/60/1 (Sept. 16, 2005).

[48] McMahan, *supra* note 10, at 494.

[49] *See* INT'L LAW ASS'N, USE OF FORCE COMM., FINAL REPORT ON THE MEANING OF ARMED CONFLICT IN INTERNATIONAL LAW (2010), www.ila-hq.org/en/committees/index.cfm/cid/1022.

[50] Israel bombed an alleged weapons of mass destruction development site in September 2007 in Syria. Syria did not counterattack. *See* Ben Piven, *Timeline: Israeli Attacks on Syrian Targets*, AL JAZEERA (May 5, 2013), www.aljazeera.com/indepth/features/2013/05/20135512739431489 .html.

[51] Melisa Goh, *Red Cross Declares Civil War in Syria*, NAT. PUB. RADIO (July 15, 2012), www.npr .org/sections/thetwo-way/2012/07/15/156808427/red-cross-declares-civil-war-in-syria.

capabilities of non-state actors and even individuals. The nature of modern security threats makes it virtually impossible to draw neat lines between war and peace, foreign and domestic, emergency and normality.[52]

She offers no proof that it is more difficult today than previously to draw "neat lines between war and peace." Whether difficult or not, in the era of human rights, our legal and ethical principles teach that when in doubt, characterize situations as peace and apply the law of peace. Defaulting to war conflicts with the priority we give to human rights. [53]

Brooks is plainly aware that during armed conflict protection of human life is less stringent. She is also aware, or should be, of the international legal definition of armed conflict. She recognizes that two U.S. presidential administrations have claimed the right to kill with military force far from actual combat zones. Yet, she is willing to defend this killing because of what she sees as new security threats that fall outside existing legal categories. In her words: "In a war against a geographically diffuse terrorist network, the spatial boundaries are necessarily arbitrary."[54]

It is unclear why "diffuse networks" render spatial boundaries arbitrary. The international law of boundaries supplies sufficient principles for understanding the location of physical boundaries. If Brooks means that terrorists are actors who move across international boundaries or use the Internet and other means to have an impact without leaving the places where they live, and that these facts eliminate the obligation on States to respect boundaries, she has stated facts and a conclusion without providing the rule or reasoning linking them. These facts do not make a case that the use of force rules should be relaxed. Nor do they indicate why the applicable rules with respect to killing cannot be applied. When it comes to killing, if any factual elements are uncertain respecting the exception to the right to life, international human rights law mandates erring on the side of life.

Brooks's argument against boundaries is part of her advocacy of "perpetual war." While she has criticized some drone strikes in the past,[55] she also finds fault with current international law, believing, like McMahan, that it is obsolete in significant areas. She served as a political appointee for two years

---

[52] Brooks, *There is No Such Thing as Peacetime, supra* note 11.

[53] This Section draws on Mary Ellen O'Connell, The Future of Peace, Weapons, and War, The Frans van Hasselt Lecture at the Technical University of Delft, The Netherlands (May 5, 2015).

[54] *Id.*

[55] *See The Law of Armed Conflict, the Use of Military Force, and the 2001 Authorization for Use of Military Force Hearing Before the S. Comm. on Armed Services*, 113th Cong. 53, 58–59 (2013) (statement of Rosa Brooks), www.armed-services.senate.gov/imo/media/doc/ lawofarmedconflict_useofmilitaryforce_2001aumf_hearing_051613.pdf.

in the Obama Pentagon and shares an all-too-common view found in the U.S. military, academic, legal, and philosophical circles that circumstances have so changed that international law should be interpreted or modified to allow a greater legal right to use military force. This view apparently only applies to certain States. Brooks and McMahan seem to argue from the perspective of U.S. policy. It is critical, however, to understand that the *jus ad bellum* applies to all sovereign States on a basis of legal equality.

During the Cold War, the existence of the Soviet Union reminded U.S. government officials and academics to take care in arguing for new rules on the use of force. The same consideration seems to have influenced the Soviets. Both superpowers tended to manipulate the facts to fit the law rather than the law to fit the facts in attempting to publicly justify uses of force. The 1956 Soviet invasion of Hungary was justified by an invitation, which the Soviets obtained by plotting with a high-ranking member of the Hungarian government, János Kádár, to claim he was the legitimate head of government, moving aside the choice of the reformers, Imre Nagy.[56] The Soviets followed a similar approach in obtaining invitations to intervene in Czechoslovakia in 1968[57] and Afghanistan in 1979.[58] The United States characterized Vietnam as two separate countries. The United States claimed to be joining South Vietnam in collective self-defense against the North. In 1983, the United States obtained an invitation to intervene in Grenada, where it replaced the government. The invitation was obtained from the British Governor-General. He likely did not have the authority to issue it and had to backdate it.[59]

When Bill Clinton became U.S. President after the Soviet Union collapsed, attitudes started to change. The use of airpower to protect Kurds and Shiites in Iraq in the aftermath of the liberation of Kuwait indicated to some human rights organizations that the international law against the use of force should be reinterpreted to allow the use of force for humanitarian purposes. This was an old argument, dating to at least the 1970s when Richard Lillich advocated for it, meeting stiff resistance from Ian Brownlie and others. A central opposing argument concerned the indeterminate nature of Lillich's proposal. Brownlie asked how many innocent people could be allowed to die in a war fought for human rights. At the end of the Cold War, the Clinton

---

[56] Charles Gati, Failed Illusions: Moscow, Budapest, and the 1956 Hungarian Revolt 17, 233 (2006).

[57] Philip Windsor & Adam Roberts, Czechoslovakia 1968: Reform, Repression and Resistance (1969).

[58] Mary Ellen O'Connell, *Soviet Prisoners in the Afghan Conflict*, 23 Colum. J. Transnat'l L. 483 (1985).

[59] Christopher C. Joyner, *Reflections on the Lawfulness of Invasion*, 78 Am. J. Int'l L. 131 (1984).

Administration took the apparent position that U.S. leaders were uniquely positioned to make the subjective determinations involved in humanitarian intervention. The decision to intervene in the Kosovo crisis was made with no official legal justification.[60]

Clinton also extended the use of military force to targeted killing in terrorism cases. During the Reagan Administration, force was used against Libya as a state sponsor of terrorism under an attenuated self-defense argument. Clinton did that too, bombing Afghanistan and Sudan following the 1998 al-Qaeda attacks on U.S. Embassies in Kenya and Tanzania. Then the President was presented with a reconnaissance drone that had been adapted by adding two Hellfire missiles. Clinton modified the Reagan executive order banning assassination and authorized the CIA to hunt for and kill Osama bin Laden using the new technology.[61]

The CIA failed, but the episode demonstrates that the development of new weapons systems that kill without posing a threat to the operator has further encouraged the trend toward loosening law against military force. The French philosopher Grégoire Chamayou has written:

> [L]arge-scale intellectual maneuvers are in the offing and semantic coups are being plotted. In fact, a whole collection of theoretical offensives are being launched with the aim of appropriating, twisting, and redefining concepts that, by naming and theorizing violence, allow it to be legitimately exercised.... Bringing about this moral conversion and transmutation of values is the task to which philosophers working within the confined field of military ethics today devote themselves.... But the offensive is also and perhaps above all pushing into the field of legal theory.[62]

For Chamayou, we in the West had a better understanding of the need for restrictions on war when we conceived that the risks were reciprocal. During the Cold War, the risks could be total annihilation. If our populations and soldiers faced death by the use of force, we wished to try to restrict that force by all available means, including legal and moral norms protecting the right to

---

[60] The United States and other NATO members did put forward arguments in justification when Serbia brought a case in the International Court of Justice against them during the intervention. Interestingly, only Belgium argued that it had the right to intervene under a newly crystallized customary international law right of humanitarian intervention. Legality of the Use of Force (Yugoslavia v. Belg.), Verbatim Record, 1999 I.C.J. Doc. CR 99/15 (May 10, 1999, 3 p.m.).

[61] CHRIS WOODS, SUDDEN JUSTICE 37 (2015).

[62] GRÉGOIRE CHAMAYOU, A THEORY OF THE DRONE 16–17 (2015). *See also* Mary Ellen O'Connell, Comment, *Seductive Drones: Learning from a Decade of Lethal Operations*, 21 J.L. INFO. & SCI. (Special Edition) 116 (2012), http://ssrn.com/abstract=1912635.

life. New weapons have removed the risk. Substantial evidence indicates that following a decade and a half of lethal operations with drones, many view drone attacks as less serious than killing carried out by ground troops, piloted planes, manned naval vessels, or a CIA agent using a knife, all of which pose some level of risk to the one doing the killing. One U.S. official has observed: "People are a lot more comfortable with a Predator strike that kills many people than with a throat-slitting that kills one."[63] The possession of such technology lowers the political and psychological barriers to killing, making it easier to overlook the legal and ethical limits as well as longer-term strategic goals.[64]

Given the political and psychological lures to killing and destroying with new technology, rather than urge the loosening of rules or characterizing facts as favorable to killing, ethical considerations instead support strict fidelity to the law and accuracy as to the facts. It is also essential that academics and government officials fully understand what international law says about the *jus ad bellum*, international boundaries, and the definition of armed conflict.

V. EQUAL APPLICATION OF THE *JUS IN BELLO*

It is well known that the *jus in bello* rules apply equally to States party to an armed conflict. The conduct rules do not distinguish between parties that have resorted to war unlawfully under the *jus ad bellum* and those that have not. Moral philosophers debate this rule.[65] Recall that McMahan believes the party resorting to force in compliance with his view of a "just war" should have advantages under the *jus in bello*. There are historical, ethical, and pragmatic reasons, however, for why parties to a conflict have the same obligations. Whether moral philosophers find these reasons persuasive or not, the rule of equal application of the law is the current, binding principle.

---

[63] Jane Mayer, *The Predator War: What Are the Risks of the C.I.A.'s Covert Drone Program?*, NEW YORKER (Oct. 26, 2009), www.newyorker.com/reporting/2009/10/26/091026fa_fact_mayer.

[64] We saw another example of the impact of technology on July 8, 2016, in Dallas, Texas, when police used a robot for the first time to deploy a bomb to kill a criminal suspect. The police had the suspect cornered in a parking garage for hours. It is not known why the police did not shoot the man, but using a drone would have made the killing easier to carry out than would have been the case for an individual police officer using a gun in a situation that may not have necessitated lethal force. *See* Ken Dilanian, *Experts: Robot Bomb Used Against Dallas Suspect Was 'Reasonable'*, NBC NEWS (July 8, 2016), www.nbcnews.com/storyline/dallas-police-ambush/police-used-robot-bomb-kill-dallas-suspect-micah-xavier-johnson-n606181. *See also infra*, text accompanying notes 67–70.

[65] *See* Dannenbaum, *supra* note 9.

Even if the world were to attempt to change the rule, it is not at all clear how McMahan's proposition would work as a practical matter. At the height of the Holy Roman Empire, it might have been possible within Europe to ask the Pope to judge who was fighting a just war and even, perhaps, whether those fighters should have some advantage in how they attacked unjust opponents. The Pope, of course, no longer has this authority in the world. The world does have a common code of international law universally recognized for its authority. In changing the law, what precise advantage would McMahan give the just fighter over the unjust one? If McMahan's point in granting an advantage is to coerce compliance with just war analysis, it should be noted that international law does not need this sort of coercion to enforce the *jus ad bellum*. Direct and indirect sanctions are used against the State resorting to war in violation of international law. Recall how few States aided the United States, Britain, and Australia in the 2003 invasion of Iraq compared with the overwhelming support to liberate Kuwait in 1991. And today national leaders may be held criminally accountable for aggression.[66]

Moreover, to alter the *jus in bello* rules to impose greater restrictions on one side versus another would require shaping new rules in conflict with centuries of moral formation. The four most important principles of the *jus ad bellum* are the principles of distinction, necessity, proportionality, and humanity. The principle of distinction forbids the intentional targeting of civilians. During an armed conflict, regular members of the armed forces who respect the law of war will not be prosecuted for the deaths they cause if in conformity with the *jus in bello*. These combatants are sometimes referred to as "privileged" combatants. Privileged combatants have the privilege to kill enemy fighters without warning.[67] Absent an armed conflict, law enforcement officials may only use lethal force in self-defense or the defense of others in the face of an imminent threat.

Altering the rule of distinction to give an advantage to the party resorting to force lawfully might entail giving greater latitude on the battlefield in deciding that an individual who appears to be a civilian is actually an enemy fighter. Such a change would alter the *jus cogens* norm that civilians and persons *hors de combat* may not be intentionally killed. Killing an individual who presents herself as a civilian depends on whether she is directly participating in armed

---

[66] Amendments on the Crime of Aggression to the Rome Statute of the International Criminal Court, arts. 8 *bis*, 15 *bis*, 15 *ter* (June 11, 2010), https://treaties.un.org/pages/viewdetails.aspx?src=treaty&mtdsg_no=xviii-10-b&chapter=18&lang=e.

[67] *See* Knut Ipsen, *Combatants and Non-Combatants, in* THE HANDBOOK OF INTERNATIONAL HUMANITARIAN LAW 301 (Dieter Fleck ed., 2d ed. 2008).

conflict hostilities. If so, she may be targeted "for such time as" the participation continues.[68] In 2009, the International Committee of the Red Cross (ICRC) in its *Interpretative Guidance on Direct Participation in Hostilities* bowed to pressure for greater flexibility in determining who may be targeted and introduced the term "continuous combat function" (CCF) to allow for the killing of civilians who are no longer directly participating in hostilities but are likely to resume participation. The ICRC also made it clear, however, that killing someone suspected of having a continuous combatant function is only justifiable in a situation of necessity.[69] The ICRC described the necessity justifying killing in the case of someone having a continuous combatant function as aligned with the one governing police use of lethal force. This shift from a battlefield to a peacetime principle was required so that killing would be based only upon objective evidence. Without it, the rule of civilian immunity would be based upon such things as intelligence gathered prior to the killing that the target would in the future rejoin armed conflict hostilities. Such assessment does not have the value of the public and open facts of a situation where killing is based on the need to save a life immediately.[70]

---

[68] Protocol I, *supra* note 7, art. 51(3).

[69] *Interpretive Guidance on the Notion of Direct Participation in Hostilities under International Humanitarian Law*, 90 INT'L. REV. RED CROSS 991 (2008), www.icrc.org/eng/assets/files/other/irrc-872-reports-documents.pdf.

[70] See the following special provisions from the U.N. High Commissioner for Human Rights' Basic Principles on the Use of Force and Firearms by Law Enforcement Officials:

> 9. Law enforcement officials shall not use firearms against persons except in self-defence or defence of others against the imminent threat of death or serious injury, to prevent the perpetration of a particularly serious crime involving grave threat to life, to arrest a person presenting such a danger and resisting their authority, or to prevent his or her escape, and only when less extreme means are insufficient to achieve these objectives. In any event, intentional lethal use of firearms may only be made when strictly unavoidable in order to protect life.
>
> 10. In the circumstances provided for under principle 9, law enforcement officials shall identify themselves as such and give a clear warning of their intent to use firearms, with sufficient time for the warning to be observed, unless to do so would unduly place the law enforcement officials at risk or would create a risk of death or serious harm to other persons, or would be clearly inappropriate or pointless in the circumstances of the incident.

Office of the U.N. High Comm'r for Human Rights, Basic Principles on the Use of Force and Firearms by Law Enforcement Officials, adopted by the Eighth United Nations Congress on the Prevention of Crime and the Treatment of Offenders, Havana, Cuba, 27 August to 7 September 1990, www.ohchr.org/EN/ProfessionalInterest/Pages/UseOfForceAndFirearms.aspx; *see also* Tennessee v. Garner, 471 U.S. 1, 11–13 (1985).

To allow the troops of one party to a conflict to kill suspected enemy fighters under a lower standard because the national leadership of their opponent went to war unlawfully imposes a greater risk of death on human beings who had no role in the decision to use force unlawfully. Such a two-level rule would require training forces to know when they are permitted to use the more flexible standard in distinguishing civilians and when they are not. International law does not generally hold troops responsible for violations of the *jus ad bellum* committed by national leaders. The McMahan approach, however, would require knowledge at the level of the individual soldier that his State is fighting lawfully (justly), and, therefore, that he is free to target certain civilians while his opponent may not. If it turns out that the soldier is wrong, he could be liable for the serious war crime of intentionally killing civilians. A conviction would depend on that particular soldier's knowledge of the *jus ad bellum* rules as applied in a particular conflict.

Dannenbaum argues that international law should require knowledge of the *jus ad bellum* by soldiers.[71] He rejects arguments that this international law is too difficult for such general understanding, writing persuasively that in recent wars, such as the Iraq War that began in 2003, few had difficulty understanding that the invasion by the United States, Britain, and Australia was unlawful. His point, however, is to support the right of troops to refuse to fight in unlawful wars. He does not argue for prosecuting the vast number of troops or the civilian populations of States whose leaders have violated Article 2(4). Such prosecutions might be necessary if troops decide the *jus ad bellum* is on their side and act on that belief by targeting civilians.

Nor is it clear that more flexible rights to kill or destroy would actually provide a true advantage. The conduct rules have developed to encourage fighters to focus on the military objective. Killing enemy fighters is the standard way of doing this. Killing civilians is not. Indeed, it has long been thought that killing civilians is counterproductive to the military goal. It is an effort that wastes resources and enflames a desire for revenge, even encouraging civilians who are being attacked to take up arms. Killing without a focus on the military objective has been seen to result in an undisciplined force that fails to see the point in following orders, putting superiors and fellow troops at risk.

Finally, McMahan, Brooks, and others who share their views are out of step with the overall structure and purpose of international law, as well as the more recent trends in human rights law. A variety of peacetime human rights rules

---

[71] Dannenbaum, *supra* note 9.

are being extended to the battlefield and occupation zones. For example, a single rule for the use of lethal force based on necessity whether in combat or peacetime policing was proposed at the end of the Cold War.[72] It is now the core concept incorporated into the ICRC's innovative CCF status.[73] Unlike giving advantages to soldiers fighting on the lawful side in an armed conflict as determined by the *jus ad bellum* or the Just War Doctrine, requiring all soldiers to kill only when necessary is considered by the ICRC to be a practical possibility.

In a major decision of the European Court of Human Rights on this subject in a 2011 case brought by an Iraqi against the United Kingdom, the Court found that the European Convention on Human Rights applied to his detention by U.K. troops in Iraq. The United Kingdom argued that only international humanitarian law applied.[74] United Kingdom courts have extended peacetime law in a similar fashion to U.K. military detention during the civil war in Afghanistan. Both a trial court and court of appeals held that the United Kingdom must base detention on national legislation or be held in violation of the European Convention on Human Rights. International humanitarian law alone was insufficient.[75]

The United States has resisted the view that it must observe its obligations under the International Covenant on Civil and Political Rights in action beyond U.S. territory, whether in armed conflict or peace. The U.N. Human Rights Committee has investigated uses of lethal force by the United States despite U.S. protests that such investigations are beyond the Committee's jurisdiction. In 2002, when the United States first used a drone to kill individuals outside the armed conflict in Yemen, a U.N. human rights rapporteur investigated and concluded that the strike constituted "a clear case of extrajudicial killing."[76] United States State Department lawyer Michael Dennis published an article taking issue with the U.N. finding and defending the "Global War on Terror." Dennis wrote: "The United States' response to the... Yemen allegations has been that its actions were appropriate under

---

[72] *See, e.g.,* Francisco Forrest Martin, *Using International Human Rights Law for Establishing a Unified Use of Force Rule in the Law of Armed Conflict*, 64 SASK. L. REV. 347 (2001); Theodor Meron & Allan Rosas, *Current Development: A Declaration of Minimum Humanitarian Standards*, 85 AM. J. INT'L L. 375 (1991).

[73] *See supra* notes 69–70 and accompanying text.

[74] *See* Al-Skeini v. United Kingdom, App. No. 55721/07, 53 Eur. Ct. H.R. 589 (2011).

[75] Serdar Mohammed v. Ministry of Defence, [2015] EWCA (Civ) 843.

[76] Asma Jahangir (Special Rapporteur on Extrajudicial, Summary or Arbitrary Executions), *Report on Civil and Political Rights, Including the Questions of Disappearances and Summary Executions*, ¶¶ 37–39, U.N. Doc. E/CN.4/2003/3 (Jan. 13, 2003).

the international law of armed conflict and that the Commission and its special procedures have no mandate to address the matter."[77]

Investigations nevertheless continued.[78]

VI. CONCLUSION

The evidence makes clear that international law continues to distinguish the law applicable in war and peace. This distinction grew up for the most pragmatic of reasons. Law restricts the use of violence within societies for use by law enforcement and in rare circumstances of personal self-defense. Humanity has striven over time to mitigate the suffering in war. In exchange for leaving virtually unchanged the right to kill the enemy without warning, to intercept war material, and to detain enemy combatants for the duration of fighting, every government has accepted limitations on other aspects of war fighting. The rights or privileges to kill, intercept, and detain continue to be tolerated in the delicate *quid pro quo* of humanitarian law and in the firm understanding that they are invoked in only the most exceptional circumstances – significant armed conflict in which the application of criminal law is unworkable. These privileges are available under the limited conditions of armed conflict and are available only to lawful combatants and parties to armed conflict.[79]

Absent an armed conflict, international human rights law protects criminal suspects. Individuals may not be killed on suspicion of membership in a group. Rather, authorities must at least make the attempt to arrest a suspect and not simply kill her. The moral philosopher Jeremy Waldron has written with respect to U.S. claims to a right to engage in targeted killing away from armed conflict zones:

> It seems that our first instinct is to search for areas where killing is already "all right" – killing in self-defense or killing of combatants in wartime – and then to see if we can concoct analogies between whatever moral reasons we presently associate with such licenses and the new areas of killing that we want to explore. In my view, *that is how a norm against murder unravels.* It unravels in our moral repertoire largely because we have forgotten how

---

[77] Michael J. Dennis, *Human Rights in 2002: The Annual Sessions of the UN Commission on Human Rights and the Economics and Social Council*, 97 Am. J. Int'l L. 364, 367 n.17 (2003).

[78] *See, e.g.,* Philip Alston (Special Rapporteur on Extrajudicial, Summary or Arbitrary Executions), *Rep. of the Special Rapporteur on Extrajudicial, Summary or Arbitrary Executions, Addendum: Study on Targeted Killings,* U.N. Doc. A/HRC/14/24/Add.6 (May 28, 2010).

[79] This Section is adapted from Mary Ellen O'Connell, *To Kill or Capture Suspects in the Global War on Terror,* 35 Case W. Res. J. Int'l L. 325 (2003).

deeply such a norm must be anchored in light of the military and political temptations that it faces and how grudging, cautious, and conservative we need to be – in order to secure that anchorage – with such existing licenses to kill as we have already issued.[80]

---

[80] Jeremy Waldron, *Justifying Targeted Killing with a Neutral Principle? Three Possible Models, in* TARGETED KILLINGS: LAW AND MORALITY IN AN ASYMMETRICAL WORLD (Claire Finkelstein et al. eds., 2012) (emphasis added).

20

The Urgent Imperative of Peace

LEILA NADYA SADAT

I. INTRODUCTION

When and under what conditions States may lawfully employ force currently preoccupies government decision makers, academics, journalists, and policy makers. As war in Syria rages, the seemingly endless conflicts in Afghanistan and Iraq metastasize into new forms of violence, North Korea threatens Seoul and the United States by launching and testing nuclear-armed missiles, the 45th U.S. President threatens "fire and fury like the world has never seen" in response, ISIS-affiliated individuals launch deadly attacks against civilians in European capitals, increasing number of incidents involving naval forces are taking place in the South China Sea, and Russia invades and annexes portions of Ukraine, there is growing concern that the Post–World War II international legal order is under terrible stress.

This unease is exacerbated by positions taken by the United States government and many in the academy,[1] where distinguished scholars have announced the "death" of Article 2(4) of the U.N. Charter prohibiting the use of force,[2] and war-talk has become so normalized that prominent academics like Rosa Brooks have suggested that human rights lawyers insisting upon clear distinctions between war and peace (under the *jus*

---

[1] This Chapter focuses largely on U.S. shifts in practice and perspective, which seems apt, or at least defensible, given that the United States was instrumental in the creation of the post-war legal order that it is now, itself, challenging. *See generally* Elizabeth Borgwardt, A New Deal for the World: America's Vision for Human Rights 233 (2005); *see also* Leila Nadya Sadat, *The Nuremberg Trial, Seventy Years Later*, 15 Wash. U. Global Stud. L. Rev. 575 (2016).

[2] Michael Glennon, *How International Rules Die*, 93 Geo. L. J. 939–91 (2005); Michael Glennon, *Why the Security Council Failed*, 82 Foreign Aff. 12–35 (2003).

ad bellum) and well-established applications of the laws of war (the *jus in bello*),[3] are "wast[ing] time and energy" and engaging in "self-deception" because "events march inexorably on."[4] Instead, she suggests that we should "develop laws, politics, and institutions premised on the assumption that we will forever remain unable to draw sharp boundaries between war and peace, and that we will frequently find ourselves in the space between."[5] A *space between* that allegedly constitutes the new normal – a normality based upon the Colossus that is the American military and its "war" against terror, which, in the views of some, is unlikely to diminish over time.

This thesis, and the assumptions that underlie it, causes others to believe that the "greatest threat to world peace today is Washington's imperial power."[6] And this power is formidable. The United States spent close to 36 percent of the global total of military spending,[7] and in terms of arsenal, has more nuclear weapons, aircraft carriers, and intelligence capabilities than the rest of the world combined.[8] Although many have noted the excessive burden that military spending places on the American economy,[9] and others have critiqued U.S. projection of its "hard power" as counterproductive and

[3]   Such as rules regarding the applicability of the Geneva Conventions to all individuals taken prisoner by the United States in the so-called "war on terror" and the peremptory nature of the international norm prohibiting torture.

[4]   Rosa Brooks, How Everything Became War and the Military Became Everything 344 (2016).

[5]   *Id.* at 353.

[6]   Chandra Muzaffar, Global Ethic or Global Hegemony? Reflections on Religion, Human Dignity and Civilizational Interaction 157 (2005). Under President Obama, 64 percent of people surveyed in 37 countries had confidence that he would "do the right thing regarding world affairs," as opposed to 22 percent with respect to Trump. *Pew Poll: More people in the world have confidence in Putin than Trump*, CNN (June 27, 2017), www.cnn.com/2017/06/27/politics/putin-trump-confidence/.

[7]   *See, e.g.,* Nan Tian, Aude Fleurant, Pieter D. Wezeman & Siemon T. Wezeman, *Trends in World Military Expenditure, 2016*, SIPRI 1, 2 (Apr. 2017), www.sipri.org/sites/default/files/Trends-world-military-expenditure-2016.pdf.

[8]   *See* Skye Gould & Paul Szoldra, *The 25 Most Powerful Militaries in the World*, Business Insider (Mar. 15, 2017), www.businessinsider.com/the-worlds-most-powerful-militaries-2017-3; James Bamford, *Commentary: The World's Best Cyber Army Doesn't Belong to Russia*, Reuters (Aug. 4, 2016), www.reuters.com/article/us-election-intelligence-commentary/commentary-the-worlds-best-cyber-army-doesnt-belong-to-russia-idUSKCN10F1H5.

[9]   *See* Dana Priest & William M. Arkin, *A Hidden World, Growing Beyond Control*, Wash. Post (July 19, 2010), http://projects.washingtonpost.com/top-secret-america/articles/a-hidden-world-growing-beyond-control/print/; Robert Pollin, *Economic Prospects: Why Militarism Hurts the U.S. Economy*, 17 New Lab. F. 134 (2008); M. Ishaq Nadiri, *Increase in Defense Expenditure and Its Impact on the U.S. Economy, in* Constraints on Strategy: The Economics of Western Security 27 (David Denoon ed., 1986).

problematic in a variety of ways,[10] many U.S. legal academics see U.S. military dominance as inevitable, benign, or both.

Brooks does not engage in a moral assessment of this new "reality" (and in fact notes her own discomfiture with U.S. policy in several regards) nor does she provide a legal framework for its guidance – but surely her book, written prior to Trump's election, does not take seriously the possibility that the U.S. Commander-in-Chief would be neither experienced nor benign. Indeed, nor did she (or in fairness, did she propose to) parse out what the world would actually look like if ten or twenty or thirty States engaged in cross-border drone strikes and military operations on the same basis proposed to justify U.S. uses of force. Instead, she postulates current efforts to rewrite the laws of war and the laws relating to the use of force as a necessary and inevitable acquiescence to U.S. government practice and military power, a sort of "tribute" that reason must pay to power, in a perverse reversal of Justice Jackson's famous plea to the International Military Tribunal at Nuremberg.[11]

So what is the "new reality" of which Brooks speaks? Article 2(4) of the U.N. Charter provides that Members of the United Nations "shall refrain in their international relations from the threat or use of force against the territorial integrity or political independence of any state, or in any other manner inconsistent with the Purposes of the United Nations."[12] This prohibition on the use of force is generally considered absolute – with the exception of force authorized by the Security Council, with the consent of the territorial State, or under the rubric (and constraints) of self-defense.[13] Yet the U.S. government is currently conducting military operations – including large-scale air strikes and drone missile attacks – in several countries with which it is not technically at war. The government's theory is that it is engaging in lawful self-defense under Article 51 of the U.N. Charter, because those States apparently have terrorist organizations – or individuals – operating on their territories and are "unable or unwilling" to effectively confront them.[14]

---

[10] JOSEPH NYE, SOFT POWER: THE MEANS TO SUCCESS IN WORLD POLITICS (2004).
[11] *See, e.g.,* Opening Statement for the United States of America by Robert H. Jackson, Chief Counsel for the United States, at the Palace of Justice, Nuremberg, Germany on November 21, 1945. ("That four great nations, flushed with victory and stung with injury stay the hand of vengeance and voluntarily submit their captive enemies to the judgment of the law is one of the most significant tributes that Power has ever paid to Reason.").
[12] U.N. Charter art. 2, ¶ 4.
[13] U.N. Charter art. 42; U.N. Charter art. 51.
[14] Brian J. Egan, State Department Legal Advisor, Keynote Address at the 110th ASIL Annual Meeting: Charting New Frontiers in International Law (Mar. 30- Apr. 2, 2016), www.asil.org/resources/video/2016-annual-meeting. *See also* Office of the President, Report on the Legal and Policy Frameworks Guiding the United States' Use of Military Force and Related National

Article 51 provides that "nothing in the present Charter shall impair the inherent right of individual or collective self-defense if an armed attack occurs against a Member of the United Nations, until the Security Council has taken measures necessary to maintain international peace and security." The September 11 attacks were declared by NATO to be an "armed attack" within the meaning of the U.N. Charter and the NATO Charter in 2001.[15] On September 14, 2001, Congress authorized the use of "necessary and appropriate" military force against

> [T]hose nations, organizations, or persons he determines planned, authorized, committed, or aided the terrorist attacks that occurred on September 11, 2001, or harbored such organizations or persons, in order to prevent any future acts of international terrorism against the United States by such nations, organizations or persons.[16]

This Resolution is specifically tied to and constrained by its connection to the armed attack of September 11. Although President Obama asserted just before leaving office that the AUMF (Authorization for Use of Military Force) continues to provide authorization for U.S. military force directed against "Al-Qaeda, the Taliban, certain other terrorist or insurgent groups affiliated with Al-Qaeda or the Taliban in Afghanistan; AQAP; al-Shabaab; individuals who are part of Al-Qaeda in Libya; Al-Qaeda in Syria; and ISIL,"[17] sixteen years following the September 11 attacks, it is hard to argue that continued military action in Syria, Yemen, Pakistan, Libya, Somalia, and even Afghanistan itself against groups and individuals that had little or nothing to do with the attacks themselves (and in fact are not supported by or connected with Al-Qaeda or the Taliban in any way, like ISIS) is still related in any reasonable way to "self-defense" conducted following that terrorist attack and supported

Security Operations, The White House 10 (Dec. 2016) [hereinafter December 2016 Presidential Report]. *See also* Permanent Rep. of the U.S. to the U.N., Letter dated 23 September 2014 from the Permanent Representative of the United States of America to the United Nations addressed to the Secretary-General, U.N. Doc. S/2014/695 (Sept. 23, 2014) (relying upon the unwilling or unable standard to justify U.S. strikes on ISIL in Syria) [hereinafter September 2014 U.S. Letter]. Note that this letter and other early iterations of the standard used the language "unwilling or unable"; however, the most documents including the December 2016 Presidential Memorandum reverse the locution to "unable or unwilling," which is therefore what this Chapter employs.

[15] Leila Nadya Sadat, *Terrorism and the Rule of Law*, 3 Wash. U. Global Stud. L. Rev. 135, 137 n.6 (2004) (*citing* statement of NATO General Secretary Lord Robertson) [hereinafter Sadat, *Terrorism*].

[16] Authorization for Use of Military Force, S. J. Res. 23, 107th Cong. (2001) [hereinafter AUMF].

[17] December 2016 Presidential Report, *supra* note 14, at 6.

by the AUMF.[18] A Presidential Memorandum published just prior to Obama
leaving office provides that "self-defense" may be used by States in response to
"*imminent* attacks before they occur," but the definition of *imminent* in the
Memorandum itself is so broad that it completely neuters the concept.[19]

The current international law justification for continued U.S. self-defense
operations around the world in its "war" against alleged terrorists is controversial for several reasons.[20] First, it assumes that non-State actors – and not just
States – can carry out an armed attack under Article 51, to which a State can
respond militarily in self-defense; second, it has expanded geographically away
from the original situs of the September 11 attacks – Afghanistan – where there
was a genuine connection between Al Qaeda and the then-extant Afghan
government, which made it more reasonable to hold Afghanistan responsible
as a nation for the launch of the attacks themselves, to surrounding countries
with which the United States is not at war; third, it has expanded temporally
beyond any credible actual connection to the September 11 attacks and
become, for all practical purposes, Brooks' "perpetual war;"[21] fourth, the
loosening of the rules regarding the *jus ad bellum* went hand in hand with

----

[18] *See, e.g.*, Jennifer Daskal & Stephen I. Vladeck, *After the AUMF*, 5 HARV. NAT'L. SECURITY J.
     115, 117 (2014); Olivier Corten, *The 'Unwilling or Unable' Test: Has It Been, and Could It be,
     Accepted?*, 29 LEIDEN J. INT'L L. 777 (2016).

[19] Although the Memorandum cites the *Caroline* incident for the proposition that self-defense
     is lawful against non-State actors, it does not cite the test for imminence in that case, which
     was when an armed attack presents a "necessity of self-defence, instant, overwhelming,
     leaving no choice of means, and no moment for deliberation." *See* Note of U.S. Secretary of
     State Daniel Webster (Apr. 24, 1841), in *The Caroline Case*, 29 BRITISH & FOREIGN STATE
     PAPERS 1137–38 (1841). Instead, the test cites five broad factors, only one of which is the "nature
     and immediacy of the attack." The others essentially allow the administration to balance
     immediacy with other factors such as whether the anticipated attack is part of a pattern, the
     likely scale of damage, and whether or not there are likely to be other opportunities to act that
     may cause "less serious collateral injury, loss or damage." It also notes that evidence need not
     be precise and that it must be understood in terms of "modern-day capabilities, techniques, and
     technological innovations of terrorist organizations." December 2016 Presidential Report, *supra*
     note 14, at 9.

[20] Brooks refers to the "war on terror" in her writings, a phrase that was coined by the Bush
     Administration but subsequently abandoned by it, and that was also not favored by the Obama
     Administration, which preferred the moniker "countering violent extremism." *See, e.g.*,
     President Barack Obama, Remarks at the Leaders' Summit on Countering ISIL and Violent
     Extremism at the United Nations Headquarters (Sept. 29, 2015), https://obamawhitehouse
     .archives.gov/the-press-office/2015/09/29/remarks-president-obama-leaders-summit-countering-
     isil-and-violent.

[21] The December 2016 Presidential Report notes that the war must end but that "[u]nfortunately,
     that day has not yet come." December 2016 Presidential Report, *supra* note 14, at 12. The Report
     adds that the United States "will degrade and dismantle the operational capacity and supporting
     networks of terrorist organizations like al-Qa'ida to such an extent that they will have been
     effectively destroyed and will no longer be able to attempt or launch a strategic attack against

the loosening of restrictions on the laws of war, including the mistreatment of prisoners and other problematic reinterpretations of international humanitarian law; fifth, the United States has expanded the conflict not only geographically and temporally, but by introducing a new weapon, the unmanned predator drone, which targets and kills individuals (and anyone near the strike site), based upon an assessment *that they might threaten the United States in the future*, abandoning any pretext that the United States was responding – until the Security Council could meet – to an actual armed attack. [22]

This expansive reinterpretation of Article 51 of the United Nations Charter – which, ironically, was proposed by U.S. conservatives who on the domestic level generally demand strict construction of legal texts such as the United States Constitution[23] – is deeply problematic. Although some scholars (including two in this volume) agree with the first proposition – that States can use force against non-State actors operating on the territory of third States in self-defense under certain circumstances – the scope and scale of U.S. actions have turned Article 2(4)'s prohibition on the use of force on its head as the self-defense "exception" has largely swallowed the prohibitory rule. Indeed,

the United States. At that point, there will no longer be an ongoing armed conflict between the United States and those forces." *Id.* at 11–12.

[22] Micah Zenko has written extensively on the U.S. drone policy. *See, e.g.*, Micah Zenko, *Reforming U.S. Drone Strike Policies*, Council Special Rep. No. 65, Council on Foreign Relations 17 (Jan. 2013); Micah Zenko, *Obama's Final Drone Strike Data*, Council on Foreign Relations (Jan. 20, 2017) (stating that President Obama authorized 542 drone strikes killing an estimated 3,797 people, including 324 civilians). *See also* Leila Nadya Sadat, *America's Drone Wars*, 45 CASE W. RES. J. INT'L L. 215, 219 (2012). President Barack Obama set forth his policies in speeches, an Executive Order, and, subsequently, a comprehensive Memorandum. *See* President Obama, Remarks by the President at the United States Military Academy Commencement Ceremony (May 28, 2014). *See also* Presidential Policy Guidance, Procedures for Approving Direct Action Against Terrorist Targets Located Outside the United States and Areas of Active Hostilities (2013; Exec. Order No. 13732, United States Policy on Pre- and Post-Strike Measures to Address Civilian Casualties in U.S. Operations Involving the Use of Force, 81 Fed. Reg. 44, 483 (July 7, 2016), and corresponding Fact Sheet: https://obamawhitehouse .archives.gov/the-press-office/2016/07/01/fact-sheet-executive-order-us-policy-pre-post-strike-measures-address [hereinafter Exec. Order No. 13732]. For President Obama's latest drone policy, *see* December 2016 Presidential Report, *supra* note 14.

[23] Mary Wood, *Scalia Defends Originalism as Best Methodology for Judging Law* (Apr. 20, 2010), http://content.law.virginia.edu/news/2010_spr/scalia.htm (discussing Justice Antonin Scalia and Justice Clarence Thomas' use of originalism on the U.S. Supreme Court). Louis Henkin opposed humanitarian intervention for precisely this reason. Louis Henkin, *The Use of Force: Law and U.S. Policy, in* RIGHT V. MIGHT: INTERNATIONAL LAW AND THE USE OF FORCE 37, 60 (Louis Henkin et al. eds., 2d ed. 1991).

governments now employ the self-defense argument in "every conceivable circumstance,"[24] which is, of course, the difficulty.

Many U.S. practices would be of concern, but much less objectionable, were they used sparingly, in actual emergencies or as responses to actual or truly imminent attacks, as opposed to constituting an ongoing and systematic practice. Although the Obama Presidential Memo promises that the "unable or unwilling" standard is not a "license to wage war globally or to disregard the borders and territorial integrity of other States,"[25] there appears to be no recent situation in which the United States has found itself unable to proceed with the use of military force on self-defense grounds if it wishes to. As Brooks herself notes, this reinterpretation of Article 51 led to the jettisoning of any seeming restraints by the United States, including the adoption of torture and cruel treatment as official U.S. policy toward detainees, and the launch of a war of aggression against Iraq under the pretext of preemptive self-defense. Given this abuse of military force, many governments have not agreed with many of these new U.S. positions as a general principle, even if they have accepted them in particular cases,[26] or been obliged to tolerate them. They have thus responded by endeavoring to reinforce international law regarding the unlawful use of force by adding the crime of aggression to the International Criminal Court Statute and adopting new weapons treaties including, most recently, a new United Nations treaty prohibiting nuclear weapons, both over the opposition not only of the United States, but most major powers.

---

[24] Noam Lubell, Extraterritorial Use of Force Against Non-State Actors 74 & n.27 (2017), *citing* Daniel Bethlehem, International law and the Use of Force: The Law as it is and as it should be, Written Evidence submitted to the UK Select Committee on Foreign Affairs, Minutes of Evidence (June 8, 2004).

[25] December 2016 Presidential Report, *supra* note 14, at 10.

[26] The September 2014 U.S. Letter was followed by Australia, *see* Permanent Rep. of Australia to the U.N., Letter dated 9 September 2015 from the Permanent Representative of Australia to the United Nations addressed to the President of the Security Council, U.N. Doc. S/2015/693 (Sept. 9, 2015); Canada, *see* Chargé d' affaires a.i., Letter dated 31 March 2015 from the Permanent Mission of Canada to the United Nations addressed to the President of the Security Council, U.N. Doc. S/2015/221 (Mar. 31, 2015); Germany (implicitly), *see* Chargé d' affaires a.i., Letter dated 10 December 2015 from the Permanent Mission of Germany to the United Nations addressed to the President of the Security Council, U.N. Doc. S/2015/946 (Dec. 10, 2015); and Turkey (in a different context), *see* Chargé d' affaires a.i., Letter dated 24 July 2015 from the Permanent Mission of Turkey to the United Nations addressed to the President of the Security Council, U.N. Doc. S/2015/563 (July 24, 2015). As Olivier Corten notes, however, the formulation is not used by the other 10 coalition partners (of the 15 members of the coalition). Corten, *supra* note 18, at 780. Corten further suggests that the Canadian and Australian positions may have been asserted out of convenience as opposed to a sense of *opinio juris* given that they switched from a position of "illegality" to "legality" over a brief period of time in apparent response to "political considerations." *Id.* at 782.

This Chapter examines the attempted rewriting of the *jus ad bellum* and the *jus in bello* by the United States (and others); and at the same time it chronicles the efforts of civil society, the United Nations, and other governments to continue to deepen and fortify the normative foundations of the international law relating to the use of force and the laws of war based upon U.N. Charter principles. It concludes that, in many respects, the current era is reminiscent of the period between World War I and World War II during which efforts of codification and institution building were taking place just as governments ascended to power that would challenge those efforts, and ultimately, nearly tear them to shreds.[27] Neither the League of Nations nor the Kellogg–Briand Pact could stop German aggression once Germany decided to no longer play by the rules of the international community and invoked the need for preemptive action as grounds for its aggressive invasion of Poland and, subsequently, most of Europe.

This is eerily similar to the current attacks by the Trump administration (and the Republican Party more generally) on the United Nations[28] and the government's adherence to a legal position that the need to prevent or preempt violence against U.S. persons, interests, or territory justifies preemptive strikes by the United States against persons or nations that appear to threaten those interests. The United Nations has been unable to stop the United States from undertaking drone strikes on the territory of other States, to prevent the invasion of Iraq by the U.S. coalition of the willing, to halt Russia's annexation of Crimea, to stop the war and total disintegration of Syria, or to stem the bellicose war of words (and threats of nuclear incineration) now emanating from Kim Jong-un and Donald Trump. This unhappy state of affairs is the natural result of legal and philosophical (and often racist)[29] approaches to international law that found voice during the Bush era, were never repudiated by the Obama administration,[30] and are in full throttle during the Trump era.

Although Brooks suggests that opposing this trend is naïve, that the slide into war is inevitable, harkening back to the nineteenth-century view that war, after all, is only "politics by other means,"[31] a recent study by Oona Hathaway

---

[27] Leila Nadya Sadat, *The Nuremberg Paradox*, 58. Am. J. Comp. 151, 164–69 (2010).
[28] Leila Nadya Sadat, *Global Trumpism: Week Two*, Lex Lata, Lex Ferenda, (Feb. 1, 2017), http://law.wustl.edu/harris/lexlata/?p=1287.
[29] Leila Nadya Sadat, *Do all Arabs Really Look Alike? Prejudice and the U.S. "War" on Terror*, 50 Wayne L. Rev. 69 (2004).
[30] *See, e.g.*, Jack Goldsmith, *Obama Has Officially Adopted Bush's Iraq Doctrine*, TIME (Apr. 6, 2016), http://time.com/4283865/obama-adopted-bushs-iraq-doctrine/.
[31] Carl Von Clausewitz, On War (1832).

and Scott Martin suggests that law – even law about war – may make a difference. They note that two decades after the Kellogg–Briand Pact, a remarkable normative shift took place – the conquest of territory by States fell from one every ten months to one every four years. And the "likelihood that any individual state would suffer a conquest in an average year plummeted – from 1.33 percent to 0.17 percent, or [from once in an ordinary human lifetime to] once or twice a millennium."[32] They admit that there may be other factors, but surely this stunning shift is why the Charter of the United Nations, the "constitution" of the international community,[33] built upon the Kellogg–Briand Pact and the Nuremberg precedent to prohibit war. The post-war normative framework posits the sovereign equality of States and a commitment to peace, human rights, and human dignity that overrides other values. The central pillar of the United Nations system is a commitment to peace, first and foremost.

To be effective and respected, international legal rules must acquire broad legitimacy throughout the international community as a practical and moral matter; they cannot do so unless they promote fairness, equality, and, fundamentally, peace. As a recent and important book by Steven Ratner suggests, the first pillar of global justice is peace.[34] Only by "putting peacetime first" can the United States – and international law – create and maintain the kind of stable, just, and fair world essential to humanity's survival. As the world lurches once again toward the specter of nuclear war, fueled by the paranoia, bellicose rhetoric, and poor judgment of some of its leaders, fidelity to the United Nations Charter, which was itself conceived in the ashes and devastation of a total war that took millions of lives, becomes an urgent imperative. Classic understandings about the demarcation between war and peace are not just quixotic remnants of a bygone era, but core underpinnings of the international legal system that are eroded at the peril of the entire world. This is the thesis that this Chapter explores.

---

[32] Oona Hathaway & Scott J. Shapiro, *Outlawing War? It Actually Worked*, N.Y. TIMES (Sept. 2, 2017), www.nytimes.com/2017/09/02/opinion/sunday/outlawing-war-kellogg-briand.html. *See* OONA HATHAWAY & SCOTT J. SHAPIRO, THE INTERNATIONALISTS: HOW A RADICAL PLAN TO OUTLAW WAR REMADE THE WORLD (2017).

[33] Bardo Fassbender, *The United Nations Charter as Constitution of the International Community*, 36 COLUM. J. TRANSNAT'L L. 529 (1998); Ronald St. J. Macdonald, *The Charter of the United Nations as a World Constitution*, 75 INT'L L. STUD. 263 (2000). Daskal and Vladeck make the same point in their essay, *supra* note 18, at 118.

[34] STEVEN R. RATNER, THE THIN JUSTICE OF INTERNATIONAL LAW 65 (2016).

II. HOW SEPTEMBER 11 CHANGED THE WORLD

Following the September 11, 2001, attacks, the administration of U.S. President George W. Bush did precisely what Brooks is now suggesting is needed. It endeavored to create a whole new set of rules to govern the use of force (*jus ad bellum*) by embracing the notion of "preemptive war,"[35] and reinterpreted the U.N. Charter to permit military action upon the territory of other U.N. Member States in "self-defense" in response to terrorist acts by non-State actors (actually occurring or anticipated at some time in the future) taking place or being launched anywhere or at any time. According to two authors in this volume, this understanding of Article 51 is the new "norm," and the countervailing jurisprudence of the International Court of Justice is either inconclusive (McDougall)[36] or out of touch with State practice (Trahan).[37] Many scholars agree with McDougall and Trahan; others, including this author, demur – or are at least unwilling to concede the expansion of Article 51 without clearer understandings on the limits of that expansion.[38] It likewise embraced a new set of norms to govern the *jus in bello*, creating a "space between" that would serve as a law-free zone in which U.S. forces could act unconstrained by international law. This was achieved, in part, by jettisoning adherence to the Geneva Conventions and embracing torture as

---

[35] White House, The National Security Strategy of the United States of America 6, 15–16 (2002), www.state.gov/documents/organization/63562.pdf.

[36] *See also* LUBELL, *supra* note 24.

[37] *See also* Carrie McDougall, *The Other Enemy: Transnational Terrorists, Armed Attacks and Armed Conflicts*, in this volume, n.30, 46–47 and accompanying text; Jennifer Trahan, *The Crime of Aggression and the International Criminal Court*, in this volume, n.139–141 and accompanying text. *But see* Douglas Pivnichny's Chapter, *The International Court of Justice and the Use of Force*, in this volume (setting forth the views of the Court); TOM RUYS, "ARMED ATTACK" AND ARTICLE 51 OF THE UN CHARTER 52 (2010) (noting the "considerable authority" of the ICJ in matters involving the use of force).

[38] Sadat, *Terrorism*, *supra* note 15, at 144n.30; *See also* Georges Abi-Saab, *There Is no Need to Reinvent the Law*, in A DEFINING MOMENT & INTERNATIONAL LAW SINCE SEPTEMBER 11, Crimes of War Project, www.globalpolicy.org/component/content/article/163/28256.html; Antonio Cassese, *Terrorism Is Also Disrupting Some Crucial Legal Categories of International Law*, 12 EUR. J. INT'L L. 993 (2201); Luigi Condor Elli, *Les attentats du 11 septembre et leurs suite: ou va le droit international*, 105 REVUE GENERAL DE DROIT INTERNATIONAL PUBLIC 829 (2001); Fréderic Mégret, 'War'?, *Legal Semantics and the Move to Violence*, 13 EUR. J. INT'L L. 361 (2002); Mary Ellen O'Connell, *Dangerous Departures*, 107 AM. J. INT'L L. 380 (2013); Dire Tladi, *The Nonconsenting Innocent State: The Problem with Bethlehem's Principle*, 107 AM. J. INT'L L. 570 (2013).

national policy.[39] This has been less well-accepted by the international community, but U.S. pressure on the laws of war continues.

These proposed changes were based on a political narrative that pitted the free peoples of the world against an "axis of evil" representing a new kind of enemy and a new kind of war; a war in which, inevitably, "mistakes would be made."[40] But changing a legal framework is only a good idea (if at all), if it produces positive results. When George W. Bush left office in January 2009, it had become painfully clear that the military campaign in Afghanistan had not produced either the desired rebuilding of a peaceful, friendly, and effective government in Afghanistan, the end of the Taliban,[41] or the capture or death of Osama bin Laden and dissolution of the al-Qaeda terrorist network. The Bush administration led the United States and its "coalition of the willing" into the 2003 invasion of Iraq[42] based upon this new interpretation of the *jus ad bellum*, a war which produced "regime change" as the country's longtime leader, Saddam Hussein, was toppled, tried, and killed,[43] but by any other measure can only be considered a fiasco.[44] Recent studies have suggested that

---

[39] Memorandum from Alberto Gonzales, Counsel to the President to President Bush (Jan. 25, 2002), http://nsarchive.gwu.edu/torturingdemocracy/documents/20020125.pdf.

[40] Donald H. Rumsfeld, *A New Kind of War*, N.Y. TIMES (Sept. 27, 2001), www.nytimes.com/2001/09/27/opinion/a-new-kind-of-war.html; *Text of Donald Rumsfeld's News Conference on Air Campaign*, WASH. POST (Oct. 29, 2001), www.washingtonpost.com/wp-srv/nation/specials/attacked/transcripts/rumsfeldtext_102901.html. Echoing this more than a decade later, Rosa Brooks writes, "Almost inevitably, some people will be detained by mistake: because they were in the wrong place at the wrong time . . . or because they resembled someone else or had the same name as a terror suspect. Guess how many Muslim men are named Muhammad, Ahmed, Abdullah, Ali, Omar . . . or variant of those names . . . it's little wonder that we sometimes nab the wrong guys." Brooks, *supra* note 4, at 57. It is doubtful that Americans would be equally indulgent of mistakes if they were being attacked by foreigners who couldn't seem to distinguish between names like John, Jean, Joseph, and Jack in their determinations of who might be detained, tortured, targeted, and killed.

[41] Najibullah Lafraie, *Resurgence of the Taliban Insurgency in Afghanistan: How and Why?*, 46 INT'L POL. 102 (2009); David Fox & Hamid Shalizi, *Taliban Claim Blast at NATO Base in Kabul*, REUTERS (Aug. 15, 2009), www.reuters.com/article/us-afghanistan-idUSTRE57E0D620090815; *Taleban "To Boost Afghan Attacks,"* BBC NEWS (June 27, 2008), http://news.bbc.co.uk/2/hi/americas/7478513.stm; David Rohde & David E. Sanger, *How a "Good War" in Afghanistan Went Bad*, N.Y. TIMES (Aug. 12, 2007), www.nytimes.com/2007/08/12/world/asia/12afghan.html.

[42] Office of Pub. Affairs, Dep't of Def., Fact Sheet: International Contributions to the War Against Terrorism (2002), http://archive.defense.gov/news/May2002/d20020523cu.pdf; Jesse Lorenz, *The Coalition of the Willing*, STAN. U. (June 5, 2003), https://web.stanford.edu/class/e297a/The%20Coalition%20of%20the%20Willing.htm.

[43] Kenneth Katzman, Cong. Research Serv., RL31339, Iraq: Post-Saddam Governance and Security (2008).

[44] Amy Belasco, Cong. Research Serv., RL33110, The Cost of Iraq, Afghanistan, and Other Global War on Terror Operations Since 9/11 (2014), https://fas.org/sgp/crs/natsec/RL33110.pdf; THOMAS E. RICKS, FIASCO: THE AMERICAN MILITARY ADVENTURE IN IRAQ (2006); Steven J.

the Iraqi death toll from the invasion and occupation may be as high as half a million people.[45] The death and destruction of these two wars has also fallen heavily on Americans – more than 7,000 have died in Iraq and Afghanistan since 2001, and more than 50,000 were wounded.[46] The two wars together cost the United States nearly US$4.8 trillion,[47] and arguably sparked the genesis of ISIS.[48]

Davis, Kevin M. Murphy & Robert H. Topel, *War in Iraq versus Containment*, Am. Enterprise Inst. (Feb. 15, 2006); Mark Thompson, *The True Cost of the Afghanistan War May Surprise You*, Time (Jan. 1, 2015), http://time.com/3651697/afghanistan-war-cost/. And even a war of aggression. John Hagan, Joshua Kaiser & Anna Hanson, Iraq and the Crimes of Aggressive War (2015).

[45] Dan Vergano, *Half-Million Iraqis Died in the War, New Study Says*, National Geographic, (Oct. 16, 2013), http://news.nationalgeographic.com/news/2013/10/131015-iraq-war-deaths-survey-2013/ (describing a study by researchers that polled heads of households and siblings in Iraq, and included both those directly killed as a result of shootings, bombings, airstrikes, or other violence and those who died from stress-related disease, ruined sanitation and hospitals, and including those who died as they were forced to flee Iraq). *See also Iraqi Civilians*, Watson Inst. Int'l Pub. Aff. (Apr. 2015), http://watson.brown.edu/costsofwar/costs/human/civilians/iraqi ("[A]pproximately 165,000 civilians have died from direct war related violence caused by the US, its allies, the Iraqi military and police, and opposition forces from the time of the invasion through April 2015. . . . The actual number of civilians killed by direct and indirect war violence is unknown but likely much higher – in the hundreds of thousands."); Iraq Body Count, www.iraqbodycount.org/database/ (177,799–199,056 documented civilian deaths from violence as of July 12, 2017). *See also* Sahar E. Aziz, *Global Conflict and Populism in a Post-9/11 World*, 52 Tulsa L. Rev. 395, 400–01 (2017) (noting that U.S. missteps and "fatal mistakes" in Iraq fueled terrorism and helped launch ISIS.).

[46] *US & Allied Killed*, Watson Inst. Int'l Pub. Aff. (Feb. 2015), http://watson.brown.edu/costsofwar/costs/human/military/killed ("The number of United States troops who have died fighting the wars in Iraq and Afghanistan had passed 6,800 at the beginning of 2015."); *Casualty Status*, U.S. Dep't of Defense, https://www.defense.gov/casualty.pdf (showing approximately 7,000 U.S. Military casualties in Iraq and Afghanistan as of July 12, 2017); *US & Allied Wounded*, Watson Inst. Int'l Pub. Aff. (Feb. 2015), http://watson.brown.edu/costsofwar/costs/human/military/wounded (more than 52,000 wounded).

[47] *US Budgetary Costs*, Cost of War (Sept. 2016), http://watson.brown.edu/costsofwar/costs/economic/budget ("The United States federal government has spent or obligated 4.8 trillion dollars on the wars in Afghanistan, Pakistan, and Iraq. This figure includes: direct Congressional war appropriations; war-related increases to the Pentagon base budget; veterans care and disability; increases in the homeland security budget; interest payments on direct war borrowing; foreign assistance spending; and estimated future obligations for veterans' care."); Linda J. Bilmes, *The Financial Legacy of Iraq and Afghanistan: How Wartime Spending Decisions Will Constrain Future National Security Budgets* 1 (Harvard Kennedy School Faculty Research Working Paper Series, Paper No. RWP13-006, 2013) (estimating $4–6 trillion in costs).

[48] Kristine Anderson, *ISIS and the State of Terror: The Genesis, Evolution, and Impact of the Islamic State*, Brookings (Apr. 3, 2015); Martin Chulov, *ISIS: The Inside Story*, Guardian (Dec. 11, 2014), www.theguardian.com/world/2014/dec/11/-sp-isis-the-inside-story.

Yet in spite of the stunning failure of the Bush-era rewrites of international law to produce positive outcomes (such as a diminishment of international terrorist activity and peace in Afghanistan, Iraq, and surrounding nations),[49] Barack Obama's administration embraced most of them. Some blame the bureaucracies, especially at the U.S. Department of Defense,[50] and there is no doubt that it is difficult for even the President to change "business as usual" particularly at the Colossus that is the Defense Department, with its half-trillion-dollar budget[51] and nearly three million employees worldwide,[52] not to mention educational and operational norms that operate within military communities. Obama earned praise for quickly repudiating the use of torture as official U.S. policy, but at the same time failed to pursue accountability measures that had any real bite, despite clear evidence of widespread and extensive uses of unlawful interrogation techniques gathered by Congressional committees,[53] human rights organizations,[54] the International Committee of the Red Cross,[55] and others. He also earned kudos by announcing he would close the prison at Guantanamo Bay, which he was

---

[49] Indeed, another "surge" has now been proposed by President Trump, an increase of several thousand U.S. troops in Afghanistan. Michael R. Gordon, Eric Schmitt & Maggie Haberman, *Trump Settles on Afghan Strategy Expected to Raise Troop Levels*, N.Y. TIMES (Aug. 20, 2017), www.nytimes.com/2017/08/20/world/asia/trump-afghanistan-strategy-mattis.html?mcubz=0.

[50] BROOKS, *supra* note 4, at 62–67.

[51] Press Release, U.S. Dep't of Defense, Department of Defense (DoD) Releases Fiscal Year 2017 President's Budget Proposal (Feb. 9, 2016), www.defense.gov/News/News-Releases/News-Release-View/Article/652687/department-of-defense-dod-releases-fiscal-year-2017-presidents-budget-proposal (proposing a $521.7 billion budget for FY 2017); Office of Mgmt. & Budget, Proposed Budget of the U.S. Government 17 (2017), www.whitehouse .gov/sites/whitehouse.gov/files/omb/budget/fy2018/budget.pdf (requesting "$639 billion for the Department of Defense – a $52 billion increase from the 2017 annualized continuing resolution level" for FY 2018).

[52] BROOKS, *supra* note 4, at 72. There are 25,000 working at the Pentagon alone. *Facts & Figures: Numbers*, Dep't of Defense.

[53] S. Rep. No. 113–288 (2014) (Comm. Rep.), www.intelligence.senate.gov/sites/default/files/documents/CRPT-113srpt288.pdf; S. Rep. No. 112–3 (2011) (Comm. Rep.), www.gpo.gov/fdsys/pkg/CRPT-112srpt3/pdf/CRPT-112srpt3.pdf.

[54] HUM. RTS. FIRST, TORTURED JUSTICE: USING COERCED EVIDENCE TO PROSECUTE TERRORIST SUSPECTS (2008); HUM. RTS. WATCH, GETTING AWAY WITH TORTURE: THE BUSH ADMINISTRATION AND MISTREATMENT OF DETAINEES (2011); LETTER FROM KENNETH ROTH, EXEC. DIR., HUM. RTS. WATCH TO PRESIDENT OBAMA (June 16, 2016); AMNESTY INT'L, USA CRIMES AND IMPUNITY (2015); CTR. VICTIMS TORTURE, UNITED STATES OF AMERICA: NGO ASSESSMENT OF THE IMPLEMENTATION OF THE COMMITTEE AGAINST TORTURE FOLLOW-UP RECOMMENDATIONS (2016); AM. C.L. UNION, UNITED STATES' COMPLIANCE WITH THE CONVENTION AGAINST TORTURE AND OTHER CRUEL, INHUMAN OR DEGRADING TREATMENT OR PUNISHMENT (2014).

[55] INT'L COMM RED CROSS, REP. ON THE TREATMENT OF FOURTEEN "HIGH VALUE DETAINEES" IN CIA CUSTODY (2007).

ultimately unable to do, although he reduced the number of detainees considerably.[56] And even while announcing that the United States was returning to faithful adherence to the laws and customs of war, the Pentagon was developing a new Law of War Manual, finally published in 2015, that many argue is regressive in its content and departs from international legal norms.[57]

In terms of the use of force, Obama accelerated to an unprecedented degree the use of drone strikes to kill individuals living in Afghanistan, Iraq, Libya, Pakistan, Somalia, and Yemen whom the U.S. government suspected of affiliation with a "terrorist" organization. Although some of these strikes took place in a "war zone," as part of an armed conflict between the United States and another party, hundreds have not, and thousands of individuals appear to have been killed in strikes on the territories of countries with which the United States is not "at war."[58] As concern and even opposition to the drone campaign grew during the Obama presidency, the administration developed policies and rules on its exercise, even having lawyers pen memos on when it would be permissible to target U.S. citizens.[59] The President

---

[56] Ensuring Lawful Interrogations, 74 FR 4893 (Jan. 22, 2009); Dep't of Def. Plan for Closing the Guantanamo Bay Detention Facility (2016); Missy Ryan & Julia Tate, *Obama Pares Down Guantanamo Population, but About 40 Inmates Will Remain*, CHI. TRIB. (Dec. 28, 2016), www.chicagotribune.com/news/nationworld/ct-obama-guantanamo-20161228-story.html; Sudha Setty, *Obama's National Security Exceptionalism*, 91 CHI. KENT L. REV. 91, 96 (2016).

[57] Office of General Counsel, Dep't of Defense, Law of War Manual (2015). For examples of criticism, *see* Adil Ahmad Haque, *Off Target: Selection, Precaution, and Proportionality in the DoD Manual*, 92 INT'L L. STUD. 31 (2016); Ryan Goodman, *The Obama Administration and Targeting "War-Sustaining" Objects in Noninternational Armed Conflict*, 110 AM. J. INT'L L. 663 (2016); Am. Bar. Ass'n, DoD Law of War Manual Review Workshop Report (2016) ("The view was expressed that the position taken in the Manual regarding the relationship between IHRL and the LOW, particularly with respect to NIAC, is both problematic and out of sync with the rest of the international community."); *but see* Charles J. Dunlap, Jr., *The DoD Law of War Manual and its Critics: Some Observations*, 92 INT'L L. STUD. 85 (2016).

[58] Sadat, *America's Drone Wars, supra* note 22, at 219; Charlie Savage & Scott Shane, *U.S. Reveals Death Toll from Airstrikes Outside War Zones*, N.Y. TIMES (July 1, 2016), www.nytimes.com/2016/07/02/world/us-reveals-death-toll-from-airstrikes-outside-of-war-zones.html; Office Dir. Nat'l Intelligence, Summary of U.S. Counterterrorism Strikes Outside Areas of Active Hostilities Between January 20, 2009 and December 31, 2015 (2016); Office Dir. Nat'l Intelligence, Summary of 2016 Information Regarding United States Counterterrorism Strikes Outside Areas of Active Hostilities (2017); Ken Dilanian, Hans Nichols & Courtney Kube, *Trump Admin Ups Drone Strikes, Tolerates More Civilian Deaths: U.S. Officials*, NBC NEWS (Mar. 14, 2017), www.nbcnews.com/news/us-news/trump-admin-ups-drone-strikes-tolerates-more-civilian-deaths-n733336. Some human rights organizations estimate the toll to be significantly higher than government figures. *See, e.g., Drone Warfare*, Bureau of Investigative Journalism, www.thebureauinvestigates.com/projects/drone-war.

[59] Memorandum for the Attorney General Re: Applicability of Federal Criminal Laws and the Constitution to Contemplated Lethal Operations Against Shaykh Anwar al-Aulaqi (July 16,

himself signed off on the most contentious targeted kills, and undoubtedly
brought a certain level of supervision and professionalism to the U.S. targeted
killing campaign.[60] U.N. officials pushed back, arguing that the drone
campaign – at least outside of "hot" battlefield areas – amounted to nothing
less than extra-judicial executions,[61] unlawful under a myriad of international
rules and principles.[62] Yet the Obama administration continued to forge
ahead by arguing that States can launch military strikes on the territory of
other States on the grounds that terrorist organizations are operating on their
territories and those States are "unable or unwilling" to do something about
their activities.[63] Thus continued a U.S. effort to unwind the constraints of the
U.N. Charter that began decades earlier when, in 1989, Abe Sofaer, then legal
advisor to the U.S. Department of State, argued that the legal rules surrounding the use of force, the concept of armed attack, and respect for territorial
integrity imposed "serious limitations on strategic flexibility," and could not be
permitted to "interfere with legitimate national security measures."[64]

The sixteen-year long slide toward loose understandings of *jus ad bellum*
(and *jus in bello*) constraints on American power begun by Bush and continued by Obama[65] appears likely to worsen under Donald Trump, who is
apparently seeking to "open the throttle on using military force."[66] It is
perhaps unsurprising, given Trump's volatile temperament, that "war talk"
and bellicose rhetoric would increase with respect to every real and perceived
threat the United States might face. Just seven days following Trump's inaug-
uration, the new U.S. ambassador to the United Nations, Nikki Haley,
immediately threatened States not signing onto the U.S. agenda with

2010), www.aclu.org/legal-document/aclu-v-doj-foia-request-olc-memo?redirect=national-security/anwar-al-aulaqi-foia-request-olc-memo; Devlin Barret & Siobhan Gorman, *U.S. Memo Outlines Rationale for Drone Strikes on Citizens*, WALL ST. J. (June 26, 2014), www.wsj.com/articles/u-s-can-kill-citizens-abroad-under-certain-circumstances-memo-says-1403542004. *See also* Memorandum from Jennifer K. Elsea, Legislative Attorney, Cong. Research Serv. (May 4, 2012); Sadat, *America's Drone Wars, supra* note 22, at 218–19.

[60] *See* sources cited, *supra* note 59.
[61] Rep. of the Special Rapporteur on Extrajudicial, Summary or Arbitrary Executions, U.N. Doc. A/HRC/14/24/Add.6, at 10 (May 28, 2010).
[62] *Id.*; Rep. of the Special Rapporteur on Extrajudicial, Summary or Arbitrary Executions, U.N. Doc. A/71/372, at 13 (Sept. 2, 2016). *See also* Kevin Jon Heller, *'One Hell of a Killing Machine': Signature Strikes and International Law*, 11 J. INT'L CRIM. JUST. 89 (2013).
[63] *See supra* note 22 and accompanying text.
[64] Abraham D. Sofaer, *Terrorism, the Law and National Defense*, 126 MIL. L. REV. 89, 90–122 (1989).
[65] *See* Goldsmith, *supra* note 30. *See also* Exec. Order No. 13732, *supra* note 22.
[66] *See* Charlie Savage & Eric Schmitt, *Trump Administration Is Said to Be Working to Loosen Counterterrorism Rules*, N.Y.TIMES (Mar. 13, 2017), at A15. *See also* Micah Zenko, *Trump Could Take Obama's Drone Policy Further into the Shadows*, FOREIGN POL'Y (Feb. 2, 2017).

retaliation when presenting her credentials.[67] Just a few months later, the U.S. military conducted strikes against an airfield in Syria from which a chemical weapons attack on civilians in the town of Khan Sheikhoun was allegedly launched by the Syrian government.[68] In the official statement read from Mar-a-Lago, Florida, Trump stated, in pertinent part:

> On Tuesday, Syrian dictator Bashar al-Assad launched a horrible chemical weapons attack on innocent civilians. Using a deadly nerve agent, Assad choked out the lives of helpless men, women, and children. It was a slow and brutal death for so many. Even beautiful babies were cruelly murdered in this very barbaric attack . . .

> Tonight, I ordered a targeted military strike on the airfield in Syria from where the chemical attack was launched. It is in this vital national security interest of the United States to prevent and deter the spread and use of deadly chemical weapons. There can be no dispute that Syria used banned chemical weapons, violated its obligations under the Chemical Weapons Convention, and ignored the urging of the U.N. Security Council.

> Years of previous attempts at changing Assad's behavior have all failed . . . as a result, the refugee crisis continues to deepen and the region continues to destabilize, threatening the United States and its allies.[69]

Although there was undoubtedly a sense of relief that Assad was receiving his comeuppance and hope that the United States might help put an end to the devastating conflict in Syria,[70] the strike met none of the criteria for the

---

[67] Ambassador Nikki Haley, U.S. Perm. Rep. to the United Nations, Remarks to Press before the Presentation of Credentials to the UN Secretary-General (Jan. 27, 2017) (noting that she was "taking names" of non-compliant States).

[68] On the attack on Khan Sheikhoun *see Syria chemical "attack": What we know*, BBC WORLD NEWS (Apr. 26, 2017), www.bbc.com/news/world-middle-east-39500947.

[69] Statement by President Trump on Syria, Mar-a-Lago, Florida, 9:43 P.M. EDT, April 6, 2017, http://heavy.com/news/2017/04/trump-syria-statement-transcript-attack-missiles-bombing-airfield-war-assad-shayrat-pentagon/.

[70] Bethan McKernan, *UK: US Missile Strike on Syrian Air Base 'Appropriate Response to Barbaric Chemical Weapons Attack,'* INDEPENDENT (Apr. 7, 2017), www.independent.co.uk/news/world/middle-east/syria-missile-strike-chemical-weapons-attack-latest-donald-trump-uk-response-a7671511.html; Patrick Donahue, *Merkel, Hollande Say Assad Alone to Blame for U.S. Syria Strike*, BLOOMBERG (Apr. 7, 2017), www.bloomberg.com/news/articles/2017-04-07/merkel-hollande-say-assad-alone-to-blame-for-u-s-syria-strike; *but see* Gregor Aisch, Yonette Joseph & Anjali Singhvi, *Which Countries Support and Which Oppose the U.S. Missile Strikes in Syria*, N.Y. TIMES (Apr. 9, 2017), www.nytimes.com/interactive/2017/04/07/world/middleeast/world-reactions-syria-strike.html?mcubz=0. A U.N. Commission recently concluded the chemical attack of April 4, 2017, was indeed perpetrated by the Assad regime. *See* Rep. of the Independent International Commission of Inquiry on the Syrian Arab Republic, U.N. Doc. A/HRC/36/55, at 16, ¶ 77 (Aug. 8, 2017).

use of force under the U.N. Charter, as it was neither an act of self-defense nor authorized by the Security Council. It could possibly have been characterized as a case of humanitarian intervention, if it met the criteria for that, by at least some authorities, but again, there was no Security Council authorization, and the five criteria set forth by the International Commission on Intervention and State Sovereignty indicating when a case might be made for a "coercive humanitarian intervention,"[71] are not present. Although there may have been just cause, it is not clear that there was "right intention," that the strike was "proportional," and that there were "reasonable prospects" that the military action would be successful.[72] The strike itself did very little damage, but seemed more in the guise of a shot across the bow; the war continued and the targeted airfield was in use by the next day.[73] Trump subsequently threatened that Assad and his military will "pay a heavy price" if there are future chemical attacks in Syria.[74] Likewise, as of this writing, the President has also threatened "pretty severe things," against North Korea if it does not end its nuclear ambitions,[75] including "fire and fury";[76] has threatened to use military force against Venezuela, stoking anger at the United States and rattling other Latin American nations;[77] and has renewed war talk regarding Iran.[78]

This is appalling. Seventy years after the Nuremberg trials, and sixteen years after the September 11 attacks and the launch of "Operation Enduring

---

[71] Gareth Evans, *From Humanitarian Intervention to the Responsibility to Protect*, 24 Wis. Int'l L. J. 703, 703–15 (2006).

[72] *Id.* The five criteria are (1) just cause, (2) right intention, (3) last resort, (4) proportional means, and (5) reasonable prospects of success.

[73] *Syrian Governor Confirms Air Base Operating Again*, Reuters (Apr. 8, 2017), www.reuters .com/article/us-mideast-crisis-syria-airbase/syrian-governor-confirms-air-base-operating-again-idUSKBN17A0SO.

[74] Office of the Press Sec'y, Statement from the Press Secretary on Identified Potential Preparations for Another Chemical Weapons Attack (June 26, 2017), www.whitehouse.gov/the-press-office/2017/06/26/statement-press-secretary; Michael D. Shear, Helene Cooper & Eric Schmitt, *Syria Will 'Pay a Heavy Price' for Another Chemical Attack, White House Says*, N.Y. Times (June 26, 2017), www.nytimes.com/2017/06/26/us/politics/syria-will-pay-a-heavy-price-for-another-chemical-attack-trump-says.html.

[75] *President Trump Threatens North Korea with "Severe Things,"* Sky News (July 6, 2017), http://news.sky.com/story/trump-threatens-north-korea-with-severe-things-10938710.

[76] Editorial, *The North Korean Missile Crisis*, Wall St. J. (July 4, 2017), www.wsj.com/articles/the-north-korean-missile-crisis-1499188198. *See also* Bret Stephens, Editorial, *A 'New Approach' to North Korea*, Wall St. J. (Mar. 27, 2017), www.wsj.com/articles/a-new-approach-to-north-korea-1490655924.

[77] Nicholas Casey, *Trump's Words Rattle a Fragile Alliance*, N.Y. Times (Aug. 15, 2017), at A4.

[78] Trita Parsi, *War with Iran Is Back on the Table – Thanks to Trump*, Guardian (July 17, 2017), www.theguardian.com/commentisfree/2017/jul/17/war-with-iran-possible-donald-trump-foreign-policy.

Freedom" by the United States,[79] the United States – and those copying the U.S. rationales for war articulated over the past sixteen years, which include both U.S. allies[80] and adversaries[81] – are moving away from the understanding that military force is a tool of last, not first, resort. Instead of putting peacetime first, they appear to have embraced the notion of "perpetual war,"[82] in which there is little or no legal accountability for the unlawful use of force, or even the breach of peremptory norms of the *jus in bello* like the prohibition against torture. They have used the excuse of future terror attacks by shadowy (mostly Muslim) non-State actors in far off countries to rewrite the rules of international law enshrined in the Charter and the laws of war in all cases and for all circumstances. Upset about North Korea? Never mind that this is a classic state–state paradigm for which the "new rules" allegedly needed to fight international terrorists should be irrelevant. Preemption applies to it, just as it did to Iraq. The United States – now imitated by other States – has asserted that it is judge, jury, and executioner in a variety of situations involving individuals,[83]

[79] The operation was initially code-named "Infinite Justice," but was changed to "Enduring Freedom" on September 25, 2001, after objections that the initial term could be seen as anti-Muslim. Sadat, *Terrorism*, *supra* note 15, at 137 n.8 (2004).

[80] *See, e.g.,* Iraq Inquiry, Report of the Iraq Inquiry: Executive Summary (2016), www.iraqinquiry .org.uk/media/247921/the-report-of-the-iraq-inquiry_executive-summary.pdf (detailing the process and reasoning of using military force against Saddam Hussein's regime in Iraq); Op-Ed., Barack Obama, David Cameron & Nicolas Sarkozy, *Libya's Pathway to Peace*, N.Y. TIMES (APR. 14, 2011), www.nytimes.com/2011/04/15/opinion/15iht-edlibya15.html (noting a collective "duty" and "mandate" under U.N. Security Council Resolution 1973 to protect civilians in Libya and the need for the Gaddafi regime to be removed); W. Michael Reisman & Andrea Armstrong, *The Past and Future of the Claim of Preemptive Self-Defense*, 100 AM. J. INT'L L. 525, 538–46 (2006) (describing other world governments' positions on preemptive self-defense).

[81] *See, e.g.,* Reisman & Armstrong, *supra* note 80, at 544–46 (noting the positions of China, Russia, and North Korea); *Transcript: Putin Defends Russian Intervention in Ukraine*, WASH. POST (Mar. 4, 2014), www.washingtonpost.com/world/transcript-putin-defends-russian-intervention-in-ukraine/2014/03/04/9cadcd1a-a3a9-11e3-a5fa-55f0c77bf39c_story.html?utm_term=.8fcead29b4f1 ("if I do decide to use the Armed Forces, this will be a legitimate decision in full compliance with both general norms of international law, since we have the appeal of the legitimate President ... Protecting these people is in our national interests. This is a humanitarian mission.").

[82] *See* Rosa Brooks, *There's No Such Thing as Peacetime*, FOREIGN POL'Y (Mar. 13, 2015).

[83] Lizzie Dearden, *Osama Bin Laden Could "Absolutely" Have Been Captured Alive, Says US Military Commander*, INDEPENDENT (July 18, 2017), www.independent.co.uk/news/world/middle-east/osama-bin-laden-capture-alive-us-military-admiral-william-mcraven-al-qaeda-navy-seal-team-pakistan-a7847286.html.

non-State actors,[84] and States[85] – and that the United Nations Charter is to be respected only insofar as it serves the goals of the current U.S. administration.

Is this inevitable? In her book, Brooks writes of the sheer enormity of the Pentagon – the complex of shopping malls, offices, meeting rooms, and daunting military capacity.[86] And for Americans who are probably not, for the most part, likely to be the target of a hell-fire missile fired by a drone or even sent into harm's way, it is easy to forget the pain and trauma of the violence inflicted by war. Yet war is not the result of some invisible hand, but the consequence of conscious political choices. It is important to constrain those choices in favor of peace. This work is ongoing: as new interpretations of international law are being proffered by the United States and some of its allies (and other States that find them convenient), a different group of States has been erecting norms they hope will constrain the use of force, including the incorporation of the crime of aggression into the Rome Statute for the International Criminal Court in 2010[87] and the adoption of a new United Nations treaty banning nuclear weapons.[88] It is to these efforts that this Chapter now turns.

III. RESTRAINING COLOSSUS

Although war was historically a tool of statecraft, as several Chapters in this volume remind us, subsequently natural law and positive law prohibitions grew increasingly robust with the passage of time. During the inter-war period, from 1919 until 1939, there was a flurry of norm and institution building that

---

[84] Spencer Ackerman & Sune Engel Rasmussen, *36 ISIS Militants Killed in US 'mother of all bombs' Attack, Afghan Ministry Says*, GUARDIAN (Apr. 14, 2017), www.theguardian.com/world/2017/apr/13/us-military-drops-non-nuclear-bomb-afghanistan-islamic-state; Dominic Tierney, *The Twenty Years' War*, ATLANTIC (Aug. 23, 2016), www.theatlantic.com/international/archive/2016/08/twenty-years-war/496736/; *U.S. Air Strike Hits Al Shabaab; Somalia Says Base Destroyed*, REUTERS (June 11, 2017), www.reuters.com/article/us-somalia-attack/u-s-air-strike-hits-al-shabaab-somalia-says-base-destroyed-idUSKBN1920RR.

[85] Peter Baker & Choe Sang-Hun, *Trump Threatens 'Fire and Fury' Against North Korea if It Endangers U.S.*, N.Y. TIMES (Aug. 8, 2017), www.nytimes.com/2017/08/08/world/asia/north-korea-un-sanctions-nuclear-missile-united-nations.html?mcubz=0.

[86] Brooks, *supra* note 4, at 39–40; Rosa Brooks, *How the Pentagon Became Walmart*, FOREIGN POL'Y (Aug. 9, 2016).

[87] Review Conference of the Rome Statute of the International Criminal Court, *The crime of aggression*, Res. RC/Res.6 (June 11, 2010).

[88] *UN Conference Adopts Treaty Banning Nuclear Weapons*, UN NEWS CTR. (July 7, 2017), www.un.org/apps/news/story.asp?NewsID=57139#.WWZqjlTyvcs.

took place, including the establishment of the League of Nations,[89] draft Statutes for a new International Criminal Court,[90] adoption of the Kellogg–Briand Pact,[91] a new Treaty banning the use of Asphyxiating Gases,[92] new Geneva Conventions in 1929,[93] and even a treaty to create an international terrorism court[94] – which never entered into force. Although these institutions and treaties were not able to stop either German or Japanese aggression, they were critical to the construction of the post-war international legal order, as well as, more immediately, the success of the Nuremberg trials, which included the charge of crimes against peace as one of the three charges leveled against the Nazis.

This charge was defined as the "planning, preparation, initiation or waging of a war of aggression or a war in violation of international treaties, agreements or assurances. . . ."[95] Although there had initially been fierce internal debate in the United States as to whether the Nazis should be tried for aggressive war,[96] ultimately the U.S. prosecutorial team, led by Supreme Court Justice Robert H. Jackson, vigorously pursued the Nazis for crimes against peace, arguing that the aggressive war itself was "the crime which comprehends all lesser crimes. . . ."[97] The International Military Tribunal agreed, famously opining that aggression "is not only an international crime; it is the supreme international crime differing only from other war crimes in that it contains within itself the accumulated evil of the whole."[98] That pronouncement was enshrined in Article 2(4) of the U.N. Charter, not as a

---

[89] Office of the Historian, *The League of Nations, 1920*, History, https://history.state.gov/milestones/1914-1920/league.

[90] Leila Sadat, *The Proposed Permanent International Criminal Court: An Appraisal*, 29 CORNELL INT'L L.J. 665 (1996) (formerly Wexler).

[91] Office of the Historian, *The Kellogg-Briand Pact, 1928*, History, https://history.state.gov/milestones/1921–1936/kellogg.

[92] Protocol for the Prohibition of the Use of Asphyxiating, Poisonous or Other Gases, and of Bacteriological Methods of Warfare, *adopted on* June 17, 1925, 94 L.N.T.S. 65 (entered into force February 8, 1928).

[93] Convention relative to the Treatment of Prisoners of War, *adopted on* July 27, 1929.

[94] Sadat, *The Proposed Permanent International Criminal Court, supra* note 90.

[95] Charter of the International Military Tribunal art. 6, Annex to the Agreement for the Prosecution and Punishment of the Major War Criminals of the European Axis, Aug. 8, 1945, 82 U.N.T.S. 279.

[96] William Schabas, *Origins of the Criminalization of Aggression: How Crimes Against Peace Became the "Supreme International Crime," in* THE INTERNATIONAL CRIMINAL COURT AND THE CRIME OF AGGRESSION 17, 25–26 (Mauro Politi & Giuseppe Nesi, eds., 2004).

[97] TELFORD TAYLOR, THE ANATOMY OF THE NUREMBERG TRIALS 54 (1992) (quoting Robert Jackson).

[98] *International Military Tribunal (Nuremberg), Judgment and Sentences*, 41 AM. J. INT'L L. 172, 186 (1947).

matter of criminal law, but as a fundamental – indeed, peremptory – norm of international law binding on all States.[99]

Yet defining aggression either as a matter of State or individual responsibility – and ensuring its prohibition – has turned out to be difficult. The ambivalence that plagued the drafting of the Nuremberg Charter continued to bedevil international efforts to definitively prohibit the unlawful use of force. The International Law Commission, charged with developing a draft code of crimes, struggled for fifty years with the task, only to include the crime of aggression, without definition, in its 1996 Draft Code.[100] The General Assembly fared somewhat better, adopting Resolution 3314 in 1974, which included both a general definition of aggression and a list of prohibited acts.[101]

The International Court of Justice has periodically been seized of disputes involving allegations of unlawful uses of force, and there have also been arbitral disputes,[102] fact-finding commissions, human rights adjudications, and even some national legislation (and case law) defining and adjudicating situations involving the unlawful use of force. Many of these are also the subject of Chapters in this volume. In spite of this growing corpus of authority, however, enforcing the notion that prohibitions on the unlawful use of force represent *binding legal norms* – and even *jus cogens* norms – rather than *political objectives* or even *wishful thinking*, has been a constant struggle of the modern era.

A case in point is the struggle to include the crime of aggression in the Statute of the International Criminal Court (ICC). Aggression was not included in the jurisdiction of the International Criminal Tribunal for the former Yugoslavia, and the fight over its inclusion in the ICC Statute threatened to derail the Rome Conference.[103] Through the perseverance of many, and in spite of the fierce opposition of the major powers, the ICC Statute included aggression, in Article 5(1) (setting forth the crimes within the jurisdiction of the Court); but left it undefined. Article 5(2) added:

---

[99] U.N. Charter art. 2, ¶ 4.
[100] Draft Code of Crimes Against the Peace and Security of Mankind art. 16, Int'l L. Comm'n, U.N. GAOR, 48th Sess., U.N. Doc. A/CN.4/L.532 (1996).
[101] Definition of Aggression, G.A. Res. 3314 (XXIX), 29 U.N. GAOR Supp. No. 31, at 142, U.N. Doc. A/9631 (Dec. 14, 1974).
[102] Alabama Claims Arbitration (U.S. v. U.K.) (1872); The Dogger Bank Case (U.K. v. Russia) (1908), I.C.I. Rep. (Feb. 26, 1905); Eritrea-Ethiopia Claims Commission (Eritrea v. Ethiopia) (Perm. Ct. Arb., 2004).
[103] Leila Nadya Sadat & S. Richard Carden, *The New International Criminal Court: An Uneasy Revolution*, 88 GEO. L. J. 381, 437 (2000).

The Court shall exercise jurisdiction over the crime of aggression once a provision is adopted in accordance with articles 121 and 123 defining the crime and setting out the conditions under which the Court shall exercise jurisdiction with respect to this crime. Such a provision shall be consistent with the relevant provisions of the Charter of the United Nations.[104]

As a practical matter, therefore, this compromise (proposed by Germany during the Rome negotiations)[105] postponed the fight about the crime of aggression to another day.

In 2002, after the Rome Statute entered into force, the Assembly of States Parties revived the discussion regarding the crime of aggression, and ultimately established a Special Working Group to fulfill the promise of Article 5(2).[106] The Special Working Group concluded its work in 2009, and developed a text that was ultimately submitted to the Assembly of States Parties meeting in Kampala, Uganda, at a seven-year mandated "Review Conference" of the Statute.[107] After difficult negotiations during which, once again, the five permanent members of the Security Council, in particular, evinced particular hostility toward the idea of aggression as a justiciable crime,[108] the Review Conference adopted amendments to the Rome Statute on the crime of aggression (the Kampala Amendments) that represent an important step forward in achieving accountability for the unlawful use of force. They define the crime of aggression and give the ICC jurisdiction over it in limited circumstances. Yet because States can opt out of the amendments if they wish to (which is not a possibility for the other crimes), and certain "understandings" were adopted in conjunction with the text that constrain the applicability and enforcement of the aggression amendments,[109] their inclusion in the

[104] Rome Statute of the International Criminal Court art. 5, *adopted on* July 17, 1998, 2187 U.N.T.S. 91 (entered into force July 1, 2002) [hereinafter Rome Statute].
[105] RONEN STEINKE, THE POLITICS OF INTERNATIONAL CRIMINAL JUSTICE: GERMAN PERSPECTIVES FROM NUREMBERG TO THE HAGUE 126–27 (2012).
[106] Stefan Barriga, *Against the Odds: The Results of the Special Working Group on the Crime of Aggression, in* THE PRINCETON PROCESS ON THE CRIME OF AGGRESSION 1 (Stefan Barriga, Wolfgang Danspeckgruber & Christian Wenaweser eds., 2009). An important point to note is that participation in the SWGCA was open to States Parties and Non-States Parties to the Rome Statute. *Id.* at 5.
[107] Rep. on the First Review Conference on the Rome Statute, Kampala, Uganda (May 31–June 11, 2010), www.iccnow.org/documents/RC_Report_finalweb.pdf.
[108] *See, e.g.,* Harold Hongju Koh & Todd F. Buchwald, *The Crime of Aggression: The United States Perspective,* 109 AM. J. INT'L L. 257 (2015).
[109] Jocelyn Getgen Kestenbaum, *Closing Impunity Gaps for the Crime of Aggression,* 16 CHI. J. INT'L L. 51, 61–62 (2016); FRITS KALSHOVEN & LIESBETH ZEGVELD, CONSTRAINTS ON THE WAGING OF WAR: AN INTRODUCTION TO INTERNATIONAL HUMANITARIAN LAW 257–58 (4th ed. 2011).

ICC Statute came with costs as well as benefits.[110] As of this writing, thirty-five States have ratified the Kampala Amendments,[111] and the Court's jurisdiction was "activated" at the sixteenth meeting of the ICC's Assembly of States Parties on December 14, 2017, through the adoption of a consensus, compromise Resolution that preserved British and French objections to the amendments' jurisdictional regime, but allows other States to apply the Court's jurisdiction to their territory and nationals.[112]

Restraining aggressive war takes on even greater urgency in an era dominated by nuclear and thermo-nuclear weapons. The world's stockpile of nuclear weapons has admittedly declined significantly since its peak of approximately 70,300 during the Cold War.[113] Yet the nuclear weapons States' pledge to reduce their stockpiles in exchange for the pledge of the non-nuclear weapons States agreement not to acquire or use nuclear weapons in the 1970 Nuclear Non-Proliferation Treaty has not been fulfilled,[114] and today's nuclear weapons are much more powerful than those of yesteryear.[115] Of the approximately 14,935 in current inventory, 92 percent are owned by either the United States (6,800) or the Russian Federation (7,000).[116] The Bulletin of Atomic Scientists, known for its continuing assessment of threat levels to world peace, has set the Doomsday Clock at two and a half minutes to midnight for 2017, based upon the assessment that

---

[110] *See generally* Mark A. Drumbl, *The Push to Criminalize Aggression: Something Lost Amid the Gains*, 41 CASE W. RES. J. INT'L L. 291 (2009); THE CRIME OF AGGRESSION: A COMMENTARY (Claus Kreß & Stefan Barriga eds., 2016).

[111] Status of Treaties, *Amendments on the Crime of Aggression to the Rome Statute of the International Criminal Court*, UNTC (Sept. 5, 2017), https://treaties.un.org/Pages/ViewDetails.aspx?src=TREATY&mtdsg_no=XVIII-10-b&chapter=18&lang=en.

[112] Res. ICC-ASP/16/Res.5, Activation of the jurisdiction of the Court over the crime of aggression (Dec. 14, 2017). It also permits referral of a case involving aggression by the United Nations Security Council. *Id.*

[113] Hans M. Kristensen & Robert S. Norris, *Status of World Nuclear Forces, Federation of American Scientists*, https://fas.org/issues/nuclear-weapons/status-world-nuclear-forces/.

[114] Treaty on the Non-Proliferation of Nuclear Weapons, *adopted on* Jan. 7, 1968, 729 U.N.T.S. 161 (entered into force Mar. 5, 1970) [hereinafter NPT]. After twenty-five years, NPT parties met in May 1995 and agreed to extend the treaty indefinitely. With 191 ratifications, the treaty has arguably slowed, but not halted, the spread of nuclear weapons. *But see* Matthew Fuhrmann & Yonatan Lupu, *Do Arms Control Treaties Work? Assessing the Effectiveness of the Nuclear Nonproliferation Treaty*, 60 INT'L STUD. Q. 530 (2016).

[115] Jay Bennett, *Today's Nukes Are Thousands of Times More Powerful Than WWII A-Bombs*, PM (Oct. 10, 2016), www.popularmechanics.com/military/a23306/nuclear-bombs-powerful-today/.

[116] Kristensen & Norris, *supra* note 113. *See also* Alana Abramson, *Here's How Many Nuclear Weapons the U.S. Has*, TIME (Aug. 9, 2017), http://time.com/4893175/united-states-nuclear-weapons/; *Nuclear Weapons: Who Has What at a Glance*, ARMS CONTROL ASS'N (July 5, 2017), www.armscontrol.org/factsheets/Nuclearweaponswhohaswhat.

[W]orld leaders were failing to act with the speed and on the scale required to protect citizens from the extreme danger posed by climate change and nuclear war. During the past year, the need for leadership only intensified – yet inaction and brinkmanship have continued, endangering every person, everywhere on earth.[117]

Frustrated with the slow progress on nuclear disarmament, and alarmed at threatening statements by some States, in July 2017 a new treaty was adopted by the United Nations on the prohibition of nuclear weapons. Endorsed by 122 States, the treaty negotiations were polarizing, as all of the States possessing nuclear weapons[118] and many others that come under their protection or host weapons on their soil refused to participate.[119] The Netherlands participated but then voted *against* the treaty (the only "no" vote). Several other countries, including the United States, Britain, and France noted that they would never "sign, ratify or ever become party to it."[120] The treaty negotiations were led by a coalition of diverse States including Austria, Brazil, Mexico, South Africa, and New Zealand. The treaty opened for signature starting in September 2017 during the annual meeting of the General Assembly. It requires fifty ratifications, a large number,[121] to enter into force, and provides that

---

[117] *It is two and a half minutes to midnight*, Bulletin of the Atomic Scientists, 2017 Doomsday Clock Statement, http://thebulletin.org/sites/default/files/Final%202017%20Clock% 20Statement.pdf.

[118] The nine countries generally recognized as having nuclear weapons are China, France, India, Israel, North Korea, Pakistan, the Russian Federation, the United Kingdom, and the United States.

[119] *Treaty Banning Nuclear Weapons Approved at UN*, GUARDIAN (July 7, 2017), www .theguardian.com/world/2017/jul/07/treaty-banning-nuclear-weapons-approved-un.

[120] Rick Gladstone, *A Treaty Is Reached to Ban Nuclear Arms. Now Comes the Hard Part*, N.Y. TIMES (July 7, 2017), www.nytimes.com/2017/07/07/world/americas/united-nations-nuclear-weapons-prohibition-destruction-global-treaty.html. The statement noted that "a purported ban on nuclear weapons that does not address the security concerns that continue to make nuclear deterrence necessary cannot result in the elimination of a single nuclear weapon and will not enhance any country's security, nor international peace and security." Christopher Ford called it a "mess of a treaty [that is] only likely to make things worse," in a recent speech to the Carnegie Endowment for International Peace. Christopher Ford, Special Assistant to the President and NSC Senior Director for WMD and Counterproliferation, *Briefing on Nuclear Ban Treaty*, Carnegie Endowment for Int'l Peace (Aug. 22, 2017). *But see UN Conference Adopts Treaty Banning Nuclear Weapons*, UN (July 7, 2017), www.un.org/apps/news/story.asp? NewsID=57139#.WbMHgLKGOUk.

[121] Treaty on the Prohibition of Nuclear Weapons art. 15, *adopted on* July 7, 2017 [hereinafter TPNW]. This treaty was adopted more than twenty years after the (unsuccessful) struggle to operationalize the Comprehensive Nuclear-Test Ban Treaty, which although it currently has 183 signatories and 166 parties, has yet to take effect because pursuant to Article XIV of the

Each State Party undertakes never under any circumstances to:

(a) Develop, test, produce, manufacture, otherwise acquire, possess or stock-
    pile nuclear weapons or other nuclear explosive devices ...

(b) .... Use or threaten to use nuclear weapons or other nuclear explosive
    devices.[122]

The new treaty fills the gap identified by the International Court of Justice
in its 1996 Advisory Opinion on Nuclear Weapons[123] by making it clear that *no
circumstances whatsoever* will justify either the use or threat of nuclear
weapons. In 1993 and 1994, the World Health Organization and the General
Assembly of the United Nations referred, independently, two questions to the
ICJ regarding nuclear weapons. Although the Court refused to give a decision
on the question raised by the WHO,[124] it did answer the General Assembly's
question, to wit: "Is the threat or use of nuclear weapons in any circumstance
permitted under international law?"[125]

The Court found that no specific treaty expressly prohibited the use of
nuclear weapons, although many treaties suggested that specific uses would
certainly violate international law. Likewise, the Court found no specific
prohibition, either conventional or under customary law, that suggested that
possession, development, acquisition, deployment, or testing were *per se*
unlawful. Ultimately the Court concluded, by a vote of seven in favor, seven
opposed, with the President of the Court (Mohammed Bedjaoui) casting the
deciding vote, that

> The threat or use of nuclear weapons would generally be contrary to the rules
> of international law applicable in armed conflict, and in particular the

---

treaty, it will only enter into force after all 44 States listed in Annex 2 to the treaty have ratified
it.. Comprehensive Nuclear Test-Ban Treaty, *adopted on* Sept. 10, 1996, 35 I.L.M. 1439. *See
also* Preparatory Commission for the Comprehensive Nuclear-Test-Ban Treaty Organization,
Status of Signature and Ratification, CTBTO, www.ctbto.org/the-treaty/status-of-signature-and-
ratification/. Thus far, the following Article XIV States have not yet ratified the treaty: China,
Democratic People's Republic of Korea, Egypt, India, Iran, Israel, Pakistan, and the United
States. United Nations Office for Disarmament Affairs, *Comprehensive Nuclear-Test-Ban
Treaty*, UN, www.un.org/disarmament/wmd/nuclear/ctbt/.

[122] TPNW, *supra* note 121, art. 1(1).

[123] Legality of the Threat or Use of Nuclear Weapons, Advisory Opinion, 1996 I.C.J. Rep. 226 (July
8) [hereinafter Nuclear Weapons Advisory Opinion].

[124] The WHO "requested the International Court of Justice to give an advisory opinion on
whether the use of nuclear weapons by a State in war or other armed conflict would be a
breach of its obligations under international law, including the Constitution of the World
Health Organization ..." *Id.* at 228. The Court found that the question did not fall within the
organization's activities, and therefore could not confer jurisdiction on the Court.

[125] *Id.*

principles and rules of humanitarian law. However, in view of the current state of international law, and the elements of fact at its disposal, the Court cannot conclude definitively whether the threat or use of nuclear weapons would be lawful or unlawful in an extreme circumstance of self-defense, in which the very survival of a State would be at stake.[126]

In so opining, the Court found that the "most directly relevant applicable law" was that relating to the "use of force enshrined in the United Nations Charter" (the *jus ad bellum*) and "the law applicable in armed conflict which regulates the conduct of hostilities, together with any specific treaties on nuclear weapons."[127] It also found that it needed to account for "certain unique characteristics of nuclear weapons," [128] in particular, "their destructive capacity, their capacity to cause untold human suffering, and their ability to cause damage to generations to come."[129] The Court noted the adoption of General Assembly Resolution 1653, and its subsequent reiteration each year, as providing evidence of the "desire of a very large section of the international community" to take a "significant step forward along the road to complete nuclear disarmament," but declined to find that prohibition had acquired sufficient force of law to declare such a rule *lex lata*.[130] Resolution 1653, which has been recalled and reiterated at every session of the General Assembly since its adoption in 1961, provides in relevant part, that

(a) The use of nuclear and thermo-nuclear weapons is contrary to the spirit, letter and aims of the United Nations and, as such, a direct violation of the Charter of the United Nations;

(b) The use of nuclear and thermo-nuclear weapons would exceed even the scope of war and cause indiscriminate suffering and destruction to mankind and civilization and, as such, is contrary to the rules of international law and to the laws of humanity;

(c) The use of nuclear and thermo-nuclear weapons is a war directed not against an enemy or enemies alone but also against mankind in general, since the peoples of the world not involved in such a war will be subjected to all the evils generated by the use of such weapons;

(d) Any State using nuclear and thermo-nuclear weapons is to be considered as violating the Charter of the United Nations, as acting contrary to

---

[126] *Id.* ¶ 105(2)(E).
[127] *Id.* ¶ 33.
[128] *Id.* ¶ 35.
[129] *Id.* ¶ 36.
[130] *Id.* ¶ 73.

the laws of humanity and as committing a crime against mankind and civilization.[131]

It is interesting, in this Resolution, to note the echoes of the Martens Clauses of the 1899 and 1907 Hague Conventions, and the Nuremberg Trial and Judgment. Some members of the Court, and in particular Judge Christopher Weeramantry, agreed with Resolution 1653 and found that the majority did not go far enough in its pronouncements. He concluded that "not *generally* but *always*, the threat or use of nuclear weapons would be contrary to the rules of international law, and, in particular, to the principles and rules of humanitarian law."[132]

Although Weeramantry's magisterial opinion is too long to be summarized in the short space of this Chapter, essentially he drew an absolute prohibition on the threat or use of nuclear weapons from their ability to "imperil all that humanity has ever stood for, and humanity itself,"[133] cataloging their explosive potential; their ability to destroy the "entire ecosystem of the planet"; their deleterious impact on future generations; their indiscriminate damage to civilian populations; the possibility of a "nuclear winter"; the potential to destroy social institutions, infrastructure, economic structures, cultural treasures, and to produce an electromagnetic pulse incapacitating all electronic devices; the potential medical effects including loss of life, the effects of heat and blast, and congenital deformities. Additionally, Weeramantry noted a more existential threat to humankind – the "shadow of the mushroom cloud," that pervades all of society, creating a climate of fear and despair, of lives being "snuffed out in an instant, or their health destroyed, along with all they cherish, in a war to which their nation may not even be a party."[134]

Of course, others – particularly the United States and the United Kingdom – argued that nuclear weapons would not necessarily have effects on third-party States, would not necessarily have indiscriminate effects upon civilians, and would not necessarily cause unnecessary suffering. Judge Schwebel issued a separate opinion to that effect.[135] Judge Weeramantry dismissed the notion of

---

[131] Declaration on the Prohibition of the Use of Nuclear and Thermo-Nuclear Weapons, G.A. Res. 1653, U.N. Doc. A/RES/1653(XVI) (Nov. 24, 1961).

[132] Nuclear Weapons Advisory Opinion, *supra* note 123, Dissenting Opinion of Judge Weeramantry, at 213 [hereinafter Weeramantry Dissenting Opinion].

[133] *Id.* at 225.

[134] *Id.* at 248.

[135] Nuclear Weapons Advisory Opinion, *supra* note 123, Dissenting Opinion of Vice-President Schwebel, at 320–22.

a "limited" nuclear war, observing that not only was such a notion "impossible," but that "the use of nuclear weapons in self-defense would result in a cataclysmic nuclear exchange."[136]

Following the Court's 1996 decision, there were renewed efforts to fill the gap between the majority view (that there was not as of yet a complete prohibition) and Judge Weeramantry's perspective. These included many additional efforts to bring cases to the Court relating to nuclear weapons,[137] further General Assembly Resolutions, and general advocacy efforts.[138] The balance sheet on these efforts has been mixed: although the Obama administration was successful in adopting a new nuclear weapons reduction treaty in 2010,[139] as a general matter, the number of nuclear weapons States and their assorted arsenals have increased rather than been reduced in the past two decades. The adoption of this new treaty, then, is an effort to stem the slide into proliferation by endeavoring to make it impossible to argue that international law does not conclusively prohibit the use or threatened use of nuclear weapons.[140] Obviously if the treaty is not widely ratified, it may allow others to draw the opposite conclusion.

IV. CONCLUSION: INTERNATIONAL LAW IN AN AGE OF GLOBAL TRUMPISM

In this short Chapter I have tried to make the case for reinforcing the current United Nations system, rather than abandoning it for some new codification

[136] Weeramantry Dissenting Opinion, *supra* note 132, at 294.
[137] Pallavi Kishore, *Using the Unprecedented Nuclear Weapons Advisory Opinion as Precedent in the Marshall Islands Cases*, 5 KATHMANDU L. REV. 136, 137 (2017).
[138] United Nations Office for Disarmament Affairs, *Nuclear Weapons*, UN, www.un.org/disarmament/wmd/nuclear/.
[139] Treaty between the United States of America and the Russian Federation on Measures for the Further Reduction and Limitation of Strategic Offensive Arms, *adopted on* Apr. 8, 2010, T.I.A.S. 11–205 (entered into force Feb. 5, 2011).
[140] The U.S. position appears to be that the treaty undermines the global non-proliferation regime and neither supports the existence of an existing ban on possession, nor crystallizes a new rule of non-possession. Ford, *supra* note 120. The U.S. legal arguments are not particularly clear, and seem to miss the point which is to completely eliminate – and render unlawful – the possession, use, and threatened use of nuclear weapons. As a practical matter, it is true that the elimination of nuclear weapons is already a goal of the NPT, but that the United States and Russia, in particular, have not been compliant with that treaty. *The Global Nuclear Nonproliferation Regime*, Council on Foreign Relations (May 21, 2012) (the "United States and other nuclear powers reaffirmed their commitment to nuclear disarmament. But despite major cuts in the numbers of U.S. and Russian operationally deployed nuclear warheads, both countries still retain massive stockpiles that account for more than 90 percent of the world's nuclear weapons.").

of law in a new and unbounded *space between*. Rejecting the paradigm of perpetual war, this requires the international community to "put peacetime first," rather than viewing the world through the lens of military force and its projection. The creators of the post-war world understood that to prevent the next war, the world needed rules, institutions, and enforcement. Brooks herself concedes as much, noting that,

> In theory, all these tensions could be resolved if we had more robust, responsible, and accountable forms of international governance. In the age of globalization, we need, more than ever, a strong global referee committed both to stability and to human dignity – a global referee that could make those difficult decisions about when and where to use force, so it wouldn't just be one state's views against another's. Only such a system could prevent the inevitable erosion of traditional norms of sovereignty from leading to a slide toward conflict and instability, at the expense of basic human rights.[141]

This is the work that needs to be done, not the insistence of a world in perpetual war, in which a "boundary-less battlefield" pushes the laws of war and the prohibition on the use of force to the breaking point, making everyone, everywhere, liable to be killed as collateral damage.[142] Particularly with war talk now including the possibility of incinerating Guam (Kim Jong-un) or North Korea (threatened by Donald Trump with a "massive military response" and "fire and fury"), the "cataclysmic nuclear exchange" warned of by Judge Weeramantry seems more and more probable unless drastic measures to put peacetime first are taken soon.

As noted in the introductory section of this Chapter, the first pillar of an ethical standard of global justice is whether a norm promotes the advancement of peace.[143] The notion of a perpetual war, in which the U.S. military – or the military of any nation – can strike whenever, whatever, and whomever they wish subject only to whatever internal constraints might be imposed by their own national leaders, works harm to the fundamental importance of peace as the presumptive framework for international relations and the existence of the emerging "human right to peace."[144] It is not a plausible system for maintaining international peace and security in a world in which nuclear

---

[141] Brooks, *supra* note 4, at 253.

[142] Naz Modirzadeh, *International Law and Armed Conflict in Dark Times: A Call for Engagement*, 96 Int'l Rev. Red Cross 737, 746 (2014).

[143] Ratner, *supra* note 34.

[144] *See, e.g.*, Douglas Roche, The Human Right to Peace (2003); Anwarul K. Chowdhury, *Human Right to Peace: The Core of the Culture of Peace, in* Contribuciones regionales para una Declaracion Universal del Derecho Humano a la Paz 125 (Carlos Villán Duran & Carmelo Faleh Perez eds., 2010).

weapons and their potential use threaten to undermine the entire system, and cannot be said to provide a "legal" framework for the conduct of international relations, as the notion of law requires objectively ascertainable and enforceable standards.

It is true that building peace is in many ways more difficult than promoting war. Domestic political constituencies are easily aroused and enthused by patriotic and jingoistic language promising national glory and honor at the expense of international cooperation. National leaders promoting peace have to ensure that domestic political constituencies not only understand how peace benefits them on a personal level, but why it is important to work across borders to promote it. International lawyers need to do the same, using their position and influence to promote peace and human rights, especially in powerful countries like the United States. It is perhaps easier – and even more rewarding in terms of influence and authority – to yield to Colossus rather than oppose its will. But the predictable outcome of yielding will be a world destroyed by war. If everything can be justified as a matter of "self-defense" and the notion of "self-defense" has virtually no limits, there is no longer a system of law, but simply the existence of power. As Oscar Schacter wrote some years ago:

> [T]he right of self-defense, "inherent" though it may be, cannot be autonomous. To consider it as above or outside the law renders it more probable that force will be used unilaterally and abusively. No state or people can face that prospect with equanimity in the present world.[145]

[145] Oscar Schacter, *Self-Defense and the Rule of Law*, 83 AM. J. INT'L. L. 259, 277 (1989).

Epilogue

BENJAMIN B. FERENCZ

An elementary principle of law and justice holds that those responsible for the illegal use of force should be brought to personal account in a court of law. The learned contributors to this book have noted that what is right is not always or easily attainable. The world continues to be awash with massive killings of innocent people while perpetrators remain immune. Important treaties remain ignored as "scraps of paper." We have not yet found a satisfactory way to deter such crimes and convince the public that it is in their own self-interest to behave toward others in a more peaceful and humane way. Perfectionists say: "It can't be done, so why bother trying?" Others insist that peace is mandatory or all life on Planet Earth may be destroyed. It was the hope of the Nuremberg trials that the force of law might replace the law of force. Without effective accountability, law loses its power and meaning. As the sole surviving Nuremberg war crimes prosecutor, having spent most of my ninety-seven years trying to prevent crimes against humanity, allow me to share some personal experiences and views that may enlighten the distant horizon.

The war crimes trials following World War II marked a significant step forward in the evolution of international criminal law. The judicial determination by highly respected jurists was that illegal war-making described as a "crime against peace" was punishable by an international tribunal. It would be unjust to allow the leading perpetrators to go unpunished. The fairness of the open trials gave credence to the fact that deeds which had been hailed in the past as heroic patriotism would in the future be condemned as "the supreme international crime." As a U.S. combat soldier in World War II (awarded battle stars for not having been killed or wounded in five major battles), I can testify of my personal knowledge that war becomes the breeding ground for every possible atrocity. There has never been a war without genocide, massive rapes, torture, and similar crimes against humanity. The horrors I personally witnessed as a liberator of several Nazi concentration camps are inconceivable to any rational mind. I learned that war can make murderers out of otherwise decent people.

The U.N. Charter authorizes the Security Council to legalize the use of force for the maintenance of peace and security. Unfortunately, the Council has been less than successful in carrying out the people's primary goal: "to save succeeding generations from the scourge of war." It has been paralyzed by the inability of its Permanent Members to agree on enforcement action that does not further their own perception of their national interests. Self-defense has long been recognized as an inherent right, but there is no accepted international authority with power to settle disputes peacefully or decide when killings constitute lawful self-defense or the crime of aggression. Disputants – be they nations, groups or individuals driven by fear – are often willing to kill and die for their particular cause. They see no viable alternative other than the use of force to protect their values by every conceivable means.

In desperation and as a last resort, political leaders send young people out to kill the presumed adversaries, including other young people they don't even know who may have done no harm to anyone. The death of innocent bystanders is brushed aside as "collateral damage" as though it was merely a passing wind. Innocent victims' cries for vengeance are met by counterattacks. When belligerents get tired of mutual slaughter, each side declares victory, rests awhile then resumes a rampage of crimes against humanity. This usual process would be ludicrous were it not so tragic. Decision makers fail to recognize that you cannot kill a cherished ideal with a gun. Under the current state of world disorganization, war, genocide, and other crimes against humanity are unavoidable.

Creating a new system of accountability for the illegal use of force is a fundamental responsibility of the legal profession. At Nuremberg I prosecuted twenty-two high-ranking and well-educated German defendants. They were convicted of deliberately murdering more than a million innocent men, women, and children. The victims were slaughtered because they did not share the race, religion, or ideology of their executioners. I did not ask for the death penalty; it would have seemed inadequate. Instead, I argued for a new rule of law that would protect the right of all people everywhere to live in peace and human dignity regardless of their race or creed. It was a plea of humanity to law. I was then twenty-seven years old and it was my first case. The ideals of my youth have never left me.

Accountability requires more than punishment of only a small sample of varied wrongdoers. Concern for the destitute victims who had lost everything also cried out for urgent relief. I remained in Germany for several years after the trials ended to help negotiate and implement unprecedented new German legislation offering some measure of restitution and compensation to the survivors of Nazi atrocities. Despite the novelty, difficulty, and duration of the tasks, the obvious justice of the cause lent strength to my endeavors.

It was the dream of Nuremberg that war could be replaced by the rule of law. These hopes were shared by a wide variety of political and military leaders, regardless of political affiliation. It was reaffirmed for many years by many learned scholars. There is no doubt that restraining the unlawful use of force is the desired goal of many people in many lands and circumstances. Skeptics continue to recite many of the obstacles still to be overcome. Optimists see success around the corner. I view myself as a Realist who is keenly aware of the countless problems, but I cannot ignore the encouraging progress. There is no quick or easy path to the desired goal. It takes courage not to be discouraged. Doing nothing solves nothing. Hope drives human endeavor and can be a catalyst to inspire the countless efforts needed to bring about the needed changes.

The law is not static. One should not expect perfection. To be effective, law must change sufficiently to meet the needs of the society it is designed to protect. The ancient notion of absolute state sovereignty is now absolutely obsolete. Contemporary society recognizes that sovereignty belongs not to a distant monarch but to the people. Leaders are more sensitive than ever to public opinion. Governments' capacity to kill has outpaced their capacity to protect innocent human lives. We are ignoring the wisdom of Dwight D. Eisenhower, my Supreme Commander in World War II, who, as president of the United States, warned about the power of the military-industrial complex. He put it bluntly on April 30, 1958: "*In a very real sense, the world no longer has a choice between force and law. If civilization is to survive, it must choose the rule of law.*" One cannot expect rules laid down centuries ago to be adequate for human protection in the current Internet and cyberspace age. We need new institutions and new thinking. Accountability for the unlawful use of force can only be effective when peace has been restored and there is a court willing and able to punish the offenders.

The first U.N. General Assembly called for the creation of an international criminal court to follow the footsteps of the International Military Tribunal at Nuremberg (IMT). U.N. committees were tasked with creating a new code of crimes including a definition of aggression. However, as every good lawyer knows, it is not difficult to find problems with any solution your client does not wish to accept. The fact is that the International Criminal Court (ICC) today still has no jurisdiction to try what the IMT correctly characterized as "the supreme international crime." It is not credible to believe that hundreds of competent lawyers, meeting in hundreds of sessions over a period of more than seventy years still remain incapable of agreeing on an actionable definition of the word "aggression." Enough is enough!

The truth is that a few powerful States (led by the United States) are not willing to accept the jurisdiction of any foreign court to determine whether their own use of force is illegal. What is lacking is the ability to change traditions that have been idolized for centuries. Accountability has been blocked by the conservative views of a politically powerful American minority. Other States, including the most powerful ones, were not ready to accept the rule of law as long as it was rejected by the United States. The U.N. Charter provisions for an international military force to protect the peace soon floundered in political dissentions. Instead of universal disarmament, as advocated in the U.N. Charter and many treaties, nations wasted their resources in an endless and increasingly perilous arms race. Fortunes spent inventing and constantly improving killing machines absorbed funds urgently needed to relieve the discontents that generate desperate violence. Counterproductive plans for security led to more insecurity. The absence of effective means to maintain peace remains a glaring and increasingly dangerous gap in the present international legal order.

Whether the use of force is illegal or criminal should not depend upon technical and obtuse nomenclature but on facts. It should be a moral and legal imperative that those responsible for the use of armed force that is not in self-defense and not mandated by the Security Council should have to justify their deeds in open court. The public has been fed the spurious excuse that aggression has not been adequately defined. It should be much easier to gain general acceptance for punishing a crime that has already been universally condemned in the public eye. In addition to amorphous charges of aggression, perpetrators can also be charged with *crimes against humanity* as already mandated in the existing ICC Statute as well as many national criminal codes. No prior approval from the Security Council is required, and there is no statute of limitations for such offenses.

Deeds that shocked the human conscience have faced public opprobrium and punishment since the early days of piracy. Scholarly Latin phrases such as *jus cogens* and *hostis humani generis* reflected general standards of decency that could be enforced wherever and whenever perpetrators could be apprehended. Actions that offended the "dictates of the human conscience" became subject to universal jurisdiction, with no derogation. The ICC Statute and many similar codes already contain catchall provisions condemning genocide, murder, rape, and "other inhumane acts." Surely, those responsible for using armed force that is not in self-defense or based on a Security Council mandate, knowing that large numbers of innocent people will inevitably be killed, are committing inhumane acts that should render them subject to criminal accountability. Tradition and the desirability of certainty in law should not be allowed to override common sense. Laws must be interpreted expansively rather than restrictively if they are to do justice and protect against current dangers. Law, morality, and accountability must go hand in hand.

The principles of Nuremberg were intended to apply equally to all persons – including those who sat in judgment. Crimes are committed by individuals. Self-granted immunities are obviously evasions of justice and should be declared invalid and ignored as reflective of bygone days when the king could do no wrong. Surely there will be situations where the prohibited "interference in the internal affairs of States" seems mandatory to halt ongoing atrocities that the local regime is unwilling or unable to stop. Crimes do not become lawful because they are done with good intentions. Unauthorized intervention may be morally justified if done for humanitarian purposes only and limited to the extent necessary to halt unrestrained cruelties. Justice is not blind. Judges and prosecutors are bound by law to take all circumstances into account; they are not likely to condemn and punish genuine good Samaritans. It should not be left to the protagonists themselves to decide whether their deeds are morally and legally justifiable. The "Responsibility to Protect" may be valid under the U.N. Charter but only if pursued by peaceful means. Accountability before an impartial tribunal is the best way to assure that justice will prevail.

The unlawful use of force is usually generated by fear that cherished values such as religion, nationality, or economic security are being jeopardized. If these causes can be ameliorated, the need for legal accountability will be diminished. Improving existing laws is vital but not sufficient to bring about significant changes in human behavior. Wise legal decisions can help shape new norms of what is permissible. Tolerance and compassion must be taught at every level of education. People everywhere must learn that compromise is not a sign of weakness or cowardice. In the interests of peace-loving people everywhere, and particularly those brave young men and women who must do the fighting, we must stop glorifying war. We need to change the hearts and minds of the public, the politicians, the diplomats and other decision makers to convince them that there will be legal and financial accountability for the unlawful use of force that kills large numbers of innocent people. We owe it to the memory of the many millions who have perished in combat, and those who still remain threatened, to do all we can to stop future genocides and crimes against humanity.

Despite all of the shortcomings of current efforts to curb the unlawful use of force, the enormous progress toward a more humanitarian world governed by law must be recognized. Human rights too numerous to mention have been protected in ways considered inconceivable not too long ago. Widely hailed universal declarations of human rights laid foundations for "freedom, justice and peace in the world." Before Nuremberg there was no such thing as international criminal law. Today humanitarian law is taught in universities throughout the world. Dozens of little-noted criminal courts try perpetrators of crimes against humanity. The International Criminal Court in The Hague, despite countless travails, is carrying out Nuremberg traditions. Genocide and "hate crimes" are increasingly being declared unlawful. Such radical transformations illustrate that minds can be changed on issues long considered immutable. Despite countless shortcomings, there has been a gradual awakening of the human conscience.

Changing hearts and minds has been a very slow, inadequate, and difficult process, but that is no cause for despair. Setbacks have been unavoidable, but progress toward a more humane world has been slowly spiraling upward. The new communication revolution holds forth the promise of speedier change. In the near future, every village on the planet will be linked by high technologies that can bring news and education into every home. The faith of Tycho Brahe, as described in the Introduction to this book by my son Don, is slowly being realized as astronauts now land in outer space and search the farthest reaches of the unfathomed universe. New knowledge carries both a promise and a threat. The hazard of annihilation from cyberspace makes it even more imperative that nations seek accountability to prevent the unlawful use of force. Compromise, compassion, creativity, determination, and courage will be needed to reach the goal of universal peace. Though my eyes be shut forever in an iron sleep, it is my fervent hope that new generations will see the kingdom of the law.

Benjamin B. Ferencz
March 6, 2017
(My views are detailed on my website www.Benferencz.org)

Index

For cases cited, see the table of cases.

attempts to codify, 54
and command responsibility, 390n 16
and crime of aggression, 285
criminalization of, 21–9, 23n 57, 58–60
and individual punishment, 80
and international criminal court, 131–3
and International Military Tribunals, 160
and Judge Bernard's Tokyo dissent, 91–2
and Judge Pal's Tokyo dissent, 93–5
and Judge Röling's Tokyo dissent, 95–6
and Nuremberg Tribunal, 285–91, 567–8, 578
penalties for, 77–9
prosecution of, 24–5n 61
and Tokyo Tribunal, 83–4
criminal combatants, 164–5
Croatia, 43n 131, 239n 80, 403–4n 73, 403–4
cross-border conflict, 223n 27, 235–8, 515–18,
    549–50
customary international law
    and aggression, 20–1, 21n 47
    and aggressive war, 302
    and collective self-defense, 515–20
    and crime of aggression, 341
    and crimes against humanity, 363n 95, 366
    and crimes against peace, 25–6
    and definition of aggression, 311n 40
    and definition of attack, 399–400
    and equity, 118–19
    and Geneva Conventions, 161
    and humanitarian principles, 528–9n 8
    and immunities from jurisdiction, 19n 43
    and Kampala Amendments, 97–8
    and Kellogg-Briand Pact, 19–20
    and London Charter, 288
    and non-state actors, 345n 31
    and non-use of force, 205
    and Nuremberg Tribunal, 97
    and other inhumane acts, 396–7, 410
    and self-defense, 494
    and use of force, 527–8
    and World War II–era jurisprudence,
        390–1n 20
cyber warfare, 13n 16, 57n 187, 239, 314, 331–2,
    336, 456n 14, 583
Cyprus, 43n 131, 227n 39, 239n 80
Cyrus the Great, 105–6, 113
Czechoslovakia, 22–4, 26–9, 28n 70, 128, 539
    Soviet invasion of, 140

Daesh. *See* Islamic State of Iraq and Syria (ISIS)
Darfur, 187–8, 314n 61, 519–20

Davids Commission, 182n 63, 182–4
Davis, Norman, 126
de Baer, Marcel, 62–3, 65, 67–8
Declaration of Basic Principles of Justice for
    Victims of Crime and Abuse of Power,
    39–40, 40n 112
Declaration on Friendly Relations, 212, 215, 226
Declaration on Principles of International
    Law Concerning Friendly Relations, 205,
    290
declarations of war, 43–4n 132, 63–4, 76,
    81–2, 123–6, 129–30, 137–8, 151–3, 291–5,
    312–14
Deeks, Ashley, 225–6, 233–4
de facto organs, 57, 190–2, 338–9, 342, 376,
    485–6
defenses admissible, 418–19
definition of aggression, 14–15, 30n 77, 40–4,
    43–4n 132, 153, 312–14. *See also* aggression
    gaps and loopholes in, 388–93
    and gravity, 361–2
    and Kampala Amendments, 54–5
    and manifest threshold, 311n 40, 311n 44,
        312n 45
    and Non-Aligned States, 147–50
Definition of Aggression (UN General
    Assembly)
    criteria for, 136–7
    debates over, 137–9
    drafting of, 135–6
    and international criminal law, 291–5
    and Kampala Conference, 341
    and non-state actors, 226
    and Ukraine conflict, 278–82
definition of war crimes, xxviii, 426
de minimis clause, 136–7, 298, 310–11, 324–6
de Mistura, Staffan, 276–7
Democratic Republic of the Congo, 199,
    228–9, 477–8
de Moor, J.M., 69–71, 73
Denmark
    and humanitarian intervention, 327–8n 118
    and ICC jurisdiction, 319n 83
    and IMT, 348n 42
    and Iraq War, 182
    and ISIS, 222–3, 230–1, 239n 80
    and Red Crusader Inquiry, 171
Dennis, Michael, 545–6
Department of Defense (US)
    budget of, 560n 51
    and definition of aggression, 140–1